Encyclopedic Liberty

Jean Le Rond d'Alembert

Denis Diderot

ENCYCLOPEDIC LIBERTY

Political Articles in the Dictionary of Diderot and D'Alembert

Edited and with an Introduction by Henry C. Clark

Translated by Henry C. Clark and Christine Dunn Henderson

LIBERTY FUND

Indianapolis

This book is published by Liberty Fund, Inc., a foundation established
to encourage study of the ideal of a society of free and responsible individuals.

The cuneiform inscription that serves as our logo and as a design motif in Liberty Fund books is the earliest-known written appearance of the word "freedom" (*amagi*), or "liberty." It is taken from a clay document written about 2300 B.C. in the Sumerian city-state of Lagash.

The portrait of Denis Diderot used for the frontispiece and the exterior of the book was painted in 1767 by Louis Michel van Loo and is from the Louvre, in Paris, France. Photo credit: Erich Lessing / Art Resource, New York.

The portrait of Jean Le Rond d'Alembert used for the frontispiece and the exterior of the book was painted in 1753 by Maurice-Quentin de La Tour and is from the Louvre, in Paris, France. Photo credit: Erich Lessing / Art Resource, New York.

(Page 779 constitutes an extension of this copyright page.)

Printed in the United States of America

20 19 18 17 16 C 5 4 3 2 1
20 19 18 17 16 P 5 4 3 2 1

Library of Congress Cataloging-in-Publication Data

Names: Diderot, Denis, 1713–1784. | Alembert, Jean Le Rond d', 1717–1783. | Clark, Henry C., editor.

Title: Encyclopedic liberty : political articles in the Dictionary of Diderot and d'Alembert / edited and with an introduction by Henry C. Clark ; translated by Henry C. Clark and Christine Dunn Henderson.

Description: Indianapolis : Liberty Fund, Inc., 2016. | Includes bibliographical references and index.

Identifiers: LCCN 2015048808 | ISBN 9780865978546 (hardcover : alk. paper) | ISBN 9780865978560 (pbk. : alk. paper)

Subjects: LCSH: Political science—Encyclopedias.

Classification: LCC JA62 .E64 2016 | DDC 320.03—dc23

LC record available at http://lccn.loc.gov/2015048808

Liberty Fund, Inc.
8335 Allison Pointe Trail, Suite 300
Indianapolis, IN 46250–1684

Contents

Volume 4 (1754)

Volume 5 (1755)

Volume 6 (1756)

Volume 7 (1757)

Volume 8 (1765)

Volume 9 (1765)

Volume 10 (1765)

Volume 11 (1765)

Volume 12 (1765)

Volume 13 (1765)

Volume 14 (1765)

Volume 15 (1765)

Volume 16 (1765)

Volume 17 (1765)

Alphabetical List of Articles

Introduction

"Whoever takes the trouble of combining the several political articles, will find that they form a noble system of civil liberty." So wrote the English legal expert Owen Ruffhead in 1768, referring to the seventeen-volume *Encyclopédie,* edited by Denis Diderot and Jean Le Rond d'Alembert, whose publication had been completed three years before.[1] One volume per year had rolled off the presses from 1751 until 1757; the remaining ten volumes emerged all at once in 1765. The present anthology brings together as many of the politically themed articles as could comfortably fit within a single volume, so readers may decide for themselves whether a "noble system of civil liberty" or, indeed, any system at all emerges from them.

The worthiness of the project will be well known to students of the period. The editors described their compendium in terms that made clear their intention not only to provide a uniquely comprehensive reference work, but to "change the way men think," to supply a "war machine" by which to overcome what they considered the entrenched, institutionalized resistance to new knowledge all around them. In his celebrated *Preliminary Discourse,* an introduction to the whole compilation, d'Alembert traced an entire history of modern philosophy and science designed to chart the way toward a sweeping Baconian project of improving the world through usable knowledge.[2]

And yet, for all the bold-sounding language that accompanied the prospectus and the first volume, the treatment of political subjects was problematic throughout the work's publishing history. Diderot had already

1. See *Monthly Review* 29 (1768): 545, cited in Arthur M. Wilson, *Diderot* (New York: Oxford University Press, 1972), 491.

2. Jean Le Rond d'Alembert, *Preliminary Discourse to the Encyclopedia of Diderot,* trans. and intro. Richard N. Schwab (Indianapolis: Bobbs-Merrill, 1963).

spent some months in prison for his writings in the late 1740s before working on the *Encyclopédie* and had not enjoyed the experience. But some of the biggest early controversies came from his own political contributions—in substantial articles such as POLITICAL AUTHORITY, CITIZEN, and NATURAL RIGHT, all of them included in this volume. The resulting firestorm, in combination with the plausible threat of further incarceration, evidently led him to delegate most political topics later in the work to other contributors.

In a more general sense, the tortured character of political coverage in the work was no doubt a function of the sheer fragility of the editors' rights to publication. At the very time when the second volume was appearing, in 1752, a Sorbonne thesis by an abbé Martin de Prades, who had contributed the entry CERTITUDE to the *Encyclopédie,* was condemned for unorthodoxy.[3] Diderot's dictionary was briefly suppressed by a royal order in council; there was even talk of putting its editors to death. The dauphin's Jesuit preceptor, Bishop Jean-François Boyer, received the king's permission to take action. The royal censor, Chrétien-Guillaume Lamoignon de Malesherbes, a man generally sympathetic to the enlightenment project who held this important office from 1752 to 1763, devised a compromise whereby the *Encyclopédie* would continue publication. In exchange, Bishop Boyer was able to choose the censors assigned to its volumes.

In 1758, after the appearance of volume 7 the previous November, a larger crisis developed. The global war that had begun in 1756 (eventually called the Seven Years' War) was not going well for France, and wartime censorship was in full operation by 1758. There was also an attempt on the life of King Louis XV by the psychotic Damiens (1757) and a trial that led to his drawing and quartering (1758). The article GENEVA (reproduced here) had in the meantime caused an international incident with the Genevan government's declaration of orthodoxy in February 1758. For these reasons Diderot came under increasing personal pressure during this time; d'Alembert himself made the decision between December 1757 and February 1758 to discontinue his editorial association with the project.

3. See Jeffrey D. Burson, *The Rise and Fall of Theological Enlightenment: Jean-Martin de Prades and Ideological Polarization in Eighteenth-Century France,* with a foreword by Dale Van Kley (South Bend: Notre Dame University Press, 2010), especially chaps. 7–9.

Voltaire was among those urging Diderot to take the enterprise abroad for safety's sake.

In the summer of 1758 Rousseau precipitated a long-brewing breach with the encyclopedic party through the publication of his *Letter to d'Alembert on the Theatre*, a work containing a personal attack against Diderot. Also that summer (July 1758) Claude-Adrien Helvétius's materialist treatise *De l'Esprit* was published. For numerous reasons, including the prefatory dedication by Diderot's close friend Friedrich-Melchior Grimm, the work quickly became a flashpoint for mounting hostility against the *Encyclopédie* itself.

Finally, in November 1758, the archbishop of Paris condemned the book; the pope followed two months later. The Parlement of Paris—the chief judicial body in the realm, which also exercised administrative functions—resolved to launch a full-scale investigation of all scandalous literature and decided upon an immediate ban on the sale of the *Encyclopédie* itself, a judgment confirmed by the Royal Council in March 1759. The pope enjoined any Roman Catholic who possessed a copy of the work to bring it to a local priest for burning.

"Where they burn books," Heinrich Heine once wrote, "they end up burning men." The ending to this story, though, was less gruesome. Diderot's files were empty when the police searched his home because Malesherbes, the royal censor, had himself taken them into safe custody. Although the publishing project had seemingly reached a dead end by July of 1759 when the parlement ordered the editors to cease operations and repay subscribers, a confidential and unwritten arrangement allowed Diderot and the chevalier Louis de Jaucourt, a Protestant nobleman who had by now in effect replaced d'Alembert as co-editor, to continue their work in private, with an expectation that the last volumes would appear at an opportune moment. That moment finally arrived in 1765.

Among the reasons that government officials eventually allowed the enterprise to go forward was the calculation that too much had been invested, by producers and buyers alike, to allow such a lucrative venture to migrate to Prussia or Holland, as would otherwise have been likely. The contrast with Diderot's Chinese counterpart, Sung Ying-hsing, is stark. That redoubtable late Ming scholar brought out a comparably ambitious and wide-ranging compendium of practical knowledge, *The Making and Wonders of the Works of Nature*, in 1637; but despite an enthusiastic reception by its readers, the work had all but disappeared from circulation within a few years—victim of a remarkably successful government suppression—only to be fitfully reconstructed from rare surviving copies centuries later.[4] The eventual publication of the last ten volumes of Diderot's work may accordingly be seen as a triumph of (partially) free expression, political pluralism, and commercial enterprise.

Properly speaking, neither Diderot nor his fellow contributors of political articles would have been recognized as political philosophers. But Diderot's dictionary was not meant to be a collection of original essays. "Woe betide such a vast work," the editors wrote, "if we wanted to make the whole thing a work of invention!"[5] It was designed as a general reference work, and modern research has established how extraordinarily successful it was in this ambition.[6]

It was also designed, however, as a dynamically interactive, aggressively cross-referenced compendium of the new knowledge and new ways of thinking in all fields of study. Both the prospectus and d'Alembert's "Preliminary Discourse," as well as Diderot's important article ENCYCLOPÉDIE itself, emphasized the intention to propagate this new approach to a larger audience. The question that would have hovered over the political articles, therefore, was: what do the new learning and the new ways of reasoning that the editors wished to disseminate have to say about the origins, nature, and ends of political order? Although some of the articles featured here are indeed distinguished for their originality, a contributor's main task would have been skillful synthesis of recognized authorities. The problem was that the selection and citation of such authorities was fraught with con-

4. For an English translation and textual history, see Sung Ying-hsing, *T'ien-kung k'ai-wu: Chinese Technology in the Seventeenth Century*, trans. E-tu Zen Sun and Shiou-chuan Sun (University Park: Pennsylvania State University Press, 1966).

5. Denis Diderot and Jean Le Rond d'Alembert, eds., *Encyclopédie, ou Dictionnaire raisonné des sciences, des arts et des métiers, par une Société de gens de lettres* [Encyclopedia, or critical dictionary of the sciences, arts and trades, by an Association of men of letters] (Paris: Briasson, David, Le Breton, Durand, 1751–72), 3:vii.

6. See Robert Darnton, *The Business of Enlightenment: A Publishing History of the "Encyclopédie," 1775–1800* (Cambridge: Harvard University Press, 1979).

troversy, as we have seen, which furnishes a not insignificant part of the interest of this volume.

Contributors resorted to a gamut of strategies in finessing this problem. They could lift material from an author without acknowledgment (see Jaucourt's use of Bolingbroke in PATRIOT, for example); they could quote material without identifying either author or work (see Jaucourt's use of Addison's *Cato* at the beginning of the same entry); they could refer to an author obliquely ("a talented English author") without naming him; they could mention a work or author once while drawing on him more often throughout the entry; or they could summarize their general reliance upon a source by mentioning it at the beginning or end of an entry. There is some reason to believe there was at least a loose correlation between citation practice and publication status: that is, in the complexly graded system of publishing permissions available under the French monarchy—everything from a full royal privilege to a complete ban, with other options in between—the more officially respectable a work's publication status was, the more overt the citation might be. Montesquieu's political work was more likely to be cited explicitly than Locke's or Bolingbroke's, Bossuet's than Montesquieu's. Different contributors, of course, had different risk thresholds, and the perceived riskiness of a work could change over time.[7]

Although no full-scale critical study has yet been attempted of the sources used in the political articles of the *Encyclopédie*,[8] it is clear enough that the main modern authorities utilized and cited for the entries presented in this volume would include the following: Hobbes; Grotius, Pufendorf, and the recently published Jean Burlamaqui (1747) for the natural-law tradition; Locke and Sidney for the English, as well as Mandeville, Shaftesbury, Addison, Bolingbroke, Gordon, and Hume; Voltaire—especially his *Letters on the English* (known today as the *Philosophical Letters*) and his *Essai sur l'histoire universelle* (more commonly known since the mid-twentieth century

7. For some of these last points, see Dan Edelstein, Robert Morrissey, and Glenn Roe, "To Quote or Not to Quote: Citation Strategies in the *Encyclopédie*," *Journal of the History of Ideas* 74 (April 2013): 213–36.

8. Those interested in this topic can follow the progress of scholarship on the *Encyclopédie* as a whole at http://www.zotero.org/groups/encyclopedie/items, the George Mason University website for this subject.

as *Essai sur les mœurs* [Essay on manners]); and, above all, Montesquieu's *Spirit of the Laws.* That last polyglot masterpiece, which had just appeared in 1748, possessed an authority in the political articles that would be difficult to exaggerate. Jaucourt relied on it almost exclusively for many of his entries. But even authors who explicitly took issue with Montesquieu's ideas—such as Boulanger in POLITICAL ECONOMY, Saint-Lambert in HONOR and LEGISLATOR, or Damilaville in POPULATION and FIVE PERCENT TAX—often take their starting point from a question or proposition advanced by him.

Rousseau, for his part, is relatively and perhaps surprisingly unimportant for understanding the *Encyclopédie.* His long entry ECONOMIE OU ŒCONOMIE in volume 5, widely available today as *Discourse on Political Economy* and not reproduced in this volume, was an early forerunner of his more developed political theory. And his signature concept of the "general will" is used in Diderot's NATURAL RIGHT, Saint-Lambert's LEGISLATOR, and Damilaville's FIVE PERCENT TAX, which do appear in this volume, and occasionally in entries that do not, for example, GRECS (PHILOSOPHIE DES) [Greek Philosophy] and VERTU [Virtue]. D'Alembert does defend the dictionary against Rousseau's two discourses of 1750 and 1754, with their indictment of the corrupting influences of the modern arts and sciences on human mores.[9] But the *Social Contract,* Rousseau's main political work, did not appear until 1762 and finds little echo in these pages.

Even more conspicuous by his nearly complete absence is Bishop Bossuet (1627–1704), the leading exponent of the political theory of divine-right absolute monarchy under the reign of Louis XIV.[10] Nothing could more vividly illustrate the sea change in political thinking that had taken place between 1680 and 1750.

On the other side of the Atlantic, Americans did not know much about this most seminal of reference works. Unlike Montesquieu's *Spirit of the*

9. See *Encyclopédie,* 1:xxxiii; also found in d'Alembert, *Preliminary Discourse,* 103–4.

10. I have found 111 references to Bossuet in the work (plus a handful of others when searching under the term "Meaux," his place of origin), but these cite almost exclusively his oratory or his religious works, such as his *Histoire des variations des églises protestantes* [*History of the variations in the Protestant churches*]. The lone instance when his political theory, contained mainly in his *Politique tirée des propres paroles de l'Ecriture sainte* [*Politics drawn from the very words of Holy Scripture*], is even mentioned, it is disparaged by Damilaville in FIVE PERCENT TAX, below.

Laws, the works of Diderot and d'Alembert, including their great dictionary itself, were not widely disseminated in the American colonies. Neither the New York book lists nor the magazines and newspapers of the period mentioned Diderot frequently, nor were his writings widely available here—and those of d'Alembert even less.[11] It would appear that Diderot was mainly known for his creative literature, that this was seen as having an irreligious tendency, and that the rest of his corpus was judged in this light. Not surprisingly, then, Americans tended later on to lump him with the regicides and atheists of the radical French Revolution, sometimes along with Rousseau and Voltaire, as Timothy Dwight, President of Yale College, did in a 1798 sermon.

Again unlike *The Spirit of the Laws*, the *Encyclopédie* was never translated into English in the eighteenth century, although a number of attempts were announced by the book publishers.[12] That it was quite expensive would also have put a damper upon its distribution. On the other hand, Franklin, Adams, Jefferson, Madison, John Randolph, and William Short were among those who owned copies, and it was available in at least some institutional libraries of the time. Hamilton cited the article EMPIRE in Federalist No. 22.[13]

The English-speaking world's engagement with the *Encyclopédie* was slight in the nineteenth century and not much fuller in the twentieth. To my knowledge, there have been only two anthologies of articles translated into English since 1900: Nelly S. Hoyt and Thomas Cassirer's *Encyclopedia: Selections* and Stephen J. Gendzier's *Denis Diderot's The Encyclopedia: Selections*. Of the eighty-one articles in the present volume, thirteen have appeared (in whole or in part) in these previous collections. There are also a few political articles to be found in the first thirty pages or so of John Hope Mason and Robert Wokler's *Political Writings*.[14]

11. See Paul Merrill Spurlin, *The French Enlightenment in America: Essays on the Times of the Founding Fathers* (Athens: University of Georgia Press, 1984), 110, 111.

12. See John Lough, *The "Encyclopédie" in Eighteenth-Century England, and Other Studies* (Newcastle: Oriel Press, 1970), 7–8. See also Darnton, *Business of Enlightenment*, 19 and passim, for the publishing history.

13. See Spurlin, *French Enlightenment*, 112–19.

14. Nelly S. Hoyt and Thomas Cassirer, ed. and trans., *Encyclopedia: Selections* (Indianapolis: Bobbs-Merrill, 1965); Stephen J. Gendzier, ed. and trans., *Denis Diderot's "The*

French-language anthologies of political writings include *Diderot: Textes politiques, Diderot: Œuvres politiques,* and *Politique,* volume 3 of *Diderot, Œuvres,* edited by Yves Benot, Paul Vernière, and Laurent Versini, respectively. John Lough's *Encyclopédie of Diderot and D'Alembert* is a French-language compendium that includes several political entries.[15]

Starting in the late 1990s, a major collaborative effort centered at the University of Michigan aimed to make available on the worldwide web an English translation of as many articles as the sponsors could find translators for.[16] This project, undertaken in the capaciously collegial spirit of the original eighteenth-century enterprise, is an inspiration to the world of teaching and scholarship. But perforce, the Michigan Collaborative Translation Project does not have the present volume's focused sense of purpose.

The present volume is therefore unique. It provides a wide-angle window onto virtually every aspect of the political thought and political imagination of the most ambitious collaborative enterprise of the eighteenth century. There is iconography, biography, and history. There are philosophical reflections and topical interventions. There is broad constitutional analysis as well as detailed coverage of legal, economic, and administrative affairs. Religion, morality, family, and sexuality on the one hand, and war, slavery, and fiscality on the other, all come in for treatment of some sort in the present collection. In short, the full sweep of what it meant to think about politics in the eighteenth century is represented here in as eclectic, open-ended, and capacious a manner as was feasible between the covers of a single volume.

Encyclopedia": Selections (New York: Harper and Row, 1967); John Hope Mason and Robert Wokler, ed. and trans., *Political Writings,* by Denis Diderot (Cambridge: Cambridge University Press, 1992).

15. Yves Benot, ed., *Diderot: Textes politiques* (Paris, 1960), vol. 6 of the "Textes choisis" series published by Editions Sociales; Paul Vernière, ed., *Diderot: Œuvres politiques* (Paris: Garnier Frères, 1963); and Laurent Versini, ed., *Diderot, Œuvres,* vol. 3, *Politique* (Paris: Robert Laffont, 1995). John Lough, ed., *The "Encyclopédie" of Diderot and D'Alembert: Selected Articles* (Cambridge: Cambridge University Press, 1954).

16. *The Encyclopedia of Diderot and d'Alembert Collaborative Translation Project.* Ann Arbor: Michigan Publishing, University of Michigan Library: http://quod.lib.umich.edu/d/did/.

Contributors

Jean Le Rond d'Alembert, 1717–83 (1,309 articles). Born illegitimately to the salon hostess Madame de Tencin and the military officer Chevalier Destouches, d'Alembert had a brilliant mathematical mind and became a member of the Royal Academy of Sciences in 1742 at the age of twenty-four. While Diderot sought out the convivial atmosphere of the cafés, d'Alembert, with his high voice and attention to fashion detail, preferred the quieter and more controlled ambience of the salons. He collaborated with Diderot on the early volumes of the *Encyclopédie,* and his major contribution was the *Preliminary Discourse,* a lengthy treatise (forty-eight thousand words) that has sometimes been seen as the single most lucid and competent summary of European Enlightenment thought in the entire eighteenth century. The controversy with Rousseau and the authorities over the article Geneva (1758–59) took its toll on him, however, and he disengaged from the project shortly thereafter. In this volume, d'Alembert's contribution, in addition to Geneva itself, is the eulogy for the recently deceased Montesquieu, which reveals his skill at editorial selection and concise summation and which provides one picture of how Montesquieu's *Spirit of the Laws* tended to be viewed in the years after its appearance.

Antoine Gaspard Boucher d'Argis, 1708–91 (4,268 articles). Born in Paris, where his father was a lawyer, Boucher d'Argis was admitted to prac-

Among the standard sources of information on this subject are John Lough, *The Contributors to the "Encyclopedie"* (London: Grant & Cutler, 1973), and especially Frank A. Kafker and Serena L. Kafker, *The Encyclopedists as Individuals: A Biographical Dictionary of the Authors of the "Encyclopédie,"* Studies on Voltaire and the Eighteenth Century 257 (Oxford: Voltaire Foundation, 1988). The number of articles refers to the author's total contribution to the *Encyclopédie.*

tice in 1727. He wrote several works on rural and property law from 1738 to 1749 and in 1753 received the post of councillor in the sovereign court of Dombes, which conferred hereditary nobility. That same year he became the legal expert on the *Encyclopédie*, subsequently becoming one of its most prolific contributors. Though not known for particularly reformist proclivities, he continued to write for Diderot's work even after it was officially banned in 1758, and he participated in the case of the widow Calas after the execution of her husband in the 1760s. In 1767 he became an alderman of Paris, but afterwards, little is known about his activities, including during the early part of the French Revolution. His son was an active royalist in the Revolution and was executed in 1794.

Nicolas Antoine Boulanger, 1722–59 (5 articles). Born in Paris into a mercantile family, he was sent to the Jansenist *collège* (secondary school) of Beauvais for his studies, where he was more interested in mathematics and architecture than in Latin. He worked in the army as a private engineer during the War of the Austrian Succession (1743–44) and entered the *ponts et chaussées* (roads and bridges) corps in 1745. He began to correspond with naturalists such as Buffon and to develop non-Biblical theories of early history. Named subengineer in 1749, he was assigned to the Paris district in 1751. He stopped working due to illness in 1758, when he moved in with his friend Helvétius, whose recently published *De l'Esprit* had triggered controversy. The few published writings in his lifetime included much of the long *Encyclopédie* article Déluge (Flood) as well as the article Corvée (Forced labor), which called for reform rather than abolition of the practice, but which still displeased his superiors.

His ambitious unfinished manuscript on the early universal flood and how it shaped human religions and political systems up to modern times was published as *Recherches sur l'origine du despotisme oriental* [Research on the origins of Oriental despotism] (1761) and *Antiquité dévoilée par ses usages* [Antiquity unmasked by its customs] (1765) by d'Holbach and his friends, who were impressed with Boulanger's thought. The latter part was translated into English by John Wilkes, a popular journalist and political figure. The philosophe André Morellet said of him, "Despite all his interest in his (often extravagant) discoveries, he was not at all put off by those who did not accept them; he was the first to laugh at a risky or foolish conjecture he had made the night before, and when he communicated with me, he found it good that I laughed my head off at it."[1]

Etienne Noël Damilaville, 1723–68 (3 articles). He was born, it seems, in a Norman village. His brother was a noble controller of the *vingtième* (5 percent) tax, but the rest of his family life is obscure. He received an uneven education before joining the army during the War of the Austrian Succession as a member of the king's elite cavalry (the *gardes du corps*). Afterward followed a stint as a lawyer in Paris, leading to a position with the controller-general of finance. By 1755 he was a high official (*premier commis*) administering the *vingtième* tax himself, giving him insight into the subject of the long article that concludes our volume.

Around 1760 he came to know both Diderot and Voltaire and used his government position to advance their interests—distributing their illegal works, arranging mail service, supplying them with information. Both *philosophes* came to regard his talents highly. Voltaire called him a "soul of bronze—equally tender and solid for his friends," and he became a trusted member of Diderot's social circle. With d'Alembert gone by that time, moreover, Damilaville's eager contributions to the *Encyclopédie,* both as writer and as editorial collaborator, were most welcome. On the other hand, d'Holbach, referring to some of his more speculative opinions, called him "philosophy's flycatcher," and Grimm saw him as dyspeptic and socially awkward. He had a reputation for religious heterodoxy, which may have affected his career advancement. For example, he was said to have attempted to convert Voltaire to atheism. Aside from his two long and important articles for the dictionary, Damilaville wrote little, though he was apparently preparing to do more writing when he retired in 1768, shortly before falling ill and dying at the age of forty-five.

Alexandre Deleyre, 1726–97 (2 articles). Born in Portets, near Bordeaux, into a longtime local family of merchants and professionals, Deleyre entered the Jesuit order at age fourteen, failed to find contentment,

1. See Jacques Proust, *Diderot et "l'Encyclopédie"* (Paris: Albin Michel, 1995), 518n39.

and left both the order and his faith at age twenty-two. After legal studies, he pursued a literary career with the help of his fellow Bordelais Montesquieu, moving to Paris in 1750, where he met Rousseau and, through him, Diderot and d'Alembert. In the 1750s, he edited anthologies of the works of Francis Bacon and of Montesquieu and contributed anonymously to a running polemic against the anti-Encyclopedist journalist Elie Fréron. He then pursued work in journalism, first with the *Journal étranger* (as editor), after with the *Journal encyclopédique* and the *Supplément aux journaux des savants et de Trévoux*—all of them open to religious and political reform.

He left journalism in 1760 and spent eight years as a tutor to the prince of Parma, where his supervisor was Etienne de Bonnot, abbé de Condillac. The latter rejected the English history textbook that he had asked Deleyre to prepare, because of its excessively favorable treatment of Cromwell. Returning to Paris in 1768, Deleyre wrote a work on northern European geography and exploration and contributed most of volume 7, book 19, of abbé Raynal's *History of the two Indies* (1774). In that work, he defended a flexible approach toward political regimes with a marked preference for English limited government. In a 1772 will, moreover, he wrote that "France . . . has fallen because of moral corruption under the yoke of despotism."

During the Revolution, he was the mayor of Portets for a time and helped draft the *cahier* for the Third Estate at the electoral assembly of the Bordeaux region. He was elected to the Convention from the Gironde in 1792 and voted for the king's execution in January 1793. Educational reform was his most frequent area of interest. When the Convention was assaulted by rioters on March 20, 1795, he reportedly said, "I am a representative of the people, I must die at my post."

Denis Diderot, 1713–84 (5,394 articles). Born in Langres, in eastern France, into a cutler's family, Diderot at first took his religion very seriously, attending perhaps both a Jansenist and a Jesuit secondary school in Paris. When a religious life did not work out, he drifted toward a bohemian life of letters in Paris. In the 1740s, he lived mainly by translating several works, the most important of which was the Earl of Shaftesbury's *Inquiry Concerning Virtue and Merit* (1745), a seminal work of sentimentalist moral theory cited several times in the present collection. By this time, he had developed a heterodox philosophy that included elements of fatalism, materialism, and at least deism if not atheism. One of his works, *Letter on the Blind* (1749), earned him a stay in the prison at Vincennes, where he was famously visited by Rousseau.[2] His selection as the editor of the *Encyclopédie* in 1747, which brought an end to his near-poverty, probably grew out of his previous associations with the publishers in his translation work.

Diderot quickly became the driving force behind the project as writer, editor, propagandist, and recruiter of collaborators. There formed around him a whole social network that contemporaries called the "encyclopedic party," and that helped make the *Encyclopédie* unique among eighteenth-century reference works. Also unique was the extensive interest shown by Diderot and his collaborators in the world of the arts and trades, reflected in the eleven volumes of plates that appeared from 1761 to 1772, as well as in some of the articles on economic policy anthologized here.

In between his editorial duties, Diderot wrote voluminously, including plays in a new tradition of *drame bourgeois* or "bourgeois drama" that he promoted—*Le Fils naturel* [The natural son] (1757) and *Le Père de famille* [The father of the family] (1758); regular art criticism in *Les Salons* for Grimm's journal *Correspondance littéraire* starting around 1760; and numerous works that he chose not to publish in his lifetime, three of which have done the most to secure his later reputation as a writer, namely, *Rameau's Nephew* (begun in 1761), *D'Alembert's Dream* (1769), and *Supplement to the voyage of Bougainville* (1772). He received a pension from the Russian Empress Catherine II the Great, who bought his library in 1765. He supported the Physiocrats for a long time but sided with Galiani in the latter's polemic with them in 1769 and afterward.

After the last plates for the *Encyclopédie* were published in 1772, Diderot traveled in 1773 to Russia, where he advised Empress Catherine on her new reform program. "There is no true sovereign except the nation," he wrote; "there can be no true legislator except the people." Catherine

2. Rousseau claims in his autobiography that the inspiration for his First Discourse appeared to him en route to this visit.

was unhappy and may have destroyed her copy of the work.[3] During the American Revolution, Diderot supported the colonists. It is as difficult to summarize Diderot's political views as it is that of the dictionary that he edited, partly because his public statements were clearly affected by the experience of imprisonment and by his running tension with French religious and political authorities. These problems are both reflected and generated by important articles of his such as POLITICAL AUTHORITY and NATURAL RIGHT in this volume.

JOACHIM FAIGUET DE VILLENEUVE, 1703–80? (15 articles). Not much is known about his early life except that he hailed from a Breton family of businessmen and was himself a pig merchant in Paris for a period of time. In 1748 he was director of a boarding school in Paris, and in 1756 he bought a government office as treasurer in the finance bureau in Châlons, a position that offered the prospect of nobility. It is not clear how he came to write for the *Encyclopédie;* he does not appear to have been a friend of either Diderot or d'Alembert. It would seem that his collaboration ended with the government's suppression of the project in early 1759, since his last article, USURY, although appearing in 1765, was composed in 1758.

In the following decade, he took his writing interests to a different arena, writing the following five books: *Discours d'un bon citoyen sur les moyens de multiplier les forces de l'Etat et d'augmenter la population* [Discourse of a good citizen on the means of multiplying the strength of the State and increasing population] (1760); *L'Econome politique* [The political Steward] (1763); *Légitimité de l'usure légale* [Legitimacy of legal usury] (1770); *Mémoires politiques sur la conduite des finances et sur d'autres objets intéressans* [Political memoirs on the management of finances and other interesting topics] (1770); and *L'Utile emploi des religieux et des communalistes, ou Mémoire politique à l'avantage des habitans de la Campagne* [The Useful employment of the religious and villagers, or political Memoir for the benefit of the inhabitants of the Countryside] (1770).

3. "Observations on the Instruction of the Empress of Russia to the Deputies for the Making of the Laws," in Denis Diderot, *Political Writings,* ed. and trans. John Hope Mason and Robert Wokler (Cambridge: Cambridge University Press, 1992), 78, 81.

All of these works contain the forthright approach to the reform of French social, economic, and political institutions—redolent of the long reformist career of the abbé St. Pierre (1658–1743)—that are found in the two articles reproduced in this anthology, MASTERSHIPS and SAVINGS.

FRANÇOIS VÉRON DE FORBONNAIS, 1722–1800 (10 articles). From an old and distinguished cloth-making family in Le Mans, Forbonnais (or Fortbonnais) attended a Jansenist secondary school in Paris before joining the family business, traveling to Spain, Italy, and elsewhere as an agent. In his twenties he pursued a career in letters, writing poems, tragedies, and in 1750 a critical study of Montesquieu's *Spirit of the Laws.* When Vincent de Gournay, another distinguished merchant, became royal intendant of commerce in 1751, Forbonnais became a member of his circle and found his niche, becoming perhaps the leading writer on economic matters in the 1750s before the Physiocrats emerged to prominence. He was the author of *Considérations sur les finances d'Espagne* [Considerations on Spanish finances] (1753); *Recherches et considerations sur les finances de France depuis l'année 1595 jusqu'à l'année 1721* [Studies and considerations on French finances from the year 1595 to the year 1721] (1758), which was widely cited; and *Elémens du commerce* [Elements of commerce] (1754), partly drawn from his *Encyclopédie* articles, which was one of the leading statements of economic theory available at that time.[4]

For unknown reasons, Forbonnais stopped writing for the *Encyclopédie* with volume 5, in 1755, and in the late 1750s, he had a falling out with Diderot and Grimm. By then he was flirting with a career in government service, becoming an important adviser to the controller-general Silhouette in 1759 and achieving a reputation for both probity and prickliness. But in the end, he did more in the coming years as an informal adviser than as the holder of specific offices. After 1759 he mainly returned to business, investing in glass manufacture and becoming a gentleman farmer. In 1762 he established a model farm based on renunciation of his personal tax exemption and imposition of taxes on the basis of land possession rather

4. See Joseph A. Schumpeter, *A History of Economic Analysis,* ed. Elizabeth Boody Schumpeter (New York: Oxford University Press, 1954), chap. 3, 174, for one account.

than income, thereby illustrating a reformist theme discussed in Quesnay's article CEREALS and in Damilaville's FIVE PERCENT TAX in this volume. In 1763 he purchased a judgeship in the Parlement of Metz, which led to nobility after twenty years.

Forbonnais was active during the Revolution as a Third Estate deputy, as a supporter of reforms in government finances, and as a royalist until the summer of 1792, at which time he retreated from the scene, calling Robespierre's republic a "sanguinary tyranny." He died in March 1800, optimistic at the prospect of Napoleon's rule.

PAUL-HENRI THIRY, BARON D'HOLBACH, 1723–89 (414 articles). Born Paul Heinrich Dietrich, d'Holbach moved from his native Palatinate, a region close to Lorraine and influenced by French culture, to Paris at the age of twelve. In the 1740s, he studied law in Leiden, returning to Paris to become a lawyer (*avocat*) and a naturalized French subject in 1749. He received family property in 1750, was conferred the title of baron of the Holy Roman Empire in 1753 upon the death of his uncle, and bought a nobility-conferring office, *secrétaire du roi*, in 1755; he also had real estate in France and Holland. By the end of the 1750s, he was a wealthy man.

In the middle of that decade, he began to host his salon, one of the most brilliant and sought-after in Paris, which met every Thursday and Sunday. Regulars included Diderot, Grimm, Morellet, Saint-Lambert, Chastellux, Galiani, Helvétius, and Raynal. Less-regular participants included d'Alembert, Boulanger, Damilaville, Jaucourt, Rousseau, Turgot, and many others.

His intellectual interests were complex and wide-ranging. His translations of German chemical work into French helped prepare the way for Lavoisier's breakthroughs in the 1770s. Probably recruited by his friend Diderot into the *Encyclopédie,* he wrote voluminously, though often anonymously, for it, accelerating his production after the government crackdown of March 1759. At first he wrote on science and German culture, then increasingly on political and religious matters. From 1766 until 1776, he poured out a number of anonymous or pseudonymous works on these controversial topics: *Le Christianisme dévoilé* [Christianity unmasked] (1766); *Théologie portative* [Portable theology] (1767); *La Contagion sacrée*

[The Sacred contagion] (1768); *Système de la nature* (1769); *La Politique naturelle* (1773); *Système sociale* (1773); *Ethocratie, ou le gouvernement fondé sur la morale* [Ethocracy: or Government founded on morality] (1776), and *La Morale universelle* [Universal morality] (1776). These works, on which he received help from Naigeon and perhaps others, marked him as a man of bold, indeed even atheistic views and wide-ranging criticism of current political regimes, leavened by a certain conservative skepticism about the alternatives. His article REPRESENTATIVES, included in this volume, is one of the most important sustained statements of political theory in our compendium.

His writing stopped in 1776; it is not clear what he thought of the American Revolution or the French pre-Revolution. He died just months before the French Revolution began in earnest.

LOUIS, CHEVALIER DE JAUCOURT, 1704–80 (17,288 articles). Author of no fewer than forty-three of the eighty-one articles translated here, Louis de Jaucourt was born in Paris on September 26, 1704, into a family of traditional sword nobility of Huguenot (Calvinist) background. Jaucourt's father had officially reconverted to Catholicism but secretly raised his family in the old faith. Though there is some disagreement about how active the family's Protestant professions were by the eighteenth century, there is little doubt that the Jaucourts were well connected in international Protestant circles and that Louis's education profited from these connections. At the age of eight, he was sent to Geneva, where he stayed with an aunt and a Protestant uncle and received an education at the Academy of Geneva (1719) and at the University of Geneva. By this time, he could speak several modern European languages.

In 1727 he went to London, where his sister had married John Carmichael, a Scottish gentleman. It seems that he briefly entertained the prospect of becoming a Calvinist pastor, but his parents counseled strongly against it, and his religious fervor seems to have waned precipitously while in the eclectic and skeptical ambience of his English friends. Most of the rest of his life he appears to have spent as a kind of deist. One of his best friends from Geneva, Theodore Tronchin, joined him both in abandoning plans for a pastoral vocation and in deciding to study medicine instead, a profession almost as disappointing to the Jaucourt family as the ministry.

To pursue this education he went to Holland, studying in Leiden under the great Hermann Boerhaave, whom he praised in some of his *Encyclopédie* articles. While there, he also fell in with some of the remarkable community of émigré Protestant scholars of the period. When the *Bibliothèque raisonnée* was founded in 1728, he collaborated on it with Jean Barbeyrac, the editor and translator of the natural-law classics of Pufendorf and Grotius, and remained associated with the project until 1740. In 1734, under his assumed academic name L. de Neufville, he appended a well-regarded biography of Leibniz to his edition of *Essais de Théodicée* [Essays on Theodicy]. He was already on cordial terms with Voltaire in the 1730s and was elected to the Academy of Bordeaux in 1747, thanks partly to Montesquieu's influence as well as to his own scientific experiments. By the end of his travels through Geneva, England, and Holland, he returned to France with a worldview not of a nobleman from Catholic France but of a Protestant, middle-class burgher with an indelible sympathy for the cause of civil and political liberty that each of these places had in its own way featured.

His great ambition in this pre-Encyclopedic phase was to make an international name as the leading expert on medical science in Europe. Toward this end, he worked for the better part of ten years, starting around 1740, on the compilation of a six-volume *lexicon medicum universale*. In June 1750 he concluded the arrangements with his Amsterdam publisher. But when he sent the only copy of the manuscript to the publisher by boat, sometime in late 1750 or early 1751, the boat capsized and the manuscript was lost forever.

Looking for alternatives after losing a decade of labor, he noticed the advertisement for contributors to the new project of Diderot and d'Alembert, sent in a few sample articles to Le Breton, the publisher, and the collaboration, announced in the third volume (1753), was begun. Although he began with topics close to his specialties in botany and natural history, he gradually expanded his range, using his Dutch gazetteer experience to turn out competent if not sparkling entries on every kind of topic.

A respected scholar with elections to the royal academies of Bordeaux, Sweden, and Berlin, and to London's Royal Society, Jaucourt was viewed by some as a mere compiler. Others, such as Voltaire, admired his work, and it is doubtful that the *Encyclopédie* had a more stalwart friend or defender. Jaucourt sold his house (to the publisher) to pay for his small staff of secretaries. In a letter to Sophie Volland, Diderot wrote of Jaucourt that "this man has for six or seven years been in the middle of four or five secretaries—reading, dictating, working thirteen to fourteen hours a day, and that situation has not yet bored him."[5] When Diderot announced to him the impending conclusion of the work, Jaucourt is reported to have responded with a long face of dismay. It is at least clear that he wrote nothing after the completion of the project in 1765 until his death, in 1780, after having turned out nearly a quarter of all the articles—most of them signed, and totaling nearly five million words—in Diderot's dictionary.

ABBÉ EDME-FRANÇOIS MALLET, 1713–55 (1,925 articles). Born in Melun to a family of pewterers, Mallet received early instruction from a local priest before being sent to a Barnabite secondary school in Montargis. He then pursued his studies in Paris, completing his doctorate in theology in 1742. There followed stints as a tutor (1742–44) and as a parish priest in a small church near Melun. During this period, he wrote two works, *Principes pour la lecture des poëtes* [Principles for reading the poets] (1745) and *Essai sur l'étude des belles-lettres* [Essay on the study of literature] (1747), which promote classical French aesthetic theory and express skepticism about Locke's sensationalist philosophy of knowledge as well as about the influence of English letters more generally.

In 1751 he was appointed to a chair of theology at the University of Paris, where he wrote two works on oratory, a work on Dutch diplomacy under Louis XIV and a translation of an Italian work on the French religious wars—in which he defended the assassination of the Duke of Guise but condemned the St. Bartholomew's Day massacre.

The nearly two thousand articles that he wrote for the *Encyclopédie* in the few years of collaboration allotted to him before his untimely death included large numbers on commerce (five hundred or so, mostly com-

5. Denis Diderot to Sophie Volland, November 10, 1760, in *Diderot: Œuvres*, ed. Laurent Versini, vol. 5, *Correspondence* (Paris: Robert Laffont, 1994–97), 316.

pilations from earlier reference works) and even more on theology and religion, where his erudition was more fruitful. His views are difficult to summarize. He affirmed the existence of Hell, sided with the Jesuits against the Jansenists over the bull *Unigenitus* (in an article suppressed by Malesherbes, the book trade director), and defended the Revocation of the Edict of Nantes by Louis XIV (in an unpublished draft of the article PACIFICATION). On the other hand, he denied rational proof of eternal punishment, opposed the Sorbonne's condemnation of the controversial thesis by abbé de Prades (which precipitated the first government censorship of the *Encyclopédie*), and won the trust of d'Alembert, whose eulogy in volume 6 depicts him as a fine scholar, a mild and modest man, and an "enemy of persecution."

FRANÇOIS QUESNAY, 1694–1774 (3 articles). The founder of the Physiocratic school of economists, Quesnay was born into a farming family in Normandy. Marrying a grocer's daughter in 1717, he practiced as a master surgeon in Mantes from 1718 to 1734, where he became a civic leader. The Duke of Villeroy and the first surgeon to the king, La Peyronie, learned about him and brought him to Paris, making him Villeroy's personal surgeon and heaping honors and offices on him. He became an active participant in the surgeons' continuing attempt to enhance their status relative to the physicians. One of his patients, the Countess d'Estrades, recommended him to Madame de Pompadour, who made him a resident royal physician in 1749. From there, he became a trusted confidant at court as well as a helpful agent for Diderot, Voltaire, Marmontel, and other men of letters in their dealings with the government.

His chief importance lay in his development of the school of theory that came to be known as Physiocracy. From 1758 until about 1770, he was the acknowledged master of this school, combining the most robust free-market theorizing of the period with a resolutely non-Montesquieuan political model the school called "legal despotism." The Physiocrats were supported by the vigorous and concerted writing and journalistic efforts of such talented figures as Pierre-Samuel Du Pont de Nemours, Pierre-Paul Le Mercier de La Rivière, abbé Nicolas Baudeau, and the Marquis de Mirabeau. Diderot himself generally supported the school through the 1760s, when the leading agenda item was complete freedom for the grain trade, a proposal partially adopted by the French government in 1763 and 1764. By the time of abbé Galiani's stinging parody of the rigid dogmatism and universalism of the school in his *Dialogues on the grain trade* (1770), with its appeal for a more Montesquieuan flexibility in treating the different liberty-interests of different regimes, Diderot, like many others, had had second thoughts about the Physiocrats.

For the *Encyclopédie,* Quesnay wrote an important anonymous article, EVIDENCE, as well as two lengthy entries on economic topics, CEREALS and FERMIERS (Farmers), which were early precursors of his Physiocratic doctrine, appearing as they did a few years before the formation of the school. By the time of the government crackdown in 1759, Quesnay, who had always been cautious about his association with the Encyclopedists because of his court position, was asking d'Alembert to withdraw his manuscripts for HOMMES (Men), IMPÔTS (Taxes), and INTÉRÊT DE L'ARGENT (Interest Rates), and his collaboration ceased. But many of the articles that appeared on economic topics in the *Encyclopédie* bore the imprint of his influence, including Damilaville's FIVE PERCENT TAX.

JEAN-FRANÇOIS, MARQUIS DE SAINT-LAMBERT, 1716–1803 (17 articles). The future poet was born in Nancy into a poor and obscure noble family. After a Jesuit education, he served in the infantry and for the king of Poland. Stationed at Lunéville, he became acquainted with Voltaire, fell in love with the latter's mistress Emilie du Châtelet, and fathered a child with her. When she died in childbirth (1749), he gained notoriety and moved to Paris, where his poetry began to attract attention. Voltaire described his now-obscure *Les Saisons,* an idyll to rural life that urged noblemen to return to their country estates and revitalize the countryside, as "the only work in our age that will make it into posterity." In the Seven Years' War, he became a colonel in the French army, though an attack of paralysis led him to leave the military for good in 1758 and instead pursue a life of letters.

He was friendly with the *Encyclopédie* circle, including Diderot, Mme. Geoffrin, d'Holbach, Grimm, Mme. d'Epinay, and, especially, Mme. d'Houdetot, with whom he had an affair celebrated for its dignity and fidelity until his death nearly half a century later. His association with the

Encyclopédie project began in 1756 with volume 6, and he wrote at least sixteen articles, all anonymous, most on political and philosophical subjects. His essay LUXURY, which was published as a separate tract immediately after its appearance in Diderot's dictionary (1765), became one of the most influential statements on that popular theme before the Revolution.[6]

His plays and especially his highly scientific and philosophic poetry led to his selection by the Académie Française in 1770, where he became a force. His *Catéchisme universel*, a lengthy work on the origins and nature of human morality, won the grand prize for *morale* at the Institut de France in 1810. Saint-Lambert died in 1803.

ANNE-ROBERT-JACQUES TURGOT, Baron of Aulne, 1727–81 (5 articles). Turgot hailed from one of France's oldest and most prestigious families. Born in Paris, he distinguished himself at the Sorbonne and became one of the leading protegés of the liberal controller-general Vincent de Gournay. His first publication, a translation of part of the Englishman Josiah Tucker's *Reflections on the expediency of a law for the naturalization of foreign Protestants* (1755), grew out of that association. In the early 1750s he drafted a number of highly original works on the historical evolution of the human mind and on economic development among other topics, and soon acquired the reputation as a polymath genius. By 1755 he was collaborating with the *Encyclopédie*.

His articles, all anonymous, were few but important. His essay ETYMOLOGY is a sophisticated application of recent epistemology to the question of the origins and history of language. EXISTENCE is a searching critique of Cartesian metaphysics, and EXPANSIBILITY is a precursor of Lavoisier's work on the chemical properties of air. He also wrote FOIRE (Fairs), on the marketplaces of old Europe. He dissociated himself from Diderot's project in the aftermath of the controversy of 1758 that led to its temporary suppression, perhaps for a variety of reasons: a prudent regard for his government position, a concern that the enterprise was becoming dogmatic,

6. It can be found not in this book, but in Henry C. Clark, ed., *Commerce, Culture, and Liberty: Readings on Capitalism Before Adam Smith* (Indianapolis: Liberty Fund, 2003), 477–501.

and the defection of d'Alembert, who had been his main friend and contact there.

In 1761, he became provincial intendant for Limousin, where he remained for thirteen years, developing a reputation for reformist vigor and effectiveness in an undynamic province. During that period, he became the leading exponent of free trade in grain, though his relations with the Physiocratic school usually associated with that policy were cool. He also found time for some writing, including his *Reflections on the formation and distribution of wealth* (1766), a short tract that was one of the most far-reaching works in economic theory before Adam Smith.[7] Smith himself knew and greatly respected Turgot's work.

In 1774 he was elevated to controller-general of France, where he attempted to implement on a national scale the reforms he had reflected on, described, and attempted locally for many years. His far-reaching changes such as the abolition of the guilds and of *corvée* (compulsory labor) on public roads met with a backlash, and he was disgraced and forced from office nineteen months later in early 1776, after which he mainly ceased both his writing and his government service. One exception is a long 1778 letter he wrote to the English philosopher Richard Price in which he praised the new American republic as "the hope of the human race." "It should give the example," he continued, "of political freedom, religious freedom, and freedom of commerce and industry. The asylum that it offers to the oppressed of all nations should console the earth."[8] But he also warned against the lack of centralization in the Articles of Confederation and against the comfort given to vested interests in the system of checks and balances built into each of the states, prompting John Adams to write three volumes in refutation a few years later (*A Defence of the Constitutions of Government*, 1787–88). He died in 1781.

7. See the lengthy excerpt in Clark, *Commerce*, 518–63.

8. Translation in R. R. Palmer, "Turgot: Paragon of the Continental Enlightenment," *Journal of Law and Economics* 19 (October 1976): 619. The original French version of the letter can be found in *Œuvres de Turgot et documents le concernant*, ed. Gustave Schelle, 5 vols. (Paris: Alcan, 1913–23), 5: 532–40.

A Note on the Text

The articles in this volume are drawn from the original twenty-eight-volume edition, the so-called first Paris folio, whose full title was *Encyclopédie, ou Dictionnaire raisonné des sciences, des arts et des métiers, par une Société de gens de lettres.* It was edited by Denis Diderot and Jean Le Rond d'Alembert and published in Paris, in 1751–72, by Briasson, David, Le Breton, Durand. The eleven volumes of plates were produced from 1762 to 1772, while the seventeen volumes of text appeared from 1751 to 1765. All citations are from this edition, which is accessible online from the ARTFL database (Project for American and French Research on the Treasury of the French Language), a collaborative effort of the University of Chicago and the Centre National de la Recherche Scientifique (CNRS), at http://encyclopedie.uchicago.edu. That website contains both a scanned electronic version of each entry and image links to a photographic reproduction of every page in the work.

The entries in this collection are arranged in alphabetical order by their original French titles. This has the advantage of presenting them in the chronological order in which they appeared off the press in the first edition.

Where it seemed necessary or appropriate, an entry that we have translated is introduced by a brief editorial note in italics. Within the text of an item that we have translated, we have used brackets for clarification, though sparingly. For the fifteen entries translated in whole or in part by others, we use brackets to indicate where we have completed the translation (if applicable). Any note that has been added to those offered by the original editor is followed by the initials HC. The 1751 *Encyclopédie* did not contain a great many footnotes; virtually all notes in the present volume are either by the present editor or by the translator of the article, and the few exceptions are clearly marked.

In using the 1751–65 edition, the aim has been to provide modern readers with as much of the experience of their eighteenth-century counterparts as possible. Toward that end, many of the features of the original publication have been duplicated. Perhaps the most important of these concerns the identification of contributors. Those authors who agreed to have identifying markers alongside their entries did so in various ways. In the early volumes, for example, there was a systematic effort to place an asterisk before the title of any article by Diderot, a practice adopted in this edition. There are other articles missing the asterisk but known to be by Diderot. For his part, Jaucourt's articles are almost always signed, though in inconsistent ways: sometimes his name appears in full, other times only his initials in parentheses appear (*D. J.*), the latter being a method also deployed by Véron de Forbonnais (*M.* V.D.F.). For other authors, a one-letter code was developed; among those included in *Encyclopedic Liberty* are Boucher d'Argis (A), Mallet (G), and d'Alembert himself (O). Italics and capital letters are often used to set off the author identifications at the end of articles, and we follow that practice as well as the practice of citing article titles themselves in capital letters.

Because one of the pleasures of reading the *Encyclopédie* is to observe the subtle ways in which the editors and their collaborators were continually trying to outwit the censors, and because some authors were more willing to identify themselves to the public than others, we have chosen to preserve as much of this original apparatus as possible.

Translators' Note

Schleiermacher once wrote, "Either the translator leaves the author in peace, as much as possible, and moves the reader towards him; or he leaves the reader in peace, as much as possible, and moves the author towards him."[1] Since the intended audience for the *Encyclopédie* was, in eighteenth-century parlance, mainly *mondain* (worldly) rather than narrowly *érudit* (learned), and since the intended readership for Liberty Fund editions is similar, we have generally made the authors do the moving in our translation.

Thus, we have often simplified syntax and broken up long sentences rather than try to duplicate the authorial eccentricities of the contributors. Within these constraints, we attempt to be as editorially unobtrusive and unambiguous as possible. On those occasions where alternative interpretations have been inescapable, we have indicated this in the footnotes. Because a significant share of the content of the entries was derived more or less directly from such earlier authors as Locke and Montesquieu, and because the original project was conceived as a reference work, the number of such ambiguous passages is relatively small.

On the other hand, our volume represents the original contributions of at least thirteen French authors (one entry remaining anonymous), and these authors do present differences in style along with corresponding translation problems. The Chevalier de Jaucourt, author of by far the largest number of our selections, writes in a fairly plain and direct style that poses relatively few problems. That is more or less true of other authors too, such as Boucher d'Argis and Forbonnais. Faiguet de Villeneuve writes in a pugnaciously chatty prose that is also mostly free of mystery. But other

1. Friedrich Schleiermacher, "On the Different Methods of Translating," in *Translating Literature: The German Tradition from Luther to Rosenzweig,* ed. André Lefevere (Assen: Van Gorcum, 1977), 74.

writers are not so straightforward. Diderot himself was an inveterate ironist whose multiple tonalities are often elusive for the unwary translator. Saint-Lambert, a celebrated poet in his own time, has a sometimes mannered style calling for special adjustments. Boulanger, author of one of our longer titles (POLITICAL ECONOMY), writes in a ponderous French full of portentous abstractions and labored transitions. Damilaville, who penned the two lengthiest articles in our collection (POPULATION and FIVE PERCENT TAX), was an ungainly stylist whose many pronouns and awkwardly structured sentences create a number of ambiguities. All told, however, the differences among these styles are somewhat greater in the original French than in our translations.

Foreign-language titles of works referred to by the contributors in text or notes have been translated into English where cognates did not make the translation obvious.

The French texts that we used contain a number of terms and concepts that pose special translation problems. Some of the more problematic and recurring cases are as follows:

commerce. If the context is economic, "trade" or "commerce," although sometimes the term seems to include all productive nonagricultural activity; see INTENDANTS for this meaning. In French, there is frequently a social meaning as well, as in "the commerce between the sexes" or "the commerce among men"; see MANNERS for this latter connotation.

droit. Usually translated as "law." Depending on the context, it can also mean "a right" (as in NATURAL RIGHT), "a tax," "a tariff," "a duty," "a fee." As a moral or political adjective, the word can mean "what is right or just." We often translate it as "law," as in "divine law," "civil law," "natural law," "canon law," or "the law of nations." See *loi,* below, for a different set of connotations.

économie. Meaning "frugality," "household economy," "management of resources," the term was not used in our modern sense as a description of a distinct field of study (economics), or of the sum total of productive activity in a given society.

état. The "regime" or "government" when used politically, and is usually capitalized in our volume. Sometimes, and notably in Damilaville's FIVE

PERCENT TAX, the word is deliberately used to encompass the whole collectivity of the society, so it does not mark as clear a distinction between government and governed as later generations would do. Juridically, the term means "estate" as in the phrase *états généraux* (Estates General), which designates the official hierarchy of French society at the time of writing; see d'Holbach's REPRESENTATIVES for this usage. Socially, the term tends to mean "status" or "condition."

franchise. Generally "exemption," "privilege," or "immunity," it can also mean "freedom." When referring to personal qualities, it can mean "openness," "candor," or "sincerity." The term is used in SAVINGS, SLAVERY, HONOR, MASTERPIECES, and FIVE PERCENT TAX.

génie. Translated as "talent" in most cases. Its English cognate "genius" generally connotes a more extraordinary ability than its eighteenth-century equivalent tended to convey.[2]

les grands. Literally "the great." The word was usually applied to the nobility during this period. To avoid ambiguity, we have generally adopted "grandees" in spite of its somewhat archaic flavor.

industrie. Generally a moral rather than economic category in this period, meaning a quality such as "resourcefulness," "ingenuity," or "industriousness." Rarely does the term apply to manufacturing as a sector in our modern sense, and still less to factory industry, despite the fascination felt by Diderot and others for modern technology. We sometimes use the term "human industry" to avoid anachronism.

liberté. Normally "liberty," although the specific context sometimes seemed to make "freedom" more advisable. There is no real French equivalent to "freedom," although see *franchise*, above.

loi. Unlike *droit*, *loi*, translated as "law," has more consistently the connotation of a command or prohibition, either divine or human, as in our phrase "laying down the law," although it too broadened out metaphorically to include scientific regularities such as the "laws of motion."

2. For a fuller discussion, see Darrin M. McMahon, *Divine Fury: A History of Genius* (New York: Basic Books, 2013).

mœurs. "Manners," "morals" or "customs," depending on the context. Sometimes we use "mores" when all of these meanings seem to be included.

morale. Sometimes "morality" as a practical code, sometimes "morals" as a subject of study.

pays and *patrie. Pays* is a general term for any distinct territory, whether city or region or province or nation. *Patrie* can also refer to these geographically diverse entities, but since it always means "natal land," it emphasizes their human rather than their merely physical dimension and often carries a more emotional resonance. "Homeland" or "fatherland," which are often used to translate *patrie,* strike us as strained and awkward options for a mainly American readership. Accordingly, in this anthology "country" will usually be used for either *pays* or *patrie,* but to preserve the distinction between them, we capitalize "Country" to indicate *patrie* and leave it uncapitalized for *pays.*

police. If it refers to an entire state, "administration" or even "government"; "regulations" if it refers to a specific institution within a state. Culturally, it can mark off the broader difference between civilized and precivilized societies, so a general term such as "civilization" or "law and order" sometimes seems best. "Police" occurs frequently in our selections, appearing in no fewer than nineteen of our entries.

pouvoir; puissance. In *Synonymes françois* [French synonyms] (Paris: Houry, 1736), 449–55, cited by Diderot in his grammar article AUTORITÉ [Authority], abbé Gabriel Girard distinguished between the French words *pouvoir* and *puissance,* both of which would generally be translated as "power." *Puissance,* he suggested, refers to the combination of moral legitimacy (*autorité*) and force. It tends to be more abstract, impersonal, and inclusive than *pouvoir;* it is the word used to denote the branches of government—the executive, legislative, and judicial powers. *Pouvoir* on the other hand is exercised by subordinates; Diderot says it evokes fear rather than the grandeur evoked by *puissance* and that it arises from the personal attachment and connections between the subject and the holder of power.

It is not always clear how conscious the authors represented in this volume are of such niceties. In any case, the context is usually adequate to illuminate the intended inflection of meaning. For this reason, we have generally stuck with the English word "power" without further comment. There are occasions, however, such as in Boucher d'Argis's PUBLIC LAW and in Damilaville's FIVE PERCENT TAX, when the author's usage has been distinctive enough to merit our highlighting it.

qualité. Meaning "status," "title," "nobility," or "quality," depending on context.

république. Sometimes "government by the people" as with the cognate term "republic," but other times it is a generic category term, best conveyed by words like "polity" or "commonwealth." We have attempted to avoid confusion by not overusing the former option. As might be imagined, it appears frequently in our collection, in no fewer than thirty-one entries.

revenu. Either "private income" or "public revenue," depending on the context; the word appears in POLITICAL ARITHMETIC, FOUNDATION, GENEVA, CEREALS, ENGLISH PARLIAMENT, and RUTLAND.

revolution. Most often "revolution," although with different and more diffuse connotations before 1789, meaning more like "vicissitudes" or "transformations" than the willful upheaval of an entire social and political system. The word appears in DESPOTISM, EULOGY FOR PRESIDENT MONTESQUIEU, and POLITICAL ECONOMY.

sauvage. "Savage," which some authors distinguished carefully from "barbaric." See Jaucourt's entry SAVAGES.

société. Most often "society." In some contexts, "company"; in others, "association," where it has a more active connotation (see CITIZEN); and "firm" in a commercial context (see TRADING COMPANY for an example).

taille. Tax on persons or on property, depending upon the part of the country that is being referred to, but always a tax on the individual; translated in this edition with the cognate "taille." See CEREALS, TAX, and INTENDANTS for this term.

A Note on Currency

In the eighteenth century, the French pound (or *franc,* an older term still used for accounting purposes in the eighteenth century) was equal to twenty sols or sous, and a sol or sou was equal to twelve *deniers* (from L., *denarius*). On the high end, an *écu,* translated either as "silver crown" (for the recent period) or as "gold crown," was the equivalent of three French pounds and a gold *louis* was worth twenty-four pounds. In England, one pound sterling was twenty shillings and one shilling equaled twelve pence. As a rough measure of cost of living, a Parisian construction worker in the middle of the eighteenth century would typically make about fifteen to twenty sous per day, or a very few hundred French pounds per year.[1]

1. See Jan de Vries, *The Economy of Europe in an Age of Crisis, 1600–1750* (Cambridge: Cambridge University Press, 1976), 186.

Acknowledgments

This project was initiated during the academic year 2005–6 while I was a visiting scholar at Liberty Fund in Indianapolis. Without the encouragement of that splendid organization, and the thoroughly agreeable surroundings they offered, the present volume would not have been possible.

My co-translator, Christine D. Henderson, and I have worked with the version of the *Encyclopédie* made available to the public by ARTFL (the Project for American and French Research on the Treasury of the French Language) on its website at the University of Chicago. I am especially grateful to Glenn Roe and Mark Olsen for their helpful and timely responses to my various inquiries over the years.

For a few of the entries, as noted on the copyright page, we have elected to profit from translations already posted to the University of Michigan's website *The Encyclopedia of Diderot and d'Alembert: Collaborative Translation Project* (http://quod.lib.umich.edu/d/did/). At the Michigan site itself, I owe thanks to Kevin Hawkins and Jennifer Popiel for answering many questions over the long development of this project.

Unless otherwise indicated, all translations of classical Greek and Latin texts are drawn with permission from the Loeb Classical Library, a registered trademark of the President and Fellows of Harvard College. For the other Latin passages, Kathy Alvis has kindly reviewed each text and offered her recommendations. I alone am responsible for all those translations. On those occasions where an author reproduces an approximation of the original Latin text, the translation is presented from the correct text unless otherwise indicated.

A number of individuals have encouraged this project over the years by making suggestions, answering inquiries, or reviewing some of our translations. It is a pleasure to acknowledge Keith M. Baker, David W. Carrithers,

Sterling Joseph Coleman, Aurelian Craiutu, Dan Edelstein, Andrew Jainchill, Erin Kidwell, Robert Kreiser, Thomas Martin, Noah McCormack, Sue Peabody, John Scott, and no doubt others whose names we omit out of negligence rather than malice. As usual, my wife, Kathleen Wine, has been a steady inspiration throughout the whole enterprise, sharing her expertise on the art of translation in innumerable ways.

My former employer, Canisius College, kindly granted me a sabbatical and generous release time during the long gestation of this volume. A visiting appointment at Clemson University, made possible by C. Bradley Thompson, was also helpful in the progress of this work. Since the summer of 2014, I have been able to finalize the editing in the friendly confines of the Political Economy Project at Dartmouth College, whose director Doug Irwin has been a welcome source of support.

The interlibrary loan services and technical support staffs of Canisius College, Dartmouth College, Liberty Fund, and Clemson University, as well as the rare-book librarians at the Rauner Library of Dartmouth College, have been unfailingly helpful from start to finish. At Dartmouth, I particularly single out for thanks Rebecca M. Torrey and Laura K. Graveline.

Finally, let me state what a pleasure it has been, as usual, to work with the expert and friendly staff of the Liberty Fund publication department. Colleen Watson, Patti Ordower, Madelaine Cooke, and Kate Mertes have shown patience beyond the call of duty in preparing the text and index. And my special thanks go to my co-translator Christine D. Henderson, whose professionalism and friendship have made this collaboration both instructive and altogether agreeable.

Henry C. Clark
Hanover, N.H.
December 2015

Volume 1
(1751)

The Divine Voice
(*Aius-Locutius*)

*AIUS-LOCUTIUS, *God of speech*, whom the Romans honored by this extraordinary name. As it is also necessary to hold one's tongue, they also had the god of silence. When the Gauls were about to invade Italy, a voice coming from the wood of Vesta was heard to cry out: "If you do not raise the walls of the city, it will be taken." This advice was disregarded. The Gauls arrived and Rome was taken. After their retreat, the oracle was recalled and an altar was raised for him under the name that we are discussing. A temple was then constructed in Rome at the very place where he had made himself heard for the first time. Cicero says in the second volume of his study *On Divination* that this god spoke when he was not known by anyone but kept quiet the moment he had a temple and altars. The god of speech became mute as soon as he was worshiped.[1] It is difficult to reconcile the singular veneration that the pagans had for their gods with the patience that they also had for the discourses of certain philosophers. Did the Christians whom they persecuted so much say anything stronger than we can read in Cicero? The books *On Divination* are merely irreligious treatises. But what an impression must have been made on the people by certain pieces of oratory in which the gods were constantly invoked and called forth to witness events, in which Olympian threats were recalled to mind—in short, where the very existence of the pagan deities was presupposed by orators who

"The Divine Voice" was translated by Stephen J. Gendzier in *Denis Diderot's "The Encyclopedia": Selections*, ed. and trans. Stephen J. Gendzier (New York: Harper and Row, 1967), 57–58, and is reprinted by permission of the translator.

This article can be found at 1:241 in the original edition of the *Encyclopédie*.

1. See Cicero, *De Divinatione* [*On Divination*], II.xxxii.69.—HC

had written a host of philosophical essays treating the gods and religion as mere fables! Can we not find the solution to all these difficulties in the scarcity of manuscripts in ancient times? In those days the people hardly read: they heard the discourses of their orators and these discourses were always filled with piety toward the gods, but they were ignorant of what the orator thought and wrote about them in the privacy of his own house. These works were available only to his friends. Since it will always be impossible to prevent men from thinking and writing, would it not be desirable to allow them to live among us as they did among the ancients? The works of incredulity are not to be feared, for they only affect the masses and the faith of simple people. Those who really think know what to believe; and a pamphlet will certainly not lead them off a path which they have carefully chosen and follow by preference. It is not by trivial and absurd reasoning that a philosopher can be persuaded to abandon his God. Impiety is therefore not to be feared except for those who let themselves be guided. But a way to reconcile the respect we owe to the faith of the masses and to public worship with freedom of thought, which is extremely desirable for the discovery of truth, and with public harmony and peace without which there cannot exist any happiness for either the philosopher or the people, would be to forbid all the works against the government and religion that are in the vernacular, to allow those people to publish who write in a scholarly language, and to prosecute only the translators thereof. It seems to me that if we deal with the situation in this way, the nonsense that is written by certain authors will not harm anyone. Moreover, this arrangement will permit the greatest amount of freedom that can be granted in an orderly society. Wherever this privilege is not enjoyed in a similar manner, the country will still be properly governed. But corruption will certainly exist in a society where this freedom becomes more extensive. This is the case, I believe, of the English and the Dutch: it seems that the people in these countries think that they are not free unless they can be unrestrained and write with impunity. [The following sentence is an erratum that Diderot placed in volume 3 of the *Encyclopedia*.] If what we say in this article does not appear to be true and offends people, although this was not our intention, then we refer them to the article Casuist where our thoughts are explained in a manner that should satisfy everyone.

Political Arithmetic (*Arithmétique Politique*)

William Petty, the late seventeenth-century Englishman on whom Diderot draws in this article, was himself working expressly within the empirical and inductive tradition of Francis Bacon, one of the patron saints of the Encyclopédie *as a whole.*[1] *For other quantitative political analysis in this volume, see* CEREALS, POPULATION, *and* FIVE PERCENT TAX. *A later article very similar to this and more directly derivative of Chambers's* Cyclopedia *appeared unsigned under the title* POLITIQUE ARITHMETIQUE *[Arithmetical Politics], 12:919–20.*

*POLITICAL ARITHMETIC is the kind whose purpose is research that would be useful for the art of governing peoples, such as research on the number of men who inhabit a country, the quantity of food they must consume, the work they may have, their life-expectancy, the fertility of the land, the incidence of shipwreck, etc. It is easy to imagine that from these discoveries and many others of the same nature, acquired by calculations based on well-confirmed tests, a skillful minister would derive countless results useful in the perfection of agriculture, commerce (internal as well as external), colonies, the circulation and employment of money, etc. But often ministers (I don't mean to speak without exception) think they do not need to go through arithmetical combinations and sequences. Many imagine themselves to be endowed with great natural genius, which exempts them

This article can be found at 1:678–80 in the original edition of the *Encyclopédie*.

1. On this connection, see Peter Buck, "Seventeenth-Century Political Arithmetic: Civil Strife and Vital Statistics," *Isis* 68 (March 1977): 67–84.

from such a slow and laborious process—besides which, the nature of affairs hardly ever permits or demands geometric precision. Nonetheless, if the nature of affairs demanded and allowed it, I have no doubt we would manage to convince ourselves that the political world, as well as the natural world, can in many ways be ordered by weight, number, and measure.

Lord Petty, an Englishman, is the first who published essays under this title. The first is on the multiplication of the human race and on the growth of the city of London—its extent, its phases, its causes and consequences. The second is on the houses, the inhabitants, deaths, and births in the city of Dublin. The third is a comparison of the city of London and the city of Paris. Lord Petty tries to prove that England's capital is overtaking that of France in all these ways. M. Auzout has attacked this essay with many objections, to which Lord Petty has offered responses.[2] The fourth aims to show that about three thousand sick people per year die in the Hotel-Dieu in Paris because of mismanagement. The fifth is divided into five parts: the first is in response to M. Auzout; the second contains the comparison of London and Paris on many points; the third estimates the number of parishioners in London's 134 parishes at 696,000. The fourth is an inquiry into the inhabitants of London, Paris, Amsterdam, Venice, Rome, Dublin, Bristol, and Rouen. The fifth has the same purpose, but with regard to Holland and the rest of the United Provinces. The sixth covers the extent and value of land, the people, houses, industry, economy, manufactures, commerce, fishing, artisans, sailors or seamen, land troops, public revenue, interest rates, taxes, profits, banks, companies, the value of men, the growth in the navy and in the armed forces; residences, locales, the construction of vessels, naval forces, etc., relative to all countries in general, but especially to England, Holland, Zeeland, and France.

This latter essay is addressed to the king, which is as much as to say that its conclusions are favorable to the English nation. It is the most important of all Lord Petty's essays. Nonetheless, it is very short if compared with the multitude and complexity of the topics. Lord Petty claims to have demon-

2. Sir William Petty (1623–87), *Five Essays in Political Arithmetick* (London: Mortlock, 1687; repr. 1699), printed in English and in French, on facing pages, was a response to the objections of Adrien Auzout (1622–91) to Petty's *Two Essays in Political Arithmetick* the previous year.

strated, in about a hundred small pages in duodecimo, big letters: (1) that by its situation, its commerce, and its administration, a small country with a small number of inhabitants can equal a large and populous country—whether compared by strength or by wealth—and that there is nothing that tends more effectively to establish this equality than the navy and maritime commerce; (2) that all kinds of taxes and public charges tend to enhance rather than to weaken society and the public good; (3) that there are some natural and permanent obstacles to France becoming more powerful at sea than England or Holland (our Frenchmen will not bring favorable judgment upon Lord Petty's calculations on this proposition, and I believe they will be right); (4) that by its soil and its natural produce, the people and territory of England are virtually equal in wealth and capacity to the people and territory of France; (5) that the obstacles to the greatness of England are only contingent and removable; (6) that for forty years, the power and wealth of England have greatly increased; (7) that a tenth of all the expenditures of the king's subjects would suffice to maintain a hundred thousand infantrymen, thirty thousand cavalrymen, forty thousand seamen, and to pay for all the other state expenses, both ordinary and extraordinary—on the sole supposition that this tenth be well-taxed, well-collected, and well-employed; (8) that the number of unemployed subjects is greater than the number needed to procure two million per year for the nation, were they appropriately employed; and these employments are all ready, awaiting only the workers to fill them; (9) that the nation has enough currency to sustain its commerce; (10) finally, that the nation has all the means at its disposal to embark upon the whole world's commerce, of whatever sort.

There you have some rather excessive claims; be that as it may, the reader will do well to examine the experience and reasoning on which Lord Petty bases his work. In making this examination, one must not forget that revolutions occur—whether for good or ill—that change the face of states in an instant, and that modify and even destroy presuppositions; and that calculations and their results are not less variable than events. Lord Petty's work was composed before 1699. According to that author, although Holland and Zeeland contain no more than a million acres of land and France contains at least 8 million, nonetheless the former country has almost a third of the wealth and power of the latter. Landed income in Holland is about seven or eight times what it is in France. (Observe that it is here a question of the state of Europe in 1699, and that all of Lord Petty's calculations, good or bad, refer to that year.) The inhabitants of Amsterdam number two-thirds those of Paris or London, and according to the same author, the difference between these two latter cities is only about one-twentieth. The carrying capacity of all the vessels belonging to Europe amounts to about 2 million tons, of which the English have 500,000, the Dutch 900,000, the French 100,000, the Hamburgers, Danes, Swedes, and inhabitants of Danzig 250,000; Spain, Portugal, Italy, etc. about the same. The value of the merchandise that leaves France annually for the use of other countries amounts in all to about 5 million pounds sterling; that is, four times as much as enters England alone. The merchandise exported from Holland to England is worth 300,000 pounds sterling, and what leaves there to be spread throughout the rest of the world is worth 18 million pounds sterling. The money that the king of France levies annually in time of peace is about 6.5 million sterling. The sums levied in Holland and Zeeland are about 2.1 million pounds sterling, and those coming from throughout the United Provinces make altogether about 3 million pounds sterling.

England's inhabitants number about 6 million, and their outlays, at 7 pounds sterling per person per year, make 42 million pounds sterling, or 80,000 pounds sterling per week.[3] Landed income in England is about 8 million sterling, and the interest and profits on personal property about the same. Housing income in England: 4 million pounds sterling. The profit from the labor of all the inhabitants amounts to 26 million pounds sterling per year. Ireland's inhabitants number 1.2 million. The wheat consumed annually in England, including the premium wheat at 5 shillings a bushel and the barley at 2.5 shillings, amounts to 10 million sterling. In 1699—that is, in Lord Petty's time, or at the end of the last century—England's navy needed 36,000 men for vessels of war and 48,000 for merchant vessels and others; France's entire navy needed only 15,000 men. In France, there are about 13.5 million souls, and in England, Scotland, and Ireland, about 9.5 million. In the three realms of England, Scotland, and Ireland, there are around 20,000 ecclesiastics; in France, there are more than 270,000.

3. Clearly either a misprint or a miscalculation for 800,000.

England's realm has more than 40,000 sailors, but France has no more than 10,000. In England, Scotland, Ireland, and their dependencies, there were at that time vessels whose capacity amounted to around 60,000 tons, which is worth about 4.5 million pounds sterling. The coastline around England, Scotland, Ireland, and the adjacent islands is about 3,800 miles. In the whole world, there are about 300 million souls, of whom there are only about 80 million with whom the English and Dutch trade. The value of all commercial assets does not exceed 45 million sterling. English manufactures exported from the realm amount to about 5 million sterling annually. Lead, tin, and coal amount to 500,000 pounds sterling per year. The value of French merchandise that enters England does not exceed 1.2 million pounds sterling per year. Finally, there are about 6 million sterling in hard currency in England. All these calculations, as we have said, are relative to the year 1699, and must surely have changed quite a bit since then.

M. Davenant, another originator of *political arithmetic*, proves that one must not rely absolutely on many of dear Petty's calculations; he offers others that he has made himself, and that are found to be based upon the observations of Mr. King.[4] Here are a few of them.

England, he says, contains 39 million acres of land. According to his calculations, the inhabitants number about 5.545 million souls, and that number increases every year by about 9,000—after deducting those who may die of the plague, diseases, war, the navy, etc., and those who go to the colonies. He counts 530,000 inhabitants in the city of London, 870,000 in the other cities and towns, and 4.1 million in the villages and hamlets. He estimates annual landed income at 10 million sterling; that of houses and buildings at 2 million per year; the produce of all types of grain, in a passably abundant year, at 9.075 million pounds sterling; the income from land on which wheat is cultivated, at 2 million, and its net product above 9 million sterling; the income from pasture, meadow, woods, forests, dunes,

4. Charles Davenant (1656–1714), *Discourse on the publick revenues, and on the trade of England* (London: Knapton, 1698); for King (1648–1712) and Graunt (1620–74), discussed below, see Peter Laslett, ed., *The Earliest Classics: Natural and political observations made upon the bills of mortality (1662) [by] John Graunt; Natural and political observations and conclusions upon the state and condition of England 1696 (1804); "The L.C.C. Burns journal," a manuscript notebook containing workings for several projected works (composed c. 1695–1700) [by Gregory King]* (Farnborough, England: Gregg, 1973).

etc., at 7 million sterling; the annual produce of livestock in butter, cheese, and milk can amount, according to him, to about 2.5 million sterling. He estimates the annual value of shorn wool at about 2 million sterling; that of horses bred every year at around 250,000 pounds sterling; the annual consumption of meat for food at about 3.35 million pounds sterling; that of suet and hides around 600,000 pounds sterling; that of hay for the annual feeding of horses, around 1.3 million pounds sterling, and for that of other livestock, a million sterling; the wood cut annually for building, 500,000 pounds sterling; the wood for burning, etc., about 500,000 pounds sterling. If all of England's land were equally distributed among all the inhabitants, everyone would have about 7.25 acres as his share. The value of the premium wheat, the rye, and the barley necessary for England's subsistence amounts to at least 6 million sterling per year. The value of the manufacture of finished wool in England is about 8 million per year, and all the wool merchandise exported annually from England exceeds the value of 2 million sterling. England's annual income, from which all the inhabitants feed and maintain themselves, and pay all taxes and charges, amounts (according to him) to about 43 million; that of France, to 81 million, and that of Holland to 18.25 million pounds sterling.

In his observations on the *mortuary lists*, Major Grant reckons that England has 39,000 square miles of land; that there are 4.6 million souls in England and the principality of Wales; that the inhabitants of the city of London number about 640,000—that is, a fourteenth of all the inhabitants of England; that there are about 10,000 parishes in England and Wales; that there are 25 million acres of land in England and Wales—that is, about 4 acres for each inhabitant; that of 100 children born, only 64 reach the age of six; that out of 100, only 40 remain alive at the end of sixteen years; that out of 100, only 25 who live past the age of twenty-six; 16 who live to be thirty-six, and only 10 out of 100 live to the end of their forty-sixth year; that of that same number, there are only 6 who reach the age of fifty-six, 3 of 100 who reach the age of sixty-six, and only one out of 100 who is still alive at the end of seventy-six years. The inhabitants of the city of London have turned over twice in the course of about sixty-four years. See *Life* [*Vie*], etc. Messrs. de Moivre, Bernoulli, de Montmort, and de Parcieux have exerted themselves on subjects relative to *Political arithmetic*; one may consult *The doctrine of chance*, by M. Moivre; *The art of conjecture* by M. Bernoulli; *The analysis of games of chance* by M. de Montmort; the work *On lifetime annuities and tontines*, etc. by M. de Parcieux; and several reports by M. Halley, scattered in the *Philosophical transactions*, along with the articles in our Dictionary, HASARD [Chance], JEU [Game], PROBABILITÉ, COMBINAISON [Combination], ABSENT [Missing], VIE [Life], MORT [Death], NAISSANCE [Birth], ANNUITÉ, RENTE [Income], TONTINE, etc.

Political Authority
(*Autorité Politique*)

This important article by Diderot, which was at first attributed to Toussaint, stirred up perhaps as much controversy as any single political article throughout the entire publishing history of the Encyclopédie. *Attacks on it continued for more than a decade. In 1752, publication of the dictionary was suspended temporarily, partly because of the storm surrounding this particular essay. Singled out for criticism in the article was the author's general argument for popular sovereignty, and the specific ideas that liberty is a gift from heaven, and that Paul's letter to the Romans should be viewed as legitimating limited government. With the resumption of publication (volume 3, in 1753), the editors defended and explained this article by echoing arguments for limited government that the Parlement of Paris had recently made in its controversy with the Crown concerning the church's withholding of sacraments from the Jansenists.*[1]

"Political Authority" was translated in an abridged version by Stephen J. Gendzier in *Denis Diderot's "The Encyclopedia": Selections*, ed. and trans. Stephen J. Gendzier (New York: Harper and Row, 1967), 185–88, and is reprinted by permission of the translator. We have added our own translations of the omitted material, indicated by square brackets, and some notes. The article is also abridged and anthologized in Denis Diderot, *Political Writings*, ed. John Hope Mason and Robert Wokler (Cambridge: Cambridge University Press, 1992), 6–11.

This article can be found at 1:898–900 in the original edition of the *Encyclopédie*.

1. See John Lough, *Essays on the "Encyclopédie" of Diderot and d'Alembert* (London: Oxford University Press, 1968), 272, 304, 330, and 424–63 passim; Lough, *The "Encyclopédie"* (New York: McKay, 1971), 288–89.—HC

Political Authority. No man has received from nature the right to command others. Liberty is a gift from heaven, and each individual of the same species has the right to enjoy it as soon as he enjoys the use of reason. If nature has established any authority, it is paternal control; but paternal control has its limits, and in the state of nature, it would terminate when the children could take care of themselves. Any other authority comes from another origin than nature. If one seriously considers this matter, one will always go back to one of these two sources: either the force and violence of an individual who has seized it, or the consent of those who have submitted to it by a contract made or assumed between them and the individual on whom they have bestowed authority.

Power that is acquired by violence is only usurpation and only lasts as long as the force of the individual who commands can prevail over the force of those who obey; in such a way that if the latter become in their turn the strongest party and then shake off the yoke, they do it with as much right and justice as the other who had imposed it upon them. The same law that made authority can then destroy it; for this is the law of might. Sometimes authority that is established by violence changes its nature; this occurs when it continues and is maintained with the express consent of those who have been brought into subjection, but in this case it reverts to the second case about which I am going to speak; and the individual who had arrogated it then becomes a prince, ceasing to be a tyrant.

Power that comes from the consent of the people[2] necessarily presupposes certain conditions that make its use legitimate, useful to society, advantageous to the republic, and that set and restrict it between limits: for man must not and cannot give himself entirely and without reserve to another man, because he has a master superior to everything, to whom he alone belongs in his entire being. It is God, whose power always has a direct bearing on each creature, a master as jealous as absolute, who never loses

2. This is the fundamental idea of Rousseau's *Contrat social,* published ten years later; however, the two friends drew different political consequences from their initial premise of a social contract.

his rights and does not transfer them.[3] He permits for the common good and for the maintenance of society that men establish among themselves an order of subordination, that they obey one of them, but he wishes that it be done with reason and proportion and not by blindness and without reservation, so that the creature does not arrogate the rights of the creator. Any other submission is the veritable crime of idolatry. To bend one's knee before a man or an image is merely an external ceremony about which the true God, who demands the heart and the mind, hardly cares and which he leaves to the institution of men to do with as they please the tokens of civil and political devotion or of religious worship. Thus it is not these ceremonies in themselves, but the spirit of their establishment that makes their observance innocent or criminal. An Englishman has no scruples about serving the king on one knee; the ceremonial only signifies what people wanted it to signify. But to deliver one's heart, spirit, and conduct without any reservation to the will and caprice of a mere creature, making him the unique and final reason for one's actions, is assuredly a crime of divine lèse-majesté of the highest degree. Otherwise this power of God about which one speaks so much would only be empty noise that human politics would use out of pure fantasy and which the spirit of irreligion could play with in its turn; so that all ideas concerning power and subordination coming to the point of merging, the prince would trifle with God, and the subject with the prince.

[True and legitimate power, then, necessarily has limits. Thus, Scripture tells us: "let your submission be reasonable (*sit rationabile obsequium vestrum*)." "All power that comes from God is an orderly power (*omnis potestas à Deo ordinata est*)."[4] For this is how these words must be understood, consistent with right reason and with the literal sense, not with the sort of interpretation prompted by servility and flattery that claims that any power of whatever kind comes from God. After all, aren't there unjust powers? Aren't there authorities which, far from coming from God, establish them-

3. In the original text, Diderot makes it quite clear that there are no intermediate powers between God and His creatures, thereby refuting without explicitly naming those political theoreticians who defended the divine right of kings.

4. The first passage is adapted from Romans 12:1, the second from Romans 13:1–2; Diderot's interpretation caused an outcry.—HC

selves against his orders and against his will? Do usurpers have God for themselves? Do we have to obey the persecutors of the true religion in everything? Will silencing idiocy legitimize the power of the Antichrist? It will still be great power. In resisting this power, are Enoch and Elie seditious rebels who have forgotten that all power comes from God? Or are they reasonable men, firm and pious, who know that all power ceases to exist as soon as it goes beyond the boundaries that reason has prescribed for it and strays from the rules that the sovereign of princes and subjects has established—men, in short, who think as St. Paul does that all power is from God only insofar as it is just and orderly?]

The prince owes to his very subjects the authority that he has over them; and this authority is limited by the laws of nature and the state. The laws of nature and the state are the conditions under which they have submitted or are supposed to have submitted to its government. One of these conditions is that, not having any power or authority over them but by their choice and consent, he can never employ this authority to break the act or the contract by which it was transferred to him. From that time on he would work against himself, since his authority could only subsist by virtue of the right that established it. Whoever annuls one, destroys the other. The prince cannot therefore dispose of his power and his subjects without the consent of the nation and independent of the option indicated in the contract of allegiance. If he proceeded otherwise, everything would be nullified, and the laws would relieve him of the promises and the oaths that he would have been able to make, as a minor who would have acted without full knowledge of the facts, since he would have claimed to have at his disposal that which he only had in trust and with a clause of entail, in the same way as if he had had it in full ownership and without any condition.

Moreover the government, although hereditary in a family and placed in the hands of one person, is not private property, but public property that consequently can never be taken from the people, to whom it belongs exclusively, fundamentally, and as a freehold. Consequently it is always the people who make the lease or the agreement: they always intervene in the contract that adjudges its exercise. It is not the state that belongs to the prince, it is the prince who belongs to the state: but it does rest with the prince to govern in the state, because the state has chosen him for that purpose: he has bound himself to the people and the administration of affairs, and they in their turn are bound to obey him according to the laws. The person who wears the crown can certainly discharge himself of it completely if he wishes, but he cannot replace it on the head of another without the consent of the nation who has placed it on his. In a word, the crown, the government, and the public authority are possessions owned by the body of the nation, held as a usufruct by princes and as a trust by ministers. Although heads of state, they are nonetheless members of it; as a matter of fact the first, the most venerable, and the most powerful allowed everything in order to govern, allowed nothing legitimately to change the established government or to place another head in their place. The sceptre of Louis XV necessarily passes to his eldest son, and there is no power that can oppose this; nor any nation because it is the condition of the contract; nor his father for the same reason.

The depository of authority is sometimes only for a limited time, as in the Roman republic. It is sometimes for the life of only one man, as in Poland; sometimes for all the time a family exists, as in England; sometimes for the time a family exists only through its male descendants, as in France.

This depository is sometimes entrusted to a certain class in society, sometimes to several people chosen by all the classes, and sometimes to one man.

The conditions of this pact are different in different states. But everywhere the nation has a right to maintain against all forces the contract that they have made; no power can change it; and when it is no longer valid, the nation recovers its rights and full freedom to enter into a new one with whomever and however it pleases them. This is what would happen in France if by the greatest of misfortunes the entire reigning family happened to die out, including the most remote descendants; then the scepter and the crown would return to the nation.

It seems that only slaves whose minds are as limited as their hearts are debased could think otherwise. Such men are born neither for the glory of the prince nor for the benefit of society; they have neither virtue nor greatness of soul. Fear and self-interest are the motives of their conduct. Nature only produces them to improve by contrast the worth of virtuous men; and Providence uses them to make tyrannical powers, with which it chastises as a rule the people and the sovereigns who offend God; the latter for usurping, the former for granting too much to man of supreme power, that the Creator reserved for Himself over the created being.

The observation of laws, the conservation of liberty, and the love of country are the prolific sources of all great things and of all beautiful actions. Here we can find the happiness of people, and the true luster of princes who govern them. Here obedience is glorious, and command august. On the contrary, flattery, self-interest, and the spirit of slavery are at the root of all the evils that overpower a state and of all the cowardice that dishonor it. There the subjects are miserable, and the princes hated; there the monarch has never heard himself proclaimed the beloved; submission is hateful there, and domination cruel. If I view France and Turkey from the same perspective, I perceive on the one hand a society of men united by reason, activated by virtue, and governed by a head of state equally wise and glorious according to the laws of justice; on the other, a herd of animals assembled by habit, driven by the law of the rod, and led by an absolute master according to his caprice.

[But in order to give to the principles disseminated in this article all the authority they are able to accommodate, let us support them with the testimony of one of our greatest kings. His speech at the opening of the assembly of notables in 1596, full of a sincerity that is mostly unknown to sovereigns, was quite worthy of the feelings he brought there.[5]

"Convinced," says M. de Sully, pag. 467, in quarto, vol. 1, "that kings have two sovereigns, God and the law; that justice must preside over the throne and mildness must be seated by its side; that since God is the true proprietor of all realms and kings merely their administrators, kings must therefore represent to their people the one whose place they are taking; that they will reign as he does only insofar as they reign as fathers; that in hereditary monarchical states, there is a delusion that one may also call hereditary, namely, that the sovereign is master of the lives and properties of all his subjects; that by means of these four words—'such is our pleasure'—he is exempt from indicating the reasons for his conduct, or

5. The reference is to King Henry IV and the assembly that he convoked at Rouen in 1596–97.—HC

even from having any; that even if he were, there is nothing so imprudent as making oneself hateful to those to whom one is obliged to entrust one's life at every moment, and that taking everything away by naked violence is a way of falling into this misfortune. Being convinced (as I say) of these principles, which all the courtier's artifice will never banish from the hearts of those who resemble him, this great man declared that in order to avoid any hint of violence and coercion, he did not want the assembly to be made up of deputies named by the sovereign and always blindly subservient to all his wishes; but that his intention was that all sorts of persons of whatever status or condition be freely admitted there, so that knowledgeable and meritorious people would have the means to propose without fear what they think necessary for the public good; that even at that moment, he did not mean to be prescribing any limits to them; that he was merely enjoining them not to abuse this allowance for the humiliation of that royal authority which is the nerve center of the state; to restore unity among its members; to relieve the people; to discharge the royal treasury of many debts to which it was subject without having contracted them; to moderate excessive pensions with the same justice (without harming the necessities), in order to establish a clear and adequate fund for the future maintenance of military men. He added that he would have no difficulty submitting to measures that he would not have thought of himself, as soon as he sees they have been dictated by a spirit of equity and disinterestedness; that he would not be found seeking in his age, experience, and personal qualities a pretext (quite a bit less frivolous than the one princes are accustomed to use) to evade the agreements; that on the contrary, he would show by his example that these agreements concern the king (in causing them to be observed) no less than the subject (in submitting to them). If I prided myself," he continued, "on passing for an excellent orator, I would have brought here more fine words than good will; but my ambition has something loftier about it than speaking well. I aspire to the glorious title of liberator and restorer of France. Thus, I have not summoned you, as my predecessors used to do, to oblige you to blindly approve my wishes. I have assembled you to receive your counsel, to believe it, to follow it—in a word, to place myself under your tutelage. This is a desire that rarely comes over kings, graybeards, and victors like me. But the love I bring to my subjects and the extreme desire I have to preserve my state cause me to find everything easy and everything honorable."[6]

Having finished this speech, Henry got up and left, leaving only M. de Sully in the assembly, to share with it the accounts, papers, and memoranda that they might need.

One does not presume to propose this conduct as a model, because there are occasions when princes may show less deference, without however deviating from the sentiments that cause the sovereign to be regarded in society as the father of his family, and his subjects as his children. The great monarch we have just cited will again provide us with the example of this sort of mildness mixed with firmness (so requisite on occasion), where reason is so manifestly on the sovereign's side that he has the right to strip his subjects of freedom of choice and leave them with obedience as the sole option. Once the Edict of Nantes had been verified, after many difficulties on the part of the Parlement, the clergy, and the University,[7] Henry IV said to the bishops: "You have urged me to my duty; I urge you to yours. Let us rival each other in doing good. My predecessors have given you fine words; but as for me with my jacket,[8] I will give you good results. I will look over your formal proposals and will respond to them as favorably as possible." And he responded to the Parlement, which had come to make remonstrances to him: "You see me in my private office where I come to speak to you not in royal costume, or in cloak and dagger like my predecessors, but dressed like a father, in a doublet, to speak informally with his children. What I have to tell you is that I am asking you to verify the edict that I have granted to those of the Religion.[9] What I have done is for the good of the peace. I have done it abroad; I intend to do it within my own kingdom." After explaining to them the reasons he had for issuing the edict, he added: "Those who prevent my edict from taking effect want war. I will declare war tomorrow on those of the Protestant

6. Sully, *Mémoires de Maximilien de Béthune, duc de Sully* (London: 1747), entry for the year 1597.

7. The Edict of Nantes (1598) guaranteed a degree of toleration to the Huguenots, the French Protestants; the University in question is the University of Paris.—HC

8. *Jaquette,* connoting rustic and lower-class apparel.—HC

9. *La religion,* a contemporary colloquialism for the French Protestants.—HC

Religion, but I will not wage it. I will send them packing. I have issued the edict; I want it to be observed. My will ought to serve as reason; in an obedient state, such reasons are never demanded of the prince. I am king. I am speaking to you as king. I intend to be obeyed." (*Mém. de Sully*, in-4°, p. 594. vol. I)[10]

There you have the proper way for a monarch to speak to his subjects when it is clear that he has justice on his side. And why couldn't he do what any man who has equity on his side is able to do? As for the subjects, the first law that religion, reason, and nature impose upon them is for them to respect the conditions of the contract they have made, and never to lose sight of the nature of their government. In France, it means not to forget that so long as the ruling family survives by the male line, nothing will ever exempt them from obeying, honoring, and fearing their master, as the one by whom they have expected the image of God to be present and visible to them on earth.[11] Nor are they exempt from being attached to these sentiments by a motive of gratitude for the tranquility and the benefits they enjoy under protection of the royal name. Nor, if they ever happen to have an unjust, ambitious, and violent king, are they exempt from opposing this misfortune by a single means: namely, by appeasing him with their submission and swaying God by their prayers. For this remedy is the only legitimate one, according to the contract of submission formerly sworn to the reigning prince and his descendants through the male line, whoever they may be. And they are to consider that all those motives that are imagined for resisting are on close inspection nothing more than subtly colored pretexts for infidelity; that by this conduct, men have never corrected princes or abolished taxes; that they have merely added a new measure of misery to the misfortunes they were already lamenting. There you have the foundations on which peoples and those who govern them could establish their mutual happiness.]

10. Sully, *Mémoires*, entry for the year 1599.—HC

11. There was disagreement among contemporaries over whether this conclusion was ironic or a genuinely cautious retreat on the author's part from the popular sovereignty claims early in the article.—HC

Volume 2
(1752)

Brownists
(*Brownistes*)

BROWNISTS (*Ecclesiastical history*), name of a sect that formed out of the Puritans' sect about the end of the 16th century: it was named after Robert Brown, its leader.

This Robert Brown, who wrote many books to support his views, was not, as Moréri claims, a schoolmaster from Southwark, but a man of good mores, and even learned. He was from quite a good family in Rutlandshire and was allied to the Lord Treasurer Burleigh. He did his studies at Cambridge and began to publish his opinions and rail against the ecclesiastical government in Norwich in 1580, which attracted the resentment of the bishops. He himself took pride in having been for this reason put in thirty-two different prisons—all of them so dark that he could not make out his hand in them, even in broad daylight. Afterward, he left the realm with his co-religionists and retired to Middleburg in Zeeland, where he and his followers obtained permission from the Estates[1] to build a church and worship God in their own way. A short time later, division arose in his little flock. Many split off, which so disgusted Brown that he resigned his office, returned to England in 1589, abjured his errors, and was raised to the position of rector in a Northamptonshire church. He died in 1630.

Brown's move led to the ruin of the Middleburg church, but the seeds of his system were not so easy to destroy in England. Sir Walter Raleigh, in an essay composed in 1592, already counts upward of twenty thousand persons imbued with Brown's opinions.

This article can be found at 2:446 in the original edition of the *Encyclopédie*.

1. The local governing authority in the United Provinces.

It was not over articles of faith that they broke off from other communions, but because of ecclesiastical discipline, and especially the form of government in the Anglican church—of which the *Brownists* strongly disapproved, though without adopting that of the Presbyterians, since they assigned equal blame to the consistories and the synods, the bishops and the ministers. They did not want to join any reformed church, since they said they were not assured of the sanctity and regeneration of the members of those churches, because the latter put up with sinners and communicated with them—which, according to the *Brownists*, was the height of impiety. They condemned the solemn celebration of marriage—which they said was merely a civil engagement, and thus needed the intervention of only the secular magistrate, not at all the ecclesiastical. Nor did they want children to be baptized by Anglican priests or Presbyterian ministers, whom they did not regard as members of the church, and who, they added, took no care of those they had baptized. They rejected every kind of prayer, saying that the Lord's Prayer ought not to be regarded as a prayer but merely as a model for a prayer that J. C. has given us. See SEPARATISTES and NON-CONFORMISTES.

They established an ecclesiastical government of democratic form. When one of their churches was assembled, whoever wanted to be incorporated into their society made a profession of faith and signed a form by which he committed himself to follow the Gospel in the same sense as they did. The power to admit or exclude members, and to decide all conflicts, belonged to the entire society. They selected their officers and ministers from among themselves to preach and care for the poor. These ministers were established and their different functions were distributed to them by the fasting, prayer, and laying on of hands of some members of the society—without, however, their believing that they possessed the title or dignity of ordination. For they sometimes reduced their ministries to the status of the laity—persuaded that in this regard, they could destroy their own work. And since they taught that a church was only an assembly of a certain number of persons in the same place, they therefore believed that the power of the minister appointed in that place was so limited to it that he could neither administer communion nor baptize nor exercise any other function in a church other than his own. All members of the sect, even the laity, were permitted to make exhortations[2] to the assembly, to propose questions after the sermon, and to debate what had been preached. In a word, each *Brownist* church was an assembly in which each member had the freedom to strive for the general good of the society without being accountable for his actions before any superior, synod or tribunal. The independents who formed themselves afterward from among the *Brownists* adopted a portion of these opinions. See INDEPENDENTS.

Queen Elizabeth actively went after this sect. Under her reign, the prisons were full of *Brownists;* there were even some hanged. The ecclesiastical commission and the Star Chamber raged against them with such vigor that they were obliged to leave England. Many families retreated to Amsterdam, where they formed a church and chose Johnson for pastor, and after him, Aynsworth, known for a commentary on the Pentateuch.[3] Also counted among their leaders: Barrow and Wilkinson.[4] Their church was maintained for about a hundred years. (G)

2. *Dictionnaire de l'Académie Française* (Paris, 1694) defines "exhortation" as "a Christian and pious speech made in informal style to excite one to devotion and to serve God well."

3. Francis Johnson (1562–1618), author of, among other things, *Certayne reasons and arguments proving that it is not lawfull to heare or to have any spirituall communion with the present ministerie of the Church of England* (Amsterdam: Thorp, 1608); Henry Ainsworth (1571–1622?), *Annotations upon the five bookes of Moses* (London: Bellamy, 1627).

4. See Henry Barrow (1550?-1593), *A True description out of the Word of God of the visible church* (Amsterdam, 1589), and William Wilkinson, *A very godly and learned treatise, of the exercise of fasting* (London: Daye, 1580), for examples.

Celibacy
(*Célibat*)

*CELIBACY (*Ancient and modern history, and Morality*) is the state of a person who lives without becoming committed to marriage. This state can be considered in itself under three different aspects: (1) with regard to the human race; (2) to society; (3) to Christian society. But before considering *celibacy* in itself, we are going to present in a few words its situation and its changing circumstances among men. M. Morin, of the Academy of Belles-lettres,[1] reduces its history to the following propositions: *Celibacy* is as old as the world; it is as widespread as the world; it will last as long as, and infinitely longer than, the world.

Abridged history of celibacy. Celibacy is as old as the world, if it is true—as is claimed by some authors of the old and new law—that our first parents lost their innocence only by ceasing to preserve their celibacy and that they would never have been expelled from paradise if they had not eaten the forbidden fruit, an act that in the modest and metaphorical style of scripture indicates nothing else (they say) but a violation of celibacy. They derive the evidence for this grammatical interpretation from the feeling of nudity that immediately followed the sin of Eve and Adam; from the notion of irregularity attached to the carnal act virtually everywhere in the

The unattributed notes in this article are translated from *Diderot: "Encyclopédie,"* ed. John Lough and Jacques Proust, vol. 6 of *Denis Diderot: Œuvres complètes*, ed. Hans Dieckmann and Jean Varloot (Paris: Hermann, 1976), 289–305, and are used with permission. All others are by the present editor. For historical context, see Claire Cage, *Unnatural Frenchmen: The Politics of Priestly Celibacy and Marriage, 1720–1815* (Charlottesville: University of Virginia Press, 2015).—HC

This article can be found at 2:801–6 in the original edition of the *Encyclopédie*.

1. Henri Morin (1655–1728).

world; from the shame that accompanies it; from the remorse that it causes; from the original sin that is communicated in this way; finally, from the state to which we will return upon departing this life, in which it will not be a question of husbands and wives, and which will be an eternal celibacy.

It is not up to me, says M. Morin, to assign the appropriate qualifications to this opinion. The opinion is odd; it seems contrary to the letter of scripture; that's enough to reject it. Scripture teaches us that Adam and Eve lived in paradise as brother and sister, as the angels live in heaven and as we will live there one day. That's good enough; there you have the first and perfect celibacy. To know how long it lasted is a question of pure curiosity. Some say several hours; others several days. There are those who—on the basis of mystical reasons, on who knows what traditions from the Greek church, on the era of Cain's birth—push this interval to thirty years.

The Jewish doctors would have another, even longer celibacy follow upon this original one. For they claim that Adam and Eve, ashamed of their crime, did penance for a hundred years without having any dealings together—a conjecture they base on the birth of Seth, their third son, whom Moses attributes to them only at the age of a hundred and thirty. But to be precise, it is only to Abel that one can assign the honor of having preserved his celibacy throughout his whole life.

To know whether his example was imitated in the following generations, whether the sons of God who allowed themselves to be corrupted by the daughters of men weren't a religious sort who lapsed into disorder—that's what we can't know, although it's not impossible. If it's true, as appears to be the case from the supposed book of Enoch, that there were at that time women who made a practice of sterility, there may well have also been men who did so. But the likelihood here is not high. At that time it was a question of populating the world; God's law and that of nature imposed on all kinds of persons a sort of necessity to work at the increase of the human race. It's to be supposed that those who lived in that time made it an essential matter for themselves to obey that precept. M. Morin says that everything history teaches us about the Patriarchs of those times is that they took and gave away women; that they brought into the world sons and daughters, and then died as if they had had nothing more important to do.

It was much the same thing in the first centuries that followed the flood. There was much clearing to do and few workers; it was up to whoever begot the most. At that time, men's honor, nobility, and power consisted in the number of children. One was certain in that way of attracting great esteem, of making oneself respected by one's neighbors, and of having a place in history. The Jews' history has not forgotten the name of Jair, who had thirty sons in service;[2] nor has the Greeks' history forgotten the names of Danaüs and Egyptus,[3] of whom one had fifty sons and the other fifty daughters. Sterility passed in those days for a kind of infamy in the two sexes, and for an unequivocal sign of the curse of God. On the other hand, to have a great number of children around one's table was regarded as an authentic mark of his benediction. Celibacy was a kind of sin against nature; today, it is no longer the same thing.

Moses hardly left men the freedom to marry or not. Lycurgus branded the celibate with infamy. There was even a special solemnity in Lacedemon, where the women brought them forth all naked to the foot of the altars, and had them make a full apology to nature, which they accompanied with very harsh punishment. Those republicans pushed the precautions further by publishing regulations against those who married too late, *ὀψιγαμία*, and against husbands who abused these precautions with their wives, *κακογαμία*.

In the course of time, men being less rare, these penal laws were mitigated. Plato tolerated celibacy up to thirty-five years in his republic; beyond that age, he prohibited only employment-related celibacy, and assigned them the last rank in public ceremonies.[4] The Roman laws, which succeeded the Greek, were also less rigorous against celibacy; nonetheless, the censors were charged with preventing that sort of solitary life, harmful to the state, *coelibes esse prohibento.*[5] To make it odious, they did not allow the celibate to either make a will or serve as witness. And here is the first question posed to those who presented themselves to swear an oath: *ex*

2. Judges 10:3–5.

3. Danaüs, father of the fifty Danaïds; Egyptus was his twin, who sired fifty sons and commanded them to marry the Danaïds.

4. Plato, *Laws,* IV, 721d.

5. "Whom they prohibited from being celibate."

animi tui sententiâ, tu equum habes, tu uxorem habes? "On your soul and conscience, do you have a horse, do you have a wife?" But the Romans were not content to afflict them in this world; their theologians also threatened them with extraordinary punishments in the underworld. *Extrema omnium calamitas & impietas accidit illi qui absque filiis à vita discedit, & daemonibus maximas dat poenas post obitum.* "It is the greatest of impieties and the utmost misfortune to depart the world without leaving children in it; the demons make those people suffer cruel pains after their death."

Despite all these precautions—temporal and spiritual—the celibate did not stop making their way in the world; the laws themselves prove it. One doesn't venture to pass laws against disorders that live on only notionally. To know how and where celibacy began, history says nothing about that. It's to be supposed that simple moral reasons and individual tastes won out over so many penal laws, emergency fiscal laws, laws that brought infamy, and over the anxieties of conscience. In the beginning, there must surely have been more pressing motives and sound physical reasons. Such were those happy and wise constitutions that nature exempts from reducing the great rule of multiplication to practice; they have existed in all times. Our authors give them withering names; the Orientals, on the other hand, call them *eunuchs of the sun, eunuchs of heaven, made by the hand of God*—honorable titles that are supposed not only to console them for the misfortune of their condition but also to authorize them before God and men to pride themselves in it, as if because of a special grace that discharges them from a goodly portion of the solicitudes of life and transports them suddenly into the midst of the path of virtue.

But without seriously examining whether it is an advantage or disadvantage, it is quite apparent that these saints[6] were the first to choose the celibacy option. That way of life is doubtless indebted to them for its origin, and perhaps its denomination. For the Greeks called the infirm in question κολοβοι, which is not far removed from *coelibes*. In fact, celibacy was the only option that the κολοβοι had to choose in order to obey the orders of nature—for their repose, their honor, and under the rules of good faith. If they did not make this determination themselves, the laws imposed it upon

6. *Béat*, usually but not always ironic.—HC

them by necessity; that of Moses was explicit. The laws of other nations were scarcely more propitious; if they allowed them to have wives, the wives were also permitted to abandon them.

The men of this condition—ambiguous and rare in the beginning, scorned equally by the two sexes—found themselves exposed to many mortifications, which reduced them to an obscure and secluded life. But necessity soon suggested to them different means of getting out of it and making themselves commendable. Detached from the anxious movements of alien love and self-love, they submitted to others' wills with a strange devotion, and they were found so accommodating that everyone wanted to have some of them. Those who had none of them got some by one of the boldest and most inhumane of operations: fathers, masters, and sovereigns arrogated to themselves the right to reduce their children, their slaves, and their subjects to that ambiguous condition. And the whole world, which in the beginning knew only two sexes, was astonished to find itself imperceptibly divided into three fairly equal portions.

These scarcely voluntary celibates were followed by free ones, who substantially increased the number of the former. Men of letters and philosophers by taste; athletes, gladiators, and musicians by reason of status; countless others by libertinage; some by virtue—all chose the option that Diogenes found so sweet that he was surprised that his expedient did not become more fashionable. Some professions were obliged to do so, such as that of the scarlet dyers, *baphiarii*. Ambition and politics also enlarged the corps of the celibate. Those bizarre men were handled carefully even by the great, eager to have a place in their will. And contrariwise, the paternal heads of household of whom nothing was expected were forgotten, neglected, scorned.

Up to now, we have seen celibacy prohibited, then tolerated, then approved, and finally advocated. It took little time to become an essential condition in most of those who devoted themselves to altar service. Melchizideck was a man without family and without genealogy. Those who set their sights on temple service and on the rites of the law were dispensed from marriage. Girls had the same freedom. We are assured that Moses dismissed his wife when he had received the law from God's hands. He ordered the priests whose turn to preside at the altar was approaching to sequester themselves from their wives for several days. After him, the prophets Elie, Elisha, Daniel and his three companions lived in continence. The Nazarenes, and the sounder part of the Essenes, are presented to us by Josephus as a marvelous nation, which had found the secret that Metellus Numidicus was striving for—to perpetuate themselves without marriage, without childbirth, and without any female company.

Among the Egyptians, the priests of Isis and most of those dedicated to the service of their divinities made a profession of chastity. And to be on the safe side, they were prepared for it from childhood by the surgeons. The gymnosophists, the Brahmins, the Athenian hierophants, a good portion of Pythagoras's disciples, those of Diogenes, the true Cynics—and in general, all those, male or female, who devoted themselves to the service of the goddesses—engaged in the same practice. In Thrace, there was an important association of celibate religious called *κτισαι*, or *creators*, from the faculty of producing themselves without the assistance of women. Among the Persians, the obligation of celibacy was imposed on the girls designated for the service of the sun. The Athenians had a house of virgins. Everyone knows about the Roman vestals. Among our ancient Gauls, nine virgins, who passed for having received extraordinary light and grace from heaven, guarded a famous oracle in a little island called *Sené*, on the Armorican coasts. There are authors who even claim that the entire island was inhabited by only the girls, some of whom made occasional trips over neighboring coasts, whence they brought back little embryos to preserve the species. All of them didn't go there; it is to be supposed, says M. Morin, that this was decided by lot, and that those who had the misfortune to draw a black ticket were forced to step into the fatal boat that exposed them throughout the continent. Those consecrated girls were highly venerated; their house had singular privileges, among which may be included the inability of being punished for a crime without having first lost the title of girl.

Celibacy has had its martyrs among the pagans, and their histories and myths are full of girls who have generously preferred death to loss of honor. The adventure of Hippolytus is well known, as well as his resurrection by Diana, protectress of the celibate. All these episodes, and countless others, were supported by principles of belief. The Greeks regarded chastity as a supernatural grace; the sacrifices were not thought to be complete without the intervention of a virgin. They might well be begun, *libare*, but they could not be consummated without her, *litare*. Regarding virginity, they had magnificent words, sublime ideas, speculations of great beauty. But digging deeper into the secret conduct of all those celibate people and all those *virtuosi* of paganism, one discovers (says M. Morin) only disorders, charlatanism, and hypocrisy. To begin with their goddesses, Vesta, the earliest, was represented with a child. Where did she get it? Minerva had before her Erichthonius, an adventure with Vulcan, and temples (as a mother). Diana had her knight Virbius and her Endymion; the pleasure she got in contemplating the latter sleeping says much about her, too much for a virgin. Myrtilus accused the muses of having strong predilections for a certain Megalion and gave these predilections to all the children that he named—name by name. It is perhaps for this reason that abbé Cartaud calls them *the girls of Jupiter's opera*. The virgin gods were scarcely worth more than the goddesses, witness Apollo and Mercury.

The priests, not excepting those of Cybelus, did not pass in the world for being folks of particularly regular conduct. Not all the sinful vestals would have been buried alive. For the sake of their philosophers' honor, M. Morin is silent, and concludes the history of celibacy in this way, such as it was in the cradle, in childhood, in nature's arms—a condition quite different from the high degree of perfection in which we see it today. This change is not surprising: the latter is the work of grace and the Holy Spirit; the former was merely the imperfect runt of a disordered, depraved, debauched nature—sad castoff of marriage and virginity. *See the Memoirs of the Academy of Inscriptions, vol. IV, page 308. Critical history of celibacy.*

In absolute terms, all the preceding is merely an analysis of that memoir. We have cut some of its long passages but have scarcely allowed ourselves the liberty of changing a single expression in what we have employed. It will be likewise in what remains of this article: we take nothing upon ourselves, we are content solely to report faithfully not only the opinions but even the speech of the authors and to draw here only on sources approved by all honorable men.[7] After having shown what history teaches us about

7. *La Religion vengée* (XI, 198) sees very clearly that Diderot's attitude on this question is far from being truly objective: "To be honest about it, he declares that he is merely reporting what others have written about this before him, but he is approving it."

celibacy, we are now going to think about that condition with the eyes of philosophy, and display what different writers have thought on the subject.

On celibacy considered in itself: (1) With regard to the human species: If a historian or some traveler gave us a description of a thinking being, perfectly isolated, without superior or equal or inferior, sheltered from everything that might move the passions—in a word, alone in his species—we would say without hesitating *that this singular being must be plunged in melancholy; for what consolation could he find in a world that for him would be but a vast solitude?* If it were added that despite appearances, he enjoys life, feels the happiness of existence, and finds some felicity within himself, we could then agree *that he is not a complete monster, and that relative to himself his constitution is not entirely absurd, but we would never go so far as to say that he is good*. Yet if one were insistent, and objected that he is perfect among his kind, and consequently that we are wrong to refuse him the epithet *good* (for what difference does it make whether he has something or nothing to sort out with others?), then we would have to call a spade a spade and acknowledge that *this being is good—if, however, it is possible that he is perfect in himself, without having any relationship, any connection with the world in which he is placed.*

But if some system in nature were eventually discovered to which the species of automaton in question could be thought to belong; if links were perceived in his configuration that attached him to beings similar to him; if his configuration indicated a chain of useful creatures that could grow and endure only by the use of faculties received from nature; he would immediately lose the name *good* with which we have dignified him. For how could this name fit an individual who, by his inaction and his solitude, would be tending so directly toward the ruin of his species? Isn't the preservation of the species one of the essential duties of the individual? And doesn't every well-formed, reasoning individual make himself guilty by failing in this duty, unless he is exempted from it by some authority superior to that of nature? See *The Essay on merit and virtue*.[8]

8. The reference is to Shaftesbury's work "An Inquiry Concerning Virtue and Merit" in *Characteristicks of Men, Manners, Opinions, Times* (Indianapolis: Liberty Fund, 2001), 2:1–100, which Diderot had translated into French in 1745. See Gordon B. Walters, *The*

I add, *unless he is exempted from it by some authority superior to that of nature*, so that it will be very clear that this in no way concerns *celibacy consecrated by religion*, but only that which imprudence, misanthropy, frivolity, or libertinage cause every day; that in which the two sexes, corrupting each other by means of natural sentiments themselves or needlessly smothering these sentiments within themselves, flee a union bound to make them better in order to live either in distant sterility or in unions that always make them worse. We are not unaware that the one who gave man all his members may dispense him from the use of some of them, or even prohibit this usage and attest that this sacrifice is agreeable to him. We are not denying that there is a certain corporal purity which nature, abandoned to itself, would never have thought of, but which God has judged necessary for a more dignified approach to the holy places that he inhabits and for a more spiritual manner of attending to the ministry of his altars. If we do not find within ourselves the seed of this purity, this is because it is, so to speak, a revealed virtue and one of faith.

On celibacy considered: (2) with regard to society. As we have just demonstrated, the celibacy that religion has not sanctified cannot be contrary to the propagation of the human species without being harmful to society. It harms society by impoverishing it and by corrupting it. *By impoverishing it:* if it is true, as can scarcely be doubted, that the lion's share of a state's wealth consists in the number of subjects;[9] that in commerce, the multitude of hands must be counted among the objects of first necessity; and that new citizens—who can't all be soldiers (because of Europe's balance of peace) and who can't wallow in idleness (because of good governance)—would work the land, populate manufactures, or become sailors. *By corrupting it:* Because it's a rule drawn from nature, as the illustrious author of *The Spirit of the Laws* has well noted, that the more you reduce the number of possible marriages, the more you harm those marriages that have already taken place; and that the fewer married people there are, the less fidelity there is in marriage, just as when there are more robbers there are more robberies.[10]

Significance of Diderot's "Essai sur le mérite et la vertu" (Chapel Hill: University of North Carolina Press, 1971).—HC

9. See POPULATION, in this volume.—HC

10. *Spirit of the laws,* 23.21.

The ancients were so familiar with these advantages, and placed such a high price on the natural faculty of marrying and having children, that their laws had provided that this faculty not be taken away. They regarded that deprivation as a certain means of diminishing the resources of a people and increasing debauchery among them. Thus, when one received a bequest on condition of preserving celibacy, when a patron had his emancipated slave swear that he would not marry, the Papinian Law annulled both the condition and the oath among the Romans. They had understood that wherever celibacy had preeminence, there could scarcely be any honor for the married state. Consequently, one encounters among their laws none that contain an express abrogation of the privileges and honors they had accorded to marriage and to the number of children.

On celibacy considered: (3) with regard to Christian society. Since the worship of the gods demands constant attention and purity of body and of a singular soul, most peoples have been inclined to make of the clergy a separate corps. Thus, among the Egyptians, the Jews, and the Persians, there were families dedicated to the service of the divinity and the temples. But they thought not only of removing ecclesiastics from the business and company of the worldly; there were religions in which the decision was to spare them the trouble of a family. It is claimed that such was especially the spirit of Christianity, even at its origin. We are going to offer an abridged exposition of its regular discipline, so the reader can judge for himself.

It must be admitted that the law of celibacy for bishops, priests, and deacons is as old as the church. Nonetheless, there is no written divine law prohibiting the ordaining of married persons as priests, or priests from getting married. Jesus Christ had no precepts about it. In his epistles to Timothy and Titus, what St. Paul says on the continence of bishops and deacons aims solely to prohibit the bishop from having several wives at the same time or successively: *oportet episcopum esse unius uxoris virum.* Even the practice of the first centuries of the church is definite on this point: no difficulty was raised over ordaining married men as priests and bishops; it was only marrying after promotion to orders, or remarrying after the death of the first wife, that was prohibited. There was a special exception for widows. It cannot be denied that the church's spirit and its devout wish have been for its leading ministers to live in great continence, and that it has always worked to establish the law of continence. Nonetheless, the practice of ordaining married persons as priests has existed and still exists in the Greek Church, and has never been explicitly disapproved of by the Latin church.

Some believe that the third canon of the first Council of Nicaea imposes on major clerics—that is, on bishops, priests, and deacons—the obligation of celibacy.[11] But Fr. Alexander[12] proves in a special dissertation that the council did not mean to prevent clerics from the company of women that they had wedded before their ordination; that what the canon put forth concerns only wives called *subintroductae & agapetae*,[13] not legitimate wives; and that it is not only major clerics but also inferior clerics that the council prohibits from cohabiting with *agapetes*. Whence that learned theologian concludes that it was concubinage that the council was prohibiting, not the practice of marriage legitimately contracted before ordination. He also draws advantage from the well-known story of Paphnutius, which other authors seem to have rejected as a myth only because it is in no way favorable to clerical celibacy.[14]

Thus, by all appearances, the Council of Nicaea spoke only of marriages contracted since ordination, and of concubinage. But the Council of Ancyra expressly permits those ordained as deacons, and unmarried, to contract marriage afterward, provided they had protested against the obligation of celibacy during the time of ordination. It is true that this indulgence was not extended to either bishops or priests, and that the Council of Neocaesarea, held shortly after that of Ancyra, pronounced explicitly: *presbyterum, si uxorem acceperit, ab ordine deponendum*,[15] although the

11. *Dictionnaire de l'Académie Française* (Paris, 1762) lists the three major clerics as priests, deacons and subdeacons.—HC

12. Noël Alexandre, a Dominican (1639–1724). His treatise on priestly celibacy appeared in 1678 in his *Dissertationum ecclesiasticarum trias* [Three essays on church affairs].

13. Women in the early church who took a vow of chastity and lived with clerics or with laymen, respectively.—HC

14. The elderly Bishop Paphnutius of Thebes was a respected celibate clergyman when he argued successfully at the Council of Nicaea (325) for requiring only postordination celibacy in the church.—HC

15. "That a priest, if he has taken a wife, has to be defrocked."

marriage was not null, according to the remark by Fr. Thomassin.[16] The Council in Trullo, held in the year 692, confirmed the practice of the Greek church in its 13th canon, and the Latin church did not demand at the Council of Florence that it renounce this. Nonetheless, it must not be concealed that many of the Greek priests are monks and observe celibacy, and that the patriarchs and bishops are normally obliged to make a public commitment to the monastic life before being ordained. It is also germane to say that in the Occident, celibacy was prescribed to clerics by the decrees of popes Siricius and Innocent; that the first is from the year 385; that St. Leo extended this law to subdeacons; that St. Gregory had imposed it on the deacons of Sicily; and that it was confirmed by: the Councils of Elvira toward the end of the third century; canon XXXIII of Toledo in the year 400, of Carthage in 419; canon III and IV of Orange in 441, canon XXII and XXIII of Arles in 452; of Tours in 461; of Agde in 506; of Orleans in 538; by our kings' capitularies and various councils held in the Occident, but mainly by the Council of Trent—although via the respectful remonstrances[17] of the emperor, the Duke of Bavaria, the Germans, and even the king of France, people didn't stop proposing the marriage of priests, and urging this on the pope after the holding of the council. Clerical celibacy had had adversaries for a long time beforehand: Vigilantius and Jovinian rose up in opposition under St. Jerome; Wycliff, the Hussites, the Bohemians, Luther, Calvin, and the Anglicans threw off its yoke; and in the period of our wars of religion, Cardinal Chatillon, Spifame the Bishop of Nevers, and some ecclesiastics of the second order dared to marry publicly. But these examples had no sequel.

When the obligation of celibacy was general in the Catholic church, those among the ecclesiastics who violated it were immediately banned for life from the functions of their order and placed in the ranks of the laity. Justinian, *leg. 45. cod. de episcop. & cler.*[18] then made their children illegitimate and incapable of succeeding and of receiving bequests. Finally, it was

16. Louis Thomassin (1619–95). His *Ancienne et nouvelle discipline* [Old and new discipline] appeared between 1678 and 1681.

17. *Représentations.*—HC

18. *Leges 45 Codex Justinianus De episcopis et clericis* (Law 45 Justinian Code, "Concerning bishops and clerics").—HC

ordained that those marriages would be annulled and the parties subjected to punishment, whence it is seen how the infraction became more serious as the law became more deeply rooted. In the beginning, if a priest happened to get married, he was deposed and the marriage remained. Over time, orders were considered as a nullifying obstacle[19] to marriage. Today, a simple tonsured cleric who marries no longer enjoys the ecclesiastical privileges concerning jurisdiction and exemption from public burdens.[20] By his marriage, he is considered to have renounced the clerical estate and its rights. Fleury, *Institutes of Ecclesiastical Law. Tom. I. Anc. & nouv. Discipline of the Church by* Fr. Thomassin.

It follows from this review, says the late abbé St. Pierre (speaking not as a religious polemicist, but as a simple Christian man of politics and a simple citizen of a Christian society), that priestly celibacy is merely a point of discipline; that it is not essential to the Christian religion; that it has never been regarded as one of the foundations of the schism we have with the Greeks and the Protestants; that it has been voluntary in the Latin church; that since the church has the power to change all points of discipline that are of human origin, then if the estates of the Catholic church got big benefits from returning to that ancient liberty, without undergoing any real harm, it would be desirable for that to happen; and that the question of these benefits is less theological than political, and concerns more the sovereigns than the church, which would have nothing more to do than pronounce upon it.[21]

But are there benefits in restoring[22] ecclesiastics to the ancient liberty of marriage? This is a phenomenon that the czar found so striking when he traveled throughout France *incognito*[23] that he couldn't understand how, in a state where he encountered such good laws and such wise establishments, a practice had been allowed to last for so many centuries which, on the one hand, was of no importance to religion, and on the other hand, was so

19. *Empêchement dirimant,* a technical term from Canon law.—HC

20. *Charges publiques,* means both taxes and public service.—HC

21. See "Observations sur le Celibat des Prêtres" in St. Pierre's *Ouvrajes de politique* (Political works) (Rotterdam: Beman, 1733–40), 2:150–83, esp. 166ff.—HC

22. *Restituer,* which sometimes has a juridical connotation of rightful restoration.—HC

23. Peter the Great made a trip to Paris in 1717.

harmful to Christian society. We will not render a verdict on whether the czar's astonishment was well-founded, but it is not useless to summarize abbé St. Pierre's memoir, and that is what we are going to do.

Benefits of priestly marriage: (1) If forty thousand parish priests in France had eighty thousand children, since those children would unquestionably be better raised, the state would gain subjects and good people, and the church would gain faithful. (2) Ecclesiastics being by their status better husbands than other men, there would be forty thousand women happier and more virtuous. (3) There are few men for whom celibacy is not difficult to observe, which is how it can happen that the church suffers a great scandal from a priest who falls short of continence, whereas no utility redounds to other Christians from the man who lives continently. (4) A priest would scarcely be less meritorious before God in putting up with the shortcomings of his wife and children than in resisting the temptations of the flesh. (5) The problems of marriage are useful to the man who puts up with them; the difficulties of celibacy are useful to no one. (6) The parish priest who is a virtuous head of household would be useful to more people than the one who practices celibacy. (7) Some ecclesiastics for whom the observation of celibacy is very difficult would believe they had not fully met its conditions, when they have nothing to blame themselves for in this regard. (8) A hundred thousand married priests would form a hundred thousand families, which would provide more than ten thousand inhabitants per year; even if you counted only five thousand, this reckoning would still produce a million Frenchmen in two hundred years. Whence it follows that without priestly celibacy, we would have today four million more Catholics (counting only since Francis I), which would form a substantial sum of money if it is true, as an Englishman has calculated, that one man is worth nine pounds sterling to the state. (9) Noble houses would find in the bishops' families offshoots to prolong their existence, *&c. See the polit. works of abbé St. Pierre, vol. II, p. 146.*

Means of returning freedom of marriage to ecclesiastics. We must: (1) form a body to meditate on the obstacles and to work on removing them; (2) negotiate with the princes of the Roman communion and form a confederation with them; (3) negotiate with the court of Rome. For abbé St. Pierre claims it is better to use the pope's intervention than the authority of a national council—even though, according to him, the national council no doubt shortens the proceedings, and even though, according to many theologians, that tribunal is adequate for an affair of this nature. Here now are the objections that abbé St. Pierre himself put forth against his scheme, along with his responses to them.

First objection: The Italian bishops could thus be married, like St. Ambrose, and the cardinals and the pope, like St. Peter.

RESPONSE: Most certainly. Abbé St. Pierre sees no problem in following these examples, nor disadvantage in the pope and cardinals having good wives, virtuous children, and a well-ordered family.

Second objection: The people have a habitual veneration for those who maintain celibacy, which it is appropriate to preserve.

RESPONSE: Among the Dutch and English pastors, those who are virtuous are no less respected by the people for being married.

Third objection: In celibacy, priests have more time to give to the functions of their estate than they would if married.

RESPONSE: The Protestant ministers find plenty of time to have children, to raise them, to be governors of their families, and to watch over their parishes. It would be an insult to our churchmen not to assume as much from them.

Fourth objection: Young parish priests of thirty years would have five or six children—sometimes little payback for their estate, little fortune, and consequently a lot of trouble.

RESPONSE: Whoever is put forward for orders is acknowledged as a wise and able man; he is obliged to have a patrimony; he will have his benefice; his wife's dowry may be respectable. Experience shows that those parish priests descended from poor parents are not, for all that, more of a burden to the church or to their parish. Moreover, why is it necessary that one portion of churchmen live in opulence while the other languishes in poverty? Wouldn't it be possible to imagine a better distribution of ecclesiastical revenues?

Fifth objection: The Council of Trent regards celibacy as a state more perfect than marriage.

RESPONSE: There are ambiguities to avoid in the words *state, perfect, obligation*. Why claim that a priest is more perfect than St. Peter? The objection proves too much, and therefore it proves nothing. My thesis, says abbé St. Pierre, is purely political, and consists in three propositions: (1) Celibacy is a matter of pure ecclesiastical discipline, which the church can change; (2) it would be advantageous to Roman Catholic states for this discipline to be changed; (3) while waiting for a national or general council, it is appropriate for the court of Rome to receive a specified sum to expedite exemptions from celibacy—payable by those requesting the exemption.

Such is the system of abbé St. Pierre, which we present because the design of our work demands it, and on which we leave the verdict to those whose place it is to judge these important matters. But we cannot refrain from remarking in passing that it was only in a Dutch edition based on a faulty copy that this philosopher-citizen put forth an objection that presents itself quite naturally, and that is not one of the least important ones: namely, the disadvantage of benefices rendered hereditary, a disadvantage that is only too strongly felt and that would become even more widespread. What then, are all resignations of benefices and all coadjutories to be extinguished, and the conferment of all benefices referred to superiors? Perhaps that would not be worse; a bishop who knows his diocese and its good subjects is certainly as well situated to name someone to a vacant position as a half-dead churchman pestered by a crowd of relations and friends with vested interests—how many simonies and scandalous trials prevented!

To complete this article, it would remain for us to speak of *monastic celibacy*. But we will content ourselves with observing, along with the celebrated M. Melon,[24] (1) that it would be enormously advantageous for society and individuals for the prince to use strictly the power that he has to enforce the law that prohibits the monastic state before the age of twenty-five; or, to use the idea and the expression of M. Melon, that doesn't permit the alienation of one's liberty before the age when one can alienate one's estate. *See the rest in the articles* MARIAGE, MOINE [Monk], VIRGINITÉ, VOEUX [Vows], *&c.* (2) We will add with a modern author, whom one cannot either read too much or praise too highly,[25] that celibacy can become

24. Jean-François Melon (?–1738), in his *Essai politique sur le commerce* [Political essay on commerce] (N.p., 1734), 42–43.

25. Montesquieu. See *Spirit of the laws,* 23.21, and 25.4.

harmful in proportion as the corps of the celibate is too extensive, and thus the corps of the laity is not extensive enough; (3) that human laws, made to speak to the mind, must give precepts but not counsel; and that religion, made to speak to the heart, must give much counsel but few precepts. That when, for example, religion offers rules not for the proper but for the best, not for what is good but for what is perfect, it is fitting that these rules be counsel and not laws. For perfection does not concern the universality of men or of things. That what's more, if they are laws, then countless others will be needed to enforce the first ones; that experience has confirmed these principles; that when celibacy, which used to be only counsel in Christianity, became an explicit law within it for a certain order of citizens, new ones were needed every day to reduce men to the observation of the latter; and consequently, that the legislator wore himself out and wore out society making men perform by precept what those who love perfection would have performed themselves as counsel. (4) That by the nature of the human understanding, in religious affairs we like everything that presupposes an effort, just as in moral matters we have a speculative liking for everything that bears the imprint of severity; and so celibacy was bound to be, as has in fact happened, more agreeable to those peoples for whom it seemed least suitable, and for whom it could have the most deplorable effects; to be retained in Europe's southern countries, where by the nature of the climate it was more difficult to practice; to be proscribed in the countries of the north, where the passions are less lively; to be accepted where there are few inhabitants and rejected in areas where there are many.

These observations are so fine and so true that they cannot be repeated in too many places. I have drawn them from the excellent work of Président de M . . . ; What preceded is either from M. Fleury, or from Fr. Alexandre, or from Fr. Thomassin. Add to that what the *Memoirs of the academy of Inscriptions* & the political works of abbé de St. Pierre and M. Melon have furnished me, and a scant few sentences are left to me in this article, and even those are drawn from a work that one can find praised in the *Journal de Trevoux, Feb. 1746.*[26] Despite these authorities, I would not be surprised

26. In the *Journal de Trévoux* for February 1746 (pp. 197–220), one finds a quite laudatory review of the *Essay on merit and virtue,* on which, see n. 8, elsewhere in this article.

if it were to find critics and opponents. But it might also happen that, just as at the Council of Trent, it was (it is said) the young ecclesiastics who most doggedly rejected the proposal for priestly marriage, it may be those among the celibate who most need women, and who have least read the authors I have just cited, who will criticize their principles most openly.

Volume 3
(1753)

Masterpiece
(*Chef-d'Œuvre*)

For other entries on early manufacturing, see INDUSTRY, INNOVATION, INVENTION, *and* MASTERSHIPS, *below.*

*MASTERPIECE (*Arts, Crafts*), one of the most difficult works in a profession, executed by candidates wishing to join a guild or corporation, after completing a period as an apprentice and journeyman, according to the rules of the guild. Each corporation has its own masterpiece, which is carried out in the presence of doyens, syndics, senior members, and other officers and dignitaries of the corporation. It is presented to the guild's members, who examine it before it is registered. Some corporations allow the aspiring master craftsman to choose between several different masterpieces, while others ask for more than one. See the rules of these corporations concerning the prevailing norm for the reception of master craftsmen. The masterpiece in architecture is a classic exercise, such as designing a slanting arch, the top and sides of which hold up a cylindrical ceiling; the carpenters' masterpiece is a curved stair stringer; silk weavers, whether to be received as companions or as masters, must restore a loom to its working order, after the masters and syndics have brought about whatever changes to it they see fit, as, for example, untying the strings or breaking the threads of the

The present translation is lightly adapted from one made by Malcolm Eden, available from the University of Michigan's website *Encyclopedia of Diderot and d'Alembert: Collaborative Translation Project*, http://quod.lib.umich.edu/d/did, and reprinted by permission of the translator.

This article can be found at 3:273 in the original edition of the *Encyclopédie*.

chain at irregular intervals. It is hard to see the utility of the masterpiece. If the candidate can do his job well, then it is a waste of time examining him. If he cannot do his job well, then it should not stop him from joining a corporation, since he will only be harming himself. A reputation as a bad worker will soon force him to give up a job in which he will inevitably face ruin if he finds no work. To be convinced of the truth of these remarks, one needs only know a little of what happens at examinations. Nobody can be a candidate who has not passed through the preliminaries, and it is impossible for anyone not to have learned something of the trade in the four or five years that the preliminaries last. If the candidate is the master's son, he is generally exempted from doing a masterpiece. Everyone else, even the town's most skillful workers, will find it hard to produce a masterpiece that is acceptable to the guild, if ever they are disliked by the guild.[1] If they are liked, on the other hand, or if they have money, even if they know nothing whatsoever about the job, then they can either bribe the people supervising them during the execution of the masterpiece, carry out a poor piece of work that will be received as a masterpiece or present an excellent piece of work done by someone else. It is clear that such practices do away with any advantages that can be claimed for the masterpiece or for guilds, and yet guilds and corporate bodies for manufacturing continue to exist all the same.

1. *Communauté*, generic term meaning any body of individuals who share property. Here and in the last sentence, it is this word that Diderot uses to indicate the guilds he is discussing.—HC

Citizen
(*Citoyen*)

*CITIZEN (*Ancient and modern history, Public law*) is someone who is a member of a free association[1] of many families, who shares in the rights of this association, *and* who benefits from its liberties.[2] *See* SOCIÉTÉ [Society or Association], CITÉ [City], VILLE FRANCHE [Free Town], FRANCHISES [Liberties]. Someone who resides in such a society for certain business, and who has to go away after his business is done is not a *citizen* of this society; he is only a temporary subject. Someone who makes it his usual abode, but who plays no role in these rights and liberties, is also not a *citizen*. Someone who has been divested of these rights and liberties has ceased to be a *citizen*. Strictly speaking, one only accords this title to women, young children, and servants as family members of a *citizen*, but they are not truly *citizens*.

One may identify two types of *citizens*, the *originary* and the *naturalized*. The *originary* are those who are born *citizens*. The *naturalized* are those to whom society allows participation in these rights *and* liberties, even though they were not born among them.

The unattributed notes are adapted from *Diderot: "Encyclopédie,"* ed. John Lough and Jacques Proust, vol. 6 of *Denis Diderot: Œuvres complètes*, ed. Hans Dieckmann and Jean Varloot (Paris: Hermann, 1976), 463–67, and are used by permission. All others are by the present editor.

This article can be found at 3:488–89 in the original edition of the *Encyclopédie*.

1. *Société;* below, we usually translate this word as "society," but in the opening sentence it is being used in a more general and active sense that makes "association" seem a better option.—HC

2. The starting point for this article is Pufendorf, *Of the Law of Nature and Nations*, VII. ii.20. [The references below to Hobbes and Aristotle also come from Pufendorf.—HC]

The Athenians were very cautious about according the title of *citizen* of their city to foreigners; they invested much more dignity in this than did the Romans. With them, the title of *citizen* never came to be held in contempt; but from their high opinion of it, they have not reaped what is perhaps its greatest benefit, namely, that of growing by means of all those who have aspired to it. There were not many *citizens* in Athens who were not born to parents who were *citizens*. When a young man had reached the age of twenty, he was registered in the ληξιαρχικον γραμματειον;[3] the state counted him among its members. In an adoption ceremony, they made him recite, while facing the sky, the following oath: *Arma non dehonestabo; nec adstantem, quisquis ille fuerit, socium relinquam; pugnabo quoque pro focis et aris, solus et cum multis; patriam nec turbabo, nec prodam; navigabo contrà quamcumque destinatus fuero regionem; solemnitates perpetuas observabo; receptis consuetudinibus parebo, et quascumque adhuc populus* prudenter *statuerit, amplectar; et si quis leges susceptas sustulerit, nisi comprobaverit, non permittam; tuebor denique, solus et cum reliquis omnibus, atque patria sacra colam. Dii Cognitores, Agrauli, Enyalius, Mars, Jupiter, Floreo, Augesco duci.* Plut. *In peric.*[4] Notice a *prudenter* [a prudent man] who, in abandoning judgment on the new laws to each individual, was capable of causing much trouble. Otherwise, this oath is very noble and very wise.

One became a *citizen* of Athens, however, through adoption by a *citizen*, and through the consent of the people: but this benefit was not widespread.

3. *Lexiarchikongrammateion*, "the register of citizens." [It was kept by each deme or subdistrict of Attica; after the reforms of Cleisthenes in 508 B.C., it was necessary to be on the register to be a citizen.—HC]

4. This passage is taken not from Plutarch's *Parallel Lives* but from the *Onomasticon* of Julius Pollux (see the Latin version in the edition provided by J. H. Lederlin and T. Hemsterduis, Amsterdam, 1706, 2 vols., 2:925–26). "I will not dishonor my arms, nor abandon my comrade at my side, whoever he may be. I will also do battle for our hearths and our altars, alone or with many others. I will not bring disorder to the fatherland, nor will I betray it. I will sail to all regions where I am sent. I will observe the universal solemnities. I will submit to the accepted customs and will embrace all those which to this point the people will have *wisely* ordained. And if someone annuls the received laws or does not recognize them, I will not allow it. Finally, I will protect and observe, alone and with all others, the rites of our ancestors. As my witness, I take the gods Agraulus, Enyalius, Mars, Jupiter, Prosperity, multiplication, command."

If one was not judged to be a *citizen* before twenty years of age, one was considered to no longer be one when advanced age prevented him from attending to public functions. It was the same for the exiles and the banished, unless they had become so through ostracism; those who had suffered that judgment were only sent away.

To constitute a true Roman *citizen*, three things were needed: to have one's residence in Rome, to be a member of one of the thirty-five tribes, and to be able to attain the honors of the republic. Those who through concession but not birth possessed some of the rights of a *citizen* were strictly speaking only honorary. *See* CITÉ [City], JURISPRUDENCE.

When people say that there were more than four million Roman *citizens* in the census Augustus carried out, it is clear that they are including both those who were presently residing in Rome and those who, having spread out across the empire, were only honorary.

There was a great difference between a *citizen* and a resident. According to the law *de incolis*,[5] *citizens* were created and were given all the privileges of citizenship[6] through birth alone. These privileges could not be acquired by length of residence. Under the consuls it was only the benefaction of the state, and under the emperors it was only their will, which could remedy in this case a defective descent.

It was the first privilege of a Roman *citizen* to be judged only by the people. The law *Portia* prohibited a *citizen* from being put to death. Even in the provinces, he was not subjected to the arbitrary power of a proconsul or a propraetor. The *civis sum* [I am a citizen] stopped these subaltern tyrants in their tracks. In Rome, says M. de Montesquieu, in his book *The Spirit of the Laws, Book XI, Chapter XIX*, as well as in Lacedemon, liberty for the *citizens* and servitude for the slaves was extreme.[7] However, in spite of the privileges, the power, and the grandeur of these *citizens*—of whom Cicero was moved to write *(or. pro M. Fonteio) an qui amplissimus Gallia cum infino cive Romano comparandus est?*[8]—it seems to me that the government of that

5. "On inhabitants."—HC

6. *Bourgeoisie.*—HC

7. Montesquieu, *The Spirit of the Laws,* 11.19, 185.—HC

8. "Can one compare the most distinguished man in Gaul—I will not say with the leading figures of our city, but with the least of our Roman citizens?"

republic was constituted in such a way that in Rome one had a less precise idea of a *citizen* than in the canton of Zurich. To be convinced of this, it is only a matter of paying attention to what we are going to say in the rest of this article.

Hobbes does not distinguish between subject and *citizen*[9]—which is true, if you take the term *subject* in its strict sense and *citizen* in its broadest sense, and consider that the latter is to laws alone what the former is to a sovereign. They are both commanded, but one by a moral being and the other by a physical person. The term *citizen* fits neither those who live subjugated, nor those who live isolated. Whence it follows that those who live absolutely in the state of nature, as do sovereigns, and those who have completely renounced that state, as do slaves, cannot be regarded as *citizens*—unless one claims that there is no society based on reason where there is no being that is moral, immutable, and above the sovereign physical person. Overlooking this exception, Pufendorf divided his work on duties into two parts—one the duties of man, the other the duties of the *citizen*.[10]

Since the laws governing the free associations of families are not the same everywhere and since most societies have a hierarchical order constituted by dignities, the *citizen* can again be looked upon both in relation to the laws of his society and in relation to the rank he occupies in the hierarchical order. In the second case, there will be some difference between the *citizen* as magistrate and the *citizen* as bourgeois; and in the first, between the *citizen* of Amsterdam and of Basel.

While acknowledging the distinctions of civil societies and the order of *citizens* in each society, Aristotle nonetheless recognized as true *citizens* only those who have a role in the judiciary, and who could expect to pass from the state of simple bourgeois to the first ranks of the magistracy, which fits only pure democracies. It must be acknowledged that it is almost always someone who enjoys these prerogatives who is truly a public man, and that one has no clear distinction between subject and *citizen* unless the latter is

9. See Hobbes, *De Cive* (On the citizen).

10. Samuel Pufendorf, *The Whole Duty of Man According to the Law of Nature* (1673); trans. Andrew Tooke (1691); ed. and intro. Ian Hunter and David Saunders (Indianapolis: Liberty Fund, 2003).—HC

supposed to be a public man, and unless the role of the former could never be anything but that of a private man, *de quidam*.[11]

In restricting the term *citizen* to those who have founded the state through the first union of families, and to their successors from father to son, Pufendorf introduces a frivolous distinction that sheds little light in his work and that can plunge a civil society into a great deal of trouble, by distinguishing the originary from the naturalized *citizens* via a misconceived notion of nobility. The *citizens* in their capacity as *citizens*, that is to say, in their societies, are all equally noble, because nobility comes not from ancestry but from the common right to the leading honors of the magistracy.

Since the moral, sovereign being is to the *citizen* what the physical despotic person is to the subject, and since the most perfect slave does not cede his whole being to his sovereign, *a fortiori* does the *citizen* have rights that he reserves to himself and from which he never desists. There are occasions in which he finds himself in line, I don't say with his fellow *citizens*, but with the moral being who commands them all. This being has two titles: one private and the other public. The former should find no resistance, while the latter can experience resistance on the part of individuals, and even succumb to them in contestation. Since this moral being has properties, commitments, farms, farmers, etc., it is also necessary to distinguish in him, so to speak, the sovereign and the subject of sovereignty. In these cases, he is both judge and party. This is doubtless a drawback, but it affects all government in general, and by itself, it proves nothing for or against except by its rarity or its frequency. It is certain that subjects or *citizens* will be less exposed to injustices, to the extent that the sovereign being, physical or moral, is more rarely judge and party, on those occasions where he is attacked as a private individual.

In times of trouble, the *citizen* will take the side of the party that is for the established system. During the dissolution of a system, he will follow the party of his city if it is unanimous; if there is division in the city, he will embrace the party that is for the equality of its members and the liberty of all.

The more the *citizens* approach equality in ambition and in wealth, the more peaceful the state will be. This benefit seems to belong to pure democracy,

11. "A certain person," suggestive of a legal formula.—HC

exclusive of all other governments. But in even the most perfect democracy, complete equality among the members is a chimerical thing, and that is perhaps the principle of dissolution for that form of government—unless it is remedied by all the injustices of ostracism. It is with government in general as it is with animal life: each step in life is a step toward death. The best government is not the one that is immortal, but the one that lasts the longest and is the most peaceful.

Trading Company
(*Compagnie de Commerce*)

TRADING COMPANY. This term means an *association formed* for undertaking, implementing, or managing any commercial operations.

These *companies* are of two kinds, either private or privileged.

Private companies are normally formed by a small number of individuals who each furnish a portion of the capital, or simply their time and advice, and sometimes both, on the conditions agreed to in the partnership contract. These *companies* more commonly bear the denomination of *firms* [*sociétés*]. See SOCIÉTÉ [Society or Association].

Usage has nonetheless preserved the name *company* for private firms or partnerships when there are a large number of members, substantial capital, and enterprises distinguished by their risk or their scale. These sorts of *company-firms* are most often composed of persons from various occupations who, being inexperienced in trade, entrust the direction of operations to partners or to competent agents under a general plan. Although the operations of these *companies* receive no public preference over private operations, they are nonetheless always regarded askance in commercial locales, because any competition reduces profit. But that reason itself ought to make them very agreeable to the state, whose commerce can be extended and perfected only through the merchants' competition.

Even in general, these *companies* are useful to traders because they extend a nation's knowledge of, and interest in, that sector that is always envied and often despised—despite its being the sole source of all others.

This article can be found at 3:739–44 in the original edition of the *Encyclopédie*. It concludes with a mathematical supplement by d'Alembert, which has been omitted here.

Abundant money, low interest rates, sound public credit, the growth of luxury—all clear signs of public prosperity—are the usual results of these sorts of establishments. They contribute in turn to that prosperity, by multiplying the various kinds of occupation for the people, their ease, their consumption, and finally the revenues of the state.

There is one case, however, in which they might be harmful: that is when dividends are distributed as shares that are traded and transferred without further formality. By this means, foreigners may elude that wise law that in civilized states prohibits non-naturalized or non-domiciled foreigners from participating in armaments companies. Thanks to these shares, peoples who have a better rate of interest than their neighbors can attract from afar all the profit from the trade of these neighbors—sometimes even ruin them, if it is in their interest. It is only then that merchants have a right to complain. Another general rule: anything that can be subject to speculation is dangerous in a nation that pays a higher rate of interest.

The usefulness of these associations to investors is much more ambiguous than to the state. Nonetheless, it is unfair to be biased against all schemes just because most of those that have been seen to hatch at various times have failed. The usual pitfalls are lack of thrift (inseparable from large operations), lavish expense on establishments before being assured of profit, impatience to see gain, hasty loss of appetite for the project, and finally, discord.

Credulity, daughter of ignorance, is imprudent, but it is contradictory to abandon an enterprise one knew to be risky simply because its risks have been unfurled. Fortune seems to take pleasure in making those who solicit her pass through trials; her largesse is not reserved for those discouraged by her first whims.

There are some general rules by which people who are not acquainted with commerce but would like to become interested in it can protect themselves: (1) At a time when a nation's capital stock has increased among all classes of people—although with some disproportion among them—the types of commerce that have raised up great fortunes, and that sustain brisk merchant competition, never procure substantial profits; the more this competition increases, the more noticeable the disadvantage becomes. (2) In distant and risky trade, it is imprudent to employ capital whose revenue is not superfluous to subsistence. For if the stakeholders annually withdraw either their dividends or simply their interest (if it is at any tolerably substantial rate), any losses that might occur fall immediately on the capital. Sometimes, this capital itself is found to be already diminished by the extraordinary expenses of the first few years. Operations languish or lack boldness; the plan as conceived cannot be fulfilled, and the dividends will certainly be mediocre, even if things go well. (3) Any plan that shows only profits is drawn up by a man lacking either prudence or sincerity. (4) An excellent commercial operation is one in which, following the ordinary course of events, capital runs no risk. (5) The gains from trade are almost always proportional to the uncertainty of success; the operation is good if this proportion is very clear. (6) The selection of individuals who should be assigned the conduct of the enterprise is the most essential item in its success. The one who is capable of taking in a broad overview of things and of directing each particular operation to the common benefit will do quite poorly on the details; aptitude for the latter indicates talent, but often only that. Without understanding commerce, one can be enriched by its means. If the laws were not burdened with formalities, a skillful merchant would surely be a good judge; he would in every case be a great financier. But just because a man knows the laws, just because he has administered the public revenues well or has profited much in one type of trade, it does not follow that his judgment ought to prevail in all commercial deliberations.

There have never been so many plans and projects of this kind since the return of peace,[1] and it is noteworthy that virtually everyone has turned his sights toward Cadiz, Martinique, and St. Domingue.[2] That did not require much skill, and however little discussion one may have wanted to engage in, it was easy to predict the fate that the stakeholders have experienced. The result is that much more capital has left this trade than has entered into it as surplus.

If one had been busy discovering new mines or establishing solid factories in lesser-known cities such as Naples or Hamburg; if *companies* had employed a great deal of capital, wisely managed, in the trade of Louisiana

1. The reference is to the end of the War of the Austrian Succession in 1748.

2. Cadiz, the southwestern Spanish port that carried much of the Spanish-American trade during this period; Martinique and St. Domingue, two profitable slave-based sugar islands in the French Caribbean.

or the North; if they had set up enterprises in our Antilles (which are conducive to them), as in Guadeloupe and Cayenne,[3] they would soon have recognized that there are even bigger and more solid fortunes to be made in the branches of commerce that are not open than have been made up to now. Means of subsistence for the people and wherewithal for families would have doubled in less than ten years.

These details would perhaps not be suitable for an ordinary dictionary, but the purpose of the *Encyclopédie* is to instruct, and it is important to absolve commerce of the faults of those who have engaged in it.

Privileged *companies* or guilds are those that have received from the state special favors or rights for certain enterprises, to the exclusion of other subjects. They began in times of barbarism and ignorance, when the seas were covered with pirates, the art of navigation was crude and uncertain, and the use of insurance was not well known. At that time, it was necessary for those who tried their luck in the midst of so many perils to diminish these by sharing them, to engage in mutual support, and to band together in political bodies. The advantage that states derived from them led states to grant encouragements and special protection to these bodies; afterward, the needs of those states and the merchants' greed imperceptibly perpetuated these privileges, under the pretext that trade could not be carried on otherwise.

This prejudice has not entirely dissipated as people have become more civilized and the human sciences more perfected, because it is easier to imitate than to reason. And even today, many people think that it is useful to restrict competition in certain cases.

One of these special cases that people cite is that of an enterprise that is new, risky, or costly. Everyone will no doubt agree that cases of this type require the special favor and encouragement of the state.

If these favors and encouragements are fiscal exemptions, it is clear that the state loses nothing from the fact that a larger number of subjects will profit from them, since it is a new industry that it is favoring. If it is outlays, bonuses, whatever is more certain and even indispensable, it is clear that three infallible consequences result from competition. First, a greater num-

3. French Caribbean colonies.

ber of men are enriched; the state's investment brings returns more surely and promptly. Second, the establishment will be brought to its perfection (which is the purpose of the outlays) to the extent that greater efforts contribute to it. Third, the outlays will cease sooner.

The reader will be better instructed on this matter if I place before him the opinions of one of England's most skillful men of commerce. I speak of Mr. Josiah Child, *ch. iii* of one of his treatises entitled, *Trade, and interest of money considered.*[4]

No one is justified in flattering himself that he thinks any better; and what I will say, when supported by such an authority, will be less open to criticism. It is good to observe that the author was writing in 1669, and that many things have changed since then, but virtually all of them in extension of his principles.[5]

> Companies of Merchants [says Mr. Child] are of two sorts, viz., Companies in joynt Stock, such as the *East-India-Company*, the *Morea-Company* (which is a Branch of the *Turkey-Company*) and the *Greenland-Company*, which is a Branch of the *Muscovia-Company;* the other sort are *Companies* who trade not by a *joynt Stock*, but only are under a Government and Regulation, such are the *Hambrough-Company*, the *Turkey-Company*, the *Eastland-Company*, the *Muscovia-Company*.
>
> It hath for many Years been a moote case, whether any Encorporating of *Merchants*, be for publik Good or not.
>
> For my own part I am of Opinion:

4. Title in English in the original; the English merchant and tract writer Josiah Child (1630–99) was of great interest to the French trade official Vincent de Gournay and to his circle of translators and publicists, including Forbonnais. Indeed, virtually the only publication by Gournay himself was a translation and commentary of the work that Forbonnais excerpts here. See Henry C. Clark, ed., *Commerce, Culture and Liberty: Readings on Capitalism Before Adam Smith* (Indianapolis: Liberty Fund, 2003), 37–53, for more on Child. See also Paul Slack, *The Invention of Improvement: Information and Material Progress in Seventeenth-Century England* (Oxford: Oxford University Press, 2015), 7, 132–35, 192–93, and passim.

5. What follows is the full text of chapter 3 from Josiah Child, *A Discourse about Trade wherein the reduction of interest in money to 4 l. per centum, is recommended* (London, 1690), a much expanded version of the 1668 title alluded to by Forbonnais; material in brackets is by Forbonnais. The spelling, punctuation, and italicization of the original have been preserved. The translation into French by Forbonnais is somewhat loose in places but not inexact in substance.

I. That for *Countries* with which his *Majesty* hath no *Allieance,* nor can have any by reason of their distance, or Barbarity, or non-Communication with the *Princes* of *Christendom,* &c., where there is a necessity of Maintaining Forces and Forts (such as *East-India* and *Guinia*), *Companies* of *Merchants* are absolute necessary.

II. *It seems evident to me that the greatest part of these two Trades ought for publick Good, to be managed by joynt Stock.*

[Since that time the English have found the secret of reconciling the liberty and protection of commerce on the coast of Africa. See GRANDE BRETAGNE, its commerce.[6]]

III. *It's questionable to me, whether any other Company of Merchants are for publick good or hurt.*

IV. I conclude however, *that all restrictions of Trade are naught,* and consequently that no *Company* whatsoever, whether they Trade in a *Joynt Stock* or under *Regulation,* can be for publick Good, except it may be easie for all, or any of his *Majesty's Subjects* to be admitted into all, or any of the said *Companies,* at any time for a very inconsiderable Fine, and that if the Fine exceed 20 l. including all Charges of admission, it is too much, and that for these Reasons.

1. Because the *Dutch* who thrive best by Trade, and have the surest rules to thrive by, *admit not only any of their own* People, *but even* Jews *and all kind of* Aliens, *to be Free of any of their Societies of* Merchants, *or any of their Cities or Towns Corporate.*

2. *Nothing in the World can enable us to coape with the* Dutch *in any Trade, but encrease of Hands and Stock, which a general admission will do;* many Hands and much Stock being as necessary to the Prosperity of any Trade, as Men and Money to warfare.

3. There is no pretence of any good to the *Nation* by *Companies*, but only *Order and Regulation* of Trade; and if that be preserved (which the admission of all that will come in and submit to the *Regulation,* will not prejudice) all the good to the *Nation* that can be hoped for by *Companies,* is obtained.

4. The *Eastland,* besides our *Native Commodities,* spend great quantities of *Italian, Spanish, Portugal,* and *French Commodities,* viz. *Oyle,*

6. There is a short entry entitled BRETAGNE (GRANDE), which refers to ANGLETERRE, where its commerce is briefly discussed.

Wine, Fruit, Sugar, Succads, Shoomack, &c. Now, in regard our *East-Country Merchants* of *England* are few, compared with the *Dutch,* and intend principally that one Trade out and home, and consequently are not so conversant in the aforesaid *Commodities,* nor forward to adventure upon them, and seeing that by the *Companies Charter* our *Italian, Spanish, Portugal* and *French Merchants,* who understand those *Commodities* perfectly well, are excluded those Trades, or at least, if the *Company* will give them leave to send out those Goods, are not permitted to bring in the Returns; it follows, that the *Dutch* must supply *Denmark, Sweeden,* and all parts of the *Baltique,* with most of those *Commodities,* and so it is in fact.

5. The *Dutch* who have no *Eastland-Companies,* yet have ten times the Trade to the *Eastern parts* as we have; and for *Italy, Spain* and *Portugal,* where we have no *Companies,* we have yet left full as much, if not more Trade, then the *Dutch.* [If, in this situation, English trade was equal to that of Holland in the countries just named, it is evident that either this trade was increased by the liberty of Northern shipping, or that England resold to Holland a part of its return cargo, and thereby deprived itself of a substantial portion of its benefit. It is an effect of all restricted shipping, because large stocks alone procure large sales.] And for *Russia* and *Greenland* where we have *Companies* (and I think Establisht by *Act* or *Acts* of *Parliament*) our Trade is in effect wholly lost, while the *Dutch* have, without *Companies,* encreased theirs to above *forty* times the Bulk of what the residue of ours now is.

From whence may be inferred:

1. *That restrained limitted Companies* are not alone sufficient to preserve and encrease a Trade.

2. *That limitted Companies, though Established by Act of Parliament, may lose a Trade.*

3. *That Trade may be carried on to any part of Christendom, and encreased without* Companies.

4. *That we have declined more, at least have encreased less, in those Trades limitted* to Companies, *then in others where all his Majesties Subjects have had equal freedom to Trade.*

The common *Objections* against this easie admission of all his *Majesties Subjects* into *Companies* of *Merchants*, are:

Object. 1. If all persons may come into any *Company of Merchants* on such easie terms, then young *Gentlemen, Shop-keepers* and divers others will turn *Merchants,* who through their own unskillfulness will pay dear for our native *Commodities* here, and sell them cheap abroad; and also buy Foreign *Commodities* dear abroad, and sell them here for less then their cost, to the Ruin of themselves, and Destruction of *Trade.*

I answer, first, *caveat emptor,* let particular Men look to themselves,[7] and so doubtless they will in those Trades for which there are now *Companies,* as well as they do in others for which there are no *Companies.*

It is the care of *Law-makers* first and principally, to provide for the *People* in gross, not particulars, and if the consequence of so easie an admission, should be to make our *Manufactures* cheap abroad, and *Foreign Commodities* cheap here (as is alledged), our *Nation* in general would have the advantage both ways.

Object. 2. *If all should be admitted &c. Shop-keepers, being the Retailors, of the same* Commodities *the* Company *Imports, would have so much the advantage of the Merchant, that he would beat the Merchant wholly out of the Trade.*

I answer, first, *We see no such thing in Holland, nor in the open Trades,* viz. *France, Spain, Portugal, Italy,* and all our own *Plantations,* neither can that well be, for to drive a *retail Trade* to any purpose, requires a Mans full Stock, as well as his full attendance, and so doth it to drive the Trade of a *Merchant,* and therefore few can find Stock and time to attend both; from whence it follows, that of the many Hundreds which in memory have turned *Merchants,* very few continued long to follow both, but commonly after two or three Years Experience, betake themselves wholly to *Merchandizing,* or returned to the sole Exercise of their *Retail way;* but whether they do, or do not, concerns not the *Nation* in general, whose common Interest is to buy cheap, whatever appellation the *Seller* hath, whether that of a meer *Merchant, Gentleman,* or a *Shop-keeper.*

Object. 3. If *Shop-keepers* and other unexperienced persons may turn *Merchants,* &c. they will through Ignorance neglect buying and sending out our *Native Manufactures,* and will send out our *Money,* or *Bills of Exchange* to buy *Foreign Commodities,* which is an apparent National loss.

I answer, that *Shop-keepers* are, like all other Men (led by their profit) and if it be for their Advantage to send out Manufactures, they will do it without forcing; and if it be for their Profit to send over Money or

7. Forbonnais does not repeat the Latin expression.

Bills of Exchange, they will do that, and so will *Merchants* as soon and as much as they.

Object. 4. *If any may be admitted, &c. what do we get by our seven Years Service, and the great Sums of Money our Parents gave to bind us Apprentices to* Merchants? *&c. And who will hereafter bind his Son to a* Merchant?

I answer, *The end of Service and giving of Money with Apprentices, I have always understood to be the Learning of the Art or Science of Merchandizing, not the purchasing of an Immunity or Monopoly to the prejudice of our Country;* and that it is so, is evident from the practice, there being many general *Merchants* that are free of no particular *Company,* who can have as large Sums of Money with *Apprentices,* as any other that are free of one or more particular *Companies of Merchants;* and many *Merchants* that are free of particular *Companies,* unto whom few will have any considerable sums of Money with *Apprentices;* the proportion of Money given with *Apprentices* not following the *Company* a *Merchant* is free of, but the condition the *Master,* as to his more or less reputed skill in his Calling, Thriving or going backward, greater or lesser Trade, well or ill Government of himself and Family, &c.

Obj. 5. *If all should be admitted on such easie terms, will not that be manifest Injustice to the* Companies of Merchants, *who by themselves or Predecessors have been at great Disburstments to purchase Priviledges & Immunities abroad, as the* Turkey-Company, *and the* Hambrough-Company *have done.*

I answer, That I am yet to learn that any Company of Merchants not trading with a joynt Stock, such as the *Turkey, Hambrough, Muscovia* and *Eastland* Companies ever purchased their Priviledges, or built and maintained Forts, Castles or Factories, or made any Wars at their own charge; but I know the *Turkey* Company do maintain an Embassador and two Consuls, and are sometimes necessitated to make Presents to the *Grand Senior,*[8] or his great Officers; and the *Hambrough* Company are at some charge to maintain their Deputy, and Minister at *Hambrough;* and I think it would be great Injustice that any should trade to the places within their Charters, without paying the same Duties or Leviations towards the Companies charge as the present Adventurers do pay, but I know not why any should be barred from trading to those places, or forced to pay a great Fine for admition, that are willing to pay

8. The reference is to the Sultan of the Ottoman Empire.

the Companies Duties, and submit to the Companies regulation and orders in other respects.

Obj. 6. *If all may be admitted as aforesaid, then such numbers of Shopkeepers and others would come into the Society of* Merchants, *as would by the Majority of Votes so much alter the Governours, Deputy and Assistants of the respective Companies, that Ignorant Persons would come into those ruling places, to the general prejudice of those Trades.*

I answer, *Those that make this Objection, if they be Merchants, know there is very little in it, for that it is not to be expected that twenty Shopkeepers will come into any one Company in a Year;* and therefore can have no considerable influence upon the Elections; but if many more should come in, it would be the *better* for the *Nation,* and not the worse for the *Company,* for that all men are lead by their Interest, and it being the common Interest of all that engage in any Trade, that the Trade should be regulated and governed by wise, honest and able men, there is no doubt but most men will Vote for such as they esteem so to be, which is manifest in the *East-India-Company,* where neither *Gentlemen nor Shopkeepers were at first excluded,* neither are they yet kept out; any *English-man whatsoever being permitted to come into that Company that will buy an Action, paying only five Pounds to the Company for his admission;* and yet undeniable experience hath convinced all Gain-sayers in this matter; that *Company*, since its having had so large and National a Foundation, having likewise had a succession of much better *Governours, Deputies* and *Assistants* then ever it had upon that narrow bottom it stood formerly, when none could be admitted to the freedom of that *Company*, for less than a Fine of *Fifty Pounds;* and the success hath been answerable, *For the first Company settled upon that narrow limitted Interest, although their Stock was larger, then this, decayed and finally came to ruin and destruction;* Whereas on the contrary, this being settled on more rational, and consequently more just, as well as more profitable Principles, *hath through Gods Goodness thriven and encreased to the trebling of their first Stock.*

What concerns the various companies of Europe is relegated to the commerce of each state. *This article is by M.* V.D.F.

Competition
(*Concurrence*)

COMPETITION, *in matters of commerce*. This word sets out the idea of several persons aspiring to one preference: thus, when various individuals undertake to sell the same commodity, each one strives to offer it better or at a lower price, to obtain the preference of the buyer.

One immediately sees that *competition* is the soul and the spur of industry, and the most active principle of commerce.

This *competition* is either external or internal.

The external *competition* of a nation's commerce consists in being able to sell abroad the products of its land and industry in the same quantity as other nations sell theirs—proportional to their respective populations, their capital stock, and the extent and fertility of their lands. The nation that does not sustain this *competition* in the proportion that we have just discussed will inevitably possess power that is inferior to that of others, because its men are less employed, less rich, less happy, thenceforth relatively fewer—in short, in less of a position, relatively speaking, to support the commonwealth. It cannot be too often repeated: the balance of trade is truly the balance of power.

This external *competition* is not obtained by force; it is the value of the efforts that human industry makes to grasp the tastes of the consumer, even to predict them and stimulate them.

Internal *competition* is of two kinds: one, between domestic commodities and foreign commodities of the same nature or the same use; and another type, depriving the people of the means of subsistence, should in general

This article can be found at 3:832–33 in the original edition of the *Encyclopédie*.

be proscribed. Those who contribute to introducing it—either by buying or selling—are genuinely guilty of increasing or maintaining the number of poor with which society is burdened.

The other type of internal *competition* is that of work among subjects: it consists in the fact that each of them has the capacity to be employed in the manner that he believes most lucrative, or that is most agreeable to him.

This is the principal basis of the freedom of trade: it alone contributes more than any other means to bringing to a nation that external *competition* which enriches it and makes it powerful. The reason is very simple. I won't, perhaps, say that every man is so unfortunate as to be naturally inclined to work, but he is naturally inclined to procure his ease; and this ease, the wages of his labor, then makes his occupation agreeable to him. Thus, as long as no internal vice in the state's administration sets obstacles to human industry, this industry enters by itself into the lists. The more substantial the number of its products, the more moderate is their price; and this price moderation obtains the preference of foreigners.

However, as money enters a state in this way, as the people's means of subsistence multiply and the number of, or *competition* among, consumers increases, commodities must be represented by a larger sum. This increase in the price of everything is real, and is the first effect of the progress of human industry. But a fortunate circle of new *competitions* ushers in appropriate arrangements. The commodities subject to consumption become daily more abundant, and that abundance partly moderates their price increase; the other part is distributed imperceptibly among all those who produce things, or who exchange them, by the reduction in their profits. The reduction in this profit is itself compensated for by the reduction in interest rates, since, as the number of borrowers is found to be fewer than the number of lenders, money loses its value by unanimous agreement, like any other merchandise. This lowering of interest is, as we see, the result of active trade. Thus, we will observe in passing that in order to know whether a nation that has no mines is engaging in as much commerce as others—relative to the respective facility that each has to engage in commerce—it is enough to compare the rates of interest in each. For it is certain that if the *competition* in these rates is not equal, there will be no equality in the external *competition* in sales and shipping.

When, by these manifest signs, one perceives a constant increase in a state's commerce, all of its parts act and transmit equal movement to each other; it enjoys the full vigor of which it is capable.

A similar situation is inseparable from great luxury. It extends over diverse classes of the people because they are all prosperous. But the luxury that produces public ease, through increase of work, is never to be feared; external *competition* constantly checks its excess, which would otherwise soon be the fateful end of all prosperity. Human industry then opens new routes; it perfects its methods and its works. Frugal use of time and energy in some sense multiplies men; needs give birth to the arts, *competition* lifts them up, and the artists' wealth makes them knowledgeable.

Such are the prodigious effects of this principle of *competition*—so simple at first sight, as are virtually all the principles of commerce. This one in particular seems to me to have a very rare advantage, namely to be subject to no exceptions. *This article is by M.* V.D.F.

Conquest
(*Conquête*)

Conquest (*Law of nations*), acquisition of sovereignty by the superior arms of a foreign prince, who forces the defeated to submit to his dominion.

It is very important to establish the just power of the right of *conquest*—its laws, its spirit, its effects—and the foundations of the sovereignty acquired in this manner. But in order not to get lost on dark and untrod paths from lack of illumination, I will take on enlightened guides, known to all the world, who have newly and attentively traversed these tricky routes and who, holding me by the hand, will prevent me from falling.[1]

The right of *conquest* may be defined as a necessary, legitimate, and unfortunate right, which always leaves an immense debt to be discharged if human nature is to be repaid.[2]

From the right of war derives that of *conquest*, which is its consequence.[3] When a people is conquered, the right of the conqueror follows four sorts of laws: the law of nature, which makes everything tend toward the preservation of species; the law of natural enlightenment, which has us do to others what we would want to have done to us; the law that forms political societies, which are such that nature has not limited their duration; lastly, the law drawn from the thing itself.

Thus, a state that has conquered another treats it in one of these four ways: either it continues to govern its conquest according to its own laws and takes for itself only the exercise of the political and civil government;

This article can be found at 3:899–901 in the original edition of the *Encyclopédie*.

1. The reference is to Montesquieu.
2. See Montesquieu, *The Spirit of the Laws,* 10.4, 142 for this definition.
3. The next two paragraphs are from Montesquieu, *Laws,* 10.3, 139.

or it gives its conquest a new political and civil government; or it destroys the society and scatters its members off into other societies; or, finally, it exterminates all the citizens.

The first two ways conform to the law of nations that we presently follow.[4] I would merely observe on the second that it is a risky enterprise on the conqueror's part to want to give his laws and customs to the conquered people; there is no good in that, because one is capable of obeying in all sorts of governments. The last two ways[5] conform to the law of nations among the Romans; on which, one can judge how much better we have become. Here homage must be paid to our modern times, to contemporary reasoning, to the religion of the present day, to our philosophy, to our mores. We know that *conquest* is an acquisition, and that the spirit of acquisition carries with it the spirit of preservation and use, not that of destruction.

When the authors of our public law, for whom ancient histories provided the foundation, have no longer followed cases strictly, they have lapsed into big mistakes.[6] They have moved toward the arbitrary; they have presupposed among conquerors a right, I know not which one, of killing. This has made them draw consequences as terrible as the principle, and establish maxims that the conquerors themselves, when they have had the slightest sense, have never adopted. It is clear that, once the conquest is made, the conqueror no longer has the right to kill, because it is no longer for him a case of natural defense and of his own preservation.

What has made our political authors think this way is that they have believed the conqueror had the right to destroy the society; whence they have concluded that he had the right to destroy the men composing it, which is a consequence falsely drawn from a false principle. For it would not follow from the annihilation of the society that the men forming that society should also be annihilated. The society is the union of men and not the men themselves; the citizen may perish, and the man remain.

From the right to kill during *conquest*, political men have derived the right to reduce to servitude, but the consequence is as ill founded as the principle.

4. Montesquieu had said "the first way" only; 10.3, 139.

5. Montesquieu says the last way only; 10.3, 139.

6. The next six paragraphs are taken from *Laws*, 10.3, 140.

One has the right to reduce a people to servitude only when it is necessary for the preservation of a *conquest.* The purpose of *conquest* is preservation. Servitude is never the purpose of *conquest,* but it is sometimes a necessary means for achieving preservation.

In this case, it is against the nature of the thing for this servitude to be eternal. It must be possible for the enslaved people to become subjects. Slavery is accidental to *conquest.* When, after a certain length of time, all the parts of the conquering state are bound to those of the conquered state by customs, marriage, laws, associations, and a certain conformity of spirit, servitude should cease. For the rights of the conqueror are founded only on the fact that these things do not exist and that there is a distance between the two nations, such that the one cannot trust the other.

Thus, the conqueror who reduces a people to servitude should always reserve for himself means—and these means are innumerable—for allowing them to leave it as soon as possible.[7]

These are not, adds M. Montesquieu, vague things here; these are principles, and our forefathers who conquered the Roman Empire put them in practice. They softened the laws that they had made in the heat, the activity, the impetuosity, the arrogance of victory; their laws had been hard, they made them impartial. The Burgundians, the Goths, and the Lombards always wanted the Romans to be the defeated people; the laws of Euric, of Gundobad, and of Rotharis made the barbarian and the Roman fellow citizens.

Instead of drawing such fatal consequences from the right of *conquest,* political men would have done better to speak of the advantages this right can sometimes confer on a vanquished people.[8] They would have been more sensitive to these advantages if our law of nations were followed exactly and if it were established around the earth. Sometimes the frugality of the conquering nation has put it in position to leave the defeated people the necessities that their own prince had taken from them. One has seen states whose oppression by tax collectors was relieved by the conqueror, who had neither the commitments nor the needs of the legitimate prince.

7. The final phrase, "as soon as possible," was added by Jaucourt.

8. With this sentence, *Laws,* 10.4, becomes Jaucourt's main source.

A *conquest* can destroy harmful prejudices, and, if one dares to say it, can put a nation under a better tutelary spirit. What good could the Spanish not have done for the Mexicans? And what harm did they not bring them by their destructive *conquests*? I pass over in silence the details on the rules of conduct that the various conquering states should observe for the preservation and the good of their *conquests;* they will be found in the illustrious author of the *Spirit of the Laws*.

There would be many remarks to make on *conquest* considered as a means of acquiring sovereignty; I must again limit myself to the main ones.[9]

(1) *Conquest* considered in itself is rather the occasion for the acquisition of sovereignty than the immediate cause of that acquisition. The immediate cause of the acquisition of sovereignty is always the consent of the people, either express or tacit. Without that consent, the state of war still exists between two enemies, and it cannot be said that one is obliged to obey the other; it is merely that the consent of the vanquished is extorted by the superiority of the victor.

(2) Every legitimate *conquest* assumes that the victor had just cause to make war on the vanquished; without this, *conquest* is not itself a sufficient title, for one cannot grab the sovereignty of a nation by the law of the strongest, and by seizing possession alone, as with something that belongs to no one. Let no one speak of the prince's glory in making *conquests*. His glory is his pride; it is a passion, not a legitimate right. Thus, when Alexander waged war on the most distant peoples, peoples who had never heard of him, such a *conquest* was certainly no more just title to the acquisition of sovereignty than brigandage is a legitimate means of becoming rich. The number and quality[10] of the persons does not change the nature of the action; the offense is the same, the crime is identical.

But if the war is just, the *conquest* is as well; for first of all, it is a natural result of the victory, and the defeated who surrenders to the victor is merely paying ransom for his life. Besides, since the defeated have engaged in an unjust war by their own fault, rather than granting the just satisfaction they owed, they are held to have tacitly consented in advance to the

9. The following discussion relies on Pufendorf, *Of the Law of Nature and Nations: Eight Books* (VII.vii.3 and VII.vii.4).

10. *Qualité;* alternatives would be "title," "nobility," or "status."

conditions that the victor might impose on them, provided these contain nothing unjust or inhuman.

What to think of unjust *conquests* and of submission extorted by violence? Can it bestow a legitimate right? Pufendorf (*Bk. VII, ch. vii*) responds that one must distinguish whether the usurper has changed a republic into a monarchy, or instead has dispossessed the legitimate monarch. In the latter case, he is absolutely obliged to return the crown to the one he has stripped of it, or to his heirs, until one can reasonably assume that they have renounced their pretentions. And this is what one always assumes when a substantial amount of time has flowed by without their having been willing or able to make an effort to recover the crown.

Thus, in relation to sovereignty, the law of nations admits of a kind of prescription between kings and free peoples; it is what the interest and tranquility of societies demands. The peaceful and sustained possession of sovereignty has to put it definitively beyond attack; otherwise there would be no end of disputes concerning realms and their limits, which would be a source of perpetual war. And there would hardly be a sovereign today who possessed authority legitimately.

It is in reality the people's duty to resist the usurper at the beginning with all their might and to remain faithful to their sovereign. But if, despite all their efforts, their sovereign gets the worst of it and is no longer in a position to validate his law, they have no further obligations and can provide for their own preservation.

Peoples cannot do without government. And since they are not bound to expose themselves to perpetual war in order to uphold the interests of their first sovereign, they may render the right of the usurper legitimate by their consent. In these circumstances, the dispossessed sovereign should find consolation for the loss of his state as for a misfortune without remedy.

With regard to the first case, if the usurper has changed a republic into a monarchy, if he governs with moderation and equity, it is enough for him to have reigned peacefully for some time in order to give occasion to believe that the people are adjusting to his domination, and thus to erase what was vicious in the manner by which he had acquired it. This is what one may apply to the reign of Augustus, or if one does not want to apply it to him, one must nonetheless accept our maxim, that by the lapse of time,

Usurpers of provinces become just princes by giving just laws. But if, on the other hand, the prince who has made himself master of the government of a republic drives it tyrannically, if he mistreats the citizens and oppresses them, one is then not obliged to obey him. In these circumstances, even the longest possession entails nothing else but a long continuation of injustice.

For the rest, nothing should better cure princes of the folly of distant usurpations and *conquests* than the example of the Spanish and Portuguese, and of all other less distant *conquests*—their uselessness, their uncertainty, and their reversals of fortune. Countless examples teach us how little these sorts of acquisition should be relied on. It happens sooner or later that a superior power uses the same means to take these acquisitions away from the one who has made them, or from his children. This is how France lost under John's reign what Philip Augustus and St. Louis had conquered from the English, and how Edward III lost the *conquests* he had himself made in France. Then one finds one of Edward's successors (Henry V) favorably restoring all of his predecessors' losses, and the French in their turn recovering a short time afterward everything that prince had taken from them.[11]

Conquests are easily made, because they are made with all one's forces and because one profits from the opportunity. They are difficult to preserve, because they are defended with only a part of these forces. The aggrandizement of a conquering prince's state reveals new areas by which it can be taken, and favorable conjunctures are chosen to this effect. It is the fate of heroes to ruin themselves conquering countries that they lose afterward. The reputation of their arms may extend their state, but the reputation of their justice would increase its strength more solidly. Thus, just as monarchs must have wisdom to legitimately increase their power, they must have no less prudence in order to limit it. *Article by Ch.* DE JAUCOURT

11. The references are to the French kings Philip II Augustus (1180–1223), Louis IX (1226–70), and John II (1350–64), and to Edward III (1327–77) and Henry V (1413–22) of England.

Volume 4
(1754)

Public Corruption
(*Corruption Publique*)

*PUBLIC CORRUPTION (*Politics and Morality*). It has two sources: the nonobservance of good laws; the observance of bad laws. It has always seemed to me more difficult to have good laws be observed rigorously than to abrogate bad ones. Abrogation is the result of public authority. Observation is the result of private integrity.

This article can be found at 4:278 in the original edition of the *Encyclopédie*.

Democracy
(*Démocratie*)

Pons writes that "like Montesquieu, de Jaucourt does not believe that democracy is possible in a large state" (205). But Pons's edition includes only the first two paragraphs of the article. A reading of the full article, as translated below, will provide a fuller opportunity to gauge the author's endorsement of democracy. See also the article FEDERAL REPUBLIC, *below, for further discussion of the possibilities of popular government in large states.*

DEMOCRACY (*Political law*) is one of the simple forms of government, the one in which the people as a body have sovereignty. Every republic in which sovereignty resides in the hands of the people is a *democracy;* and if the sovereign power is found in the hands of only part of the people, it is an aristocracy. See ARISTOCRACY.

Although I do not think that *democracy* is the most convenient or most stable form of government, although I am persuaded that it is disadvantageous for large states, I nonetheless believe it to be one of the most ancient forms among nations that have followed as equitable this maxim:

"That whatever the members of the society have an interest in should be administered by all in common."[1]

The natural equity that exists among us, says Plato (speaking of Athens, his Country), makes us seek in our government an equality consonant with

This article can be found at 4:816–18 in the original edition of the *Encyclopédie*.

1. For this Canon law maxim, originating in Roman private law, see Gaines Post, "A Romano-Canonical Maxim, *Quod omnes tangit,* in Bracton and in early Parliaments," in *Studies in Medieval Legal Thought* (Princeton: Princeton University Press, 1964), 163–238.

the law, while at the same time making us submit to those among us who have the most ability and wisdom.

It seems to me not without reason that *democracies* boast of being nurseries of great men.[2] In fact, since there is no one in popular governments who does not have a part in the administration of the state—each according to his status[3] and his merit—since there is no one who does not participate in the fortunes or misfortunes of events, all individuals vie with each other in applying themselves and interesting themselves in the common good, because there are no revolutions that are not useful or harmful to all. Moreover, *democracies* lift spirits, because they show the way to honors and glory, which are more open to all citizens, more accessible and less limited than under government of a few or government of one, in which countless obstacles prevent them from appearing. It is these happy prerogatives of *democracy* that fashion men, great deeds and heroic virtues. To be convinced of it, one need only cast one's eyes over the republics of Athens and Rome, which by their constitutions raised themselves above all the world's empires. And wherever one follows their conduct and their maxims, they will produce virtually the same effects.

It is thus not a matter of indifference to seek the fundamental laws that constitute *democracies,* and the principle that alone can preserve and maintain them; this is what I propose to sketch here.[4]

But before going any further, it is necessary to remark that in a *democracy,* each citizen does not have the sovereign power, or even a part of it; that power resides in the general assembly of the people convoked according to the laws. Thus, the people in a *democracy* are in certain respects sovereign, and in other respects they are subjects.[5] They are sovereign by their votes, which are their wills; they are subjects as members of the assembly vested with sovereign power. Since, therefore, *democracy* is only properly formed when each citizen has entrusted the right of settling all common

2. Similar praise can be found in Jean-Jacques Rousseau's first discourse (1750) and in his *Encyclopédie* article ECONOMIE, usually translated as "Discourse on Political Economy."

3. *Qualité;* see the translators' note.

4. For this approach, and for much of the analysis that follows, see Montesquieu, *The Spirit of the Laws,* esp. 2.2.

5. Montesquieu, *Laws,* 2.2, 10.

affairs to an assembly composed of all, there arise several things absolutely necessary for the constitution of this sort of government.

(1) There must be certain settled times and places for common deliberation over public affairs. Otherwise, the members of the sovereign council might not assemble at all, and then nothing would be dealt with; or else they would assemble in different times and different places, giving birth to factions that would rupture the essential unity of the state.

(2) It must be established as a rule that the plurality of votes will be considered the will of the whole body; otherwise, no affair can ever be brought to conclusion, because it is impossible that a large number of persons will always be of the same opinion.

(3) It is essential to the constitution of a *democracy* that there be magistrates charged with convoking the assembly of the people in extraordinary cases, and with having the decrees of the sovereign assembly executed. Since the sovereign council cannot always be on the alert, it is obvious that it cannot deal with everything by itself. For as concerns pure *democracy*—that is, the one in which the people in themselves and by themselves perform alone all the functions of government—I know of none like that in the world, unless perhaps it's a little dump[6] like San-Marino in Italy, where five hundred peasants govern a wretched rock whose possession is envied by no one.[7]

(4) It is a necessary part of the democratic constitution to divide the people into certain classes, and upon this the duration and prosperity of *democracies* have always depended. Solon divided the people of Athens into four classes. Guided by the spirit of *democracy*, he created these four classes to determine not those who could elect, but those who could be elected. And leaving to each citizen the right of suffrage, he decreed that judges could be elected in each of these four classes, but only magistrates in the first three, composed of leisured[8] citizens.

6. *Bicoque*, a pejorative term that connotes military defenselessness.

7. San Marino, a small mountainous republic nestled in northeastern Italy near the Adriatic Sea; it remains an independent republic as of this writing.

8. *Aisé*, referring to the classical view that only citizens with enough free time for public affairs should hold public office.

The laws establishing the right to vote are therefore fundamental in this government. Indeed, it is as important in this case to regulate how, by whom, for whom, and on what issues votes should be cast, as it is in a monarchy to know the monarch and how he should govern. At the same time, it is essential to set the age, condition, and number of citizens that have the right to vote; otherwise, it might not be known whether the people have spoken, or only a part of the people.

The method of casting one's vote is another fundamental law of *democracy*. One may cast one's vote by lot or by choice, and even by both. Lot leaves to each citizen a reasonable expectation of serving his Country. But since it is imperfect by itself, the great legislators have always applied themselves to remedying it. With this in mind, Solon determined that only those who presented themselves could be elected; that whoever was elected would be examined by judges, and that each one could accuse him without being unworthy.[9] This applied to both lot and choice. On completing his term, the magistrate had to go through a second judgment regarding the way in which he had conducted himself. People without ability, M. de Montesquieu observes here,[10] must have been very reluctant to offer their names to be drawn by lot.

The law that determines the way votes are cast is a third fundamental law in *democracy*. A great question is debated on this score, namely, whether the votes should be public or secret, for both practices are in use in different *democracies*. It seems they cannot be too secret (to maintain their liberty), nor too public (to make them authentic), so that the lesser people may be enlightened by the leaders and contained by the gravity of certain eminent men. In Geneva, in the election of first magistrates, the citizens cast their votes in public but write them in secret, so that order is then maintained with liberty.[11]

The people, who have sovereign power, should do by themselves everything they can do well; and what they cannot do well, they should have done by their ministers. But the ministers are not theirs if they do not name

9. See the slightly different account at Montesquieu, *Laws,* 2.2, 13.

10. Montesquieu, *Laws,* 2.2, 14.

11. This last sentence probably reflects Jaucourt's personal experience living in Geneva earlier in his life.

them. It is thus a fourth fundamental law of this government that the people name their ministers—that is, their magistrates. Like monarchs, and even more so, they need to be guided by a council or senate. But to have confidence in it, they must elect its members, either by choosing them themselves as in Athens, or through some magistrate they have established to elect them, such as was practiced in Rome on occasion. The people are quite fit to choose those in whom they are to entrust some part of their authority. If there could be doubts about their capacity to discern merit, one need only remember that continual series of excellent choices made by the Greeks and Romans, which will surely not be attributed to chance. However, just as most citizens who have enough capacity to elect do not have enough to be elected, so too the people, who have enough capacity to call others to account for their management, are not fit to manage by themselves, nor to conduct public business, which proceeds at a pace with a certain movement that is neither too slow nor too fast. Sometimes with a hundred thousand arms they upset everything; sometimes with a hundred thousand feet they move only like insects.

Finally, it is a fundamental law of *democracy* that the people be the legislator. However, there are countless occasions when it is necessary for the senate to be able to enact laws; it is often even appropriate to test a law before establishing it. The constitutions of Rome and Athens were very wise. The decrees of the senate had the force of law for a year; they became permanent only by the will of the people.[12] But although every *democracy* must inevitably have written laws, ordinances, and stable rules and regulations, nonetheless nothing prevents the people who have provided these from revoking them, or changing them any time they think it necessary, unless they have sworn to observe them in perpetuity. And even in that case, the oath obliges only those citizens who have themselves taken it.

Such are the main fundamental laws of *democracy*. Let us speak now of the spring or principle that is appropriate for the preservation of this type of government.[13] This principle can only be virtue, and it is only by means of this that *democracies* are maintained. Virtue in a *democracy* is love of

12. This is the last sentence in Montesquieu, *Laws*, 2.2, 15; the next sentence is Jaucourt's contribution.

13. Montesquieu, *Laws*, 5.1 and esp. 5.3.

the laws and love of Country. Since this love demands self-renunciation, a constant preference of the public interest to one's own produces all the private virtues; they simply are that preference.[14] This love leads to good mores, and good mores lead to love of Country.[15] The less we are able to satisfy our private passions, the more we give ourselves up to passions for the general good.

Virtue in a *democracy* also includes love of equality and of frugality.[16] Since everyone there has the same happiness and the same advantages, everyone is bound to taste the same pleasures and form the same hopes, things that can be expected only from a generalized frugality. Love of equality limits ambition to the happiness of rendering greater services to one's Country than other citizens do. They cannot all render it equal services, but they should equally render it services. Thus, distinctions in a democracy arise from the principle of equality, even when equality seems to be erased by successful services or superior talents. Love of frugality limits the desire of possession to the concern required by what is necessary for one's family, and even by what is surplus for one's Country.

Love of equality and love of frugality are strongly aroused by equality and frugality themselves, when one lives in a state in which the laws establish both.[17] There are nonetheless cases in which equality among democracy's citizens can be taken away for democracy's utility.[18]

The ancient Greeks, persuaded that peoples who lived in a popular government must of necessity be brought up in the practice of the virtues necessary to maintain *democracies*, created distinctive institutions to inspire these virtues.[19] When you read in the life of Lycurgus the laws he gave the Lacedemonians, you think you are reading the history of the Sevarambes.[20] The laws of Crete were the originals for the laws of Lacedemon, and Plato's laws were their correction.

14. Montesquieu, *Laws*, 4.5, 36.
15. Montesquieu, *Laws*, 5.2, 42.
16. This paragraph is mainly adapted from Montesquieu, *Laws*, 5.3.
17. Montesquieu, *Laws*, 5.4, which cites "society" instead of "state."
18. Montesquieu, *Laws*, 5.5, 47.
19. Adapted from Montesquieu, *Laws*, 4.6, 36.
20. A reference to a rationalistic utopia based on Denis Veiras's (or Vairasse's) *L'Histoire des Sévarambes* (1677–79), often translated and reprinted.

Private education should also be extremely attentive about inspiring the virtues we have discussed. But there is one sure way for children to have them, and that is for the fathers themselves to have them.[21] One is ordinarily in charge of giving one's knowledge to one's children, and even more in charge of giving them one's passions. If this does not happen, it is because what was done in the father's house is destroyed by impressions from the outside. It is not young people who degenerate; they are ruined only when grown men have already been corrupted.

The principle of *democracy* is corrupted when love of the laws and of Country begins to deteriorate, when general and individual education are neglected, when honest desires change their goals, when work and duty are called obstacles. From then on, ambition enters those hearts that can admit it, and avarice enters them all.[22] These truths are confirmed by history. Athens had in its midst the same forces when it dominated with so much glory as when it served with so much shame. It had twenty thousand citizens when it defended the Greeks against the Persians, when it disputed for empire with Lacedemon, and when it attacked Sicily. It had twenty thousand when Demetrius of Phalereus enumerated them as one counts slaves in a market. When Philip dared dominate in Greece, the Athenians feared him as the enemy not of liberty but of pleasure. They had passed a law to punish by death anyone who might propose that the silver destined for the theaters be converted to the uses of war.

Finally,[23] the principle of *democracy* is corrupted not only when the spirit of equality is lost but also when the spirit of extreme equality is taken up and everyone wants to be the equal of those chosen to command. At that point, the people, finding intolerable even the power they entrust to others, want to do everything themselves: deliberate for the senate, execute for the magistrates, and cast off all the judges. This abuse of *democracy* is with reason called a veritable *ochlocracy. See this word.* In this abuse, there is no more love of order, no more mores—in a word, no more virtue. Corrupters then emerge, petty tyrants having all the vices of a single one. Soon, a

21. This paragraph is from Montesquieu, *Laws,* 4.5, 36; throughout the discussion of education, Jaucourt changes Montesquieu's "virtue" into "the virtues."

22. This paragraph is adapted from Montesquieu, *Laws,* 3.3.

23. For this and the next paragraph, see Montesquieu, *Laws,* 8.2.

single tyrant rises up over the others, and the people lose everything, even the advantages they thought to derive from their corruption.

It would be a fortunate thing if popular government could preserve mores, frugality, love of virtue, execution of the laws; if it could avoid the two excesses—I mean the spirit of inequality that leads to aristocracy, and the spirit of extreme equality that leads to the despotism of one. But it is quite rare that a *democracy* is able to save itself for long from these two shoals. It is the fate of this government, admirable in its principle, to become almost inevitably the prey of the ambition of some citizens, or of some foreigners, and thereby to pass from a precious liberty into the greatest servitude.

There you have virtually an extract of the book *The Spirit of the Laws* on that topic, and in any other work but this one, it would be enough to refer to it. I leave it to readers who would like to extend their views still further, to consult Lord Temple in his *Posthumous Works*, Locke's *Treatise of civil government*, and the *Discourse on government* by Sidney.[24] *Article by Chevalier* DE JAUCOURT

24. The references seem to be to Sir William Temple, *Œuvres postumes de chevalier Temple* (Utrecht: Van de Water, 1704); John Locke, *Du gouvernement civil,* translation of *Two treatises of government,* by David Mazel in numerous editions, 1691; and Algernon Sidney, *Discourses concerning government* (London, 1698; trans. Peter A. Samson, 1702).

Despotism
(*Despotisme*)

DESPOTISM (*Political law*), tyrannical, arbitrary, and absolute government of a single man: such is the government of Turkey, the Mogol, Japan, Persia, and virtually all of Asia. Following some celebrated writers, let us unfold its principle and its character, and let us give thanks to heaven for causing us to be born under a different government, where we obey with joy a monarch that it makes us love.

The principle of despotic states is that a lone prince governs everything according to his will, having absolutely no other law to dominate him but that of his whims. It is in the nature of this power that it passes entirely into the hands of the person in whom it is entrusted.[1] This person, this vizir, becomes the *despot* himself, and each individual officer becomes the vizir. The establishment of a vizir flows from the fundamental principle of *despotic* states.[2] When eunuchs have weakened the hearts and minds of the eastern princes, and have often left them ignorant even of their status, these princes are withdrawn from the palace to be placed on the throne. They then appoint a vizir, in order to give themselves up in their seraglio to all the excesses of their most stupid passions. Thus, the more people the prince has to govern, the less he thinks about government; the greater the matters of business, the less he deliberates about them, since this concern belongs to the vizir. The latter, incompetent in his position, can neither express his fears about a future event to the sultan nor blame his lack of success on the

This article is available at 4:886–89 in the original edition of the *Encyclopédie*.

1. Montesquieu, *The Spirit of the Laws,* 3.9, and esp. 5.16.
2. Here the references are to Montesquieu, *Laws,* 2.5.

caprice of fortune.[3] In such a government, the lot of men is no different from that of beasts: instinct, obedience, punishment. In Persia, when the Sophi[4] has dismissed someone from favor, it would show a lack of respect to present a petition on the latter's behalf. When he has condemned him, no one may speak to him further about it or ask for a pardon. If he were drunk or mad, the decree would have to be carried out just the same; otherwise, he would be contradicting himself, and the Sophi cannot contradict himself.

But if, in *despotic* states, the prince is made a prisoner, he is supposed dead, and another ascends the throne.[5] The treaties he makes as a prisoner are null; his successor would not ratify them. Indeed, since he is the law, the state, and the prince, and since as soon as he is no longer the prince he is nothing, if he were not considered dead, the state would be destroyed. The preservation of the state rests only in the preservation of the prince, or rather of the palace in which he is enclosed. This is why he rarely wages war in person.

Despite so many precautions, the succession to dominion in *despotic* states is no more assured by them, and indeed it cannot be.[6] It would be vain to establish inheritance by the eldest; the prince can always choose another. Since each prince of the royal family is equally entitled to be elected, it happens that the one who ascends to the throne has his brothers strangled immediately, as in Turkey; or blinded, as in Persia; or driven mad, as with the Moguls; and if these precautions are not taken, as in Morocco, then each time the throne is vacated a horrible civil war ensues. In this way, no one is monarch except by fact in *despotic* states.

It is clear that neither natural law nor the law of nations is the principle of such states, nor is honor.[7] As the men there are all equal, one cannot prefer oneself to others; as the men there are all slaves, one cannot prefer oneself to anything. Still less would we look there for some spark of magnanimity—would the prince give out a share of what he is so far from

3. Montesquieu, *Laws,* 3.10, 29.
4. Persian monarch.
5. For this paragraph, see Montesquieu, *Laws,* 5.14.
6. The rest of this paragraph is from Montesquieu, *Laws,* 5.14, 62.
7. Montesquieu, *Laws,* 3.8.

having?[8] Neither grandeur nor glory are found in him. The whole support of his government is based on fear of his vengeance; this beats down all courage; it extinguishes the least feeling of ambition.[9] Religion, or rather superstition, does the rest, because this is a new fear added to the first.[10] In the Mohammedan empire, the people derive the principal part of the respect they have for their prince from religion.

Let us go into more detail, to better unveil the nature of and problems with the *despotic* governments of the Orient.

First of all, since *despotic* government is exercised over peoples that are timid and beaten down, everything turns on a small number of ideas; education is limited to putting fear in their hearts, and servitude in practice. Knowledge is dangerous there, emulation lethal. It is equally pernicious whether one reasons well or badly; that one is reasoning is enough to offend this kind of government.[11] Education is therefore nothing there; one could only make a bad subject by wanting to make a good slave:

Knowledge, talents, public liberty, All is dead under the yoke of despotic power.[12]

Women are slaves there, and since having many of them is permitted, countless considerations oblige them to be enclosed. Since sovereigns take as many as they want, they have such a large number of children by them that they can scarcely have affection for them, nor the latter for their brothers.[13] Moreover, there are so many intrigues in their seraglios—those places where artifice, wickedness, and deceit reign in silence—that the prince himself, becoming daily more imbecilic, is in fact only the first prisoner of his palace.

It is an established custom in *despotic* countries not to approach any superior without giving him presents.[14] The emperor of the Moguls does not accept requests from his subjects unless he has received something from them. This is bound to be the way in a government where one is filled with

8. Montesquieu, *Laws,* 5.12.

9. Montesquieu, *Laws,* 3.9.

10. For the rest of the paragraph, see Montesquieu, *Laws,* 5.14.

11. Montesquieu attributes this "reasoning" to the English in *Laws,* 19.27, 332.

12. The passage seems to come from P.-J. Crébillon's play *Catalina,* in *Oeuvres,* T.2. (1749; Paris, Didot, 1818), 227.

13. The remainder of the paragraph is from Montesquieu, *Laws,* 5.14, 63.

14. For this paragraph, see Montesquieu, *Laws,* 5.17.

the idea that the superior owes nothing to the inferior, in a government where men believe themselves bound only by the punishments that the former mete out to the latter.

Poverty and the uncertainty of fortunes naturalizes usury there, as each one increases the price of his money in proportion to the peril involved in lending it.[15] Destitution is omnipresent in these miserable countries; everything is taken away, including the recourse to borrowing. Government could not be unjust without hands to inflict its injustices. Now it is impossible for these hands not to be used on their own behalf; therefore, embezzlement is inevitable there. In countries where the prince declares himself owner of all the land and heir to all his subjects, cultivation of the land is always abandoned. All is fallow, all is deserted.[16]

> When the Savages of Louisiana want fruit, they cut down the tree and gather the fruit.[17]

There you have *despotic* government, says the author of the *Spirit of the Laws;* Raphael did no better in painting the School of Athens.

In a *despotic* government of that nature, there are no civil laws on landed property, since it all belongs to the *despot.*[18] Nor are there any on inheritance, because the sovereign has the sole right of succession. Because trade belongs exclusively to the despot in some countries, all types of laws concerning commerce are rendered useless. Since extreme servitude cannot be increased, new laws to increase taxes in wartime do not make their appearance in the *despotic* countries of the Orient, as they do in republics and monarchies, where the science of government can procure an increase in wealth for the government in time of need.[19] Because marriages are contracted with female slaves in Oriental countries, there are scarcely any civil laws about dowries or the privileges of wives.[20] In Masulipatam,[21] the

15. For this and what follows, see Montesquieu, *Laws,* 5.15.

16. Montesquieu, *Laws,* 5.14, 61.

17. Montesquieu, *Laws,* 5.13.

18. For this and what immediately follows, see Montesquieu, *Laws,* 6.1.

19. This sentence seems loosely adapted from Montesquieu, *Laws,* 13.13.

20. Montesquieu, *Laws,* 6.1, 74.

21. Modern-day Bandar, on the eastern coast of India; it was the British East India Company's first trading post.

existence of written laws has not been discovered; the Vedas and other similar books contain no civil laws. In Turkey, where people are equally unbothered about the fortune, life, or honor of the subjects, all disputes are speedily concluded in one way or another. The pasha has canings under the soles of the pleaders' feet meted out at whim, and sends them back home.[22]

If pleaders are punished in this way, how rigorous must the penalties be for those who have committed some offense? Thus, when we read in history about examples of the atrocious justice of the sultans, we feel with a kind of sorrow the sickness in human nature. In Japan it is even worse; there, almost all crimes are punished by death. There, it is not a question of correcting the guilty but of avenging the emperor. A man who risks some money in gambling is punished by death because he has neither the ownership nor the usufruct of his property; it is the kubo who does.[23]

The people, who possess nothing of their own in the *despotic* lands we have depicted, have no sense of attachment to Country, and are bound by no obligation to its master. Thus, following M. La Loubère's observation (in his *Historical account of Siam*),[24] since the subjects have to suffer the same yoke no matter the prince, and since they cannot be made to bear a heavier one, they never take any part in the fortunes of whoever is governing them. At the least sign of disturbance or unrest, they placidly let the crown go to whoever has the most strength, nimbleness, or political savvy, whoever it may be. A Siamese man happily exposes himself to death to avenge a private insult, to escape from a burdensome life, or to avoid a cruel torture; but to die for prince or Country is a virtue unknown in that land. They lack the motives that animate other men; they have neither liberty nor property. Those imprisoned by the king of Pegu[25] remain tranquilly in the new habitation assigned them, because it cannot be worse than

22. Montesquieu, *Laws*, 6.2, 75.

23. In the article Dairi, or Dairo (4:612), Jaucourt explains that the kubo is the secular ruler of Japan, namely, the emperor.

24. Simon de Loubère (1643–1729); the work appeared in 1691 in French, and in 1693 in English, and was frequently reprinted.

25. Modern Bago, port city in southern Burma (Myanmar); in Jaucourt's time, it had again recently (in 1740) been made capital of the Mon kingdom, first established in the sixth century. In 1757, shortly after Jaucourt's article, the king of Burma destroyed Pegu and its independence.

the prior one. The inhabitants of Pegu act in the same way when they are taken by the Siamese. Those wretches—equally crushed in their country by servitude, equally indifferent toward the change of residence—have the good sense to say with the ass in the fable:

Fight it out and let us pasture, Our enemy, he is our master.[26]

The rebellion of Sacrovir brought joy to the Roman people; the universal hatred Tiberius had attracted by his *despotism* made people wish for a happy outcome for the public enemy:[27] *multi odio praesentium, suis quisque periculis laetabantur*, says Tacitus.[28]

I know that the kings of the Orient are regarded as the adoptive children of heaven. Their souls are thought to be celestial, and to surpass others in virtue as much as the prosperity of their condition surpasses that of their subjects. Nonetheless, once the subjects revolt, the people come to harbor doubts on which is the worthier soul, that of the legitimate prince or that of the rebel subject, and on whether the celestial adoption hasn't passed from the person of the king to that of the subject. Moreover, in those countries there are no small revolts;[29] there is no space between murmur and sedition, sedition and catastrophe. The malcontent goes straight to the prince, strikes him, overthrows him—he erases even the thought of him. In an instant the slave is the master; in an instant he is the usurper and is legitimate. Great events are not prepared by great causes there; on the contrary, the least accident produces a great revolution, often as unforeseen by those who effect it as by those who suffer it. At the time when Osman, emperor of the Turks, was deposed, he was only being asked to give justice on some grievances; a voice arose from the crowd by chance, pronouncing the name of Mustapha, and suddenly Mustapha was emperor.

26. From La Fontaine, "Le Vieillard et l'Ane" (The Old Man and the Ass), in his *Fables,* which began to appear in 1668.

27. Julius Sacrovir of Gaul; the revolt occurred in A.D. 21, in the reign of Tiberius. It ultimately failed and Sacrovir killed himself.

28. Tacitus, *Annals,* III.xliv, "in many hatred of the existing order . . . [was] such that they exulted even in their own perils."

29. From here until the end of the paragraph, see Montesquieu, *Persian Letters,* trans. George R. Healy (Indianapolis: Hackett, 1999), LXXXI, 137.

Father Martini[30] claims that the Chinese have convinced themselves that in changing the sovereign they are conforming to the will of heaven, and they have sometimes preferred a bandit to the prince who was already on the throne. But, he says, aside from the fact that this *despotic* authority is deprived of defense, since its exercise terminates entirely in the prince, it is weakened for not being shared and transmitted to other persons. Whoever wants to dethrone the prince has scarcely anything else to do but play the role of sovereign and capture its spirit. Authority, being contained within a single man, passes easily from one man to another, for lack of people in positions who have an interest in preserving royal authority. It is thus only the prince who is interested in defending the prince, whereas countless hands have an interest in defending our kings.

Thus, far from a *despot's* being assured of maintaining himself on the throne, he is only closer to falling from it. Far from his even being secure in his life, he is only more exposed to seeing its course cut short in a violent and tragic manner, like his reign. The person of a sultan is often torn to pieces with less formality than that of a malefactor from the dregs of the people. If they had less authority, they would have more security: *nunquam satis fida potentia, ubi nimia.*[31] Caligula, Domitian, and Commodus, who reigned *despotically*, were assassinated by those whose deaths they had decreed.

Let us conclude that *despotism* is equally harmful to princes and peoples in all times and all places, because it is everywhere the same in its principle and in its effects. It is particular circumstances—religious opinion, prejudice, received examples, established customs, manners, mores—that make up the differences one encounters among them throughout the world. But whatever these differences, human nature always rises up against a government of this kind, which is the misery of prince and subjects.[32] And if we still see so many idolatrous and barbarous nations subject to this government, it is because they are enchained by superstition, education, habit, and climate.

30. Martino Martini (1614–61), Austrian-born Jesuit and author of *Novus Atlas Sinensis* [New Chinese atlas] (Vienna, 1653).

31. "When a man has excessive power, he never can have complete trust." Tacitus, *Histories,* II.xcii. Jaucourt may be drawing here on the English Whig Thomas Gordon, *Discourses on Tacitus,* 2nd ed. (London: T. Woodward, 1737), Discourse V, sect. III, para. 2, for his citation is identical to Gordon's and slightly different from the original.

32. For a less categorical statement, see Montesquieu, *Laws,* 5.14, 63.

In Christianity, on the other hand, there cannot be an unlimited sovereignty, because however absolute that sovereignty may be supposed, it cannot include an arbitrary and *despotic* power, with no other rule or reason than the will of the Christian monarch. Look, how could the creature claim such a power, since the sovereign himself does not have it? His absolute domain is not founded on blind will; his sovereign will is always determined by the immutable rules of wisdom, justice, and goodness.

Thus, to echo La Bruyère,

> to say that a Christian prince is the arbiter of the lives and property of his subjects is to say simply that men, by their crimes, become naturally subject to the laws and justice of which the prince is the depository. To add that he is the absolute master of all the property of his subjects—without consideration, without account or discussion—this is the language of flattery, it is the opinion of a favorite who will recant at the hour of death. (*Chap. X du Souverain*)[33]

But one may suggest that a king is master of the lives and property of his subjects because, loving them with a paternal love, he preserves them and takes care of their fortunes as he would something that was most proper to him. In this fashion, he conducts himself as if everything belonged to him, taking absolute power over all their possessions in order to protect and defend them. It is by this means that, winning the hearts of his people and thereby everything they have, he can declare himself their master, even though he never causes them to lose their ownership of it, except in cases ordained by law.

> "It does not," says a councilor of state (M. La Mothe le Vayer, in a book entitled *The Household management of the Prince*,[34] which he dedicated to Louis XIV, ch. ix), "it does not, Sire, set harmful limits to your sovereign will, to set them in conformity with those by which God has intended to limit his own. If we say that Your Majesty owes protection

33. See Jean de La Bruyère (1645–96), *Characters,* trans. Henri Van Laun, intro. Denys C. Potts (1688; London: Oxford University Press, 1963), X.28, 169–70, for a nearly identical version.

34. François de La Mothe le Vayer (1583–1672) was an important intellectual in the skeptical tradition; this work, *L'Economique du prince* (Paris, 1653), is part of a six-part series of studies (1651–69) designed for Louis XIV.

> and justice to his subjects, we add at the same time that Your Majesty is made accountable for this obligation, and for all of your actions, only to the one by whom all kings on earth are exalted. Finally, we do not attribute any personal property to your people except to thereby further exalt the dignity of your monarchy."

Also, Louis XIV always recognized that he could do nothing contrary to the laws of nature, the laws of nations, or the fundamental laws of the state. In the treatise *Of the rights of the Queen of France*, published in 1667 by order of that august monarch to justify his claims over a part of the Catholic Low Countries, one finds these fine words:

> That kings have that happy impotence, of being unable to do anything against the laws of their country. . . . It is (adds the author) neither imperfection nor weakness in a supreme authority to submit to the law of his promises, or to the justice of his laws. The necessity of doing well and the powerlessness to fail are the highest means of all his perfection. God himself, according to the thought of Philo the Jew, cannot go further. And it is this divine impotence that sovereigns, who are his images on earth, should particularly imitate in their states. (*Page 279 of the edition printed according to the Royal printer's copy*.)

> Let it not be said, therefore (continues the same author, who speaks in the name of, and with the approbation of, Louis XIV), let it not be said that the sovereign is not subject to the laws of his state, since the contrary proposition is a truth of the law of nations, which flattery has sometimes attacked, but which good princes have always defended as the tutelary divinity of their states. How much more legitimate is it to say with the wise Plato that the perfect felicity of a realm is for a prince to be obeyed by his subjects, for the prince to obey the law, and for the law to be upright and always directed toward the public good?

The monarch who thinks and acts in this way is indeed worthy of the name of Great, and he who can only augment his glory by continuing a dominance that is full of clemency, doubtless merits the title of WELL-LOVED.[35] *Article by Chevalier* DE JAUCOURT.

35. The references are to Louis XIV (*le grand*, r. 1660–1715) and Louis XV (*le Bien-aimé*, r. 1726–70).

Volume 5
(1755)

Natural Right
(*Droit Naturel*)

This article was controversial in its time and continues to be interpreted in different ways. Praised by the friendly Journal encyclopédique *(February 15, 1756), it was attacked by Abraham Chaumeix in his* Préjugés légitimes, *II, 78–80, for attempting to free human beings of their obligations to God and country, leaving them with merely a vague duty to the "human species." "You are a citizen of the world, and a patriot of nowhere. You have to do nothing, conceive of nothing, meditate on nothing except the temporal interests of yourself and other men," he sums up Diderot's pernicious doctrine. Some later commentators have seen Diderot's "general will" in the light of Rousseau's, but others see it as more like Adam Smith's universal principle of sympathy in* The Theory of Moral Sentiments. *For his part, Rousseau criticized this article in the first version of the* Social Contract *(bk. 1, chap. 2), though the chapter was deleted in the definitive version.*[1]

*NATURAL RIGHTS[2] (*Morality*). These words are used so frequently that almost everyone is convinced that they are clearly understood. This feeling

"Natural Right" was translated by Stephen J. Gendzier, in *Denis Diderot's "The Encyclopedia": Selections*, ed. and trans. Stephen J. Gendzier (New York: Harper and Row, 1967), 171–75, and is reprinted by permission of the translator. Gendzier translates the title as "Natural Rights." On this point, see the entry for *droit* in the translators' note.

This article can be found at 5:115–16 in the original edition of the *Encyclopédie*.

1. For these points, see *Diderot: "Encyclopédie,"* ed. John Lough and Jacques Proust, vol. 7 of *Denis Diderot: Œuvres complètes*, ed. Hans Dieckmann and Jean Varloot (Paris: Hermann, 1976), 29.—HC

2. *Droit natural* is generally translated as "natural law," but the word *droit* used by Diderot in this article means what is rightful as well as what is lawful, and in this context Diderot is more concerned with natural rights.

is common to the philosopher and to the man who does not think, with the only difference that in regard to the question "What are rights?" the latter, in that moment lacking both terms and ideas, refers you to the tribunal of conscience and remains silent, while the first is only reduced to silence and to more profound reflections after having turned in a vicious circle that brings him back to the very point from which he departed or draws him to some other question that is not less difficult to resolve than the one he thought he was rid of by its definition.

The philosopher under question says: "Rights are the foundation or the primary object of justice." But what is justice? "It is the obligation to render to each person what belongs to him." But what belongs to one rather than to another in a state of things where everything belongs to everyone and where perhaps the distinct idea of obligation would not yet exist? And what would an individual owe to others if he were to allow them everything and ask nothing of them? It is here that the philosopher begins to feel that of all the notions of morality, that of natural rights is one of the most important and most difficult to determine. Therefore we believe we will have accomplished a great deal in this article if we have succeeded in clearly establishing a few principles that might assist someone to resolve the most considerable difficulties customarily proposed against the notion of natural rights. For this purpose it is necessary to discuss the question thoroughly and to advance nothing that is not clear and evident, with at least the kind of evidence that moral questions permit and that satisfy every sensible man.

(1) It is evident that if man is not free or if his instantaneous resolutions or even his indecision arise from something material that is external to his soul, then his choice is not the pure act of an incorporeal substance or of a simple faculty of that substance; there will therefore be neither rational benevolence nor rational malevolence, although it is possible to be both benevolent and malevolent at an animal level; there will be neither good nor evil in the moral sense, neither right nor wrong, neither obligation nor privilege. Hence we see, although we say it in passing, how important it is to establish firmly the reality, I do not say of what is voluntary, but of freedom, which is too often confused with the former.

(2) We live in a state of being that is poor, contentious, and anxious. We have passions and needs. We want to be happy; and at every moment the

unjust and passionate man feels inclined to do to others what he would not wish to have done to himself. This is a judgment he makes at the bottom of his soul and that he cannot avoid. He sees his own malevolence and must admit it to himself, or grant to everyone the same authority that he arrogates to himself.

(3) But with what can we reproach a man who is tormented by passions so violent that even life becomes an onerous burden if he does not satisfy them and that in order to acquire the right to dispose of the existence of others, abandons to them his own? What shall we answer him if he intrepidly says, "I feel that I bring terror and disorder in the midst of mankind, but I must either be unhappy or make others unhappy; and nobody is dearer to me than I am to myself. Let no one reproach me with this abominable predilection: it is not free. It is the voice of nature that never explains itself more powerfully than when it speaks to me in my favor. But is it only in my heart that it makes itself heard with the same violence? O men! it is to you I appeal: which one among you who on the point of death would not buy back his life at the expense of the greater part of the human race if he could count on impunity and secrecy? But he will continue: I am fair and sincere; if my happiness demands that I destroy the lives of all those who disturb me, it is also necessary for an individual, whoever he may be, to be able to destroy mine if he is similarly disturbed; reason requires this, and I subscribe to it; I am not so unjust as to insist upon a sacrifice from another person that I do not wish to make for him."

(4) I perceive first of all one thing that seems to me acknowledged by the good and the evil person, that we must apply reason in all matters, because man is not only an animal but an animal who reasons; that there are consequently, in regard to the question under discussion, ways to discover the truth; that the person who refuses to search for it renounces his human condition and must be treated by the rest of his species as a wild beast; and that the truth once discovered, whoever refuses to conform to it is mad or evil practicing a morality of malevolence.

(5) What shall we therefore answer our violent reasoner before we stifle him? That his entire discourse is reduced to knowing if he acquires the right over the lives of others by abandoning his own to them; because he does not want only to be happy, he wants to be fair and by his fairness

brush far away from him the epithet of evil person; without which it would be necessary to stifle him without an answer. We shall therefore draw his attention to the fact that even if what he abandons would belong to him so completely that he were able to dispose of it at will, and that the condition that he proposes to others would be even advantageous to them, he has no legitimate authority to make them accept it; that the person who says "I want to live" has as much justification as the person who says "I want to die"; that the latter has only one life and by abandoning it makes himself the master of an infinity of lives; that his exchange would be hardly equitable if there were only himself and another evil person on the entire surface of the earth; that it is absurd to make others desire what one desires; that it is uncertain that the peril in which he places his fellow man is equal to the one to which he really wishes to be exposed; that what he allows to chance cannot be of proportionate value compared to what he forces me to chance; that the question of natural rights is much more complicated than it appears to him; that he appoints himself as judge and plaintiff, and that this matter would certainly not fall within the competence of his court.

(6) But if we take away from the individual the right of deciding about the nature of right and wrong, where shall we place this great question? Where? Before the entire human race; for only they may decide the issue, since the good of all is the only passion they have, particular wills are suspect; they can be good or evil, but the general will is always good: it is never wrong, it never will be wrong. If animals were on an approximate level with us, if there were certain means of communication between them and us, if they were able to convey clearly their feelings and thoughts and know ours with the same clarity: in a word, if they were able to vote in a general assembly, it would be necessary to summon them there, and the cause of natural rights would no longer be pleaded before humanity but before the animal kingdom [*animalité*]. But animals are separated from us by invariable and eternal barriers; and it is a question here of a category of knowledge and ideas peculiar to mankind which emanate from its dignity and which constitute it.

(7) It is to the general will that the individual must address himself to know up to what point he must be a man, a citizen, a subject, a father, a child, and when it is suitable to live or to die. The general will determines

the limits of all duties. You have the most sacred natural rights in everything that is not contested by the entire species. They will enlighten you on the nature of your thoughts and your desires. Everything that you will conceive, everything that you will contemplate will be good, noble, exalted, and sublime if it is in the general and common interest. The only essential quality in your species is what you demand from all your fellow men for your happiness and for theirs. It is this conformity of you with all of them and all of them with you that will mark you when you go beyond or stay within the limits of your species. Therefore never lose sight of it; otherwise you will see the notions of benevolence, justice, humanity, and virtue blurred in your understanding. Say often to yourself: I am a man, and I do not have any other truly inalienable rights than those of humanity.

(8) But you will say to me, where is the depository of this general will? Where could I consult it? In the principles of law written by all civilized nations; in the social practices of savage and barbaric peoples; in the tacit conventions between enemies of mankind among themselves; and even in the feelings of indignation and resentment, these two passions which nature seems to have placed even in animals to compensate for the deficiency of laws in society and the blemish of public vengeance.

(9) If you therefore meditate carefully on the foregoing, you will remain convinced: (i) that the man who listens only to his particular will is the enemy of the human race; (ii) that the general will in each individual is a pure act of understanding that reasons in the silence of the passions about what man can demand of his fellow man and about what his fellow man can rightfully demand of him; (iii) that this consideration of the general will of the species as well as the common desire is the rule of conduct relating one individual to another in the same society, one individual to the society of which he is a member, and the society of which he is a member to other societies; (iv) that the submission to the general will is the bond of all societies, without excluding those formed by crime (alas! virtue is so beautiful that thieves respect its image in the very center of their dens!); (v) that the laws must be made for all and not for one, otherwise this solitary being would resemble the violent reasoner whom we have stifled in section 5; (vi) that since of the two wills, the one general and the other particular, the general will never falls into error, it is not difficult to see on which one,

for the happiness of the human race, the legislatures ought to depend, and what veneration we owe the august mortals whose particular wills reunite both the authority and the infallibility of the general will; (vii) that if one were to assume the notion of the species being in perpetual flux, the nature of natural rights would not change, since it would always be related to the general will and to the common desire of the entire species; (viii) that equity is to justice as cause is to its effect, or that justice cannot be anything else than declared equity; (ix) that all these inferences are evident to the person who reasons, and that the person who does not wish to reason, renouncing his human condition, must be treated as an unnatural being.

Natural Law
(*Droit de la Nature*)

This article is by Boucher d'Argis; in the third volume of the Encyclopédie, *he is introduced to the readers in the following terms: "Thanks to the care of M. Boucher d'Argis, well known for his excellent works, jurisprudence, which is unfortunately a necessary science as well as an extensive one, will now appear in the* Encyclopédie *with all the detail it deserves." The article on natural law is the second one on this topic in the* Encyclopédie. *The article which precedes this, entitled simply "Natural Right" (Droit Naturel), is by Diderot. Whereas Diderot's article deals extensively with the moral issues involved and presents his personal views on justice, good, evil, and general will, the present article approaches the problem essentially from a historical point of view and offers a good introduction to the main authorities to whom eighteenth-century thinkers turned for definitions of natural law.*

Law of Nature, or Natural Law, in its broadest sense, is taken to designate certain principles which nature alone inspires and which all animals as well as all men have in common. On this law are based the union of male and female, the begetting of children as well as their education, love of liberty, self-preservation, concern for self-defense.

It is improper to call the behavior of animals natural law, for, not being endowed with reason, they can know neither law nor justice.

The headnote, translation, and unattributed footnotes for Natural Law are from Nelly S. Hoyt and Thomas Cassirer, *The Encyclopedia: Selections [by] Diderot, d'Alembert and a Society of Men of Letters* (Indianapolis: Bobbs-Merrill, 1965), 193–202.

This article can be found at 5:131–34 in the original edition of the *Encyclopédie*.

More commonly we understand by natural law certain laws of justice and equity which only natural reason has established among men, or better, which God has engraved in our hearts.

The fundamental principles of law and all justice are: to live honestly, not to give offense to anyone, and to render unto each whatever is his. From these general principles derive a great many particular rules which nature alone, that is, reason and equity, suggest to mankind.

Since this natural law is based on such fundamental principles, it is perpetual and unchangeable: no agreement can debase it, no law can alter it or exempt anyone from the obligation it imposes. In this it differs from positive law, meaning those rules which only exist because they have been established by precise laws. This positive law is subject to change by right of the same authority that established it, and individuals can deviate from it if it is not too strict. Certain people improperly mistake natural law for the law of nations. This latter also consists in part of rules which true reason has established among all men; but it also contains conventions established by men against the natural order, such as wars or servitude, whereas natural law admits only what conforms to true reason and equity.

The principles of natural law, therefore, form part of the law of nations, particularly the primitive law of nations; they also form part of public and of private law: for the principles of natural law, which we have stated, are the purest source of the foundation of most of private and public law. But public and private law contain rules based on positive laws. See LAW OF NATIONS, POSITIVE LAW, PUBLIC LAW, PRIVATE LAW (*Droit des Gens, Droit Positif, Droit Public, Droit Privé*). From these general ideas on natural law it becomes clear that this law is nothing other than what the science of manners and customs calls morality.

This science of manners or of natural law was known only imperfectly to the ancients; their wise men and their philosophers have spoken of it most often in a very superficial way; they introduced into it errors and vices. Pythagoras was the first to undertake a discussion of virtue. After him Socrates gave the best and broadest treatment, but he wrote nothing, being content to teach his disciples by means of simple conversations. Nevertheless he is considered the father of moral philosophy. The entire ethics of Plato, the disciple of Socrates, is contained within ten dialogues, several of which deal specifically with natural law and politics. This is the case with Plato's treatises on the republic, on laws, on politics. Aristotle, Plato's most celebrated disciple, was the first among ancient philosophers to have given a somewhat methodical system of ethics; but he deals more with the duties of the citizen than with those of man in general and with the reciprocal duties of those who are citizens in a well-run state.

The best treatise on morality that we have from the ancients is the *De Officiis* by Cicero which contains a summary of the principles of natural law. Still, a great many subjects are missing. They may have been contained in his treatise on the republic of which only fragments remain. There are also some good things in his treatise on laws, where he attempts to prove that there is a natural law independent of the institutions of men, which has its origins in the will of God. He demonstrates that this is the basis of all just and reasonable laws; he shows the importance of religion in civil society and concludes at length on the reciprocal duties of citizens.

The principles of natural equity were not unknown to Roman jurisconsults: some even claimed to follow them rather than the severe laws; this was the case for the sect of the Proculeans, whereas the Sabinians followed the letter of the law rather than the principles of equity.[1] But in what has remained of the works of this great number of jurisconsults, one does not see that they treated *ex professo* either of natural law or of the law of nations.

Even the books of Justinian contain at most a few definitions and some very rudimentary notions about these two laws. We find these in the digest *De justitia et jure* and in the institutes *De juri naturali: gentium et civili.*

Among modern authors, Melanchthon gives a sketch of natural law in his *Ethics.* Benedict Winkler also sometimes mentions it in his *Principes de droit*, but he often mistakes man-made law for natural law.[2]

The famous Grotius is the first to have drafted a system of natural law in a treatise in three books entitled *De jure belli et pacis.* The title suggests merely the subdivisions of the law of nations, and it is true that the greatest

1. The sects were named after the first-century jurists Proclus and Massurius Sabinus.—HC

2. The references are to Luther's leading collaborator, Philip Melanchthon (1497–1560), *Epitome philosophiae moralis* (Epitome of moral philosophy) (1538), and the University of Leipzig law professor Benedict Winckler (1579–1648), a precursor to Grotius for his 1615 work *Principiorum juris libri quinque* (Principles of law in five books).—HC

part of the work deals with the law of war. In spite of this, the principles of natural law are laid down in the Preliminary Discourse, on the certitude of law in general, as well as in the first chapter. In this chapter, after having given the outline of the whole work and having defined the meaning of war and the ways in which one can understand the term *law,* Grotius explains that law taken as meaning a certain rule can be divided into natural law and arbitrary law. Natural law, according to him, consists in certain principles of true reason, which make us realize that a certain action is honest or dishonest, depending on whether it is or is not in accord with a reasonable and sociable nature. God, who is the creator of nature, therefore approves or condemns such action. Grotius examines how many different kinds of natural law exist, and how they can be distinguished from rules to which the name is applied erroneously. He maintains that neither the instinct men have in common with animals nor the instinct characteristic of all men, properly speaking, constitutes natural law. Finally he examines how the maxims of natural law can be proven.

The remainder of his work is mainly concerned with the laws of war and therefore with political law and the law of nations. Nevertheless a few topics can also be related to natural law, such as justifiable self-defense, rights common to all peoples, the original acquisition of property, other ways of acquiring property; the law concerning paternal power, marriage, legal and religious bodies, the power of sovereigns over their subjects, and masters over their slaves; territorial possessions, alienation of property; inheritance *ab intestat,* promises and contracts, oaths, royal promises and oaths, public treaties promulgated by the sovereign without his order, damages caused unjustly and the obligations which result; the rights of embassies, the right of burial, penalties, and how they are transmitted.

Shortly after the appearance of Grotius's treatise, John Selden, the famous English jurisconsult, published a treatise on all the Hebrew laws concerning natural law. He entitled it *De jure naturae et gentium apud Hebraeos.*[3] This is an erudite but unsystematic work, written in obscure language. In addition, this author does not derive the natural principles from the light of reason only. He simply deduces them from the seven supposed precepts

3. On Selden, see the entry SUSSEX, in this volume.—HC

given to Noah, the number of which is uncertain and which are based on a very dubious tradition. Often he even contents himself with relating the decisions of the rabbis, without examining whether they are well founded.

Thomas Hobbes was one of the greatest geniuses of his century, though unfortunately prejudiced by the indignation aroused in him by the seditious persons then fomenting troubles in England. In 1642 he published, in Paris, a treatise about the citizen[4] where, among other dangerous opinions, he tries to establish, in accordance with Epicurus's ethics, that the basis of society is self-preservation and private interest. This leads him to conclude that men have the desire, the strength, and the power to inflict evil upon each other, and that the state of nature is a state of war of all against all. He assigns to kings a limitless authority not only in matters of state, but also in matters of religion. Lambert Velthuisen, the Dutch philosopher, published a dissertation attempting to justify the way in which natural laws are presented in the treatise about the citizen. But he could only do it by either abandoning Hobbes's principles or attempting to give them a favorable interpretation.[5] Hobbes published still another work, called *Leviathan*,[6] which states, in summary, that without peace there can be no security in a state; that peace cannot exist without control, and control cannot exist without weapons, and that weapons are useless unless they are in the hands of one person, etc. He openly maintains that the will of the sovereign not only creates the just and the unjust but also religion; that any divine revelation can become obligatory only after the sovereign, to whom he attributes arbitrary powers, has proclaimed it as law.

Since then Spinoza had the same ideas about the state of nature and has based them on the same principles.

We shall not attempt here to refute the pernicious systems of these two philosophers. It is easy to perceive their errors.

4. *Elementorum Philosophiae, sectio tertia, de Cive* (1642). A French translation of this appeared in 1649 under the title *Elemens philosophiques du citoyen, Traité politique où les fondemens de la societé civile sont découverts, par Thomas Hobbes. . . .*

5. The reference is to Lambert van Velthuysen (1622–85), *Epistolica dissertatio De principiis iusti et decori: continens apologiam pro tractatu clarissimi Hobbaei, "De Cive"* (On the principles of the just and proper: containing an apology for Hobbes's "De Cive") (Amsterdam: Elzevier, 1651).—HC

6. Spelled *Le viathan* in the article.

Baron Puffendorf, having conceived the plan of a system of the law of nature and of nations, followed the spirit of Grotius; he examined things at their origin and took advantage of the knowledge of those who preceded him. To this he added his own discoveries and published a first treatise under the title of *Elements of Universal Jurisprudence.* This work, even though not perfect, gave such evidence of the great quality of the author that the following year[7] the Elector Palatine Charles-Louis called him to his University of Heidelberg and founded for him the chair of Professor of Natural Law and the Law of Nations.

Barbeyrac in his Preface to the translation of Puffendorf's treatise mentions another German professor called Buddaeus, who had been Professor of Natural Law and Ethics at Hall [*sic,* Halle] in Saxony and who was the author of a history of natural law.[8]

M. Burlamaqui, author of the principles of natural law of which we shall speak in a minute, used to be Professor of Natural and Civil Law in Geneva. This gives us a chance, in passing, to note that in several states of Germany and Italy the usefulness of establishing public schools dealing with natural law and the law of nations has been recognized. This law is the basis of civil, public, and private law. It would be well if the study of natural law and the law of nations and that of public law were held in equally high esteem everywhere. Let us return to Puffendorf whom we left for a moment.

The *Elements of Universal Jurisprudence* is not his only work on natural law. Two years later he produced his legal treatise *De jure naturae et gentium* which was translated and annotated by Barbeyrac; Puffendorf has also published an abridgment of this treatise, entitled *The Duties of Man and the Citizen.* Though his great work is called *Of the Law of Nature and of Nations,* he deals far more extensively with the law of nations than of nature. It has been analyzed under LAW OF NATIONS (*Droit des Gens*), to which we refer the reader.

7. 1662; *Elements* was published in 1661.—HC

8. Johann Franz Buddeus (1667–1729), prolific theologian and author, professor at Halle 1693–1705; his *Tractatus de juris natura et gentium* (Treatise of the law of nature and nations) appeared in 1705.—HC

The most recent, the most precise, and the most methodical work that we have on natural law is the one which we have already mentioned by J. J. Burlamaqui, Councillor of State and formerly professor of Natural and Civil Law in Geneva. In 1747 in Geneva this work was printed in quarto. It is entitled *Principles of Natural Law* and is divided into two parts.[9]

The first part deals with general principles of law, the second with natural laws. Each of the two parts is divided into several chapters, and each chapter into several paragraphs.

In the first part, which relates to general principles of law, after having defined natural law, the author seeks the principles of this science in man's nature and in his condition; he examines man's actions, in particular as they concern the law; he explains that understanding is necessarily just, that its perfection consists in the knowledge of truth, and that ignorance and error are two obstacles to this knowledge.

From there he goes on to man's will, to his instincts, inclinations, passions; to the use man makes of his freedom when he is dealing with truth and self-evident things, with good and evil, and with things not easily defined.

Man is capable of direction in his behavior, and he is accountable for his own actions.

The distinctions of the various conditions of man also enter into the knowledge of natural law; man has to be considered in his original state in relation to God, in relation to society or by himself. There have to be considerations of accessory and adventitious[10] conditions resulting from war and peace, from birth and marriage. The weakness of man at birth puts children in a natural position of dependence on their parents; the situation of man vis-à-vis property and government brings about still other related conditions.

It would not be proper for men to live without rules; rules presuppose a final goal; that of man is to aspire to happiness; this is the system of Providence; it is the essential desire of man, inseparable from reason which is man's basic guide. Since true happiness cannot be incompatible with the

9. The next seven paragraphs summarize the contents of Burlamaqui, *Principles,* I.I.i–x.—HC

10. These are terms of Roman law pertaining to indirect inheritance.

nature and condition of man, rules of conduct consist in a distinction between good and evil, in a comparison of past and present, in not seeking a good that may give rise to greater evil, in accepting a small evil if it is followed by a great good, in giving preference to the greatest good, in certain cases in being persuaded only by probability or verisimilitude and finally in acquiring the inclination toward the truly good.

In order really to know natural law, one has to understand what is meant by obligation in general. Law taken as power produces obligations; rights and obligations are several: some are natural, others are acquired; some are such that they cannot be rigidly fulfilled, others cannot be renounced. These obligations are also distinguished by their object. For instance, there is the right we have over ourselves, which is called liberty; the right of property or estate over things that belong to us; the right one has over the person or actions of another, which is called sovereignty or authority; finally the right one can have over things belonging to someone else, which is also of several kinds.

Man, by nature a dependent being, must take law as the rule of his action, for law is nothing other than a rule set down by the sovereign. The true foundations of sovereignty are power, wisdom, and goodness combined. The goal of laws is not to impede liberty but to direct properly all man's actions.

In substance these are the topics considered by M. Burlamaqui in the first section of his work. In the second, which deals specifically with natural law, he defines it as the law God imposes on all men, which they can come to know by the light of their reason alone when they examine their nature and condition.[11]

Natural law is the systematization, the collection, or the body of these same laws. Natural jurisprudence is the art of arriving at the knowledge of the laws of nature, of developing them, and of applying them to man's actions.

We cannot doubt realities of natural law, since everything contributes to proving the existence of God. He has the right to prescribe laws to men,

11. The next several paragraphs are a selective summary of Burlamaqui, *Principles*, I.II.i–v, I.II.ix., I.II.xii–xiii.—HC

and it is a consequence of His power, wisdom, and goodness to give men rules of conduct.

The ways by which one can distinguish what is just and unjust or what is dictated by natural law are:

(1) Instinct or a certain inner feeling that makes us lean toward certain actions or away from them.

(2) Reason, which confirms instinct; it develops principles and deduces consequences.

(3) God's will, made known to man—and so becoming the supreme rule.

Man cannot arrive at a knowledge of natural laws except by examining his nature, his make-up, and his condition. All natural laws are concerned with three objects: God, the self, and others.

Religion is the principle of the laws which concern God.

Self-love is the principle of natural laws relating to ourselves.

The spirit of society is the basis of those laws which relate to others.

God has sufficiently revealed the natural laws to man; men can still help each other to know them. These laws are the work of God's goodness. They do not depend upon an arbitrary institution; therefore they oblige all men to conform to them. They are perpetual, immovable, and admit no exceptions.

To apply natural law to actions, that is, to render equitable judgment, one has to consult one's conscience, which is nothing else but one's reason. When the question arises whether someone can be held responsible for the consequences of a bad action, it must be ascertained whether he knew the law and the fact or whether forces beyond his control constrained him to act contrary to natural law.

The authority of natural laws stems from the fact that they owe their existence to God. Men submit to them because to observe them leads to the happiness of men and society. This is a truth demonstrated by reason. It is equally true that virtue by itself is a principle of inner satisfaction, whereas vice is a principle of unrest and trouble. It is equally certain that virtue produces great external advantage, while vice produces great ills.

Yet virtue does not always have for those who practice it as happy outward effects as it should have. One can frequently observe the good and evil of nature and of fortune distributed unequally and not according to the merits of each individual. Evils resulting from injustice fall upon the innocent as well as upon the guilty, and often virtue itself is subject to persecution.

All man's prudence is not sufficient to relieve such disorders. Still another consideration is necessary to force men to observe the natural laws, namely, the immortality of the soul and the belief in the future, where what might be missing in the sanction of natural laws will be carried out if divine wisdom deems it necessary.

This is how our author proves the authority of natural law over reason and religion, which are the two great lights given by God for man's conduct.

The Preface of the book announces that this treatise is merely the beginning of a more extensive work, or a complete system of the law of nature and of nations, which the author intends to publish. However, since his plans were thwarted by other commitments and by ill health, he was determined to publish this first part. Though this is an excellent summary of natural law, one cannot help hoping that the author will complete the work he has undertaken, where the subject will be treated to the fullest extent.[12]

One can also refer to what is said on natural law in several places by the author of *The Spirit of the Laws*.[13] (A)

12. Burlamaqui had died in 1748, a fact of which Boucher d'Argis may have been unaware, although see the editor's introduction to Burlamaqui, *Principles*, x–xiv, for the lively afterlife of his lecture notes.—HC

13. Montesquieu.

Public Law
(*Droit Public*)

This article contains a lucid summary of the proper scope of government, as seen by a mainstream establishment lawyer well versed in both French law and the natural-law tradition. See also Boucher d'Argis's entry NATURAL LAW *[Droit de la Nature] above.*

PUBLIC LAW is law established for the common utility of the people considered as a political body, as distinct from private *law,* which is created for the utility of each person considered individually and independent of other men.

Public law is either general or particular.

That *public law* is called *general* which regulates the foundations of civil society that are common to most states, and the interests that these states have with each other.

Some people confuse general *public law* with the *law* of nations, which is not accurate, at least without making distinctions. For the *law* of nations, which has (as all *law* in general does) two purposes, public utility and private utility, is divided into the *public law* of nations and the *private law* of nations. Thus, the general *public law* is indeed a part of the *law* of nations and is the same thing as the *public law* of nations. But it does not include the whole *law* of nations, since it does not include the private *law* of nations. See below, DROIT DES GENS [Law of Nations].

Note that we have translated *puissance* as "power" here and *pouvoir* as "capacity"; see the translators' note for these terms.

This article can be found at 5:135–36 in the original edition of the *Encyclopédie.*

Particular *public law* is the law that regulates the foundations of each state; it differs in this respect both from general *public law* (which concerns the relations that the different states can have with each other) and from private or particular *law* per se (which concerns each of the members of a state separately).

Particular *public law* is composed, in part, of precepts from divine *law* and from natural *law*, which are invariable; in part, from the *law* of nations, which changes little (except over a long series of years); and finally, it is also composed of part of the civil *law* of the state concerned—that is, of the part of that *law* that has as its purpose the body of the state. Thus, a part of the particular *public law* is founded on ancient customs (written or unwritten), on laws, ordinances, edicts, declarations, charters, diplomas,[1] etc. Being founded on positive human *law,* this part of particular *public law* can be changed according to time and circumstance by those who have the public power.

The purpose of the particular *public law* of each state is generally to establish and maintain that general administration[2] necessary for the good order and tranquility of the state; to procure what is most beneficial to all the members of the state, considered collectively or separately—whether it concerns the goods of the soul, the goods of the body, or the goods of fortune.

The destiny of men in the providential order is to cultivate the earth and aspire to the sovereign good. Men inhabiting the same country, having sensed the necessity they were under to lend each other mutual assistance, joined together in society; this is what formed the different states.

To maintain good order in each of these societies or states, a certain form of government had to be established. And to make this form or general administration be observed, the members of each society or state were obliged to establish a public power above them.

This power was bestowed upon one man or several or all those who compose the state. In some places, it is perpetual; in others, those who are vested with this power exercise it for only a certain time fixed by the laws.

1. *Diplômes,* a general term for certain public, usually princely acts.

2. *Police;* see the translators' note.

Whence arises the distinction between monarchical, aristocratic, and democratic or popular states.[3]

The *rights*[4] of the public power are: the legislative power; the *right* of causing the laws to be executed or dispensed with; of rendering and causing the rendering of justice; of granting favors, distributing employments and honors; establishing officers and dismissing them, having a fisc or a public patrimony, imposing taxes, coining money, allowing certain persons to form a political body together, regulating the social orders, making treaties of alliance, navigation, and commerce with foreigners; creating fortified places, levying troops and disbanding them, making war and peace.

These *rights* extend not only over those who are members of a state; most of these same *rights* extend also over foreigners, who are subject to the general laws of state administration during the whole time they live there, and to the laws concerning the property they possess there even when they are not living there.

The commitments of the person or persons on whom the public power is bestowed are to maintain good order in the state.

For their part, the members of the state must be subject to the public power, and to the persons who represent it in some section of government; likewise, they must be subject to the laws and observe them.

The common and particular good of each member of the state, which forms in general the object of the particular *public law,* includes within itself many objects belonging to the latter, which form some more or less substantial portion of it.

Everything connected to civil ecclesiastical government, military justice, or finance belongs therefore to the *public law*.

Thus, it is up to *public law* to regulate everything concerning religion, to prevent the disorders that the diversity of opinion can cause, to make people respect the holy places, observe the saints' days, and other rules of discipline relative to religion; to preserve a fitting order and decency in pious ceremonies; to prevent abuses that can be committed during the

3. Here, the author follows Aristotle's traditional typology of monarchy, aristocracy, or democracy, on the basis of the number of holders of political power.

4. *Droits;* Boucher d'Argis seems to be drawing on another of its meanings in this section; see the translators' note.

holiest practices, and to prevent the formation of any new establishments in religious matters without approval by those who have the capacity to do this. One must merely pay heed that the task of maintaining religion in its purity, and of making its external ritual be observed, is entrusted to the two powers, spiritual and temporal—each according to the extent of its capacity.

From this standpoint, one must also include what concerns the clergy in general, the different bodies and individuals of which it is composed (whether secular or regular), and everything that has some connection to religion and piety, such as the universities, the secondary schools and academies for the instruction of youth, the poorhouses, etc.[5]

Likewise, *public law* has in view everything related to mores, such as luxury, intemperance, prohibited games, decency in public spectacles, debauchery, frequenting of bad places, swearing and blasphemy, judicial Astrology, and the imposters known by the name of *soothsayers, witches, magicians,* and those weak enough to allow themselves to be abused by these.

Just as *public law* provides for the goods of the soul—that is, for what touches religion and mores—it also provides for bodily goods. Whence the laws that have health as their object—that is, preserving or restoring the salubriousness of the air and the purity of the water, the good quality of the other things that nourish the body, the choice of remedies, the competence of doctors and surgeons; the precautions taken against contagious diseases.

It is also a continuation of the same object to provide for what concerns living provisions—such as bread, wine, meat, and the other foods—whether related to the husbandry (for those who need it) or to their protection, transportation, sale, and preparation, even for what is used in the feeding of the animals that serve in the cultivation of the land or in the transport.

Distinguishing among costumes according to the status and condition of persons, and the task of repressing luxury, are likewise objects of *public law* in every state.[6]

5. See Poorhouse, below.

6. This is a reference to the sumptuary laws that were still prevalent in Europe in the eighteenth century, on which Boucher d'Argis wrote a substantial article in the *Encyclopédie,* 9:672–77.

The laws also contain many rules relating to clothing, such as whatever concerns the quality that the materials are supposed to have, the distinction among costumes according to status, and what tends toward the repression of luxury.

It also provides that buildings be constructed in a solid manner, and that nothing be made that is contrary to the decor of the city; that the streets and public ways be made secure and convenient, and not obstructed. This has produced a multitude of particular regulations whose object is to prevent sundry accidents that might occur due to the imprudence of the workers or the drivers of horses or wagons, etc.

One of the greatest objects of the *public law* of every state is the administration of justice in general. But not everything related to this belongs equally to *public law*. In this regard, one must distinguish form and content, civil matters and criminal matters.

The form of the administration of justice belongs to *public law,* in civil matters as well as in criminal matters. This is why individuals are not allowed to deviate from it.

But in substance, the arrangement of the laws concerning what touches individuals in civil matters belongs to *private law*. Thus, individuals can deviate from it by agreement—unless there is some contrary law, in which case this law forms part of *public law*.

As for the punishment of crimes and misdemeanors, it is entirely in the jurisdiction of *public law*. One does not include in this category certain acts that interest only individuals, but solely those that disturb public order, directly or indirectly—such as heresy, blasphemy, sacrilege, and other impieties; the crime of lèse-majesté, rebellions against justice, illicit assemblies, bearing of arms, and assaults;[7] duels, the crime of embezzlement, extortion, and other official malfeasance; the crime of counterfeiting, assassination, homicide, poisoning, parricide, and other attacks on the life of others or one's own; the exposure of children, robbery and larceny, fraudulent bankruptcy, the crime of forgery, attacks against modesty, slander, and other acts injurious to the government, etc.

7. *Voies de fait,* lit. "the way of action," distinguished in French legal language of the time from *voies de droit* or "the way of law"—that is, having recourse to the legal system.

It is clear from what has just been said that whatever concerns the functions of judicial officials and other public officials is likewise a matter of *public law*.

The *public law* of each state also has as its object everything belonging to the governing of finances, such as the assignment and levying of taxes, the proportion that is to be maintained in their distribution, and the abuses that might slip into these operations or in the collection.

Finally, this same *law* embraces everything related to the common utility, such as shipping and commerce, colonies, manufactures, the sciences, arts and trades, workers of every kind, the power of masters over their servants and domestics, and the submission that the latter owe their masters, and everything that concerns the public tranquility, such as regulations made for the relief of the poor, for obliging able-bodied mendicants to work, for the confinement of vagabonds and vagrants.[8]

It would be very curious to detail all these matters, but since this could not be done without repeating part of the subject matter of the articles Crime, Gouvernement, Puissance Publique [Public Power], and other similar ones, it will be enough to refer to those articles. (A)

8. *Gens sans aveu,* "people lacking recognition," as by a feudal lord in earlier times; the phrase is sometimes rendered "masterless men."

Natural Equality
(*Egalité Naturelle*)

Natural Equality (*Natural law*) is that which is found among all men solely by the constitution of their nature. This equality is the principle and foundation of liberty. Natural or moral equality is therefore based on the constitution of human nature common to all men, who are born, grow, live, and die in the same way.

Since human nature is the same in all men, it is clear according to natural law that each person must value and treat other people as so many individuals who are naturally equal to himself, that is to say, as men like himself.

Several consequences ensue from this principle of the natural equality of men. I shall rapidly examine the principal ones.

(1) It follows from this principle that all men are naturally free and that the faculty of reason could only make them dependent for their own welfare.

(2) That in spite of all the inequalities produced in the political government by the differences in station, by nobility, power, riches, etc., those who have risen the most above others must treat their inferiors as being naturally equal to them by avoiding any insults, by demanding nothing beyond what is required, and by demanding with humanity only what is unquestionably due.

(3) That whoever has not acquired a particular right, by virtue of which he can demand preferential treatment, must not claim more than others

"Natural Equality" was translated by Stephen J. Gendzier, in *Denis Diderot's "The Encyclopedia": Selections,* ed. and trans. Stephen J. Gendzier (New York: Harper and Row, 1967), 169–71, and is reprinted by permission of the translator.

This article can be found at 5:415 in the original edition of the *Encyclopédie.*

but, on the contrary, allow them to enjoy equally the same rights that he assumes for himself.

(4) That anything which is a universal right must be either universally enjoyed or alternately possessed, or divided into equal portions among those who have the same right, or allotted with equitable and regulated compensation; or finally if this is possible, the decision should be made by lot: a quite suitable expedient that removes any suspicion of contempt and partiality without diminishing in any way the esteem of those people not immediately favored. Finally, to go even further, I base on the incontestable principle of natural equality, as did the judicious Hooker,[1] all the duties of charity, of humanity, and of justice which all men are obliged to practice toward one another, and it would not be difficult to demonstrate this.

The reader will derive other consequences that arise from the principle of the natural equality of men. I shall observe only that it is the violation of this principle that has established political and civil slavery. The result is that in the countries subject to arbitrary power, the princes, the courtiers, the principal ministers, those who control the finances, possess all the riches of the nation, while the rest of the citizens have only the necessaries of life, and the great majority of people groan in poverty.

Nevertheless let no one do me the injustice of supposing that with a sense of fanaticism I approve in a state that chimera, absolute equality, which could hardly give birth to an ideal republic. I am only speaking here of the natural equality of men.

I know too well the necessity of different ranks, grades, honors, distinctions, prerogatives, subordinations that must prevail in all governments. And I would even state that natural or moral equality are not contrary to this. In the state of nature men are truly born into equality but do not know how to remain so. Society forces them to lose it, and they only become equal again by laws. Aristotle relates that Phaleas of Chalcedon had imagined a way to equalize the fortunes of the republic: he would have the rich give dowries to the poor and not receive any in their turn, and the poor receive money for their daughters and not give any to others. "But," as the

1. Richard Hooker (1553–1600), English theologian who examined the philosophical foundations of law and political power. He was called "the judicious Hooker" for his attempt to reconcile divergent theological points of view and adjust them to Anglicanism.

author of the *Spirit of Laws* has observed, "has any republic ever accommodated itself to such a regulation? It places the citizens in conditions of such striking discrimination that they would hate even that equality that one would attempt to establish, and that would be foolish to try to introduce."[2]
Article by Chevalier DE JAUCOURT.

2. Montesquieu, *The Spirit of the Laws,* 5.5, 46, commenting on Aristotle, *Politics,* 2.7 (1266a39–1266b5).—HC

Eulogy for President Montesquieu
(*Eloge de M. le Président de Montesquieu*)

Though twenty-eight years his junior, d'Alembert, the author of this entry, had become not only an admirer but a friend of Montesquieu's. He was present at Montesquieu's deathbed in February 1755. Diderot, for his part, was the only member of the philosophic community to attend his funeral. The editors then took the unusual step of beginning the next volume of the work, volume 5, which appeared in November of that year, with a lengthy eulogy with a title set in a large typeface. The eulogy contains both an appreciation of Montesquieu's life and career and an editorial summary of the doctrine contained in his Spirit of the Laws*—a work that would loom so large in the political articles of the dictionary throughout its publication history that it seemed appropriate for inclusion in this anthology. The eulogy provides a revealing glimpse into how the Encyclopedists viewed the place of Montesquieu and his work in the encyclopedic project itself, and into their perceptions of the kind of criticism then being made of Montesquieu's powerful but complex new doctrine. It appeared in English translation for the first time in the London, 1777, edition of Montesquieu's works published by T. Evans, though we have offered a new translation here. Most of the merely biographical information in it has been omitted. It should also be noted that the summary of* The Spirit of the Laws *appears in the* Encyclopédie *as a note, but for the sake of convenience it is reproduced here as text.*

This article can be found at 5:ii, vii–xiii, in the original edition of the *Encyclopédie*.

EULOGY FOR PRESIDENT MONTESQUIEU

The interest that good citizens take in the *Encyclopédie,* and the great number of men of letters who devote their works to it, would seem to allow us to regard it as one of the most appropriate monuments to serve as depositories of the sentiments of the Country, and of the homage that it owes to the celebrated men who have honored it. Convinced, nonetheless, that M. Montesquieu had the right to expect panegyrists other than ourselves and that the public grief would have merited more eloquent spokesmen, we would have contained within ourselves the just regrets and respect that we have for his memory. But the acknowledgment of what we owe him is too precious for us to leave responsibility for it to others. Benefactor of humanity by his writings, he deigned also to be a benefactor of this work, and our gratitude wishes only to trace some lines at the foot of his statue.

[A summary of Montesquieu's life and early writings follows; at 5:viii, d'Alembert appends a lengthy footnote discussing *The Spirit of the Laws;* its translation follows here.]

Since most men of letters who have spoken of *The Spirit of the Laws* have been more fond of criticizing it than of providing an accurate notion of it, we are going to attempt to fulfill what they ought to have done and to unfold its plan, character, and purpose. Those who find the analysis too long will perhaps consider, after reading it, that this was the only means of enabling one to grasp the author's method. One should remember, moreover, that the history of celebrated writers is only the history of their thoughts and their works, and that that part of their eulogy is the most essential and the most useful part, especially at the head of a work such as the *Encyclopédie.*

Men in the state of nature—abstracted of all religion, knowing no other law [*loi*] in the disagreements they may have except that of the animals, the right of the stronger—one should regard the establishment of societies as a kind of treaty against this unjust law [*droit*], a treaty designed to establish among the different parts of the human race a sort of scale. But with natural equilibrium as with moral, it is rare for it to be perfect and durable, and the treaties of the human race are like the treaties among our princes—a constant seed of divisions. Interest, need, and pleasure have brought men closer together, but those same motives constantly push them to want to enjoy the advantages of society without bearing its burdens. It is in this sense that one may say with the author that men, as soon as they are in society, are in a state of war. For war assumes in those who wage it, if not equality of strength, at least the opinion of that equality, whence arises the desire and mutual expectation of defeating each other. Now in the social state, if the balance is never perfect among men, it is not too unequal, either. On the contrary, they would either have no conflicts in the state of nature, or, if necessity drove them to it, one would find weakness fleeing before strength, oppressors without combat, and the oppressed without resistance.

Thus, there you have men, brought together and armed all at the same time—embracing each other on the one hand, if one may speak in this way, and looking to do mutual harm on the other. The laws are the more or less efficacious bonds designed to suspend or restrain their blows. But since the vast expanse of the globe we inhabit and the natural differences in the regions of the earth and in the peoples who cover it do not permit all men to live under one and the same government, the human race has had to distribute itself into a certain number of States, distinguished by the differences in the laws they obey. A single government would have made of the human race but one body, languishing and attenuated, extended without vigor over the surface of the earth. The different States are so many agile and robust bodies which, extending their hands to each other, form but one, whose reciprocal action everywhere fosters movement and life.

One may distinguish three sorts of government: the republican, the monarchical, the despotic. In the republican, the people as a body have sovereign power; in the monarchical, one person governs by fundamental laws; in the despotic, no other law is known but the will of the master, or rather of the tyrant. This is not to say that there are only these three types of States in the world; it is not even to say that there are States that belong solely and rigorously to one or another of these forms. Most are, so to speak, half and half, or shaded blends of these forms: here monarchy inclines to despotism; there, monarchical government is combined with republican; elsewhere, it is not the whole people, it is a part of the people who make the laws. But the foregoing division is nonetheless exact and precise. The three species of government that it includes are distinguished in such a way that they have, properly speaking, nothing in common, and yet all States that we know of partake of one or the other of them. It was thus necessary to form particular classes out of these three species and to apply oneself to determining the laws appropriate to them. It will be easy afterward to modify these laws in their application to whatever government it may be, according to whether it belongs more or less to these different forms.

In the various States, the laws should be relative to their *nature,* that is, to what constitutes them, and to their *principle,* that is, what supports them and gives them their activity—an important distinction, the key to countless laws, and the author derives many conclusions from it.

The principal laws relative to the *nature* of democracy are that the people be in some respects the monarch and in others the subject, that they elect and judge their magistrates, and that the magistrates make the decisions on certain occasions. The nature of monarchy demands that there be many intermediate powers and ranks between the monarch and the people, and a body that is depository of the laws and mediator between the subjects and the prince. The nature of despotism demands that the tyrant exercise his authority either by himself alone or through one person who represents him.

As for the *principle* of the three governments, that of democracy is love of the republic, that is, of equality; in monarchies, where one alone is the dispenser of distinctions and rewards, and where people are accustomed to confuse the State with this one man, the principle is honor—that is, ambition and love of esteem; under despotism, finally, it is fear. The more vigorous these principles are, the more stable the government; the more they are altered and corrupted, the more the government tends toward its destruction. When the author speaks of equality in democracies, he does not mean an equality that is extreme, absolute, and therefore chimerical; he means that happy equilibrium that makes all citizens equally subject to the laws, and with an equal interest in observing them.

In each government, the laws of education should be relative to the *principle.* What is meant here by *education* is the one received on entering the world, not the one given by parents and masters, which is often contrary to it, especially in certain States. In monarchies, education should have as its object urbanity and reciprocal esteem; in despotic States, terror and abasement of spirits. In republics, one needs all the power of education; it should inspire a noble but painful sentiment: self-renunciation, whence is born love of Country.

The laws that the legislator enacts should be in conformity with the *principle* of each government: in a republic, to maintain equality and frugality; in a monarchy, to support nobility without crushing the people; under despotic government, to keep all estates equally silent. One must not accuse M. de Montesquieu here of tracing out for sovereigns the principles of arbitrary power, whose very name is so odious to just princes, and all the more so to the wise and virtuous citizen. To show what has to be done to preserve such power is to work toward annihilating it. The perfection of this government is its ruin. And the exact code of tyranny, such as the author presents it, is simultaneously the satire and the most fearsome scourge of tyrants. As for the other governments, they each have their advantages: the republican is more appropriate for small States, the monarchical for large ones; the republican is more subject to excesses, the monarchical to abuses; the republican brings more maturity into the execution of the laws, the monarchical more dispatch.

The different principles of the three governments are bound to produce differences in the number and purposes of the laws, in the form of the sentences and the nature of the punishments. Since the constitution of monarchies is unchanging and fundamental, it requires more civil laws and tribunals so that justice may be rendered in a more uniform and less arbitrary manner. In moderate States, whether monarchies or republics, one cannot bring too many formalities to bear on the criminal laws. Punishment must be not only in proportion with the crime, but also as mild as possible, especially in a democracy; the opinion attached to punishments will often have more effect than their actual scale. In republics, one must judge according to the law, because no individual is in command of changing it. In monarchies, the sovereign's clemency can sometimes soften the law; but crimes must never be judged except by the magistrates expressly charged with knowing about them. Finally, it is mainly in democracies that the laws should be rigorous against luxury, the relaxation of mores, and the seduction of women. The mildness of women and even their weakness renders them fit enough to govern in monarchies, and history proves that they have often worn the crown with glory.

Having surveyed each government in particular, M. de Montesquieu next examines them in the relationship they may have with each other, but only from the most general viewpoint—that is, the viewpoint uniquely related to their nature and their principle. Envisioned in this manner, States can have no other relationships but that of defending or attacking. Confined by nature to a small State, republics cannot defend themselves without allies, but it is with other republics that they should be allied; the defensive strength of monarchy consists mainly in having frontiers out of attack range. Like men, States have the right to attack for their own preservation: from the right of war derives the right of conquest, a right that is necessary, legitimate, and unfortunate, *which always leaves an immense debt to be discharged if human nature is to be repaid*,[1] and whose general law is to do the least harm possible to the vanquished.[2] Republics are less able to conquer than monarchies; immense conquests presuppose despotism, or ensure it. One of the great principles of the spirit of conquest should be to improve the condition of the conquered people as much as possible. This simultaneously satisfies the natural law and the maxim of State. Nothing is more noble than Gelon's peace treaty with the Carthaginians, by which he prohibited them from immolating their own children in the future.[3] In conquering Peru,[4] the Spanish ought likewise to have obliged the inhabitants to no longer immolate men to their gods, but they thought it more beneficial to immolate these very peoples. They had nothing more for a conquest than a vast desert; they were forced to depopulate their country, and they weakened themselves forever by their own victory. One may sometimes be obliged to change the laws of the defeated people; nothing can ever oblige one to take away their mores or even their customs, which are often their whole mores. But the surest means of preserving a conquest is, if possible, to put the vanquished people on the level of the conquering people, to accord them the same rights and privileges. This is the means the Romans often used; this is especially the means Caesar used with respect to the Gauls.

1. Montesquieu, *The Spirit of the Laws*, 10.4, 142.
2. *Laws*, 1.3.
3. For this episode, see *Laws*, 10.5.
4. Under the conquistador Francisco Pizarro in the early 1530s.

In considering each government both in itself and in its relation with others, we have thus far been concerned neither with what they ought to have in common, nor with the particular circumstances drawn either from the nature of the country or from the genius of the people. This is what now needs to be explored.

The common law of all governments, at least of moderate and therefore just governments, is the political liberty that each citizen should enjoy.[5] This liberty is not the absurd license of doing what one wants, but the power to do everything the laws permit. It can be envisioned either in its relation with the constitution, or in its relation with the citizen.[6]

In the constitution of each State, there are two sorts of powers, the legislative and the executive power. This latter has two objects, the internal affairs of the State and its external ones. The degree of perfection in a constitution's political liberty depends on the legitimate distribution and the appropriate allocation of these different kinds of power. M. de Montesquieu brings in as evidence the constitution of the Roman republic and that of England. He finds the principle of the latter in the fundamental law of the ancient Germans' government: that unimportant affairs were decided by the chieftains, and that great affairs were brought to the tribunal of the nation after being debated by the chieftains. M. de Montesquieu does not examine whether the English do or do not enjoy that extreme political liberty which their constitution provides them;[7] it suffices for him to say that it is established by their laws. He is even further from intending to satirize other States.[8] On the contrary, he believes that an excess even of good things is not always desirable, that extreme liberty has its disadvantages as does extreme servitude, and that in general, human nature adjusts better to a middling condition.[9]

Political liberty considered in relation to the citizen consists in the security that he is sheltered by the laws, or at least he is of the opinion that he

5. *Laws,* 11.4, for Montesquieu's slightly different formulation.

6. *Laws,* 11.1 and 11.3, for these two sentences.

7. *Laws,* 11.6, 166.

8. This echoes *Laws,* 3.6, where Montesquieu seeks to avoid the appearance of demeaning monarchy in his definition of virtue as the principle solely of republics.

9. *Laws,* 11.6, 166.

has that security which causes one citizen not to fear another.[10] It is mainly through the nature and proportion of the punishments that this liberty is established or destroyed.[11] Crimes against religion should be punished by privation of the goods that religion procures; crimes against mores, by shame; crimes against public tranquility, by prison or exile; crimes against security, by corporal punishment. Writings should be less punished than actions; simple thoughts should never be punished. Nonjudicial accusations, spies, anonymous letters: all these expedients of tyranny, equally shameful to those who are their instruments and to those who use them, should be proscribed in a good monarchical government. It is not permissible to accuse except in the face of the law, which always punishes either the accused or the slanderer. In every other case, those who govern should say with Emperor Constans:[12] *We cannot suspect a man who has no accuser even though he does not lack enemies*. It is very good to have established a public party who is charged in the name of the State to prosecute crimes, and who has all the usefulness of the informant without having the vile interests, the disadvantages, and the infamy.[13]

The level of taxes should be in direct proportion with liberty.[14] Thus, in democracies, they can be greater than elsewhere without being onerous, because every citizen regards them as a tribute[15] he pays to himself, which ensures the tranquility and the lot of each member. Moreover, in a democratic State, the unfaithful use of public revenue is more difficult, because it is easier to know about and punish, since the agent owes an account, so to speak, to the first citizen who demands it.

In any government, the least onerous type of tax is the one established on merchandise, because the citizen pays without being aware of it.[16] The excessive number of troops in time of peace is only a pretext to burden

10. *Laws,* 11.6, 157.

11. For what follows, see *Laws,* 12.4.

12. Constans (Flavius Julius Constans), coemperor from 337 until he was killed by Magnentius in 350; this is from *Laws,* 12.24.

13. *Laws,* 6.8.

14. This is the subject of book 13 of *Laws.*

15. *Tribut,* meaning either "tribute" or "tax." See TAX and FIVE PERCENT TAX, below.

16. This is Montesquieu's argument in *Laws,* 13.14. For the contrary argument, see the article FIVE PERCENT TAX, below.

the people with taxes, a means of enervating the State, and an instrument of servitude. The direct collection[17] of taxes, which brings the whole yield into the public fisc, is incomparably less burdensome to the people, and therefore more advantageous (when it can take place) than the farming of these same taxes, which always leaves a portion of State revenues in the hands of some private individuals. All is lost especially (these are the terms of the author) when the profession of tax-farmer becomes honorable,[18] and it becomes honorable as soon as luxury is in force. To let a few men feed on the public sustenance in order to fleece them in their turn, as has been practiced in the past in certain States, is to remedy one injustice by another, and to do two bad things instead of one.

Let us move now, with M. Montesquieu, to the particular circumstances that are independent of the nature of the government and that are bound to modify its laws. The circumstances that come from the nature of the country are of two sorts: some are related to the climate, others to the terrain. No one doubts that climate has an influence on the customary arrangement of bodies, and therefore on characters.[19] This is why the laws should be in conformity with the nature of the climate in indifferent matters, and conversely, should combat them when the effects are vicious. Thus, in countries where the use of wine is harmful, the law that prohibits it is a very good one. In countries where the heat of the climate leads to laziness, the law that encourages work is a very good one. The government may thus remedy the effects of the climate, and this suffices to safeguard *The Spirit of the Laws* from the very unjust criticism made of it, that it attributes everything to cold and heat. For besides the fact that heat and cold are not the only things by which climates are distinguished, it would be as absurd to deny certain effects of climate as to want to attribute everything to it.

The use of slaves, established in the warm countries of Asia and America but condemned in the temperate climates of Europe, gives the author occasion to treat of civil slavery.[20] Since men have no more right over the liberty than over the lives of one another, it follows that slavery, generally

17. The word is *Régie,* and the contrast that follows is the topic of *Laws,* 13.19.

18. Perhaps the reference is to the last sentence in *Laws,* 13.8.

19. Montesquieu explores the role of climate in *Laws,* bks. 14–17.

20. That is the topic of bk. 15 of *Laws.*

speaking, is contrary to natural law. In fact, the right of slavery cannot come from war—since then, it could be based only on the ransoming of one's life, and there is no right over the lives of those who are no longer attacking. Nor can it come from a man's sale of himself to another—since every citizen, being indebted to the State for his life, is all the more indebted to it for his liberty, and therefore is not in charge of selling it. Besides, what would be the price of this sale? It cannot be the money given to the seller, since the moment one turns oneself into a slave, all one's possessions belong to the master. Now, a sale without a price is as chimerical as a contract without conditions. There has perhaps been only one just law in favor of slavery: this was the Roman law that made the debtor a slave of the creditor. In order to be equitable, even this law had to limit the servitude as to degree and time. Slavery can at most be tolerated in despotic States, where free men, too weak against the government, seek for their own utility to become the slaves of those who tyrannize the State; or else in climates whose heat so enervates the body and so weakens morale that men are brought to perform an arduous duty only by the fear of punishment.[21]

Alongside civil slavery, one may place domestic servitude—that is, the servitude in which women are held in certain climes.[22] It can take place in those Asian countries where they are living with men before being able to make use of their reason: nubile by the law of climate, a child by the law of nature. This subjection becomes even more necessary in countries where polygamy is established—a custom that M. Montesquieu does not pretend to justify insofar as it is contrary to religion, but which, in the places where it is accepted (and speaking only politically), can be well-founded up to a certain point, either on the nature of the country, or on the relationship between the number of women and the number of men. On this occasion, M. Montesquieu speaks of renunciation and of divorce, and he establishes on good grounds that once it is allowed, renunciation ought to be permitted to women as well as to men.[23]

If climate has so much influence over domestic and civil servitude, it has no less over political servitude—that is, over the servitude that sub-

21. *Laws,* 15.7, 251.
22. For this paragraph, see *Laws,* bk. 16.
23. *Laws,* 16.15.

jects one people to another. The peoples of the North are stronger and hardier than those of the South. Thus, the latter in general are bound to be subjugated, the former are bound to be conquerors; the latter slaves, the former free. It is also what history confirms: Asia has been conquered eleven times by the peoples of the North; Europe has suffered many fewer revolutions.[24]

With regard to the laws in their relationship with the nature of the terrain,[25] it is clear that democracy is more appropriate than monarchy for sterile countries, where the earth needs all of men's industry. Moreover, liberty is in that case a kind of compensation for the harshness of the work. More laws are needed for an agricultural people than for a people who raise flocks; more for the latter than for a hunting people; more for a people who make use of money than for those unfamiliar with money.

Finally, one should consider the particular genius of the nation.[26] The vanity that enlarges objects is a good resource for government; the pride that devalues them is a dangerous resource. The legislator should respect prejudices, passions, abuses up to a certain point. He should imitate Solon, who gave the Athenians not the best laws in themselves, but the best ones they could have. The gay character of those people demanded easier laws; the hard character of the Lacedemonians, more rigorous laws. The law is a bad means of changing manners and customs; it is by reward and example that one must try to achieve this end. At the same time, however, it is true that a people's laws, when one is not bent on grossly and directly offending their mores, are bound to imperceptibly influence these mores—either to reinforce them or to change them.

After thoroughly exploring in this manner the nature and the spirit of the laws relative to the different types of country and people, the author returns anew to consider States in their relations to each other. At first, in comparing them among themselves in a general manner, he had been able to envision them only in relation to the harm they could do each other. Here, he envisions them in relation to the mutual assistance they can give

24. See *Laws,* 17.1–4, for Montesquieu's version of this argument.

25. This is the subject of *Laws,* bk. 18.

26. See bk. 19 of *Laws* for this theme.

each other; as it happens, this assistance is mainly founded on commerce.[27] If the spirit of commerce naturally produces a spirit of interest opposed to the sublimity of the moral virtues, it also renders a people naturally just, and it banishes laziness and brigandage. Free nations that live under moderate governments are bound to engage in more commerce than slave nations. One nation should never exclude another nation from its trade without very good reasons.[28] Nonetheless, liberty in this area is not an absolute faculty granted to traders to do what they want, a faculty that would often be harmful to them; it consists only in hampering traders to the benefit of trade.[29] In a monarchy, the nobility should not devote themselves to it, still less the prince. Finally, there are nations for which commerce is disadvantageous—not those that need nothing, but those that need everything, a paradox the author makes concrete by the example of Poland, which lacks everything except wheat, and which, through the commerce it engages in, deprives the peasants of their sustenance in order to satisfy the luxury of the lords. On the subject of the laws that commerce requires, M. Montesquieu presents the history of these different revolutions, and this part of his book is neither the least interesting nor the least curious. He compares the impoverishment of Spain by the discovery of America to the fate of that imbecilic prince of the fable—ready to die of hunger for having asked the gods that everything he touched be converted into gold.[30] Since the use of money is a substantial part of the topic of commerce, and its main instrument, he thus thought he should treat the operations on the currency, on exchange, on the payment of public debt, on lending at interest—upon which he defines the laws and limits, and which he in no way confuses with the so justly condemned excesses of usury.[31]

The population and the number of inhabitants have an immediate relationship with commerce.[32] Since the purpose of marriage is population, M. Montesquieu thoroughly examines that important matter here. What most

27. Commerce is the subject of *Laws,* bks. 20–21.

28. *Laws,* 20.9.

29. *Laws,* 20.12.

30. *Laws,* 21.22.

31. These topics are the concern of *Laws,* bk. 22.

32. See *Laws,* bk. 23, for population.

encourages propagation is public continence; experience proves that illicit unions contribute little, and indeed are harmful. It is with justice that the consent of the father has been established for marriage; however, restrictions ought to be placed on this, for the law ought in general to encourage marriage. The law that prohibits the marriage of mothers with sons is (independent of the precepts of religion) a very good civil law. For aside from many other reasons, since the contracting parties are of very different ages, these sorts of marriages can rarely have propagation as their purpose. The law that prohibits the marriage of father and daughter is based on the same motives; however (speaking only from the perspective of civil law), it is not as indispensably necessary as the other to the purpose of population, since the capacity for procreation ends much later in men. Thus, the contrary custom has occurred among certain peoples upon whom the light of Christianity has not shone. Since nature brings itself to bear on marriage, it is a bad government that would need to encourage it. Liberty, security, moderate taxes, and proscription of luxury are the true principles and the true supports of population. Nonetheless, one may successfully enact laws to encourage marriage when, despite the corruption, there still remain resources in the people that attach them to their Country. Nothing is finer than Augustus's laws for encouraging the propagation of the species; unfortunately, he passed these laws during the decay, or rather the fall, of the republic. The demoralized citizens must have foreseen that they would no longer be bringing anyone into the world but slaves; thus, the execution of these laws was quite weak during the entire time of the pagan emperors. Constantine in the end abolished them in becoming a Christian, as if Christianity's purpose was to depopulate society by recommending the perfection of celibacy to a small number.

The establishment of poorhouses,[33] depending on the spirit with which it is done, can harm population or encourage it. There may, and even should be, poorhouses in a State in which most of the citizens have only their resourcefulness as an asset, because that resourcefulness may sometimes fall short through misfortune. But the assistance that these poorhouses give should be only temporary, in order not to encourage mendicancy

33. *Hôpital;* see the article by that title, below.

and idleness. One must begin by making the people rich, and afterward build poorhouses for pressing, unforeseen needs. Woe betide the countries in which the multitude of poorhouses and of monasteries (which are only perpetual poorhouses) makes everyone comfortable except those who work.

M. Montesquieu has thus far spoken only of human laws. He now passes to the laws of religion,[34] which in almost all States form such an essential object of government. He everywhere praises Christianity, he shows its advantages and its greatness, he seeks to make it loved. He maintains that it is not impossible, as Bayle claimed,[35] for a society of perfect Christians to form a durable and coherent State. But he also thought it permissible for him to examine what the different religions (humanly speaking) might have that is in conformity with, or contrary to, the genius and situation of the peoples who profess them. It is from this point of view that one must read everything he wrote on this matter, which has been the subject of so many unjust rantings. It is especially surprising that in an age that calls so many other ages barbarous, what he said about tolerance should have been made a crime against him, as if to tolerate a religion was to approve of it, as if even the Gospel did not proscribe every other means of spreading itself but mildness and persuasion. Those in whom superstition has not extinguished every feeling of compassion and justice will be unable to read without being moved to pity the remonstrance to the inquisitors—that odious tribunal which outrages religion while appearing to avenge it.[36]

Finally, after treating individually the different types of law that men may have, it remains only to compare them all together, and to examine them in their relationship with the things they ordain.[37] Men are governed by different types of law: by natural law, common to each individual; by divine law, which is that of religion; by ecclesiastical law, which is that of the administration of the religion; by civil law, which is that of the members of the same society; by political law, which is that of the government

34. *Laws,* bks. 24–25.

35. Pierre Bayle, a Huguenot refugee to Holland whose *Historical and Critical Dictionary* (1697) had a far-reaching skeptical influence on the *Encyclopédie* itself.

36. The remonstrance appears at the beginning of *Laws,* 25.13.

37. See *Laws,* bk. 26, for this theme.

of that society; by the law of nations, which is that of societies' relations with each other. These laws each have their distinctive objects, which must not be confused. One must never regulate by one type of law what belongs to another, so as to avoid sowing disorder and injustice in the principles that govern men. The principles that prescribe the type of law, and that circumscribe its purpose, must also prevail in the manner of drafting them.[38] As far as possible, the spirit of moderation must dictate all its clauses and provisions. Well-made laws will be in conformity with the spirit of the legislator, even when appearing to be opposed to it.[39] Such was the famous law of Solon, by which all those who took no part in an act of sedition were declared infamous. It either prevented seditions or made them useful by forcing all members of the republic to attend to its true interests. Ostracism itself was a very good law. For on the one hand, it treated the affected citizen honorably, and on the other, it made provision against the effects of ambition. Moreover, a great many votes were necessary, and banishment was only possible every five years. Often, laws that seem the same have neither the same motive nor the same effect nor the same level of equity: the form of government, the specific conjunctures, the character of the people change everything. Finally, the style of the laws should be simple and serious. They can dispense with motivating, because the motive is assumed to exist in the mind of the legislator. But when they do motivate, it should be on evident principles; they should not resemble that law which, prohibiting the blind from pleading, adduces as a reason that they cannot see the ornaments of the magistracy.[40]

To show by examples the application of his principles, M. de Montesquieu chose two different peoples, the most celebrated on earth and the one whose history interests us the most: the Romans and the French.[41] He devotes himself to only a part of the jurisprudence of the former, that which concerns inheritance. As for the French, he goes into the greatest detail on the origin and revolutions of their civil laws, and on the different customs, abolished or still extant, that have resulted from them. He mainly covers

38. This is the topic of *Laws,* bk. 29.
39. For this section, see *Laws,* 29.3.
40. *Laws,* 29.16.
41. The reference is probably to *Laws,* bks. 27–28, 30–31.

the feudal laws—that type of government which was unknown to all of antiquity, which will perhaps be unknown forever to future ages, and which did so much good and so much harm. He especially discusses these laws in their relationship to the establishment and the revolutions of the French monarchy. He proves, against Abbé Du Bos,[42] that the Franks truly entered as conquerors into Gaul, and that it is not true, as that author claims, that they had been called by the people to succeed to the rights of the Roman emperors who were oppressing them. He does so in detail that is profound, exact, and remarkable, though it is impossible for us to follow it here, and in any case, its principal points will be found scattered throughout different parts of this dictionary, in related articles.

Such is a general analysis—though very imperfect and ill-formed—of the work of M. de Montesquieu; we have separated it from the rest of his eulogy in order not to interrupt the order of our account too much.

[D'Alembert completes his obituary, emphasizing the criticisms of *The Spirit of the Laws* and Montesquieu's response; along the way, he cites a brief notice that occurred in the English newspaper the *Evening Post,* which it seemed appropriate to include here as it appears in d'Alembert's text, in English. It is at 5:xvi.]

> On the 10th of this month, died at Paris, universally and sincerely regretted, Charles Secondat, Baron of Montesquieu, and President a mortier of the Parliament of Bourdeaux. His virtues did honour to human nature, his writings justice. A friend to mankind, he asserted their undoubted and inalienable rights with freedom, even in his own country, whose prejudices in matters of religion and government [it must be remembered that it is an Englishman who is speaking][43] he had long lamented, and endeavoured (not without some success) to remove. He well knew, and justly admired the happy constitution of this country, where fix'd and known Laws equally restrain monarchy from Tyranny, and liberty from licentiousness. His Works will illustrate his name, and

42. Montesquieu had a long-running dispute with abbé Jean-Baptiste Dubos (1670–1742), like him a member of the Académie Française. Dubos was the author of *Critical history of the establishment of the French monarchy in Gaul* (1742); see esp. *Laws,* 30.23–25.

43. Note by d'Alembert.

survive him, as long as right reason, moral obligation, and the true spirit of laws, shall be understood, respected and maintained.

[D'Alembert finishes the eulogy in the following way.]

Death prevented him from giving us any further benefits. And combining our own regrets with those of all Europe, we might write on his tomb: *Finis vitae ejus nobis luctuosus,* Patriae *tristis, extraneis etiam ignotisque non sine curâ fuit.*[44]

44. Tacitus, *Agricola,* 43: "The end of his life brought mourning to us, melancholy to his friends, anxiety even to the bystander and those who knew him not." D'Alembert changed Tacitus's word "friends" to "Country," as the font change in the original indicates.

Child
(*Enfant*)

Contemporary political criticism of the Encyclopédie *included the claim that its authors were undermining paternal authority. See especially Jaucourt's article* GOVERNMENT, *below. The present article was also criticized for its political implications.*[1]

CHILD, *son* or *daughter* (*Natural Law, Morality*): Relation of a son or daughter to his or her father and mother. Roman Law extends the word "child" to grandchildren as well, be they of male or female descent.

Children, because of their close relationship to those who beget, feed, and educate them, have certain indispensable obligations toward their father and mother, such as deference, obedience, honor, and respect. They should also always be of service and give aid commensurate with their situation and gratitude.

Due to the state of weakness and ignorance into which children are born, they find themselves naturally subject to their father and mother, to whom nature gives all the necessary power to govern those for whom they must procure every advantage.

The article "Child" is a lightly adapted version of the translation by Emily-Jane Cohen from the University of Michigan's website *Encyclopedia of Diderot and d'Alembert: Collaborative Translation Project*, http://quod.lib.umich.edu/d/did. It is reprinted by permission of the translator. The headnote is by the present editor.

This article can be found at 5:652–54 in the original edition of the *Encyclopédie*.

1. See John Lough, *Essays on the "Encyclopédie" of Diderot and d'Alembert* (London: Oxford University Press, 1968), 282.—HC

As a result, *children*, for their part, must honor their mother and father in word and in deed. They owe them obedience, not a limitless obedience but one as extensive as this relationship demands and one as great as possible, given the dependency either party may have on mutual superiors. Children must feel affection, esteem, and respect for their father and mother and must testify to these sentiments in all their conduct. They must render their parents all services of which they are capable, advise them in business matters, console them in their misfortunes, patiently tolerate their bad moods and their defects. There is neither age, nor rank, nor position that can exempt a child from these sorts of duties. Finally, a child must aid, assist, and feed his mother and father, should the latter become needy or indigent. Solon was praised for having taxed with infamy all those who fail in this last duty, though it be infrequent in comparison with the need of fathers and mothers to nourish and raise their *children*.

However, to better understand the nature and the appropriate limits of the duties we have just discussed, we must carefully distinguish the three estates [*états*] of *children*, in accordance with the three phases of their lives.

In the first, their judgment is imperfect, and they lack discernment, as Aristotle says.

At the second, when their judgment is mature, they are still members of the paternal family; or, put another way and according to the same philosophy, they are not yet on their own.

The third and last occurs when they have left the family through marriage at an appropriate age.

All the actions of children of the first estate are subject to direction by their father and mother, for it is right that those not capable of managing themselves be governed by others, and only those who gave birth to a child are naturally responsible for governing him.

In the second phase, that is to say when children have attained the age where their judgment is fully developed, only matters important to the welfare of the paternal or maternal family depend on the will of the father and mother, and for the following reason: it is right that the interest of one party conform to the interests of all. With regard to all other actions, children have the moral power to do what they deem appropriate. Nevertheless, they should always strive to conduct themselves in a manner agreeable to their parents.

Still, since this obligation is not founded on a right that the parents can exert to its full effect, but rather on what is demanded by natural affection, respect, and gratitude toward those who bestow life and education, then if a child fails in these duties, what he does against his parents' wishes is no more null and void than a donation by a legitimate property owner made in violation of the rules of frugality becomes invalid solely for that reason.

In the third and last phase, the child is absolute master of himself in all respects, but he does not cease, for the rest of his life, to be obliged to have sentiments of affection, honor, and respect, whose foundations subsist forever. It follows from this principle that the acts of a king cannot be annulled simply because his father or mother has not authorized them.

If a child never acquires a sufficient degree of reason to govern himself, as happens with idiots and those born insane, he will always depend on the will of his father and mother. But these examples are rare and outside the ordinary course of nature. The bonds of *children*'s subjection thus resemble their swaddling clothes: they are necessary only because of the frailty of childhood. Age, which brings reason, places them outside paternal power and makes them masters of themselves. They have as much liberty vis-à-vis their father or mother as does a charge who, once his legally determined minority reaches its term, becomes the equal of his guardian.

The liberty of *children* arrived at the age of complete men, and the obedience they owe their father and mother beforehand, are not incompatible. Similarly, according to the most zealous defenders of absolute monarchy, the subjection of a prince during his minority to the queen regent, his wet nurse, his tutors, or his governors is not incompatible with the right to the crown he inherited from his father, or the sovereign authority which will one day be vested in him when age will have made him capable of ruling himself and others.

Although *children*, once they find themselves at an age to know what nature's laws or civil society ask of them, are not obliged to violate these laws to satisfy their parents, a *child* is always obliged to honor his father and mother in recognition of the care they took of him, and nothing will exempt him from this. I say that he is forever obliged to honor his father and his mother, because the mother has as much right as the father, and should the father ever order the contrary, the *child* should not obey him.

At the same time, I add, and most expressly, that the duties of honor, respect, attachment, and gratitude due the father and the mother may be more or less extensive on the part of children and may be proportional to the care parents invested in educating them, and to parental sacrifices. Otherwise, a child does not have much obligation to parents, who, after having brought him into the world, neglected to provide for him according to their situation, to furnish him the means to one day live happily or usefully, while they gave themselves up to their pleasures, tastes, passions, and the dissipation of their fortune, those vain and superfluous expenditures of which we see so many examples in the lands of luxury. "You deserve nothing from our country for having given it a citizen," rightly states a Roman poet, "if as a result of your care he is not useful to the republic in times of war and peace and if he is not capable of making the most of our lands."

> Gratum est, quod patriae civem, populoque dedisti;
> Si facis ut patriae sit idoneus, utilis agris
> Utilis & bellorum, & pacis rebus agendis.
> Juvenal, *Sat.*, xiv. 70 & seqq.[2]

It is therefore easy to decide the long-debated question as to whether the perpetual obligation of children toward their father and mother is principally founded on birth or on the benefits of education. In effect, in order to reasonably claim that someone is greatly accountable to us for a good received, we have to have known to whom we were giving, at what cost, and if it had been our intent to render service to the beneficiary rather than to procure something useful or pleasurable for ourselves. We must know if we were compelled to act by reason, by our senses, or to satisfy some desire, and finally, if what we give can be useful to the recipient without our doing him other favors.

Many important questions related to this subject are still bandied about, though the majority can be resolved according to the principles we have established. Nevertheless, here are the main ones:

2. "Thank you for producing a citizen for your fatherland and your people, just so long as you make him an asset to his fatherland, capable of farming, capable of action in war and peace alike." Juvenal, *Satires*, XIV.70–72.—HC

(1) It may be asked whether or not the promises and engagements of a child are valid. I answer that the promises and engagements of a child who finds himself in the first category of childhood we defined are null and void, since all consent supposes (a) the physical power to consent; (b) the moral power to consent, that is, the use of reason; (c) a serious and free use of these two sorts of power. Now *children,* who cannot reason, fulfill neither of these conditions. But when the faculty of judgment is perfectly formed, it is likely that according to natural law, the *child* who freely committed himself to something, say, a loan, without having been surprised or deceived, must pay back this loan without having recourse to the benefits of civil law.

(2) It may be asked if a *child,* having grown up, may not leave his family without his mother and father's acquiescence. I answer that in the *independent state of nature,* the heads of families cannot retain a child against his will when he gives good reasons for wanting to separate from his parents and to live free.

It follows that *children,* once they are mature, can marry without the consent of their father and mother, because the obligation to listen to and to respect the advice of one's superiors does not detract from the right to dispose of one's property and oneself. I know that the right of fathers and mothers is legitimately founded on their power, their love, and their reason. All this is true insofar as the *child* is in a state of ignorance and drunk with passion, but when *children* have attained the age of their reason's maturity, they can dispose of themselves when taking a step where liberty is absolutely essential—that is to say, marriage. One cannot love through the heart of another. In a word, paternal power consists of raising and governing one's children for as long as they are not in a state to govern themselves, but, according to natural right, it does not extend any further. See FATHER, MOTHER, PATERNAL POWER.

(3) It is asked if *children,* even those who are still in their mother's belly, can acquire and maintain a right of property for goods transferred to them. Civilized nations have established that this be the case. Moreover, reason and natural equity authorize such a practice.

(4) Finally, it may be asked if *children* may be punished for a crime committed by their father or their mother. But that is a shameful question.

Nobody can be reasonably punished for a crime committed by another when he himself is innocent. All merits and demerits are personal and depend on the individual's will, which is the most personal and inalienable of life's possessions. Human laws that condemn children for the crimes of their fathers are therefore as unjust as they are barbarous. "It is despotic furor," aptly says the author of *The Spirit of the Laws,* "that demands that the disgrace of the father lead to that of the children and women: they are unfortunate enough without being criminals. Moreover, it is necessary that the prince allow supplicants to mediate between the accused and himself so that they may move him to clemency or enlighten his justice."[3] *Article by Chevalier* DE JAUCOURT

3. A close paraphrase of Montesquieu, *The Spirit of the Laws,* 12.30.—HC

Savings
(*Epargne*)

SAVINGS (*Morality*), signifies sometimes *the treasury of the prince, savings treasurer, savings revenue.*

Savings in this sense is hardly in use any more; today, one instead says *royal treasury.*

Savings, the law of savings, expression used by some modern scientists to express the decree by which God regulates, in the simplest and most constant manner, all the movements, all the alterations, and the other natural changes. *See* ACTION, COSMOLOGY, *&c.*

Savings, in the most common sense, is a function of economy; properly speaking, it is the care and skill necessary to avoid superfluous expenses, and to incur those expenses that are indispensable at little cost. The observations one is going to read here could have gone *with the word* ECONOMY, which has a broader sense, and which embraces all legitimate means, all the efforts necessary to preserve and increase any possession, and especially to dispense it appropriately. It is in this sense that one says *family economy, bees' economy, national economy*. Notwithstanding, the terms *savings* and *economy* express virtually the same idea, and they will be employed indiscriminately in this essay, according as how they appear more convenient for exactness of expression.

Economic *savings* have always been regarded as a virtue, both under paganism and by Christians; there have even been heroes who have practiced it with perseverance. Nonetheless, we must admit that this virtue is too modest, or if you will, too obscure to be essential to heroism; few heroes

This article can be found at 5:745–50 in the original edition of the *Encyclopédie*.

Res Domestica (Frugality)
A woman with compasses (for measuring resources) in her right hand and a wand and ship's rudder (for household leadership) in her left (alongside beehive). In the background, a rich dissolute household is depicted on the left, a modest and frugal household on the right.

are capable of reaching that far. Economy accords much better with politics; it is its basis, its support, and one may say in a word that it is inseparable from it. Indeed, the government ministry is properly the concern of public economy; thus, M. de Sully, that great minister, that such wise and zealous steward, entitled his memoirs, *Royal Economies, &c.*[1]

Economic *savings* therefore join forces perfectly with piety; they are its faithful companion. It is there that a Christian soul finds resources assured for so many good works prescribed by charity.

In any case, there is perhaps no people today less fond of, nor less acquainted with, *savings* than the French. As a result, there is scarcely a people more agitated or more exposed to the sorrows and miseries of life. Despite this, the indifference, or rather the contempt, we have for this virtue is inspired in us from childhood by a bad education, and especially by the bad examples that we constantly see. We are forever hearing praise for sumptuous meals and feasts, magnificence in clothes, apartments, furniture, *&c.* All of this is represented not only as the purpose and reward of work and talent, but especially as the fruit of taste and genius, as the mark of a noble soul and an elevated mind.

Furthermore, whoever has a certain air of elegance and tidiness in everything around him, whoever knows how to do the honors in his house and at his table, will surely pass for a man of merit and a sophisticate, even if he lacks the essentials in everything else.

In the midst of these praises poured out to luxury and expense, how to plead the case for *savings?* Nowadays we don't take care in studied speeches, education, or sermons to recommend work, *savings,* or frugality as useful and worthy qualities. It is unheard of to exhort young people to renounce wine, rich food, finery, to know how to do without vain superfluities, to adapt early on to simple necessities. Such exhortations would seem base and offensive. They are nonetheless quite consistent with the maxims of wisdom, and would perhaps be more efficacious than any other morality in making men orderly and virtuous. Unfortunately, they are not fashionable among us; we are becoming daily more alienated from them.

1. The Protestant Maximilien de Béthune, Duke of Sully (1560–1641), became a symbol of prudent stewardship for his work as minister under King Henry IV, as recounted in his 1638 *Mémoires.*

Everywhere the reverse is insinuated: flabbiness and the comforts of life. I remember that in my youth, young people who were too preoccupied with their finery were observed with a sort of contempt: today, those who have a simple and unaffected air would be regarded with contempt. Education ought to teach us to become useful, sober, disinterested, beneficent citizens: how it estranges us from that great goal today! It teaches us to multiply our needs, and it thereby makes us more grasping, more burdensome to ourselves, harsher and more useless to others.

If a young man has more talent than fortune, one will at most say to him in a vague manner that he should think seriously about his advancement, that he should be faithful in his duties, avoid bad company, debauchery, *&c.* But no one will say to him what in fact needs to be said and repeated constantly: that to ensure the necessities of life and advance by legitimate means, to become an honorable man and a virtuous citizen, useful to himself and his Country, he must be hardy and patient, he must work without respite, avoid expense, contemn both pain and pleasure, and finally, rise above the prejudices that encourage luxury, dissipation, and flabbiness.

The efficacy of these means is well-enough known: nonetheless, since a certain idea of baseness is wrongly attached to everything that smacks of *saving* and economy, one would not dare give such advice, which would seem like preaching avarice—on which point, I would observe in passing that of all the vices combated by morality, none is less clearly defined than that one.

Misers are often depicted to us as people without honor and without humanity, people who live only to enrich themselves, and who sacrifice everything to the passion for accumulation; indeed, as unfeeling people who, in the midst of abundance, push far away from them all the sweet pleasures of life, and who deny themselves even the strict necessities. But few people would recognize themselves in this frightful painting, and if all these circumstances were necessary to constitute the miserly man, there would hardly be any on earth. To truly merit this odious characterization, it is enough to have a violent desire for wealth and few scruples about the means of acquiring it. Avarice is not essentially connected to stinginess; perhaps it is not even incompatible with splendor and prodigality.

Nonetheless, by a lack of justice that is only too ordinary, the sober, attentive, and hardworking man who, by his work and *savings,* lifts himself imperceptibly above his fellows is commonly labeled a *miser;* but would to heaven that we had more misers of that kind. Society would find itself much better off that way, and we would not suffer as many injustices on men's part. In general these men—repressed, if you will, but more economizers than misers—are almost always good company; sometimes, they even become compassionate. And if they are not found to be generous, they are at least found to be quite fair-minded. Finally, one almost never loses anything with them, whereas one loses more often than not with the spendthrifts. These economizers, in a word, function within the framework of honest *saving,* on which we wrongly lavish the word *avarice.*

The ancient Romans, more enlightened than us on this matter, were quite far from acting this way. Far from regarding *parsimony* as base or vicious conduct—an error that is too common among the French—they identified it, on the contrary, with the most complete probity. They considered these virtuous habits so inseparable that the well-known expression *vir frugi* signified at the same time *the sober and economizing man, the honest man, the good man.*

The Holy Spirit presents us with the same idea; in countless passages he sings the praises of economy, and everywhere he distinguishes it from avarice. He marks the difference in a quite concrete manner when he says, on the one hand, that there is nothing more wicked than avarice and nothing more criminal than the love of money (*Ecclesiast. x.9.10.*),[2] and on the other when he exhorts us to work, to *savings,* to sobriety, as the sole means of enrichment; when he shows us ease and wealth as desirable goods, as the happy fruits of a sober and industrious life.

Go, he says to the lazy man, go to the ant, and look at how she collects in the summer enough to live on during the other seasons. *Prov. vi.6.*

Whoever, says he again, is slothful and negligent in his work is hardly better than the spendthrift. *Prov. xviii.9.*

He likewise assures us that the lazy man who does not want to plow during the cold will be reduced to begging in the summer. *Prov. xx.4.*

2. See, perhaps, Ecclesiastes 5:10.

He tells us in another place: however little you may give way to the sweet pleasures of rest, indolence, and laziness, poverty will come and establish itself in your midst and will make itself strongest there. But, he continues, if you are active and industrious, your harvest will be like an abundant spring, and dearth will fly far away from you. *Prov. vi.10.11.*

He recalls the same lesson a second time by saying that he who plows his field will be satisfied, but that he who loves idleness will be overtaken by indigence. *Prov. xxviii.19.*

He warns us at the same time that the worker subject to drunkenness will never become rich. *Ecclesiastes, xix.1.*[3]

That whoever loves wine and rich food will not only not become wealthy, but will even fall into poverty. *Prov. xxi.17.*

He prohibits us from looking at wine when it is shining in a glass, for fear that that liquor may make impressions on us that are agreeable but dangerous, and that in the end, like the snake and the basilisk, it will kill us with its poison. *Prov. xxiii.31.32.*

Cut back, he says elsewhere, cut back on the wine to those who are charged with public office, for fear that, inebriated on that treacherous beverage, they may come to forget justice, and may alter the rights of the poor. *Prov. xxxi.4.5.*

Be content, he says again, with goat's milk for your food, and let it furnish the other needs of your house, *&c. Prov. xxvii.27.*

What instruction and encouragement to *savings* and frugal work do we not find in his eulogy to the strong woman! He depicts her as a careful and economizing mother and family woman, who brings sweetness to the life of her husband and spares him countless anxieties; who launches important enterprises and sets herself to work on them; who gets up before sunrise to distribute the work and food to her domestics; who augments her domain by new acquisitions; who plants vines; who makes fabric to furnish her house and for outside trade; who has no other finery but a simple and natural beauty; who nonetheless will on occasion put on the richest clothes; who offers only words of mildness and wisdom; who, finally, is compassionate and kindly toward the less fortunate. *Prov. xxxi.10.11.12.13.14.15. &c.*

3. See, perhaps, Ecclesiastes 10:17–18.

To these precepts, to these examples of economy so well traced in the books of wisdom, let us add a word from St. Paul, and let us confirm the whole by an act of *saving* that J. C. has left us. Writing to Timothy, the apostle wants bishops to be capable, among other qualities, of raising their children and ordering their domestic affairs—in a word, of being good stewards. Indeed, he says, if they cannot run their house, how can they run the affairs of the church? *Si quis autem domui suae praeesse nescit, quomodò ecclesiae Dei diligentiam habebit?* First epistle to Timothy, *chap. iii.4–5.*

The Savior himself also gives us an excellent lesson in economy when, after multiplying five loaves and two fishes to the point of satisfying a crowd of people following him, he then has the remaining pieces—which fill twelve baskets—collected, so that, as he says, nothing will be lost: *colligite quae superaverunt fragmenta ne pereant.* John *vi.12.*[4]

Despite these authorities, so respectable and so sacred, the taste for vain pleasures and foolish expenses is the dominant passion with us—or rather, it is a type of mania which possesses great and small, rich and poor, and for which we often sacrifice a goodly part of our necessities.

Nonetheless, only someone with no experience of the world would seriously propose the total abolition of luxury and superfluities; that is not my intention. The common run of men are too weak, too much the slaves of custom and opinion, to resist the torrent of bad example. But if it is impossible to convert the multitude, it is perhaps not difficult to persuade the people in office—enlightened and judicious people to whom one can exhibit the abuse of a thousand essentially useless expenses, whose suppression would in no way impede the public's liberty; expenses, moreover, that have no properly virtuous end and that could be employed with more wisdom and utility: fireworks and other firecrackers, public balls and banquets, ambassadors' ceremonial entrances, *&c.* What mummery, what child's play, what millions are lavished in Europe to pay tribute to custom! Whereas there are real and pressing needs which cannot be satisfied because we are not faithful to the national "economy."[5]

4. "Gather up the fragments left over, that nothing may be lost."

5. This term has been placed in quotation marks to indicate that the author seems to be metaphorically applying the household term to the nation, rather than using the term in the modern sense.

But what am I saying? We began to sense the futility of these expenses and our ministry already recognized it when, after heaven gratified our wishes with the birth of the Duke of Burgundy[6]—that young prince so dear to France and to all of Europe—we preferred, in expressing the common joy at this happy event, we preferred, I say, to light up on all sides the flame of Hymen and show the people his laughter and his games for encouraging population through new marriages, than to follow custom by engaging in ill-advised extravagances or lighting up useless and expensive fireworks that shine for a moment and then go out.

This quite reasonable conduct returns perfectly in the thought of a wise Swede who, when he was giving a sum of money two years ago to begin an establishment useful to his Country, expressed himself in this way in a letter he wrote on the subject:

> May heaven grant that the fashion be established among us, that for any event that causes public rejoicing, our joy may break out only in acts useful to society! Soon we would see numerous honorable monuments to our reason, which would much better perpetuate the memory of deeds worthy of passing into posterity, and would be much more glorious for humanity, than all those tumultuous trappings of festivals, banquets, balls, and other diversions commonly used on such occasions. (*Gazette de France, 8 December 1753. Sweden.*)

The same proposal is well confirmed by the example of an emperor of China who lived in the last century, and who, during one of the great events of his reign, forbade his subjects to engage in the ordinary rejoicings consecrated by custom, whether to spare them the useless and misplaced costs, or to engage them more plausibly in effecting some durable good—more glorious for himself, more advantageous to his whole people than the frivolous and passing amusements of which no visible utility remains.

Here is another striking example I should not forget:

6. Louis, Dauphin of France and Duke of Burgundy (1682–1712), briefly in line to succeed Louis XIV as king of France before his death from measles at the age of 29. A circle of reform-minded advisers, including his erstwhile tutor Fénelon, planned to turn France under him into a limited and decentralized monarchy.

> "The ministry of England," says a gazette . . . from the year 1754, "had a thousand guineas counted out for M. Wal, ex-ambassador of Spain in London, which is, it is said, the normal present that the state gives to foreign ministers on leaving Great Britain."

Who doesn't see that a thousand guineas or a thousand louis make for a more useful and reasonable present than would a jewel, designed solely for the adornment of an office?

After these great examples of political *savings,* would anyone dare blame that Dutch ambassador who, receiving upon his departure from a foreign court a portrait of the prince bedecked with diamonds, but finding this magnificent present quite meaningless, frankly asked what it might be worth? When he was assured that the whole thing cost forty thousand gold crowns, he said: "couldn't I have been given a bill of exchange for a similar sum to draw on an Amsterdam banker?" This Dutch naïvete makes us laugh at first, but in examining it closely, sensible people will manifestly consider that he was right, and that a good bill for forty thousand crowns is much more serviceable than a portrait.

In following the same taste for *saving,* how many cutbacks, how many useful and practicable establishments of so many different kinds! What *savings* are possible in the dispensing of justice, in administration and in finance, since it would be easy, by simplifying the collection of taxes and other matters, to employ many fewer people in all those things than at present! This item is important enough to merit specific treatises; we have many on this subject that one may very fruitfully read.

What *savings* are possible in the discipline of our troops, and what advantages could be drawn from it for king and state, if we devoted ourselves as the ancients did to occupying them usefully! I will talk about it on some other occasion.

What *savings* are possible in the administration of the arts and commerce, by lifting the obstacles found at every turn to the transport and sale of merchandise and commodities—but especially by restoring little by little the general liberty of the crafts and trades, such as it existed in the past in France, and such as it still exists today in many neighboring states; for that reason abolishing the onerous formalities of masterships, initiations, notarized letters of apprenticeship, and other such practices that stop the activity of workers, often alienating them completely from useful occupations and then consigning them to miserable extremities; practices, finally, that the spirit of monopoly introduced into Europe and that are only maintained in these enlightened times by the inattentiveness of legislators. All of us have only too much aversion to arduous work; we must not increase its difficulty, nor generate occasions or pretexts for our laziness.[7]

Moreover, independent of the masterships, there are countless abusive and ruinous customs among the workers that ought to be abolished pitilessly: such, for example, as all rights of *compagnonnage*,[8] all feasts of the workers' community, all assembly fees, cameos, wax candles, feasts, and drinking parties—perpetual occasions of idleness, excess, and waste, which inevitably redound against the public, and which do not accord with national economy.

What *savings* would be possible, finally, in the exercise of religion, by abolishing three-quarters of our feast days, as has been done in Italy, in Austria, in the Low Countries, and elsewhere. France would gain millions every year; besides which, many expenses incurred these days in our churches would be saved. On this score, may the reader pardon a citizen animated by love of the public good for the following details.

What relief and what *savings* for the public if the distribution of consecrated bread were cut back![9] It is one of the most useless expenses, a nonetheless substantial expense that makes plenty of people complain aloud. It is said that certain parish officers make petty exactions from them—doubtless unknown by the police—and that since there is no settled law on it, they fleece the citizens with impunity according to how easy it is to do so. Be that as it may, it is demonstrated by an exact calculation that consecrated bread costs many millions per year in France. And yet there is no need for

7. See Faiguet de Villeneuve's article MASTERSHIPS in this volume.

8. The *compagnon* was a worker who belonged to a sort of association of similar workers; the term refers to the period when the worker continues to work for his master after completing his apprenticeship. The institution, and many of the customs cited by Faiguet de Villeneuve in this paragraph, were in fact abolished by the French Revolution, especially the Le Chapelier Law of 1791.

9. This proposal was attacked for being too Protestant. See John Lough, *Essays on the "Encyclopédie,"* 317–18.

it, indeed there are regions in the realm where it is not given out at all. In a word, it carries no more benediction than the water employed in blessing it, and consequently, one could stick to the water that costs nothing, and abolish the expense of the consecrated bread as being onerous to plenty of people.

After pointing to the abolition of consecrated bread, I don't think I need to spare most of the collection plates in use among us, especially for the location of seats. All trafficking is prohibited in the temple of the Lord; he himself proscribed it loudly, and I see nothing in the Gospel on which he spoke out more forcefully. *Domus mea domus orationis est, vos autem fecistis illam speluncam latronum*. Luke, *xix.46.*[10] It seems to me that this is a lesson both for pastors and for magistrates.

Nothing more indecent than selling places in church. Our ecclesiastical gentlemen take great care to place themselves comfortably and properly, seated and kneeling; it is fitting for all the faithful to do likewise—conveniently, and without ever paying up for it. For this, there should be benches suited to the purpose, benches that would fill the nave and the sides and that would leave only simple passageways. I have seen something approaching this in a province of the realm, but much better in England and Holland, where one is seated in the church without cost, and without being interrupted by beggars, collectors, or seat renters. Here, the Protestants give us a fine example to follow, if we were reasonable enough and disinterested enough for that.

It will doubtless be asked: how to provide for ordinary expenses, given this cutback in receipts? Here is the sure and easy means: cut out a good part of these expenses completely, and moderate where possible those believed to be indispensable. What is the necessity for so many cantors and other officers in the parishes? What good are so many lanterns, so many ornaments, so many bells, *&c.?* If one were a bit more reasonable, would there have to be so much display, so many lamps, so much ringing to bury the dead? One could say the same about countless other onerous superfluities, which bespeak more love of loot (in some) and love of ostentation (in others) than zeal for religion and true piety.

10. "'My house shall be a house of prayer'; but you have made it a den of robbers."

What's more, it is not always possible for simple individuals to remedy such abuses. Each person knows the tyranny of custom, each person even groans under it as an individual; nonetheless, everyone bears the yoke. The man-child fears censure and the "what will they say?" and no one dares resist the torrent. Thus, it is up to government to determine once and for all, depending on differences in social condition, all funerary expenses, marriage and baptism expenses, *&c.* I think we could reduce them to about a third of what they cost today, to the great benefit of the public, in such a way that it would be a firm rule for all families, and it would be absolutely forbidden to individuals and priests to make or bear any expense beyond that.

Some modern political men have wisely observed that the excessive number of clergy is manifestly contrary to national opulence, which is mainly true of the regular clergy of both sexes. In fact, except for those who have a useful and recognized ministry, all the others live at the expense of the true workers, without producing anything profitable to society; they do not even contribute to their own subsistence, *fruges consumere nati;* Hor. *bks. I. ep. ii.v.29.*[11] And though born for the most part into the most modest circumstances, and subject by their condition to the rigors of penitence, they find means of eluding the ancient law of work, and of leading a sweet and tranquil life without being obliged to wipe away the sweat from their faces.

To arrest such a big political problem, only the number of subjects necessary for the service of the church ought to be admitted to orders. As for the cloistered who have a public ministry, one can only praise their zeal in fulfilling their arduous functions, and one should regard them as precious subjects for the state. As for those who have no important occupations, it would seem appropriate to reduce their number in the future, and to look for ways of making them more useful.

There you have many means of *saving* that political men have already lighted upon. But here is another one of which they have not yet scratched the surface, though it is among the most interesting: I am talking about gambling casinos,[12] which are manifestly contrary to the national good.

11. "Born to consume earth's fruits." See Horace, *Satires, Epistles, and Ars Poetica*, Ep. I.ii.27.

12. *Académies de jeu,* where from the seventeenth century, gamblers went to participate in one of numerous kinds of games.

But I am talking especially about the taverns which have so multiplied and are so harmful among us that they are the most common cause of the poverty and disorder of the people.

The taverns,[13] properly understood, are a constant occasion for excess and waste, and it would be very useful, from a religious and a political perspective, to abolish the greater portion of them as they come to be vacant. It would be no less important to forbid all settled and recognized persons in each parish to frequent them during work days; to close them with strict precision at nine o'clock in the evening in every season, and finally, to subject all violators to a stiff fine, half of which would go to the informers and half to the inspectors.

It will be said that these regulations, although useful and reasonable, would diminish the yield on the excise taxes. But firstly, the realm is not made for excise taxes, excise taxes are made for the realm; they are properly speaking a resource for meeting its needs. If, however, by whatever cause it may be, they become harmful to the state, there is no doubt they must be rectified or other less ruinous measures sought—somewhat as we change or discontinue a remedy when it becomes harmful to the sick person.

Moreover, the proposed regulations should not alarm royal budget officials for the very good reason that what is not consumed in the taverns will be consumed even more—and more universally—in private homes, though ordinarily without excess and without waste of time; whereas the taverns, always open, disrupt our workers so much that one cannot usually count on them or see the end of a work once begun. We complain constantly about the harshness of the weather; why don't we rather complain about our imprudence, which leads us to make and to tolerate countless expenses and waste?

Another proposal that belongs to public *saving* would be to found state pawnshops in all our big cities, where people could procure money on collateral and without interest, or perhaps one could get two percent per year to provide for administrative costs. The lender-usurers are known to be very harmful to the public, and thus quite a few losses would be avoided if

13. *Cabarets;* at this time, French taverns were more likely to feature violence, prostitution, and other disorders than their English counterparts.

one could bypass their services. It would thus be very desirable for pious souls and kindly hearts to think seriously about effecting the auspicious foundations of which we speak.

Aside from the general convenience of free and easy loans for the people, I regard it as one of the advantages of these establishments that they would be so many known offices where one could with confidence deposit sums that one is not always in a position to place usefully, and that one sometimes finds awkward. How many misers are there who, fearing for the future, don't dare part with their money, and who, despite their precautions, always have to fear theft, fire, pillage, *&c.?* How many workers, how many domestics and other isolated people are there who, having saved a small sum—ten pistoles (a hundred crowns, more or less)—do not in fact know what to do, and are with reason apprehensive about dissipating or losing it? I thus find it advantageous in all these cases to be able to deposit any sum whatsoever with certainty, and to be free to withdraw it at will. Countless sums, small and large, that today remain inactive would thereby be made to circulate throughout the public. On the other hand, the individual depositors would avoid many anxieties and swindles; moreover, they would be less liable to lend their money unsuitably or spend it foolishly. Thus, each person would recover his funds or his savings if his business was in order, and most workers and domestics would become more orderly and economizing.

This habit of economy in the smallest matters is more important to the general good than people think, and on this count we are far behind neighboring nations, which are almost all more accustomed than we are to *saving* and to the economizing mentality. Here we see an item that is distinctive of the English and that deserves to be reported. We are assured that in most of their big houses, there is what they call *a saving-man*[14]—that is, a careful and thrifty domestic who is on constant alert that nothing is out of place, nothing gets lost or wasted. His sole job is to wander around at all hours through the nooks and crannies of a big house, from the cellar to the attic, in the courtyards, stables, gardens, and other appendages, to put back in its place everything he finds displaced, and to bring into its pantry everything he encounters that is scattered and abandoned—all sorts of used metal,

14. The term is in English in Faiguet de Villeneuve's text.

the ends of boards and other wood, rope, leather, candles, all sorts of rags, furniture, utensils, tools, *&c.*

Aside from countless small things—each of little value, though together amounting to something and being saved from loss by this economizing—he just as often saves things of value, which the masters, domestics, or workers leave out of place by forgetfulness or by whatever other reason it may be. His vigilance stirs the attentiveness of the others, and his position makes him the antagonist of mischief and the repairer of negligence.

I already indicated above that it is a question here of public *savings,* and that I would be touching hardly at all on the conduct of private individuals. Many people, however, have only countered me with the supposed disadvantages of totally abolishing our luxury, a charge which does not attack my thesis and which therefore goes awry. Nonetheless I will attempt to respond to the objection as if I found that it had some solid basis.

If, it is said, so many projects of reform and perfection were followed, such that on the one hand, useless expenses were abolished, and on the other, people dedicated themselves on all sides to fruitful enterprises—in a word, such that economy became fashionable among the French—one would indeed soon see our opulence noticeably increase. But what would be done with so much accumulated wealth? Moreover, most subjects, less employed in the arts of splendor, would scarcely have a share in such opulence and would no doubt languish in the midst of the general abundance.

It is easy to respond to this difficulty. If economic *savings* took root among us and we gave more attention to the necessities and less to superfluities, I agree that there would indeed be fewer frivolous and misplaced expenses, but there would also be many more reasonable and virtuous ones. The rich and the great, being less indebted, would be more likely to pay off their creditors. Moreover, being more powerful and more flush with cash, they would find it easier to marry off their children. Instead of placing one in marriage, they would place two, and instead of two, they would place four, so that fewer reversals of fortune and extinctions of family lines would be seen. We would pay less attention to splendor, caprice, and vanity, but more to justice, beneficence, and true glory. In a word, many fewer subjects would be employed in sterile arts, arts of amusement and frivolity, but many more in worthwhile and necessary arts. At that point, if there were fewer artisans of luxury and pleasure, fewer useless domestics at loose ends, there would in recompense be more cultivators and other precious instruments of true wealth.

It has been demonstrated, to whoever reflects on it, that subjects' differences in occupation produce national opulence or scarcity—in a word, what is good or bad for society. It is perfectly well known that if someone can keep a man on a wage basis, it will be more advantageous to him to have a good gardener than to maintain an ornamental domestic. Some jobs, then, are infinitely more useful than others. And if most men were employed more intelligently and usefully, the nation would be more powerful, and individuals more comfortable.

Moreover, since the habitual practice of *savings* would produce, at least among the rich, a superabundance of goods that are almost never seen here, a noticeable relief for the people would ensue, in that the lower classes would then feel less anxiety and would be less crushed by the great. Let the wolf cease to be hungry and he will no longer ravage the sheepfolds.

Be that as it may, the proposals and actions articulated above would seem more attractive to us if bad habit, ignorance, and flabbiness had not made us indifferent to the advantages of *savings*, and especially if such a precious habit had not been confused, more often than not, with avarice—an error we find exemplified in the mostly unfavorable judgment in our own time toward a virtuous and disinterested citizen, the late M. Godinot, canon of Rheims.

A passionate lover of agriculture, he dedicated all the leisure left over from his official duties to the study of natural science and rural pastimes. He was especially fond of perfecting the cultivation of vines, and even more the making of wines, and he soon found the art of making them so superior and so perfect that he later furnished them to all the potentates of Europe.[15] That gave him the means to accumulate, in the course of a long life, prodigious sums of money. This Christian philosopher meditated for a long time over the noblest and worthiest use of his beneficence.

Moreover, he lived in the greatest simplicity, in the faithful and constant practice of visible *savings*, which even seemed excessive. Thus, common

15. Jean Godinot (1661–1749), doctor of theology and canon of the Rheims cathedral, author of *Manière de cultiver la vigne et de faire le vin en Champagne* [The way to cultivate vineyards and make wine in Champagne] (Langres: Guéniot, 1990 [1722]).

minds, who judge only by appearances, and who did not understand his grand designs, regarded him for many years with merely a sort of contempt. And they continued on in the same vein until, educated and completely won over by the useful establishments and constructions by which he decorated the city of Rheims, and especially by the immense projects he undertook at his own expense to bring abundant and salubrious water there which had been lacking before, they—along with the rest of France—finally lavished him with the praise and admiration they could no longer refuse to his generous patriotism.[16]

Such a splendid model will doubtless touch the hearts of Frenchmen, encouraged as well by the example of many societies established in England, Scotland, and Ireland—societies concerned solely with economizing views, which annually make substantial gifts out of their own funds to husbandmen and artisans[17] who distinguish themselves by the superiority of their works and their discoveries. The same taste has spread to Italy. Last year, we learned about the new establishment of an academy of agriculture in Florence.

But it is mainly in Sweden that the economizing science seems to have fastened the seat of its empire. In other countries it is cultivated only by some amateurs, or by weak companies still little known and of little repute. In Sweden, it has a royal academy devoted solely to it, made up and maintained, moreover, by all the most learned and distinguished elements of the state—an academy that sets aside everything that is merely erudition, amusement, and curiosity, and that allows only research and observations tending toward palpable, physical utility.[18]

It is by this abundant source that our economizing journal is most often enriched—a new production whose purpose makes it worthy of the ministry's full attention, and whose utility would make it win out over all those academy compendia of ours if the government put in charge men perfectly familiar with the economizing sciences and arts; and if these precious men, animated and guided by an enlightened superior, were never at the mercy

16. In 1945, the new cancer facility built in Rheims was christened the Centre Jean-Godinot.

17. *Artistes;* an excellent artisan or one skilled at combining the mind and the hand (Féraud).

18. Perhaps a reference to the Royal Swedish Academy of Sciences, founded by the naturalist Carl Linnaeus (1707–78), the merchant and industrial innovator Jonas Alströmer (1685–1761), and the mechanical engineer Marten Triewald and others in 1739.

of the enterprisers and thus never deprived of the just honoraria so much owing to their work.

It would in fact be entirely consistent with justice and public economy not to abandon the majority of subjects to the rapacity of those who employ them and whose main goal, or rather only goal, is to profit from the labor of another without regard to the workers' good. On this, I observe that in this conflict of interests, the government ought to abrogate every concession[19] of exclusive rights, to close its ears to every representation which, dressed up as the public good, is in essence suggested by the spirit of monopoly, and that it ought to effect without manipulation what is equitable in itself and favorable to the openness and liberty of the arts and of commerce.

Be that as it may, we can congratulate France for the fact that in the midst of so many academy members devoted to the craze for sophistication but mostly untouched by useful research, she counts some superior talents, men accomplished in every kind of science, who have continued to combine beauty of style and even the graces of eloquence with the most solid studies. These men, having dedicated themselves for quite a few years now to economizing works and experiments, have enriched us, as is well known, with the most important discoveries.

Finally, it appears that since the peace of 1748,[20] the taste for *public economy* is imperceptibly winning over all of Europe. More enlightened than in the past, princes today are much less ambitious about aggrandizing themselves through war. Both history and experience have taught them that it is an uncertain and destructive path. The improvement of their states shows them another way, shorter and more assured. Thus, they are virtually competing with each other for improvements and seem more disposed than ever to profit from the many works published in our time on commerce, shipping, and finance, on the exploitation of the land, on the establishment and progress of the most useful arts. These are favorable inclinations, which would contribute to make the subjects more frugal, healthier, happier, and I even think more virtuous.

19. *Concession*, has the specific sense of a royal grant.

20. The Peace of Aix-la-Chapelle ended the War of the Austrian Succession begun in 1740. This article was published in 1755, a year before the outbreak of the Seven Years' War.

Indeed, true economy, which is equally unknown to the miser and the spendthrift, holds a golden mean between the opposing extremes. It is to the lack of that much reviled virtue that one must attribute most of the evils that cover the face of the earth. The only-too-frequent taste for amusements, superfluities, and delights brings about flabbiness, idleness, expense, and often scarcity, but always at least a thirst for riches, which become all the more necessary as one becomes subject to more needs. These then produce ruses and detours, rapacity, violence, and so many other excesses that arise from the same source.

Thus, I am loudly preaching public and private *savings*, but it is a wise and disinterested *savings*, one that brings courage against pain, firmness against pleasure, and that is in the end the best resource of beneficence and generosity. It is that honest parsimony that was so dear in the past to Pliny the Younger, and that enabled him, as he said himself, to make large public and private liberalities out of a modest fortune. *Quidquid mihi pater tuus debuit, acceptum tibi ferri jubeo; nec est quod verearis ne sit mihi ista onerosa donatio. Sunt quidem omnino nobis modicae facultates, dignitas sumptuosa, reditus propter conditionem agellorum nescio minor an incertior; sed quod cessat ex reditu, frugalitate suppletur, ex quâ velut a fonte liberalitas nostra decurrit.* Letters of Pliny, *book II. letter iv.* Countless gestures of beneficence are found in all these letters. *See* especially *bk. III. lett. xi., bk. IV. lett. xiii.,* &c.[21]

Nothing ought to be more strongly recommended to young people than this virtuous habit, which would become for them a protection against all the vices. This is where ancient education was more coherent and more reasonable than our own. They accustomed children early on to household management, as much by their own example as by the nest egg[22] they gave them, which the latter, although young and dependent, turned to good

21. "I entirely acquit you of the debt which your father owed me. Do not scruple to receive this present at my hands, upon the supposition that I can ill spare so large a sum. It is true, my fortune is but moderate: the expenses which my station in the world requires are considerable; while the yearly income of my estate, from the nature and circumstances of it, is as uncertain as it is small; yet what I want in revenue, I make up by economy, the fountain, so to speak, that supplies my bounty" (Pliny, *Letters,* vol. I, II.iv.).

22. *Peculium,* a term in Roman law, primarily concerning relations between slave and master but also between father and son. For other uses of the term, see Jaucourt's essay Slavery, in this volume.

account. This light administration gave them the beginnings of diligence and solicitude, which became useful for the rest of their lives.

How different from the ancients' is our thinking about these things! Today, one wouldn't dare turn young people toward economy; it would be thought unfeeling to inspire them with a taste and esteem for it: a quite common error in our age, but a pernicious error that does endless harm to our mores. Prizes for eloquence and poetry have been established in countless places; who among us will establish prizes for *saving* and frugality?

What's more, these proposals have no other goal but to enlighten men on their interests, to make them more attentive to necessities, less ardent for superfluities—in a word, to apply their ingenuity to more fruitful purposes, and to employ a greater number of subjects for the moral, physical, and palpable good of society. May heaven grant that such mores take the place of interest, luxury, and pleasure among us; what ease, what happiness and peace would result for all our citizens! *This article is by M.* FAIGUET.

Pin
(*Epingle*)

Pinmaking had an honored place among eighteenth-century commentators. In his Cyclopedia *article for "pin," Chambers had already written that "the number of artificers employed" in their manufacture was "incredible."*[1] *Adam Smith was already using the example of pin manufacturing to illustrate the modern division of labor in the early draft of* The Wealth of Nations *and in his lectures on jurisprudence in the 1760s before he made the example famous in* The Wealth of Nations *itself. It would seem that Smith had Deleyre's* Encyclopédie *article mainly in mind rather than Chambers's earlier entry, since he attributes to pinmaking "about eighteen distinct operations" rather than the twenty-five that appear in the Englishman's work.*[2] *Another difference between Chambers and Deleyre is the Baconian flourish that Diderot appends to the latter's article.* *See the entry on Deleyre in Contributors, above, pp. xxvii–xxviii.*

PIN (*Mechanical art*), a small straight metal tool, pointed at one end, used as a detachable clip on linen and fabrics to fix the different shapes given to them when dressing, working, or packing.

Of all mechanical works, the *pin* is the thinnest, commonest, and cheapest. And yet, it is one of those that demand perhaps the most combinations.[3]

This article can be found at 5:804, 807 in the original edition of the *Encyclopédie*.

1. Ephraim Chambers, *Cyclopaedia*, 2 vols. (London: Knapton, 1728), 2:814.

2. Adam Smith, *Wealth of Nations* (London, 1776), I.i.3.

3. *Combinaison*, which the *Dictionnaire de l'Académie Française* (Paris, 1762) defines as "assembly of many things arranged two by two; and by extension assembly of many things arranged together in a certain order."

Thus it happens that art as well as nature displays its prodigies in small objects, and that industry is as limited in its focus as it is wondrous in its resourcefulness. For a *pin* undergoes eighteen operations before becoming an item of trade.

[Deleyre next describes the eighteen operations in detailed numbered paragraphs. Then, in his remaining six long paragraphs, he distinguishes pin types by length and width and by materials (brass vs. iron), treating the preparation of the raw materials in some detail. We omit these paragraphs and include only Diderot's editorial identification at the end.]

This article is by M. Delaire, who was describing the manufacture of the *pin* in the workers' actual workshops, based on our designs, at the same time that he was publishing in Paris his analysis of Chancellor Bacon's sublime and profound philosophy. Bacon's work, combined with the foregoing description, will prove that a good mind can sometimes enjoy the same success rising to the highest contemplations of philosophy as it does descending to the most minutely detailed mechanics. Moreover, whoever has some acquaintance with the views the English philosopher held as he was composing his works will not be surprised to see his disciple pass without disdain from his research on the general laws of nature to the least important use of nature's productions.

Slavery
(*Esclavage*)

Although organized abolitionist movements, often under religious inspiration, did not begin until the 1770s and 1780s in France and England, authors such as Montesquieu and Voltaire had begun to criticize the institution earlier in the century. And Diderot had had a hand in the wide-ranging attack on the slave trade that Raynal included in his Philosophical and political history of the settlements and trade of the Europeans in the East and West Indies, *which appeared in 1770.*[1] *Here, Jaucourt draws mainly on Montesquieu for his critique. See also* TRAFFIC IN BLACKS, *below.*

SLAVERY (*Natural law, Religion, Morality*). *Slavery* is the establishment of a right founded on force. This right makes a man belong to another man so much that the latter is the absolute master of his life, his goods, and his liberty.

This definition is almost equally suitable for civil *slavery* and political *slavery*. To outline its origin, its nature, and its foundation, I will borrow many things from the author of the *Spirit of the laws*, without stopping to praise the solidity of his principles, because I can add nothing to his glory.[2]

All men are born free. In the beginning, they had but one name, one condition. In the time of Saturn and Rhea, says Plutarch, there were neither

This article can be found at 5:934–39 in the original edition of the *Encyclopédie*.

1. See Henry C. Clark, ed., *Commerce, Culture, and Liberty: Readings on Capitalism Before Adam Smith* (Indianapolis: Liberty Fund, 2003), 610–23.

2. Montesquieu discussed slavery in numerous places in *The Spirit of the Laws*, notably in bks. 15 and 16.

masters nor slaves.[3] Nature had made them all equal. But this natural equality was not preserved for long; men strayed from it little by little, servitude was introduced by degrees, and it seemed to have been founded on free conventions, even though necessity was its source and origin.

When, as an inevitable result of the multiplication of the human race, men began to tire of the simplicity of the early centuries, they sought new means of enhancing the comforts of life and acquiring superfluous goods. It seems clear that rich people engaged the poor to work for them, in exchange for a certain wage. Since this expedient seemed very convenient to both sides, many decided to ensure their status and enter forever on the same footing into someone's family, on condition he furnish them food and all the other necessities of life. Thus, servitude was at first created by free consent, and by a contract to do in order that one give to us: *do ut facias*.[4] This association was conditional, or only for certain things, according to the laws of each country, and the conventions of the interested parties. In a word, such slaves were properly speaking only servants or mercenaries, quite similar to our domestics.

But men did not leave things there; they found so many advantages in making another do what they would have been obliged to do themselves, that to the extent that they wanted to expand, arms in hand, they established the custom of granting life and corporal liberty to prisoners of war, on condition that they forever serve as slaves those into whose hands they had fallen.

Since they preserved some vestige of an enemy's resentment toward the wretches they reduced to *slavery* by right of arms, they ordinarily treated them with much harshness. Cruelty seemed excusable toward people at whose hands they risked experiencing the same fate, so they imagined being able to kill such slaves with impunity by an angry impulse or for the slightest fault.

Once this license had been authorized, they extended it under an even less plausible pretext to those who were born slaves, and even those bought

3. See Plutarch's comparison of Lycurgus, Spartan lawgiver of the seventh century B.C., with Numa Pompilius in the *Parallel Lives;* Montesquieu, *Laws,* 15.7.

4. *Do ut facias,* "I give so that you may do," a form of contract in Roman law, along with *facio ut des,* "I do so that you may give." See Hugo Grotius, *The Rights of War and Peace,* ed. Richard Tuck (Indianapolis: Liberty Fund, 2005), 2:730–31, for a discussion.

or acquired by whatever other means. Thus, servitude came to be naturalized, so to speak, by the fate of war. Those that fortune favored and left in the state in which nature had created them were called *free;* those on the contrary whom weakness and misfortune subjected to the victors were called *slaves*. And the philosophers themselves—judges of the merit of men's actions—regarded the conduct of this victor, who made his victim into a slave instead of wresting his life away, as an act of charity.

The law of the strongest, the right of war harmful to nature, ambition, the thirst for conquest, the love of domination and of indolence—these introduced *slavery*, which, to the shame of humanity, has been accepted by virtually all the world's peoples. In fact, we cannot cast our eyes over sacred history without discovering the horrors of servitude. Profane history—the history of the Greeks, the Romans, and all other peoples that pass for the most civilized—are so many monuments to that ancient injustice engaged in with more or less violence over the whole face of the earth, varying with the times, places, and nations.

There are two types of *slavery* or servitude, real and personal. Real servitude is that which attaches the slave to the land; personal servitude concerns the care of the house and is more related to the person of the master. The extreme abuse in *slavery* is when it is found to be simultaneously personal and real. Such was the servitude of foreigners among the Jews, who engaged in the harshest treatment of them. In vain did Moses cry out to them, "You have no rigorous dominion over your slaves; you will not oppress them." He could never manage through his exhortations to soften the harshness of his ferocious nation; thus, he tried to bring some remedy through his laws.

He began by fixing a term to *slavery,* and by ordaining that it would last at most until the jubilee year for foreigners, and for the space of six years for the Hebrews. *Levit. ch. xxv. V.39.*

One of the main reasons for his institution of the Sabbath was to procure some respite for servants and slaves. *Exodus, ch. xx. and xxiii.*[5] *Deuteronomy, ch. xvi.*

He also established that no one would be able to sell his liberty unless he was reduced to having absolutely nothing more to live on. He prescribed

5. Exodus 20:10 and 23:12.

that when slaves were redeemed, their service would be taken into account, in the same way the income already derived from a sold property entered in compensation into the price of the resale when the ex-owner recovered it. *Deuteron. ch. xv., Levitic. ch. xxv.*

If a master had gouged out an eye or broken a tooth of one of his slaves (and *a fortiori,* no doubt, if he had done something worse), the slave was to have his liberty, in compensation for this loss.

Another one of that legislator's laws provides that, if a master strikes his slave and the slave dies as a result of the blow, the master must be punished as being guilty of homicide. It is true that the law adds that if the slave lives for a day or two, the master is exempt from the punishment. The reason for this law was perhaps that when the slave did not die on the spot, it was presumed that the master did not intend to kill him. And at that point, it was thought that he was punished enough by losing what the slave had cost him, or the service he would have gotten from him. At least this is what we are given to understand by the words that follow the text, *for this slave is his money.*

In any case, it was quite a strange people, following M. de Montesquieu's remark, whose civil law ceased to adhere to natural law.[6] This is not how St. Paul thought of the matter when, in preaching the light of the Gospel, he offered this precept from nature and from religion, which ought to be deeply engraved on the hearts of all men: *Masters* (Ep. to the Coloss. iv.1), *treat your slaves justly and fairly, knowing that you also have a Master in heaven*—that is, a master who has no regard for this distinction of conditions, forged by pride and injustice.

The Lacedemonians were the first Greeks who introduced the use of slaves, or who began to reduce to servitude the Greeks they had taken as prisoners of war. They went even further (and I greatly regret being unable to draw the curtain over this part of their history): they treated their Helots in the most barbarous fashion. These people, inhabitants of the territory of Sparta who had been defeated in their revolt by the aristocratic Spartans,[7] were condemned to perpetual *slavery,* and masters were prohibited from emancipating them or selling them outside the country. Thus, the Helots

6. Montesquieu, *Laws,* 15.17.

7. The term is *spartiates,* who are distinguished from the *plebs,* or commoners, who were Lacedemonians.

saw themselves subject to all the work outside the house, and to all sorts of insults inside the house. Their excessive misery reached the point where they were the slaves not only of a citizen, but also of the public. Many peoples have only a real *slavery,* because their women and children do the domestic work. Others have a personal *slavery,* because luxury demands service from the slaves within the house. But here, real *slavery* and personal *slavery* were combined in the same persons.

It was not the same with the other Greek peoples. There, *slavery* was vastly milder, and even slaves who were too roughly treated by their masters could ask to be sold to another. This is what Plutarch teaches us, *de superstitione, p. 66. v. I ed. of Wechel.*[8]

According to Xenophon, the Athenians in particular acted with great mildness toward their slaves. They punished severely, sometimes even with death, whoever had beaten another's slave. With reason, Athenian law did not want to add the loss of security to the loss of liberty. Thus, we don't see the slaves disturbing that republic in the way they convulsed Lacedemon.

It is easy to understand that in a moderate government, the humanity shown toward slaves can alone prevent the dangers that could be feared from there being too many of them. Men grow accustomed to servitude, provided their master is not harsher than the servitude itself.[9] Nothing is better suited to confirm this truth than the slaves' status among the Romans in the republic's heyday, and this status deserves to attract our attention for a few moments.

The early Romans treated their slaves with more decency than any other people have done. Masters regarded them as their companions; they lived, worked, and ate with them. The greatest punishment they inflicted on a slave who had committed some offense was to attach a pitchfork on his back or his chest, stretch his arms over both ends of it, and lead him around that way in public places. It was an ignominious punishment and nothing more. Mores sufficed to maintain the slaves' fidelity.

Far from preventing by coercive laws the multiplication of these living, animated organs of household economy, they encouraged it with all their

8. Plutarch, "Superstition," in *Moralia* 166d.

9. For this and the next paragraph, see Montesquieu, *Laws,* 15.16.

might, joining their slaves together by a kind of marriage, *contuberniis*. In this manner they filled their houses with domestics of both sexes, and went far toward populating the state. The slaves' children, who over time made the wealth of a master, were born in an atmosphere of trust around him. He alone was charged with their upkeep and their education. The fathers, free of this burden, followed the penchant of nature and multiplied without fear of a large family. Without jealousy, they looked upon a happy society of which they regarded themselves as members. They felt that their soul could rise up like that of their master, and they did not feel the difference between the condition of a slave and of a free man. Often, indeed, generous masters arranged instruction in exercises,[10] music, and Greek letters. Terence and Phaedrus are quite good examples of this kind of education.[11]

The republic made use of this people of slaves, or rather of subjects, to its great benefit. Each of them had his *peculium*—that is, his little treasure, his little purse, which he possessed on conditions his master imposed on him.[12] With this nest egg, he worked wherever his talent carried him. This one did banking, that one went in for sea trade; one sold retail merchandise, another applied himself to some mechanical art, or else leased or exploited lands. But there was no one who did not dedicate himself to profiting from this nest egg, which simultaneously procured him comfort in his present servitude and the hope of future liberty. All these measures spread abundance and animated the arts and industry.

Once they were enriched, these slaves had themselves enfranchised and became citizens. The republic constantly replenished itself, receiving new families in its midst as the old ones were destroyed. Such were the best days of *slavery*, as long as the Romans preserved their mores and their integrity.

But when they had aggrandized themselves by their conquests and their plunder, when their slaves were no longer the companions of their labor but were employed to become the instruments of their luxury and their

10. The French term *exercices* can cover a range of activities from horsemanship to dancing associated with the life of a gentleman.

11. Terence, the Roman comic playwright, who died young in 159 B.C., and Gaius Iulius Phaedrus (ca. 15 B.C.–ca. A.D. 50), the fabulist from Thrace.

12. For another discussion of the *peculium*, see the article SAVINGS, above.

pride, the slaves' condition totally changed its face.[13] They came to be regarded as the basest part of the nation, and consequently no one had any scruples about treating them inhumanely. By reason of the fact that mores were gone, men had recourse to the law. And indeed, some terrible ones were needed to establish the security of these cruel masters, who lived amidst their slaves as if amidst their enemies.

Under Augustus—that is, at the beginning of the tyranny—the senatus-consultum Silanianum was passed,[14] along with many other laws that ordained that when a master was killed, all the slaves who were under the same roof or within earshot would be condemned to death. In this case, those who gave refuge to a slave in order to save him were punished as murderers. Even the slave whose master had ordered him to kill him and who had obeyed would be guilty. The one who had not prevented the master from killing himself would be punished. If a master was killed on a trip, those who remained with him and those who fled were both put to death. Let us add that during his life, this master could kill his slaves with impunity and subject them to torture. It is true that afterward, there were emperors who diminished this authority. Claudius decreed that sick slaves abandoned by their masters would be free if they returned to health. In rare cases, this law assured their liberty; it should also have secured their life, as M. de Montesquieu has very well said.[15]

Moreover, all these cruel laws we have just been talking about were applicable even to those whose innocence was proven.[16] These laws arose not from the civil government, but from a defect in the civil government. They were not derived from the equity of the civil laws, since they were contrary to the principle of the civil laws. Properly speaking, they were founded on the principle of war, except that the enemies were within the bosom of the state. The senatus-consultum Silanianum is said to derive from the law of nations, which states that a society, even an imperfect one, must preserve itself. But an enlightened legislator avoids the frightful misfortune of becoming a terrifying legislator. In the end, the barbarism toward slaves was

13. For this and the next paragraph, see Montesquieu, *Laws,* 15.16.
14. C. Junius Silanus and P. Cornelius Dolabella, ca. A.D. 10; see also Montesquieu's note.
15. See Montesquieu, *Laws,* 15.17, for a slightly different version.
16. For most of this paragraph, see Montesquieu, *Laws,* 15.16.

pushed so far that it produced the slave wars which Florus compared to the Punic wars, and which, by their violence, shook the Roman Empire to its foundations.[17]

I like to imagine that there are still happy climes on earth whose inhabitants are gentle, tender, and compassionate—such as the Indians of the peninsula on this side of the Ganges. They treat their slaves as they treat themselves. They take care of their children, marry them off, and easily grant them their liberty. In general, the slaves that belong to simple and hardworking people of open and sincere mores are happier than anywhere else. They suffer only real *slavery,* which is less hard for them and more useful for their masters. This was the case with the slaves of the ancient Germans. Tacitus says these peoples did not keep them in the house to make each one work at a certain task, as we do. Instead, they assigned each slave his private manor in which he lived as a head of household. The only servitude the master imposed on him was to oblige him to pay an annual land rent in cereal, livestock, hides, or fabrics. In this way, adds the historian, you could not distinguish the master from the slave by their earthly delights.

When they had conquered the Gauls under the name of *Franks,* they sent their slaves to cultivate the lands that fell to them by lot. They were called *people under power, gentes potestatis* in Latin, attached to the glebe, *addicti glebae.*[18] And it is from these serfs that France has been populated ever since. Their multiplication created almost as many villages out of the farms they cultivated (and these lands retained the name *villae*) as the Romans had given them. Hence have arisen the words *village* and *villein,* in Latin *villa & villani,* to mean *country folk of low extraction.* Thus, two kinds of slaves were seen in France, those of the Franks and those of the Gauls, and they all went to war, whatever M. de Boulainvilliers might say about it.[19]

17. Florus, *Epitome rerum Romanorum,* 2.7.2, is cited at Montesquieu, *Laws,* 15.16.

18. Henry, Count of Boulainvilliers, *Histoire de l'ancien gouvernement de la France* [History of the former government of France], 3 vols. (The Hague, 1727), 3:34.

19. Boulainvilliers was noted for his theory that only the Franks were warlike and thus the legitimate rulers of the French nation, in the form of an aristocratic caste. See Montesquieu, *Laws,* 30.10, for an influential critique of his theory.

These slaves belonged to their patrons, of whom they were reputed to be *men of the body*, as they used to say back then. With time, they became subject to harsh corvée labor and were so attached to their masters' land that they seemed like part of it, so that they could not set up elsewhere or even get married on another lord's land without paying what was called the *fors-mariage* or *mé-mariage* fee.[20] Even the children brought forth by the union of two slaves who belonged to different masters were distributed; or else one of the patrons, to avoid this distribution, gave another slave in exchange.

A military government, in which authority was parceled out among many lords, was bound to degenerate into tyranny—and this did not fail to happen. Ecclesiastical and lay patrons everywhere abused their power over their slaves. They overwhelmed them with so many labors, annual payments, corvées, and so many other kinds of mistreatment that in 1108, the miserable serfs, no longer able to bear the harshness of the yoke, brought on that famous revolt described by historians, which eventually ended up procuring their enfranchisement. For up to that time, our kings had tried without any success to soften the condition of *slavery* by their edicts.

Nonetheless, as Christianity began to gain ground, more humane sentiments were embraced. Moreover, our sovereigns, determined to humble the lords and rescue the lower orders from the yoke of their power, made the decision to enfranchise the slaves. Louis the Fat[21] was the first to give an example, and in enfranchising the serfs in 1135, he partly succeeded in taking back the authority over his vassals that they had usurped. In 1223, Louis VIII[22] distinguished the beginning of his reign by a similar enfranchisement. Finally, Louis X, called the *Headstrong*,[23] offered an edict on this subject that seems to us worthy of being reported here:

> Louis, by the grace of God, king of France and of Navarre: to our friends and trusty companions . . . since, according to the law of nature, each person must be born free . . . we, considering that our realm is

20. This was a payment due to a lord when a man of servile condition married a free woman or a woman from another domain without the lord's permission.

21. Louis VI (r. 1108–37).

22. Louis VIII (r. 1223–26).

23. Louis X (r. 1314–16).

> named and called *the realm of the Franks,*[24] and wanting the thing in truth to be in accordance with the name . . . by deliberation of our grand council, have ordained and do ordain that everywhere in our realm . . . freedom [*franchise*] be given on good and legally valid conditions . . . and so that all the lords who have men of the body will follow our example in restoring to freedom, *&c.* Given in Paris the third of July, the year of grace 1315.[25]

Still, it was only around the 15th century that *slavery* was abolished in the greater part of Europe. And yet, only too many vestiges of it still exist in Poland, Hungary, Bohemia, and many parts of lower Germany; *see the works of* Messrs. Thomasius and Hertius; there are even some sparks of it in our customaries; *see* Coquille.[26] In any case, almost within the space of the century following the abolition of *slavery* in Europe, the Christian powers, having made conquests in countries where they thought it advantageous to have slaves, permitted the buying and selling of them and forgot the principles of nature and Christianity, which render all men equal.

After surveying the history of *slavery* from its origins to our day, we are going to prove that it wounds the liberty of man, that it is contrary to natural and civil right, that it is offensive to the best forms of government, and finally, that it is useless in itself.

The liberty of man is a principle that was accepted long before the birth of J. C. by all nations that profess generosity. The *natural* liberty of man—this is to recognize no sovereign power on earth and to be subject to no legislative authority whatsoever, but only to follow the laws of nature. Liberty *in society* is to be subject to a legislative power established by the consent of the community, and not to be subject to the whim or to the fickle, uncertain, and arbitrary will of a single man in particular.

24. The tribal name *Francs* [Franks] and the word *franc* [free] were often related in this way by French authors.

25. See François-André Isambert et al., *Recueil général des anciennes lois françaises* [General collection of former French laws], 29 vols. (Paris, 1822–33), 3:102–4 for the text of the ordinance.

26. Christian Thomasius (1655–1724) and Johannes Nicolaus Hertius (ca. 1651–1710), German philosophers broadly in the natural-law tradition of Pufendorf; Guy Coquille (1523–1603), author of *Institution au droit des françois* [Establishment of French law] (1607) and other works.

Such liberty, by which one is not subjected to an absolute power, is so tightly bound up with the preservation of man that it can be separated from it only by whatever simultaneously destroys his preservation and his life. Thus, whoever tries to usurp an absolute power over someone thereby places himself in a state of war with him, so that the latter can regard the conduct of the former only as a manifest attack on his life. In fact, from the moment a man wants to subject me to his domination against my will, I have reason to presume that if I fall into his hands, he will treat me according to his whim and will not scruple to kill me when the fancy strikes him. Liberty is, so to speak, the rampart of my preservation and the foundation of all other things that belong to me. Thus, whoever wants to make me a slave in the state of nature authorizes me to repulse him by any means, in order to secure my person and my property.

Since all men naturally have equal liberty, they cannot be stripped of this liberty without their having occasioned this by some criminal acts. Certainly, if a man in the state of nature has deserved death at the hands of someone whom he has offended, and who has become in this case master of his life, the latter, when he has the guilty party in his hands, can make a deal with him and employ him in his service; in this, he does him no wrong. For ultimately, when the criminal finds that his *slavery* is more burdensome and more troublesome than the loss of his existence, it is within his power to attract the death that he desires by resisting and disobeying his master.

What makes the death of a criminal lawful in civil society is that the law punishing him was made in his favor.[27] A murderer, for example, has benefited from the law that condemns him. It has preserved his life at every moment; therefore, he cannot complain about that law. It would not be the same with the law on *slavery*. The law establishing *slavery* would be against him in every case without ever being for him, which is contrary to the fundamental principle of all societies.

Property rights over men and over things are two quite different rights. Although every lord says of whoever is subject to his domination, *that person belongs to me,* his property over such a man is not the same as the property he can claim when he says, *that thing belongs to me*. Property in a

27. For this paragraph, see Montesquieu, *Laws,* 15.2.

thing brings with it a full right to use it, consume it, and destroy it, whether because it is found profitable or out of pure whimsy, so that however one disposes of it, no wrong is done to it. But the same expression applied to a person signifies only that the lord has a right, exclusive of anyone else, to govern this person and prescribe laws to him, while at the same time he is himself subject to many obligations in relation to that same person, so that in any case his power over that person is very limited.

Whatever great injuries we have received from a man, once we have become reconciled with him, humanity does not permit us to reduce him to a condition in which no trace of the natural equality of all men remains, and thus to treat him like a beast of which we are the master, able to dispose of him at our whim. The peoples who have treated slaves as a good that they could dispose of at will have been nothing but barbarians.

Not only is it the case that one cannot, properly speaking, have a property right in persons. But in addition, it is repugnant to reason for a man who has no power over his own life to be able to give to another, either by his own consent or by any kind of agreement, the right that he does not have himself. Thus, it is not true that a free man can sell himself.[28] A sale presupposes a price. If the slave sold himself, all his goods become the property of the master; thus, the master would give nothing and the slave would receive nothing. He would have a nest egg, someone will say; but the nest egg is attached to the person. The liberty of each person is a part of the public liberty. This status, in the popular state, is even a part of sovereignty. If liberty has a price for the one who buys it, it is priceless for the one who sells it.

Civil law, which has permitted the division of property among men, could not have ranked among that property a portion of the men who are to take part in the division. Civil law, which makes restitution in contracts that contain some sort of damage, cannot keep from making restitution for an agreement that contains the most enormous of all damages. Thus, *slavery* is no less contrary to civil law than to natural law. What civil law could keep a slave from saving himself from servitude, since he is not in society, and thus, no civil law affects him? He can be restrained only by a family law, by the master's law—that is, by the law of the strongest.

28. For the rest of this paragraph and into the next, see Montesquieu, *Laws,* 15.2.

If *slavery* is offensive to natural and civil law, it is also harmful to the best forms of government. It is contrary to monarchical government, in which it is supremely important neither to beat down nor to debase human nature.[29] In democracy, where everyone is equal, and in aristocracy, where the laws should put their effort into making everyone as equal as the nature of the government can permit, slaves are contrary to the spirit of the constitution; they would serve only to give citizens a power and a luxury they should not have.

Moreover, in every government and in every country, however arduous the work that society requires, one can do anything with free men—by encouraging them with rewards and privileges, by adjusting the work to their strength, or by replacing it with machines invented and applied by art, depending on location and need. *See* the evidence for this in M. de Montesquieu.[30]

Finally, we may again add with that illustrious author that *slavery* is useful to neither master nor slave:[31] not to the slave, because he can do nothing from virtue; not to the master, because he contracts all sorts of vices and bad habits from his slaves that are contrary to the laws of society, because he grows imperceptibly accustomed to neglecting all the moral virtues, because he becomes proud, curt, angry, harsh, voluptuous, and barbarous.

Thus, everything favors leaving man the dignity that is natural to him. Everything cries out to us that we cannot deprive him of that natural dignity which is liberty; the rule of the just is not founded on power but on what conforms to human nature. *Slavery* is a humiliating condition not only for the one who suffers it, but for humanity itself, which is degraded by it.

Since the principles just stated are unassailable, it will not be difficult to demonstrate that *slavery* can never be sugarcoated by any reasonable cause—not by the right of war, as the Roman jurisconsults used to think, nor by the right of acquisition or the right of birth, as some moderns have wanted to persuade us. In a word, nothing in the world can render *slavery* legitimate.[32]

29. See Montesquieu, *Laws,* 15.1, for this paragraph.

30. This seems a more categorical rejection of slavery than is found at Montesquieu, *Laws,* 15.8, where a climatic exception is noted. But see Jaucourt's discussion below.

31. See Montesquieu, *Laws,* 15.1, for this paragraph.

32. For this and most of the next paragraph, see Montesquieu, *Laws,* 15.2.

In past centuries, people said that the right of war authorizes the right of *slavery*. It prescribed that prisoners be slaves, so that they would not be killed. But today, we are disabused of this generosity, which consisted of making your conquered into your slave rather than massacring him. We have come to understand that this supposed charity is nothing but the charity of a brigand, who glories in giving life to those he has not killed. Nowadays, it is only the Tartars who put to the sword their prisoners of war and who think they are doing them a favor when they sell them or distribute them to their soldiers.[33] Among all other peoples who have not shed every generous sentiment, killing in war is only permissible in cases of necessity. But as soon as one man has made another a prisoner, one cannot say that he was under necessity to kill him, since he has not killed him. The only right that war can give over captives is the right to secure them sufficiently so that they are in no position to do harm.

The acquisition of slaves by means of money is even less able to establish a right of *slavery*, because money, and all that it represents, cannot confer a right to deprive someone of his liberty. Moreover, the traffic in slaves, for the purpose of deriving a vile profit as if from brute beasts, is repugnant to our religion, which came for the purpose of erasing all traces of tyranny.

Slavery is certainly not better founded on birth. This supposed right falls with the other two. For if a man could not sell himself or be bought, still less could he sell his unborn child. If a prisoner of war could not be reduced to servitude, still less his children. In vain would one object that if the children are conceived and brought into the world by a slave mother, the master does them no wrong in appropriating them and reducing them to the same condition; that because the mother has nothing of her own, her children can be raised only from the master's goods, which furnish them food and the other necessities of life before they are in a position to serve him. These are but frivolous ideas.

If it is absurd for a man to have a property right over another man, he is *a fortiori* unable to have one over his children. Moreover, nature, which has given milk to mothers, has provided adequately for the children's nourishment, and the remainder of their childhood is so close to the age at which

33. Montesquieu, *Laws,* 18.20.

they have the greatest capacity to make themselves useful that it could not be said that whoever nourishes them in order to be their master is giving them anything. If he has furnished something for the upkeep of the child, the thing is so modest that any man, however mediocre the faculties of his soul and body, can earn enough to pay off that debt within a few years. If *slavery* were founded on nourishment, it would have to be reduced to persons incapable of earning their living. But no one wants those slaves.

There can be no justice in a convention, express or tacit, by which the slave mother subjects the children she has brought into the world to the same condition into which she has fallen, because she cannot stipulate for her children.

To sugarcoat this pretext for child *slavery,* it has been said that they would not be in the world if the master had wanted to use the right given him by war of putting their mother to death. But the assumption is false that all who are taken in war, even the most just war in the world—and especially women, who are at issue here—can be legitimately killed. *Spirit of the laws, bk. XV.*[34]

It was an arrogant presumption on the part of the ancient Greeks to imagine that since the barbarians were slaves by nature (that is how they spoke) and the Greeks free, it was just for the former to obey the latter. That being the case, it would be easy to treat as barbarians all peoples whose mores and customs are different from our own, and (without other pretext) to attack them in order to place them under our laws. It is only the prejudices of pride and ignorance that make us renounce the virtue of humanity.

Thus, it goes directly against nature and the law of nations to believe that the Christian religion gives those who profess it a right to reduce to servitude those who do not profess it, in order to work more easily toward its propagation. It was this way of thinking, however, that encouraged the destroyers of America in their crimes, and this is not the only time that men have used the religion against its own maxims, which teach us that the status of neighbor[35] extends throughout the world.

It is playing with words, or rather engaging in mockery, to write, as one of our modern authors has done, that it is small-minded to imagine that

34. Montesquieu, *Laws,* 15.2.

35. *Prochain,* as in, "love your neighbor as yourself." Lev. 19:18.

having slaves degrades humanity, because the liberty that each European thinks he enjoys is nothing but the power to break his chains in order to give himself a new master—as if the chain of a European was the same as that of a slave from our colonies.[36] It is clear that this author has never been placed in *slavery*.

Still, are there no places or situations in which *slavery* derives from the nature of things? I respond to this question, firstly, that there are none. I next respond, with M. de Montesquieu, that if there are countries in which *slavery* seems based on a natural cause, it is those in which the heat enervates the body and so weakens the sense of spirit that men are led to an arduous duty only by the fear of punishment. In those countries, since the master is as craven toward his prince as his slave is toward himself, *civil slavery* is accompanied by *political slavery*.

Under arbitrary governments, it has been very easy to sell oneself, because *political slavery* in some sense destroys civil liberty.[37] Dampier says that everyone seeks to sell himself in Achim.[38] Some of the leading lords have no fewer than a thousand slaves, who are the leading merchants, who also have many slaves under them, and these latter many others; they are inherited and there is a traffic in them. There, the free men, who are too weak to oppose the government, seek to become the slaves of those who tyrannize the government.

Notice that in despotic states, where men are already under *political slavery, civil slavery* is more bearable than elsewhere.[39] Each person is happy enough to have his sustenance and his life. Thus, the slave's condition is scarcely more burdensome than the subject's condition; these are two conditions that converge. But although *slavery* in these countries is based, so to speak, on a natural cause, it is nonetheless true that *slavery* is contrary to nature.

In all Mohammedan states, servitude is rewarded by the idleness that those slaves are enabled to enjoy who serve in sensual pleasure.[40] It is this

36. The reference may be to Jean-Jacques Rousseau, *Discourse on the Sciences and the Arts* (1750), third paragraph of part 1.

37. For this paragraph, see Montesquieu, *Laws*, 15.6.

38. William Dampier (1652–1715), *Voyages and Descriptions* (1699).

39. For the first part of this paragraph, see Montesquieu, *Laws*, 15.1.

40. For this paragraph, see Montesquieu, *Laws*, 15.12.

idleness that makes the seraglios of the East places of delight even for those against whom they are created. People who fear only work can find their happiness in these tranquil places. But it is clear that in this way, one runs counter even to the purpose for which *slavery* is established. These latter reflections are from *The Spirit of the laws.*

Let us conclude that *slavery*—founded by force, by violence, and in certain climates by an excess of servitude—can perpetuate itself in the world only by the same means. *Article by Chevalier* DE JAUCOURT.

Volume 6
(1756)

State of Nature
(*Etat de Nature*)

STATE OF NATURE (*Natural law*). Generally and properly speaking, this is the state of man at the moment of his birth, but in common usage this word has different acceptations.

This *state* can be envisioned in three ways: in relation to God; in imagining each person as he would be found alone and without the aid of his fellows; and finally, according to the moral relation that exists among all men.

From the first perspective, the *state of nature* is the condition of man considered as God made him, the most excellent of all animals. Whence it follows that he should recognize the Author of his existence, admire his works, offer up a worship worthy of him, and conduct himself as a being endowed with reason, so this *state* is contrary to the life and condition of the animals.

From the second perspective, the *state of nature* is the sad situation to which one imagines man would be reduced if he were abandoned to himself upon entering into the world. In this sense, the *state of nature* is contrary to the life that has been civilized by human industry and service.

From the third perspective, the *state of nature* is the state of men insofar as they have no other moral relations but those founded on the universal ties resulting from the resemblance in their nature, independent of all subjection. At this level, those said to live in the *state of nature* are those who are neither subject to the dominion of each other, nor dependent upon a common master. Thus, the *state of nature* is in that case opposed to the civil *state,* and it is in this latter sense that we are going to consider it in the present article.

This article can be found at 6:17–18 in the original edition of the *Encyclopédie.*

This *state of nature* is a *state* of perfect freedom, a state in which men can do what they please and dispose of themselves and their possessions as they see fit without depending on the will of anyone, provided they stay within the bounds of the natural law.[1]

This *state* is also a *state* of equality, such that all power and all jurisdiction are reciprocal. For it is evident that beings of the same species and the same rank, who share in nature's same advantages and who have the same faculties, ought likewise to be equal among themselves, without any subordination. This *state* of equality is the foundation of the duties of humanity. *See* EQUALITY.

Although the *state of nature* is a *state* of liberty, it is in no way a *state* of license,[2] for a man in this *state* does not have the right to destroy himself, any more than to destroy another. He must make the best use of his liberty that his own preservation demands of him. The *state of nature* has the law of nature as a rule. Reason teaches all men, if they would but consult it, that being all equal and independent, no one must do harm to another concerning his life, his health, his liberty, and his property.

But in order that no one in the *state of nature* undertakes to do harm to his neighbor, each person, being equal, has the power to punish the guilty with penalties that are proportional to their offences and that strive to make amends for the harm and to prevent something similar from happening in the future.[3] If each individual lacked the power to repress the wicked in the *state of nature*, it would follow that the magistrates of a political society would be unable to punish a foreigner, because in relation to such a man, those magistrates can have no more right than each person can have naturally in relation to another. This is why each individual in the *state of nature* has a right to kill a murderer, in order to deter others from homicide. If someone sheds the blood of a man, his blood will also be shed by a man, says the great law of nature. And Cain was so fully convinced of it that he cried out, after killing his brother: *Quiconque me trouvera me tuera.*[4]

1. For this and the next paragraph, see John Locke, *The Second Treatise of Government* (1690; Cambridge: Cambridge University Press, 1960), chap. 2, para. 4.

2. For this paragraph, see Locke, *Second Treatise,* chap. 2, para. 6.

3. See Locke, *Second Treatise,* chap. 2, paras. 8 and 11, for this paragraph.

4. "Whoever finds me will slay me." Gen. 4:14.

For the same reason, a man in the *state of nature* can punish the various infractions of the laws of nature in the same manner they can be punished in any civilized government. Most domestic laws are just only insofar as they are founded on natural laws.

It has often been asked where and when men are or have been in the *state of nature*.[5] I answer that since the princes and magistrates of independent societies that are found throughout the earth are in the *state of nature*, it is clear that the world has never been and will never be without a certain number of men in the *state of nature*. When I speak of princes and magistrates of independent societies, I consider them in themselves abstractly. For what puts an end to the *state of nature* is solely the convention by which men enter voluntarily into the body politic. All other kinds of commitments that men may make together leave them in the *state of nature*. For example, the promises and compacts for truck between two men on a desert island that Garcilaso de la Vega speaks of in his *History of Peru*, or between a Spaniard and an Indian in the American deserts, must be exactly performed, even though these two men are on this occasion in the *state of nature* vis-à-vis each other. Honesty and faith-keeping are things that men must observe religiously as men, not as members of the same society.

Thus, the *state of nature* must not be confused with the *state* of war.[6] These two *states* seem to me as contrary to one another as a *state* of peace, assistance, and mutual preservation is to a *state* of enmity, violence, and mutual destruction.

When men live together in conformity with reason, without any superior on earth who has the authority to judge their differences, they find themselves to be precisely in the *state of nature*. But the violence of one person against another, in a situation in which there is no common superior on earth to whom to appeal, produces the *state* of war. Absent a judge before whom a man can call out an aggressor, there is no doubt that he has the right to wage war on this aggressor, even though both of them are members of the same society and subjects of the same *state*.

5. For this paragraph, see Locke, *Second Treatise*, chap. 2, para. 14.

6. See Locke, *Second Treatise*, chap. 3, para. 19, for these three paragraphs.

Thus, I can kill on the spot a thief who besets me, who seizes the reins of my horse or stops my coach. This is because the law made for my preservation, if it can be interposed to assure my life against a present and sudden attack, gives me the liberty to kill this thief, since there is not enough time to call him before our common judge and have the laws decide a case in which the harm may be irreparable. The lack of a common judge vested with authority puts all men in a *state of nature,* and the unjust and sudden violence that I just spoke of produces the *state* of war, whether or not there is a common judge.

Thus, let us not be surprised if history tells us little about men who have lived together in the *state of nature.*[7] The inconveniences of such a state (which I am about to explain) and the desire and need for society have obliged individuals to join together early on in a civil body that would be fixed and durable. But if we cannot suppose that men have ever been in the *state of nature,* because we lack historical accounts in this regard, we could also doubt whether the soldiers who composed Xerxes' armies had ever been children, since history does not indicate as much, and speaks of them only as grown men bearing arms.

Government always precedes records. Rarely are belles-lettres cultivated among a people before a long continuation of civil society has, by other more necessary arts, provided for its safety, ease, and plenty. Men begin to search the history of the founders of that people and to research its origins when the memory of them has been lost or grown obscure. Societies have this in common with individuals: they are usually quite ignorant in their birth and their infancy. If they know something afterward, it is only by means of monuments that others have preserved. Those monuments that we have of political societies make us see clear examples of the beginnings of some of these societies, or at least they make us see their manifest footsteps.

One can scarcely deny that Rome and Venice, for example, took their beginnings from independent people, among whom there was no superiority, no subjection.[8] The same thing is found already established in the

7. For this paragraph and the next, see Locke, *Second Treatise,* chap. 8, para. 101.
8. For this paragraph, see Locke, *Second Treatise,* chap. 8, para. 102.

greater part of America, in Florida and in Brazil, where there is no question of king or community or government. In a word, it is probable that all political societies have been formed by a voluntary union of persons in the *state of nature*, who have agreed on the form of their government and who have been led to this union by consideration of the things that are wanting in the *state of nature*.

First, there want laws that are established, accepted, and approved by common consent, as the standard of right and wrong, of justice and injustice.[9] For though the laws of nature be plain and intelligible to all rational people, yet men, through interest or ignorance, evade or ignore them without scruple.

In the second place, there wants in the *state of* nature a known and impartial judge who has authority to terminate all differences in conformity with established laws.

In the third place, there often wants in the *state of nature* a coercive power for executing a sentence. Those who have committed some crime in the *state of nature* employ force if they can to bolster the injustice, and their resistance sometimes makes their punishment dangerous.

Thus, weighing the advantages of the *state of nature* with its defects, men soon preferred to join together in society. Hence it comes to pass that we seldom find any number of people living together for long in the *state of nature*. The inconveniences they find there force them to seek in the established laws of a government a sanctuary for the preservation of their properties. And in this we have the source and the limits of legislative power and executive power.

Aside from the freedom to enjoy innocent pleasure, men have in fact two sorts of power in the *state of nature*. The first is to do what they find fitting for their preservation and that of others, following the spirit of the laws[10] of nature. If it were not for human depravity, it would not be necessary to abandon the natural community in order to create smaller ones. The other power that men have in the *state of nature* is to punish the crimes

9. For these next five paragraphs, see Locke, *Second Treatise,* chap. 9, paras. 124–28 and 131; Locke does not use the phrase "justice and injustice."

10. This last phrase is not in Locke; Jaucourt doubtless takes it from Montesquieu's work of the same title.

committed against the laws. In entering a society, these same men merely remit to that society the powers they had in the *state of nature*. Thus, the legislative authority of any government can never extend beyond what the public good demands. Consequently, this authority must be reduced to preserving the properties that each person keeps from the *state of nature*. Thus, whoever has the sovereign power of a community is obliged to follow no other rules in his conduct but the tranquility, security, and property[11] of the people—*quid in toto terrarum orbe validum sit, ut non modò casus rerum, sed ratio étiam, causaeque noscantur*. Tacit. *history. lib. I. Article by Chevalier* DE JAUCOURT.[12]

11. "Bien," so that "good" would be an alternative translation.

12. Tacitus, *Histories,* I.4. Jaucourt's truncated version would read: "the elements of strength . . . in the entire world, that we may understand not only the incidents of events . . . but also their reasons and causes."

Compound States
(*Etats Composés*)

Jaucourt here follows Pufendorf in seeking an alternative to Hobbes's theory of absolute unitary sovereignty.[1]

COMPOUND STATES (*Political law*). Term used for those states formed by the union of several simple *states*. One may define them, with Pufendorf, as an assemblage of *states* tightly bound by some particular tie, so that they seem to be but a single body in relation to the matters that concern them in common, even though each one of them preserves full and complete sovereignty independent of the others.

This assemblage of *states* is formed either by the union of two or several distinct *states* under one and the same king, as for example England, Scotland, and Ireland were before the union of Scotland and England in our time;[2] or else when several independent *states* confederate in order to form

This article can be found at 6:19–20 in the original edition of the *Encyclopédie*.

1. For Pufendorf, see Severinus de Monzambano [Samuel von Pufendorf], *De statu Imperii Germanici* [On the imperial German states] (1667), and Peter Schröder, "The Constitution of the Holy Roman Empire After 1648: Samuel Pufendorf's Assessment in his *Monzambano*," *Historical Journal* 42, no. 4 (1999): 961–83. For the related concept of a federal republic, see the entry FEDERAL REPUBLIC [Republique Fédérative], also by Jaucourt, below. For a more recent examination of the same kind of problem, see Vincent Ostrom, *The Political Theory of a Compound Republic*, 2nd ed. (San Francisco: Institute for Contemporary Studies, 1987).

2. The reference is to the period from the Union of the Crowns in 1603, which placed Scotland and England under the same monarch, until the Acts of Union passed by the Scottish and English Parliaments in 1707, creating a single Kingdom of Great Britain.

but a single body; such are the United Provinces of the Low Countries, and the Swiss Cantons.

The first type of union can be made either on the occasion of a marriage, or in virtue of a succession, or when a people chooses as king a prince who was already sovereign of another realm, so that those different *states* come to be united under a prince who governs each one singly by its fundamental laws.

As for *composite states* that are formed by the permanent confederation of several *states*, it must be remarked that this confederation is the sole means by which several small *states*, too weak for each of them individually to maintain themselves against their enemies, may preserve their liberty.

These confederated *states* make a mutual commitment to exercise certain parts of sovereignty only by common accord, especially those that concern their mutual defense against external enemies. But each of the confederates retains complete liberty to exercise as it sees fit the parts of sovereignty not mentioned in the act of confederation as having to be exercised in common.

It is absolutely necessary in confederated *states:* (1) that specific times and places of ordinary assembly be indicated; (2) that some member be named who would have power to convoke the assembly for extraordinary affairs not admitting of delay. Or, in making a resolution, they might set up an assembly composed of deputies from each *state,* which is always in a condition of readiness and which dispatches the common business according to the orders of their superiors. Such is the assembly of the Estates General at the Hague, and perhaps no other example could be cited.

It is asked whether the decision on common affairs must depend on the unanimous consent of the whole body of confederates, or only on the majority. It seems to me that in general, since the liberty of a *state* is the power to decide in the last resort on the affairs that concern its own preservation, one cannot consider a *state* to be free by the treaty of confederation when it can be constrained by proper authority to do certain things. If, however, in the assemblies of the confederated *states,* there happened to be one state that refused—out of an insane stubbornness—to yield to the deliberation of the others in very important affairs, I believe one could either break the confederation with this *state* that is betraying the common cause, or even use against it all the means permitted in the state of natural liberty against the violators of alliances.

Composite states are dissolved (1) when some of the confederates separate to govern their affairs apart, which ordinarily happens because they think that union is more of a burden than a benefit to them. (2) Internecine wars among the confederates also break their union—unless, with the return of peace, the confederation is renewed at the same time. (3) From the moment one of the confederated *states* is subjugated by a foreign power or becomes the dependent of another *state,* the confederation no longer exists for it—unless, after being constrained to surrender to the victor by force of arms, it later comes to be delivered from this subjection. (4) Finally, a *composite state* becomes a simple *state* if all the confederated peoples submit to the sovereign authority of one person alone, or if one of these *states*, by the superiority that its forces give it, reduces the others to the status of province. *See* on this matter the *Latin essay* by Pufendorf, *de systematibus civitatum, in-4°.*[3] *Read* also *the history of the United Provinces* and that of *the Swiss Cantons;*[4] there, you will find some remarkable things on their respective unions and confederations. *Article by Chevalier* DE JAUCOURT.

3. The reference is to Pufendorf's early essay, "De Systematibus Civitatis," in *Dissertationes academicae selectiores* . . . (1668; Frankfurt and Leipzig, 1678), 264–330; see also Montesquieu, *The Spirit of the Laws,* 9.1.

4. Possibly a reference to *Histoire abregée des provinces-unies des païs bas* [Abridged history of the United Provinces of the Low Countries] (Amsterdam: Malherbe, 1701), and to Charles-Guillaume Loys de Bochat (1695–1754), *Memoires critiques, pour servir d'eclaircissemens sur divers points de l'histoire ancienne de la Suisse* [Critical memoirs, to serve in illuminating various points in the ancient history of Switzerland] (1727–49), which Jaucourt also cites in SUISSE, below.

Volume 7
(1757)

Foundation
(*Fondation*)

This important article by Turgot (1727–81), the future royal administrator and controller-general under Louis XVI, was written in 1756, when he was a Wunderkind and protegé of Vincent de Gournay, intendant of commerce and leading propagandizer for a more open trade policy.[1]

FOUNDATION (*Politics and Natural law*). [The words *found, fundament, foundation,* are applied to every durable and permanent establishment by a quite natural metaphor, since the very word *establishment* is based on precisely the same metaphor. In this sense, one says *the foundation of an empire, a republic.* But in this article, we will not speak of such great objects. What we could say about them concerns the original principles of political law, the first institution of governments among men. *See* GOVERNMENT, CONQUEST & LEGISLATION. One also says *found a sect.* V. SECT. Finally, one says *found an academy, a high school, a poorhouse, a convent, masses, prizes to distribute, public games, &c. To found* in this sense] is to assign a fund or

The present translation is adapted from the abridged version of "Endowments" in *The Life and Writings of Turgot: Comptroller-General of France, 1774–76,* ed. and trans. W. Walker Stephens (London: Longman's, 1895), 219–28. Our principal adaptation consists in changing the term "endowments" to "foundations" in most of the places it appeared. Bracketed material is that part of the text omitted in the Stephens edition and supplied by the present translators in order to complete Turgot's original.

This article can be found at 7:72–75 in the original edition of the *Encyclopédie.*

1. See Henry C. Clark, *Commerce, Culture, and Liberty: Readings on Capitalism Before Adam Smith* (Indianapolis: Liberty Fund, 2003), 448–76, for Turgot's summary of Gournay's career.—HC

a sum of money in order to its being employed in perpetuity for fulfilling the purpose the founder had in view, whether that purpose regards divine worship, or public utility, or the vanity of the founder, often the only real one, even while the two others serve to veil it.

[The formalities necessary to transfer to those charged with fulfilling the intentions of the founder; the property or use of funds the latter has designated; the precautions to take in assuring the perpetual execution of the commitment entered into by these persons; the compensation due those who may have an interest in this transfer or property (as, for example, the suzerain deprived forever of the fees he was collecting on the fund at each change of owner); the limits that policy has wisely meant to place on the excessive multiplication of these imprudent liberalities—in short, different circumstances, essential or subordinate to the *foundations,* have given rise to different laws, whose detail does not belong to this article, and for which we would refer the reader to the *articles* FOUNDATION (*Jurisp.*), MORTMAIN, AMORTIZATION, *&c.* In this one, our goal is only to examine] the utility of *foundations* in general, in respect to the public good, and chiefly to demonstrating their impropriety. May the following considerations concur with the philosophic spirit of the age, in discouraging new foundations and in destroying all remains of superstitious respect for the old ones!

(1) A founder is a man who desires the effect of his own will to endure forever. Now, even if we suppose him to be actuated by the purest motives, how many reasons there are to question his enlightenment! How easy it is to do harm in wishing to do good! To foresee with certainty that an establishment will produce only the effect desired from it, and no effect at variance with its object; to discern, beyond the illusion of a near and apparent good, the real evils which a long series of unseen causes may bring about; to know what are the real sores of society, to arrive at their causes, to distinguish remedies from palliatives; to defend oneself against the prestige of a seductive project, to take a severe and tranquil view of it amidst that dazzling atmosphere in which the praises of a blind public, and our own enthusiasm, show it [to be] surrounded; this would need the effort of the most profound genius, and perhaps the political sciences of our time are not yet sufficiently advanced to enable the best genius here to succeed.

By these institutions support is often given to a few individuals against an evil the cause of which is general, and sometimes the very remedy opposed to the effect increases the influence of the cause. We have a striking example of this kind of abuse in the establishment of houses designed as asylums for repentant women. In order to obtain entrance, proof of a debauched life must be made. I know well that this precaution has been made in order to prevent the *foundation* being diverted to other objects; but that only proves that it is not by such establishments, powerless against the true causes of libertinage, that it can be combated. What I have said of libertinage is true of poverty. The poor have incontestable claims on the abundance of the rich; humanity and religion alike make it a duty on us to relieve our fellow-creatures when under misfortune. It is in order to accomplish these indispensable duties that so many charitable establishments have been raised in the Christian world to relieve necessities of every kind, that so many poor are gathered together in hospitals[2] and are fed at the gates of convents by daily distributions. What is the result? It is that precisely in those countries where gratuitous resources are most abundant, as in Spain and some parts of Italy, there misery is more common and more widely spread than elsewhere. The reason is very simple, and a thousand travelers have observed it. To enable a large number of men to live gratuitously is to subsidize idleness and all the disorders which are its consequences; it is to render the condition of the ne'er-do-well preferable to that of the honest workingman. Consequently it diminishes for the State the sum of labor and of the productions of the earth, a large part of which is thus left necessarily uncultivated. Hence frequent scarcities, the increase of misery, and depopulation. The race of industrious citizens is displaced by a vile populace, composed of vagrant beggars given up to all sorts of crime. [To see the abusive character of these ill-directed alms, imagine a state so well administered that no poor people are found there (doubtless a possibility for any state that has colonies to populate; see MENDICITY). The establishment of free assistance for a certain number of men would immediately create poor people there—that is, it would give a certain number of men an interest in becoming poor by abandoning their occupations. From this would result

2. See the article POORHOUSE for the contemporary meaning of this term.—HC

a loss] of the labor and wealth of the State [and] a great increase of public burdens, thrown on the shoulders of the industrious man, and an increase of all the disorders we see in the present constitution of society. It is thus that the purest virtues can deceive those who surrender themselves without precaution to all suggestions that they inspire. But if these pious and respectable designs contradict in practice the hopes that were conceived for them, what must we think of those endowments (undoubtedly numerous) whose only motive and object is the satisfaction of a frivolous vanity? I do not fear to say that were we to weigh the advantages and the disadvantages of all the *foundations* in Europe, perhaps there would not be found one which would stand the test of an enlightened scrutiny.

(2) But of whatever utility a *foundation* might be at its conception, it bears within itself an irremediable defect which belongs to its very nature—the impossibility of maintaining its fulfillment. Founders deceive themselves vastly if they imagine that their zeal can be communicated from age to age to persons employed to perpetuate its effects. There is no body that has not in the long run lost the spirit of its first origin [even if it had that spirit for a certain time]. There is no sentiment that does not become weakened, by mere habit and by familiarity with the objects which excite it. What confused emotions of horror, of sadness, of deep feeling for humanity, of pity for the unfortunates who are suffering, does that man experience who for the first time enters the ward of a hospital! Well, let him open his eyes and look around. In this very place, in the midst of these assembled human miseries, the ministers provided to relieve them walk about with an air careless and expressionless; they mechanically and without interest distribute from invalid to invalid the food and the remedies prescribed, and sometimes do so even with a brutal callousness; they give way to heedless conversation, and sometimes to ideas of the silliest and the grossest; vanity, envy, hatred, all the passions reigning there, as elsewhere, do their work, and the groans from the sickbed, the cries of acute pain, do not disturb the *habitués* any more than the murmur of a rivulet interrupts an animated conversation. [It is hard to imagine, but we have seen the same bed be simultaneously a death bed and a bed for debauchery. *See* POORHOUSE.] Such are the effects of habit in relation to objects the most capable of moving the human heart. Thus it is that no enthusiasm can be constantly sustained. And how without

enthusiasm can ministers of a *foundation* fulfill its purpose always and with precision? What interest, in their case, can counteract idleness, that weight attached to human nature which tends constantly to retain us in inaction? The very precautions which the founder has taken in order to ensure for them a constant revenue dispenses them from meriting it by exertion. Are there superintendents, inspectors, appointed to see the work of the foundation carried out? It will be the same with these inspectors [as with anyone set up to maintain any rule whatsoever]. If the obstacle to the right working comes from idleness, the same idleness on their part will prevent them from exposing it; if the abuse proceeds from pecuniary interest, they will too readily share in it. [*See* INSPECTEURS.] Supervisors themselves would need to be supervised, [and where would this ridiculous progression stop? It is true that canons have been obliged to be assiduous about offices, reducing virtually their entire revenue to manual distributions. But this measure can only oblige one to a purely corporal assistance, and what use can that be for all the *foundations'* other and much more important goals?] Thus almost all old foundations have degenerated from their primitive institution. Then the same spirit which had devised the first has created new ones on the same plan, or a different plan, which, after having degenerated in their turn, are displaced in the same manner. Measures are ordinarily so well taken by the founders to protect their establishments from exterior innovations, that generally it is found to be easier to found new establishments than to reform the old; but, through these double and triple renovations, the number of useless mouths in society and the sum of wealth kept from general circulation are continually increased.

[Certain *foundations* cease to be fulfilled by a still different reason, and through the mere lapse of time: these are the *foundations* based on money and on annuities. It is well-known that every kind of annuity has lost virtually all of its value in the long run, because of two causes. The first is the gradual and progressive increase in the face value of the silver mark, which means that whoever originally received one pound—worth twelve ounces of silver—today receives only one of our pounds, which is not worth one seventy-third of those twelve ounces. The second cause is the increase in the quantity of silver, which means that today, one can procure with three ounces only what could be had for one ounce before America was discovered.

There would not be a big disadvantage in this if those *foundations* were entirely destroyed. But the body of the *foundation* endures nonetheless; it is only the conditions that are no longer fulfilled. For example, if the revenues of a hospital suffer this decrease, then they get rid of sickbeds, and they content themselves with providing for the upkeep of chaplains.]

(3) I will suppose that a *foundation* has had at its origin an incontestable utility, that sufficient precautions have been taken against its degeneration through idleness and negligence, that the nature of its funds has sheltered it from the revolutions of monetary changes, then I say that the very immutability which the founders have succeeded in giving it is still a substantial disadvantage, because time brings about new revolutions which sweep away the utility it might have had at its origin, and which can even render it harmful. Society has not always the same needs; the nature and dispositions of properties, the divisions between different orders of the people, opinions, manners [*mœurs*], the general occupations of the nation or of its different sections, the climate even, the maladies, and the other accidents of human life—all experience a continual variation. New needs arise, others cease to be felt. The proportion of those remaining declines from day to day, and along with them the utility of the foundations designed to relieve them diminishes or disappears. The wars of Palestine gave rise to innumerable *foundations* whose utility ceased with the wars. Without speaking of the military religious orders, Europe is still covered with leper hospitals (*maladreries*), although for long leprosy has been almost unknown. The greater number of foundations long survive their utility: first, because there are always men who profit by them, and who are interested in maintaining them; secondly, because even when we become convinced of their inutility, we make long delays before deciding either upon the measures or the formalities necessary to overthrow establishments consolidated for many centuries, [which are often connected to other establishments we are afraid to overthrow,] or deciding upon the use or the distribution we should make of their property; [thirdly, because we make long delays in convincing ourselves of their inutility, so that they sometimes have the time to become harmful before we have suspected that they are not useful.

[There is every reason to presume that a *foundation*, however useful it may appear, will one day become at least useless, perhaps harmful, and will be that way for a long time. Isn't this reason enough to stop any founder who proposes any other goal but that of satisfying his vanity?]

(4) I have said nothing of the splendor of the buildings and of the pomp connected with some of the grand foundations. It would be perhaps to value very favorably the utility of these objects if we estimated them at one-hundredth part of the whole cost.

(5) Woe to me if my object be, in presenting these considerations, to concentrate man's motives in his mere self-interest, and to render him insensible to the sufferings or the happiness of his fellow-creatures, to extinguish in him the spirit of a citizen, and to substitute an indolent and base prudence for the noble passion of being useful to mankind. In place of the vanity of founders, I desire that humanity, that the passion of the public good, should procure for men the same benefits, but more surely, more completely, and at less cost, and without the drawbacks of which I have complained.

Among the different needs of society intended to be fulfilled by means of durable establishments or *foundations,* let us distinguish two kinds. One belongs to society as a whole, and is just the result of the interest of each of its members, such as the general needs of humanity, sustenance for everyone, the good manners [*mœurs*] and education of children, for all families. [And this interest is more or less pressing for different needs, for a man feels the need for sustenance more strongly than his interest in giving his children a good education.] It does not require much reflection to be convinced that the first kind of social needs is not of a nature that can be fulfilled by *foundations,* or by any other gratuitous means, and that, in this respect, the general good ought to be the result of the efforts of each individual for his own interests. Every able-bodied man ought to procure his subsistence by his work, because if he were fed without working, it would be so at the cost of those who work. What the State owes to all its members is the destruction of the obstacles which impede them in their industry, or which trouble them in the enjoyment of the product which is its recompense. While these obstacles subsist, particular benefits will not diminish the general poverty, for the cause will remain untouched. For the same reason every family owes education to the children who are born to it; [they all have an immediate interest in it,] and it is only from the efforts of each in particular that the general perfection of education can arise. If you amuse yourself in endowing masters and bursaries in high schools, the utility of which will be felt only by a small number of men, favored by chance, who have not perhaps the necessary talents to profit by them, that will be, for the whole nation, but a drop of water spread on a vast sea, and you will have procured, at very great expense, very small results. And then, do you have to accustom people to be asking for everything, receiving everything, never owing anything to themselves? This sort of mendicancy, spread out over all conditions of men, degrades a people and substitutes for the high impulses a character of lowness and intrigue. Are men powerfully interested in that good which you would procure for them? Leave them free to attain it;[3] this is the great, the only principle. Do they appear to you to be actuated by less ardor toward it than you would desire to see? Increase their interest in it. You wish to perfect education—propose prizes for the emulation of parents and children, but let these prizes be offered to whosoever can *merit* them, offered at least to every order of citizens; let employments and places become the recompense of merit, and the sure prospect of work, and you will see emulation struck up at once in the heart of all families. Your nation will soon be raised above its old level, you will have enlightened its spirit, you will have given it character [*mœurs*], you will have done great things, and you will have done all at less expense than founding one college.

The other class of public needs intended to be provided for by *foundations* comprises those regarded as accidental, which, limited to particular places and particular times, enter less into the system of general administration, and may demand particular relief. It is desired to remedy the hardships of a scarcity, or of an epidemic, to provide for the support of some old men, or of some orphans, for the rescue of infants exposed, for the working or maintaining works to improve the amenity or the salubrity of a town, for the improving of agriculture or some arts in a backward condition in a locality, for rewarding the services rendered by a citizen to the town of which he is a member, to attract to it men celebrated for their talents, etc. Now, it is above all necessary that the means taken by public establishments or *foundations* should be the best in order to procure for their subjects all

3. *Laissez-les faire.*

these benefits as fully as possible. The free employment of a part of the revenues of a community (or the contribution of all its members) in cases where the need is pressing and general; a free association and voluntary subscriptions by several generous citizens, in cases where the need is less urgent and less generally felt—that would be the true means of fulfilling all kinds of schemes really useful, and this method would have the inestimable advantage over *foundations* of being subject to no great abuse. As the contribution of each is entirely voluntary, it is impossible for the funds to be diverted from their destination. If they were, their source would be soon dried up. There would be no money sunk in useless expenses, in luxury, or in construction. It is a partnership of the same kind as those made for business [*commerce*], with the difference that its object is only the public good; and as the funds are employed only under the eyes of the shareholders, these are able to see them employed in the most advantageous manner. Resources would not be permanent for needs that are temporary; succor would be given only to the portion of society that suffered, to the branch of commerce that languished. If the need ceased, the liberality would cease, and its course would be directed to other needs. There would never be useless repetitions of schemes, because the generosity of the public benefactors would be determined only by the actual utility recognized. In fine, this method would withdraw no funds from general circulation, the lands would not be irrevocably possessed by idle hands, and their productions under the hands of an active proprietor would have no limit except that of their fecundity. Is it said that these ideas are chimerical? England, Scotland, Ireland are full of such voluntary associations, and they have experienced from them, for many years, the happiest effects. What has taken place in England can take place in France, and [whatever is said about it,] the English have not the exclusive right to be citizens. We have already in some provinces examples of such associations, which prove their possibility. I would cite in particular the city of Bayeux, whose inhabitants are associated in order to banish begging entirely from their town, and have succeeded in providing work for all able-bodied mendicants, and alms for all those unfit for work. This fine example deserves to be proposed for the emulation of all our towns. Nothing would be so easy, if we really willed it, as to direct to objects of certain and general utility the emulation and the tastes of a nation so sensible to honor as ours is, and so easy to lend itself to all the impressions which the government might know how to give.

(6) These reflections ought to strengthen our approval of the wise restrictions which the king, by his edict of 1749, has made to the liberty of creating new *foundations*.[4] Let us add that they ought to leave no doubt on the incontestable right possessed by the government—in the first place, in the civil order, next, by the government and the church, in the order of religion—to dispose of old *foundations*, to extend their funds to new objects, or, better still, to suppress them altogether. Public utility is the supreme law, and it ought not to be nullified by any superstitious respect for what we call the *intention of the founder*—as if ignorant and short-sighted individuals had the right to chain to their capricious wills the generations that had still to be born. Neither should we be deterred by the fear to infringe upon the pretended rights of certain bodies—as if private bodies had any rights opposed to those of the State. Citizens have rights, and rights sacred for the very body of society. They exist independent of that society. They are its necessary elements. They enter into it with all their rights, solely that they may place themselves under the protection of those same laws to which they sacrifice their liberty. But private bodies do not exist of themselves, nor for themselves; they have been formed by society, and they ought not to exist a moment after they have ceased to be useful.

We conclude. No work of man is made for immortality; and since *foundations,* always multiplied by vanity, would in the long run, if uninterfered with, absorb all funds and all private properties, it would be absolutely necessary at last to destroy them. If all the men who have lived had had a tombstone erected for them, it would have been necessary, in order to find ground to cultivate, to overthrow the sterile monuments and to stir up the ashes of the dead to nourish the living.

4. The so-called Edict of Mortmain, August 1749, severely curtailed the establishment of new foundations; earlier monarchs had also tried to accomplish this. See François-André Isambert et al., *Recueil général des anciennes lois françaises* [General collection of former French laws], 29 vols. (Paris, 1822–33), 22:226–33.—HC

Gallantry
(*Galanterie*)

The author, who is unidentified but who modern scholars suggest may have been Diderot, hints in this article at a political typology of gallant manners, stretching both from primitive to civilized societies across time and from "free peoples" to the government of one across regime types.

GALLANTRY (*Morals*). One may consider this word under two general acceptations: (1) in men, it is a marked attention to telling women, in a refined and delicate manner, things that please them and that give them a good opinion of themselves and of us. This art, which could improve and console them, too often serves only to corrupt them.

It is said that all courtiers are polite; assuming this is true, it is not true that all are gallant.

Worldly practice may produce common politeness, but nature alone produces that seductive and dangerous characteristic that makes a man gallant, or that disposes him to become so.

It has been claimed that *gallantry* is the light, delicate, perpetual lie of love. But perhaps love lasts only because of the assistance lent to it by *gallantry*; is it only because *gallantry* no longer takes place between the spouses that love ceases?

Unhappy love excludes *gallantry;* the ideas *gallantry* inspires require a free spirit, and it is happiness that affords this.

This article can be found at 7:427–28 in the original edition of the *Encyclopédie*.

Truly gallant men have become rare; they seem to have been replaced by a kind of opportunist. Bringing only affectation to bear on what they do (because they have no grace) and jargon to what they say (because they have no wit), they have substituted a vapid boredom for the charms of *gallantry.*

Among savage peoples, who have no ordered government and live almost without clothing, love is only a need. In a state where everyone is a slave, there is no *gallantry,* because men lack liberty and women lack dominion. Among a free people, one will find great virtues but a politeness that is coarse and rough-hewn; a courtier from the court of Augustus would be quite an odd man for one of our modern courts. In a government in which one alone is charged with the affairs of all, the idle citizen, placed in a situation that he cannot change, will at least think of making it bearable. From this common necessity, a more extended social circle will emerge: women will have more liberty there; men will form a habit of pleasing them; and little by little, we see taking shape an art that will be the art of *gallantry*. Then, *gallantry* will spread a general hue over the mores of the nation and its productions in every genre. The latter will lose grandeur and force, but they will gain mildness, sweetness, and a certain original charm that other peoples will try to imitate, but that will give them a gauche and ridiculous air.

There are men whose mores have always been more redolent of particular systems than of the generally prevailing conduct—these men are the philosophers. They have been criticized for not being gallant, and it must be admitted that it was difficult for them to combine *gallantry* with their rigid idea of the truth.

However, the philosopher sometimes has this advantage over the man of the world: if a word escapes him that is truly gallant, the contrast between the word and the person's character makes it come out all the more like flattery.

(2) *Gallantry,* considered as a vice of the heart, is only libertinage on which an honorable name has been bestowed. In general, peoples rarely fail to mask common vices by honorable designations. The words *gallant* and *gallantry* have other acceptations. *See the preceding article.*[1]

1. That is, GALANT, not included in this volume.

Geneva
(*Genève*)

When this article by d'Alembert appeared in 1757, Diderot's friend Friedrich Melchior Grimm inserted the following comment in his Correspondance littéraire, *an account of the latest events in the literary world of Paris, which he regularly sent to various German princes: This article "is causing a great stir: its author very rashly asserts that the theologians of Geneva are Socinians, and even deists; this represents a particularly bad blunder by M. d'Alembert since he surely had no intention of incurring the displeasure of the Republic of Geneva."*[1]

It may seem surprising that such an attack on one of the editors of the Encyclopédie *should come from a close friend of Diderot and appear in a periodical to which Diderot himself frequently contributed. Yet even if this comment was not inspired by Diderot, it certainly expressed his own reactions, for* GENEVA *proved to be the single most controversial article of the* Encyclopédie, *and the storm of controversy it provoked did much to endanger Diderot's cherished enterprise.*

The article owes a great deal to Voltaire. The previous year d'Alembert had visited Voltaire in Geneva, and Voltaire had profited from this opportunity

The headnote, translation, and footnotes for GENEVA are from Nelly S. Hoyt and Thomas Cassirer, *The Encyclopedia: Selections [by] Diderot, d'Alembert and a Society of Men of Letters* (Indianapolis: Bobbs-Merrill, 1965), 122–39; the translation is reproduced on *The Encyclopedia of Diderot & d'Alembert Collaborative Translation Project* (Ann Arbor: Michigan Publishing, University of Michigan Library, 2003): http://hdl.handle.net/2027/spo.did2222.0000.150 (accessed June 3, 2015). The translation is lightly adapted for the present volume.

This article can be found at 7:578–578D in the original edition of the *Encyclopédie.*

1. *Correspondance littéraire,* December 15, 1757 (vol. 3, p. 458, in edition by Maurice Tourneux; Paris, 1878).

to further his own designs in the city in which he had recently taken up residence. It was Voltaire who was convinced that the ministers of Geneva were really no longer Calvinists but enlightened Unitarians and even deists, though perhaps without knowing it themselves. He was anxious to help them shed the vestiges of their Calvinist past and, in particular, their aversion to the theater, which was and had always been his passion. He felt that d'Alembert's article would provide welcome reinforcement for his campaign to turn Geneva into the city of philosophy, and his first reaction on receiving the seventh volume of the Encyclopédie *was enthusiastic: "My dear courageous philosopher," he wrote to d'Alembert, "I have just been reading and rereading your excellent article 'Geneva.' I feel that the Council and the people should be profoundly grateful to you; and you deserve to be thanked even by the ministers."*[2]

As it turned out, the Genevans proved most ungrateful for d'Alembert's somewhat tactless suggestions on how to improve their city, and the ministers in particular were outraged at the suggestion that they no longer upheld the teachings of Calvin. A committee of nine was appointed by the city to draw up a declaration refuting d'Alembert's assertions; it also sent letters of protest to d'Alembert and Diderot, and tried, unsuccessfully, to get d'Alembert to retract his controversial remarks.

The article displeased not only the Genevans, it also aroused the Catholics in France who rightly saw d'Alembert's praise of Genevan institutions as an indirect attack on Catholic orthodoxy. It was d'Alembert's misfortune that GENEVA *appeared at the very time when the* philosophes *were under intense attack as a result of the attempted assassination of Louis XV, and the unhappy editor saw his article used by his adversaries as a convenient club with which to destroy the* Encyclopédie. *A third onslaught from still another quarter followed in 1758: Jean-Jacques Rousseau, until recently a contributor himself to the* Encyclopédie, *came to the defense of his native city in his* Lettre à M. d'Alembert sur les spectacles *(Letter to d'Alembert on the theatre). Unlike d'Alembert's other critics, Rousseau was not aroused by the former's remarks on the religious opinions of the Genevans, but by the suggestion that Geneva needed a theater. This he rejects indignantly on*

2. *Voltaire's Correspondence*, ed. Th. Besterman, vol. 32, p. 257 (December 29, 1757).

the grounds that the theater corrupts the moral fiber of a nation; d'Alembert, he implies, could scarcely have suggested anything more likely to bring about the downfall of Geneva.

In the midst of all this controversy d'Alembert resigned as coeditor of the Encyclopédie. *He himself maintained that his decision had nothing to do with* GENEVA, *but it is certain that Diderot's displeasure, Rousseau's attack, and the violent criticism he received from both Protestants and Catholics were all persuasive arguments in favor of abandoning his exposed position. This "desertion," as Diderot called it, was a heavy blow: the* Encyclopédie *was deprived of an illustrious editor who was a member of the French Academy as well as of the academies of Berlin, London, Stockholm, and Bologna; and many, among them Voltaire, expected that this resignation would mark the end of the* Encyclopédie. *That this did not happen is largely due to Diderot's decision to ride out the storm.*[3]

GENEVA (*History and Politics*). This city is situated on two hills, at the foot of the lake which today is named after the city but formerly was called Lake Leman. It is very pleasantly situated. On one side one sees the lake, on the other the Rhone, and all around, the smiling countryside. Along the lake there are hills dotted with country houses, while a few miles away rise the Alpine peaks, which are always covered with ice and look as if they are made of silver when on a fine day the sun shines on them. As a rich and busy trading center, Geneva owes its prominence to the harbor, with its jetties, its boats, its markets, etc., as well as to its location between France, Italy, and Germany. The city has several fine buildings and attractive promenades. The streets are lighted at night, and on the banks of the Rhone a very simple pumping machine has been installed that provides water even for the highest quarters, located a hundred feet above. The lake is approximately eighteen leagues long and four to five across at its widest point. It is a kind of little sea with storms and other remarkable phenomena. See TROMBE (Waterspout), see SEICHE (Tidal Wave), etc., and the

3. Arthur M. Wilson's *Diderot, the Testing Years* (New York: Oxford University Press, 1957), 280–90, gives a full account of this episode in the history of the *Encyclopédie.*

Histoire de l'académie des sciences for the years 1741 and 1742. Geneva lies on latitude 46°12′, longitude 23°45′.

Julius Caesar mentions Geneva as a city of the Allobroges, who were then already under Roman dominion. He came to the city to oppose the passage of the Helvetii, today called the Swiss. As soon as Christianity was introduced, the city became a bishopric suffragan to Vienne.[4] At the beginning of the fifth century Emperor Honorius ceded it to the Burgundians. These were driven out by the Frankish kings in 534. When toward the end of the ninth [*sic*] century Charlemagne set out to war against the Lombard kings in order to free the pope (who rewarded him with the imperial crown), he passed through Geneva and chose it as the meeting place of all his armies. Later the city was annexed to the German Empire, and it was here that Conrad assumed the imperial crown in 1034. Succeeding emperors, however, neglected to keep their eyes on the city, since for three hundred years they were preoccupied with the great difficulties in their relationship with the popes. This enabled Geneva gradually to throw off its yoke and to become an imperial city whose bishop was its prince, or rather its lord, for the authority of the bishop was tempered by the authority of the citizens. The coat of arms which it chose at that time gave expression to this mixed constitution: on one side an imperial eagle, on the other a key representing the power of the church, with the device *Post tenebras lux* [Light after darkness]. The city of Geneva kept these arms when it renounced the Roman Church. The keys [*sic*] in its coat of arms are now all it holds in common with the papacy. It is actually rather strange that Geneva retained them after having broken, with a sort of superstitious zeal, all the bonds that could possibly bind it to Rome. Geneva apparently thought that the device, *Post tenebras lux*, expressed so perfectly its present attitude to religion, that there was no need to change anything in its coat of arms.

The dukes of Savoy, neighbors of Geneva, repeatedly made covert attempts, sometimes with the aid of the bishops, to establish their authority over the city, but the latter resisted courageously, supported by its alliance with Fribourg and Berne. At that time, that is to say, around 1526, the Coun-

4. French city on the Rhone, capital of a province of Gaul in Roman times.

cil of Two Hundred was established. The ideas of Luther and Zwingli were beginning to penetrate. Berne had rallied to them; Geneva received them favorably and was finally converted to them in 1535. The papacy was no longer recognized, and since that time the bishop resides in Annecy. He still carries the title "Bishop of Geneva" but has no more jurisdiction over the city than the bishop of Babylon has in his diocese.

Between the two doors of Geneva's city hall one can still see a Latin inscription commemorating the abolition of the Catholic religion. In it the pope is called "Antichrist." This name, which the Genevans' fanatic love of liberty and innovation gave him in a century that was still half barbarous, today seems scarcely worthy of a city so imbued with the philosophic spirit. We venture to suggest that the Genevans replace this insulting and vulgar monument with an inscription that is truer, nobler, and simpler. For Catholics the pope is the head of the true church, for reasonable and moderate Protestants he is a sovereign whom they respect as a prince without obeying him, but in a century such as ours there is no one for whom he is still the Antichrist.

In order to defend its liberty against encroachment by the dukes of Savoy and by its bishops, Geneva strengthened its position still more by an alliance with Zurich and, above all, with France. Thanks to this aid it resisted the weapons of Charles-Emmanuel and the wealth of Philip II, a prince whose memory is assured of the execration of posterity because of his ambition, his despotism, his cruelty, and his superstition. Henri IV, who had sent three hundred soldiers to help Geneva, soon thereafter himself needed the city's help: it was of some use to him in his wars with the League[5] and on other occasions. This is the origin of the privileges which the Genevans, like the Swiss, enjoy in France.

The Genevans, wishing to bring fame to their city, called in Calvin. He enjoyed a great and well-deserved reputation because he was a man of letters of the first rank, who wrote Latin as well as a dead language can be written, and French with a purity of style that was exceptional for

5. League, or Holy League, an association of important nobles; founded in 1576, revived in 1584, led by the Guise family. It played an important political role during the Religious Wars, consistently opposed the monarchy under Henri III, and came to an end only after Henri IV renounced Protestantism.

his time. This purity, which our grammarians still admire today, renders his writings far superior to almost all others written in his century, just as today the works of the Messieurs of Port-Royal[6] still seem far superior to the barbarous rantings of their adversaries and contemporaries. Calvin was both an excellent jurist and as enlightened a theologian as a heretic can be, and together with the magistrates he drew up a compendium of civil and ecclesiastical laws that was approved in 1543 by the people and has become the basic code of the republic. The excess of ecclesiastical property, which before the Reformation fed the luxury of the bishops and their subordinates, was now used to found a hospital, a college, and an academy; but the wars in which Geneva had to engage for almost sixty years prevented the arts and commerce from flourishing as much as the sciences. In 1602 the failure of the attempt by the Duke of Savoy to scale the walls brought peace to the republic. The Genevans repulsed their enemies, who had attacked by surprise, and they hanged thirteen of the leading enemy generals in order to give the Duke of Savoy a distaste for such undertakings. They thought they were justified in treating men who attacked their city without a declaration of war as if they were highwaymen. The strange new policy of waging war without having declared it was not yet known in Europe; and even if it had then been followed by the great states, it would still be true that it is too much against the interest of small states ever to gain favor among them.

When Duke Charles-Emmanuel saw himself repulsed and his generals hanged, he gave up the idea of conquering Geneva. His example served as a lesson for his successors, and since that time the city has been at peace and has not ceased to grow in population, in wealth, and in beauty. From time to time the tranquility of the republic has been slightly disturbed by internal dissensions, of which the last broke out in 1738,[7] but peace was luckily restored by means of the mediation of France and the Swiss Confederation, while external security is today more firmly established than ever with two

6. Seventeenth-century Jansenist writers who lived in retreat at the convent of Port-Royal. Pascal was the most famous member of this group.

7. These were disputes between the patrician government and the more democratic bourgeois party.

new treaties, one concluded with France in 1749, the other with the king of Sardinia[8] in 1754.

It is very remarkable that a city, which scarcely counts twenty-four thousand souls and has a fragmented territory containing fewer than thirty villages, is nevertheless a sovereign state and one of the most prosperous cities of Europe. Geneva is rich because of its liberty and its commerce and often sees everything around it in flames without being in any way affected. The events that disturb Europe are only a spectacle for this city from which it profits without taking any part. Because it is linked to France by treaties and commerce and to England by commerce and religion, it maintains an impartial opinion on the rights and wrongs of the wars which those two powerful nations wage against each other, and at the same time it is too prudent to take any part in these wars. Geneva judges all the sovereigns of Europe without flattery, insult, or fear.

The city is well fortified, especially on the side facing the prince it fears the most, the king of Sardinia. The side bordering France has been left almost completely open and undefended. Military service, however, is performed as in a fortress city. The arsenals and military storehouses are well stocked, and every citizen is a soldier, as in Switzerland or in ancient Rome. Genevans are permitted to serve in foreign armies, but the state does not supply any power with bodies of troops, and no recruiting is allowed on its territory.

While the city is wealthy, the state is poor because of the people's aversion to all new taxes, even the least burdensome. The revenue of the state comes to less than five hundred thousand *livres* in French money, but the admirable economy with which this is administered makes it quite sufficient for all the needs of the city and even produces reserves for emergencies.

There are four classes of inhabitants in Geneva: the citizens who are the sons of bourgeois and were born in the city; they alone can become magistrates. The bourgeois who are the sons of bourgeois or of citizens but were born in a foreign country, or who are foreigners to whom the magistracy has granted the rights of a bourgeois, which it has the power to do; these can be members of the General Council and even of the Grand Conseil,

8. The Duke of Savoy. The house of Savoy had acquired Sardinia in 1718.

called the "Council of the Two Hundred." The residents are foreigners who have the permission of the magistrate to reside in the city but do not exercise any function. Lastly the natives are the children of residents; they have some privileges which their forefathers did not possess, but they are excluded from the government.

The government is headed by four syndics who can hold this position for only one year and must wait at least four years before holding it again. They are aided by the Petit Conseil, composed of twenty counselors, a treasurer, and two secretaries of state, and by another body called Le Corps de la Justice. These two bodies deal with the daily business that demands immediate action, whether criminal or civil.

The Grand Conseil is composed of two hundred and fifty citizens or bourgeois. It judges major civil suits, it grants pardons, coins money, elects the members of the Petit Conseil, and decides what matters should be brought before the General Council. This General Council comprises all citizens and bourgeois, with the exception of those under twenty-five years of age, and of those who are bankrupt or have incurred censure of some sort. This assembly holds the legislative power; it has the right of decision over war and peace, the right to form alliances, levy taxes, and elect the principal magistrates. The election is conducted with orderly decorum in the cathedral, even though there are about fifteen hundred electors.

This fact shows us that the government of Geneva has all the advantages and none of the drawbacks of democracy: everything is under the direction of the syndics; everything is originally discussed in the Petit Conseil, which also has the ultimate executive responsibility. Thus it seems that the city of Geneva has taken as its model the very wise law of the ancient Germanic government: *De minoribus rebus principes consultant, de majoribus omnes; ita tamen, ut ea quorum penes plebem arbitrium est, apud principes praetractentur.*[9]

The civil law of Geneva is almost entirely drawn from Roman law, with some modifications: for example, a father can leave no more than half his

9. "On little matters the chiefs consult, on larger questions the community; only with this limitation, that even those subjects, the decision about which rests with the people, are first handled by the chiefs" (Tacitus, *Germania* 11). D'Alembert omitted *quoque* between *ut* and *quorum* of the original.

property to any heir he wishes to designate; the rest is equally divided between his children. This law on the one hand guarantees the independence of the children and on the other forestalls any injustice by the fathers.

M. de Montesquieu is right to give the name of "beautiful law" to the law that excludes from responsible positions in the republic all citizens who do not pay their father's debts after his death, and, of course, also all those who do not pay their own debts.[10]

The degrees of family relationship that prohibit marriage do not go beyond those laid down in Leviticus: thus first cousins are allowed to marry, but on the other hand no dispensation can be obtained in forbidden cases. Divorce is granted, upon declaration in a court of law, in cases of adultery or intentional desertion.

Criminal justice is dispensed scrupulously rather than harshly. Torture, which has already been abolished in several states and should be abolished everywhere because it is useless cruelty, is forbidden in Geneva. It is administered only to criminals who are already condemned to death, in order to discover their accomplices, if that is necessary. The accused has the right to ask for a transcript of the proceedings and to be assisted by his relatives and a lawyer who defends his case before the judges in open court. Criminal sentences are rendered by the syndics in the public square with great ceremony.

Hereditary titles are unknown in Geneva. The son of a first magistrate remains lost in the crowd if he does not rise above it by his merit. Neither nobility nor wealth carry with them rank, prerogatives, or easy access to public office. Corrupt practices are strictly forbidden. Offices carry so little remuneration that they do not tempt cupidity. Only noble souls are tempted, because of the high esteem in which these offices are held.

There are few lawsuits. Most of them are settled out of court by the efforts of mutual friends, by the lawyers themselves, and by the judges.

Sumptuary laws prohibit the use of jewels and gold, limit funeral expenses, and oblige all citizens to go on foot on the city streets. Carriages are used only for trips to the countryside. In France these laws would be considered too strict and almost barbarous and inhuman, but they do not

10. Montesquieu, *The Spirit of the Laws*, 20.16.

restrict the true comforts of life which can always be obtained at little expense. The laws only eliminate lavishness, which does not bring happiness and bankrupts us without being useful.

There exists no city perhaps where there are more happy marriages. On this point there is a gap of two hundred years between Geneva and our morals. Thanks to the regulations against luxury, no one is afraid to have many children. In Geneva luxury is not, as in France, one of the chief obstacles to population increase.

No theater is permitted in Geneva. There is no objection to plays in themselves, but it is feared that troops of actors would spread the taste for adornment, dissipation, and loose morals among the youth. Would not, however, a series of laws, strictly applied, on the conduct of the actors counteract this undesirable effect? In this way Geneva would possess both theater and good morals and would enjoy the advantages of both. Theatrical performances would educate the taste of the citizens and endow them with a delicacy of tact and a subtlety of feeling, which it is very difficult to acquire otherwise. Literature would profit while morals would not decline, and Geneva would add to the wisdom of Sparta the civility of Athens. There is another consideration, worthy of a republic that is so wise and enlightened, which might induce it to allow a theater. One of the principal causes of the loose morals for which we reproach actors is undoubtedly the barbarous prejudice against the acting profession. These men who are so indispensable to the progress and the vitality of the arts have been forced to live in a state of degradation. They seek in pleasures compensations for the esteem their estate cannot bring them. An actor whose morals are good should be doubly respected, but he is given scarcely any credit for his morality. The tax farmer who is an affront to the penury of the nation from which he draws his wealth, the courtier who fawns and does not pay his debts, those are the types of men we honor most highly. It would be better if actors were not only tolerated in Geneva, but if they were first restrained by wise regulations, then protected, and even granted respect as soon as they were worthy of it. In short, if they were treated exactly like other citizens, the city would soon enjoy the advantage of having a company of honorable actors, something that we believe to be so rare and yet is rare only by our own fault. I might add that such a company would soon be the best in Europe. Many people would hasten to Geneva who have great inclination and talent for the theater but who at present fear they would be dishonored by acting. There they would cultivate a talent that is so pleasing and so unusual, not only without shame but even in an atmosphere of respect. While many Frenchmen now find a stay in Geneva depressing because they are deprived of seeing plays, the city, which is already the abode of philosophy and liberty, would then also be the abode of respectable pleasure. Foreigners would no longer be surprised that in a city where regular performances of decent plays are forbidden, vulgar and stupid farces, as offensive to good taste as to good morals, may be presented. This is not all. Little by little the example of the Genevan actors, their steady conduct, and the esteem it would bring them would serve as a model to the actors of other nations and as a lesson to those who until now have treated them so inconsistently and even harshly. We would no longer see them being on the one hand pensioners of the government and on the other the objects of anathema. Our priests would lose the habit of excommunicating them, and our bourgeois of viewing them with disdain. Then a small republic could claim the glory of having reformed Europe in this respect, and this is perhaps more important than one thinks.

Geneva has a university called the Académie, where the young people are taught free of charge. The professors can become magistrates, and in fact several have held the office. This does much to stimulate the zeal and the fame of the Academy. A few years ago a school of design was founded as well. The lawyers, the notaries, and the doctors belong to associations to which one is admitted only after public examination, and all the craft guilds also have their regulations, their apprenticeships, and masterpieces.

The public library contains a good selection of books. It contains twenty-six thousand volumes and quite a number of manuscripts. These books can be borrowed by all citizens. Thus everyone reads and becomes enlightened, and the Genevans are much better educated than any other people. There is no suggestion that this might be bad, as some people maintain it would be for our country. Perhaps the Genevans and our politicians are equally right.

After England, Geneva was the first to practice smallpox inoculation, which is so difficult to introduce in France and which nevertheless will be introduced,[11] although a number of our doctors still fight it, as their predecessors fought the circulation of the blood, emetics, and so many other incontrovertible truths and useful practices.

All the sciences and almost all the arts have been so well cultivated in Geneva that one would be surprised to see the list of scholars and artists of all kinds produced by the city during the last two centuries. Sometimes it has even had the good fortune to have famous foreigners choose to live in Geneva because of its pleasant location and the freedom enjoyed by its inhabitants. M. de Voltaire, who took up residence in Geneva three years ago, is now accorded the same tokens of esteem and respect by these republicans which he formerly received from several monarchs.

The most flourishing manufacture in Geneva is watchmaking. It employs more than five thousand persons, that is to say, more than a fifth of the citizens. Nor are the other arts neglected, particularly agriculture: painstaking cultivation compensates for the lack of fertile land.

All the houses are built of stone. This often prevents fires, which are also promptly contained because of the good arrangements for extinguishing them.

Genevan hospitals are not, as elsewhere, merely a retreat for the poor who are sick or crippled. While they offer shelter to the homeless poor, they provide above all a great many small pensions that are distributed to poor families to help them live at home and continue working. Every year the hospitals spend more than three times their revenues, so generous are charitable gifts of every kind.

We must still speak of religion in Geneva. This is the section of the article that is perhaps of greatest interest to philosophers. We are now going to take up this subject, but we beg our readers to remember that we are writing only as historians, not as partisans. Our theological articles are intended to serve as antidote to the present article, and, besides, to recount is not

11. Most French doctors still opposed inoculation at this time. The *Encyclopédie* contains a lengthy article on the subject (INOCULATION) by the famous Genevan doctor Théodore Tronchin, who had successfully inoculated the children of the Duke of Orléans in 1756. Tronchin also became involved in the controversy occasioned by GENEVA since he acted as secretary to the committee of nine and wrote the letter to d'Alembert asking him to retract his allegations on the religious opinions of the Genevan clergy. Nonetheless, he always remained a good friend of both Voltaire and Diderot.

to approve. We refer our readers to the words EUCHARISTIE [Eucharist], ENFER [Hell], FOI [Faith], CHRISTIANISME [Christianity], etc., to caution them beforehand against what we are going to say.[12]

The ecclesiastical constitution of Geneva is purely presbyterian. There are no bishops, not to speak of canons. Not that there is objection to the institution of episcopacy, but the Genevans do not grant it any divine right and are of the opinion that a small republic is better served by ministers who are not as rich and influential as the bishops.

The ministers are either pastors, like our parish priests, or postulants, like those of our priests who do not have a living. The minister's income does not exceed twelve hundred livres, and there are no perquisites. The state provides the income since the church owns nothing. No one is accepted into the ministry before the age of twenty-four and only after examinations that are very strict in respect to knowledge and to morality. One would wish that most of our Catholic churches would follow this example.

The clergy plays no role in funerals. These are a purely administrative matter and are performed without any pomp. The Genevans believe that to put on a display after death is ridiculous. The dead are buried in a large cemetery quite far from the city, a custom that should be followed everywhere. See EXHALASION [Exhalation].[13]

The clergy of Geneva have exemplary morals. The ministers live in great concord. One does not see them, as in other countries, quarrel bitterly among themselves about unintelligible subjects, persecute each other, and accuse each other in unseemly fashion before the magistrates. Yet they are far from all thinking alike on the articles that elsewhere are considered the most essential to religion. Several no longer believe in the divinity of Jesus Christ, which Calvin, their leader, defended with such zeal that he had Servetus

12. Three of the articles to which d'Alembert refers the reader are perfectly orthodox, but ENFER [Hell], by the abbé Mallet, is in great part a paraphrase from the seventeenth-century English archbishop Tillotson, a precursor of the English deists, and dwells at length on Tillotson's argument that belief in hell is incompatible with belief in a just and merciful God.

13. This article is also by d'Alembert. In it he refers to the dangerous vapors produced by the presence of cemeteries within the confines of the city. Voltaire repeatedly advocated the removal of cemeteries from the city. Also noteworthy is the article AIR, on the dangers to health from the impure air in the cities.

burned at the stake.[14] When anyone speaks to them about this execution, which mars the charity and moderation of their patriarch, they do not attempt to justify him. They admit that Calvin's action was very reprehensible, and they confine themselves (if it is a Catholic who speaks with them) to contrasting the execution of Servetus with that dreadful Saint Bartholomew's Day, which every good Frenchman would wish to erase from our history with his own blood. They also compare it to the execution of John Hus, which even the Catholics, they remind their interlocutor, no longer attempt to justify; it was an action that equally violated humanity and good faith and should cover the memory of the emperor Sigismund[15] with opprobrium for all time.

"It is no small sign of the progress of human reason," writes M. de Voltaire, "that it was possible to publish in Geneva, with public approval, the statement (in the *Essai sur l'histoire universelle* by the same author) that Calvin had a cruel soul as well as an enlightened mind. The murder of Servetus today seems abominable."[16] We believe that the praise which this noble freedom of thought and of writing deserves should be addressed equally to the author, to his century, and to Geneva. How many countries are there where philosophy has made just as much progress but where truth is still captive, where reason does not dare raise her voice to thunder against abuses she condemns in silence, where we find only too many pusillanimous writers, called "wise men," still respecting prejudices they could combat with complete propriety and safety!

14. Servetus, a Spanish theologian, was burned at the stake in 1553 for preaching against the doctrine of the Trinity and against child baptism.

15. Sigismund (1368–1437) was Holy Roman Emperor and King of Hungary and Bohemia. He granted Hus a safe-conduct to the Council of Constance but did not act when the council imprisoned Hus and condemned him to be burned at the stake.

16. This is quoted from a letter by Voltaire to Nicholas Thieriot which was printed in the *Mercure de France* in May 1757 (pp. 35–38). The *Essai sur l'histoire universalle* is better known today as *Essai sur les Moeurs.*

Voltaire was quite upset that d'Alembert gave such wide publicity to opinions he had expressed in a letter. Mme Denis, Voltaire's niece, wrote in a letter to Tronchin on January 5, 1758: "My uncle has been very worried since he read the article on Geneva, because he thinks that d'Alembert has quoted him quite inopportunely. But he has told me: 'I will not write a word about it unless our friend Tronchin tells me to do so.' Be assured that you will never perform any miracle for humanity that will be as remarkable as to cure my uncle of this article, something none of his friends have been able to accomplish so far." *Voltaire's Correspondence* (Besterman ed.), vol. 33, p. 17 (January 5, 1758).

Hell, one of the principal tenets of our faith, is no longer given such importance by several ministers in Geneva. According to them it would be an insult to the divinity if we imagined that this Being full of goodness and justice were capable of punishing our offenses with eternal torments. They explain as best they can the passages in the Bible which are explicitly contrary to their opinion and assert that in the Holy Scriptures one must never take anything literally if it seems to go against humanity and reason. They believe that there is punishment in the afterlife, but that it is only temporary. Thus purgatory, once one of the principal causes of the separation of the Protestants from the Roman Catholic Church, is today the only punishment after death that many of the former will accept. Here is another item to add to the history of human contradictions.

In short, many of the ministers of Geneva have no other religion than a perfect Socinianism;[17] they reject everything called "mystery" and imagine that the first principle of a true religion is not to propose any belief that conflicts with reason. When they are pressed on the question of the "necessity" of revelation, a dogma that is so basic to Christianity, many substitute the term "utility," which seems more agreeable to them. If they are not orthodox in this, at least they are true to their principles. See Socianisme [Socinianism].

A clergy holding these opinions must needs be tolerant and is tolerant enough to be viewed with disfavor by the ministers of the other reformed churches. One might add further, without any intention of approving the religion of Geneva, that there are few countries where the theologians and the clergymen are more opposed to superstition. As a result, because intolerance and superstition serve only to increase the number of unbelievers, one hears less complaint in Geneva than elsewhere about the spread of unbelief, and this should not surprise us. Here religion consists almost entirely in the adoration of a single God, at least among all classes other than the common people. Respect for Jesus Christ and for the scriptures is perhaps all that distinguishes the Christianity of Geneva from pure deism.

The clergymen of Geneva are not merely tolerant: they remain entirely within their province and are the first to set an example for the citizens by

17. A unitarian doctrine based on the writings of the Italian theologian Fausto Paolo Sozzini (1539–1604).

submitting to the laws. The Consistory, charged with watching over morals, inflicts only spiritual punishment. The great quarrel between the priesthood and the empire, which in the age of ignorance imperiled the crown of many an emperor, and which—we know this only too well—causes troublesome disturbances in more enlightened times, is unknown in Geneva where the clergy does nothing without the approval of the magistrates.

Worship is very simple in Geneva. The churches contain no images, no lights or ornaments. However, a portal in very good taste has just been added to the cathedral; little by little the interior of the churches will perhaps be embellished. Indeed, what objection could there be to having paintings and statues? If one wishes, the common people could be told not to worship them and to look on them only as monuments destined to recount in a striking and pleasing manner the principal events of religion. This would be to the advantage of the arts yet would bring no profit to superstition. The reader surely realizes that we are speaking here according to the principles of the ministers of Geneva, and not those of the Catholic Church.

The divine service includes both sermons and singing. The sermons are almost entirely concerned with morality and are all the better for that. The singing is in rather bad taste, and the French verses that are sung are in even worse taste. It is to be hoped that Geneva will become reformed on these two points. An organ has just been placed in the cathedral, and perhaps God will now be praised in better language and in better music. We must admit, however, that the Supreme Being is honored in Geneva with a seemliness and calm that is not noticeable in our churches.

Perhaps we will not devote articles of such length to the greatest monarchies, but in the eyes of the philosopher, the Republic of the Bees is no less interesting than the history of great empires. It may be that the model of a perfect political administration can be found only in small states. If religion does not allow us to believe that the Genevans have successfully worked for their happiness in the next world, reason forces us to believe that they are perhaps as happy as one can be in this world:

O fortunatos nimium, sua si bona norint![18] (*O*)

18. "Oh how very happy they are if they know their blessing!" (Virgil, *Georgics* II. 458).

Government
(*Gouvernement*)

This article, written during the Seven Years' War, shortly before the controversy that brought publication of the Encyclopédie *to an end, is one of the more ambitious and wide-ranging of Jaucourt's many political articles. It was also one of the most frequently attacked of the political articles. Drawing on a combination of Locke and Sidney, as well as Pufendorf and Montesquieu, the author addresses the origins and functions of government in historical and philosophical fashion. Critics especially condemned Jaucourt's use of the Lockean argument that children are born under no government, and that the age of reason brings with it the right to choose one's government.*[1]

GOVERNMENT (*Natural and political law*), manner in which sovereignty is administered in each state. Let us examine the origin, the forms, and the causes of the dissolution of *governments*. This subject merits the close attention of peoples and sovereigns.

In earliest times, the father was by rights the prince and the born governor of his children. For it would have been quite difficult for them to live together without some kind of *government*. And what simpler and more suitable *government* could be imagined than the one in which a father administers the executive power of nature's laws within his family!

It was difficult for children, once they had become grown men, not to continue assigning the authority of this natural *government* to their father

This article can be found at 7:788–91 in the original edition of the *Encyclopédie*.

1. See John Lough, *Essays on the "Encyclopédie" of Diderot and d'Alembert* (London: Oxford University Press, 1968), 278, 280–82, 304–5, 312, 453–55.

by tacit consent. They were accustomed to see themselves guided by his concern and to bring their conflicts before his tribunal. Since community property was established between them, and the sources of the desire to possess were still unknown, no disputes caused by greed sprouted up. And if one arose over other topics, who could better judge them than a father full of enlightenment and tenderness?

In those days, no distinction was made between minority and majority. And if a child was old enough to dispose of his person and the possessions his father gave him, he had no desire to escape from his tutelage, because nothing held him there. Thus, the *government* to which each person freely submitted always carried on to the satisfaction of each, and was much more a protection and safeguard than a brake and subjection. In a word, children could not elsewhere find a greater security for their peace, their liberty, or their happiness than in paternal guidance and *government.*

This is why fathers became the political monarchs of their families. And since they lived for a long time and normally left able heirs worthy of succeeding them, they thereby laid the foundations of hereditary or elective realms, which since have been organized by various constitutions and various laws, according to the country, place, circumstance, and situation.

If, after the father's death, the nearest heir was not capable of *government* because of lack of age, wisdom, prudence, courage, or some other quality; or if various families agreed to unite and live together in a society, let there be no doubt that at that point, all who composed those families were using their natural liberty to place over them whomever they judged most capable of governing them. We see that the peoples of America who live at a distance from the conquerors' sword and from the sanguinary domination of the two great empires of Peru and Mexico, still enjoy their natural liberty and conduct themselves in that manner. Sometimes they choose the last governor's heir as their leader, sometimes the most valiant and brave among them. It is thus likely that every people, however populous they may have become, however vast the country they may occupy, owes their beginning to one or several families associating together. One cannot assign conquest as the origin of the establishment of nations; conquests arise from the corruption of peoples' primitive condition, and from their immoderate desires. *See* CONQUÊTE.[2]

Since it is certain that every nation owes its beginnings to one or several families, it must have preserved, at least for a certain time, the paternal form of *government*. That is, it must have obeyed only the laws of a feeling of affection and tenderness that the example of a leader excites and stimulates between brothers and relatives—a mild authority that gives them every shared good, and that claims no property for itself.

Thus, every people on earth, at its birth and in its native country, has been governed as we see the small tribal peoples of America governed today, and as the ancient Scythians—who were virtually the breeding ground of other nations—are said to have been governed. But as these peoples grew in the number and extent of their families, the feelings of fraternal union were bound to weaken.

The families of those nations that through particular causes remained the least numerous, and that stayed the longest in their native land, have been the most consistent in preserving their original form of entirely simple and natural *government*. But those nations that, too cramped in their own country, saw themselves obliged to transmigrate have been forced by circumstances and by the complications of travel, or by the nature and situation of the country to which they moved, to establish by free consent the forms of *government* most suitable to their character, their position, and their number.

All public *governments* seem manifestly to have been formed by deliberation, consultation, and agreement. Who doubts, for example, that Rome and Venice began with men who were free and independent of each other, among whom there was no natural superiority or subjection, and who agreed to form an association of *government?* Taking nature in itself, however, it is not impossible for men to be able to live without any public *government*.

2. See CONQUEST, above. Robert Filmer's theory of the paternal basis of power in *Patriarcha* (1680) was attacked by John Locke in his *Two Treatises of Government*. The first of these focused on Adam and the divine institution of government, but Jaucourt bypasses this religious framework and deals only with the natural origins of government explored in the *Second Treatise*.

The inhabitants of Peru had none; even today, the Cheriquanas, the Floridians, and others live in bands without rules or laws. But since other less savage peoples must have repulsed private injuries more efficaciously, they generally made the decision to choose a type of *government* and submit to it. They had recognized that the disorders would never end if they did not give authority and power to someone or to several among them to resolve all disputes, since no one lacking that authority had a right to pose as lord and judge of anyone else. That was the conduct of those who came from Sparta with Pallanta, mentioned by Justin.[3] In a word, all political societies have begun by a voluntary union of individuals, who have made the free choice of a type of *government*. Then, the formal disadvantages of some of these *governments* obliged the same men who were members of them to reform them, change them, and establish different ones.

In these sorts of establishments, if it happened at first (as was possible) that men were content to refer everything to the wisdom and discretion of the one or several who were chosen as the first governors, experience showed that this arbitrary *government* destroyed the public good, and far from remedying the problem, aggravated it. That is why men made laws, in which each person could read his duty and know the punishments due to those who violate them.

Of these laws, the principal one was that each person would have and possess with security that which properly belonged to him. This law is from natural right. Whatever power may be granted to those who govern, they have no right to seize the possessions that belong to any subject, not even the least portion of these possessions, against the consent of the owner. Not even the most absolute power, albeit absolute when it is necessary to exercise it, is arbitrary on this point. The well-being of an army and of the state demand blind obedience to superior officers; a soldier who signals his opposition is punished with death. And yet, the general himself, with all his power of life and death, does not have the power to dispose of a penny of that soldier's possessions, or to seize the smallest part of what belongs to him as property.

3. Marcus Junianus Justinus, third-century Roman historian and author of *Historiarum Philippicarum libri XLIV*, a compendium of the earlier work of Pompeius Trogus, now lost. I have not been able to determine the meaning of Jaucourt's reference.

I know that that general can make conquests, and that there are authors who regard conquests as the origin and foundation of *governments*.[4] But conquests are as far from being the origin and foundation of *governments* as the demolition of one house is from being the true cause of the construction of another house on the same site. In truth, the destruction of one state does prepare for a new state. But the conquest that establishes it by force is only one more injustice. All legitimate sovereign power must emanate from the free consent of the people.

Some peoples have placed this sovereign power in all the heads of household, assembled and united in a council, upon which is devolved the power to make laws for the public good, and to have these laws executed by magistrates delegated for the purpose. Then, the form of this *government* is named a *democracy*. *See* DEMOCRACY.[5]

Other peoples have assigned all sovereign authority to a council composed of the leading citizens, and then the form of this *government* is called *an aristocracy*. *See* ARISTOCRATIE [Aristocracy].

Other nations have entrusted sovereign and undivided power, and all the rights essential to it, to the hands of one man—king, monarch, or emperor—and then the form of this *government* is a monarchy. *See* MONARCHY.[6]

When power is placed in the hands of this one man, and afterward to his heirs, it is a hereditary monarchy. If it is conferred on him only during his life, on condition that after his death the power return to those who have given it to him and that they name a successor, it is an elective monarchy.

Other peoples, making a kind of division of the sovereignty and mixing, so to speak, the forms of *government* we have just discussed, have entrusted different parts of it to different hands, have tempered monarchy with aristocracy and at the same time have granted the people some share in the sovereignty.

It is certain that a society has the freedom to form a *government* in the manner it pleases, to mix it and combine it in different ways. If the legislative

4. See Hobbes, *Leviathan,* chap. 20, for one possible target of Jaucourt's comment.

5. In this volume.

6. Here, Jaucourt adopts Aristotle's traditional regime typology, based on the number of members of the ruling group, rather than Montesquieu's innovative replacement of aristocracy with despotism.

power has been given by a people to one person, or to several persons for life or for a limited time, then when that time is up, the sovereign power returns to the society from which it emanated. Once it has returned there, society may dispose of it anew as it pleases, placing it again in the hands of those it finds good, in the manner it judges appropriate, and thus setting up a new form of *government*. Pufendorf may say what he likes about how all types of mixed *government* are *irregular*, but true regularity will always be that which is most consistent with the good of civil society.[7]

Some political writers claim that since all men are born under a *government*, they do not have the freedom to set up a new one. They say each person is born a subject of his father or his prince, and consequently, each is in a perpetual obligation of subjection or fidelity. This reasoning is more specious than solid. Never have men regarded any natural subjection in which they are born, with respect to their father or their prince, as a tie that obliges them to submit without their own consent. Sacred and profane history furnish us frequent examples of a multitude of people who have withdrawn from the obedience and the jurisdiction under which they were born, from the family and the community in which they had been raised, in order to establish new societies and new *governments* elsewhere.

It is these emigrations, at once free and legitimate, that have produced such a large number of small societies which have spread out to different countries, expanded, and settled there to the extent they found subsistence; or until the strongest, swallowing up the weakest, established large empires on their remains, which in turn were smashed and dissolved into various small dominions. If it were true that men did not have the natural liberty to separate themselves from their families and their *government*, whatever it may be, in order to set up others as they desire, then instead of numerous realms, only a single monarchy would have been found in the earliest ages.

It is clear by the practice of *governments* themselves, as well as by the laws of right reason, that a child is born as a subject of no country and of no *government*. He remains under the tutelage and authority of his father until he has reached the age of reason. At that age of reason, he is a free

7. The reference is to Pufendorf's "De Republica irregulari" in *Dissertationes Academicae Selectiores* (Upsala, 1677), 301–57.

man, he has the authority to choose the *government* under which he finds it good to live, and to join the political body that he likes the best. Nothing but his sole consent is capable of reducing him to the subjection of any power on earth. The consent that subjects him to some *government* is either express or tacit. Express consent makes him unquestionably a member of the society that he adopts. Tacit consent binds him to the laws of the *government* in which he enjoys possession. But if his obligation begins with his possessions, it also ends with their enjoyment. Then, proprietors of this kind have the freedom to incorporate themselves into another community, or to set up a new one *in vacuis locis* (as they say in legal terms), in a desert or in some area of the world that is without possessors and without dwellings.[8]

Nonetheless, although men are free to leave one *government* in order to submit to another, it must not be concluded from this that the *government* they prefer to submit to is more legitimate than the one they have left. Governments of whatever sort that have as their foundation the free acquiescence of the people—either express, or justified by long and peaceful possession—are equally legitimate, at least as long as the sovereign's intention is to strive for the people's happiness. Nothing can degrade a *government* like real and open violence, either in its establishment or in its exercise—I mean usurpation and tyranny. *See* USURPATION and TYRANNY.

But the question that most divides minds is to determine what is the best form of *government*.[9] From the meeting held on this subject by the seven noble lords of Persia until our own day, men have come to different conclusions on this great question—discussed already in Herodotus—and have almost always resolved it by a taste based on habit or inclination, rather than by an enlightened and reflective taste.

It is certain that each form of *government* has advantages and disadvantages which are inseparable from it. There is no perfect *government* on earth. And however perfect it may appear in speculation, it will always be accompanied in practice and in the hands of men by instability, revolutions,

8. See Locke, *Second Treatise*, chaps. 6, 18; Locke's phrase "in vacuis locis" means "in empty spaces."

9. Much of the discussion that follows, including the emphasis upon moderation as a standard of regime evaluation, comes from Montesquieu, *The Spirit of the Laws*, 11.6 and passim.

and vicissitudes. In the end, the best will be destroyed, as long as it is men who govern men.

In general, however, one could respond to the question put forth by saying that the image of the best form of *government* ought to be drawn from a moderation fit for repressing license without degenerating into oppression. This is the one which, in avoiding extremes, will be able to provide for good order and for internal and external needs, while leaving the people sufficient guarantees that it will not stray from these ends.

Lacedemon's legislator, seeing that the three types of simple *government* each had great disadvantages—that monarchy degenerated easily into arbitrary power, aristocracy into an unjust *government* of some individual, and democracy into a blind domination without rules—Lycurgus, I say, thought he ought to introduce these three types of *government* into that of his Country, and blend them, so to speak, into a single one, so that they might use each other as balance and counterweight. That wise mortal was not mistaken—at least no republic has preserved its laws, its customs, and its liberty for as long as the republic of Lacedemon.

In Europe, there is a thriving state in which the three powers are even better blended than in the republic of the Spartans. Political liberty is the direct purpose of the constitution of that state, which, by all appearances, can perish only when legislative power is more corrupt than executive power.[10] No one has given a better exposition of the fine system of *government* in the state that I am speaking of than the author of *The Spirit of the Laws.*

Nonetheless, it is quite necessary to observe that no government is equally suitable for every people. Their form must endlessly depend on locale and climate as well as on the mind, the genius, and the character of the nation, and on its extent.

Whatever form one prefers, there is always a primary goal in any *government,* which must be taken from the general good of the nation. On this principle, the best *government* is the one that makes the greatest number of people happy. Whatever the form of political *government,* the duty of whoever is charged with it, in whatever manner it may be, is to work to render

10. This sentence combines elements from Montesquieu, *Laws,* 11.5, and the end of 11.6, 166.

the subjects happy—by procuring them, on the one hand, the amenities of life, security, and tranquility; and on the other, all the means that might contribute to their virtues. The sovereign law of every good *government* is the public good, *salus populi, suprema lex esto:* thus, amidst the differences of opinion over the forms of *government,* everyone unanimously agrees on this latter truth.

In starting from this principle, it is doubtless important to research what would be the most perfect *government* one could establish in the world, even though others serve the purposes of the societies for which they have been created. And although it is not as easy to found a new *government* as it is to build a ship on a new theory, the subject is nonetheless among the worthiest for our curiosity. Even in a situation where the question concerning the best form of *government* has been decided by the universal consent of the political class, who knows if, several centuries later, an occasion might not arise for reducing theory to practice, either by the dissolution of an ancient *government* or by other events that demand the establishment somewhere of a new *government?* In every situation, it is bound to be advantageous for us to know what is most perfect within a given type, in order to be in a position to bring all *government* constitutions as close to this point of perfection as possible—by new laws, imperceptible alterations in the prevailing laws, or innovations conducive to the good of society. The passing of the centuries has served to perfect many arts and many sciences; why would it not serve to perfect the different types of *government,* and give them the best form?

In a new constitution or a reformed *government,* enlightened principles and known experience would already enable one to avoid all the palpable defects that are opposed—or that could not fail to be opposed—to its growth, strength, and prosperity.

A *government* would be defective if the laws and customs of a state were not consistent with the people's nature or with the characteristics and situation of the country—for example, if the laws tended to turn toward arms a people suited for the arts of peace; or if these same laws neglected to encourage and honor commerce and manufactures, in a country favorably situated for drawing great profit from them. A *government* would be defective if the constitution of the fundamental laws were advantageous only to the great, or if it tended to make the dispatch of public business at once slow and difficult. Such are the laws to be reformed in Poland, where on the one hand, whoever kills a peasant gets off with a fine, and on the other, the opposition of a single member of the assembly breaks up the Diet, which in any case is limited to too short a time for the dispatch of public business.[11] Lastly (for I have no intention of satirizing existing states), a *government* is substantially defective wherever regulations and customs are found that are contrary to the essential maxims of good politics. And if, as ill luck would have it, one were able to gloss over these defects under the specious pretext of religion, their effects would be much more pernicious.

It is not enough to abrogate the laws that are mistakes in a state; the good of the people must also be the great end of *government*. Governors are named to fulfill this end, and the civil constitution that vests them with this power is committed to it by the laws of nature and the law of reason, which has determined this end in every form of *government* as the motive force of its good fortune. The greatest good of the people is their liberty. Liberty is to the body of the state what health is to each individual. Without health, man cannot taste pleasure; without liberty, happiness is banished from states. A patriotic governor will therefore see that the right to defend and maintain liberty is the most sacred of his duties.

Next, the principal concern that ought to occupy him is to work to prevent all the sorry causes of the dissolution of *government*. This dissolution can occur by disorders from within and by violence from without.

(1) This dissolution of *government* can occur when the legislative power is altered.[12] Legislative power is the soul of the body politic; this is where the members of the state derive everything necessary for their preservation, their union, and their happiness. Thus, if the legislative power is ruined, the dissolution and death of the entire body politic follow.[13]

(2) A *government* may be dissolved when whoever has supreme executive power abandons his post, so that the laws already made cannot be executed.[14]

11. For part of this account, Jaucourt may be drawing on Voltaire, *Essay sur l'histoire générale* (Geneva: Cramer, 1756), chap. 98.

12. The discussion of dissolution of governments that follows is drawn from Locke, *Second Treatise,* chap. 19.

13. Locke, *Second Treatise,* chap. 19, para. 212.

14. For this paragraph, see Locke, *Second Treatise,* chap. 19, para. 219.

These laws are not established for their own sake; they have been created only to be the bonds of society that continue each member in his function. If the laws cease, the *government* ceases at the same time; the people become a confused multitude, without order or restraint. When justice is no longer administered and therefore the rights of each person are no longer secure, there remains no more *government*. Once the laws are no longer enforced, it is as if there are no laws. A *government* without laws is a political mystery, inconceivable to man's mind and incompatible with human society.

(3) *Governments* can be dissolved when the legislative or executive power acts by force, beyond the authority delegated to them and in a manner opposed to the confidence people placed in them. This is what happens, for example, when those who are vested with these powers usurp the citizens' possessions and make themselves absolute arbiters of things that properly belong to the community—I mean the life, liberty, and wealth of the people. The reason men enter a political society is to preserve their own possessions, and the end for which they invest certain persons with legislative authority and executive power is to have laws and power that will protect and preserve what properly belongs to the whole society.

If it happens that those who hold the reins of *government* find resistance when they use their power for the destruction and not the preservation of the things that belong properly to the people, they should blame only themselves, because the public good and society's benefit are the purpose of the institution of *government*. Whence it necessarily arises that power cannot be arbitrary and that it must be exercised according to the established laws, so that the people may know their duty and find their security in the shadow of the laws, and so that the governors may at the same time be restrained within just limits and not be tempted to employ the power they have at hand to do things harmful to political society.

(4) Finally, a foreign force, foreseen or unforeseen, may entirely dissolve a political society; when that society is dissolved by a foreign force, it is certain that its *government* can exist no more.[15] Thus, the conqueror's sword overthrows, confounds, destroys all things, and the society and *government* are thereby broken in pieces, because those who are subjugated are

15. For this paragraph, see Locke, *Second Treatise*, chap. 19, para. 211.

deprived of the protection of that *government* which they used to depend upon, and which had been designed to defend them. Everyone easily understands that when society is dissolved, *government* can no longer last. At that point, it is as impossible for *government* to last as it is for the structure of a house to last after the materials with which it had been constructed have been dispersed by a hurricane, or scrambled pell-mell in a heap by an earthquake.

Independent of these misfortunes, it must be agreed that there is no absolute stability in humanity. For what exists immutably exists necessarily, and this attribute of the Supreme Being cannot belong to man or his works. The best-instituted *governments*, like the best-constituted animal bodies, carry within them the principle of their destruction. Establish with Lycurgus the best laws; imagine with Sidney the means of founding the wisest republic;[16] bring it about, with Alfred, that a populous nation finds its happiness in a monarchy[17]—all this will last only a certain time. After growing and expanding, states then tend toward their decline and their dissolution. Thus, the only way of prolonging the life of a flourishing *government* is to bring it back, on every favorable occasion, to the principles on which it was founded. When these occasions present themselves often and when they are grasped appropriately, *government*s are happier and more durable. When these occasions arise rarely or when they are not taken advantage of, the political body fades, dries out, and perishes. *Article by Chev.* DE JAUCOURT.

16. The reference is to Algernon Sidney, the Whig republican author of *Court Maxims* and especially *Discourses Concerning Government* (1698; see the 1996 version edited by Thomas G. West for Liberty Fund), a work that helped convict him of treason and send him to his death. Jaucourt was the only contributor who cited Sidney by name in the *Encyclopédie;* see his articles DEMOCRACY and TYRANNY in this volume for the other references.

17. The reference is probably to King Alfred the Great (r. 871–99), whose successful defense of his realm of Wessex against the Vikings had made him the dominant ruler in the British Isles by the time of his death and a later hero of English unification.

Cereals
(*Grains*)

This 1758 article is one of the earliest and most important statements of the theories of a group of political economists who subsequently called themselves the Physiocrats, a term coined in the 1760s after the Greek for "the rule of nature." Quesnay was the acknowledged leader of the group. The Physiocrats had a theory not only of economics, but of government, and were keenly interested in the effects of wealth on fiscal and military strength, as is seen in this article. For the present volume, only the introductory material and the final pages on the "Maxims of Economic Government" are included, along with the one footnote supplied by Quesnay for that text. The bulk of the remainder, which comprises two-thirds of the entire entry and which consists of a detailed quantitative analysis of agricultural productivity, is omitted.

CEREALS (*Political economy*). The main items of commerce[1] in France are *cereals*, wines and brandies, salt, hemp and flax, wool, and other animal products. The manufacture of cloth and common fabrics can greatly increase the value of hemp, flax, and wool, and can procure subsistence for many men employed in such profitable work. But it is perceived today that the production and trade of most of these commodities are almost annihilated in France. For a long time, luxury manufactures have seduced the nation. We have neither the silk nor the wool suitable for making nice fabrics

This article can be found at 7:812, 826–31 in the original edition of the *Encyclopédie*.

1. We translate *commerce* as "commerce" and "trade" interchangeably in this entry.—HC

and fine cloth. We have devoted ourselves to an industry that is foreign to us, and we have employed a multitude of men in it at a time when the realm was being depopulated and the countryside was becoming deserted. We have brought down the price of our wheat so that manufacturing and manual labor will be less expensive than abroad. Men and wealth have accumulated in the cities.

Agriculture, the most fertile and the noblest part of our commerce, the source of the revenues of the realm, has not been envisioned as the primary source of our wealth; it has seemed to interest only the farmer and the peasant. Their work has been limited to the subsistence of the nation, which pays the expenses of agriculture through the purchase of commodities. And it has been believed that this was a trade or traffic built upon industry, which was bound to bring gold and silver into the realm. Planting of vines has been prohibited; cultivation of mulberry trees has been recommended; the sale of agricultural products has been stopped, and landed income has been reduced, all to encourage manufactures that are harmful to our own commerce.

France can produce in abundance all materials of primary necessity. Luxury merchandise is the only thing it can buy from abroad. Mutual traffic between nations is necessary to support commerce. But we have become mainly attached to the fabrication and trade of commodities that we can get from abroad. And by an overly avid commercial rivalry, we have wanted to harm our neighbors and deprive them of the profit they would derive from us by the sale of their merchandise.

Through this policy, we have extinguished a reciprocal trade between them and us that was entirely to our advantage. They have prohibited the import of our commodities, and we buy from them in contraband and at high cost the materials that we employ in our manufactures. To earn a few million to manufacture and sell fine fabric, we have lost billions on the produce of our land; and the nation, decked out in gold and silver, thought it enjoyed a flourishing commerce.

These manufactures have plunged us into a disordered luxury that has spread a little to other nations and has excited their emulation. We have perhaps surpassed them by our human industry, but that advantage has mainly been sustained by our own consumption.

The subjects' consumption is the source of the sovereign's revenue, and the sale of the surplus abroad increases the subjects' wealth. The prosperity of the State depends on the convergence of these two advantages. But the consumption that is maintained by luxury is too limited; it can support itself only by opulence. Men who are little favored by fortune can engage in it only to their detriment and to the disadvantage of the State.

The most enlightened ministry knows that the consumption which can procure large revenues for the sovereign, and which brings happiness to his subjects, is that general consumption which satisfies the needs of life. Only indigence can reduce us to drinking water, eating bad bread, and covering ourselves in rags. All men strive through their work to get themselves good food and good clothing. Their efforts cannot be too strongly encouraged, for these are the revenues of the realm, the profits and expenses of the people that create the wealth of the sovereign.

The detail with which we are going to treat the income procured by abundant *cereal* harvests, and freedom of trade for this commodity, will sufficiently prove how far the production, sale, and consumption of materials of primary necessity interest all the different estates of the realm, and will enable us to decide what we should expect today of the government's views on the restoration of agriculture.

[The author then offers a detailed analysis of the grain trade, omitted here.]

Maxims of Economic Government

I. *The works of human industry do not multiply wealth.* The works of agriculture compensate for its costs, pay the manual labor of cultivation, and procure gains for the husbandmen; moreover, they produce real-estate income. Those who buy the products of industry pay for the merchants' expenses, manual labor, and profit, but these works produce no revenue beyond that.

Thus, all the expenses for works of human industry are drawn only from real-estate income, for the works that do not produce income can exist only through the wealth of those who pay for them.

Compare the profit of the workers who manufacture works of industry with that of the workers whom the cultivator employs in cultivating the land, and you will find that the profit in both cases is limited to the upkeep of those workers, that this profit is not an increase in wealth, and that the value of the industrial works is proportional to the value itself of the upkeep that the workers and merchants consume. Thus, the artisan destroys as much in upkeep as he produces through his work.

There is therefore no multiplication of wealth in the production of industrial works, since the value of those works rises only from the price of the upkeep that the workers consume. The merchants' large fortunes should be viewed in no other way; they are the results of large commercial enterprises, which combine profits similar to those of the petty merchants, in the same way that the enterprises of large work projects bring about large fortunes by the small profits drawn from the work of a large number of workers. All these contractors make fortunes only because others incur expenses. Thus, there is no increase in wealth.

It is the source of men's subsistence that is the origin of wealth. It is human industry that prepares this wealth for men's use. The proprietors pay for the works of industry in order to enjoy them. Their income thereby becomes common to all men.

Men are therefore multiplied in proportion to real-estate income. Some generate wealth by cultivation, others get it ready for enjoyment, and those who enjoy it pay both.

Real estate, men, and wealth are therefore necessary in order to have wealth and men. Thus, a State populated only by merchants and artisans could survive only by the real-estate income of foreigners.

II. *The works of industry contribute to population and to the increase of wealth.* If a nation gains a million from abroad by its manual labor on domestically manufactured merchandise, and if it also sells abroad a million's worth in foodstuffs from its crop, both of these results are equally an increase in wealth for it and are equally advantageous for it, provided that it has more men than the income from the kingdom's soil can maintain. For then, a portion of these men can subsist only through the products of manual labor that they sell abroad.

In that case, a nation is getting all the output from men and the soil that it can get. But it gains much more on the sale of a million in merchandise from its crop than on the sale of a million in products of manual labor, because in the latter case it gains only the price of the artisan's work, while in the former it gains the price of the work of cultivation and the price of the contents produced by the soil. Thus, in the equality of the amounts derived from the sale of these different kinds of merchandise, the crop trade is always proportionally much more profitable.

III. *The works of industry that employ men to the detriment of the cultivation of real estate are harmful to population and to the increase of wealth.* If a nation that sells abroad a million's worth in products of manual labor and a million's worth in merchandise from its crop does not have enough men busily bringing returns on its real estate, it loses much on the employment of men tied up in the manufacture of products of manual labor that it sells abroad. For then, men can engage in this work only to the detriment of the income from the soil, and the work yield of the men who cultivate the earth can be double or triple that of the manufacture of products of manual labor.

IV. *The wealth of the cultivators generates the wealth of cultivation.* The work yield of cultivation can be nil or almost nil for the State when the cultivator cannot defray the expenses of good cultivation. A poor man whose work draws from the earth only foodstuffs of little value (like potatoes, buckwheat, chestnuts, etc.)—who lives on them, who buys nothing and sells nothing—works only for himself alone. He lives in destitution; he and the land he cultivates bring no returns to the State.

Such is the effect of indigence in the provinces where there are no husbandmen in a position to employ peasants, and where these very poor peasants can by themselves obtain only bad food and bad clothes.

Thus, the employment of men in agriculture can be unfruitful in a realm in which they do not have the wealth necessary to prepare the earth to yield rich harvests. But real-estate income is always assured in a realm well populated with rich husbandmen.

V. *Works of industry contribute to the increase in real-estate income, and real-estate income supports the works of industry.* A nation which, by the fertility of its soil and the difficulty of its transport, had an annual surplus of foodstuffs that it could not sell to its neighbors, and which could sell them easily transportable products of manual labor, would have an interest in attracting many manufacturers and artisans who would consume the foodstuffs of the country, sell their works abroad, and increase the wealth of the nation by their profits and their consumption.

But then, this arrangement is not easy, because manufacturers and artisans gather in a country only in proportion to the real income of the nation—that is, in proportion as there are proprietors or merchants who can buy their works at almost as good a price as they would sell them for elsewhere, and who would procure their sale as they manufactured them. This is hardly possible in a nation that does not itself have the turnover of its foodstuffs, and where the low value of these same foodstuffs does not presently produce enough income to establish manufactures and manual-labor works.

Such a plan can be executed only very slowly. Many nations that have tried it have even found it impossible to achieve it.

It is the only situation, however, in which the government might usefully involve itself in the progress of industry in a fertile realm.

For when the farm trade is easy and free, the manual-labor works are always unfailingly assured by the real-estate income.

VI. *A nation that has a brisk trade in domestic foodstuffs can always maintain, at least for itself, a brisk trade in products of manual labor.* For it can always pay, in proportion to the income from real estate, the workers who manufacture the manual-labor works that it needs.

Thus, the trade in works of industry belongs as surely to that nation as the trade in domestic foodstuffs.

VII. *A nation that has little commerce in domestic foodstuffs and is reduced to getting by on a commerce in industry is in a precarious and uncertain state.* For its commerce can be taken away from it by other rival nations that engage with more success in this same commerce.

Moreover, such a nation is always a dependent of nations that sell it materials of primary need. It is reduced to a severe economy because it has no revenue to dispense, and because it cannot extend and support its trade, its industry, and its shipping except by savings, whereas those that have real estate increase their revenues by their consumption.

VIII. *An extensive internal commerce in products of manual labor can exist only by real-estate revenues.* One must examine the proportion of external to internal trade in the industrial works of a realm. For if the internal commerce of products of manual labor was worth, for example, three million, and the external commerce one million, then three-quarters of this entire commerce of products of manual labor would be paid for by the real-estate income of the nation, since the foreigner would be paying for only a quarter of it.

In this case, the real-estate income would be the main wealth of the realm. Then the main object of the government would be to attend to the maintenance and increase of the real-estate income.

The means consist in the freedom of commerce and in the preservation of the cultivators' wealth. Without these conditions, the income, the population, and the products of industry are destroyed.

Agriculture produces two sorts of wealth: namely, the annual yield on the proprietors' income, and the restitution of the expenses of cultivation.

The income must be spent, in order to be distributed annually to all citizens and to provide for the tax revenues of the State.

The wealth employed in the cost of cultivation should be reserved to the cultivators and exempt from all taxes. For if one takes it away, one destroys agriculture, abolishes the gains made by the residents of the countryside, and halts the source of State revenues.

IX. *A nation with a large territory that lowers the prices of its domestic foodstuffs to encourage the manufacture of manual-labor works destroys itself on all sides.* For if the cultivator is not compensated for the great expenses that agriculture demands and if he does not make a profit, agriculture perishes. The nation loses the income from its real estate. The labor from the manual-labor works diminishes, because this labor can no longer be paid for by real-estate proprietors. The country is depopulated by poverty and by the desertion of the manufacturers, artisans, day-laborers, and peasants, who can subsist only in proportion to the gains procured them by the nation's income.

Then the forces of the realm are destroyed. Wealth is wiped out, taxes overburden the people, and the revenues of the sovereign decline.

Thus, such poorly understood management would alone suffice to ruin a State.

X. *The advantages of external commerce do not consist in an increase in monetary wealth.* The surplus wealth procured by the external commerce of a nation may not be a surplus in monetary wealth, because external commerce with foreigners may take place by the exchange of other merchandise consumed by that nation. But for that same nation, this is nonetheless a source of wealth that it enjoys, and that it might convert (through economizing) into monetary wealth for other uses.

Viewed as merchandise, moreover, foodstuffs are a combination of monetary wealth and real wealth. A husbandman who sells his wheat to a merchant is paid in money; with this money, he pays the proprietor, the taxes, his domestics, and his workers, and he buys the merchandise he needs. The merchant who sells the wheat to the foreigner and buys other merchandise from him, or who trades with him through exchange, resells in his turn the merchandise he has brought in, and with the money he receives, he buys some more wheat. Therefore, the wheat viewed as merchandise is a source of monetary wealth for the sellers, and real wealth for the buyers.

Thus, the foodstuffs that can be sold should always be regarded indifferently in a State as monetary and real wealth, which the subjects can use as it suits them.

The wealth of a nation is not determined by the supply of monetary wealth. The latter can increase or decrease without being noticed, because it is always effective in a State by its quantity, or by the celerity of its circulation, in proportion to the abundance and value of the foodstuffs. Spain, which enjoys the treasures of Peru, is always exhausted by its needs. England supports its opulence by real wealth; the paper that represents its money has a value assured by the commerce and the property income of the nation.

It is thus not the greater or lesser monetary wealth that decides the wealth of a State, and the prohibitions on the export of money from a realm to the detriment of profitable trade can be founded only on some harmful prejudice.

For the support of a State, real wealth is necessary—that is, wealth that is always regenerating, always sought after, and always being paid for, in order to enjoy it, to obtain commodities, and to satisfy the needs of life.

XI. *One cannot know the commercial advantages or the state of each nation's wealth by the balance of trade between various nations*. For some nations may be richer in men and real estate than others, and the latter may have less internal commerce, less consumption, and more external commerce than the former.

Moreover, some of these nations may have more merchandise trade than others. The trade that brings in the selling price of merchandise they resell is a larger share of the balance, without the core of this trade being as profitable to them as a lesser trade engaged in by other nations selling their own products abroad.

The commerce in products of manual labor is deceptive as well, because people include in the end result the price of raw materials, which should be distinguished from the cost of the manufacturing work.

XII. *It is by the internal and external commerce, and especially the state of the internal commerce, that one may judge the wealth of a nation.* For if it has high consumption of its foodstuffs at high prices, its wealth will be proportional to the abundance and the prices of the foodstuffs it consumes, because these same foodstuffs are real wealth by reason of their abundance and their expensiveness. Because of the opportunities that exist to sell them, they can be susceptible to any other employment in times of extraordinary need. It suffices to have the basis of them in real wealth.

XIII. *A nation should not envy the commerce of its neighbors when it gets the best yield possible from its soil, its men, and its shipping.* For it could not undertake any ill-intentioned initiatives against the commerce of its neighbors without disturbing its state and doing itself harm, especially in the reciprocal trade it has established with them.

Thus, commercial nations that are rivals or even enemies should be more concerned with maintaining or if possible expanding their own trade than with seeking to directly harm others' trade. They should even encourage it, because nations' reciprocal trade is mutually supported by the wealth of sellers and buyers.

XIV. *In reciprocal trade, the nations that sell the most necessary or useful merchandise have the advantage over those that sell luxury merchandise.* A nation whose real estate assures it a trade in its domestic foodstuffs, and therefore also an internal commerce in products of manual labor, is independent of other nations. It trades with other nations only to maintain, facilitate, and extend its external commerce. And to preserve its independence and its advantage in the reciprocal trade, it should as much as possible get only luxury merchandise from them, and should sell them merchandise that is necessary for life's needs.

By the real value of these different kinds of merchandise, they will think that this reciprocal trade is more favorable to them. But the advantage is always with the nation that sells the most useful and necessary merchandise.

For then its trade is based on the needs of others; it sells them only its surplus, and its purchases show only its opulence. The others have more interest in selling to it than it needs to buy. And it is easier for it to cut back on luxuries than for others to economize on necessities.

It must even be observed that States that dedicate themselves to luxury manufactures experience difficult vicissitudes. For when times are tough, the luxury trade languishes and the workers find themselves without bread and without employment.

If trade were free, France could produce an abundance of foodstuffs of first necessity that would suffice for a high level of consumption and a brisk external commerce, and that could support a large trade in manual-labor works within the realm.

But the condition of its population does not permit it to employ many men in luxury work. And to facilitate the external trade in domestically grown merchandise, it even has an interest in undertaking a reciprocal commerce abroad by the purchase of luxury merchandise.

Besides, it should not completely aspire to a general commerce. It should sacrifice some of the less important branches in favor of other parts that are more profitable to it, and that would increase and ensure the real-estate income of the realm.

Nonetheless, all commerce should be free, because it is in the merchants' interest to apply themselves to the most certain and profitable branches of external trade.

It is enough for the government: to attend to the increase in property income in the realm, to not obstruct human industry, and to leave citizens with the facility and choice of expenses.

To reinvigorate agriculture by the activity of commerce in the provinces where foodstuffs go unsold.

To abolish prohibitions and impediments detrimental to internal trade and to reciprocal external trade.

To abolish or moderate excessive river and transit tolls, which destroy the income of distant provinces, where foodstuffs can be traded only after long transport. Those who own these tolls will be sufficiently compensated by their part in the general increase in the propertied income of the realm.

It is no less necessary to extinguish the privileges usurped by provinces, cities, or communities for their particular advantage.

It is also important everywhere to facilitate the communication and transportation of merchandise by the repair of roads and the navigation of rivers.[2]

Again, it is essential not to subject the commerce of provincial foodstuffs to prohibitions and transitory or arbitrary permissions, which ruin the countryside on the captious pretext of assuring abundance in the cities. The cities survive on the expenditures of the proprietors who inhabit them. Thus, destroying real-estate income neither encourages the cities nor procures the good of the State.

The governance of the nation's income should not be abandoned to the discretion or authority of subordinate and particular administration.

One must not limit the export of *cereals* to particular provinces,[3] because they run out before other provinces can resupply them. The inhabitants can be exposed for several months to a scarcity that is rightly attributed to the exportation.

But when the freedom to export is general, the gathering up of *cereals* is not perceptible, because the merchants get it from all parts of the realm, and especially from provinces where the price of *cereals* is low.

2. The rural roads or roads that connect to the great highways, cities, and markets are missing or in bad shape almost everywhere in the provinces, which is a big obstacle to commercial activity. Nonetheless, it seems possible to remedy this within a few years. The proprietors have too great an interest in the sale of commodities produced by their estates not to want to contribute to the expense of these road repairs. Thus, you could levy a small tax on them of one sou per pound on their farmers' taille—the farmers and peasants would be exempt from this. Which roads to repair would be decided by Messrs. the intendants in each district after consulting the inhabitants, who would afterward have the repairs carried out by contractors. The most impassible places would be repaired first, and the roads would be perfected successively; the farmers and peasants would then be charged with maintaining them. Similar arrangements could be made with the provinces for rivers that can be made navigable. There are provinces that have so clearly recognized the utility of these projects that they have themselves asked to be authorized to make expenses for them. But State needs have sometimes taken away the funds earmarked for them. These bad outcomes have stifled dispositions so beneficial to the well-being of the State.

3. A reference to the actual practice in France at that time.—HC

Then, there are no more provinces where foodstuffs remain unsold.

Commerce and agriculture progress together. Export never removes more than a surplus that would not exist without it, and that always maintains abundance and increases incomes within the realm.

This increase in income augments population and consumption, because expenses increase while procuring profits that attract men.

By this progress, a realm may arrive in short order at a high degree of power and prosperity. By quite simple means, a sovereign may thus make much more profitable conquests in his own State than those he would launch against his neighbors. The progress is rapid; under Henry IV, the kingdom, exhausted and burdened with debt, soon became a country of abundance and wealth. *See* TAX.

Observations on the necessity of wealth for the cultivation of cereals. It must never be forgotten that this state of prosperity to which we can aspire is much less the fruit of the farmer's work than the result of the wealth he is able to employ in the cultivation of the land. It is the manure that procures rich harvest; it is the livestock that produce the manure; it is the money that provides the livestock and that furnishes the men to manage them. It has been seen in the detailed analysis above that the expenses for thirty million acres of land treated by small-scale farming are only 285 million, while the expenses for 30 million well-treated acres in large-scale farming would be 710 million. But in the first case, the yield is only 390 million, while in the second it would be 1,378,000,000. Greater expenses would yield still greater profits. For their part, the extra men and expenses demanded by good farming for the purchase and management of livestock get a yield that is scarcely less substantial than that of the harvests.

Notwithstanding, bad farming demands a lot of work; but since the cultivator is unable to make the necessary expenses, his labors are unfruitful. He succumbs, and the imbecile bourgeois attribute his failure to laziness. They doubtless believe it is enough to plow, to torment the earth in order to force it to bear good harvests. People applaud when someone says to a poor man who is not employed, *go plow the earth.* It is the horses and the oxen, not the men, that must plow the earth. It is the flocks that must fertilize it; without this aid, the earth does little to reward the cultivators' labors. Do they not know, moreover, that the earth does not make the investments, that on the contrary it makes one wait a long time for the harvest? What then could be the fate of that poor man who is told, *go plow the earth?* Can he cultivate on his own behalf? Will he find work with the farmers if they are poor? The latter, powerless to pay the expenses of good farming and in no position to pay the wages of domestics and workers, cannot employ the peasants. The earth, without fertilizer and almost uncultivated, can only leave both groups to languish in poverty.

It must again be observed that all the inhabitants of the realm have to profit from the advantages of good farming, in order for it to support itself and yield much in revenues for the sovereign. By increasing the proprietors' income and the farmers' profits, it procures gains for all the other estates, and maintains a level of consumption and expense that support it in turn. But if the sovereign's taxes are fixed on the cultivator himself, if they take away his profits, agriculture withers and the proprietors' income diminishes. This results in an unavoidable saving that influences the wage-earners, the merchants, the workers, the domestics. The general system of expenses, works, profits, and consumption is disturbed; the State is weakened; the imposition of taxes becomes more and more destructive. A realm can thus be flourishing and imposing only because of production that is being renewed or regenerated constantly from the wealth itself of a large and active people whose human industry is supported and animated by the government.

It has been imagined that the disorder that government can cause in the fortunes of private individuals is a matter of indifference to the State, because, it is said, if some become rich at the expense of others, the wealth exists equally throughout the realm. This idea is false and absurd, for a State's wealth is not maintained by itself. It is preserved and increased only insofar as it is renewed by being employed, and managed with intelligence. If the cultivator is ruined by the royal budget official, then the incomes in the realm are wiped out, and trade and industry languish. The worker lacks work; the sovereign, the proprietors, the clergy are deprived of revenue; expenses and profits are abolished. Wealth enclosed in the coffers of the budget official is unfruitful—or if it is lent out at interest, it overburdens the State. The government must therefore be very mindful about preserving the wealth necessary to all the productive professions for the production and increase of the wealth of the realm.

Observations on the population supported by the cultivation of cereals. Finally, it must be recognized that the produce of the earth is not wealth in itself; it is wealth only insofar as it is necessary for men, and insofar as it is tradable. It is thus wealth only in proportion to its consumption and to the number of men who need it. Each man who lives in society does not apply his work to all his needs, but by the sale of what his work produces, he procures what he is lacking. Thus, everything becomes tradable; everything becomes wealth by a mutual traffic among men.[4] If the number of men falls by a third in a State, its wealth must fall by two-thirds, because each man's expenditures and product form a double wealth in the society. There were around 24 million men in the kingdom a hundred years ago. After virtually constant wars for forty years, and after the Revocation of the Edict of Nantes,[5] the census of 1700 still found nineteen million, five hundred thousand. But the ruinous war of the succession to the crown of Spain,[6] the realm's fall in incomes caused by the obstruction of commerce and by arbitrary tax impositions, the wretched poverty of the countryside, the desertion abroad, the throng of domestics that poverty and the military oblige to retreat into the large cities where debauchery replaces marriage for them; the disorders of luxury (which are compensated, unfortunately, by economizing on propagation)—all these causes give only too much sanction to the opinion of those who today would reduce the number of men in the realm to sixteen million. And there are a great number in the countryside who are reduced to procuring their food by the cultivation of buckwheat or other low-cost *cereals;* thus, they are of as little use to the State by their work as by their consumption. The peasant is useful in the countryside only to the extent that he produces and earns by his labor, and to the extent that his consumption, in good food and good clothing, contributes to support the price of foodstuffs and the income from property, and to increase the number of manufacturers and artisans and make them

4. "Every man thus lives by exchanging, or becomes in some measure a merchant, and the society itself grows to be what is properly a commercial society." Adam Smith, *Wealth of Nations,* I.iv.1.—HC

5. This 1685 act denied French Protestants (Huguenots) the limited tolerance afforded them in the original edict of 1598.—HC

6. From 1701 to 1714.—HC

profitable—all of whom can pay the king levies in proportion to production and profits.

Thus, it should be understood that whether poverty increases or the kingdom loses still a few more million men, present wealth would diminish excessively, and other nations would draw a double advantage from this disaster. But if the population were reduced to half of what it should be—that is, half of what it was a hundred years ago—the realm would be devastated. Only a few cities or a few commercial provinces would be inhabited; the rest of the realm would be uncultivated. Property would no longer yield income; there would be an overabundance of lands everywhere, and they would be abandoned to whoever would like to use them—without paying or knowing the proprietors.

I repeat, land is wealth only because its produce is necessary to satisfy men's needs, and because it is these needs themselves that establish wealth. Thus, the more men there are in a realm whose territory is extensive and fertile, the more wealth there is. Cultivation animated by men's needs is the most fecund source of this wealth, and the main support of population. It furnishes the materials necessary for our needs, and procures revenues for the sovereign and income for the proprietors. Population increases much more by income and expenses than by the nation's propagation itself.

Observations on cereal prices. Income multiplies expenses, and expenses attract men seeking profit. Foreigners quit their Country to come and participate in the ease of an opulent nation, and their confluence again increases its wealth, by supporting through consumption the high price of the products of agriculture, and by stimulating through this high price the abundance of these products. For not only does the high price encourage the progress of agriculture, but the wealth it procures consists in the high price itself. The value of a setier[7] of wheat considered as wealth consists only in its price. Thus, the more abundant and expensive are wheat, wine, wool, and livestock, the more wealth there is in the State. *Abundance along with unsold goods is not wealth. High prices along with penury is wretched poverty. Abundance with high prices is opulence.* I mean permanent high prices and abundance.

7. A setier was a liquid or dry measure, varying by locale and by time; in Paris, it equaled twelve bushels (roughly 150 liters).—HC

For transitory high prices would not procure a general distribution of wealth to the whole nation, nor would they increase the proprietors' income or the king's revenues. They would only be advantageous to a few private individuals who would then have foodstuffs to sell at a high price.

Foodstuffs can therefore be wealth for any nation only because of abundance and high prices maintained constantly by good farming, high consumption, and external trade. One should even recognize that relative to a whole nation, abundance and high prices that prevail abroad are great wealth for that nation, especially if that wealth consists in agricultural production. For it is wealth in property limited in each realm to the territory that can produce it. Thus, by its abundance and its high price, it is always to the advantage of the nation that has the most and that sells it to others. For the more a realm can obtain wealth in money, the more powerful it is and the more the capacities of individuals are extended—because money is the sole wealth that can lend itself to all uses and that can determine the relative strength of each nation.

Nations are poor wherever the country's produce that is most necessary to life is at a low price. This produce is the most precious and tradable good; it can go unsold only by lack of population and external trade. In these cases, the source of monetary wealth is lost in countries deprived of the advantages of commerce, where men, severely reduced to the goods necessary for survival, cannot procure those necessary to satisfy the other needs of life and the security of their Country. That is the situation of our provinces where foodstuffs are undervalued—those lands of abundance and poverty, where forced labor and extreme saving are not even resources for procuring money.

When foodstuffs are expensive, and when income and profits increase proportionally, one can make economizing arrangements to diversify expenses, pay debts, make acquisitions, get children settled, etc. The ease resulting from the high price of foodstuffs consists in the possibility of these arrangements. This is why the cities and provinces of a realm in which foodstuffs are expensive are more populous than those where all the foodstuffs are at too low a price, because this low price snuffs out income, cuts expenses, destroys commerce, and abolishes the gains from all other occupations, the works and wages of artisans and day laborers. Moreover, it wipes out the king's revenues, because the greater part of the commerce for consumption occurs through exchange of foodstuffs, and does not contribute to the circulation of money. It does not bring the king excise levies on the consumption of subsistence goods from these provinces, and very little on property income.

When trade is free, the high price of foodstuffs inevitably has its limits fixed by the very prices of the foodstuffs of other nations that are extending their trade everywhere. It is not the same with the high or low cost of foodstuffs caused by the lack of freedom of trade. These variations succeed each other in turn and irregularly. Each of them is highly disadvantageous, and they both almost always depend on a defect in the government.

The usual high price of wheat that procures so much revenue for the State is not harmful to the common people. A man consumes three setiers of wheat. If, because of the high price, he bought each setier at four pounds more, this price would increase his expenses by at most one shilling per day. His wage would also increase proportionally, and this increase would be a small matter for those who paid it, in comparison with the wealth that would result from the high price of wheat. Thus, the advantages of the high price of wheat are not destroyed by the increase in the workers' wage. For this increase is far from approaching that of the farmers' profit, the proprietors' income, the yield on the tithe, or the king's revenues. It is also easy to perceive that these benefits would not have increased by a twentieth, perhaps even by a fortieth, the price of the manual labor in manufacturing, which has led to the imprudent decision to ban the export of wheat, and which has caused an immense loss to the State. It is, moreover, a great drawback to accustom the same common people to buy wheat at too low a price; they become less industrious, they live on cheap bread and become lazy and arrogant. The independent farmers find workers and domestics with difficulty; thus, they are poorly served in abundant years. It is important for the lesser people to earn more and to be pressed by need to earn. In the last century, when wheat sold for much more, the people got used to it, they earned in proportion, and they were bound to be more industrious and more comfortable.

Thus, by the term *high cost* here, we do not mean a price that could ever be excessive, but only a common price between us and the foreigner. For assuming freedom of external trade, the price will always be determined by the competition in neighboring nations' trade in foodstuffs.

Those who do not envision the full scope of the distribution in a State's wealth may object that high prices are beneficial only to the sellers, and that they impoverish those who buy; that it therefore decreases the latter's wealth as much as it increases the former's. According to these ideas, then, high prices can under no circumstances be an increase of wealth in the State.

But don't the high prices and abundance of agricultural products increase the cultivators' profits, the king's revenue, the income of the proprietors and the benefice-holders who enjoy the tithe? Doesn't this wealth itself increase expenses and profits? Don't the day laborer, the artisan, the manufacturer, etc., have their time and their works paid for in proportion to the cost of their subsistence? The more income there is in a State, the more it happens that commerce, manufactures, the arts, the crafts, and other occupations become necessary and lucrative.

But this prosperity can exist only because of the high price of our foodstuffs. For when the government halts the turnover in landed produce, and when it lowers its price, it opposes abundance and reduces the nation's wealth in proportion to its lowering the price of foodstuffs, which are converted into money.

This condition of high prices and abundance has existed in the realm as long as our *cereals* have been an item of trade, cultivation of the land has been protected, and population has been large. But the obstruction of the grain trade, the formulation and imposition of excise levies, the poor employment of men and wealth in luxury manufactures, the constant wars, and other causes of depopulation and indigence have destroyed these advantages. And the State annually loses more than three-quarters of the yield it drew a century ago from the cultivation of *cereals,* without including the other losses that inevitably result from this enormous degradation of agriculture and of the population. *Article by M. QUESNAY, the son.*

In order not to make this article too long, we refer to NIELLE [Blight] for that which concerns grain diseases.

Volume 8
(1765)

Habeas Corpus

Habeas Corpus (*England's jurisprudence*), a law common to all English subjects, which gives a prisoner the capacity to be released on bail.

To understand this law well, one must know that when an Englishman is arrested, at least if it is not for a crime worthy of death, he sends a copy of the *mittimus* to the chancellor (or to any judge of the exchequer), who is obliged, without removal, to grant him an act called *habeas corpus*. On reading this act, the jailer or concierge must bring the prisoner and give an account of the reasons for his detention at the tribunal where the act is sent. Then the judge pronounces whether the prisoner is in the kind of situation where paying bail is an option or not. If he is not in that situation, he is sent back to prison; if it is a case where he has that right, he is sent away on bail.

This is one of the finest privileges that a free nation can enjoy. For as a result of this act, prisoners of state have the right to choose the tribunal where they want to be judged, and to be released on bail if no one brings forward the cause of their detention, or if their judgment is postponed.

This law, necessary to prevent arbitrary imprisonments that a king would employ to make himself absolute, could have deplorable consequences in extraordinary cases—for example in a conspiracy, where the precise observation of formalities would encourage those with bad intentions, and would assure suspect persons of the facility to execute their bad designs. It seems therefore that in cases of this nature, the public good demands that the law be suspended for a certain time. And in fact, since its establishment, it has at times been suspended in England.

This article can be found at 8:5–6 in the original edition of the *Encyclopédie*.

It was suspended for a year in 1722 because there were rumors of a conspiracy formed against King George I and against the state.[1] The lords who then spoke out in the high chamber for this suspension said that when an act became contrary to the public good because of rare and unforeseen circumstances, it was inevitably necessary to set it aside for a certain time; that in the Roman republic, composed of the royal power, the nobles' power, and that of the people—represented by the senate and the tribunes—the consuls had only a quite limited power, but at the first rumor of conspiracy, those magistrates were immediately vested with supreme authority, to ensure the preservation of the republic. However, other lords attacked the suspension in general, and even more its length, which they opposed with strong reasons. They maintained that such a bill granted the king of England power as great as that of a Roman dictator; that under such a bill, no one could be arrested without being told the name of the accuser who cast suspicion on him, in order to make clear that the conspiracy was not serving as a cover for other causes of discontent; that the act of *habeas corpus* has never been suspended for more than six months; that by suspending it for a year, the bill would offer a pernicious example, authorizing the sovereign to demand its prorogation for a second year or more—by means of which, the act that did more than any other to assure the nation's liberty would be imperceptibly destroyed.

"It is true," says the author of *The Spirit of the Laws* on this subject,[2] "that if the legislative power leaves to the executive the right to imprison citizens who might make bail for their conduct, there is no more liberty. But if they are arrested only to respond without delay to an accusation that the law has rendered capital, then they are truly free, since they are subject only to the power of the law. Now if the legislative power thinks itself in danger because of some secret conspiracy against the state or some correspondence with external enemies, it could, for a brief and limited time, permit the executive power to arrest suspected citizens, who would lose their liberty for a time only to preserve it forever." (*D.J.*)

1. The so-called Atterbury plot, after the Tory bishop Francis Atterbury, was a Jacobite conspiracy uncovered in April 1722 which aimed to overthrow the government of George I and return the Stuart dynasty to power. Atterbury was denied bail before his trial for treason.

2. The passage, whose syntax and diction have been somewhat altered by Jaucourt, can be found in Montesquieu, *The Spirit of the Laws,* 11.6, 159.

Man
(*Homme*)

This brief essay by Diderot is written under the influence of early Physiocratic doctrine, which highlighted a preference for agriculture over the luxury trades. For the emphasis on population, see Quesnay's essay CEREALS *and Diderot's essay* POLITICAL ARITHMETIC, *both in this volume.*

*MAN (*Politics*). There are only two true sources of wealth: man and the land. Man is worth nothing without the land, and land yields nothing without man.

The true worth of man lies in numbers; the more numerous a society is, the more powerful it will be in times of peace and the more formidable in times of war. This is why a sovereign should give serious attention to increasing the number of his subjects. The greater their number, the more merchants, workers, and soldiers he will have.

Should there be one single man among those over whom he rules who is afraid to have children, or who leaves life without regret, the state would be in a deplorable situation.

The translation for "Man" is from Nelly S. Hoyt and Thomas Cassirer, *The Encyclopedia: Selections [by] Diderot, d'Alembert and a Society of Men of Letters* (Indianapolis: Bobbs-Merrill, 1965), 245–46, and is reproduced on *The Encyclopedia of Diderot & d'Alembert Collaborative Translation Project* (Ann Arbor: Michigan Publishing, University of Michigan Library, 2003): http://hdl.handle.net/2027/spo.did2222.0000.160 (accessed June 3, 2015).

This article can be found at 8:278 in the original edition of the *Encyclopédie*.

It is not sufficient, however, for a state to have many men; they must be industrious and healthy.

Men will be healthy if their standards of morality are high and if they can easily become and remain affluent.

Men will be industrious if they are free.

The lack of commercial freedom can result, in a given province, in affluence that can become an evil as terrible as poverty. In such a case the nation is being subjected to the worst possible government. See the articles GOVERNMENT, LAWS, TAXES, POPULATION, LIBERTY, etc. [Gouvernement, Lois, Impôts, Population, Liberté].

Our children will be our men; a country, therefore, must take care of its children. This means that special attention must be given to fathers, mothers, and nurses.

The five thousand children who are abandoned each year in Paris could be a seedbed for soldiers, sailors, and tillers of the soil.

The number of those employed in the luxury trades and in domestic service should be reduced. Under certain conditions the luxury trades do not yield sufficient profit for the men whom they employ; but domestic employment always results in a loss. A tax should be levied on domestic servants in order to lighten the tax burden of the rural population.

It is the life of the rural laborers that is the most fatiguing. If they are also the least well fed, they will either leave their occupation or they will perish. Only ignorance or cruelty can prompt anyone to say that, if they were comfortably off, they would leave their occupation.

It is the hope for a pleasant existence that prompts men to choose a certain way of life. It is the enjoyment of a pleasant mode of life that calls them to it or keeps them in it.

To employ men is worthwhile when the profit exceeds the expense of the wages. The wealth of a nation is the sum total of this profit.

The bigger and the better distributed the net product is, the better the government. An equally distributed net profit may be better than a greater profit unequally distributed. Such a distribution would divide a people in two classes, of which one would have a surfeit of riches, while the other was dying of privations.

As long as land is allowed to remain untilled while men are employed in manufactures, the state sustains a loss.

We could add a great many more items to these clear and simple principles. A sovereign could find them himself if he had the courage and good will needed to put them into practice.

Honor
(*Honneur*)

Even before Montesquieu stirred controversy by claiming in The Spirit of the Laws *(3.5–7) that honor and not virtue was the motive force of monarchy, honor was sometimes seen as a political and not merely a social or individual phenomenon. In this unsigned article, Saint-Lambert, whose authorship has been determined only by recent scholarship, treats all of these dimensions together.*

HONOR (*Morals*). It's the esteem we have for ourselves as well as our opinion[1] about the right we have to others' esteem because we have not strayed from the principles of virtue and because we feel ourselves strong enough to follow those principles. That's the thinking man's *honor*, and the reason he carefully fulfills the duties of man and citizen is to preserve it.

The feeling [*sentiment*] of self-esteem is the most delicious of all. But the most virtuous man is often crushed under the weight of his imperfections, and he seeks in the looks and countenance of men the expression of an esteem that would reconcile him with himself.

Whence two kinds of *honor:* the honor inside us that is based on what we are, and the honor in others based on what they think of us.

In the man of the people—and by *people* I mean all social conditions—I single out only the man who examines the scope of his duties in order to fulfill them, and their nature in order to impose only the real ones upon

This article can be found at 8:288–90 in the original edition of the *Encyclopédie*.

1. *Sentiment,* so "feeling" is another possible translation.

himself. In the man of the people, *honor* is the esteem he has for himself, and his right to the public's esteem as a result of his exactitude in observing certain laws established by prejudice and custom.

Some of these laws are in harmony with reason and nature; others are in conflict. Even the most just are often respected only because they are established.

Among even the most enlightened peoples, the bulk of enlightenment is never widespread. The people possess only received and unexamined opinions, foreign to reason. These opinions fill up their memories and direct their mores; they obstruct, repress, reinforce, corrupt, and perfect the instinct of nature.

Among even the most polished nations, *honor* can be attached sometimes to respectable qualities and actions, often to pernicious practices, sometimes to extravagant customs, sometimes to vice.

Even today in certain parts of Europe, the most cowardly and odious acts of vengeance are honored. And almost everywhere—in spite of religion, reason, and virtue—revenge is honored.

In a polished nation full of wit and strength, laziness and gravity are held in *honor*.

In most of Europe, a mistaken application of shame, attached to what is called "never failing,"[2] forces whoever has been unjust for a moment to be unjust his entire life.

If there are governments where caprice decides independent of the law, where the arbitrary will of the prince or his ministers distributes rewards and punishments without consulting order and justice, the soul of the people, numbed by fear and beaten down by authority, rises to no noble sentiments. In that condition, man esteems neither himself nor his fellows. He fears punishment more than shame, for what shame do slaves have to fear if they consent to be slaves? But these harsh and unjust governments, cruel and offensive to humanity, either do not exist or exist only as temporary abuses.[3] We must never consider men in this humiliating condition.

2. *Se démentir,* as in "never failing in one's loyalty" or "in one's duty."

3. The apparent object of criticism is Montesquieu, for whom "despotism" is one of the three political archetypes in *The Spirit of the Laws.*

A genius of the first order has claimed that *honor* is the spring of monarchies and virtue that of republics. Is it permissible to see some errors in the works of that great man—who possessed both *honor* and virtue![4]

He does not define *honor,* and in reading him, one cannot attach a precise idea to this word.[5] He defines virtue as "the love of the laws and of Country."[6]

All men from top to bottom love their Country—that is, they love it in their family, in their possessions, and in their fellow citizens from whom they expect aid and comfort. When men are content with the government under which they live, whatever its type, they love the laws. They love the princes and the magistrates who protect and defend them. The manner by which the laws are established, executed, or avenged, and the form of government are what one calls the *political order*. I think President Montesquieu would have expressed himself with more precision if he had defined virtue as "love of the political order and of Country."

All men possess a love of order.

They love order in the works of nature. They love the proportion and symmetry in that tree whose leaves are spread out in a circle over its stalk; in the rainbow of colors distributed symmetrically over the insect, the flower, or the shell; in the assemblage of different parts that compose an animal's shape. They love order in works of art. The proportion and symmetry in a poem, in a piece of music, in a building, or in a garden give the mind the capacity to assemble quickly and easily a multitude of objects; to see things whole in a glance; to move back and forth from one part to another without getting lost; to retrace its steps at will; to turn its attention where it wants; and to be sure that the object that occupies it will not cause it to lose the object that just occupied it.

Political order, aside from the secret pleasure of collecting and keeping in the mind a lot of knowledge and ideas, also gives us the pleasure of marveling at them. It astonishes us and gives us a grand idea of our nature. We

4. The reference is to Montesquieu, *Laws,* 3.6.

5. Montesquieu writes, "Honor, that is, the prejudice of each person and each social condition. . . ." *Laws,* 3.6. Whether Saint-Lambert would consider this a "definition" is, of course, a separate question.

6. See Montesquieu, *Laws,* 4.5.

find it difficult, useful, and beautiful. We see with surprise how a multitude of effects arise from a small number of causes. We admire the harmony in the different parts of government. We are as capable in a monarchy as in a republic of loving to fanatical excess this useful, simple, and grand order which fixes our ideas, elevates our soul, enlightens us, protects us, and decides our fate. When content with their government, the farmer (whether French or Roman), the patrician, or the nobleman[7]—all of them love order and Country. In the Persian monarchy, one didn't approach the altars of the gods without invoking them for their Country. It was not allowed for the citizen to pray only for himself. The Incan monarchy was merely one immense family, whose monarch was the father.[8] The days when the citizen cultivated his field were workdays. The days when he cultivated the field of the State and of the poor were holidays.

But under monarchy as under republic, this love of Country, this virtue, is the mainspring only in some situations and some circumstances. *Honor* is everywhere a more constantly active motive. The civic and mural crowns,[9] giving victors the names of the country of conquest, the triumphs—all these things excited Roman souls to great deeds more than did love of Country. Let it not be said that I am here confusing *honor* and glory. I know the distinction, but I believe that wherever one loves glory, there is *honor*. With virtue, *honor* supports the consular fasces[10] and the royal scepter. *Honor* or virtue in either a republic or a monarchy is the mainspring—depending on the nature of the laws and the power, scope, dangers, or flourishing of the state.

In great empires, one is guided more by *honor*, by the desire and expectation of esteem. In small states, it is more the love of political order and of Country. In these latter, a more perfect order prevails. In small states, one loves one's Country because the ties of attachment to her are scarcely more than those of nature. Citizens are united among themselves by blood and

7. *Gentilhomme,* in this context "nobleman." Saint-Lambert's point here is to contrast Roman and French social elites.

8. Inca, the Peruvian empire before Pizarro's conquest in the 1530s. For the Persian custom cited, see Herodotus, *Histories,* II. 132.

9. Crowns given to Romans who were first to scale the walls in defense of a besieged city.

10. Symbol of Roman republican authority.

by mutual good offices. The state is but a family joined by all the feelings of the heart, which are always stronger in proportion as they are less extensive. Large fortunes are impossible, and because cupidity is less aroused there, it cannot hide itself in the darkness. Mores are more pure and the social virtues are political virtues.

Notice that early Rome and the small Greek republics, where enthusiasm for Country reigned, were often in danger; the slightest war threatened their constitution and their liberty. Being in great peril, the citizens naturally made great efforts. In military success, they hoped for the preservation of all that was most dear to them. Rome showed less extreme love of Country in the war against Pyrrhus than in the war against Porsena, less in the war against Mithridates than in the war against Pyrrhus.[11]

In a large state, whether republic or monarchy, wars are rarely dangerous for the constitution of the state or the fortunes of the citizenry. The people seldom have anything to fear except some frontier fortifications. The citizen has nothing to hope for from the success of the nation. He is rarely in circumstances where he can feel and manifest enthusiasm for his Country. These large states would have to be threatened by a calamity entailing that of each citizen—then patriotism will awaken. When King William had retaken Namur, the poll tax was established in France, and the citizens, delighted to see a new resource for the state, received this tax edict with cries of joy.[12] At the gates of Rome, Hannibal caused no more alarm or suffering than France feels in our time during the illness of its king.[13] If the loss of the famous battle of Hochstädt led the French to compose songs to express their discontent at the ministry, the people of Rome more

11. Lars Porsena was the Etruscan ruler who assisted Tarquin after the latter was overthrown and replaced by a republic in 509 B.C. Saint-Lambert's point is that Porsena posed a more mortal threat to the existence of Rome herself than either Pyrrhus of Epirus (late fourth, early third century B.C.) or Mithridates the Great (134–63 B.C.), despite the increasing scale of the latters' victories against Rome.

12. During the War of the League of Augsburg, King William of England retook Namur in 1695, the year the capitation was established in France.

13. Hannibal, Carthaginian commander in the Second Punic War (218–203 B.C.), who won so many important victories that "Hannibal at the gates" became a saying despite his never having reached Rome. The other reference is probably to Louis XV's illness in Metz in 1744 during the War of the Austrian Succession, when public prayers were said for his recovery.

than once enjoyed humiliating their magistrates after a defeat of the Roman armies.[14]

But why is this *honor*—almost always a leading motive under all governments—sometimes so bizarre? Why is it rated among those customs that are either puerile or pernicious? Why does it sometimes impose duties condemned by nature, virtue, and refined reason? And why is it that in certain times, it is especially attributed to certain qualities and actions, while in other times to actions and qualities of the opposite kind?

We must recall David Hume's great principle of utility. It is always utility that decides concerning our esteem.[15] The man who may be useful to us is the man that we honor, and among all peoples, the man without *honor* is the one whose character is thought to make him unable to serve society.

But certain qualities and talents are more or less useful in different times—honored at first, they are less so afterward. To find the causes of this difference, we must take society at its birth, look at *honor* in its origins, and follow the progress of society and the changes in *honor*.

In the forests where nature placed him, man is born to combat man and nature. Too weak against his fellows and against tigers, he joins with the former to combat the latter. At first, bodily strength is the principal source of merit. Debility is all the more despised, in that, before the invention of those arms with which a weak man can engage in combat without disadvantage, bodily strength was the foundation of valor. Even if violence is unjust, it does not take away from *honor*. The mildest of occupations is combat. Courage is the only virtue, and victory is the only noble deed. After courage, the most honored qualities are love of truth, candor, and good faith—qualities that presuppose it. After weakness, nothing is more shameful than lying. If common ownership of women is not established, conjugal fidelity will be women's *honor*, because they must without assistance prepare the warriors' meals, keep and defend the house, and raise

14. Battle of Hochstädt (August 1704), also known as the Battle of Blenheim, a key victory by the Austro-English allies under the Duke of Marlborough against Louis XIV during the War of the Spanish Succession.

15. See Hume, *An Enquiry Concerning the Principles of Morals,* sec. V, pt. I, "Why Utility Pleases." The work had recently been translated by Jean-Baptiste Robinet as *Essais de Morale ou Recherches sur les principes de la morale* (Amsterdam: Schneider, 1760).

the children. This is because, given the equality of conditions, marriage is decided by personal preference. Choice and commitments are free, leaving no excuse for someone to break them. This gross people is necessarily superstitious, and the superstition will determine the species of its *honor*, in the conviction that the gods give victory to the good cause. Differences will be decided by conflict, and citizen will spill the blood of citizen out of *honor*. People believe there are fairies that have relationships with the gods, and the respect felt for them is extended to their entire sex. A woman is believed to be incapable of lacking fidelity to a worthy man, and the *honor* of the husband depends on the chastity of his wife.

And yet, men in this condition are constantly feeling new needs. Some among them invent arts or machines. The entire society enjoys the use of these things. The inventor is honored, and the mind's merit begins to be respected. As society expands and becomes more polished, a multitude of connections arise between an individual and the many. Rivalries are more frequent, passions collide; countless laws are needed. These laws are harsh and they are powerful. And men, forced to engage in combat all the time, are also forced to change weapons. Deceit and dissimulation are common. There is less horror at falsity, and prudence is honored. A thousand qualities of the soul are revealed; they acquire names and pass into usage. They place men into classes that are more carefully distinguished from each other than nations were. These classes of citizens have the *honor* attached to these different ideas.

Superior enlightenment acquires the principal esteem. Strength of soul is more respected than strength of body. The attentive legislator excites the most necessary talents; it is then that he distributes what are called *honors*. These are the distinctive mark by which he announces to the nation that a certain citizen is a man of merit and of *honor*. There are *honors* for all classes. The ribbon of Saint Michael is given to the skilled merchant and the industrious artisan;[16] why not use it to decorate the intelligent, hardworking, frugal farmer who fructifies the earth?

16. Founded in 1469 as a chivalric order, the Ordre de Saint-Michel went through several changes of purpose before being abolished by the Constituent Assembly in the summer of 1791; it was resuscitated on different terms by the restored Bourbon monarchy in 1816.

After satisfying the functions of their status, many men in a society perfected in this way enjoy a repose that would be poisoned by boredom without the aid of the agreeable arts. In such an uncorrupted society, these arts support the love of virtue, the sensibility of the soul, and the taste for order and beauty. They dissipate boredom and enrich the mind. And their output, having become one of the principal needs of the leading classes of citizens, is honored even by those who cannot enjoy them.

In this extended society, pure mores seem less useful to the mass of the state than activity and great talent. These lead to *honors* and enjoy general esteem, and often it is difficult to tell whether those who possess these *honors* have virtue. Soon, one no longer blushes at being foolish or poor.

Society is corrupted day by day. At first, industry and even cupidity have been stimulated, because society needs its opulent citizens. But opulence leads to jobs, and venality is then introduced. Wealth is overly honored, jobs and wealth are hereditary, and birth is *honored*.

If the good fortune of being pleasing to princes and ministers leads to jobs and *honors* and wealth, then the art of pleasing is honored.

Soon immense and rapid fortunes arise. There are *honors* without work, dignities and jobs without functions. The arts of luxury multiply; fantasy attaches a price to that which has none. The taste for beauty is worn out in idle men who want only enjoyment. These men demand what's unique, the arts are degraded, frivolity spreads, and the agreeable is honored more than the beautiful, the useful, or the decent.

At that point, *honors* and even glory are separated from true *honor*, which no longer exists except in a small number of men who have the strength to be enlightened and the courage to be poor. The *honor* of prejudice is extinguished. And the *honor* that had sustained the vigor of the nation is no longer more prevalent in the second and lowest classes than true *honor* is in the first.

But in a monarchy—of all governments, the one that most easily reforms its abuses and its mores without changing its nature—the legislator sees the evil, learns of the remedy, and makes that remedy a practice.

By choice, let him in all areas decorate talents combined with virtue. And without virtue, let genius itself be neither advanced nor honored, however useful it may be. For nothing is as useful to a state as true *honor*.

Let vice alone be branded and let no class of citizens be degraded, so that every man in any class may think well of himself, do good, and be content.

Let the prince attach the idea of *honor* and virtue to the love and observance of all the laws. Let the warrior who fails in his discipline be as dishonored as the one who flees before the enemy.

Let him learn not to change and not to multiply his laws. They must be respected, but they must not be terrifying. Let him be loved. In a country where *honor* is to reign, the legislator must be loved; he must not be feared.[17]

Honor must give each citizen a horror of evil and a love of his duty. Let him never be a slave attached to his state, but let him be condemned to shame if he can do no good.

Let the prince be persuaded that the virtues which establish societies when they are small and poor sustain societies when they are extensive and powerful. The Mandevilles and their infamous echoes will never persuade men that courage, fidelity to one's commitments, or respect for truth and justice are not necessary in large states.[18]

Let the prince be persuaded that these virtues and all others will accompany talent when the celebrity and glory of genius do not save people from the shame of bad morals. *Honor* is active, but the day when intrigue and credit obtain *honors* is the moment when it rests.

Peoples are rarely corrupted without being enlightened. But then it is easy to bring them back to order and to *honor*. Nothing is so difficult to govern poorly, or so easy to govern well, as a thinking people. Such a people has less of the prejudice and enthusiasm of each status, but it can preserve the lively feeling of *honor*.

Let industry be stimulated by love of wealth and some *honors*. But let the virtues and the political or military talents be stimulated only by *honors* or by glory.

17. See Machiavelli, *The Prince*, chap. 17, who had given a different answer to the question, "whether it is better to be loved or feared."

18. The reference is to Bernard Mandeville, whose *Fable of the Bees: or, Private Vices, Publick Benefits* (1714) was translated into French by Jean Bertrand in 1740 under the title *La Fable des abeilles, ou Les fripons devenus honnêtes gens.*

A prince who overturns abuses in one part of the administration shatters them in all others. There is scarcely an abuse that is not the effect of vice and that does not produce vice.

Finally, when the government has revitalized *honor*, it will direct it and purify it. It will take away from *honor* whatever it carried over from barbarous times. It will restore to *honor* whatever the reign of luxury and flabbiness had taken away from it. In each citizen, *honor* will soon be the consciousness of one's love of duty and of the principles of virtue, and the recognition that he gives himself and expects from others that he is fulfilling his duties and following moral principles.

Poorhouse
(*Hôpital*)

For other discussions of this old-regime social institution, see PUBLIC LAW, EULOGY FOR MONTESQUIEU, FOUNDATION, LAW, MASTERSHIPS, POPULATION, *and* FIVE PERCENT TAX, *in this volume.*

*POORHOUSE (*Grammar, Morals, and Politics*). In the past, this word signified only *hostelry; hospitals* were public houses where foreign travelers received the aid of hospitality. There are no more of these houses; today there are places where the poor of every kind take refuge, and where they are well or poorly provided with the things necessary for the urgent needs of life.

In the early church, the bishop was charged with the immediate care of the poor of his diocese. When the ecclesiastics had assured income, a quarter of it was earmarked for the poor, and the houses of piety we call *hospitals* were founded. *See the articles* DIXMES [Tithe], CLERGÉ [Clergy].

Even in their temporal dimension, these houses were administered by priests and deacons, under the inspection of the bishop. *See* EVÊQUE [Bishop], DIACRE [Deacon].

They were later endowed by private individuals, and they had income; but in the relaxation of discipline, the clerics who possessed their administration converted them into benefices. It was to remedy this abuse that the Council of Vienne transferred the administration of the *hospitals* to lay people, who would swear an oath and answer to episcopal authority,

This article can be found at 8:293–94 in the original edition of the *Encyclopédie.*

and the Council of Trent confirmed this decree.[1] See ECONOME [Church Management].[2]

We will not go into historical detail on the different *hospitals;* instead we will substitute some general perspectives on the manner of making these establishments worthy of their purpose.

It is much more important to work to prevent poverty than to multiply sanctuaries for the poor.

A sure means of increasing the present revenues of the *poorhouses* would be to reduce the number of the poor.

Wherever moderate work suffices to provide for the needs of life, and wherever a little economizing in times of health prepares a resource for a prudent man in his age of infirmity, there will be few poor people.

In a well-governed state, there should not be poor people, except men who are born into indigence or who fall into it by accident.

I cannot count those young and vigorous lazybones as poor. Finding easier and more substantial aid in our misguided charity than in what they would procure by their own labor, they fill our streets, our churches, our highways, our towns, our cities, and our countryside. Those vermin can exist only in a state in which the value of men is unknown.[3]

To make the condition of the professional beggars and the true poor equal by mixing them up in the same houses is to forget that there are uncultivated lands to clear, colonies to populate, manufactures to support, and public works to continue.

If a society has refuges solely for the truly poor, it is consistent with religion, reason, humanity, and public health that they be the best possible.

It is not that the *poorhouses* should be fearsome to the unfortunate, but that the government should be fearsome to idlers.

Among the true poor, some are healthy and others sick.

1. The reference is to the ecumenical church councils of Vienne (1311–12), where the property of the Knights Templar was a major item of business, and of Trent (1545–63).

2. As Lough and Proust point out in their edition of this entry in *Denis Diderot: Œuvres complètes,* ed. Hans Dieckmann and Jean Varloot (Paris: Hermann, 1976), 7:426, n. 1, the article up to this point is taken directly from Ephraim Chambers, *Cyclopaedia,* 2 vols. (London: Knapton, 1728), 1:255, "Hospital."

3. On the value of men, see Diderot's article MAN, above.

There is no disadvantage in having the habitations of the healthy poor be in the cities; there are, it seems to me, several reasons requiring that the habitations of the sickly poor be distant from where healthy men live.

A *poorhouse* of sick people is a building in which architecture should subordinate its art to the views of the doctor. To mix the sick in the same place is to destroy the ones by the others.

Poorhouses are no doubt necessary everywhere; but shouldn't they all be connected by a general correspondence?

If there were a general reservoir for the alms, whence they were distributed through the whole extent of a realm, these salutary waters would be directed wherever the fire raged the most.

A sudden scarcity or an epidemic immediately multiply the poor of a province. Why not transfer the customary or momentary surplus of one *poorhouse* to another?

If one listens to those who cry out against this plan, one sees that it is for the most part horrible men who drink the blood of the poor and who find their private advantage in the general disorder.

The sovereign is the father of all his subjects. Why would he not be the general cashier of his poor subjects?

It is up to him to bring the narrow views of individual founders back to the general utility. *See the article* FOUNDATION.[4]

The fund for the poor is so sacred that it would blaspheme against royal authority to imagine that it could ever be diverted, even in times of extreme need for the state.

Is there anything more absurd than for one *poorhouse* to go into debt while another is becoming rich? What if they were all pillaged?

So many agencies have been set up, and even quite uselessly; how could this one, whose utility would be so great, be impossible? The greatest difficulty one would find, perhaps, is in discovering the revenues of all the *poorhouses*. They are, nonetheless, well known to those who administer them.

If a precise statement of the revenues of all the *workhouses* were published, with periodic lists of expenses and receipts, the relation between assistance and needs would be known. And one would have too bad an

4. The article, written by Turgot, is in the current volume.

opinion of men to believe that this would be without effect; commiseration is natural to us.

We will not enter here into a critical examination of the administration of our *poorhouses*. One may consult on this the various essays that M. de Chamousset has published under the title *Views of a citizen*.[5] It will be seen there that of the sick who enter the Hôtel-Dieu, a quarter perish, whereas only an eighth are lost at the Charity, a ninth and even a fourteenth in other *poorhouses*. Where does the frightful difference come from? *See the articles* Hôtel Dieu and Charité.

5. Claude-Humbert Piarron de Chamousset (1717–73), one of the leading humanitarian reformers whose *Vues d'un citoyen* appeared in 1757. His *Œuvres complettes de M. de Chamousset, contenant ses projets d'humanité, de bienfaisance et de patriotisme: précédés de son éloge* [Complete works by M. de Chamousset, containing his plans for humanity, beneficence and patriotism: preceded by a eulogy for him], ed. abbé Cotton Des-Houssayes, appeared in Paris in two volumes, in 1783.

Tax
(*Impôt*)

This article by Jaucourt appears under both the Political law *and* Finances *categories. It will be noted that Jaucourt did not subscribe to the Physiocratic proposal of taxing only landed property, but instead combined the political analysis of Montesquieu with the commercial and financial expertise of Véron de Forbonnais, a protégé of Vincent de Gournay and himself a contributor to the* Encyclopédie. *See Forbonnais's articles* COMPETITION *and* TRADING COMPANY, *above.*

TAX (*Political law and Finances*), contribution that individuals are expected to make to the state for the preservation of their lives and properties.

This contribution is necessary for the upkeep of the government and the sovereign. For it is only by levies that it can procure the tranquility of the citizens, and during that time they cannot refuse reasonable payment without betraying their own interests.

But how should *taxes* be collected? Should they fall on persons, on land, on consumption, on merchandise, or on something else? Each of these questions, and those related to them in any detailed discussion, would require a profound treatise that would also be adapted to different countries according to their situation, their extent, their government, their production, and their trade.

Nonetheless, we can establish some decisive principles on this important matter. Let us draw these principles from the luminous writings of excellent

This article can be found at 8:601–4 in the original edition of the *Encyclopédie*.

citizens, and let us transfer them into a work that exudes progress in knowledge, love of humanity, the glory of sovereigns, and the happiness of subjects.

The sovereign's glory is to demand only just and absolutely necessary levies, and the subjects' happiness is to pay only the same. If the prince's right to collect *taxes* is based on the state's needs, then he must demand only levies that are consistent with those needs, give them back immediately after those needs are satisfied, and employ the yield only for those same purposes—not diverting them to his private use or in lavish outlays for persons who do not contribute to the public good.

The *taxes* in a state are what the sails are on a ship—they are to guide it, secure it, and bring it to port, rather than burden it, keep it tied up at sea, and ultimately submerge it.

Since *taxes* are established to furnish indispensable necessities, and since all subjects contribute with a portion of the goods that belong to them as property, it is appropriate for them to be collected directly, without expense, and to enter promptly into state coffers. Thus, the sovereign should watch over the conduct of the people entrusted with tax collection, to prevent and punish their customary surcharges. Nero in his prime passed a very wise edict. He ordained that the magistrates of Rome and the provinces receive complaints against the public *tax* farmers at any moment, and that they judge them on the spot. Trajan decreed that judgment in doubtful cases be made against his receivers.

When all the individuals in a state are citizens, when each one possesses in his domain what the prince possesses in his dominion, *taxes* may be placed on persons, on land, on consumption, on merchandise, or on one or two of these things together—depending on the urgency of the situations that require them with absolute necessity.

The personal or head *tax* has all the disadvantages of arbitrariness, and its method is not at all popular. Nonetheless, it can serve as an expedient when there is an essential need for sums that would otherwise be unavoidably shifted onto commerce, land, or its produce. This tax is also admissible provided that it be proportional, and that it fall more heavily on prosperous folks and not at all on the bottom classes of the people. Although all subjects enjoy equally the protection of the government and the security that it procures them, the inequality in their fortunes and in the advantages they draw from them argues for impositions consistent with this inequality, and means that these impositions should be, so to speak, in geometric progression—two, four, eight, sixteen—on the prosperous. For this *tax* must not fall on the necessities.

In Athens, the citizens were divided into four classes: those who got five hundred measures of dry or liquid fruit from their property and paid the public one talent—that is, sixty minae; those who got three hundred measures owed a half-talent; those who had two hundred measures paid ten minae; those in the fourth class paid nothing. The tax was equitable; if it was not proportional to property, it was at least proportional to needs. It was considered that each person had equal physical necessities, that these physical necessities should not be taxed, that abundance should be taxed, and that superfluity should be taxed even more.

Insofar as the *taxes* in a luxury-based realm are not set up in such a way that they are collected from individuals in proportion to their prosperity, the condition of that realm cannot improve. One portion of the subjects will live in opulence and will eat the food of a hundred families in one meal, whereas the other portion will have only bread and will waste away daily. A *tax* that annually cut out five, ten, thirty, fifty gold crowns from the frivolous expenses of each prosperous family—with the cut being made in proportion to the prosperity of that family—would suffice along with current revenues to pay off the state debts, or to defray the costs of a just war, without the yeoman farmer hearing about it except in the public prayers.[1]

It is believed that in France, a tax imposed only on the cities—on glass and crystal works, silverware, coachmen, lackeys, horse-drawn coaches, sedan carriages, calico from the Indies, and other similar items—would bring in annually fifteen or twenty million.[2] This is no less necessary to put the brakes on the depopulation of the countryside than to manage an allocation of *taxes* by a method that most conforms to distributive justice. This method consists in applying them to the greatest luxury, as being the most onerous to the state. It is an incontestable truth that the weight of

1. The reference is to the use of the pulpit for public announcements in old-regime France.

2. Jaucourt seems here to be discussing pounds (*livres*), not gold crowns as in the previous paragraph; see the note on currency, above.

taxes is felt especially strongly in this kingdom because of the inequality of its assessment, and that the total forces of the body politic are prodigious.

Let us move to the tax on land, a very wise tax when it is devised according to a detailed count, a true and precise estimate. It's a matter of implementing its collection at little expense, as is done in England. In France, rolls are drawn up where the various classes of property are placed. When these classes are distinguished with justice and enlightenment, there is nothing to be said against it. But it is difficult to know well the different values of the different properties, and even harder to find people who do not have an interest in ignoring them in the preparation of the rolls. There are two sorts of injustice to fear: the injustice of man and the injustice of the matter. However, if taxes are moderate on the people, some private injustices by more prosperous people are not going to merit great attention. If, on the other hand, taxes do not leave the people with enough to live on honorably, it will be the most glaring injustice and will have the greatest implications. If some number of subjects happen to get lost in the crowd and do not pay enough taxes, the harm is tolerable. But if some number of citizens who have only the necessities pay too much, their ruin redounds against the public. When the state proportions its fortunes to the people's, the ease of the people soon raises the fortunes of the state.

Thus, the share of taxes imposed on the farmer in proportion to his industry must not be heavy or so demoralizing in its nature that he is afraid to clear a new field, increase the number of his livestock, or display a new source of industry, for fear of seeing an increase in that arbitrary tax that he cannot pay.[3] Then he would feel no more emulation to engage in acquisition, and in losing the hope of becoming rich, his interest would be in presenting himself as poorer than he really is. People who claim that the peasant should not live in ease spout a maxim that is as false as it is contrary to humanity.

It would again be bad administration to tax the industry of artisans, for this would make them pay the state precisely because they are producing value within the state that did not previously exist. It would be a means of wiping out human industry, ruining the state, and cutting off its source of levies.

3. This sort of deception was widely practiced in old-regime France.

Moderate and proportional *taxes* on the consumption of foodstuffs and merchandise are the least onerous for the people, the most lucrative for the sovereign, and the most just. They are least onerous for the people because they are paid imperceptibly and daily, without discouraging industry, insofar as they are the fruit of the will and capacity to consume. They yield more for the sovereign than any other kind because they apply to everything that is consumed every day. Finally, they are the most just, because they are proportional, because whoever possesses wealth cannot enjoy it without paying in proportion to his capacity. These truths, despite being self-evident, could be supported by the constant experience of England, Holland, Prussia, and some Italian cities, if examples were fit sources of persuasion.

But consumption *taxes* must not be added to personal *taxes* that are already substantial. This would crush the people, whereas substituting a consumption *tax* for a personal *tax* would obtain more money in a milder and more imperceptible manner.

In employing this *tax*, it must be observed that the foreigner pays a great portion of the levies added to the price of the merchandise he buys from the nation. Thus, merchandise that serves only for luxury and that comes from foreign countries should be heavily *taxed*. When this merchandise consists in things that can grow or be manufactured in the country, import duties on them will be raised and manufacturing or agriculture will be encouraged. As for merchandise that can be transported abroad, if it is publicly beneficial for them to leave, then the export duties will be lifted, and the export may even be facilitated by liberal incentives.

Finally, the *taxes* on foodstuffs and merchandise consumed in the country are the ones that the people feel the least, because a formal demand is not made of them. These sorts of levies can be so wisely handled that the people are almost unaware they are paying them.

To this end, it is of great moment that the seller of the merchandise be the one who pays the duty. He knows very well that he is not paying it for himself; the buyer who provides the funds pays it and mixes it in with the price. Moreover, when it's the citizen who pays, all kinds of difficulties arise, even including searches that are permitted in his house. Nothing is more contrary to liberty. Those who establish these sorts of *taxes* have not the good fortune of having discovered the best kind of administration.[4]

For the price of the item and the tax on the item to be mixed together in the payer's mind, there must be some relationship between the value of the merchandise and the *tax;* one must not impose an excessive levy on a foodstuff of little value. There are countries in which the levy is fifteen or twenty times the value of the foodstuff—a foodstuff essential to life. Then the prince who imposes such taxes on that foodstuff strips his subjects of their illusions; they see they are burdened by such unreasonable levies that they feel nothing any more except their poverty and their servitude. Moreover, for the prince to be able to levy a tax that is so disproportional to the value of an item, he must farm out the item; the people must be able to buy it only from his tax collectors, which brings countless disasters.

Since fraud is quite lucrative in this case, the natural punishment—the one demanded by reason, namely, the confiscation of the merchandise—becomes incapable of halting it. Thus, recourse must be had to Japanese punishments and those similar to the ones inflicted for the greatest crimes. People who could not be regarded as wicked men are punished as villains; all sense of proportion in punishment is eliminated.

Let us add that the more the people are placed under the necessity of defrauding that tax collector, the more the latter is enriched and the former are impoverished. Eager to arrest the fraud, the tax collector never stops complaining, or demanding, usurping, and obtaining extraordinary means of vexation, and then all is lost.[5]

In a word, the advantages of the consumption *tax* consist in the moderation in levies on essential commodities, the liberty in payment on consuming them, and the uniformity of imposition. Otherwise, this kind of *tax,* admirable in principle, has nothing but disadvantages. For evidence of this, *look* in the excellent work entitled *Inquiries and considerations on state finance, 1758,* in 4°, 2 vols.[6]

4. See the last paragraph of Montesquieu, *The Spirit of the Laws,* 13.7, 218.

5. These two paragraphs are slightly adapted from Montesquieu, *Laws,* 13.8.

6. *Recherches & considerations sur les finances de France, depuis 1595 jusqu'à 1721.* The reference is to the influential work by Véron de Forbonnais published with Liège or Basel imprints in 1758.

The arbitrary *tax* by head is more consistent with servitude than any other. The proportional *tax* on land is consistent with justice. The *tax* on merchandise is appropriate to the liberty of a commercial people. This *tax* is properly paid by the buyer, although the merchant advances it both to the buyer and to the state. The more moderate the government is, the more the spirit of liberty will reign, the more security fortunes will enjoy, and the easier it will be for merchants to advance substantial levies to the state and to private individuals. In England, a merchant actually lends the state fifty pounds sterling for each barrel of wine he receives from France. Where is the merchant who would dare do something of this order in a country governed like Turkey? And if he dared to do it, how could he with a fortune that was suspect, uncertain, ruined?

Most republics can increase *taxes* in time of pressing need, because the citizen, who believes he is paying to himself, has the will to pay them—and usually the power, as a result of the nature of the government. Under a moderate monarchy, *taxes* can be increased because the wisdom and skill of the government can procure wealth; it is a kind of reward to the prince for the respect he has for the laws.[7]

Nonetheless, the more he respects them, the more he is bound to limit the *taxes* he is forced to establish, to distribute them proportionally according to people's ability to pay, and to cause them to be collected with order and without charges and fees. The sense of equity in the city of Rome's levy of taxes fit the fundamental principle of the government as founded by Servius Tullius, and could not be infringed upon without the republic collapsing at the same time, as experience showed.

The tax imposed by Aristides on all of Greece to defray the costs of the war against the Persians was allocated with such mildness and justice that the taxpayers called this tax the *happy fate of Greece,* and it is in all likelihood the only time a tax has received this fine description.[8] It amounted to 450 talents; soon Pericles increased it by a third. After it was eventually tripled, without war becoming any more ruinous because of its duration or the various accidents of fortune, the weight of this *tax* arrested the

7. This paragraph is slightly adapted from Montesquieu, *Laws,* 13.13.

8. Aristides the Just (530–468 B.C.), whose assessment of the tax burden for members of the Delian League during the Persian wars (in 479 B.C.) became standard.

progress of the [Greek] conquests and emptied the veins of the people, who, having become too weak to resist Philip, fell under the yoke of his dominion.[9]

Thus, let us make it a fundamental maxim not to measure *taxes* by what the people can give, but by what they should equitably give. And if one is sometimes forced to measure *taxes* by what the people can give, this must at least be according to what they can give all the time. Without this adjustment, it will happen that one will be forced either to overcharge those unfortunate people—that is, to ruin the state—or else to float loans in perpetuity, which leads to a perpetual surcharge on the tax imposed, since the interest must be paid. In the end, disorder in state finances inevitably results, not counting innumerable drawbacks during the course of these loans. The principle that has just been advanced is much more certain, of wider effect, and more advantageous to the monarchy, than the treasures amassed by kings.

The sovereign must eliminate all *taxes* that are vicious by nature—without seeking to repress their abuses, because that is not possible. When a *tax* is vicious in itself, as all arbitrary levies are, the form of collection (however good) merely changes the name of the excesses without remedying their cause.

The maxim of the great empires of the east—to remit levies to the provinces that have suffered—ought to be taken up in all monarchical states. There are some states where it is adopted, but where it simultaneously weighs people down as much as, or more than, if it had not been, because the prince levies neither more nor less and the whole state becomes jointly liable. To relieve a village that pays poorly, another village that pays better is burdened with the debt. The first is not restored to prosperity; the second is ruined. Between the necessity of paying to avoid executions, which follow promptly, and the danger of paying for fear of surcharges, the people grow desperate.[10]

Some have dared to suggest that the joint liability of the residents of the same village is reasonable because a fraudulent plot could be assumed

9. Pericles (495–429 B.C.), Athenian leader; Philip of Macedon (r. 359–336 B.C.).
10. For this paragraph and the next, see Montesquieu, *Laws*, 13.18.

on their part. But where does the idea come from that, based on mere suppositions, something that is unjust in itself and ruinous for the state has to be established? It is said that the collection of *taxes* must be fixed in order to correspond to expenses that are fixed. Yes, the collection of *taxes* that are not unjust and ruinous. Remit such *taxes* without hesitation; they will inevitably be fruitful. Nonetheless, can't cuts be made to some of these expenses that are called *fixed?* Can't harmonization do for the administration of a state what it can do in the house of a private individual? Does a state have no expedients for economizing in times of peace, for clearing its debts, even setting up savings for unforeseen events and dedicating them to the public good—while in the meantime making them constantly circulate through the hands of the treasurers or receivers, as loans to solid companies that would establish discount banks, or by other means?

There are a hundred schemes for making the state rich, as opposed to a single one whose goal would be to enable each individual to enjoy the wealth of the state. Glory, grandeur, power of a realm! How vain and meaningless are these words next to the words liberty, ease, and happiness of the subjects! What then, would it not make a nation rich and powerful to enable each of its members to participate in the wealth of the state? Do you want to achieve this in France? A host of methods come to mind. I will cite a few of the ones by which I cannot better terminate this article.

(1) It's a matter of powerfully encouraging agriculture, population, and commerce, sources of the wealth of subject and sovereign. (2) Proportion the benefits from the affairs of state finance to the benefits from trade and from the clearing of lands in general. For then, the enterprises of state finance will work out for the best, since they will be without risk. Besides which, it must not be forgotten that the state financiers' profit is always a reduction in the people's income and in the king's revenue. (3) Restrain the immoderate resort to useless wealth and office. (4) Abolish monopolies, tolls, exclusive privileges, letters of mastership, windfall inheritance,[11] duties on franc-fief,[12] the number of tax farmers and their vexations. (5) Cut

11. The *droit d'aubaine,* by which the king or other high official inherited the goods of a foreigner who happened to die on French soil; it was subject to many exceptions.

12. The occasional levies on commoners who owned noble lands.

out the majority of feast days.[13] (6) Correct the abuses and complications of the taille, the militia burden,[14] and the salt tax. (7) Do not engage in extraordinary arrangements to diminish the value of the currency. (8) Allow the transport of specie, because it is a just and beneficial thing. (9) Keep interest rates as low as is permitted by the combined number of lenders and borrowers in the state. (10) Finally, lighten *taxes* and allocate them according to the principles of distributive justice, that justice by which kings are the representatives of God on earth. France would be only too powerful, and the French only too happy, if these methods were in practice. But is the dawn of a bright day ready to appear? (*D.J.*)

13. The reference is to the saints' days, of which the large number in Catholic eighteenth-century France faced growing opposition from, among others, common people looking to improve their material condition. See Noah Shusterman, *Religion and the Politics of Time: Holidays in France from Louis XIV Through Napoleon* (Catholic University Press, 2010).

14. The reference seems to be to the quartering duty that local populations had to fulfill in old-regime France.

Indissoluble

This brief argument for freedom of divorce under the Grammar *category is a typical example of the elusive method of approaching political questions often resorted to by Diderot and other contributors. Divorce was in fact greatly liberalized for a time during the French Revolution.*

*INDISSOLUBLE (*Grammar*), what cannot be dissolved or broken. Marriage is an *indissoluble* commitment. The wise man shudders at the very idea of an *indissoluble* commitment. The legislators who have prepared *indissoluble* ties for men have not been very familiar with his natural inconstancy. How many criminals and wretches have they created?

This article can be found at 8:684 in the original edition of the *Encyclopédie*.

Industry
(*Industrie*)

This article appears under the categories of Political law *and* Commerce. *In the previous article, by the same title and under the* Metaphysics *rubric in the* Encyclopédie, *Jaucourt expressly borrows from the Physiocrat Quesnay in redefining this traditional term to emphasize both the mechanical arts and the process of invention, as opposed to mere "imitation" or "routine." New machines for productive labor, of course, were of great interest to the Encyclopedists. It is also of note how many of the staple controversies surrounding the industrial revolution of the nineteenth century are already making their appearance in this article from the early 1760s. See the article* INVENTION, *below. On the semantic front, see the translators' note, above, for contemporary usage of the term "industrie," which is well exemplified by the illustration on the following page.*

INDUSTRY (*Political law and Commerce*). This word signifies two things: either the simple work of the hands, or the mind's inventions in useful machines, relative to the arts and crafts. *Industry* includes sometimes one, some times the other of these two things, and it often combines both of them.

It concerns the cultivation of the land, manufactures, and the arts; it fertilizes everything and spreads abundance and life everywhere. Just as destructive nations do harm that lasts longer than they do, industrious nations do good that does not even end with themselves.

This article can be found at 8:694–95 in the original edition of the *Encyclopédie*.

Industria (Industry)
In foreground, woman with spur, hourglass, rooster, and beehive (all symbols of industriousness); in background, the Roman freedman C. Furius Chresimus rebuffs witchcraft charges by showing proof of his own industrious farming.

In America, the land naturally brings forth many fruits that people live on. If the land were left uncultivated in Europe, there would scarcely appear anything but forests, oak, pine, and other sterile trees. Thus, to make the land productive in Europe, a great deal of labor, *industry,* and knowledge was necessary. This is because needs, *industry,* and knowledge always proceed at the same pace. That's why in European states, independent farmers and usefully industrious men should be highly protected and rewarded. The reason is evident: every increase in cultivation, as well as all *industry,* multiplies foodstuffs and merchandise, attracting into the state the money that is the sign of their valuations.

It is a timeworn truth almost shameful to repeat, but in certain countries, there are people who evade the ways and means offered them to make the land fruitful, and who persist in sacrificing principles of this kind to the prejudices that dominate them. They are unaware that the obstacles imposed on *industry* completely destroy it, and that on the other hand, the efforts of *industry* that are encouraged make it prosper marvelously through the emulation and profit that result. Far from imposing taxes on *industry,* one must give incentives to those who have best cultivated their fields, and to the workers who have gone furthest in making their work meritorious. No one is unaware of how far this method has succeeded in the three realms of Great Britain. In our day, by this means alone, one of Europe's most significant cloth manufactures has been set up in Ireland.

Just as the consumption of merchandise increases with the cheapness of manual labor, *industry* influences the price of this manual labor every time it can reduce the amount of work or the number of hands employed. Such is the effect of watermills, windmills, looms, and so many other machines, the fruit of precious *industry*. As examples, one may cite the machines invented by M. de Vaucanson;[1] the machine for working up raw silk that has been known in England for twenty years; sawmills for lumber—by which, under the inspection of a single man and by means of a single axle, up to forty-eight eighteen-foot boards are worked up in one hour of favorable

1. Jacques de Vaucanson (1709–82), engineer and inventor who made automatons, invented machine tools, and whose innovations helped automate the French weaving and silk industries. His bequest to Louis XVI became the basis for the Conservatoire des Arts et Métiers in Paris.

winds; the ribbon looms with multiple shuttles also have countless advantages. But all these things are so well known that it is useless to expand on them. M. Melon has said it well: to make with one man, with the help of the machines of *industry,* what one would make with two or three men without these machines is to double or triple the number of citizens.[2]

The occasions for the employment of manufacturing workers know no bounds but those of consumption; consumption in turn is limited only by the price of labor. Thus, the nation that possesses the cheapest manual labor, and whose merchants content themselves with the most moderate profit, will engage in the most lucrative commerce, all circumstances being equal. Such is the power of *industry,* when at the same time the channels of internal and external commerce are free. Then, it opens new markets to consumption, and even forces access into those that are closed to it.

Against the utility of the inventions of *industry,* let it no longer be objected that every machine that reduces manual labor by half instantly takes away the means of subsistence from half the workers in the craft; that the workers without employment would sooner become beggars burdening the state than learn another craft; that consumption has its limits, so that even assuming it doubles, via the resourcefulness we are extolling so much here, it will diminish as soon as the foreigner procures machines similar to ours; that in the end, no advantage will remain to the inventing country from its inventions of *industry.*

Such objections are typically devoid of good sense and enlightenment. They resemble the objections that the Thames boatmen put forward against the construction of the Westminster bridge. Haven't those boatmen found something to do with themselves, while the construction of that bridge has been expanding new commodities throughout the city of London? Isn't it better to anticipate the *industry* of other peoples in using machines, than to wait for them to force us to adopt the use of those machines in order to preserve our competitive position in the same markets? The surest profit will always go to the nation that has been industrious first; and all things equal, the nation whose *industry* is the freest will be the most industrious.

2. Jean-François Melon (1675?–1738), *Essai politique sur le commerce* (1734), chap. 8. The book was translated into English by the Irishman David Bindon in 1738 as *A Political Essay upon Commerce.*

Nonetheless, we do not mean to disapprove of the care that a government may take in preparing with some prudence the use of industrious machines that are capable of suddenly doing too much damage to the occupations that employ men. However, this prudence itself is only necessary in a straitened condition[3]—which is the first vice one must begin by destroying. In any event, whether invention be discouraged, whether progress in the arts takes place, *industry* seems to have reached the point where its gradations today are quite mild, and its violent shocks are very little to be feared.

In the end, we conclude that one cannot protect *industry* too much, if one considers how far it can go in yielding returns for the common good in all the liberal and mechanical arts. Witness the advantages drawn from it by Painting, Engraving, Sculpture, Printing, Clock-making, Jewelry-making, the manufactures in linen, wool, silk, gold, silver—in a word, all crafts and all occupations. (*D.J.*)

3. The phrase is *état de gêne,* which might mean in this context either financial or psychological distress.

Innovation

INNOVATION (*Political government*), novelty, or important change made in the political government of a state, against the practice and rules of its constitution.

These sorts of *innovation* are always deformities in the political order. Laws and customs that are well established and consistent with the character of a nation have their place in the scheme of things. Everything is so well linked that a novelty that has its advantages and disadvantages, and that is brought in to replace current abuses without mature reflection, will never fit with the fabric of a timeworn part, because it is not matched to the piece.

If only time would stop, to afford the leisure to remedy its ravages. . . . But it's a wheel that turns with such rapidity; the means of replacing a spoke that is missing, or that is menacing! . . .

The revolutions brought by time in the course of nature arrive step by step; one must therefore imitate this slowness in the useful *innovations* that may be introduced into the state. For it is not a question here of changes in the administration of a particular city.

But above all, when a political *innovation* needs to be supported by examples, they must be taken from times of enlightenment, moderation, and tranquility, not looked for in the days of darkness, turmoil, and austerity. These children of pain and blindness are normally monsters that bring disorder, misery, and desolation. (*D.J.*)

This article can be found at 8:755 in the original edition of the *Encyclopédie*.

Intendants
(*Intendans*)

There are several articles under this general heading, including two lengthy and historically descriptive entries by the jurist Boucher d'Argis. The unsigned article translated here, whose author remains unknown, is important because of its robust advocacy of a reform in the French political system—a system powerfully shaped by the creation of royal intendants under Richelieu in the early seventeenth century—in the direction of stronger local government and administration. Proposals to strengthen the provincial estates had been made by the circle around the Duke of Burgundy under Louis XIV (Fénelon was its leading figure) and afterward by Mirabeau, Turgot, Necker, and others. A November 12, 1764, letter by Diderot to the publisher Le Breton complains that the latter had markedly censored this entry, indicating its topical sensitivity.

INTENDANTS (*Modern history*), *assigned by H. M.*[1] *to the provinces and generalities of the realm. . . .*

The authority of the *intendants* is, as can be seen, very extensive in *pays d'élection*,[2] since they alone decide on the allocation of taxes, the quantity and time of compulsory labor, the new commercial establishments, the distribution of troops in the different provincial locations, the price and

This article can be found at 8:809–10 in the original edition of the *Encyclopédie*.

1. His Majesty.

2. *Pays d'élection* were those provinces in the old regime whose tax assessment and collection were conducted mainly by agents of the royal government (*élus*) rather than with the help of provincial estates, as in the *pays d'état*, on which, see below.

apportionment of fodder granted to the men of war; since the purchases of foodstuffs to fill the king's warehouse are made by their order and by their law; since it is they who preside at the military levies and who resolve the difficulties that arise on that occasion; since it is by them that the ministry is informed on the condition of the provinces—their production, their markets, their burdens, their losses, their resources, etc.; since in fact, under the name *intendants* of justice, police, and finances, they cover virtually every aspect of administration.

Provincial estates are the best remedy for the disadvantages of a large monarchy. They are even of the essence of monarchy, which requires not *powers* but *intermediary bodies* between the prince and the people.[3] The provincial estates do for the prince a part of what the prince's officials would do, and although they take the place of the official, they are unwilling and unable to put themselves in the prince's place. At worst, this is what one might fear of the Estates General.[4]

The prince may be knowledgeable about the general order, the fundamental laws, his situation relative to the foreigner, the rights of his nation, etc.

But without the aid of the provincial estates, he can never know the wealth, the forces, the resources, what troops and taxes he can and should levy, etc.

In France, the king's authority is nowhere more respected than in the *pays d'état*. In their august assemblies, it appears in all its splendor. It is the king who convokes and dismisses these assemblies; he names its president; he can exclude whom he wills; he is present through his agents. The limits of authority are never brought into question; only the choice of means to obey that authority is weighed, and it is usually the fastest means that are chosen. If the province is found to be in no position to pay the charges imposed upon it, it limits itself to representations, which are never more than an exposition of their present contribution, their past efforts, their current needs, their means, their zeal, and their respect. Whether the king perseveres in his will or whether he changes his will, all obey. The approbation

3. The reference is to Montesquieu's idea in *The Spirit of the Laws,* 2.4.

4. The Estates General had not met since 1614; see REPRESENTATIVES, below, for an argument in favor of convoking them. They would not meet again until Spring of 1789, when they would spearhead the French Revolution.

that the notables who make up these estates offer to the prince's demands serves to persuade the people that they were just and necessary; they have an interest in making the people obey promptly. More is given than in the *pays d'élection,* but it is given freely, voluntarily, with zeal, and everyone is content.

In the provinces enlightened by the constant discussion of public business, the taille on property has been established without difficulty; the barbarisms and injustices of the taille on persons are no longer known there. You don't see collectors followed by bailiffs or soldiers spying to see if they can bring to light some rags that were left to a poor wretch to cover his children, and get him to sell them—rags that barely escaped the exactions of the previous year. You don't see that multitude of fiscal officials who absorb a part of the taxes and tyrannize the people. There is only one general treasurer for the whole province; the collection is assigned, without remuneration, to officials appointed by the estates, or to municipal officials.

The private treasurers of the towns and villages have modest salaries; it is they who collect the taille that they are responsible for. Since it is on property, if there are delays, they do not risk losing their advances; they recover them without expense. Delays are rare, and the recoveries are almost always prompt.

In the *pays d'état,* you don't see three hundred tax collectors, sheriffs, or mayors of a single province, groaning in prison for an entire year—and in many cases dying—for not having brought in the taille from their villages, which had been made insolvent. You don't see a village whose territory yields 4000 pounds being charged 7000 pounds in taxes. The yeoman farmer is not afraid of enjoying the fruits of his labor and of appearing to increase his comfort; he knows that his additional payments will be exactly proportional to what he has acquired. He has no cause to corrupt or to sway a collector; he has no cause to plead at an election's election,[5] before the *intendant* of the *intendant* in council.

The king does not tolerate losses in the *pays d'état;* the province always furnishes exactly the sum required of it. The allocation, done equitably

5. The play on words hinges on two distinct uses of "election," the first meaning the boundaries of the royal jurisdiction, the second a tribunal that heard tax cases.

and always proportionally by wealth, does not overburden the comfortable farmer in order to relieve the unfortunate—who, however, is indemnified.

As for public works: the engineers, the contractors, the workers, the property taken away from private individuals—everything is paid for exactly and is levied without expense. No roads or bridges are built that are useful to only a few people; they are not slaves to an eternal and blind avarice.

If certain changes in the value of property or in commerce should occur, the whole province is informed, and the administration makes the necessary changes.

The different orders in the estates enlighten each other mutually. Since none of them have authority, they cannot oppress each other; they all discuss, and the king decrees. These assemblies produce men who are capable of public affairs. It was by arranging the election of the consuls of Aix and explicating the interests of Provence to the assembly that Cardinal Janson[6] became a celebrated diplomat.

You don't travel across the kingdom without perceiving the excellent administration of the estates and the pernicious administration of the *pays d'élection*. It is not necessary to ask questions, but only to look at the residents of the countryside, in order to know whether you're in a *pays d'état* or a *pays d'élection*. What an endless resource these *pays d'états* are for the realm!

Compare what the king gets from Normandy with what he gets from Languedoc. These provinces are of the same scope, but the arid sands of the latter send more money to the royal treasury than the opulent pasture and fertile countryside of the former. What would these *pays d'état* be like if the king's domains were leased out to and exploited by the estates themselves? That was the plan of the late Duke of Burgundy,[7] and to this plan he added a greater one, that of putting the entire realm into provincial estates.

6. Toussaint de Forbin-Janson (1631–1713); becoming bishop of Marseille in 1662 involved him *ex officio* in the provincial estates of Provence.

7. The Duke of Burgundy was the grandson of Louis XIV. Heir to the throne, he was the center of an important reform movement before his sudden death in 1712. Fénelon was his best-known adviser; see his enormously popular and influential work *Télémaque* (1698).

If the realm has sudden and unforeseen needs that require a prompt remedy, it is from the *pays d'état* that the prince should expect this remedy. Despite its moors and its small size, Brittany gave a third more in tax contributions in the last war[8] than vast and rich Normandy. Provence, a sterile land, gave twice as much as Dauphinois, a land abundant in every species of production.

Devastated by enemy armies and weighed down by the burdens of war, Provence proposes to levy and maintain an army of thirty thousand men at its own expense. Languedoc sends the Prince of Conti two thousand mules to enable him to profit from his victories and from his passage of the Alps.[9]

What I am saying is known to everyone, and abroad our Estates-run provinces have a reputation for opulence. They have more credit than the government; they have more than the king himself.

Let us remember that in the last war, Genoa would lend to the king only on Languedoc's guaranty.[10]

There are *intendants* in these provinces. It is desirable for them always to be men who merely watch over it for the prince. It is desirable for them never to extend their authority, and for that authority to be greatly moderated in the *pays d'élection*.

8. The reference is to the War of the Austrian Succession, 1740–48.

9. Louis François de Bourbon, Prince of Conti (1717–76), whose command during the war included a stint in Piedmont.

10. Throughout the eighteenth century, the French monarchy was increasingly dependent upon estates, municipalities, and other corporate entities for lines of credit.

Invention

This article by Jaucourt deals with a subject of great importance to the Encyclopédie. *Interest in inventions and inventors is an ever-recurring theme. D'Alembert, in* The Preliminary Discourse,[1] *and Diderot, in his article* ENCYCLOPÉDIE, *both stress the vital role of the mechanical arts and the crucial contributions of inventors to the progress and happiness of mankind. Among the three key inventions that expanded the limits of the world are the compass, the printing press, and gunpowder. Each of these inventions is treated in a long article; a complete list of articles on inventions in the* Encyclopédie *would be infinitely varied, including, among many other items,* GLASS BLOWING, METALLURGY, *and* INCUBATOR (Verre; Metallurgie; Poulets, Four à).

INVENTION (*Arts and Sciences*). A general term which can be applied to everything that is found, invented, or discovered, and which is of use or interest in the arts, sciences, and crafts. To some extent this term is synonymous with "discovery," though less striking; I should like to be permitted

The headnote, translation, and unattributed footnotes for "Invention" are from Nelly S. Hoyt and Thomas Cassirer, eds., *The Encyclopedia: Selections [by] Diderot, d'Alembert and a Society of Men of Letters* (Indianapolis: Bobbs-Merrill, 1965), 155–59; the translation is reproduced on *The Encyclopedia of Diderot & d'Alembert Collaborative Translation Project* (Ann Arbor: Michigan Publishing, University of Michigan Library, 2003): http://hdl.handle.net/2027/spo.did2222.0000.155 (accessed June 3, 2015).

This article can be found at 8:848–49 in the original edition of the *Encyclopédie.*

1. See *The Preliminary Discourse to the Encyclopedia of Diderot,* trans. R. N. Schwab (Indianapolis: Bobbs-Merrill, 1963).

here to use them interchangeably, without repeating the interesting things the reader should already have read under the word DISCOVERY.[2]

We owe inventions to time, pure chance, to lucky and unforeseen speculations, mechanical instincts, as well as to the patience and resourcefulness of those who work.

The useful inventions of the thirteenth and fourteenth centuries did not at all result from the researches of those who are known as wits in polite society, nor did they come from speculative philosophers. They were the fruit of that mechanical instinct with which nature has endowed some men, independent from philosophy. The invention of spectacles, known as *besicles,*[3] to assist the weakened sight of old men dates from the end of the thirteenth century. It is said that we owe it to Alexander Spina. In that same century the Venetians already possessed the secret of making crystal mirrors. Faience earthenware which was used in Europe instead of porcelain was discovered in Faenza; windmills date from approximately the same period. The making of paper from pounded and boiled cloth was invented in the early fourteenth century. Cortusius speaks of a certain Pax who established the first papermaking factory in Padua a century before the invention of printing. This is how early discoveries happily produce their first fruit, and often thanks to men who remain unknown.[4]

I say the first fruit, for it has to be observed that the most interesting and useful things that we possess today in the arts were not found in the state in which we see them now. Everything was discovered in rough form or in parts and has been gradually brought to greater perfection. At least this seems to be the case for those inventions of which we have spoken, and it can be proven for the invention of glass, the compass, printing, clocks, mills, telescopes, and many others.

I shall not mention the discoveries in the sciences that could have been prepared by the labors of preceding centuries; this would be a subject for

2. The article DISCOVERY is by d'Alembert. In it he differentiates between discovery, which deals with what is new, useful, and difficult, and inventions, which he considers to be less important discoveries.

3. An obsolete word used to describe a special kind of round "noseglasses" without shanks.

4. Jaucourt seems to have drawn this paragraph from Voltaire, *Essay,* chap. 69, p. 170; Gulielmus Cortusius, the Paduan chronicler, flourished in the middle of the fourteenth century.—HC

too extensive a research. Nor shall I speak of discoveries that are supposedly modern, yet are merely old theories, put forward once again, and more clearly. In any case, such discussions would prove very little. In order to remain within the framework of the arts, I shall be satisfied to observe that a shorter or longer time lapse was needed to perfect the inventions which originally, in uncivilized centuries, were the products of chance or mechanical genius.

Guttenburg [*sic*] invented only movable characters, carved in relief on wood and on metal. It was Schöfer who improved this invention and found the secret of casting these characters. How much this art has been perfected since Schöfer is well known.

The invention of the compass in the twelfth century is of the same order as the invention of printing, whether its use was first discovered by the mariner Goya, a native of Malfi, or by the English, or the French, or the Portuguese. In the beginning men knew only how to place the magnetized needle on a piece of cork floating on water; later this needle was suspended on a pivot inside a box that in its turn was suspended. Finally it was fixed onto a mariner's card or a piece of talc upon which had been traced a circle divided into thirty-two equal parts to mark the thirty-two wind directions, together with another concentric circle divided into 360 degrees, which measured the angles and separations of the compass.

The invention of windmills (perhaps originating in Asia) became successful only when geometry perfected the machine, which is based entirely upon the theory of compound movement.

How many centuries have elapsed between the moment when Ctesibius made the first watch run by a movement, probably around 613 in Rome, and the most recent pendulum clock made in England by Graham or in France by Julien Le Roi. Did not Huygens or Leibniz and many others contribute to their perfection?[5]

5. The references are to Ctesibius, ancient inventor (fl. 270 B.C.); George Graham (1674?–1751), English clockmaker and member of the Royal Society; Julien LeRoy (1686–1759), royal clockmaker in 1739; Christiaan Huygens (1629–95), Dutch scientist and author of an important 1656 work on clockmaking; Gottfried Wilhelm Leibniz (1646–1716), philosopher and inventor, one of whose interests was clocks.—HC

I could say almost as much about the development of the small telescope, from Metius to the Benedictine Dom Noël. Can there be any doubt about the difference between the rough cut of the diamond discovered by chance three centuries ago by Louis de Berquen, and the beautiful brilliant or rose cut our gem cutters are able to execute today?[6] Usage and practice have taught them all kinds of ways of cutting stones, and their eyes and their hands are the guides. It is the forty-seventh proposition of the first book of Euclid which has made possible the achievement of such beautiful proportions when cutting these precious stones into lozenges, triangles, facets, and bevels, which give them their brilliance and glittering effect. Thus those men who were fortunate enough to be born at the right time, had a perfect knowledge of mechanics, and have taken advantage of the sketchy simplicity of early inventions; and slowly, thanks to their shrewdness, they brought them to the degree of perfection where we see them today.

Inventions are the children of time, but, if I may say so, industriousness can speed the delivery. How many centuries did men walk on silk without knowing how to make use of it, how to adorn themselves with it. No doubt nature has in her storehouse treasures which are as precious and which she keeps for the moment when we least expect them; let us always be prepared to take advantage of them.

Often an invention illuminates a preceding one and throws a few flickers of light on one that is to follow. I am not saying that any invention is always productive in itself. Great rivers do not always rise in the waters of other great rivers. But inventions which seem to be without any general relationship still cross-fertilize each other; they reappear in a thousand ways that shorten and assist men's labors, and there is nothing more gratifying than the invention or perfection of arts that aim at the happiness of mankind. Such inventions have the advantage over political enterprises[7] in that they bring about the public good without harming anyone. The most spectacular conquests are bathed only in sweat, tears, and blood. He who discovers some secret useful to life, such as, for example, the dissolution of

6. Louis de Berquen, from Bruges (fl. 1450–76), said to be the inventor of modern gem-cutting.—HC

7. The French word "enterprises" here has a military connotation.—HC

stones in the bladder, would not have to fear the remorse that is inseparable from glory where crime and unhappiness are mingled. The invention of the compass and the printing press opened wider horizons and beautified and enlightened the world. If we scan history we will see that inventors were the first to be deified; the world adored them as visible gods.

After this we need not be astonished that inventors are sensitive to the honor of being discoverers. It is the last thing of which a man would want to divest himself. After Thales discovered the relationship between the sun's diameter and the circle this star describes around the earth, he communicated this discovery to someone who offered him anything he would desire for it. Thales asked only to be allowed to keep the honor of the discovery. This wise man of Greece, poor and old, was left untouched by the thought of money or profit or any kind of advantage, but he feared the injustice that might deprive him of his deserved glory.[8]

Moreover, all those who, thanks to their astuteness, their labors, their talents, and their diligence, will be able to combine research and observation, profound theory and experimentation, will continually enrich existing inventions and discoveries and will have the glory of paving the way for new ones.

If I may repeat here the words which the editors of this work wrote in the Introduction to Volume III:

> The *Encyclopédie* will write the history of our century's wealth in this subject; it will do so for our own century, which is ignorant of this history, and for the centuries to come, which thus will be able to go further. Discoveries in the arts will no longer run the danger of being forgotten; facts will become known to the philosophers, and reflection will be able to simplify and enlighten blind practice.

For the success of this enterprise, however, it is necessary that an enlightened government be willing to grant it a powerful and constant protection against injustice, persecution, and the calumny of enemies. (*D.J.*)

8. Thales of Miletus (ca. 624–ca. 546 B.C.), often viewed as the first true Greek philosopher.—HC

Volume 9
(1765)

Ars Politica (Statecraft)
Female symbol of statecraft in foreground, with scales (for justice and prudence) in her right hand and lictors' rods (for enforcement) at her feet; in background, Spartan citizens swear oath to Lycurgus to follow laws that he, as the foundational lawgiver of the community, had laid down.

Legislator
(*Législateur*)

The term "legislator" is sometimes translated as "lawgiver" for this period, connoting a somewhat wider meaning than our modern word. (See Lycurgus in the illustration for a flavor of this wider meaning.) Long thought to be the work of Diderot, the present article is now known to have been written by the Marquis de Saint-Lambert. Either way, the essay is widely agreed to be one of the most important and richly textured political articles in the Encyclopédie. *The author's wide-ranging approach to government, with its emphasis on climate, religion, manners, and liberty, evokes Montesquieu and Hume. His distinction between the* esprit de communauté *and the* esprit de propriété *is an original formulation, as is his precise way of drawing a relationship between commerce and constitutions, with its particular emphasis upon Europe's constitutional diversity.*

LEGISLATOR (*Politics*). The *legislator* is the one who has the power to make or to abrogate laws. In France the king is the *legislator;* in Geneva it is the people;[1] in Venice and Genoa, the nobility; in England there are the two houses and the king.

"Legislator" was translated in an abridged version by Stephen J. Gendzier in *Denis Diderot's "The Encyclopedia": Selections,* ed. and trans. Stephen J. Gendzier (New York: Harper and Row, 1967), 159–64, and is reprinted by permission of the translator. We have added our own translations of the omitted material, indicated by square brackets, and some notes.

This article can be found at 9:357–63 in the original edition of the *Encyclopédie.*

1. At the time of writing, Geneva was undergoing significant political upheaval. Voltaire was actively involved, eventually on the side of the democratizing reformers. For an account, see Peter Gay, *Voltaire's Politics* (Princeton: Princeton University Press, 1959), chap. 4.—HC

Every *legislator* must defend the security of the state and the welfare of the citizens.

By uniting to form a society, men sought a more fortunate condition than the state of nature, which had two advantages, equality and freedom, and two disadvantages, the fear of violence and the privation of assistance, either in obtaining primary necessities or in warding off danger. To protect themselves from these disadvantages they then consented to lose a little of their equality and freedom; and the *legislator* has fulfilled his goal when he takes away from men the least possible degree of equality and freedom, and he thereby procures for them the greatest degree of security and welfare.

[The *legislator* must make, maintain, or change the constitutive or civil law.

Constitutive law is law that constitutes the type of government. In making these laws, the *legislator* will take into account the extent of the country that the nation possesses, the nature of its soil, the power of the neighboring nations, their character, and the character of his own nation.

A small state should be republican. Its citizens are too enlightened about their interests. Those interests are not complicated enough for them to want to allow a monarch—who would be no more enlightened than they are—to decide about them. The entire state could conceive the same opinion in an instant, which would often be opposed to the king's will. The people, who cannot constantly keep themselves within the bounds of a just liberty, would be independent as soon as they want to be. This eternal discontent, attached to the condition of man—and of obedient man—would in these circumstances not be limited to murmurs; there would be no interval between the whim and the resolution.

The *legislator* will see that in a fertile country, in which the cultivation of the land occupies the largest portion of the inhabitants, the citizens are bound to be less jealous of their liberty, because they need only tranquility and because they have neither the will nor the time to occupy themselves with the details of administration. Besides, as President Montesquieu says, when liberty is not the sole possession, one is less attentive about defending it.[2] For the same reason, peoples that inhabit rocky hillsides or sterile mountains are less disposed to the government of one. Their liberty is their

2. For this whole paragraph, see Montesquieu, *The Spirit of the Laws,* 18.1–2.—HC

sole possession. In addition, if they want by means of industry and commerce to replace what nature refuses them, they need an extreme liberty.

The *legislator* will give the government of one to states of a certain expanse. It is too hard for their different parts to come together suddenly in order to make easy resolutions. Promptness in resolution and execution, which is the great advantage of monarchical government, causes orders, punishments, and assistance to move when they need to, and instantaneously, from one province to another. The different parts of a large state are united under the government of one, but in a large republic, factions would inevitably be formed, which could tear it apart and destroy it. Moreover, large states have many neighbors, they give umbrage, they are exposed to frequent wars. And here is the triumph of monarchical government; it is especially in warfare that it has the advantage over republican government. It has going for it secrecy, unity, celerity, no opposition, no slowness. The Roman victories prove nothing against me; the world they subjugated was either barbarous, or divided, or softened up. And when they waged wars that placed the republic in danger, they hastened to create a dictator, a magistrate more absolute than our kings. Holland, led in peacetime by her magistrates, has created stadholders in her wars against Spain and against France.]

The *legislator* reconciles the civil laws with constitutive law; in regard to many cases they will not be the same in a monarchy as in a republic, in an agricultural nation or in a nation devoted to commerce; they will change according to the times, the customs, and the climate. But has the climate as much influence on men as a few authors have maintained, and has it had such little influence on us as other authors have declared? This question deserves the attention of the *legislator*.[3]

[Men are everywhere susceptible to the same passions, but they can receive them by different causes and in different manners. They can receive the first impressions with more or less sensibility. And if climate can make but little difference in the type of passion, it can make much difference in sensations.

3. The chief proponent of the theory of climatic influence was Montesquieu, *Laws*, bks. 14–17.—HC

Unlike southern peoples, northern peoples do not receive lively impressions whose effects are prompt and rapid. A robust constitution, body heat concentrated by the cold, and food that has little succulence, all do much to make northern peoples feel hunger as a public privation. In some cold and humid countries, the animal spirits are numb, and violent stimuli are needed to make men feel their own existence.

Southern peoples need less food, which nature furnishes them in abundance. The heat of the climate and the liveliness of the imagination exhaust them and make labor difficult for them.

A great deal of labor and industry are needed for someone to be clothed and sheltered in such a manner as not to suffer from the rigors of the cold. But to protect oneself from the heat, only some trees, a hammock, and rest are necessary.

Northern peoples have to be occupied with the task of procuring themselves the necessities, but the southerners feel the need of amusement. The Samoyeds[4] hunt, open up a cave, prepare skins for clothing, cut and transport wood for maintaining a fire and hot drinks, whereas the African savage goes around completely naked, slakes his thirst at a fountain, collects fruit, and sleeps or dances in the shade.

The southern peoples' liveliness of sense and imagination make the physical pleasures of love more necessary to them than to the northern peoples. But, says President Montesquieu, since southern women lose their beauty at the age when reason begins, those peoples are bound to do less to bring the moral dimension into love than the peoples of the north, where intellect and reason accompany beauty.[5] The Caffres,[6] the peoples of Guyana and Brazil make their women work like beasts, while the Germans honor them like divinities.

The liveliness of each impression and the little need felt to retain and combine their ideas must be the reason why southern peoples will have little coherence and much inconsistency in their minds. They are guided by the moment; they forget time and sacrifice life to a single day. The Carib

4. Uralic-speaking peoples from northern Siberia.—HC

5. This argument is found at Montesquieu, *Laws,* 16.2.—HC

6. Perhaps a tribal people on the southeastern part of Africa, so called by the Portuguese who mistook the Muslim term *kafir* (heretic) for an ethnic term.—HC

weeps in the evening out of regret at having sold his bed in the morning to get drunk on eau-de-vie.

In the north, in order to provide for needs that demand more perseverance, industry, and combining of ideas, people must have more coherence, regularity, logic, and reason in their minds. In the south, people are bound to have sudden enthusiasms, fits of anger, terrorizing panics, groundless hopes and fears.

These climatic influences are to be sought among peoples that are still savage, and that are situated either near the equator or near the polar circle. In temperate climates, and among peoples who are only a few degrees from each other, the climatic influences are less perceptible.

The *legislator* of a savage people must pay close attention to the climate, and rectify its effects by legislation—both with respect to subsistence and commodities, and with respect to mores. There is no climate, says Mr. Hume, in which the *legislator* is unable to establish mores that are strong, pure, sublime, weak, or barbarous.[7] In our long-since civilized countries, the *legislator,* without overlooking climate, will pay more attention to prejudices, opinions, and established mores. Depending upon whether these mores, opinions, and prejudices correspond to or are contrary to his designs, he must combat them or reinforce them by his laws. Among European peoples, the causes of prejudices, customs, mores, and their opposites must be sought not only in the governments under which they live, but also in the diversity of governments under which they have lived, each of which has left its trace. Among us, one finds vestiges of the ancient Celts; one finds customs that come down to us from the Romans; others have been brought to us by the Germans, the English, the Arabs, *&c.*]

For men to feel as little as possible that they have lost the two advantages of the state of nature, equality and independence, the *legislator* in all climates, circumstances, and governments must propose to change private and property interests to community interests. Legislation is more or less perfect, according to what extent it leads to this goal; and the more it has succeeded, the more real is the possibility of general security and welfare.

7. See "Of National Characters," in Hume, *Essays, Moral, Political, and Literary,* ed. Eugene F. Miller, rev. ed. (Indianapolis: Liberty Fund, 1987), 197–215.—HC

In a nation where community interests prevail, the order of the prince or the magistrate does not seem like an order of the Country, for each man has already become, as Metastasio[8] says, *compagno delle legge e non seguace*, "the friend and not the slave of the laws." Love of Country is the only object of passion that unites competitors or antagonists; it smothers dissension; each citizen sees in another citizen only a useful member of the state; everyone proceeds together contentedly toward the public good; love of Country gives the most noble kind of courage: the sacrifice of oneself to what is loved. Love of Country enlarges one's outlook because it directs our attention to a thousand objects that interest other people as well: it raises the soul above petty interests; it purifies by making certain things obtained through injustice less necessary for our existence; it provides the enthusiasm of virtue. A state animated with this spirit does not threaten its neighbors with invasion, and they have nothing to fear from them. We have just seen that a state cannot expand without losing its freedom, and as it extends its frontiers, it must yield greater power to a smaller number of men, or to a single man, until it has become a great empire with the laws, glory, and welfare of the people bound to disappear in the rule of despotism. A state in which the love of Country reigns supreme fears this misfortune as the worst of all, remains at peace, and allows others to do so. Look at the Swiss, this country of good citizens, respected by all of Europe, surrounded by more powerful nations: they owe their tranquility to the esteem and confidence of their neighbors, who are acquainted with their love of peace, freedom, and Country. If a nation in which community interests prevail does not regret having submitted its will to the general will [*see* Natural Right], if it does not feel the weight of the law, it feels even less the burden of taxation; they pay little, they pay with joy. These happy people multiply, and the excess population becomes a new cause of security and welfare.

[In legislation, everything is linked; everything depends on everything else; the effects of a good law extend over a thousand things extraneous to that law. One good procures another; the effect reacts upon the cause; the general order maintains all parts; each part exerts influence on the other

8. Pietro Metastasio (1698–1782), Italian poet, the most celebrated librettist in Europe during the eighteenth century.

and on the general order. The spirit of community, spread throughout the whole, links and vitalizes the whole.

In democracies, the citizens are more free and equal because of the constitutive law than in other governments. In democracies, where the state is truly the possession of each individual because of the role the people play in affairs, the weakness of the Country increases patriotism, men in communal danger become necessary to each other, and the virtue of each draws profit and strength from the virtue of all. In democracies, I say, less art and less care are therefore necessary than in states where the power and administration are in the hands of a small number or of one alone.

When the spirit of community is not the necessary effect of the constitutive laws, it must be the effect of the forms, of some laws, and of the administration. Look at the seed within us of passions that pit us against our fellows—now as rivals, now as enemies. Look at the seed within us of passions that unite us to society. It is up to the *legislator* to repress the former and stimulate the latter. In stimulating these social passions, he will dispose the citizens to the spirit of community.

By means of laws that require the citizens to render each other mutual services, he can inculcate a habit of humanity in them; by means of laws, he can make of that virtue one of the mainsprings of his government. I am speaking of the possible, and I call it possible, because it has been real in the other hemisphere. The laws of Peru aimed to unite the citizens by chains of humanity. While laws in other systems of legislation prohibited men from harming each other, in Peru they constantly ordained that men do good to each other. In establishing the community of goods (as much as is possible outside the state of nature), these laws weakened the spirit of property, source of all vice. In Peru, the holidays and the first days of spring were days where people cultivated the state fields, the old man's or the orphan's field. Every citizen worked for the mass of citizens; he deposited the fruit of his labor in the state warehouses, and received the fruit of others' labor in return. That people had as enemies only men capable of evil. They attacked neighboring peoples in order to eliminate their barbarous customs. The Incas wanted to attract all nations to their amiable mores. Even in combating the cannibals, they avoided destroying them; they seemed to seek less the submission than the welfare of the vanquished.

The *legislator* can establish a relationship of benevolence between himself and his people, and between his people and himself, thereby extending the spirit of community. The people love a prince who is concerned with their welfare. The prince loves men who entrust their fate with him; he loves the witnesses of his virtues, the organs of his glory. Benevolence turns the state into a family that obeys paternal authority. What might a prince like Henry IV have done without the superstition that brutalized his age and made his people ferocious! In all times and in all monarchies, skillful princes have made use of benevolence as a resource. The greatest praise one can bestow upon a king is the one that a Danish historian bestowed upon Canute the Good: "he lived with his people like a father with his children."[9] Friendship, beneficence, generosity, and gratitude will inevitably be common virtues in a government where benevolence is one of the mainsprings. Those virtues formed Chinese morals until the reign of Chi-T-Sou.[10] When the emperors of that empire—too vast for an ordered monarchy—began to make themselves feared, when they made their authority depend less on the love of the people than on their Tartar soldiers, Chinese morals stopped being pure, but they remained mild.

One can imagine what energy, what activity, what enthusiasm, what courage this spirit of benevolence might spread among the people, and how it interests the whole nation in the community. I am glad to say that in France, we have more than once seen examples of this. Benevolence is the sole remedy for the abuses that are inevitable in those governments whose constitutions leave the least liberty to their citizens and the least equality among them. The constitutive and civil laws will inspire less the benevolence than the conduct of the *legislator*, and the forms by which his will is announced and executed.

The *legislator* will excite the sentiment of honor—that is, the desire for the esteem of self and others, the desire to be honored, to have honors. This is a necessary force in all governments. But the *legislator* will take care that this sentiment be joined to the spirit of community, as in Sparta and

9. The references would be to Henry IV (r. 1589–1610), king of France, and probably to Canute II, king of much of Scandinavia and eventually of England until his death in 1035.—HC

10. Seemingly a reference to Kublai Khan, who founded the Yuan dynasty in 1271, attributing the founding to his grandfather, Genghis Khan.—HC

Rome, and that the citizen, attached to his own honor and his own glory, be if possible even more attached to the honor and glory of his Country. In Rome, there was a temple of honor, but one couldn't enter except by passing through the temple of virtue.[11] Independent of love of Country, the feeling of honor can make the citizens capable of grand efforts for her.[12] But it does not join them together; on the contrary, it multiplies for them the objects of jealousy. The interest of the state is sometimes sacrificed to the honor of a single citizen, and honor leads all of them to distinguish themselves from each other more than to cooperate under the yoke of their duties in upholding the laws and in the general good.]

Should the *legislator* make the practice of religion one of the mainsprings in the machinery of government?

[If the religion is false, then as enlightenment spreads among men, it will make known this falsity, not to the bottom class of the people but to the first orders of citizens—that is, to the men who are destined to lead the rest and who owe them an example of patriotism and the virtues. If the religion had been the source of their virtues, then once disabused of that religion, one would see them change their morals. They would lose a bridle and a motive, and would be disillusioned.]

If the religion is the true one, then new dogmas and new opinions can be involved in political questions; and this new way of thinking can be opposed to the government. Now, if the people are accustomed to obeying by the force of religion more than by that of laws, they will follow the stream of its opinions, and they will overthrow the constitution of the state, or will no longer follow its impulses. [What ravages the Anabaptists caused in Westphalia! The Abyssinian fast weakened them to the point of rendering them incapable of sustaining the travails of war.[13] Wasn't it the Puritans who led the hapless Charles I to the scaffold?[14] The Jews didn't dare engage in combat on the Sabbath day.]

11. Possibly a reference to the temple to Honos and Virtus completed by M. Claudius Marcellus in 222 B.C.—HC

12. See HONOR, above, also by Saint-Lambert.—HC

13. The Anabaptists in Münster (Westphalia) saw their communistic experiment collapse in 1534–35; the Abyssinian fast refers to the unusually rigorous annual regime of the Coptic Christian Church.—HC

14. King Charles I was executed in January 1649.—HC

If the *legislator* makes religion one of the mainsprings of the state, it necessarily gives too much influence to priests, who will soon acquire political ambition. In countries where the *legislator* has, so to speak, amalgamated religion with the government, we have seen priests who, after they have become important, favor despotism to increase their own authority; and this authority, once established, threatens despotism and contests its power to tyrannize the people.

Finally religion would be a mainspring whose widespread consequences could never be entirely foreseen nor controlled by the *legislator*. This is a sufficient reason for him to make the principal laws (either constitutive or civil) and their execution independent of religious worship and dogmas; but he must respect and love religion and make it loved and respected.

The *legislator* must never forget the disposition of human nature for superstition. He can assume that it will exist at all times and among all peoples: it will always be blended even with the true religion. Knowledge and the progress of reason are the best remedies against this sickness of our species, but up to a certain point it is incurable and thereby deserves much indulgence.

[The conduct of the Chinese in this regard seems to me excellent. Philosophers are ministers of the prince, and the provinces are covered with pagodas and gods. Severity is never used toward those who worship the gods. But when a god has not answered the prayers of the people and they have become discontented to the point of allowing themselves some doubt about his divinity, the mandarins seize this moment to abolish one superstition; they smash the god and overturn the temple.]

The education of children will be for the *legislator* an effective means of attaching the people to the Country, of inspiring them with community spirit, humanity, benevolence, public virtues, private virtues, love of honesty, passions useful to the state, and finally of giving them and of conserving for them the kind of character, of genius that is suitable to the nation. Whenever the *legislator* was careful in encouraging the proper education for inspiring in his people the character they should have, this character had great force and endured for a long time. [In the space of 500 years, virtually no change was made in the astonishing mores of Lacedemon. Among the ancient Persians, education made them love the monarchy and their laws. It is especially to education that the Chinese owe the immutability of their mores. For a long time, the Romans taught their children only agriculture, the military art, and the laws of their country; they inspired in them only a love of frugality, glory, and Country; they gave their children only their knowledge and their passions. In any Country, there are different orders, different classes. There is virtue and knowledge that should be common to all orders and classes; there is virtue and knowledge that is more suitable to certain professions. And the *legislator* must ensure that these important details are looked after. It is especially princes and the men destined to hold our fate in the balance that must be educated in governing a nation in the manner that she wants to be and ought to be. In Sweden, the king is not in charge of his son's education. It was not long ago that at the assembly of the estates of that realm, a senator said to the governor of the heir to the throne: "Take the prince to the shacks of the industrious poor. Make him see the wretches up close, and teach him that it is not to serve the whims of a dozen sovereigns that the peoples of Europe have come into being."

[When forms, education, constitutive and civil laws have all contributed to assuring the defense and survival of the state, the tranquility of the citizens and their mores; when the people are attached to Country and have taken on the sort of character that is most appropriate to the government under which they are to live, a manner of thinking is established that comes to be perpetuated in the nation. Everything associated with the constitution and with the mores seems sacred. The spirit of the people does not allow itself to examine the utility of a law or custom. People don't discuss the relative necessity of duties; they know only how to respect and follow them. And if they do argue about their boundaries, it is less to restrict these boundaries than to extend them. That is when citizens have principles that are rules for their conduct, and the *legislator* adds the authority of opinion to the authority given him by the laws. This authority of opinion enters into all governments, and reinforces them.[15] It is because of opinion that virtually everywhere, the majority—poorly governed—do not murmur about obeying the minority. The real forces are with the subjects, but opinion constitutes the force of the masters; this is true even down to despotic

15. For a perhaps stronger statement on the priority of opinion, see "Of the First Principles of Government," in Hume, *Essays,* 32–36.—HC

states. If the emperors of Rome and the sultans of the Turks have reigned by fear over the great majority of their subjects, then to make themselves feared, they also had praetorians and janissaries whom they ruled by opinion.[16] Sometimes this opinion is merely a widespread idea that the ruling family has a real right to the throne; sometimes, it is connected to religion, sometimes to the idea people have adopted concerning the scale of the oppressive power; the only truly solid opinion is the one founded on the welfare and approbation of the citizens.

The power of opinion also increases through habit, if it is not weakened by unforeseen shocks, sudden revolutions, and great blunders.

Through administration, the *legislator* preserves the power, welfare, and genius of his people. Without a good administration, the best laws save neither states from decadence nor peoples from corruption.

Since the laws must deprive the citizens of the least liberty possible and leave as much equality as possible among them, then in governments where men are the least free and the least equal, it is by administration that the *legislator* must make them forget what they have lost of the two great advantages of the state of nature. He must constantly consult the desires of the nation. He must expose the details of administration to the eyes of the public. He must account to them for his favors. He must even enlist the people to take an interest in the government, to discuss it, to follow its operations; this is a means of making them attached to Country. "The *legislator*," says a king who writes, lives, and reigns as a philosopher, "must persuade the people that the law alone can do everything, and that fantasy can do nothing."

The *legislator* will dispose his people to humanity by the goodness and consideration with which he treats every manner of man—whether citizen or stranger: by encouraging inventions and men useful to the human race; by the pity he will evince toward the poor; by his attentiveness about avoiding war and superfluous expenses; finally, by the esteem he will himself accord to men known by their goodness.

The same conduct that contributes to spreading the sentiment of humanity among his people stimulates within himself that sentiment of

16. Praetorians and Janissaries, the bodyguards of those respective regimes.—HC

benevolence that is the bond between him and his people. Sometimes he will stimulate this sentiment by dazzling sacrifices of his personal interest to his nation's interest—by preferring in his favors, for example, the man useful to Country over the man useful only to himself. A king of China, not finding his son to be worthy of succeeding him, had his scepter passed on to his minister, and said: "I would rather my son do poorly and my people do well than my son do well and my people do poorly." In China, the kings' edicts are exhortations by a father to his children. The edicts have to instruct and exhort as much as they command. This was the practice of our kings in the past, and they have lost something by neglecting it. The *legislator* can't give all the orders of the state too many proofs of his benevolence. A king of Persia admitted the plowmen to his table, and said to them, "I am one among you. You need me, and I need you; let us live as brothers."

By distributing honors justly and fittingly, the *legislator* will animate the sentiment of honor and will steer it toward the good of the state. When honors are a reward for virtue, honor will bring virtuous actions.[17]

The *legislator* holds in his hands two reins with which he can guide the passions at will—I mean punishments and rewards. Punishments should only be imposed by the tribunals in the name of the law. But the *legislator* should reserve to himself the power to freely distribute a portion of the rewards.

In a country where the constitution of the state gives the citizens an interest in the government and where education and administration have engraved in men honor and patriotic principles and sentiments, it suffices to impose the lightest punishments on the guilty. It is enough that these punishments indicate that the punished citizen has committed an offence; the looks of his fellow citizens add to his chastisement. The *legislator* is in charge of attaching the gravest punishments to the most dangerous vices for his nation. He could make people regard real advantages as punishments, if it were useful that the nation's desires not be inclined in that direction. He could even make men regard as real punishments what in other

17. Montesquieu had argued, controversially, that honor but not virtue was essential to a monarchy such as France; see *Laws,* 3.5–7. See also Saint-Lambert's entry HONOR, above.—HC

countries might serve as rewards. In Sparta, after certain offenses, a citizen was no longer allowed to lend out his wife. Among the Peruvians, the citizen prohibited from working in the public field would have been a very unhappy man. Under these sublime bodies of laws, a man saw himself as punished when he was brought back to his personal interest and the spirit of property. Nations are degraded when torture or the privation of possessions become ordinary forms of correction; it is proof that the *legislator* is obliged to punish what the nation would no longer punish. In republics, the law should be mild, because one is never exempt from it. In monarchies, it should be more severe, because the *legislator* must make his clemency loved by pardoning in spite of the law. Nonetheless, among the Persians before Cyrus, the laws were quite mild.[18] They condemned to death or infamy only the citizens who had done more evil than good.

In countries where punishments can be light, modest rewards for virtue are sufficient. Virtue is pretty weak and pretty rare if one has to pay for it. Rewards can serve to change the spirit of property into a spirit of community: (1) when they are granted upon proof of this latter sort of spirit; (2) by accustoming citizens to regard as rewards the new occasions given them to sacrifice personal interest to the interest of all.

The *legislator* can set a boundless price on his benevolence by bestowing it only upon men who have served the state well.

If ranks, preeminences, and honors are always a prize for service, and if they impose the duty of rendering new services in turn, they will not excite the envy of the multitude, who will not feel the humiliation of ranks. The *legislator* will give them other consolations for that inequality of wealth which is an inevitable effect of large states. It must be that one can only achieve extreme opulence by an industry that enriches the state, never at the expense of the people. It must be that the burdens of society are made to fall on the rich men who enjoy the advantages of society. The taxes in the hands of a *legislator* who administers well are a means of abolishing certain abuses, or a pernicious form of industry, or vice. They can be a means of encouraging the most useful type of industry, of exciting certain talents and certain virtues.

18. Cyrus (d. 530 B.C.), Achaemenid king of Persia.—HC

The *legislator* will not regard courtly ritual[19] and ceremonies as indifferent matters; he must strike the eyesight, the sense that acts most on the imagination. The ceremonies should awaken in the people a feeling for the power of the *legislator*, but they should also be linked to the idea of virtue. They should call up the recollection of noble deeds, the memory of magistrates, illustrious warriors, good citizens. Most of the ceremonies and courtly rituals of our moderate governments of Europe would be fitting only for the despots of Asia. And many are ridiculous, because they no longer have the relationship with mores and customs that they had at the time of their institution. They used to be respectable; now they make us laugh.

[The *legislator* will not neglect manners.[20] When manners are no longer the expression of morals, they are at least their bridle; they force men to seem to be what they ought to be. And if they only imperfectly replace morals, they nonetheless often have the same effects. It is from the place of the *legislator's* residence, by his examples and by the example of respected men that manners spread throughout the people.

Public games, spectacles, and assemblies will be one of the means the *legislator* uses to join the citizens together. The Swiss brotherhoods,[21] the English coteries,[22] our spectacles, our holidays and festivals all spread the spirit of society, which contributes to the spirit of patriotism. These assemblies, moreover, accustom men to appreciate the value of the attention and judgment of the multitude; they enhance the love of glory and the fear of shame. Only timid vice or failed pretentiousness severs itself from these assemblies. And in any case, even if they had no other use than to multiply our desires, they would still merit the attention of the *legislator*.

19. *Etiquette,* the detailed schedule of daily activities taking place in the royal household, first used of Spain, eventually of other European courts (*Dictionnaire de l'Académie Française* [Paris, 1762]).—HC

20. See MANNERS, below, also written by Saint-Lambert.—HC

21. *Confrairie,* a deviant spelling of *confrérie* (confraternity or brotherhood, often religious) which placed the emphasis upon the *frairie,* that is, "a party for amusement, good food and drink, and debauchery" (*Dictionnaire de l'Académie Française,* 1694).—HC

22. *Cotterie,* which Littré defines: "old word, which signified a certain number of peasants, joined together to hold a lord's lands." More recently, it had come to be a colloquial word for any regular group of close-knit neighbors, friends, or family.—HC

In reminding himself of the purposes and principles of all legislation, he must, in proportion to what men have lost of their liberty and their equality, compensate them by a tranquil enjoyment of their possessions and a protection against authority that will prevent them from desiring a less absolute government, where the advantage of more liberty is almost always disturbed by the anxiety of losing it.]

If the *legislator* neither respects nor consults the general will; if he makes his power felt more than that of the law; if he treats men with arrogance, talent with indifference, poverty with harshness; if he sacrifices his subjects to his family, the finances to his fantasies, peace to his glory; if his favor is granted to the man who knows how to please more than to the man who can serve; if honor, if position are obtained by intrigue; if taxes increase, then the community spirit disappears; impatience overcomes the citizen of a republic; languor grips the citizen of the monarchy; he looks for the state and sees nothing else but the prey of a master; work slows down; the prudent man remains idle; the virtuous man is merely a fool; the veil of public opinion falls; national principles seem to be nothing more than prejudices, and they are in fact only that; people are drawn closer to the law of nature because legislation violates their rights; morals no longer exist; the nation loses its character; the *legislator* is astonished at the total lack of public assistance, and he increases the rewards for services rendered; but those individuals who flattered virtue have lost their value, which was maintained only by public opinion; in place of the noble passions that previously motivated the people, the *legislator* tries to substitute greed and fear, and he further increases the vice and degradation of the nation. If in his perversity he retains those phrases, those expressions of benevolence used by his predecessors to announce their good will, if he retains the language of a father with the conduct of a despot, he plays the role of a charlatan who is at first scorned and soon imitated; he introduces treachery and duplicity into the nation, and, as Guarini[23] says, *viso di carità, mente d'invidia.*[24]

[Sometimes the *legislator* sees the constitution of the state dissolve, and the genius of the people expire, because the body of laws had only one

23. Giovanni Battista Guarini (1538–1612), Italian poet and moralist, author of *Il Pastor fido* [The faithful shepherd].

24. "He has a charitable face but an envious [or spiteful] mind."

object, and as this object changes, first the mores and soon the laws could not remain the same.

Lacedemon was founded to preserve liberty in the middle of a host of petty states that were weaker than herself, because they did not have her mores. But she lacked the power to grow without destroying herself. The object of legislation in China was the tranquility of the citizens through the exercise of mild virtues. That great empire would not have been the prey of hordes of Tartars if the *legislators* there had inspired and maintained the strong virtues, and if as much thought had been given to elevating the soul as to directing it. Too much of the object of legislation in Rome was aggrandizement. Peace for the Romans was a state of turmoil, factions, and anarchy; they devoured each other when they no longer had the world to subdue. Too much of the object of legislation in Venice is to hold the people in slavery. They are either softened up or degraded, and the vaunted wisdom of that government is merely the art of surviving without power and without virtues.

Often a limited *legislator* unties the springs of the government and disrupts its principles, because he does not sufficiently see their unity, and because he gives all his attention to the part that he sees alone or that is closest to his private taste, his character.

One conqueror, greedy for conquests, will neglect jurisprudence, commerce, the arts. Another stimulates the nation to commerce and neglects war. A third does too much to promote the arts of luxury, while the useful arts are depreciated. And so on for the rest. There is no nation—at least no great nation—that cannot be, under a good government, simultaneously warlike and commercial, learned, and polite.

I am going to terminate this article, already too long, with some reflections on the present state of Europe.

The system of equilibrium, which out of a multitude of states forms but a single body, influences the decision making of all *legislators*. Constitutive laws, civil laws, and administration are more closely linked today with the law of nations, and indeed are more dependent on it than they were in the past. Nothing happens any more in one state that doesn't interest all others, and the *legislator* of one powerful state influences the destiny of all Europe.

Out of this new situation for men, there arise many consequences.

For example, there can be small monarchies and large republics. In the former, the government will be maintained by associations, alliances, and by the general system. The petty princes of Germany and Italy are monarchs, and if their people got tired of their government, they would be repressed by the sovereigns of the large states. The dissensions and parties inseparable from large republics would not nowadays be able to weaken them to the point of exposing them to invasion. No one profited from the civil wars of Switzerland and Poland.[25] Many powers will always league together against the one that wants to aggrandize itself. If Spain were a republic, and were threatened by France, she would be defended by England, Holland, *&c.*

Today in Europe there is a moral impossibility to effect conquests.[26] The result of this impossibility for the people has until now been, perhaps, more disadvantageous than advantageous. Some *legislators* have neglected the part of the administration that gives strength to states, and we've seen great kingdoms under clear skies languish without wealth and without power.

Other *legislators* have regarded conquests as merely difficult but not impossible, and their ambition has been busy multiplying the means of conquering. Some of these have given their states a purely military form, and leave their subjects hardly any job to do but that of soldier; others maintain mercenary armies even in peace, which ruins the state finances and promotes despotism. Magistrates and some lictors would make men obey the law, but immense armies are needed to make men serve a master. That's the main object of most of our *legislators,* and to fulfill it they find themselves obliged to employ the sorry expedients of debt and taxes.]

Some *legislators* have profited by the enlightenment that has rapidly spread for fifty years from one end of Europe to the other and illuminated the details of administration, the means of encouraging popula-

25. In 1733–35, there was a civil war involving numerous European powers over the succession to Poland's elective monarchy; it is less clear what the Swiss reference means.—HC

26. By "moral" here, Saint-Lambert means the opposite of "physical"—that is, everything having to do with human action and will.—HC

tion, stimulating industry, conserving the advantages of the present state of affairs, and procuring new ones. We can believe that the lights of reason and knowledge preserved by the printing press cannot be extinguished and can increase even more. If some despot wanted to plunge his nation into darkness again, some free nations will exist to restore the light for them.

During enlightened centuries it is impossible to base legislation on false beliefs or personal folly; even charlatanism and the bad faith of ministers are immediately perceived and only arouse the indignation of the people. It is equally difficult to spread destructive fanaticism, like the kind cultivated by the disciples of Odin[27] and Mohammed: you cannot make any modern nation of Europe accept prejudices that are contrary to the rights of men and the laws of nature.

All nations today have rather just ideas of their neighbors, and consequently they have less blind enthusiasm for their Country than in the Dark Ages; there is hardly any enthusiasm when there is a great deal of enlightenment; this type of patriotic zeal represents the impulses of a passionate rather than an educated soul. When people compare all the nations in regard to their laws, morals, and men of talent, they will find so few reasons to prefer one to the other that if they conserve for their Country that love which is the fruit of personal interest, they will at least no longer have that blind enthusiasm which is the fruit of exclusive esteem.

In our day and age you could not inspire by the tactics of supposition, imputation, and political artifice national hatreds as intense as those leaders previously inspired. Libel directed against us by our neighbors has hardly any effect except on the weak and vile part of the inhabitants of a capital, which includes the worst of the rabble as well as the best of the people.

Religion, which has become more enlightened from day to day, teaches us that we must not hate those people who do not think like us; we know today how to distinguish the sublime spirit of religion from the suggestions of its ministers. We have seen in our time the Protestant powers at war with the Catholic powers, and not one of them has succeeded with their

27. Odin, one of the principal gods in Scandinavian mythology, was worshiped by the Teutonic tribes as a war god.

plan of inspiring the people with that brutal and ferocious zeal that people previously had against each other, even during the peace among nations of different forms of worship.

All men from all countries have become necessary for the exchange of the fruits of industry and the products of their earth; commerce is a new bond for men; it is in the interest of every nation that another nation conserves its wealth, industry, banks, luxury, and agriculture; the ruin of Leipzig, Lisbon, and Lima[28] caused bankruptcy to spread throughout Europe and had an effect on the fortunes of millions of citizens.

Commerce, as enlightenment, diminishes the ferocious part of man, but just as enlightenment removes the enthusiasm of narrow esteem, commerce also removes perhaps the enthusiasm for virtue; it slowly extinguishes the spirit of disinterestedness, which is replaced with that of justice; it softens the customs and morals that are refined by enlightenment, but by directing men to what is useful more than to what is beautiful, to the prudent rather than to the grand, it diminishes perhaps the generosity, power, and greatness of morality.

Given the commercial outlook and the knowledge that men today have of the true interests of all nations, it follows that *legislators* must be less preoccupied with defense and conquest than they previously were; it follows that they must favor the cultivation of the land and the arts and encourage the consumption and the manufacture of their products; but they must take care at the same time that refined customs and morals do not lose their force and that the high regard of martial virtues are maintained.

For there will always be wars in Europe; we can rely here on the interests of ministers; but those wars that were fought because of a conflict between nations will be promoted in the future mainly by *legislators*.

[What is also bound to set Europe ablaze is the differences between governments. This splendid part of the world is divided into republics and monarchies. The spirit of the latter is active, and although it may not be in their interest to expand, they may initiate conquests at times when they are governed by men who are not guided by their nation's interest. The

28. Leipzig was under siege five times and occupied on four different occasions during the Thirty Years' War; Lisbon was destroyed by a great earthquake in 1755, and Lima by earthquake in 1746.

spirit of republics is pacific, but the love of liberty—or a superstitious fear of losing it—will often induce republican states to wage war in order to humble or repress monarchical states. This arrangement of Europe will sustain an emulation of the strong and warlike virtues, for the diversity of sentiments and mores that are born from different governments will counter the progress of that flabbiness, that excessive mildness in mores that is the effect of commerce, luxury, and protracted peace.]

Legislation
(*Législation*)

This short entry is typical of Diderot's practice of raising large questions in few words.

LEGISLATION (*Grammar and Politics*), the art of giving laws to peoples. The best legislation is that which is the simplest and most consistent with nature. It is not a matter of opposing men's passions, but, on the contrary, of encouraging them by applying them to the private and public interest. By this means, the number of crimes and criminals will be diminished, and the laws will be reduced to a very small number. *See the articles* LEGISLATOR *and* LAWS.

This article can be found at 9:363 in the original edition of the *Encyclopédie*.

Natural Liberty
(*Liberté Naturelle*)

This article and Civil Liberty *are unsigned and anonymous, though note that the third in what forms a sort of sequence,* Political Liberty, *is signed by Jaucourt.* Liberté Naturelle *appears before* Liberté Civile *in the* Encyclopédie.

Natural Liberty (*Natural right*), right that nature gives all men to dispose of their persons and their property in the manner they judge most conducive to their happiness, under the restriction that they do it within the terms of natural law and that they not abuse it to the detriment of other men. The laws of nature are therefore the rule and measure of this *liberty,* for although men in the primitive state of nature are in a state of independence toward each other, they are all dependent upon the laws of nature, by which they ought to direct their actions.

The first state that man acquires by nature and that is considered the most precious of all the goods he might possess is the state of *liberty.* He cannot exchange himself with another, or sell himself, or ruin himself. For all men are naturally born free—that is, they are not subject to the power of a master, and no one has a right of property over them.

By virtue of this state, all men hold from nature itself the power to do what they will and to dispose as they wish of their actions and their property, provided they not act against the laws of the government to which they are subject.

This article can be found at 9:471 in the original edition of the *Encyclopédie.*

Among the Romans, a man lost his *natural liberty* when he was taken by the enemy in an open war or when, to punish him for some crime, he was reduced to the condition of a slave. But the Christians have abolished servitude in peace and war, to the point where prisoners taken in the war on the infidels are considered free men, so that whoever kills one of these prisoners would be regarded and punished as a murderer.

Moreover, all Christian powers have judged that a servitude that gives the master a right of life and death over his slaves is incompatible with the perfection to which the Christian religion summons men. But how is it that the Christian powers have not judged that this same religion, independent of natural law, cries out against the enslavement of the Negroes? it's because they need them for their colonies, their plantations, and their mines. *Auri sacra fames!*[1]

1. Virgil, *Aeneid*, 3.57, "O accursed hunger for gold!"

Civil Liberty
(*Liberté Civile*)

This article and Natural Liberty *are unsigned and anonymous, though note that the third in what forms a sort of sequence,* Political Liberty, *is signed by Jaucourt.*

Civil Liberty (*Law of nations*). This is the natural *liberty,* stripped of that part constituting the independence of individuals and communal goods, to live under the laws that procure them security and property. This *civil liberty* consists at the same time in not being able to be forced to do a thing that the law does not decree, and one is in this state only because one is governed by civil laws. Thus, the better these laws are, the more auspicious is this *liberty.*

No word, as M. de Montesquieu says, has struck minds in so many ways as has *liberty.*[1] Some have taken it for the ease of removing the person to whom they had given tyrannical power; some, for the faculty of electing the person whom they were to obey. Others have taken this word for the right to be armed and to be able to use violence; still others, for the privilege of being governed only by a man of their own nation, or by their own laws. Many have attached this name to one form of government and excluded the others. Those who had tasted republican government put it in that government, whereas those who had enjoyed monarchical government placed it in monarchy. In short, each person has given the name of *liberty* to

This article can be found at 9:472 in the original edition of the *Encyclopédie.*

1. For the remainder of this paragraph, see Montesquieu, *The Spirit of the Laws,* 11.2–4.

the government that was consistent with his customs or his inclinations. But *liberty* is the right to do everything the laws permit, and if one citizen could do what these laws forbid, he would no longer have *liberty* because the others would also have this same power. It is true that this *liberty* is found only in moderate governments—that is, in governments whose constitution is such that no one is constrained to do the things the law does not oblige him to do, or kept from doing the things the law permits him to do.

Civil liberty is thus founded on the best possible laws. And in a state that had its fair share of them, the man who had been brought to trial under the law, and who was going to be hung the next day, would be freer than a Turkish pasha.[2] Consequently, there is no *liberty* in states in which the legislative and executive powers are in the same hands. *A fortiori,* there is no more *liberty* in those states in which the power of judging is joined to the legislative and executive.[3]

2. See Montesquieu, *Laws,* 12.2; a pasha was a Turkish dignitary, sometimes a provincial governor.

3. For these last two sentences, see Montesquieu, *Laws,* 11.6.

Political Liberty
(*Liberté Politique*)

POLITICAL LIBERTY (*Political right*). The *political liberty* of a state is formed by the fundamental laws that establish the distribution between the legislative power, the executive power over things depending on the law of nations, and the executive power over things depending on the civil law, so that these three powers are bound together.[1]

The *political liberty* of a citizen is that tranquility of mind that comes from the opinion each person has of his security, and in order for him to have this security, the government must be such that one citizen cannot fear another citizen. Good civil and political laws[2] assure this *liberty;*[3] it also triumphs when the criminal laws derive every punishment from the particular nature of the crime.[4]

There is one nation in the world whose constitution has *political liberty* as its direct purpose.[5] If the principles on which it bases this constitution are solid, its advantages must be recognized. It is on this subject that I remember hearing a fine English talent say that Corneille has better depicted the lofty sentiments that *political liberty* inspires than any of their poets, in this speech that Viriatus made to Sertorius:

> Set free the Tagus, and forget the Tiber.
> Freedom is naught when all the world is free.

This article can be found at 9:472 in the original edition of the *Encyclopédie*.

1. See Montesquieu, *The Spirit of the Laws,* 11.5–6.
2. *Lois civiles et politiques.*
3. Montesquieu, *Laws,* 12.2.
4. Montesquieu, *Laws,* 12.4.
5. Montesquieu, *Laws,* 11.5.

'Tis sweet to show one's freedom to the eyes
Of those enslaved along the Rhone or captive
In Rome, and see envied by humbled peoples
That deep respect which is the valiant's portion.
Sertorius, act. IV, sc. vi.[6]

I do not claim to determine whether the English presently enjoy the prerogative I am discussing; it is enough for me to say with M. de Montesquieu that it is established by their laws, and that after all, this extreme *political liberty* should not mortify those who have only a moderate one, because the excess even of reason is not always desirable, and men in general almost always accommodate themselves better to middle ways than to extremes.[7] (*D.J.*)

6. "Sertorius," in *Moot Plays of Corneille,* trans. Lacy Lockert (Nashville: Vanderbilt University Press, 1959), 233. The play first appeared in 1662.

7. For this paragraph, see Montesquieu, *Laws,* 11.6.

Liberty; Inscription, Medals
(*Liberté*)

LIBERTY (*Inscription, Medals*). On medals, *Liberty* holds in its right hand a bonnet, which is its symbol. Everyone knows that this was given to those who were enfranchised. Appian[1] recounts that after the assassination of Caesar, one of the murderers carried around the city a bonnet at the end of a pike, as a sign of *liberty*. On Mount Aventine, there was a famous temple dedicated to *Liberty*, with a square in front, around which ranged a portico that people called the *atrium libertatis*. Under this portico was the celebrated library of Asinius Pollio, who rebuilt that edifice.[2]

Under Tiberius, a statue to *Liberty* was built in the public square, once the death of Sejanus was known.[3] Josephus reports that after the massacre of Caius, Cassius Chaerea came to ask the consuls for the password, which had not been seen within anyone's memory, and that the word they gave him was *liberty*.[4]

Caius having died, a monument to *Liberty* was built under Claudius's reign. But Nero plunged the empire into a cruel servitude. His death again spread a general joy. All the people of Rome and the provinces took the bonnet of *liberty;* it was a universal triumph. People rushed to represent

This article can be found at 9:475 in the original edition of the *Encyclopédie*.

1. Appian, Greek historian of early second century A.D., author of *The Civil Wars*, a surviving section of his broader Roman history.

2. Gaius Asinius Pollio (76 B.C.–A.D. 4), praetor, commander in Spain, he built Rome's first public library with booty from the Parthian campaign of 39 B.C.

3. Tiberius, Roman emperor (42 B.C.–A.D. 37, r. 14–37); Sejanus (20 B.C.–A.D. 31), an ambitious military leader and associate of Tiberius.

4. Cassius Chaerea, centurion and tribune in the praetorian guard; mocked by Caius (i.e., Caligula) for his alleged effeminacy, and instrumental in the latter's murder in A.D. 41.

the image of *Liberty* everywhere on statues and coins, thinking it was being reborn.

One particular inscription tells us of a new statue of *Liberty* built under Galba.

Here it is, as it is read in Rome on the marble base that supported that statue:

> *Imaginum domus Aug. cultoribus signum Libertatis restitutae, Ser. Galbae imperatoris Aug. curatores anni secundi, C. Turranius Polubius, L. Calpurnius Zena, C. Murdius Lalus, C. Turranius Florus, C. Murdius Demosthenes.*[5]

On the left side of the base is written:

> *Dedic. id. Octob. C. Bellico Natale Cos. P. Cornelio Scipione Asiatico.*[6]

These two consuls were substituted in the year 68 of Jesus Christ.

This statue, or something similar, was the model for so many coins struck during the time of the same emperor, coins that bore on the reverse side, *libertas August. libertas restituta, libertas publica.*[7] In imitation of the capital, thc provinces erected similar statues. In the cabinet of the king of France, there is a Greek medallion of Galba, with the figure of *Liberty* and the word ELEUTERIA.[8] (*D.J.*)

5. The full text would read: "To the worshippers of the images of the Imperial House, the managers Caius Turranius Polubius, Lucius Calpurnius Zena, Caius Murdius Lalus, Caius Turrandius Florus, and Caius Murdius Demosthenes gave as a gift with their own money, in the second year, this sculpture of Liberty Restored by Servius Galba, Augustus Emperor." Servius Sulpicius Galba (3 B.C.–A.D. 69), Roman emperor, 68–69.

6. The full text would read: "Dedicated on 15 October [A.D. 68] by Caius Bellicus Natalis and Caius Cornelius Scipio Asiaticus, consuls."

7. "Augustan liberty, restored liberty, public liberty."

8. Feast of Liberty.

Liberty; Mythology, Iconology
(*Liberté*)

Liberty (*Mythology, Iconology*), goddess of the Greeks and Romans. The Greeks invoked her under the name of *Eleutheria,* and sometimes they said Theoi Eleuteroi, gods of *liberty*. The Romans, who called her *Libertas,* held this divinity in singular veneration, built her numerous temples and altars, and erected a goodly number of statues to her. On Mount Aventine, Tiberius Gracchus dedicated a magnificent temple to her, supported by bronze columns and decorated with sumptuous statues. In front of it was a courtyard called the *atrium Libertatis*.[1]

After Julius Caesar subjected the Romans to his dominion, they raised a new temple in honor of that goddess, as if their *liberty* had been restored by the one who had sapped its foundations. But on a medallion of Brutus, one sees *Liberty* in the shape of a woman, holding with one hand the hat, symbol of *liberty,* and in the other hand two daggers with the inscription, *idibus Martiis,* "on the ides of March."

The goddess was even represented by a woman dressed in white, holding the bonnet in her right hand, and a javelin or rod in her left, like the one the masters used to strike their slaves when they enfranchised them. Sometimes, there is a chariot next to her.

On other medallions, she is accompanied by two women, named *Adioné* and *Abéodoné,* regarded as her followers because *liberty* includes the power of going and coming where one wants.[2]

This article can be found at 9:475–76 in the original edition of the *Encyclopédie.*

1. The "hall of freedom."

2. The reference is to the Latin words *abeo* and *adeo.*

Some Italian cities—such as Bologna, Genoa, Florence—used to have on their flags and their coats of arms the word *liberty*, and they were right. But this fine motto no longer suits them today; it belongs to London to make a trophy of it. (*D.J.*)

Law
(*Loi*)

French dictionaries have generally distinguished between loi, *any command or rule that has the force of established authority behind it, and* droit, *a normative term meaning "right" or "correct" or "just" which comes to be used as "law" by extension. By adopting Montesquieu's definition of* loi *at the outset of this article, Jaucourt gives a specific inflection to the discussion. See the translators' note, above, for* loi *and* droit.

LAW (*Natural, moral, divine, and human law*). *Law* in general is human reason insofar as it governs all the earth's peoples, and the political and civil laws of each nation are bound to be only the particular cases to which this human reason is applied.[1]

Law may be defined as a rule prescribed by the sovereign to his subjects, either to impose upon them the obligation to do or not do certain things under the threat of some punishment, or to allow them the liberty to act or not act in other things as they find appropriate, and to assure them the full enjoyment of their right in this regard.

Men, says M. de Montesquieu, are governed by various sorts of *laws*.[2] They are governed by natural law; by divine law, which is that of religion; by ecclesiastical law (otherwise called *canonical*), which is that of the administration of religion; by the law of nations, which can be considered as the civil law of the world in the sense that each people is a citizen of it; by

This article can be found at 9:643–46 in the original edition of the *Encyclopédie*.

1. See Montesquieu, *The Spirit of the Laws*, 1.3, for this definition.
2. The following discussion can be found in Montesquieu, *Laws*, 26.1.

the general political law, whose object is human wisdom, and which has founded all societies; by the particular political law, which concerns each society; by the law of conquest founded on the fact that one people was willing or able or under some necessity to do violence to another; by the civil law of each society, which allows one citizen to defend his goods and his life against every other citizen; finally, by domestic law, which comes from the fact that a society is divided into various families needing private government. Thus, there are different orders of *laws,* and the sublimity of human reason consists in knowing well which of these orders is most suitable to the things that need to be decreed, and in not bringing confusion into the principles that ought to govern men.

A host of reflections arise on this subject. Let us articulate some of them from the profound writings of those fine talents who have enlightened the world with their works on this important matter.

The binding force that the inferior *laws* have flows from that of the superior *laws*. Thus, nothing can be prescribed within families that is contrary to the *laws* of the state of which they are a part. In each civil state, nothing can be ordained that is contrary to the *laws* that bind all peoples, such as those that prescribe not to take the property of another, to redress the damage one has done, to keep one's word, *&c.,* and these *laws* common to all nations must include nothing that is contrary to the supreme dominion of God over his creatures. Thus, once there are things in the inferior *laws* that are contrary to the superior *laws,* they no longer have the force of *laws*.

A more extensive code of laws is necessary for a people dedicated to commerce than for a people satisfied to cultivate their lands.[3] The latter people needs a greater one than a people who live by their flocks. These last need a greater one than a people who live by hunting. Thus, the *laws* should be closely related to the way in which the various peoples procure their subsistence.

In despotic governments, the despot is the prince, the state, and the *laws*.[4] In monarchical governments there is one *law*. Where it is precise, the judge follows it; where it is not, he seeks its spirit. In republican governments,

3. For this paragraph, see Montesquieu, *Laws,* 18.8.

4. For this paragraph, see Montesquieu, *Laws,* 6.3.

it is in the nature of the constitution for judges to follow the letter of the *law*. There is no citizen against whom one can interpret a law when it is a question of his property, his honor, or his life. In England the jury decides on the fact; the judge pronounces the punishment imposed by *law:* he needs only his eyes for that.

Those who have in their hands the *laws* to govern peoples must always allow themselves to be governed by the *laws*. It is the *law* and not man that must rule. The *law*, says Plutarch, is the queen of all mortals and immortals.[5] The edict of 1499 alone, issued by Louis XII, makes his memory dear to all who dispense justice in this kingdom, and to all who love justice. By that memorable edict, he decrees "that the *law* always be followed, despite the orders contrary to the *law* that importunity might wrest from the monarch."[6]

The motive and effect of the *laws* must be the prosperity of the citizens. This prosperity arises from the integrity of mores, the maintenance of the police, the uniform distribution of justice, the strength and opulence of the state; the *laws* are the sinews of good administration. When someone asked King Anaxidamus of Lacedemon who had the authority in Sparta, he answered it was the *laws*. He could have added: along with the mores that they influence, and from which they derive their force.[7] In fact, the laws and mores of the Spartans, intimately united in the hearts of the citizens, formed so to speak but a single body. But let us not expect to see Sparta reborn in the midst of commerce and the love of profit.

> "The great difference Lycurgus introduced between Lacedemon and other cities," says Xenophon, "consists in the fact that he has above all made the citizens obey the *laws*. They run when the magistrate calls them, whereas in Athens, a rich man would despair if it were thought he depended on the magistrate."[8]

5. Jaucourt is quoting a note from Montesquieu, *Laws,* 1.1, who in turn is quoting Plutarch, "To an Uneducated Ruler," in *Moralia*, 780c.

6. Louis XII, king of France (1498–1515); see the edict of December 22, 1499, found in Isambert et al., *Recueil général des anciennes lois françaises* [General collection of former French laws], 11:406–8.

7. Anaxidamus, Spartan king of the seventh century B.C.; see Pausanias, *Description of Greece*, III.7.6.

8. Xenophon, "The Constitution of the Lacedemonians," 8.2. Jaucourt is paraphrasing the text.

There's more: the first function of the Lacedemonian ephors upon taking office was a public proclamation by which they enjoined the citizens not to observe the *laws* but to love them, so that observing them would not be hard.

Nothing should be dearer to men than *laws* designed to make them good, wise, and happy. The *laws* will be precious to the people to the extent that the people regard them as a rampart against despotism, and as the safeguard of a just liberty.

Amongst the *laws,* there are excellent ones, deficient ones, and useless ones. Every good *law* should be just, easy to execute, and particularly appropriate to the government and the people who receive it.

Any equivocal *law* is unjust, because it strikes without warning. Any law that is not clear, plain, and precise is deficient.

The *laws* should begin directly with the jussive terms.[9] The preambles that are usually placed there are invariably superfluous, even though they were invented for the justification of the legislator and for the satisfaction of the people. If the *law* is bad, contrary to the public good, the legislator should certainly refrain from issuing it; if it is necessary, essential, indispensable, he has no need to justify it.

The *laws* should change, but their style should always be the same—that is, simple, precise, always conveying the antiquity of their origins, like a sacred and unalterable text.

Let the *laws* always exude candor; made to prevent or punish men's wickedness, they should have the greatest innocence.

Laws that offended the principles of nature, morality, or religion would inspire horror. In the proscription of the Prince of Orange by Philip II, the latter prince promises to whoever kills him, or to his heirs, twenty thousand gold crowns and noble status—this, on the king's honor and as a servant of God. Nobility promised for such an action! Such an action decreed in one's capacity as a servant of God! All this overthrows equally the ideas of honor, morality, and religion.[10]

9. *Jussion,* that is, in the old regime, a royal command to superior courts to do what they had previously refused to do.

10. The Catholic Philip II banished the Calvinist Prince of Orange in June of 1580. A year later, the Dutch Estates General passed the Act of Abjuration, which declared their

When one does go so far as to offer reasons for a *law,* this reason must be (1) worthy of it. A Roman *law* determines that a blind man cannot plead because he does not see the ornaments of the magistracy.[11] It is pathetic to offer such a bad reason when so many good ones present themselves. (2) The alleged reason must be true. Charles IX was declared of age at the beginning of his 14th year because, said Chancellor de l'Hôpital, the *laws* regard the year as beginning when it concerns acquiring honors; but is the government of peoples only an honor? (3) In the *laws,* one must reason from reality to reality and not from reality to image or image to reality. The *law* of the Lombards, *bk. II. tit. XXXVII,* prohibits a woman who has taken a nun's habit from marrying.[12]

"For," says this *law,* "if a husband who has engaged a woman by a ring cannot marry another without committing a crime, then all the more so for the spouse of God or of the Blessed Virgin."

Finally, once the condition of things has been fixed in a *law,* one must not add vague expressions to it. In a criminal ordinance of Louis XIV, after an enumeration of royal cases, there is added: "And those the royal judges have judged in all times."[13] This addition brings back the arbitrariness that had just been avoided.

The *laws* do not make the rule of justice.[14] Rules are general, the *laws* are not; rules guide, *laws* command; the rule serves as a magnetic compass, the *laws* as a pair of geometer's compasses.[15]

Following Solon's example, one must impose on the people less the best *laws* in themselves than the best that the people can bear in their situation.[16] Otherwise, it is better to let the disorders exist than to pretend to rectify

---

independence from Philip II in a fashion sometimes compared to the American Declaration of Independence.

11. For this paragraph, and the preceding one, see Montesquieu, *Laws,* 29.16.

12. The references are to Charles IX, king of France (1560–74), and Michel de l'Hôpital (1505–73), chancellor of France.

13. For this paragraph, see Montesquieu, *Laws,* 29.16.

14. *Règle de droit,* also translated as "rule of law," though the phrase can include custom as well as law.

15. The contrast is between *boussole* and *compas,* so there is no play on words in French, as has seemed unavoidable in English.

16. The same anecdote, which derives from "Solon," in Plutarch, *Life of Solon,* 15.2, appears in Montesquieu, *Laws,* 19.21.

them by *laws* that will not be observed. For this is to abase the *laws* without remedying the problem.

There is nothing so splendid as a state in which there are suitable *laws* and in which they are observed by reason and by passion, as was done in Rome during the earliest times of the republic. For then, all the strength a faction could have is joined to the wisdom of the government.[17]

It is true that the *laws* of Rome became powerless to preserve her, but it is a normal thing that good *laws,* which have made a small republic grow, become a burden to it when it is enlarged, because they were made only to effect its enlargement.

There is a considerable difference between *laws* that enable a people to make itself master of others, and those that maintain its power once it is acquired.[18]

Laws that cause what is indifferent to be regarded as necessary are not sensible. And they also have this disadvantage: they cause what is necessary to be considered indifferent.[19] Thus, the *laws* should only pronounce on essential things.

If indifferent *laws* are not good, useless ones are even less so, because they weaken necessary *laws*. Those that can be eluded also weaken legislation. A *law* should have its effect, and departures from it for some private agreement must not be permitted.[20]

Many *laws* that seem the same are quite different.[21] For example, Greek and Roman *laws* punished the receiver of stolen goods just as they did the robber; French *law* does likewise. The former were reasonable, the latter is not. Among the Greeks and Romans, the robber was condemned to a pecuniary punishment, so it was quite necessary to punish the receiver with the same punishment, for a man who contributes in any way whatsoever to damages should remedy them. But in France, since the punishment for robbery is capital, it has not been possible to punish the receiver like the

17. These two sentences are a slight variation on Montesquieu, *Considerations on the Causes of the Greatness of the Romans and Their Decline*, trans. David Lowenthal (New York: Free Press, 1965; repr. Indianapolis: Hackett, 1999), chap. 4, pp. 45–46.

18. The previous two paragraphs are adapted from Montesquieu, *Considerations,* chap. 9, p. 94.

19. See Montesquieu, *Laws,* 24.14.

20. For this paragraph, see Montesquieu, *Laws,* 29.16.

21. This is the topic of Montesquieu, *Laws,* 29.12.

robber without going to extremes. The one who receives stolen goods may in countless circumstances receive them innocently; the one who robs is always guilty. In truth, the receiver prevents conviction for a crime already committed, but the other commits the crime. All is passive in the one; there is action in the other. The robber must overcome more obstacles, and his soul must be hardened against the *laws* for a longer time.

Since the laws cannot foresee or trace out every case, it is up to reason to compare the omitted facts with the ones specified. When the *law* is found to be mute, the public good must decide. Custom can do nothing then, because there is a danger that it may be applied badly and that people will want to guide it instead of following it.

But bolstered by a chain and by a succession of examples, custom supplies the defect of the *law*, takes its place, has the same authority, and becomes a tacit or prescriptive *law*.

The cases that depart from the common law should be articulated by the *law*;[22] this exception is a homage that confirms the *law's* authority. But nothing taints it like the arbitrary and indeterminate extension of one case to another. It is better to wait for a new *law* for a new case than to transcend the limits of the exception already made.

It is especially in situations of rigor that sobriety is needed in multiplying the cases cited by the *law*. The kind of mental subtlety that goes around drawing inferences is contrary to the sentiments of humanity and to the perspectives of the legislator.

Laws occasioned by the alteration of things and of time should cease with the reasons that brought them into being, far from being revived by conjectural similarities, because the latter are almost never the same, and every comparison is suspect, dangerous, and capable of leading astray.

New *laws* are established either to confirm the old ones, to reform them, or to abolish them. All additions merely burden and entangle the body of *laws*. Following the Athenian example, it would be better to periodically collect the superannuated, contradictory, useless, and abusive laws, in order to purify and diminish the nation's code.

22. Here, the constrast is between the *droit commun* (common law or common right) and the *loi;* see the translators' note, above.

Thus, when it is said that no one should consider himself more prudent than the *law,* it is living *laws* that are meant, not dormant *laws.*

One must hasten to abrogate *laws* worn out by time, for fear that contempt for dead *laws* might redound against living *laws,* and that this gangrene might overtake the entire body of law [*droit*].

But if it is necessary to change the *laws,* bring to the task so many solemnities and precautions that the people will naturally conclude that the *laws* are indeed sacred, since so many formalities are needed to abrogate them.[23]

Do not change customs and manners by the *laws;* that would be tyranny. Indifferent matters are not in the law's bailiwick; customs and manners must be changed by other customs and manners.[24] If the *laws* obstructed manners in France, they would perhaps obstruct the virtues. Let this light-minded people do[25] frivolous things seriously and serious things gaily.[26] Nonetheless, the *laws* can contribute in forming the mores, manners, and character of a nation; England is an example.

Everything that concerns the rules of modesty, shame, or decency can hardly be included in a code of *laws.* It is easy to regulate by *laws* what one owes others; it is difficult to include in them all that one owes oneself.[27]

All things being equal, the multiplicity of *laws* proves the poor constitution of a government. Since they are only made to repress injustice and disorder, there must necessarily be more disorder in a state where there are more *laws.*

The uncertainty and inefficacy of *laws* proceeds from their multiplicity, from their defective composition, style, and sanction; from deadlocks among interpreters,[28] contradictory judgments, etc.

The *laws* are subject to a kind of pillaging at the hands of that long procession of jurisconsults who comment on them. The very sight of their compilations is enough to overwhelm the most indefatigable soul. Their

23. See Montesquieu, *Persian Letters,* letter 129.

24. See Montesquieu, *Laws,* 19.14.

25. Jaucourt uses the term *"laissez faire"* here.

26. Montesquieu, *Laws,* 19.5.

27. For this paragraph, see Montesquieu, *Laws,* 7.10.

28. *Partage des interprètes,* where "partage" is here a term of art meaning a tie vote between judges of a particular court on a particular case (*Dictionnaire de l'Académie Française* [Paris, 1694]).

glosses and subtleties are the snares of chicanery. All quotations, if they are not from the *law*, ought to be prohibited at the bar. These quotations are only men that one shows to other men, but doubtful cases must be judged by reasons, not authorities.

There are retroactive *laws* that come to the aid of anterior *laws*, and that extend their effect over cases they had not foreseen. There should very rarely be these dual-purpose *laws* that concern both the past and the future.

A retroactive *law* should confirm and not reform that which precedes it; reform always causes disturbances, whereas confirmatory *laws* solidify order and tranquility.

In a state with no fundamental *laws*, the succession to dominion cannot be fixed, since the successor is declared by the prince, by his ministers, or by civil war. What evils and disorders result![29]

The *laws* have wisely established formalities in the administration of justice, because these formalities are the *palladium* of liberty.[30] But the number of formalities could be so large that it would violate the purpose of the very *laws* that had established them. Then there would be no end of confusion. Ownership of property would remain uncertain, and the parties would be ruined by virtue of investigating it. There are countries in Europe in which people are in that situation.

Princes have issued good *laws* but sometimes so ineptly that they have produced only harmful effects. Louis the Debonair had the bishops rebelling against him because of the rigid *laws* he prescribed to them, which went beyond the purpose he should have set for himself in the circumstances of the times.[31]

To know and depict the character of nations and of kings, one must illuminate their history by their *laws* and their *laws* by their history.[32] The *laws* of Charlemagne reveal a prince who understands everything by his spirit of foresight, who brings together everything by the force of his genius. By his *laws*, pretexts to elude duties are eliminated, negligence is

29. For this paragraph, see Montesquieu, *Laws*, 5.14.

30. See Montesquieu, *Laws*, 26.15, where the phrase used is "palladium of property."

31. Louis I the Debonair (778–840) succeeded his father, Charlemagne, on the latter's death in 814.

32. See Montesquieu, *Laws*, 31.2, for this formulation.

corrected, abuses reformed or prevented. A head of household could learn from them how to govern his home. The king ordered that the eggs from the barnyards of his domains and the useless produce from his gardens be sold, and it is known from history that he distributed to his people all the Lombards' wealth and the immense treasures of those Huns who had ravaged the world.[33]

In every society, it is force or the *law* that dominates. Sometimes force covers itself in the *law*, sometimes the *law* relies upon force. Whence three kinds of injustice: open violence, the violence that walks in the shadow of the *law*, and the violence born from the rigors of the *law*.

Legislators' passions and prejudices sometimes seep into their *laws* and color them; sometimes they remain there and become part of them.

In a time of decadence, Justinian ventured to reform the jurisprudence of enlightened ages. But it's in enlightened days that it is fitting to correct the days of darkness.

In spite of myself, I will end all these reflections bearing on the *laws* in general. But I will speak separately of the fundamental *laws*, the civil, criminal, divine, human, moral, natural, penal, political, sumptuary laws, *&c.*, and I will try to unfold in a few words their nature, character, spirit, and principles. (*D.J.*)

33. For this paragraph, see Montesquieu, *Laws*, 31.18.

Fundamental Law
(*Loi Fondamentale*)

FUNDAMENTAL LAW (*Political law*), any primordial law on the constitution of a government.

The *fundamental laws* of a state, in their fullest extent, are not only the ordinances by which the entire body of the nation determines what should be the form of government and how one will succeed to the throne;[1] they are also the conventions between the people and the individual or group on whom sovereignty is conferred—which conventions regulate the manner by which one must govern and prescribe limits to sovereign authority.

These regulations are called *fundamental laws* because they are the basis and foundation of the state, upon which the edifice of government is raised, and because the people regard them as producing its entire strength and security.

It is nonetheless only in what might be called an abusive manner that the word *laws* is applied to them; for properly speaking, they are veritable conventions. But since these conventions are obligatory between the contracting parties, they have the force of *laws* themselves.

To assure their success in a limited monarchy, however, the entire body of the nation may reserve to itself the legislative power and the nomination of its magistrates; it may entrust the judicial power and the power of establishing taxes to a senate or a parliament; it may give the monarch the military and executive power, among other prerogatives. If the

This article can be found at 9:660 in the original edition of the *Encyclopédie*.

1. Apparent reference to the Salic Law, a part of which governed the succession to the French throne (excluding female succession) and which was widely viewed as constitutive of France's fundamental law.

government is set up on this footing by the primordial act of association, this primordial act bears the name the *fundamental laws* of the state, because they constitute its security and its liberty. What's more, such *laws* do not make sovereignty imperfect; on the contrary, they perfect it and submit the sovereign to the necessity of good conduct by making him, so to speak, impotent to engage in bad conduct.

Let us also add that there is a kind of *fundamental laws* of right and necessity that are essential to all governments, even in states where sovereignty is, so to speak, absolute, and this *law* is that of the public good, from which the sovereign cannot stray without to a certain extent failing in his duty. (*D.J.*)

Lübeck

LÜBECK, *the law* (*German law*). It is originally the law that *Lübeck* established in its jurisdiction to rule and govern it.

Since this city acquired great authority in the past by its power and its maritime trade, it happened that its laws and statutes were adopted by most of the cities situated on the North Sea. Stralsund, Rostock, and Wismar in particular obtained from their masters the freedom to introduce this law, and other cities admitted it despite their sovereigns.

Many authors trace the beginnings of this law to Frederick II, who was the first to accord liberty to the city of *Lübeck*, and also to confirm its statutes and its legatine power.[1] It is nonetheless likely that the law that governs the city was not established all at once, but that new articles were added from time to time according to the various circumstances. It was not until 1582 that the senate of *Lübeck* organized all of its statutes into one body of laws, which came into being in 1586. Even today, the authority of this code is highly respected in Holstein, Pomerania, Mecklenburg, Prussia, and Livonia. Although the cities of these countries no longer have the privilege of appealing to *Lübeck*, their trials are nonetheless judged according to the law of that city, which is observed particularly in the tribunal of Wismar.

One may consult the Latin work of Jean Sibrand on this matter, and the erudite commentary *Commentarius ad jus Lubecense* [Commentary on

This article can be found at 9:709 in the original edition of the *Encyclopédie*.

1. Frederick II, Holy Roman Emperor (r. 1220–50), made Lübeck a free imperial city in 1226 by preventing Cologne and Tiel from hindering its trade with tolls.

Lübeck law] by David Moevius, who was at first professor at Grypswald, and ultimately vice-president of the chamber of Wismar.[2] (*D.J.*)

2. The reference is to David Mevius (1609–70), whose *Commentary* was published in 1642, and, it would appear, to Johannes Sibrand, *Urbis Lubecae et Anseaticarum* [On Lübeck and the Hanseatic cities] (Rostock, 1619). The two titles appeared together in a 1744 volume on Wismar.

Machiavellianism
(*Machiavélisme*)

This article was written by Diderot.

Machiavellianism (*History of Philosophy*), an abhorrent type of politics that can be described in two words—the art of tyranny—whose principles were propagated in the works of the Florentine Machiavelli.

Machiavelli was endowed with profound genius, and was a learned scholar in many fields. He knew ancient and modern languages. He had an extensive knowledge of history. He took an interest in moral philosophy and politics. He paid due attention to literature. He wrote a few comedies which are by no means worthless. It is claimed that he taught Cesare Borgia how to rule.[1] What is for certain is that he found the despotic rule of the house of Medici repugnant, and that this hatred—that he was too firm in his beliefs to hide—exposed him to long and cruel persecutions. He was suspected of having been involved in the Soderini conspiracy.[2] He was caught and sent to prison; but the courage with which he resisted the agonizing interrogation he received saved his life. The Medici, who could not

The article "Machiavellianism," translated by Timothy Cleary, is from the University of Michigan's website *Encyclopedia of Diderot and d'Alembert: Collaborative Translation Project*, http://quod.lib.umich.edu/d/did. It has been lightly adapted here and is reprinted by permission of the translator.

This article can be found at 9:793 in the original edition of the *Encyclopédie*.

1. Cesare Borgia (1475–1507), skilled military commander during the Italian wars of King Charles VIII, and notorious as Pope Alexander VI.—HC

2. Piero Soderini was the Gonfaloniere (executive official) in 1513 when charged with conspiracy against the Medici and tortured.—HC

ruin him on this occasion, protected him and—out of charity—employed him to write history. He did it; his past experiences did not cause him to be any more cautious. He was once again caught up in a plot that a few citizens had hatched to assassinate Cardinal Giulio de' Medici, who was subsequently elevated to the rank of sovereign pontiff under the title Clement VII. All that they could put forward against him was his continual praise of Brutus and Cassius. If there was not enough evidence to condemn him to death, there was more than enough to punish him by cancelling his allowance, which happened to him. This new setback threw him into destitution, which he endured for some time. He died aged 48, in 1527, as a result of a self-administered drug he took to protect himself against illness.[3] He left behind a son called Luke Machiavelli. His final discourses, if it is to be believed, were of the utmost profanity. He said that he preferred to be in hell with Socrates, Alcibiades, Caesar, Pompey, and the other great men of antiquity, than in heaven with the founders of Christianity.

He left us eight books on the history of Florence, seven on the art of war, four on the republic, three books of discourses on Titus Livius, the life of Castruccio, two comedies, and the treatises on the prince and the senator.

Few works have caused such a stir as the treatise on the prince: it is here that he teaches sovereigns to spurn religion, the rules of justice, the inviolability of pacts and all that is sacred, when it is in one's interest to do so. The fifteenth and twenty-fifth chapters could be entitled "circumstances where it is suitable for the prince to be a villain."

How can one explain that one of the most ardent defenders of the monarchy should suddenly become a vile advocate of tyranny? Here is my explanation, and I outline my opinion only as an idea that is not entirely implausible. When Machiavelli wrote his treatise on the prince, it is as if he had said to his fellow citizens, "read this work well. If you ever accept a ruler, he will be as I portray him: this is the ferocious creature to whom you shall surrender."[4] Such was the error of his contemporaries, if they were unaware of his goal: they took satire for praise. Lord Chancellor Bacon

3. Machiavelli lived from 1469 to 1527.—HC

4. This is also the view of Jean-Jacques Rousseau in *The Social Contract*, bk. 3, chap. 6, "On monarchy."—HC

made no mistake when he said: this man teaches tyrants nothing; they are well aware of what they have to do, but he informs the common people of what they have to fear. *Est quod gratias agamus Machiavello & hujus modi scriptoribus, qui apertè & indissimulanter proferunt quod homines facere soleant, non quod debeant.*[5] Be that as it may, one can hardly doubt that at least Machiavelli had sensed that sooner or later there would be a general outcry against his work, and that his opponents would never manage to demonstrate that his prince was an unfaithful portrayal of the majority of those who have been the most impressive rulers over men.

I have heard that a philosopher, who was questioned by a great prince on a refutation of Machiavellianism he had just published, replied, "Sire, I should think the first lesson Machiavelli taught his disciple was to refute his work."[6]

5. "There is that for which we give thanks to Machiavelli and writers of that sort who openly and without dissimulation make known what men are accustomed to do, not what they ought to do." See Francis Bacon, *De augmentis scientiarum* [On the advancement of learning), VII.2.

6. Frederick II of Prussia published his *Anti-Machiavel* anonymously in French in 1739, the year before he became king of Prussia. Voltaire, who did much to popularize the work in 1740, spent three years at the court of Frederick starting in 1750. For the anecdote in question, see *Mémoires,* in *Œuvres complètes de Voltaire,* ed. Louis Moland, 52 vols. (Paris: Garnier, 1877–85), 1:267.—HC

Masterships
(*Maîtrises*)

For related entries on economic policy, see MASTERPIECE, TRADING COMPANY, COMPETITION, *and* SAVINGS, *the latter also written by Faiguet de Villeneuve.*

MASTERSHIPS (*Arts, Commerce, Politics*). People think that masterships and preferential initiations were established to certify the competence required in those who practice commerce and the arts, and even more to foster emulation, order, and equity among them. But in truth, they are merely refinements on monopoly that are truly harmful to the national interest—besides which, they have no necessary connection with the wise arrangements that ought to guide the commerce of a great people. We will even show that nothing contributes more to fortify ignorance, bad faith, and laziness in the various occupations.[1]

The Egyptians, Greeks, Romans, and Gauls preserved a great deal of order in all parts of their government. Nonetheless, one does not find that they adopted *masterships*—or the exclusive profession of the arts and commerce—as we have. They allowed all citizens to practice an art or commerce; hardly anywhere in ancient history does one find any trace of

This article can be found at 9:911–15 in the original edition of the *Encyclopédie*.

1. The debate over the guild system, the subject of this article, continues today. For orientation, see S. R. Epstein, "Craft guilds in the pre-modern economy: a discussion," *Economic History Review* 61 (2008): 155–74, and Shelagh Ogilvie, "Rehabilitating the guilds: a reply," *Economic History Review* 61 (2008): 175–82.

these privative rights that today make up the main regulatory system for mercantile bodies and communities.

Even in our day, there are many peoples that do not subject workers and traders to *masterships* and ceremonial initiations. Leaving aside the Orientals, where these are unknown, we are assured that there are virtually none in England, Holland, Portugal, and Spain. There are none at all in our colonies, any more than in certain of our modern cities, such as Lorient, St. Germain, Versailles, and others. We even have privileged places in Paris where many people work and trade without special legal status—all to the public's satisfaction. Moreover, how many occupations are there that are completely free, and that nonetheless exist to all subjects' advantage? From which I conclude that *masterships* are not necessary, since people have done without them for a long time, and do without them every day without drawback.

No one is unaware that the *masterships* have degenerated considerably since their original establishment. In the beginning, they consisted more in maintaining good order among the workers and merchants than in taking substantial sums from them. But since they have been turned into a tax, "*they are nothing more,*" says Furetiere,[2] "*than cabal, drunkenness and monopoly.*" The richest or most powerful usually manage to exclude the weakest, and thereby draw everything to themselves—a persistent abuse that can never be eradicated except by introducing competition and liberty into each occupation. *Has perniciosas pestes ejicite, refrenate coemptiones istas divitum, ac velut monopolii exercendi licentiam.* Bk. I Eutopiae Mori.[3]

I believe I can add to this what Colbert said to Louis XIV. "The rigor shown in accepting a merchant in most of the large cities of your realm is an abuse that your majesty has an interest in correcting. For it prevents many people from launching into commerce, where they would quite often be more successful than those who are in it. What is the necessity of a man going through an apprenticeship? At most, this can only be good for

2. Antoine Furetière, *Dictionnaire universel* (Paris, 1690).

3. "Banish these blights, . . . Restrict the right of the rich to buy up anything and everything, and then to exercise a kind of monopoly." Thomas More, *Utopia,* ed. and trans. George M. Logan, Robert M. Adams, and Clarence H. Miller (Cambridge: Cambridge University Press, 1995), 66–67.

the workers, so that they not undertake a craft they don't know; but the others, why make them waste their time? Why prevent people who have in some cases learned more in foreign countries than they need in order to open a business from doing so, just because they are missing a certificate of apprenticeship? If they have the industry to earn their living, is it justice to prevent them from doing so in the name of your majesty—common father of his subjects, who is obliged to take them under his protection? I therefore think that if you were to pass an ordinance by which you abolished all prior regulations on this subject, you would do no further harm." *Testam. polit. ch. xv.*[4]

No one complains about the free market fairs established in many parts of the realm, which are in some way illegitimate deviations[5] from the *masterships*. Nor does anyone complain in Paris that it is permissible to bring provisions there twice a week. Finally, all of those successful talents who have excelled in our midst in all genres of literature and science are not owing to *masterships* or privative rights.

Thus, administration and what is called *mastership* must not be confused: these ideas are quite different, and the one perhaps never leads to the other. Thus, the origin of *masterships* must not be traced either to the perfection of administration or to the needs of the state, but solely to the spirit of monopoly that normally prevails among workers and merchants. It is well understood, in fact, that *masterships* were unknown four or five centuries ago. I have looked at the administrative regulations from those times, which begin by announcing a perfect freedom in whatever concerns the arts and commerce: *It is permitted to he who wills, &c.*

The spirit of monopoly subsequently blinded workers and merchants; they believed, wrongly, that the general liberty of commerce and the arts was detrimental to them. With this conviction, they conspired together to

4. Jean-Baptiste Colbert, *Testament politique de messire Jean-Baptiste Colbert* (The Hague: H. van Bulderen, 1693). The work came out in several editions thereafter, including in a 1695 English translation. Colbert had died in 1683, and the spuriousness of this claim to authorship was immediately recognized; the true author was the memoirist and novelist Gatien de Courtilz de Sandras (1644–1712). In The Hague 1704 edition in French, the quoted passage appears on page 406.

5. *Dérogeance,* a term usually used to describe a nobleman forfeiting his status by engaging in non-noble conduct; here used by metaphorical extension.

have themselves given certain regulations that would be favorable to themselves in the future, and that would pose an obstacle to new entrants. First of all, therefore, they obtained full privileges for all those who were actually established in such and such an occupation. At the same time, they took measures to subject candidates to exams and initiation fees that were not substantial at first, but that under various pretexts increased prodigiously. On which, I must here make an observation that seems to me important: namely, that the first authors of these establishments, which would be ruinous for the public, labored—without being aware of it—against their own posterity. However little they reflected on the vicissitudes of families, they ought in fact to have considered that, since their descendants were not all going to be able to undertake the same occupation, they were going to be subject over the centuries to all the obstructions of the *masterships*. And this is a reflection that ought to be made today by those who are most obsessed by them and who think they are useful to their trade, whereas they are truly damaging to the nation. I appeal to the experience of our neighbors, who are enriching themselves in better ways by opening to everyone the career of arts and commerce.[6]

The corporate bodies and communities look only with jealousy at the large number of candidates, and consequently they do everything possible to reduce them. That is why they are constantly inflating the initiation fees, at least for those who are not masters' sons. On the other hand, when the ministry on certain occasions announces the creation of new, moderately priced *masterships*, these corporate bodies, still guided by the spirit of monopoly, prefer to acquire them for themselves under assumed names and by this means buy them up for their own benefit than to see them pass into the hands of good subjects whose work would compete with theirs.

But what I find most peculiar and most iniquitous is the practice of many corporate communities in Paris, of depriving a widow of all her rights and making her quit her shop and her trade when she marries a man who is not in a *mastership* situation. For what basis is there for causing her and her children such substantial damage—damage that should be the punishment for only some great crime? The entire crime for which she is criticized and

6. Likely a reference to the Netherlands or Great Britain.

punished with such severity is that she is taking, as they say, a husband without quality.[7] But what police or what law—indeed what power on earth—can obstruct in this way the inclinations of free persons by preventing marriages that are otherwise honorable and legitimate? Moreover, where is the justice in punishing the children of a first union, and who are master's sons—where, I say, is the justice of punishing them for their mother's second nuptials?

If the claim simply were that in marrying a master's widow, the man without quality acquired no rights for himself, and that on his wife's death he must soon cease a trade to which he was not admitted by the corporate community, I would find less to complain about. But that a widow who has freedom of trade in her own right as long as she remains in widowhood, and that this widow should come to lose this right and in some sense that of her children upon remarriage, for the sole reason that the statutes exclude her husband—this is, I say it loudly, the most rank injustice. Nothing is more opposed to what God prescribed in Exodus xxii.22: "*viduae & pupillo non nocebitis*."[8] It is obvious in fact that a custom so unreasonable and so contrary to natural law tends toward the oppression of widows and orphans. And one sees upon reflection that it could only have been brought in on the sly, without having been well discussed or well examined.

There you have the arbitrary lawmaking on *masterships*, giving rise to dubious regulations favorable to some and harmful to the majority. But is it fitting for individuals without authority, without enlightenment, and without literacy to impose a yoke on their fellow citizens, to establish for their own advantage laws that are onerous to society? And in the end, can our magistracy approve such assaults against the public liberty?

Much has been said in recent years about encouraging population, and doubtless this is the ministry's intention.[9] But unfortunately, we are in contradiction with ourselves on this, since in general there is nothing more contrary to marriage than subjecting citizens to the entanglements of the *masterships*, and obstructing widows on this matter to the point of taking

7. Without any special legal status such as the *masterships* confer.

8. "You shall not afflict any widow or orphan."

9. Promoting an increase in population is a theme in several of the articles in this volume, including CEREALS, MAN, POPULATION, and FIVE PERCENT TAX.

away from them in certain cases all the resources of their trade. This bad policy reduces quite a few people to bachelorhood, it occasions vice and disorder, and it diminishes our true wealth.

In fact, since it is difficult to become master,[10] and is hardly possible otherwise to support a wife and children, quite a few people who feel and fear this predicament renounce marriage forever and abandon themselves afterward to laziness and debauchery. Others, frightened by the same difficulties, think of looking far and wide for the best positions, and persuaded by public rumor that foreign countries are more favorable, they scramble to transfer their talent and their heart there. Moreover, it is not the deformed, the weak, or the imbeciles who think of expatriating; it is always the most vigorous and the most enterprising who go and try their fortunes abroad, and who sometimes go to the ends of the earth with the same goals in mind. These emigrations, so disgraceful to our administration, and which different causes occasion every day, can only bring a palpable weakening of the national power; this is why it is important to work to prevent them. One of the most effective means of doing this would be to award solid benefits to the conjugal union—in a word, to make the *masterships* free or of low cost to married people, whereas they would be very expensive for bachelors (if it were not considered preferable to exclude them completely).[11]

In any case, I repeat that *masterships* are not a necessary consequence of an exact administration. Properly speaking, they serve only to reinforce division and monopoly among us. Without these things, it is easy to establish order and equity in commerce.

A municipal chamber could be formed in our good cities, composed of five or six aldermen with a magistrate at their head, to regulate *gratis* everything concerning the administration of the arts and commerce. Those who wanted to make or sell some works or merchandise would have only to present themselves to this chamber, declare what they were interested in, and give their name and address so they could be overseen by juridical visits that would be fixed in number and in the salary awarded to the overseers.

10. To be received into an artisanal *mastership*.

11. See Diderot's discussion in CELIBACY, above.

With regard to the competence required to practice each occupation as a master, it seems to me this should be evaluated as a whole, without chicanery and without partiality, by the number of years of practice. I mean that whoever demonstrated, for example, eight or ten years of work with masters, would be considered at that time, *ipso facto*, without certificate of apprenticeship, without masterwork and without exam, to be reasonably conversant with his art or trade—and worthy, in a word, of achieving the *mastership* under the conditions prescribed by his majesty.

In fact, why is it necessary to subject simple journeymen[12] to dubious masterworks and countless other obstructive formalities to which masters' sons are not subjected? It is doubtless imagined that the latter are more skillful, and this ought naturally to be the case; however, experience shows the opposite clearly enough.

A simple journeyman always has great difficulties to overcome in establishing himself in an occupation. He is usually less rich and less protected, in less of a position to get settled and make himself known. Nonetheless, he is as much a member of the commonwealth as anyone else, and he should experience the protection of the laws equally. It is therefore unjust to aggravate the unhappiness of his condition, or to make it more difficult and costly for him to get established—in a word, to subject a weak and defenseless subject to ruinous ceremonies from which those with more wherewithal and more protection are exempt.

Moreover, is it really beyond doubt that masterworks are necessary for the perfection of the arts? As for me, I don't believe it in any way. To do well usually requires only exactitude and probity, and fortunately, these good qualities are within the reach of the most middling subjects. I would add that a man who is tolerably familiar with his occupation can work fruitfully for the public and for his family, without being in a position to perform prodigies of art. Is it better in that case for him to remain without employment? Heaven forbid! He will work usefully for the common and middling folk, and then his work will be paid only its correct value, whereas the same work often becomes very expensive in masters' hands. The great worker,

12. *Compagnons*, artisans or workers who have completed their apprenticeships but who are still working for another, not having become masters themselves.

the man of taste and genius, will soon be known by his talents, and he will employ them for the rich, the curious, and the delicate. Thus, whatever capacity one may have to receive masters of middling competence, one should not be afraid of lacking excellent artists if the need arises. It is not the obstructionist *masterships* that form them, it is the nation's taste and the price one might pay for beautiful work.

One may infer from these reflections that, since all subjects are equally dear and equally subject to the king, his majesty could with justice establish a uniform regulation for the initiation of workers and traders. And let it not be said that the *masterships* are necessary to assign the capitation[13] and make people pay it, since, after all, all this is done equally well in the cities where there are few or no *masterships*. Moreover, one would still preserve the corporate bodies and communities, as much to maintain order and administration as to assign the public taxes.

But from another angle, I maintain that as they operate today, *masterships* and initiations enable many subjects to evade the capitation who would pay it under any other circumstances. In fact, since the difficulty of becoming a master forces many people in commerce and the arts to grow older as shop boys, go-betweens, journeymen, etc., those folks—almost always isolated, unsettled, and little known—dodge personal taxes easily enough. Whereas if the *masterships* were more accessible, there would be many more masters as a result—people set up for the arts and for commerce who would all pay the capitation to the advantage of the public and the king.

Another advantage that might be found in the corporate bodies forged by the ties of *mastership* in our time is that, instead of burdening candidates with substantial taxes that melt in the hands of the leaders, and that are generally unfruitful, one could resort to the more prudent arrangement of procuring all members some recourse against a bankruptcy disaster. I will explain.

A young merchant commonly spends around 2,000 francs for his initiation and all appurtenances, and as we have said, this is pure loss. I would like it if, on site and after the competency exam we have indicated or some other that might be thought preferable, the candidates were made to count

13. A hearth tax instituted by Louis XIV in 1695.

out the sum of 10,000 pounds,[14] in order to confer the right and reputation of merchant upon them—a sum from which they would be paid interest at four percent for as long as they wanted to engage in trade. This money would immediately be placed at five or six percent with people who were solvent as well as very reputable. By means of the 10,000 pounds advanced by all merchants, each would have in his corporate body a credit of 40,000 francs in the bank or in the general office, so that those who furnished them with merchandise or with money would always be able to ensure their credit up to the above-mentioned sum of 40,000 pounds.

Whereas today one approaches the matter of commercial credit with fear and trembling, the new regulation would increase confidence and therefore circulation. It would also prevent most bankruptcies, mainly because one would see many fewer adventurers getting themselves into trades that would then require liquidity. This is also a principle of exclusion that would be more effective, more favorable to the old families and to those already established, than the present rigors of the *masterships,* which have no effect on commerce but to arrest its progress.

With a surplus in interest in the bank, even if placed at five percent, the bank would replace the gaps and losses it would still sometimes absorb, but these would be quite rare because commerce, as we have seen, would only be engaged in by people with known funds and resources. If, however, some loss were incurred beyond the yield, which is difficult to believe, that loss would then be borne by the entire corps, according to the capitation tax imposed on each of the members. This contribution, which would perhaps not take place once in twenty years, would become almost imperceptible to the individuals, and it would prevent the ruin of so many honorable people often crushed nowadays by even a single bankruptcy. If a man wanted to leave the trade, his 10,000 pounds would be returned to him, provided he has satisfied the creditors who had vested funds in the bank.

Moreover, what is being said here in a few words regarding the merchants could be applied commensurately to the workers. Virtually the same

14. The terms *franc* and *livre* (pound) are being used interchangeably in this example; see the note on currency, above.

arrangements could be employed to increase the credit of the notaries and the public's confidence in them.

Be that as it may, since it is natural to employ rewards and punishments in order to interest each individual (according to his own status) in making himself useful to the public, those who have distinguished themselves for some years by their vigilance, their rectitude, and their skill could be rewarded with a kind of insignia that the corporate authorities would accord them as an authentic testimony of their exactitude and their probity. On the other hand, if someone engages in proven mischief or misconduct, he will be ordered to pay a fine and will be obliged to endure a sign of infamy and reprimand on his door for some time—a much wiser practice than walling up his shop.

In a word, one may take all manner of precautions to ensure that each person fulfills the duties of his status, but everyone must be left the freedom of doing well. Far from fixing the number of subjects there must be in the useful occupations, which is absolutely unreasonable—unless we are going to simultaneously fix the number of children that must be born—what is necessary is to provide all citizens with the possibility of employing their faculties and talents appropriately.

With such regulations, each person will presumably want to pride himself on his honor, and the system will be more faithfully observed than ever—without needing recourse to cumbersome expedients, which are a source of divisions and of trials between the different bodies of the arts and commerce. Another useful result arises from the above-noted precautions, namely, that the reliable and competent people to whom one could turn are easily known—knowledge that is today acquired only after many attempts, normally at one's own expense.

To respond to what is often said against liberty in the arts and commerce, namely, that there would be too many people in each occupation: It is obvious that nobody would reason that way if they examined the matter closely. For after all, would freedom of trade make everybody quit his first condition to take up a new one? Doubtless not: each would remain in his place, and no occupation would be overburdened, because all of them would be equally free. In truth, many people who are presently too wretched to aspire to *masterships* would suddenly see themselves rescued from servitude and able to engage in work on their own account, in which there is something to be gained for the public.

"But," it is said, "don't you see that countless subjects who have no settled condition would soon pile in once they see the doors to the arts and commerce opened to everyone, and thereby disturb the harmony that we see prevailing in those activities?"

What a ridiculous objection! If access to the arts and commerce became easier and freer, too many people, it is said, would profit from the freedom. Well, wouldn't this be the greatest good that could be desired? Unless perhaps one thinks that it is better to subsist by some vicious ingenuity, or wallow in idleness, than to devote oneself to some honest labor. In a word, I do not understand how one could hesitate to open the career in commerce and the arts to all subjects, since in the end there is nothing to deliberate over, and there is more advantage in having many workers and merchants—even if some of them are found to be unskillful—than to make idleness almost inevitable, and thereby produce loafers, robbers, and rogues.

What a sorry lot is man's! At birth, most of them don't have a place to rest their heads, not the tiniest space within the great expanse that belongs to their parents and whose rent doesn't have to be paid. But it was not enough for the rich and the great to have overrun estates, lands, houses; they also had to establish *masterships,* they had to prohibit the weak and defenseless from engaging in the quite natural use of their industry and their hands.

The arrangement I point to here would soon produce a more lively and extensive commerce throughout the realm. Manufacturers and other merchants would multiply on every side and would be in a better position than they are today to offer their merchandise at a favorable price—especially if, to complete the reform, at least three-quarters of our feast days were abolished, and if the yield from the import and export duties imposed on merchandise and foodstuffs were transferred to the general capitation, at least those that are collected in the interior of the realm and from province to province.

We are sometimes surprised that certain nations offer almost everything at a better price than the French,[15] but this is not a secret they have to the

15. The reference would be to the Dutch or the English.

exclusion of ourselves. The true reason for this moral and political phenomenon is that commerce is regarded by them as the principal affair of state, and that it is more protected there than it is by us. Another reason that counts for much here is that their customs are less cumbersome and less ruinous for commerce, at least for all their manufacturing and their harvest. Moreover, these commercial peoples experience practically none of the exclusiveness involved in the *masterships* or the privileged companies; even less do they have our feast days, and this is where they have quite an advantage over us. All of this, combined with their low interest rates and with the great economy and simplicity of their manner of living and dressing, puts them in a position to sell at a modest price, and to preserve their commercial superiority. Nothing prevents us from profiting by their example and from working to imitate them; then we will soon be moving along as their equals. Let's return to our subject.

It is maintained that a general freedom in the arts and commerce would harm those who are already masters, since any man could then work, manufacture, and sell.

On this point, we should take the unbiased view that there would not be as many new masters as is imagined. In fact, there are countless difficulties in starting out. At first, one lacks knowledge and practice, and above all, one doesn't have sufficient funds at the right time for convenient lodging, for getting settled, for making an advance and taking risks, etc. Nonetheless, all this is necessary, and will always make these establishments very difficult. Thus, the existing masters would still profit for a long time from the advantage they have over all the new arrivals. And with the nation enjoying freedom of trade—and enjoying it equally—it would at worst find itself in this respect virtually at the point where it was several centuries ago, at the point where our colonies still are, and even most foreigners, who procure abundance and wealth through their freedom in the arts and commerce, as is well known.

Moreover, the interests of the old and new masters can be reconciled without anyone having cause for complaint. Here's the accommodation one could make: allow the old masters time to exploit their exclusive rights. Freedom in the arts and commerce would be granted only on condition of paying half what is disbursed today for *masterships* and initiations; this would continue for a period of twenty years. After this, one would pay in perpetuity only a quarter of what it costs—that is, a *mastership* or initiation that amounts to 1,200 pounds would be modified at first to 600 pounds, and at the end of twenty years, it would be fixed for good at 300 pounds for the whole thing, without the feast and without other ceremonies. For the space of twenty years, the sums payable by the new masters would be employed to the benefit of the old—as much to discharge the debts of their corporate community as for their private capitation—and this, to compensate them proportionally. But afterward, the sums arising from new initiations, which would be paid equally by all subjects—masters' sons and others—would be converted into city tolls, to the benefit of the inhabitants, and not dissipated as they are today in *Te deums*, consecrated bread, feasts, shindigs,[16] &c.

In any case, I believe that while waiting for this freedom, one could establish right now a free marketplace in the large cities—a marketplace that would be open four or five times a year, with complete freedom to bring all nonprohibited merchandise, but with this essential precaution: that the merchants not be constrained to set up in certain buildings, certain enclosures, where the leases and stalls are too expensive.

Besides the *masterships'* drawback in harming population, as has been shown above, they have another one that is scarcely less important: they cause the public to be much more poorly served. Since the *masterships* can in fact be obtained by favor and by money, and since they do not essentially presuppose either competence or integrity in those who obtain them, they are less fit for distinguishing merit or establishing justice and order among the workers and merchants than for perpetuating ignorance and monopoly in trade, in that they give sanction to bad subjects who afterward make us pay—I don't say for their initiation fees alone, but even for their negligence and their mistakes.

Moreover, since most masters employ a number of workers and make only a vague and general inspection of them, their works are rarely as perfect as they ought to be—a result all the more inevitable in that these subordinate workers are paid meagerly and have no strong interest in

16. The word is *frairie*, which can mean either a wild and sumptuous party or a traditional village festivity.

managing the master's practice, since they normally aim only at passing the time or else rushing through many works, if they are (as is said) by the piece. Whereas if doing well were permissible to anyone who had the will to do so, many of those who are working with masters would soon be working on their own account. And since every artisan would then be less burdened with work and would want to secure the practice, it would inevitably happen that the man who today is negligent in working for others would become more careful and more dedicated as soon as he was working for himself.

Finally, the most terrible disadvantage of the *masterships* is that they are the usual cause of the large number of idlers, bandits, and robbers that are seen in all parts. This is because they make access to the arts and commerce so difficult and so tedious that many people, repelled by these first obstacles, withdraw forever from useful occupations and usually survive thereafter only by mendicancy, counterfeiting, and contraband, by swindles, theft, and other crimes. In fact, most malefactors condemned to the galleys or to capital punishment were originally poor orphans, dismissed soldiers, fired domestics, or such other isolated subjects. Having not been placed in solid crafts, and finding constant obstacles to all the good they might do, they thereby see themselves led, as it were, into a frightful series of crimes and misfortunes.

How many other people of different sorts are there—hermits, seekers,[17] charlatans, etc.—and how many candidates for the useless and harmful professions, who have no other calling but one possessing all the difficulties now associated with the arts and commerce, many of whom are without property and employment and are only too often reduced to looking desperately for the wherewithal they don't find anywhere else?

Let commerce, agriculture, and all the necessary arts be encouraged, let all subjects be permitted to exploit their possessions and their talents, let the trades be taught to all soldiers, let the children of the poor be employed and instructed, let order, work, and commodiousness prevail in the poorhouses,[18] let all who present themselves there be admitted, let all beggars in

17. The word is *souffleur,* which in this context means someone who uses alchemy to seek the philosopher's stone.

18. See Diderot's article POORHOUSE, above.

good health be sheltered and corrected. Soon, instead of the vagabonds and thieves that are so common in our day, only hard-working men will be seen. With the people able to earn their living and avoid misery by means of work, they will never be reduced to pernicious and deplorable extremities.

Pauciores alantur otio, reddatur agricolatio, lanificium instauretur, ut sit honestum negotium quo se utiliter exerceat otiosa ista turba, vel quos hactenùs inopia fures facit, vel qui nunc errones aut otiose sunt ministri, fures nimirum utrique futuri. Bk. I Eutopiae.[19] *Article by M.* FAIGUET DE VILLENEUVE.

19. More, *Utopia*, 66–67: "Let fewer people be brought up in idleness. Let agriculture be restored, and the wool-manufacture revived as an honest trade, so there will be useful work for the idle throng, whether those whom poverty has already made thieves or those who are only vagabonds or idle servants now, but are bound to become thieves in the future."

Volume 10
(1765)

Manners
(*Manière*)

The role of manners in achieving certain political ends, particularly stability, was a topic that much interested the eighteenth century. In this essay, Saint-Lambert ranges across space and time—from ancients to moderns, from despotisms to democracies—to reflect upon the nature and effects of manners, drawing on but criticizing Montesquieu's discussion of the relationship between manners, laws, and regimes.

MANNERS (*Grammar, Politics, Morals*). In the most generally accepted sense, these are the customs established to make the commerce that men ought to have among themselves milder. They are the expression of mores, or merely the effect of submission to customs. They are to morals what the liturgy is to religion: they manifest them, preserve them, or take their place, and consequently they are of greater importance to societies than moralists have thought.

It is not well enough understood how our machinelike habit makes us engage in acts whose moral principle we no longer have within us, and how this habit contributes to preserving that principle. When certain acts or movements are connected in our minds with the ideas of certain virtues or sentiments, those acts or movements recall those sentiments and virtues within us. See LIAISON DES IDÉES [Connection of Ideas].

In China, children give their parents extraordinary honors. They constantly show them external signs of respect and love. It is likely that there

This article can be found at 10:34–36 in the original edition of the *Encyclopédie*.

is more display than reality in these external signs, but respect and love for parents is livelier and more consistent in China than in countries where the same sentiments are commanded[1] without laws prescribing the manner of manifesting them. In France, the people are far from respecting all the grandees they greet, but the grandees are more respected there than in countries where the established manners do not impose signs of respect toward them.

Among the Germans, and afterward among us in the age of chivalry, women were honored like gods. Gallantry was a liturgy, and in this liturgy as in all others, there were the lukewarm and the hypocrites. But they still honored women, and they certainly loved them and respected them more than the kaffir who makes them work while he rests, and the Asiatic who enchains them and caresses them like animals designed for his pleasures.

The habit of certain acts, certain gestures, certain movements, certain external signs maintains the same sentiments within us better than all the dogmas and all the metaphysics in the world.

I said that the machinelike habit makes us engage in acts whose moral principle we no longer have within us. I said it preserves the principle within us. It does more; it increases it and generates it.

There is no passion in our soul, no affection, no sentiment, no emotion that does not have its effect on our body, that does not raise, collapse, relax, or tighten some muscles, and that does not have a more or less specific expression in our varying exterior. Pains and pleasures, desires and fears, love and aversion—whatever may be their moral cause—have within us more or less the physical effects that are made manifest by signs that are more or less perceptible. All the affections marked on the face present a certain expression; they make up what is called the *physiognomy;* they change the body's habit; they give bearing and take it away; they cause us to make certain gestures, certain movements. This is an uncontested truth.

But it is no less true that once the movement of the muscles and nerves that is the usual effect of a certain passion is stimulated and repeated within us without the aid of that passion, it reproduces itself there to a certain point.

The effects of music on us are palpable evidence of this truth. The impression of the sonorous body on our nerves stimulates different move-

1. *Ordonnés,* possibly a reference to the fourth commandment (Exod. 20:12).

ments there, many of which are of the same kind that a certain passion would stimulate. And if these movements succeed each other, if the musician continues to bring the same sort of disturbance to the nervous system, then soon this or that passion—joy, sadness, anxiety, etc.—is transmitted into the soul. It follows from this observation, whose truth any man endowed with a little refinement in his organs can attest within himself, that if certain passions bring certain movements to the body, these movements bring the soul back to these passions. Now since *manners* consist for the most part in gestures, bodily habits, gait, then actions—which are the signs, the expression, the effects of certain sentiments—are bound not only to manifest or preserve these sentiments, but sometimes to generate them.

The ancients paid more attention than we do to the influence of *manners* on mores, and to the relations between the habits of the body and of the soul. Plato distinguishes two sorts of dance. The one is an art of imitation—properly speaking pantomime—which is the only dance appropriate to the theater. The other is the art of accustoming the body to decent bearing, to making ordinary movements with propriety. This kind of dance has been preserved by the moderns, and our dancing masters are professors of *manners*. Molière's dancing master was not as wrong as we think in, if not preferring himself, then at least comparing himself to the philosophy master.[2]

Manners should express the respect and submission of inferiors toward superiors, the marks of humanity and condescension by superiors toward inferiors, and the sentiments of benevolence and esteem between equals. They regulate deportment and prescribe it to the different orders, to the citizens of the different estates.

It is clear that manners as well as mores are bound to vary according to the different forms of government.[3] In despotic countries, marks of submission on the part of inferiors are extreme. The satraps of Persia used to prostrate themselves in the dust before their kings, and the people likewise prostrated themselves before the satraps; Asia has not changed.

2. The reference is to the dancing master in Molière's 1670 play, *Le Bourgeois Gentilhomme,* act I, sc. 2.

3. Montesquieu announces this relationship in *The Spirit of the Laws,* 1.3, and returns to it many times throughout the work.

In despotic countries, the marks of humanity and condescension on the part of superiors are reduced to very little. There is too big a gap between what a man is and what a man in office[4] is for them ever to be able to approach each other. There, superiors show inferiors only disdain and sometimes an insulting pity.

Since the equal slaves of a common master have no esteem either for themselves or for their peers, they show no marks of it in their *manners*. They have weak feelings of benevolence for each other. They expect little from each other; slaves raised in servitude do not know how to love. They are more eagerly occupied in shifting the weight of their irons onto each other than in helping each other bear them. They have more the air of imploring pity than of expressing propriety.

In democracies, in governments where the legislative power resides in the body of the nation, *manners* show only weak evidence of dependency relations—of whatever kind. There are fewer *manners* and established customs than expressions of nature. Liberty is manifested in the bearing, the character traits, and the actions of every citizen.

In aristocracies, and in countries where public liberty is no more but where civil liberty is enjoyed—in countries where the few make the laws, and especially in those where one alone rules, though by the laws—there are many *manners* and *customs* by convention. In these countries, to please is an advantage, to displease a misfortune. One pleases by one's charms and even one's virtues, and *manners* are usually noble and agreeable. The citizens have a mutual need to preserve each other, assist each other, elevate or enjoy each other. They are afraid of alienating their fellow citizens by letting their faults be seen. Everywhere, one sees hierarchy and esteem, respect and liberty, the desire to please and sincerity.

Normally in these countries, one notices at first glance a certain uniformity; the characters seem to resemble each other because their differences are hidden by *manners*. Much more rarely than in republics does one find those original characters who seem to owe nothing except to nature—not only because *manners* impede nature but because they change it.

4. *Homme en place,* referring loosely to being in a position of authority or dignity.

In countries where there is little luxury, where the people are occupied by commerce and by the cultivation of the land, where men view each other more via interests of first necessity than reasons of ambition or tastes in pleasure, the externals are simple and honest, and *manners* are more sensible than affectionate.[5] There, it is not a question of finding charms and displaying them; one promises and demands only justice. In general, in all countries where nature is not disturbed by emotions imprinted by government, where the natural is rarely forced to present itself and is fairly unfamiliar with the need to constrain itself, *manners* count for nothing; there are very few manners unless the laws have established them.

President Montesquieu criticizes the legislators of China for mixing together religion, mores, laws, and *manners*.[6] But wasn't it to eternalize the legislation they meant to enact that those sublime geniuses bound together things that in many governments are independent, and sometimes even opposed to each other? It was by supporting the moral with the natural and the political with the religious that they made the constitution of the state eternal, and the mores immutable. If there are circumstances, if the centuries bring moments when it would be good for a nation to change its character, then the legislators of China have been wrong.

I observe that the nations that have preserved their national spirit the longest are those in which the legislator has established the closest connection between the constitution of the state, religion, mores, and *manners*, and above all those in which *manners* have been instituted by the laws.

In antiquity, the Egyptians were the people that changed the most slowly, and that people was guided by rites, by *manners*. The subjects of Psammetichus and Apries are recognizable under the dominion of the Persians and the Greeks; they are recognizable under the Romans and under the Mamelukes.[7] Even today among the modern Egyptians, vestiges of their ancient customs are still seen, so powerful is the force of habit.

5. The word is *affectueux*, which may also mean "impassioned."

6. The reference seems to be to Montesquieu, *Laws*, 19.16–19, although it is not clear how critical of the Chinese the author is there; see also 14.5.

7. Psammetichus (r. 664–610 B.C.) and Apries (r. 589–570 B.C.), Egyptian pharaohs; the Mamelukes were slave soldiers who converted to Islam and ruled Egypt, 1250–1517.

After the Egyptians, the Spartans are the people who preserved their character the longest. They had a government in which mores, *manners,* laws, and religion joined together, fortified each other, and were made for each other. Their *manners* were instituted. The form and topics of conversation, the deportment of the citizens, the way in which they approached each other, their conduct during meals, the details of propriety and decency—in short, the externals—all had occupied Lycurgus's talents along with virtue and the essential duties. Thus, in the reign of Nerva, the Lacedemonians—who had been subjugated for a long time and were no longer a free people—were still a virtuous people. Nero, going to Athens to cleanse himself after his mother's murder, did not dare move on to Lacedemon. He feared the looks of its citizens, and there were no priests there who expiated parricides.[8]

I believe that the French are the modern European people whose character is most pronounced and has experienced the least alteration. They are, says M. Duclos, what they were in the time of the crusades: a lively, gay, generous, brave, sincere, presumptuous, fickle, conceited, rash nation.[9] France changes fashions but not mores. *Manners*, so to speak, made up part of her laws in the past. The code of chivalry, the customs of the old valiant knights, the rules of the old-style civility had *manners* as their purpose. More than in the rest of Europe, in France they are still one of the purposes of that second education one receives upon entering the world, which unfortunately accords too little with the first.

Manners, therefore, should be one of the goals of education, and can be established even by the laws, at least as often as by example. Morals are the interior of man, *manners* are his exterior. To establish *manners* by laws is merely to give virtue a liturgy.

One of the main effects of *manners* is to impede the first impulses within us. They take away the soaring energy of nature, but by giving us time for reflection, they also prevent us from sacrificing virtue to present pleasure—that is, the happiness of life to a moment's interest.

8. Nero (r. 54–68) and Nerva (r. 96–98), Roman emperors; the death of Nero's mother Agrippina occurred in 59.

9. Charles Pinot Duclos, *Considérations sur les mœurs de ce siècle* (1751). See the first sentence of chapter 7. An abridged, anonymous English translation of this work appeared in volume 1 of *Memoirs illustrating the manners of the present age* (Dublin: G. Faulkner, 1752).

In the imitative arts, this should not be taken too much into account. The poet and the painter should give nature all its liberty, but the citizen should often constrain it. It is quite rare that whoever puts himself above *manners* for a frivolous interest would not put himself above morals for a large one.

In a country in which *manners* are an important matter, they live on after morals, and indeed morals need to be vastly altered for any change in *manners* to be perceptible. Men still display themselves as being what they ought to be when they no longer are that way. In Europe, the interests of women have long preserved the externals of gallantry. Even today, they still place an extremely high value on polished *manners*. Therefore, they still receive homage, they never experience bad conduct, and people still rush to offer them useless services.

Manners are corporeal. They speak to the senses, to the imagination—in fact, they are palpable. That is why they survive morals; that is why they preserve them better than precepts and laws. It is for the same reason that ancient customs persist among all peoples, even though the motives that led to their establishment are no longer preserved.

In the part of Morea that used to be Laconia, people still assemble on certain days of the year to hold public feasts, even though the spirit that led Lycurgus to establish them has now quite completely died out in Morea. Cats had temples in Egypt; it would be unknown today why they have hospitals if they had not previously had temples.

If there were civilized peoples before the invention of writing, I am persuaded that they preserved their mores for a long time in the way that the government had instituted them. Since they did not have the aid of letters, they were obliged to perpetuate the principles of morals by *manners*, tradition, hieroglyphs, pictures—in short, by perceptible signs, which are etched more strongly on the heart than writing, books, and definitions. The Egyptian priests preached rarely and painted much.

Mores
(*Mœurs*)

The French word mœurs *can mean "morals," "manners," or "mores." In Saint-Lambert's foregoing article,* MANNERS, *we translated* mœurs *as "morals." Here, however, it seems more fitting to translate it as "mores." Like* MANNERS, *this brief article of uncertain attribution is informed by Montesquieu's attempt to draw systematic relationships between laws and mores, between regime types and the "general spirit" of a people.*

MORES (*Morality*), free acts of men—natural or acquired, good or bad—that are susceptible to rule and direction.

Their variety among the different peoples of the world depends on climate, religion, the laws, government, needs, education, manners, and examples. To the extent that one of these causes acts in each nation with greater force, the others give way proportionally.

To corroborate all these truths, it would be necessary to go into details that the limits of this work cannot permit. But in simply glancing over the different forms of government in our temperate climates, one figures out the *mores* of the citizens pretty accurately by this sole consideration. Thus, in a republic that can survive only on a commerce of economy,[1] simplicity in *mores,* tolerance in matters of religion, love of frugality, savings, the spirit of interest and of avarice must inevitably dominate. In a limited monarchy, where each citizen takes part in the administration of the state,

This article can be found at 10:611 in the original edition of the *Encyclopédie.*

1. The contrast between a "commerce of economy" and a "commerce of luxury" was popularized in France mainly by Montesquieu, *The Spirit of the Laws,* 20.4–6, 8, 10, 11.

liberty will be regarded as such a great good that every war undertaken to uphold it passes for a very minor evil. The people of that monarchy will be proud, generous, profound in the sciences and in politics, never losing sight of their privileges even in the midst of leisure and debauchery.[2] In a rich absolute monarchy in which women set the tone, honor, ambition, gallantry, the taste for pleasure, vanity, and laxness would be the distinctive character of the subjects. And since this government in turn produces idleness, this idleness, in corrupting *mores,* will give birth in their place to politeness of manners.[3] *See* MANNERS.

2. The reference is probably to England; see the distinctions Jaucourt makes between limited and absolute monarchy in the articles on MONARCHY that follow. This section seems loosely based on Montesquieu, *Laws,* 19.27.

3. This veiled critique of France is drawn from Montesquieu, *Laws,* 19.27.

Monarchy
(*Monarchie*)

The four articles on monarchy reproduced in this volume, all by Jaucourt, may be read separately, or together as a single argument for limited and elective monarchy. They all draw heavily on Montesquieu and Burlamaqui.

MONARCHY (*Political government*), form of government in which one person governs by fixed and established laws.

Monarchy is that state in which sovereign power, and all rights essential to it, reside indivisibly in a single man called *king, monarch,* or *emperor.*

Let us establish, following M. de Montesquieu, the principle of this government, its support, and its degeneration.

The nature of *monarchy* consists in the fact that the monarch is the source of all political and civil power, and that he rules alone by fundamental laws. For if the state featured only the momentary and capricious will of one alone without fundamental laws, this would be a despotic government, in which a single man drags along everything by his will. But *monarchy* commands by laws whose repository is in the hands of political bodies, which announce laws when they are made and recall them when they are forgotten.[1]

Monarchical government, unlike republican, does not have good mores as its principle.[2] The laws take the place of the virtues—independent of love of Country, desire for true glory, self-renunciation, sacrifice of one's dearest interests, and all the heroic virtues of the ancients that we have

This article can be found at 10:636 in the original edition of the *Encyclopédie.*

1. For this paragraph, see Montesquieu, *The Spirit of the Laws,* 2.4.

2. See Montesquieu, *Laws,* 3.5, for this controversial claim.

only heard about. Mores are never as pure in monarchies as in republican governments, and the virtues displayed there are always less what one owes others than what one owes oneself. They are not so much what calls us toward our fellow citizens as what distinguishes us from them.[3] In *monarchy*, honor—that is, the prejudice of each person and each condition—takes the place of political virtue and represents it.[4] It enters into all the modes of thought and all the ways of feeling. According to its fancy, it extends or limits duties, whether their force arises from religion, politics, or morality.[5] It can, however, inspire splendid deeds; when joined to legal forms, it can even lead toward the purpose of government just as virtue itself does.[6]

Such is the strength of monarchical government that it uses at will all the members who compose it. Since it is from the prince alone that wealth, dignities, and rewards are expected, the rush to merit them creates the mainstay for his throne. Moreover, since public affairs are guided by one person, its assured effects are order, diligence, secrecy, subordination, the greatest purposes, and the fastest execution. Even in upheavals, the prince's security is attached to the incorruptibility of all the different orders of the state at once, and the seditious, who lack both the will and the expectation of overturning the state, are neither able nor willing to overturn the prince.[7]

If the monarch is virtuous and if he dispenses rewards and punishments with justice and discernment, everyone rushes to merit his benefits, and his reign is a golden age. But if the monarch is not like this, the principle that serves to lift up the souls of his subjects to participate in his graces, to elbow their way through the crowd with noble deeds—that principle degenerates into baseness and slavery. Romans, you triumphed under the first two Caesars, but under the others you were the most abject of mortals.

The principle of *monarchy* has been corrupted when the highest dignities are marks of the greatest servitude, when the great are stripped of the people's respect and turned into instruments of arbitrary power.[8]

3. See Montesquieu, *Laws*, 4.2, for these sentences.
4. Montesquieu, *Laws*, 3.6.
5. For these two sentences, see Montesquieu, *Laws*, 4.2.
6. Montesquieu, *Laws*, 3.6.
7. See Montesquieu, *Laws*, 5.11.
8. For most of the next two paragraphs, see Montesquieu, *Laws*, 8.7.

It has been corrupted when some singularly cowardly souls grow vain from the greatness of their servitude, when they believe that what makes them owe everything to the prince makes them owe nothing to their Country, and especially when adulation, holding a face-paint container[9] in her hand, tries to persuade the one who is holding the scepter that men vis-à-vis their sovereigns are what nature as a whole is in relation to its author.

The principle of *monarchy* has been corrupted when the prince changes his justice into severity, when he puts a Medusa's head on his breast as the Roman emperors did, when he takes on that menacing and terrifying air that Commodus required in the statues made of him.

The *monarchy* is ruined when a prince believes he shows his power more by changing the order of things than by following it, when he deprives the bodies of the state of their prerogatives, when he removes the functions that are natural to some in order to give them arbitrarily to others, and when he is enamored of his frivolous fancies.

The *monarchy* is ruined when a prince, referring everything directly to himself, reduces the state to its capital, the capital to the court, and the court to his person alone.[10]

The *monarchy* is ruined when a prince misunderstands his authority, his situation, his people's love, and when he does not realize that a monarch should consider himself secure, just as a despot should think himself in peril.

The *monarchy* is ruined when a prince, deceived by his ministers, comes to believe that the poorer the subjects, the larger their families will be; and the more they are burdened with taxes, the more able they are to pay them—two sophisms that I call crimes of *lèse-majesté*, which have always

9. *Coquille de fard*, a shell-shaped container; Jaucourt, who is the only *Encyclopédie* author to use the phrase, employs it also in his article Jour de la Naissance (Birthday) at 11:9. It does not appear in the historical dictionaries or in the ARTFL database. Addison and Steele had used the phrase "shell of paint" to express the flattery metaphor in *The Spectator*, no. 460 (August 18, 1712; London: Buckley, 1713), 6:357; that phrase was translated as *coquille de fard* in the anonymous translation of their work, *Le Spectateur; ou le Socrate moderne* (Paris: Melrigot, 1755), 2:280. The epigraph to the *Spectator* entry was Horace's line "Decipimur specie recti" ("[we] deceive ourselves by the semblance of truth") in *Ars Poetica*, 25, the same passage used by Rousseau as the epigraph for the *Discourse on the Arts and Sciences* (1750).

10. Montesquieu, *Laws*, 8.6, for this section.

ruined and will always ruin *monarchies*.[11] Republics end in luxury, *monarchies* in depopulation and poverty.[12]

Finally, the *monarchy* is absolutely ruined when it tumbles into despotism, a condition that soon sends a nation into barbarism, and from there into total annihilation, where the heavy yoke that precipitated this falls with it.

Someone will say to the subjects of a *monarchy* whose principle is close to crumbling, "But a prince is born to you who will restore that principle in all its luster. Nature has endowed this successor with command of the virtues and qualities that will bring your felicity; it is only a matter of aiding in their development." Alas! People, I tremble again that the expectations you've been given will be disappointed. Monsters will dishonor and smother this lovely flower at its birth; their poisonous breath will extinguish the happy faculties of this heir to the throne, to govern him at their will. They will fill his soul with errors, prejudices, and superstitions. They will inspire their pernicious maxims in him with ignorance. They will infect this tender offspring with the spirit of domination that possesses them.

Such are the main causes of the decline and fall of the most flourishing *monarchies*. *Heu! quam pereunt brevibus ingentia causis!*[13] (*D.J.*)

11. Montesquieu, *Laws*, 23.11, for this.

12. Slightly adapted from Montesquieu, *Laws*, 7.4.

13. "Alas, in how swift ruin perish even the greatest things." "In Rufinum," in *Claudian*, trans. Maurice Platnauer (Cambridge: Harvard University Press, 1922), II.49. Jaucourt had changed *fatis* to *causis*.

Absolute Monarchy
(*Monarchie Absolue*)

The phrase "absolute monarchy" does not seem to have been widespread in eighteenth-century France. It does not appear in the writings of Montesquieu. Before the French Revolution, according to the ARTFL database of French authors, the term is found only in Vertot (Histoire des revolutions arrivées dans le gouvernement de la République romaine, *1719*), *Voltaire's* Essays, *d'Argenson* (Considerations sur l'ancien gouvernement françois, *1764*), *and two writers in the 1780s. In England and Holland, where Jaucourt had spent much time, it was a different story. In England, for example, virtually everyone across the spectrum used the term, from the Puritan revolutionary William Prynne to the Tory Bolingbroke, including most of the familiar names in between, such as Harrington, Locke, Berkeley, and Hume.*

ABSOLUTE MONARCHY (*Government*), form of *monarchy* in which the entire body of citizens has thought it necessary to entrust sovereignty to the prince, with all the latitude and absolute power that resided in him originally, and without adding any particular restriction besides that of the established laws.[1] The absolute power of such a monarchy must not be confused with arbitrary and despotic power. For the origin and nature of absolute *monarchy* is limited by its very nature, by the intentions of those

This article can be found at 10:636–37 in the original edition of the *Encyclopédie*.

1. For this definition, see Jean-Jacques Burlamaqui, *The Principles of Natural and Politic Law,* trans. Thomas Nugent, ed. Petter Korkman (Indianapolis: Liberty Fund, 2006), II.II.i.XIV, 330.

from whom the monarch holds it, and by the fundamental laws of his state. Just as the people who live under a good administration are happier than those who wander around in the forests without rules and without leaders, so too the monarchs who live under the fundamental laws of their state are happier than despotic princes, who have nothing to regulate the hearts of their people, or their own. (*D.J.*)

Elective Monarchy
(*Monarchie Elective*)

The first part of this article is mostly a reproduction of Burlamaqui's discussion of the election of sovereigns in The Principles of Natural and Politic Law, *II.II.iii.XIV–XVI, 352–53, except that Burlamaqui ends up preferring hereditary over elective succession (XXII on 354) on experiential grounds.*

ELECTIVE MONARCHY (*Political government*). This refers to any government in which royalty is attained only by election. This is without doubt a very legitimate means of acquiring sovereignty, since it is founded on the consent and free choice of the people.

The election of a monarch is that act by which the nation designates the one it considers most capable of succeeding the deceased king in governing the state, and as soon as this person accepts the people's offer, he is invested with sovereignty.

Two kinds of *elective monarchy* may be distinguished: one in which the election is entirely free, the other in which the election is restricted in certain ways. The first takes place when the people can choose as monarch whomever they deem appropriate, the other when the people are compelled by the constitution of the state to elect as sovereign a person who is from a certain nation, a certain family, a certain religion, etc. No one among the ancient Persians, says Cicero, could be elected king if he had not been instructed by the Magi.[1]

This article can be found at 10:637 in the original edition of the *Encyclopédie*.

1. Cicero, *On Divination*, I.xli.91.

But doesn't a nation that enjoys the privilege of raising one of its citizens to the monarchy, and especially a nation that is still subject to the laws of nature, have the right during his election to speak to that citizen in the following way?

> We are quite happy to place power in your hands, but at the same time we advise you to observe the conventions that have been made between us. And since these aim to maintain such perfectly reciprocal support that nothing necessary or useful is to be lacking if at all possible, we enjoin you to do your best to supervise the preservation of this order, to make it easier for us to enjoy effective means of maintaining it, and to encourage us to put them to use. Reason has prescribed this rule for us, and we urge you to remind us of it constantly. We endow you with the power and authority of the laws over each of us; we make you their organ and their herald. We commit ourselves to assist you, and to join you in constraining whoever among us is so void of sense as to disobey. At the same time, you must grasp that if you yourself went so far as to impose some yoke upon us that was contrary to the laws, those same laws declare you to be fallen from all power and all authority.
>
> We judge you to be capable of governing us; with confidence, we abandon ourselves to the instructions of your counsel. This is a first homage that we pay to the superior talents with which nature has endowed you. If you are faithful to your duties, we will cherish you as a gift from heaven, we will respect you as a father—there you have your reward, your glory, your grandeur. What happiness to be able to merit many thousands of mortals, your equals, taking a tender interest in your existence and your preservation!
>
> God is a sovereignly beneficent being. He has made us sociable; maintain us in the society that we have chosen. Just as he is the motor of all nature, where he maintains an admirable order, be the motor of our body politic; in this, you will seem to imitate the Supreme Being. Moreover, remember that with respect to what touches you personally, you have no other incontestable rights, no other powers but those that bind the common citizenry, because you have no other needs and you experience no other pleasures. If we think that one of your own is capable of the same command after you, we will give them close consideration, but by a choice that is free and independent of any claim on their part.

What imperial capitulation,[2] what ancient right of possession can prescribe against the truth of this perpetual edict, or emancipate sovereigns elected on these conditions from it? What am I saying—it would deprive them of a privilege that invests them with the power of supreme benefactors, and thereby makes them genuinely similar to the divinity. Let men draw their conclusions, based on this account, about the ordinary form of governments! (*D.J.*)

2. The term *capitulation* refers here to the specific provisions proposed by the electors of the Holy Roman Empire upon the election of a new emperor.

Limited Monarchy
(*Monarchie Limitée*)

LIMITED MONARCHY (*Government*), sort of *monarchy* in which the three powers are so blended together that they use each other as balances and counterweights. Hereditary *limited monarchy* seems to be the best form of *monarchy* because, independent of its stability, the legislative body is composed of two parts, which constrain each other by their mutual capacity for prevention. And both are bound by the executive power, which itself is bound by the legislative. Such is the government of England, whose roots—always being cut, always bloody—have after centuries at last produced, to the astonishment of nations, the equal mixture of liberty and royalty.[1] In the other European *monarchies* that we know, the three powers are not blended together in this manner; they each have a particular distribution, which makes them approach more or less closely to political liberty. It seems this precious advantage is enjoyed in Sweden to the same extent that it is far from being enjoyed in Denmark; Russia's monarchy, though, is a pure despotism.[2] (*D.J.*)

This article can be found at 10:637 in the original edition of the *Encyclopédie*.

1. This sentence is taken from Voltaire, *Essai sur l'histoire générale* (Geneva: Cramer, 1756), chap. 80.

2. The Swedish allusion is to the constitution of 1719, after the death of Charles XII, which enhanced the power of the Riksdag; the Danish reference is to the *Lex Regia* [the *Royal Law*] of 1665 which curtailed the prerogatives of the nobility and established, in effect, an absolutist constitution. Montesquieu was among those who criticized the latter, writing in *Considerations on the Causes of the Greatness of the Romans and Their Decline* (trans. David Lowenthal [Indianapolis: Hackett, 1999], chap. 15, p. 138): "No authority is more absolute than that of a prince who succeeds a republic, for he finds himself with all the power of the people, who had not been able to impose limitations on themselves. Thus we see the kings of Denmark today exercising the most arbitrary power in Europe."

Volume II
(1765)

Trade
(*Négoce*)

TRADE (*Commerce*), or traffic in merchandise or money. *See* COMMERCE.

Trade is a very honorable occupation in the Orient, where it is practiced not only by commoners, but also by the greatest lords, and even sometimes by kings in person (though always through their agents).

It is especially in Persia that the character of the merchant enjoys extraordinary honors and prerogatives. Thus, this name is not given to people who keep a shop or traffic in petty commodities but only to those who maintain agents and factors in the most distant countries. These persons are often elevated to the highest positions, and the king of Persia chooses his ambassadors from among them. The word *merchant* in Persian is *saudaguet*, which signifies *maker of profit*.

In the Orient, *trade* is engaged in by brokers, whom the Persians call *delal*—that is, *great talkers*—because of their peculiar manner of buying or selling. *See* COURTIERS (Brokers). And those maintained in foreign countries they call *vikils*. *Diction. de Com.*[1]

The surest means of ruining *trade* in a realm is to authorize state finance to its detriment. The tangle of formalities, the fees for the tax farmers and agents, the burdens, the visits, the official reports, the delays in expeditions, the takings, the discussions that result, *&c.*, all destroy in a few years the

This article can be found at 11:75 in the original edition of the *Encyclopédie*.

1. See Jacques Savary des Bruslons, *Dictionnaire universel de commerce* (Geneva: Cramer and Philibert, 1744 [1723]), vol. 1, pt. 2, 713–14, for this discussion. Savary's *Dictionary* was a standard reference work, translated by Malachy Postlethwayt as *The Universal dictionary of trade and commerce* in 2 vols. in 1751–55.

most lucrative and trusted *trade* in the provinces.[2] Thus, the pernicious liberty accorded the customs farmer in Lyon to establish bureaus wherever he wanted to was so widely employed in the last century that in less than fifty years, a hundred and sixty-seven of them were found in the Lyonnais, Dauphiné, Provence, and Languedoc, and the entire *trade* in foodstuffs abroad was thereby turned upside down. Most of the establishments pernicious to the kingdom's *trade* must be traced back to the great credit of the favorites and state financiers in the reign of Henry III.[3] (*D.J.*)

2. Montesquieu, *The Spirit of the Laws,* 20.13, is among the critics of current trade policy Jaucourt may have been drawing on here.

3. Henry III, king of France (r. 1574–89).

Political Economy
(*Œconomie Politique*)

Jean-Jacques Rousseau had already written a long article on this theme under the title ECONOMIE OU ŒCONOMIE, *which appeared in volume 5 of the* Encyclopédie *in November 1755, shortly after the publication of his* Discourse on the Origins of Inequality Among Men *(1754). But as has been aptly noted, this later article by Boulanger "was almost surely inserted by Diderot as a foil to Rousseau's more sanguine ideas about the lives of primitive peoples."*[1] *Specifically, Rousseau had argued that true public economy consists in identifying and following the "general will" (a concept made famous by his later work,* On the Social Contract*), ensuring that all particular and private wills are in synch with it through a robust regime of virtue-oriented public education, and protecting personal property by means of a state that kept its needs and its tax revenues low, the better to encourage equality of wealth among its citizens. "The voice of the people is indeed the voice of God," he had written, evoking ancient republics such as Sparta.*

Boulanger's approach was completely different. In combining Montesquieu's constitutional typology with some imaginative but controversial conjectures about prehistory, the article also provides one of the most unusual defenses of modern, law-abiding monarchy to appear in the eighteenth century. In addition, the work features a conception of "political economy" that grows directly out of the older tradition, going back to Xenophon and Aristotle, of seeing "economy" as household management. Thus, it will

This article can be found at 11:366–83 in the original edition of the *Encyclopédie.*

1. Frank A. Kafker and Serena L. Kafker, *The Encyclopedists as Individuals: A Biographical Dictionary of the Authors of the "Encyclopédie,"* Studies on Voltaire and the Eighteenth Century 257 (Oxford: Voltaire Foundation, 1988), 66.

be noted that the work has nothing to do with the new science of "political economy" that David Hume, the Physiocrats, the circle around Vincent de Gournay, and others were developing at the same time; the term "commerce" appears only once in the entire long article, for example.

One term that is frequently used in this entry is police, *which we have translated variously as "government," "administration," or the more capacious word "governance," depending on the context. For this term, see the translators' note, above.*

Political Economy (*History, Politics, Religion ancient and modern*). This is the art and science of maintaining men in society, and of making them happy—a sublime object, the most useful and interesting that exists for the human race. We will not speak here about what the powers of the earth do or should do: instructed by past ages, they will be judged by future ones. Let us restrict ourselves, then, to a historical account of the various governments that have successively appeared, and the various means that have been employed to lead nations.

All the established governments are commonly reduced to three types: (1) *the despotic,* in which authority resides in the will of one; (2) *the republican,* which is governed by the people, or by the leading classes of the people; and (3) *the monarchical,* or the power of a sovereign, unique and tempered by the laws and customs that the wisdom of monarchs and the respect of peoples have rendered sacred and inviolable, because—being useful to both parties—these laws and customs fortify the throne, defend the prince, and protect the subjects.[2]

To these three governments, we must add a fourth, the *theocratic,* which political writers have forgotten to consider. Doubtless, this is because they have been embarrassed to give a rank on earth to a government in which the officers and ministers command in the name of an invisible power and being. Perhaps that administration seemed to them too special and too supernatural to place it among the list of political governments. If, however,

2. Before Montesquieu, the standard typology was Aristotle's division into monarchy, aristocracy, and democracy—the government of one, the few, and the many. It was *The Spirit of the Laws,* 2.1, that furnished what Boulanger here calls the "common" discourse.

those writers had fixed their more reflective attention on the earliest scenes presented by antiquity, and if they had combined and brought together all the fragments that are left to us from its history, they would have recognized not only that this theocracy, albeit supernatural, was one of the earliest governments men gave themselves, but also that those governments we have just named have emerged from them in succession, have in fact been their inevitable consequences. And to begin at this end, they are all bound by a continuous chain of events that embraces virtually all the great revolutions that have occurred in the political world and in the moral world.

The theocracy that we have particularly in mind here is not, as one might at first think, the *Mosaic theocracy,* but another one more ancient and more extensive, which has been the source of some good and much more evil, of which the Hebrews' theocracy was in its time merely a renewal and a prudent reform that separated them from the human race, which the abuses of the first one had made idolatrous. It is true that this primitive theocracy is almost unknown, and that the recollection of it had grown murky even in the memories of the ancient peoples. But the analysis we will make of the history of man in society will enable that theocracy to be glimpsed and eventually even fully unveiled by those who would afterward like to study, and reflect carefully on, all the various subjects of the immense trajectory that we can but lightly touch on here.

If we wanted to seek the origin of societies and governments as metaphysicians, we would go find man from the territories of the South Pole.[3] If it were suitable for us to speak as theologians about our primitive state, we would reveal man degenerated from his first innocence. But in order to conduct ourselves as simple historians, we will consider man as escaped from the miseries of the world after the last revolutions of nature. Behold the sole and unique epoch we can return to, and there is the sole man that we ought to consult on the origin and principles of societies that have been formed since those destructive events. Despite the murkiness that one seems inevitably to encounter in transcending the limits of historical time, we have nonetheless not lacked for guides and torches in looking into and

3. *Terres Australes,* or "south lands," referring to a continent that was assumed in the past to exist in the Antarctic zone.

beyond the darkness for natural events and human institutions. We have transported ourselves into the midst of ancient witnesses of the world's calamities. We have examined how they were affected by them, and what impressions those calamities made on their minds, their hearts, and their character. We have sought to catch the human race unawares in the excess of its misery. And to study it, we have studied ourselves, distinctly aware of the fact that despite the differences in centuries and in men, there are common sentiments and uniform ideas that are awakened universally by the cries of nature—and even by the very panics by which certain centuries known to us have sometimes been frightened. After the examination of this common conscience, we have reflected on the most natural results of these impressions and on their effect with respect to men's conduct. And using our results as starting points,[4] we have related them to the customs of antiquity; we have compared them with the administration and the laws of the earliest nations, with their worship and their government. We have followed the various opinions and customs of men from one era to another, such as we have been able to know their consequences, or at least the vestiges of the primitive impressions. And everywhere, in fact, our examination has seemed to perceive in the annals of the world a continuous though unknown chain, a distinctive unity hidden beneath a thousand forms; and in our principles, the solution to a multitude of enigmas and obscure problems that concern man in all times and his various governments in all ages.

We will spare the reader the apparatus of our research; he will have only the analysis from our work. And unless we have been deluding ourselves, he will come to know the origin and nature of primitive theocracy. In the good and bad things it produced, he will recognize the golden age and the reign of the gods. He will see the successive birth of savage life, superstition and servitude, idolatry and despotism. He will observe its reformation among the Hebrews. Republics and monarchies will then appear, with their intentions of remedying the abuses of the earliest legislation. The reader will weigh each of these two governments, and if he has followed the chain of events carefully, he will conclude as we have that monarchy alone has been the effect of the total extinction of ancient prejudices, and the fruit

4. *Principes,* that is, "origins" or "beginnings."

of reason and good sense, and that it is the sole government truly made for man and for the earth.

One has to know awfully little about the human race to doubt that in the deplorable times we are supposing, and in the first ages that followed, man was very religious, and that his miseries then took the place of strict missionaries and powerful legislators, who would have turned his whole perspective toward heaven and toward morality. That multitude of austere and rigid institutions, of which such fine vestiges are found in the history of all peoples famous for their antiquity, was doubtless merely a general consequence of those first dispositions of the human mind.

The same must be true of their administration. All those admirable regulations that we find only among the most ancient peoples—on agriculture, labor, industry, population, education, and everything that concerns public and domestic economy—must doubtless have been made as a consequence of all those unfortunate events that in the past ruined the human species, its subsistence, and its abode.

It had to be during that epoch—when the unity of principle, purpose, and effect had been restored among mortals who were now reduced to small numbers and pressed by the same needs—that domestic laws became the basic, or better yet the only laws for societies, as all the most ancient legislation proves.

Just as war produces generals and soldiers, so too the extreme evils of the human race and of its great necessities gave rise in their time to the simplest and wisest laws and to primitive legislation, which, in administrative matters, had as its sovereign purpose the true and only good of humanity. Man at that time did not let himself be guided by custom; he did not seek the laws among his neighbors, but found them in his reason and his needs.

How affecting the spectacle of these earliest societies must have been! As pure in their morality as they were regular in their discipline, animated by a fervent charity toward each other, mutually sensitive and tightly united, it was then that equality shone, and that equity reigned on earth. No more thine, no more mine; everything belonged to society, which had but one heart and one mind. *Erat terra labii unius, & sermonum eorumdem. Gen. XI.1.*[5]

5. "Now the whole earth had one language and few words." Genesis 11:1.

The myth of the golden age, so celebrated by our forefathers, is thus not a myth devoid of all reality. It must have existed around the earliest epochs of the world renewed—a time, an ancient time, when justice, equality, union, and peace reigned among humans. If there is something to erase from the mythological accounts, it is likely only the smiling picture of the happy state of nature; nature must then have been much less beautiful than the heart of man. The earth offered only a desert filled with horror and misery, and the human race covered only the world's debris.

It was this situation of nature, which took many centuries to remedy and to change the frightful spectacle from its ruin into what we see today, that kept the human race for a long time in that almost supernatural condition. The golden-age morality and way of life could no longer prevail in the midst of expanded societies, because they are no more suitable to the luxury of nature than to the luxury of humanity, which was merely its aftermath and its effect. As the sojourn of man became more attractive, as societies multiplied and as they formed cities and states, the moral reign inevitably had to make room for the political reign. Thine and mine were bound to appear in the world—not at first from man to man, but from family to family and from society to society—because they became indispensable, and because they are part of that same harmony that was bound to return to the revitalized nations just as it has imperceptibly returned to nature after the last period of chaos. That golden age was therefore an age of holiness, a supernatural state worthy of our envy and justly deserving all of antiquity's regrets. Nonetheless, when subsequent legislation wanted to adopt its customs and principles indiscriminately, the good inevitably turned into evil, the gold into lead. Perhaps there would never even have been an iron age if the practices of the golden age had not been in effect when it was no longer time for it. That is what we will be able to determine from the rest of this article.

Such were the first, and we may say the fortunate effects of the misfortunes of the world. They forced man to unite. With men bereft of everything, rendered poor and miserable by the disasters that had occurred, and living in fear and expectation of those they long continued to believe were threatening them, religion and necessity gathered together the sad remnants and induced them to become inviolably united, in order to assist the effects of activity and industry. All those great resources that the human heart is reliably capable of only in adversity then had to be put to use. In our time, they are without force and without vigor, but in those sad centuries this was not the case. All the virtues were exalted; the reign and triumph of humanity appeared, because that was its moment.

We will not go into detail on all the means put into effect to remedy the evils of the human race and to restore societies. Although history has not handed them down to us, they are easy to know; when we consult nature, she enables us to discover them in the bottom of our hearts. Can it be doubted, for example, that one of the first consequences of the impression made on men by the sight of the world's ruin was to remove from the midst of the earliest families, and even the earliest nations, that destructive spirit by which they never ceased to be animated against each other later on? Violence, murder, war, and their frightful effects must have been unknown or abhorred by mortals for many centuries. Instructed by the most powerful of all lessons—that Providence has the means to exterminate the human race in the blink of an eye—they doubtless stipulated among themselves and in the name of their posterity that they would never shed blood on earth. This, in effect, was the first precept of the law of nature, to which the miseries of the world inevitably brought societies: *requiram animam hominis de manu fratris ejus quicumque effuderit humanum sanguinem, &c. Gen. ix. 5.6.*[6] The peoples who even to this day have avoided as if it were a crime the shedding or drinking of animal blood offer us a vestige of this primitive humanity. But that is only a pale shadow of it; those peoples, often barbarous and cruel toward their fellow men, make it very clear that they were looking only to evade the first and most sacred of all laws.

However, it is not yet in these earliest periods that one must look for those various political governments that afterward appeared on earth. The condition of those earliest men was an entirely religious one. Their families, steeped in fear of judgments from on high, lived for a time under the guidance of fathers who gathered their children together; these families had no other ties between them but their needs, and no other king but the God they

6. "Of every man's brother I will require the life of man. Whoever sheds the blood of man, etc." Genesis 9:5–6.

invoked. Only after multiplying did large societies need a stronger and more forceful bond than did families, in order to maintain the unity whose price was well known, and to support that spirit of religion, *economy*, industry, and peace that alone could repair the countless evils that human nature had suffered. Thus, laws were then made. In the beginning, they were as simple as the mind that inspired them. To design them, no recourse to sublime philosophers or profound men of politics was necessary; the needs of man dictated them. And when they gathered together all the parts, they doubtless did nothing more than write or engrave on stone or wood what had been done up to that happy time when the reason of individuals—being in no way different from public reason—had been the sole and unique law. Such was the origin of the first codes; they made no changes to the primitive means of governing societies. The purpose of this new precaution was merely to fortify these codes in proportion to the size and scope of the body they had to put in motion, and man submitted without difficulty. Since his needs had taught him early on that he was not a being that could live in isolation on earth, he joined together with his fellow creatures from the beginning, preferring the advantages of a necessary and reasonable engagement to his natural liberty. And since the enlargement of society then required that the tacit contract each individual had made in joining society should have a more solemn form and should become authentic, he thus consented to it again. He submitted to written laws, and to civil and political subordination. In its elders, he acknowledged superiors, magistrates, and priests. More important, he sought a sovereign, because he knew then that a large society without leader or king is only a body without a head—even a monster, whose various movements cannot have anything rational or harmonious about them.

To grasp this great truth, man had only to glance over that society which had already taken shape. At the sight of any assembly, we cannot in fact prevent ourselves from looking in it for the one who is its chief or leader. It is an involuntary and truly natural sentiment, a consequence of the secret attraction that simplicity and unity—which are the marks of order and truth—have for us. It is a precious inspiration of our reason, by which, whatever penchant we have for independence, we know enough to submit for our well-being and for the love of order. The spectacle of someone presiding over a society, far from causing any displeasure in those who compose it, cannot be viewed by private reason without a pleasant, sweet inner satisfaction. This is because it is the entire society, and we ourselves who belong to it, that we are looking at in that leader and in that organ of public reason of which he is the mirror, the image, and the august representation. The first society ordered and administered by the laws was doubtless unable to contemplate itself without admiring itself.

The idea of giving themselves a king was thus one of the first ideas of sociable and reasonable man. The spectacle of the universe itself seconded the voice of reason. Still anxious at that time, man often raised his eyes toward heaven to study the movement of the stars and their harmony, on which the tranquility of the earth and its inhabitants depended. Noticing above all that unique and brilliant star that seems to command the army of the heavens and to be obeyed by it, he thought that he saw up there the image of good government, and that he recognized the model and plan that earthly society should follow in order to make that government happy and immutable by means of a similar harmony. Religion brought support to all these motives. In all of nature, man saw but one sun; in the universe, he knew but one supreme being. Thus, he thereby saw that something was missing from his legislation, that his society had not been perfected—in a word, that a king was needed to be the father and center of that great family, and the protector and organ of the laws.

That is the advice, counsel, and example that reason, the spectacle of nature, and religion unanimously gave man from the earliest times. But he evaded them rather than following them. Instead of choosing a king from among his peers, with whom society would have made the same contract that each individual had previously made with society, man proclaimed the king from the golden age—that is, the Supreme Being. Man continued to regard him as his monarch, and crowning him in forms, he wanted there to be no other master and no other sovereign on earth, as in heaven.

The reader has doubtless not expected to see such early collapse and oblivion for those sentiments that we have been pleased to assign to the human mind, at a moment when societies were preparing to represent their unity by a monarch. If we have attributed this kind of thinking to them, it is because those earliest sentiments—true and full of simplicity—are worthy of those primitive ages, and because the supernatural governance of those societies seems to indicate that they were surprised and deceived at that fatal moment. Perhaps some will suspect that the love of independence was the motive for this approach, and that man, in refusing to take on a visible king in order to recognize one that he could not see, had a tacit design not to accept any king. This would be unfair to man in general, and in particular to man when he had escaped the miseries of the world, since he had been led more than all others to sacrifice his liberty and all his passions. If, in giving himself a king, he made such a peculiar application of the lessons he received from reason and from all of nature, this is because he had not yet purified his religion as he had his civil and domestic administration, and because he had not disengaged it from superstition, that daughter of fear and terror that absorbs reason and—taking the place and assuming the face of religion—annihilates it in order to deliver humanity over to fraud and imposture. Man was at that time cruelly duped; superstition alone presided over the election of the god-monarch, and it was then that the first epoch and source of all the evils of the human race occurred.

We have said above that the earliest families had no other king but the god they invoked, and that this same custom, consecrated by time, led expanding nations to metamorphose this religious worship into a political government. Thus, it is important here to make known the prejudices that the earliest families added to their worship, because these are the same prejudices that later perverted their posterity's religion and administration.

Among the impressions made on man by the cataclysm on earth and the great changes in nature, he had been particularly affected by fear of the end of the world. He had imagined that the days of justice and vengeance had arrived. He had expected shortly to see the supreme judge come and demand a reckoning from the world, to pronounce those formidable decrees that the wicked have always feared and that have always been the hope and consolation of the just. Man, seeing the world shattered and almost destroyed, had no doubt that the reign of heaven was very near, and that the future life that religion calls *par excellence* the *kingdom of God,* was ready to appear. This is the source of those dogmas that seize humanity through all the revolutions of nature, and that in all times return men to the same point. They are doubtless sacred, religious, and infinitely respectable in themselves. But the history of certain ages has taught us about the false principles to which they have sometimes led weak men, when those dogmas have been presented to them only after mendacious and terrorizing panics.

Although the miseries of the world in the earliest ages were only too real, they nonetheless led man to the abuses that are typical of false terrors. This is because there is always as much difference between some change in the world and its absolute end—of which only God knows the different moments—as there is between a simple renewal and a fully miraculous creation. Nonetheless, we agree that in these ancient epochs in which man was led to abuse these universal dogmas, it was much more excusable than in those later centuries when superstition had no other source but false calculations and false oracles that the very state of nature contradicted. It was nature itself, and the entire universe with its back to the wall, that seduced the primitive ages. At the sight of all the fearsome manifestations of a complete dissolution, could man have prevented himself from being struck by those religious dogmas whose precise purpose, it is true, he did not see, but all of whose signs and approaches he evidently thought he recognized? His eyes and his reason seemed to warn him of it at every instant and to justify his terrors. His sorrows and his miseries, which had reached their limit, left him no strength to doubt it. The consolations of religion were his only hope. He surrendered to it without reserve. He awaited the fatal day with resignation. He prepared for it, even desired it—so deplorable was his state on earth!

In these sorry circumstances, the arrival of the great judge and of the kingdom of heaven were thus the only vantage points that man had examined with a holy ardor. He had used them to support himself constantly during the excitement of his sojourn. These dogmas had made such profound impressions on him that nature, which doubtless recovered only gradually, was completely restored at a time when man was still waiting. During the first generations, these dispositions of the human mind served only to perfect his morality proportionally, and they produced the heroism and holiness of the golden age. Steeped in these dogmas, each family represented but a religious community that directed all its steps toward the celestial future. And no longer counting on the survival of the world, it awaited events by living solely by the ties of religion. It seems the unexpected centuries that succeeded those thought to be the last should have disabused man of what had been erroneous in his principles. But is hope discouraged? Good faith and simplicity had established those principles in the earliest ages. Prejudice and custom perpetuated them in the ages that followed, and they still animated the enlarged and expanded societies when the latter began to give ordered form to their civil and political administration. Preoccupied by heaven, they forgot at that moment that they were still on earth. Instead of giving their state a fixed and natural tie, they persisted in a government which, being only provisional and supernatural, could not suit political societies as it had suited mystical and religious societies. They no doubt thought by this sublime speculation to anticipate their glory and their felicity, to enjoy heaven on earth, and to get the jump on the celestial future. Nonetheless, this speculation was the germ of all their errors and all the evils into which the human race was later plunged. No sooner was the god-monarch elected than the principles of the reign above were applied to the reign here below. And these principles were found to be false because they were misplaced. That government was only a fiction that had inevitably to be supported by a multitude of assumptions and conventional practices. And since those assumptions were later taken literally, there resulted a host of religious and political prejudices, countless bizarre and unreasonable customs, and myths beyond number that eventually plunged religion, primitive administration, and the history of the human race into the darkest chaos. That is how the earliest nations, after drawing on their good sense and their true needs for their domestic and economic[7] laws, subjected them all to an ideal government that history has hardly known but that Mythology, which has assembled the shadows of the earliest times, has handed down to us under the name *reign of the gods*—that is, in our language, *the reign of God,* and in one word, *theocracy.*

Since the historians have always scorned the myths of antiquity, and almost always with reason, primitive theocracy is one of the most suspect ages of the world. If we had here no other authority but that of Mythology, everything we might say about this ancient government would then seem implausible in the eyes of most people. Perhaps we would have the approbation of some of those whose genius, buttressed by knowledge, is alone capable of grasping the totality of all human errors, and of perceiving the

7. *Œconomique,* which refers here to household management.

proof for an unknown incident in the credit given to a universal error, then returning from that error to the truths or events that gave rise to it by a reflective combination of all the different aspects of that same error. But since the limits of our trajectory do not allow us to employ the materials that Mythology is able to furnish us, we will not undertake here to reconstruct the theocratic annals. We would only observe that if the universality and uniformity of an error are capable of enabling the most intelligent minds to glimpse some principles of truth, where so many others, meanwhile, are seeing only the effects of ancient poets' whimsy and imagination, the traditions concerning the reign of the gods should not be totally rejected. Those traditions are universal and are found in all nations that make first the demigods and then the kings succeed them, by distinguishing these three reigns as three different forms of government. Egyptians, Chaldeans, Persians, Indians, Chinese, Japanese, Greeks, Romans, even down to the Americans—all these peoples alike have preserved the murky memory of a time when the gods came down on earth to gather men together, govern them, and make them happy by giving them laws and teaching them the useful arts. For all these peoples, the particular circumstances of the descent of these gods are the miseries and calamities of the world. One came, say the Indians, to bolster the shattered earth; another one came to wrest it from beneath the waters; another to aid the sun, to make war on the dragon, and to exterminate monsters. We will not remind the reader of the wars and victories of the Greek and Egyptian gods over the Typhons, the Pythons, the Giants, and the Titans.[8] All the great solemnities of paganism celebrated their memory. Whatever climate one examines, one finds the same constant and distinctive tradition of a theocratic age. And it must be observed that, independent of the uniformity of those prejudices that reveal a fact such as it might be, this supernatural reign is always designated as being close by the ancient revolutions, since in all places the reign of the gods is filled and embellished with literal or allegorical anecdotes on the ruin or restoration of the world. Here, I believe, you have one of the greatest authorities one could find on such an obscure subject.

8. In Greek mythology, Typhon, the son of Gaia and Tartarus, attempted to replace Zeus; Python was an earth-dragon of Delphi and enemy of Apollo.

"If men were happy in the earliest times," says Plato, *bk. IV of the Laws*, "if they were happy and just, it is because they were not then governed as we are today, but in the same manner that we govern our flocks. For just as we don't set a bull over a bull, or a goat over a goat, but instead put them under the direction of a man who is their shepherd, likewise God, who loves men, placed our ancestors under the direction of spirits and angels."[9]

Either I am mistaken or we have here that supernatural government that gave rise to the traditions of the golden age and the reign of the gods. Plato was brought to this tradition by a route quite similar to the one I am following. He says elsewhere that after the deluge, men lived under three successive states: the first, on the mountains, wandering and isolated from each other; the second, in families in the neighboring valleys, a little less terrified than in the first state; and third, in societies formed in the plains and living under laws. Moreover, if that government became so generally obscure and mythic, only the government itself can be blamed. Although formed under the auspices of religion, its supernatural principles led it to so many excesses and abuses that it became imperceptibly disfigured, and was in the end unrecognizable. But perhaps history, which has rejected it, has also partially accepted it in its splendor under the name of *sacerdotal reign*. In its time, this reign was merely one of the sequels of the original, and it cannot be denied that this form of administration was found in many quite historical nations.

To fill this large void in the annals of the world by a means other than Mythology, we have reflected on the etiquette and customs that must have been appropriate to this type of government. And after making ourselves a blueprint and a picture of it, we have again compared it with the political and religious customs of nations. Sometimes we have followed the order of the ages, and sometimes we have gone backward, in order to clarify the ancient by the modern as one clarifies the modern by the ancient. Such has been our method of finding out the known by the unknown; its exactness or inexactness will be judged by some examples, and by the result whose analysis follows.

Since supernatural government had obliged nations to have recourse to a multitude of customs and assumptions to support its edifice, one of

9. The passage is loosely adapted from Plato, *Laws*, IV (713C–D).

their first concerns was to exhibit their monarch's house in the middle of the nation, to raise a throne for him, and to give him officers and ministers. Considered as a civil palace, this house was doubtless excessive on earth, but considered as a temple, it could not suffice for the public worship of the whole nation. At first, people wanted this house to be alone and unique, because the god-monarch was alone and unique. But since all the different portions of society could not go there as often as the daily worship owed to the divinity demands, the most distant parts of the society fell into religious and political anarchy, or made themselves into rebels and culprits by multiplying the god-monarch with the houses that they too wanted to erect for him. Little by little, the ideas one ought to have about divinity shrank. Instead of regarding that temple as a place for assemblies and public prayers—an infinitely respectable purpose—men sought the master they could not see there, and in the end, they gave him a tangible face and form. The sign of authority and the scepter of dominion were not placed in specific hands. They were lodged in that house and on the seat of the celestial monarch—that is, in a temple, and in the most respectable place within that temple, namely, the sanctuary. In the earliest times, the scepter and other marks of royal authority were merely sticks and branches; temples were merely huts, and the sanctuary was just a basket and a small box. This is what is found throughout antiquity. But by an abuse of these customs, religion absorbed government, and the reign of heaven gave religion the reign on earth, thus perverting both.

Nor was the code of civil and religious law placed in the hands of the magistrate; it was lodged in the sanctuary. One had to have recourse to that sacred place to know those laws and be instructed in one's duties. The laws were buried there over time; the human race forgot them, perhaps was even made to forget them. In those festivals that among the ancients bore the name *festivals of legislation*, like the Palilia and the Thesmophoria, the holiest truths were no longer communicated except secretly to a few initiates, and the simplest governmental item, as well as the truest and most useful religious item, were turned into a mystery for the people.[10]

10. Thesmophoria, a women's harvest festival before the time of sowing, in honor of Demeter; Palilia, or Parilia, annual Roman festival in April in honor of the god of shepherds.

Since the nature of primitive theocracy necessarily demands that the repository of the laws kept in the sanctuary appear to have emanated from god himself, and that he must be thought of as men's legislator as well as their monarch, time and ignorance gave the pagan ministers space to imagine that the gods and goddesses had revealed the laws to the ancient legislators, whereas their sole and true sources had been merely the needs and the public reason of the earliest societies. By these frightful lies, they robbed man of the honor of those laws, so fine and simple, that he had originally made. And they so weakened the dignity and resourcefulness of his reason—by making him falsely believe that it was incapable of dictating those laws—that he scorned his reason and thought he was paying homage to the divinity by no longer using a gift that he had only received from the divinity for the purpose of making constant use of it.

Since the society's god-monarch was unable either to speak to it or to command it in a direct fashion, men were placed in the necessity of imagining means to know his orders and his will. Thus, an absurd convention established signs in heaven and on earth which were supposed to be looked upon, and in fact were looked upon, as the monarch's augurs. Oracles were invented, and each nation had its own. A host of seers, soothsayers, and diviners made their appearance. In government as in religion, man no longer consulted reason, but believed that his conduct, his enterprises, and all of his methods of proceeding needed as guide an order or an official opinion from his invisible prince. And since fraud and imposture dictated these things to nations gone blind, these nations all became their dupes, their slaves, their victims.

Similar abuses also arose from the taxes thought to be owed him. In the earliest times, when neither religion nor government were yet corrupted by their false trappings, societies had no other taxes or obligations toward the Supreme Being but the fruits and first goods of the earth. Also, this was only a homage of gratitude and not a civil tax, which the sovereign—dispenser of everything—did not need. It was not the same when each nation fashioned its particular king out of a universal being. He had to be given a house, a throne, some officers, and finally some revenues to maintain them. Thus, the people brought him the tithe from their property, their lands, and their flocks. They knew they owed everything to their divine king, which is clear from the fervor with which each person came to offer whatever might contribute to the splendor and magnificence of his monarch. Generous piety knew no bounds; people went so far as to offer themselves, their families, and their children. It was thought possible to acknowledge oneself a slave of the sovereign of all nature without dishonoring oneself; man made himself but the subject and slave of theocratic officers.

As religious simplicity faded away and superstition increased along with ignorance, it gradually became necessary to improve upon the ancient offerings and to seek out new ones. After the fruits, one offered animals, and when this latter custom made men familiar with the cruel idea that the divinity loves blood, it was but a short step to slitting the throats of men, in order to offer him what was doubtless in his eyes the dearest and most precious blood. Unable to rise to a higher apex, ancient fanaticism thus slit the throats of human victims. It presented the palpitating organs to the divinity as an offering that was agreeable to him. What's more, man ate of it himself, and after extinguishing his reason, he ended up overcoming nature to participate in the banquets of the gods.

It is not necessary to engage in a lengthy application of these customs to the customs of all the pagan and savage nations that have followed them. For all of them, the original purpose of the bloody sacrifices was to cover the theocratic king's table, as we cover the table of our monarchs. The priests of *Belus* made the people of Assyria believe that it was their divinities themselves who ate the meats presented to them on their altars.[11] And in times of calamity, the Greeks and Romans never failed to assemble their gods and goddesses around a magnificently covered table in the public square, to obtain by an extraordinary banquet the graces that could not be granted at the regular evening and morning meals—that is, at the ordinary daily sacrifices. That is how a custom originally established to support in all its aspects the figurative ceremonial of a supernatural government was taken literally, and how the divinity, finding himself treated as a mortal creature in every way, was debased and lost from view.

Nor can cannibalism, which has reigned and which still reigns in half the world, have any other source than the one we have glimpsed here. It is not

11. Belus, a mythic Egyptian ruler and putative founder of a colony on the Euphrates, who appointed priests.

nature that has led so many nations to this abominable excess; instead, lost and led astray by the supernatural character of his principles, it is step by step and by degrees that a cruel and senseless worship has perverted man's heart. He became a cannibal only by the example and on the model of a divinity that he believed to be a cannibal.

If humanity was ruined, then morals were also, *a fortiori,* altered and withered. In his corruption, theocratic man gave women to the god-monarch. And since he was due everything that was good and better, virginity itself was obliged to make him its offering. Hence the religious prostitutions of Babylon and Paphos.[12] Hence those shameful duties of paganism that constrained girls to dedicate themselves to some divinity before being able to enter into marriage. Hence, finally, all those children of the gods who populated Mythology and the poetic heaven.

We will pursue no further the etiquette and ceremonial of the god-monarch's court; each custom was an abuse, and each abuse produced countless others. Considered as a king, he was given horses, chariots, shields, arms, furniture, lands, flocks, and a domain that became with time the patrimony of the pagan gods. Considered as a man, he was made seductive, angry, hot-tempered, jealous, vindictive, and barbarous; he was made the example and the model for all the iniquities whose frightful legends we find in pagan theogony.

The greatest of all the crimes of primitive theocracy was undoubtedly to have plunged the human race into idolatry by the supernatural character of its principles. It is so difficult for man to conceive of a being so grand, so immense, and yet invisible like the supreme being—without the aid of some tangible expedients—that that government had almost inevitably to end up supplying its representation. It was a question of the Supreme Being much more often then than it is today. Independent of his name and his status as god, he was still king. All acts of government, like all acts of religion, spoke only of him; his orders and decrees were found everywhere; his laws were followed, his taxes were paid; his officers, his palace, all but his public dignity were seen; thus, this dignity was soon filled.

12. Paphos, the Aegean city where Aphrodite, the goddess of love, was said to have been born; the cult of Aphrodite dominated the town for centuries.

Some represented this dignity with a rough stone, others a sculpted stone—the latter an image of the sun, the former of the moon. Many nations exhibited an ox, a goat, or a cat, like the Egyptians; in Ethiopia, it was a dog. And these signs, representing the monarch, were filled with all the symbolic attributes of a god and a king. They were decorated with all the sublime qualities befitting the one of whom the emblems were made. Before these signs, prayers and offerings were brought, all acts of government and religion were performed, and the whole theocratic ceremonial was in the end fulfilled. One is doubtless thinking that this is already idolatry. No, we are not there yet; this is only the fatal door to it. We reject that frightful opinion that men were naturally idolatrous, or that they came to be that way voluntarily and with premeditated design. Never have men forgotten the divinity; never in their grossest aberrations have they completely failed to recognize his excellence and his unity. And in their favor, we would even dare to think that there has been less real idolatry on earth than profound and general superstition. Nor was it by a sudden leap that men passed from the adoration of the Creator to the adoration of the creature. They became idolatrous without knowing it and without willing it, just as we will see below that they became slaves without ever desiring to place themselves in slavery. Primitive religion was corrupted and the love of unity was obscured by the forgetting of the past and by the assumptions that had to be made by a supernatural government that confused all ideas when it confused governance with religion. We have to think that in the earliest times, when each nation made its god-monarch tangible, men still behaved vis-à-vis their emblems with an intelligent and religious circumspection. What they intended to represent was less god than monarch; that is why our magistrates in our tribunals still have before them the image of their sovereign, who at every moment, by his resemblance and by the ornaments of royalty, calls to mind the true sovereign who is not seen but who is known to exist elsewhere. This scene cannot deceive us and is for us merely a relative and commemorative object, and such was surely the original intention behind all the representative symbols of the divinity. If our forefathers were deceived, however, this is because it was not as easy for them to depict that divinity as it is for us to depict a mortal. What connection, in fact, could there have been between the reigning god and all the different effigies made of him? It could only be an imaginary and purely conventional connection—always ready, therefore, to debase the god and the monarch as soon as fitting instruction was no longer attached to him. These instructions were no doubt given in the early days, but by this means, the cult and the governance, simple though they were, became compounded and allegorical; by this means, the theocratic officer saw people's need for his profession increase. And since he became ignorant himself, the original conventions changed into mysteries and the religion degenerated into a marvelous and bizarre science, whose secret became impenetrable from one age to the next, and whose purpose was in the end lost in a labyrinth of grave puerilities and weighty bagatelles.

If all the different societies had at least taken one and the same symbol as the sign of the reigning divinity, the unity of worship, albeit degenerated, would still have been preserved on earth. But as everyone knows, some took one thing, others took another. Under countless different forms, the Supreme Being was worshipped everywhere while no longer being the same in the eyes of gross men. Each nation became accustomed to considering the symbol it had chosen as the most authentic and the most holy.

The unity was thus broken; with the general religion being extinct or misunderstood, a general superstition took its place, and it displayed its particular standard in each country, as each person regarded his god and his king as the sole authentic one, detesting his neighbors' god and king. Soon all other nations were reputed to be foreign; men separated themselves from them, closed their borders, and thereby became by birth, by condition, and by religion declared enemies of each other.

Inde furor vulgò, quod numina vicinorum / Odit uterque locus, cum solos credat habendos / Esse deos, quos ipse colit. Juvenal, *Sat. 13.*[13]

Such was the deplorable state to which the pernicious abuses of primitive theocracy had already plunged the religion of the entire human race when God, to preserve the memory of his unity among men, at last chose a special people and gave the Hebrews a wise and informed legislator to

13. "[On each side, the height] of mob fury arises because each place detests the gods of their neighbors. They think that only the gods they themselves worship should be counted as gods." Juvenal, *Satires,* ed. and trans. Susanna Morton Braund (Cambridge: Harvard University Press, 2004), XV.36–38, 491.

reform the pagan theocracy of the nations. To achieve this, that great man had only to strip it of everything that ignorance and fraud had introduced into it. Moses thus destroyed all the idolatrous emblems raised to the god-monarch; he abolished the augurs, the soothsayers, and all the false interpreters of the divinity; and he expressly prohibited his people from ever representing that divinity by any figure of brass or stone, or by any painted or graven image. It was this last law that distinguished the Hebrews in an essential way from all the peoples of the world. To the extent that they observed it, they were truly wise and religious; every time they transgressed it, they put themselves on the level of all other nations. But such was the force of prejudice and the extreme coarseness of men in those ancient times that that precept, which seems to us today so simple and so consistent with reason, was for the Hebrews painful and difficult to observe. Hence their frequent relapses into idolatry and those constant reversions toward the images of nations, which until the present could be explained only by hardness of heart and unimaginable obstinacy, but whose source and motives must now be found in the ancient prejudices and in the customs of primitive theocracy.

After surveying the religious part of this ancient government up to the idolatry that it produced and its reform by the Hebrews, let us take a look at its civil and political part, whose vice has already been glimpsed. However grand and sublime a government that took heaven as its model and its purpose may have appeared in its own time, a political edifice constructed down here on such speculation inevitably had to crumble and cause very great evils. Amidst that host of false opinions with which theocracy filled the human mind, two arose that were strongly opposed to each other, and yet each was equally contrary to the happiness of societies. The picture men painted of the felicity of the celestial reign generated false ideas on earth about liberty, equality, and independence. By contrast, the sight of such a grand and immense god-monarch reduced man virtually to nothing and led him to scorn himself and willingly abase himself because of these two extremes. The spirit of humanity and reason that ought to have forged the link between societies was inevitably lost in one half of the world—men wanted to be more than they could and more than they should be on earth. In the other half, men debased themselves below their natural condition, so that in the end, one no longer looked at man, but imperceptibly saw the appearance of the savage and the slave.

The aspiration of the human race had nonetheless been to make itself happy by theocracy, and we cannot doubt that it succeeded at least for a time. The reign of the gods has been celebrated by the poets like the golden age, as a reign of felicity and liberty. Each person was free in Israel, the Scripture also says in speaking of the beginnings of Mosaic theocracy. Each person did what he liked, went where he wanted, and lived then in independence: *unusquisque, quod sibi rectum videbatur, hoc faciebat*. Jud. *xvii. 6.*[14] Those happy times, in which the germ of future abuses should nonetheless be perceived, could exist only on the outskirts of that mystical age, when man was still in the fervor of his morality and the heroism of his theocracy. His felicity as well as his justice were bound to be transitory, because the fervor and heroism that alone could support the supernatural quality of that government are momentary virtues and religious sallies that never endure on earth. Solid and authentic theocracy is reserved only for heaven; it is there that man will one day be without passion, like the divinity. But it is not at all the same here below with an earthly theocracy in which the people can only abuse their liberty under a provisional and spineless government, and in which those who command cannot but abuse the unlimited power of a god-monarch in whose name it is only too easy to speak. Thus, it is highly likely that theocratic administration was ruined in the past by these two excesses. By one, the entire ancient Occident exchanged its liberty for brigandage and a vagabond life; by the other, the entire Orient saw itself oppressed by its tyrants.

The savage state of the earliest known Europeans and of all the peoples of America display shadows and vestiges that are still so consistent with some of the features of the golden age that one should not be surprised if we have been led to seek the origin of the state of a large part of the human race in the aftermath of the world's miseries, and in the abuse of those theocratic prejudices that spread so many errors throughout the world. In fact, the more profoundly we have examined the different traditions and customs of savage peoples, the more things we have found arising from the

14. "Every man did what was right in his own eyes." Judges 17:6.

primitive sources of myth and the customs connected to the general biases of high antiquity. We have even sometimes noticed that these vestiges were purer and better motivated among the Americans (and other barbarous or savage peoples like them) than among all the other nations of our hemisphere. To speak of these customs would be to go into too much detail. We will only say that savage life was essentially but a consequence of the impression that the spectacle of the world's past miseries made on a portion of mankind, a spectacle inspiring their contempt and disgust for the world. Having learned then about the inconstancy and fragility of the world, the most religious sector of early societies thought they should take as the basis for their earthly conduct the idea that this world is merely a passage. Thus it happened that, since societies in general had not given themselves a visible tie nor a tangible leader for their government in this world, they were never organized perfectly; and that families separated themselves early on and completely renounced the spirit of human governance, in order to live as pilgrims and to think only of a future that they desired and whose appearance they expected to see soon.

At first, these early solitary generations were as religious as they were miserable. With their eyes always lifted toward heaven and seeking only to provide for their most pressing need, they surely did not abuse their idleness or their liberty. But as they grew, they distanced themselves from the earliest times and from the bulk of society; as a result, they were no longer anything more than wandering tribes and melancholy nations who gradually became secularized into savage and barbarous peoples. Such has been the sad abuse of a dogma that in itself was very holy. The world is only a passage, it is true—and this is one of the most useful truths for society, because that passage leads to a more excellent life that each person should seek to deserve by fulfilling his duties here below. And yet, one of the greatest mistakes of primitive governance was not to have set wise limits on the effects of this truth. These effects have been highly pernicious to the well-being of societies every time events or general panics have suddenly made man forget that he is in this world because God placed him here, and that he is placed here only to discharge toward society and toward himself all the duties to which his birth and the name of man commit him. In contemplating a truth, one should never have made an abstraction of society. The holiest dogma is only true relative to the whole human race. Life is only a pilgrimage, but a pilgrim is only an idler, and man is not made for that. As long as he is on earth, there is a unique and common center to which he should be invisibly attached, and from which he cannot stray without being a deserter—and a quite criminal deserter that human governance has a right to summons. This is how primitive governance ought to have thought and acted, but could the theocratic spirit that guided it have been capable of caution in this regard? It wanted to rise but it plunged; it wanted to get a head start on the reign of the just, but it only engendered barbarians and savages; in the end, humanity was lost because one no longer wanted to be man on earth. Here, one can certainly perceive that the progress of human errors is like the course of the planets: they too have an immense orbit to travel, they too are seen in various phases and under different appearances; and yet, they are always the same and are constantly returning to the point from which they set out, to begin again a new revolution.

The provisional government that led those who separated themselves from early societies to a savage and vagabond life produced an entirely opposite effect on those who remained—it reduced them to the harshest slavery. Since societies originally had only families, which were subject more to religious discipline than to civil government; and since the excesses of their religion, which had led them to give themselves God for a monarch, had demanded along with contempt for the world the total renunciation of themselves and the sacrifice of their liberty, their reason, and all property; it inevitably happened that since those families had grown and multiplied under these principles, their religious servitude ended up changing into a civil and political servitude, and that instead of being the subject of a god-monarch, man became no more than the slave of the officers who commanded in his name.

The baskets, coffers, and symbols by which the sovereign was represented were nothing, but the ministers assigned to him were men, not celestial beings incapable of abusing a system of governance that gave them complete power. Since there is no agreement or convention to be made with a God, the theocracy over which he was assumed to preside was thus by its nature a despotic government, whose Supreme Being was the invisible sultan and whose theocratic ministers were the viziers—that is, the real despots with all the political vices of theocracy. There you have the most fatal condition for men, and the one that prepared the way for Oriental despotism.

In the early days, the visible ministers were doubtless worthy of their invisible master because of their moderation and their virtue. By the good they would have done men at first, men grew accustomed to recognizing the divine power in them. By the wisdom of their first orders and the utility of their first advice, men habituated themselves to obeying them and submitted themselves without difficulty to their oracles. Little by little, an extreme confidence produced an extreme credulity by which man—warned that it was God who was speaking, that it was an immutable sovereign who was willing, commanding, and threatening—thought he should not resist the organs of heaven even when they were doing only evil. Having gradually arrived at such a point of unreason as to no longer recognize the dignity of human nature, man in his misery no longer dared lift his eyes toward heaven, still less toward the tyrants who spoke in its name. A fanatic in everything, he worshiped his slavery and in the end thought himself obliged to honor his God and his monarch by his nothingness and his unworthiness. These wretched prejudices are still the basis of all the sentiments and all the inclinations of the Orientals toward their despots. They imagine that the latter have the power by divine right to create good and evil, and that they should find nothing impossible in the execution of their will. If these peoples suffer, if they are miserable because of the ferocious whims of a barbarian, it is also true that they worship the designs of an impenetrable providence; they recognize the rights and titles of tyranny in force and violence; they seek the solution to the cruel and illegitimate conduct of which they are the victims solely in devout and mystical interpretations—ignoring that this conduct has no other sources but the neglect of reason and the abusiveness of a supernatural government that has dragged on forever in those climes, albeit with different trappings.[15]

Having thus become despotic under cover of prejudices by which they blinded nations, the theocracies covered the earth with tyrants. For many

15. On the character of Oriental despotism in its relationship to climate, see Montesquieu, *Laws*, 14.4, and 17.3–6.

centuries, their ministers were the only true sovereigns of the world, and since nothing resisted them, they disposed of the possessions, the honor, and the lives of men, as they had already disposed of their reason and their minds. Time, which has hidden the history of that ancient government from us because it was but an age of profound ignorance and lies, has in truth thrown a thick veil over the excesses of its officers. Since the Judaic theocracy was reformed in its religion but not exempt from political abuses, it can help us unveil some of them. Scripture itself reveals to us how abominable was the conduct of the children of Heli and of Samuel, and it teaches us what the crimes were that put an end to that particular theocracy in which the true God reigned.[16] These unworthy descendants of Aaron and Levi no longer rendered justice to the people; they allowed money to redeem guilty parties; they could not be approached without gifts; their passions alone were both their law and their guide; their lives were but brigandage; they forcibly abducted and devoured the victims destined for the god-monarch, who was now no more than a figurehead. And since their incontinence equaled their avarice and their voraciousness, they slept, says the Bible, with the women who watched over the entrance to the tabernacle. *I. bk. King. ch. ii.*[17]

Scripture passes modestly over this last anecdote, which the spirit of truth, however, could not hide. But if the ministers of the true God gave themselves over to such excess, the ancient nations' theocratic ministers triumphed in this regard over the Hebrews by the fraud with which they disguised their disorders. They everywhere reached that height of impiety and insolence; they covered even their debauchery with the mantle of divinity. They are the ones who gave rise to a novel order of creatures which the minds of imbecile peoples regarded as a special and divine race. All nations then saw the appearance of demigods and heroes whose illustrious birth and exploits led men in the end to alter their first government, and to pass from the reign of those gods they had never been able to see, to that of their supposed children whom they saw in their midst. That is how the incontinent theocracy began to take on masters, and how that government was led to its ruin by crime and the abuse of power.

16. The reference seems to be to 1 Samuel 1–4.

17. See 1 Samuel 2:22.

The age of the demigods was as real as that of the gods, but being almost as obscure, it was inevitably rejected by history, which acknowledges only facts and times handed down by continuous and long-lasting annals. To judge only by the shadows of that universal Mythology that one finds among all peoples, it seems that the reign of the demigods was not as regular or as long as the reign of the gods had been, or as the reign of kings later was, and that nations were not always fortunate enough to have these extraordinary men. Since these children of theocracy could not all be born with the heroic virtues that corresponded to the portent of their birth, the majority doubtless got lost in the crowd, and it was only from time to time that talent, birth, and courage, mutually reinforcing each other, gave the languishing world protectors and useful masters. To judge again by mythological tradition, these illustrious children waged war on tyrants, exterminated brigands, purged the earth of monsters infesting it, and were incomparable knights who, like the paladins of our Gallic antiquities, ran around the world for love of the human race, restoring good order, governance, and security all over. There has surely never been a mission more splendid and more useful, especially in those times when primitive theocracy had brought forth in the world only those extreme evils: anarchy and servitude.

The birth of those demigods and their exploits thus combine to show us how frightful the disorder in government and religion was for the human race of their time. Each time a hero arose, the fate of societies seemed to become realized and to be determined toward unity. But as soon as those illustrious figures were no more, societies returned to their original theocracy and fell again into new miseries until a new liberator again came to the rescue.

Instructed, however, by their frequent relapses and by the good things they had experienced every time they had had a visible leader in the person of some demigod, societies began at last to open their eyes to the essential vice of a government that could never be solid and coherent, because nothing durable or real had ever exhibited unity in it, nor bound men together around a tangible and common center. The reign of the demigods thus began to humanize primitive prejudices, and it is this middle condition that led nations to desire the reign of kings. They became imperceptibly alienated from the yoke of theocratic ministers who had never ceased to abuse the gods' power that had been placed in their hands. And when public indignation reached its peak, they rose up against them and at last placed a mortal on the throne of the god-monarch, who had hitherto been represented only by mute and stupid symbols.

Like all the preceding events, the transition from theocracy to royalty is hidden in the darkest night. But we still have the Hebrews, whose particular conduct in a similar transformation we can examine, in order to apply it later to what had been done beforehand by all other nations, whose customs and prejudices will take the place for us of annals and monuments.

We have already observed one of the causes of the Judaic theocracy's ruin in the disorders of its ministers. We must now add a second, namely, the calamity simultaneously befalling the Ark of the Covenant when it was captured by the Philistines.[18] A government without regular order and without a master doubtless cannot last. Now, such was the government of the Hebrews in these latter instances; the Ark of the Covenant represented the seat of their supreme sovereign, in peace as in war.

The ark was his organ and his arm: it marched at the head of armies like the chariot of the god of battles, it was followed like an invincible general, and no one ever doubted victory in its train. Things were no longer this way after its defeat and capture. Although it was returned to its people, Israel's confidence had been weakened, and since the ministers' disorders had alienated the popular spirit, they rose up and compelled Samuel to give them a king who could march at the head of their armies and do them justice. It is well known what Samuel's response was at that point to the people's demand, as well as the frightful picture he drew of the enormous strength and prerogatives of sovereign power.[19] Flattery and servility found there a vast field in which to pay court to tyrants; superstition saw things worthy of its mystical reveries, but no one, perhaps, recognized the theocratic spirit that dictated it with the design of frightening the people and diverting them from their plan. Since the prior government had been a reign in which there was no middle ground between the god-monarch and the people, and in which the monarch was everything and the subject nothing, these religious

18. For this episode, see Exodus 25:10–22, Psalms 78:61, and 1 Samuel 5, among others.
19. The encounter can be found in 1 Samuel 8.

dogmas—changed over time into political prejudices—made men apply to the man-monarch all the ideas they had had of the supreme authority of the god-monarch. Moreover, since the people were seeking less to change the theocracy than to hide it from the vexations of the theocratic ministers who had abused the oracles and silent emblems of the divinity, they paid little attention to the odious picture that had been drawn solely to frighten them. And content to have a living emblem of the divinity in future, they cried out: it doesn't matter, we need a king to march before us, to command our armies, and to protect us from all our enemies.

This strange conduct might seem to show that there were nations that voluntarily submitted to slavery by authentic deeds,[20] if it weren't for the fact that this detail obviously proves that at that moment, nations still animated by all the religious bias they had always had toward theocracy were once again blinded and deceived by its false principles. Although disgusted by the sacerdotal ministry, man had, in demanding a king, no intention of abrogating his ancient government. On this score, he thought only to reform the image and the organ of the god-monarch, who was still regarded as the one true master, a fact proven by the very reign of the Hebrew kings—which was but a precarious reign in which the prophets elevated those that God had designated for them—and easily confirmed by the august title that the kings of the earth preserved: the image of the divinity.

The first election of sovereigns was therefore not a true election, nor was the government of one a new government. The original principles were merely renewed under another appearance, and the nations thought they saw in this transformation merely a change and reform in the theocratic image of the divinity. The first man of whom they created this image counted for nothing; it was not him that they esteemed directly. At first, they acted vis-à-vis him as they had originally acted with the first symbols of brass or metal, which had been only relative signs; the minds and imaginations of the people still remained fixed on the invisible and supreme monarch. But since these new trappings led men to apply their false principles and ancient prejudices in a new way, they led men to new abuses and to absolute despotism. The first age of theocracy had made the earth idolatrous,

20. "Actes authentiques," connotes being solemnly official.

because God was treated as a man. The second enslaved it, because man was treated as a god. The same imbecility that had previously given a house, a table, and some women to the divinity, now gave symbolic attributes, halos, and thunderbolts to a simple mortal—a bizarre contrast, and always deplorable conduct, which brought shame and misfortune to those societies, which still continued to seek the principles of human governance elsewhere than in nature and in reason.

The sole precaution that men ventured when they began to represent their god-monarch by one of their fellow creatures was to seek the tallest and handsomest man—this is seen in the history of all ancient nations. They paid much more attention to height and bodily qualities than to those of the mind, because in these original elections it was only a matter of representing the divinity by an appearance corresponding to the idea that people had formed of it. With respect to the management of the government, men always counted not on the spirit of the representative but on the god-monarch's spirit of inspiration. Those nations imagined that he would reveal himself to these new symbols just as they thought he had revealed himself to the old ones. They were not, however, stupid enough to believe that an ordinary mortal alone could enjoy the great privilege of being in contact with the divinity. But since they had previously invented customs to make a special and supernatural quality descend upon the stone or metal symbols, they thought they should also engage in these practices vis-à-vis the human symbols. It was only after these formalities that, with everything seeming to be regular and in order, these nations saw in the new representative nothing but a changed mortal, an extraordinary man from whom oracles were demanded and who became the object of public worship.

Thus, if we wanted to rummage through the titles of those proud Asian despots who have so often made human nature groan, we could only find titles that would shame and disgrace them. In the monuments of ancient Ethiopia, we would see that those sovereigns who only showed themselves to their people behind a veil (according to Strabo) had had dogs as predecessors, to which men had been given as officers and ministers.[21] Those

21. The first part of this account seems to come from Strabo, *Geography*, XVII.2.2. I have not found a source for the second part.

dogs had been the theocratic kings of that country—that is, the representatives of the god-monarch—for a very long stretch of time. It was in their cries, their gait, and their various movements that men looked for the orders and the will of the supreme power of which they had been made the symbol and the provisional image. Such was undoubtedly the source of that absurd cult that Egypt offered to certain animals, a cult that could be a result of only that ancient and stupid government.

And Israel's idolatry in the desert seems to give us manifest evidence of it. Since that people did not see the return of its leader who was making a long retreat on Mount Sinai, they thought he was completely lost. Rushing to Aaron, they said to him: make us a calf to march before us, for we do not know what has become of this Moses who had rescued us from Egypt[22]—bizarre reasoning, whose true spirit is not yet understood, but which seems to completely bear out the origins of idolatry and despotism that we are offering. This is because there were times when a dog, a calf, or a man placed at the head of a society were but one and the same thing for that society, and men turned toward one or the other symbol, as circumstance demanded, without thinking that they were thereby bringing any innovations to the system of government. It is in the same spirit that those Hebrews so persistently returned to the idols during their theocracy, every time they no longer saw in their midst some inspired judge or some man brought forward by God. They then had to turn toward Moloch or Chamos to find another representative,[23] as they had previously rushed to the golden calf during the disappearance of Moses.

Now that we have arrived where the history of known times begins, it will be easier for us to follow despotism and to verify its origins by its conduct and practices. The man raised to such a height of grandeur and glory as to be regarded as the organ of the god-monarch on earth, and to such an excess of power as to be able to act, will, and command sovereignly in his name, succumbed almost immediately under a burden that is not made for man. The illusion of his dignity made him misjudge what was really grand and really true within him. And the rays of the Supreme Being that

22. The story referred to is in Exodus 32.

23. See 1 Kings 11:7.

adorned his diadem dazzled him to such a point that he no longer saw the human race; he no longer even saw himself. Abandoned by public reason, which no longer wanted to see in him an ordinary mortal but rather a living idol inspired by heaven, the very feeling of his dignity ought to have dictated equity, moderation, and mildness on his part; but that very dignity led him toward all the opposite excesses. Such a man ought to have turned often within himself; but everything that surrounded him made him abandon himself and always kept him alienated from himself.

And how could a mortal know himself and recognize himself! He saw himself decorated with all the sublime titles due to the divinity and hitherto held by its idols and its other emblems. The entire ceremonial due to the god-monarch was carried out before the man-monarch. Worshipped like the one that he in turn came to represent, he was likewise regarded as infallible and immutable. The whole world owed him; he owed nothing to the world. His intentions became the decrees of heaven; his ferocities were regarded as judgments from on high; in the end, this living emblem of the god-monarch surpassed in every way the frightful picture presented to the Hebrews in the past.[24] Like Israel, all peoples subscribed to their own cruel prerogatives and their senseless privileges. They all groaned from it afterward, but this was by becoming more and more oblivious of the dignity of human nature, and by humbling their faces in the dust, or else turning toward craven and atrocious acts—all equally ignoring that reason which alone could be their mediator. One need not be well versed in history to recognize here the government of the Orient since time immemorial. Out of a hundred despots who have reigned there, hardly two or three can be found who have deserved the name of man. And what is more extraordinary is that the ancient prejudices that have given birth to despotism still exist in the minds of the Asiatics, and perpetuate it in that most beautiful part of the world, of which they have made but a wretched desert. We will abridge this sorry painting; each informed reader, in recalling the infinite evils that this government has produced on earth, will always find the same long chain of events and errors, the pernicious consequences of all the false principles of the first societies. By these principles, religion and governance

24. In 1 Samuel 8; cf. above at p. 424, n. 19.

have been imperceptibly changed into monstrous phantoms engendering idolatry and despotism, whose fraternity is so tight that they are but one and the same thing. There you have the bitter fruits of the sublime speculations of a chimerical theocracy, which, to get the jump on the celestial future, has disdained to think about the earth, whose end it thought near.

To arrive at a proof of these great truths, let us glance over the ceremonial system and leading customs of the sovereign despots who still humiliate the great majority of nations. In making recognizable the customs and principles of primitive theocracy, we will doubtless be putting the final seal of evidence on these annals of the human race. This part of our course would be immense if we did not put limits on it, as we have done with everything that we have already surveyed. Ancient and modern historians, travelers—they all concur in showing us the prerogatives of the god-monarch in the despots' court. And what is remarkable is that all these writers have acted like blind men in what they have looked at and written about in the different subjects they have tried to display to us.

"None shall appear before me empty-handed" (*Exodus, xxiii.15*), the god-monarch used to say to the theocratic societies through the mouth of his officers. No doubt, such is the unknown title of those Asiatic despots before whom no man could present himself without bringing his offering. Thus, the origins of that onerous custom must be sought not in the pride or avarice of sovereigns, but in the primitive prejudices that changed a moral lesson into political ritual. It is because all things down here come from the Supreme Being that a religious government had demanded that at every moment, it be given the homage of possessions held only from itself. One even had to offer oneself; for who is the man who is not part of his creator's domain?

All Hebrews, for example, regarded themselves as the born slaves of their supreme monarch. All those that I have rescued from the miseries of Egypt, he told them, are my slaves. They belong to me; they are my property and my heritage. And this slavery was so real that the first-born of men had to be bought back and a redemption tax paid to the public ministry. This precept was also extended over animals; man and beast had to be subject to the same law because they belonged equally to the supreme monarch. It was the same with the other theocratic laws—morally true, politically false. From the earliest times, their misapplication produced the fundamental principles of the future servitude of nations. These laws inspired only terror and spoke only of punishment because societies could not be maintained in the supernatural sphere to which they had been brought by their administration and their government without constant effort. By the hardened Jews and by all other nations, the monarch was regarded less as a father and a god of peace than as an avenging angel. The motive force of theocracy, therefore, was fear; this was also the motive of despotism:[25] the Scythians' god was represented by a sword. The true God among the Hebrews was also obliged, because of their character, to threaten them constantly. Tremble before my sanctuary, he told them; whoever approaches the place where I reside will be put to death. And this language, sometimes true in the mouth of religion, was then ridiculously adopted by Asiatic despots, in order to mimic the divinity in everything. Among the Persians and the Medes, it was impossible to see one's king—just as it was impossible to see one's god—without dying. Therein lies the origin of that invisibility that Oriental princes have affected in every age.

The Judaic superstition that imagined it could not pronounce the terrible name of *Jehovah,* which was the great name of its monarch, has thereby handed down to us one of the markers of that primitive theocracy, which has also been preserved in Oriental government. There, hiding the true name of the sovereign has always been the principle. It is a crime of lèse-majesté to pronounce it in Siam. In Persia, the prince's ordinances do not begin with his name as in Europe, but by the words *ridiculous* and *emphatic,* a commandment has issued forth from the one the world must obey, Chard. *vol. VI, ch. xi.*[26] As a result of this theocratic custom, Oriental princes are known by their subjects only through surnames. Never in the past were the Greek historians able to know the true names of the Persian kings, which were hidden to foreigners as to their subjects under epithets attached to their sovereign power. Herodotus tells us (*book V*)

25. See Montesquieu, *Laws,* 3.9, for fear as the motive of despotism.

26. The reference is to Jean Chardin (1643–1713), whose journal of his voyages to Persia and the East Indies was published in 1686 and in numerous editions thereafter; it would appear that Boulanger is referring either to the 1711 edition published by De Lorme in Amsterdam or to the 1723 edition in 10 volumes, published by Ferrand in Rouen.

that *Darius* means *exterminator*, and we can well believe it; it is a real surname for *despots*.[27]

Since there is only one God in the universe, and since this is a truth that has never been totally obscured, the first mortals who represented him also did not fail to think that there must be but one sovereign in the world. Thus, the dogma of the unity of God has also given rise to the despotic dogma of the unity of power—that is, to the title of universal monarch, which all despots have arrogated to themselves, and which they have almost always sought to fulfill by extending the boundaries of their empire, by destroying what they could not possess around them, and by scorning what the weakness of their arms could not reach. In this respect, almost all their vast conquests were wars of religion, and their political intolerance was originally but a form of religious intolerance.

If we look at some of those Oriental states whose specific origin has been the secularization of the ancient theocracies' great priests who made themselves hereditary sovereigns, we will find these theocratic images applying even to the eternity itself of the god-monarch whose throne they have usurped. It is an accepted dogma in certain parts of Asia that the great Lama of the Tartars and the kutucha of the Kalmyks[28] never die, that they are immutable and eternal like the Supreme Being of which they are the organs. This dogma, which has been supported by fraud in Asia for countless centuries, is also accepted in Abyssinia, although it is spiritually more mitigated in that case because there, the absurdity is evaded through cruelty. The chitomé, or universal priest, was prevented from dying naturally. If he was sick, he was suffocated; if he was old, he was bludgeoned. In this, he was treated like the Apis of ancient Memphis, who was drowned devoutly in the Nile when he was all used up, undoubtedly for fear that by a natural death, he would offend the eternity of the god-monarch he represented. These abominable customs reveal to us the antiquity of their origin; being contrary to the sovereigns' well-being, they are therefore not of the latter's own invention. If despots have inherited supreme advantages from theocracy, they have also been the slaves and victims of the ridicule and cruel

27. Herodotus, *Histories;* at VI.98, he says Darius's name means "doer," but it is not clear what passage Boulanger has in mind.

28. Central Asian potentates.

prejudices with which it has filled the minds of nations. Diodorus says that in the realm of Saba, princes who showed themselves and emerged from their palaces were stoned; this was because they were failing in the ritual of invisibility—new evidence for what we have just said.[29]

But what contrast are we going to present? All the despots are commanding nature itself. There, they have the indocile seas flogged, and they overturn mountains that oppose their passage. Here, they speak of themselves as the masters of all lands, seas, and rivers, and regard themselves as the sovereign god of all the gods of the universe. All the historian-moralists who have observed these traits of ancient despotism have seen in these extravagances only the individual follies of certain senseless princes. But we should see in them nothing but conduct authorized and accepted by the scheme of ancient government. These follies have had nothing personal about them, but have been the work of that general vice that had infected the governance of all nations.

America—which, no less than Asia, has preserved a multitude of these theocratic errors—shows us one of the most remarkable ones here in the oath that Mexico's sovereigns took at their coronation, and in the engagement they contracted when they mounted the throne. They swore and promised that for the duration of their reign, the rains would fall opportunely in their empire; neither the rivers nor the streams would overflow; the countryside would be fertile; and their subjects would suffer no malign influence from either heaven or the sun. How enormous, then, was the burden that man found himself bearing as soon as the image of the divinity had replaced the brutal and inanimate symbols of the first theocracy? He then had to stand surety for all the natural calamities that he could neither cause nor prevent, and be the source of goods that he could not give. Sovereigns thereby found themselves confused with those vain idols that had even less power than they did. Imbecilic nations likewise obliged them to behave as gods, whereas in putting them at the head of societies, they ought to have required them to behave only as men and never to forget that they were, by their nature and their weaknesses, equal to all those who submitted to them under the common protection of humanity, reason, and the laws.

29. Also known as Sheba; see Diodorus Siculus, *Library of History,* III.47.4.

Because these ancient peoples demanded too much of their sovereigns, they obtained nothing from them. Despotism became an unlimited authority because unlimited things were exacted. And the impossibility of performing the extreme goods demanded of it left it no other means of manifesting its enormous power but by performing extravagances and extreme evils. Doesn't all of this again prove that despotism is only an idolatry that is as stupid before the man of reason as it is criminal before the man of religion? America may have gotten this custom from Africa, where all the despots are still gods in full practice, or from the kingdoms of Totoca, Agag, Monomotapa, Loango, etc.[30] Peoples have recourse to their sovereigns to obtain rain or dryness. They beseech their sovereigns to ward off the plague, cure the sick, make sterility or famine cease. They are invoked against thunder and storms, and ultimately in all circumstances where supernatural aid is needed. Modern Asia does not grant less power to some of its sovereigns. Many still claim to restore health to the sick. The kings of Siam command the elements and maleficent demons; they prohibit them from spoiling the goods of the earth. And like certain ancient kings of Egypt, they order the overflowing rivers to return to their beds and stop their devastation.

Among the senseless privileges of primitive theocracy, we can also count the Oriental sovereigns' abuse of that weak half of the human race whom they lock up in their seraglios—less to serve in the pleasures their country's polygamy seems to permit than as a marker of superhuman power and of a supernatural grandeur in everything. In recalling what we have said previously about the women that an incontinent theocracy gave to the god-monarch and the shameful duties to which it subjected virginity, no one will doubt that the symbols of the gods have also inherited this infamous tribute: in the Indies, one still solemnly marries stone idols, and in ancient Libya, in *bk. L* of Herodotus's narrative, fathers who married off their daughters were obliged to lead them to the prince on the first night

30. Munhumutapa, a medieval kingdom in southern Africa ultimately conquered by the Portuguese in 1629; Loango, an African state in what is now the Republic of the Congo; Agag, a name for Amalekite kings in the Old Testament (Numbers 24:7, 1 Samuel 15); I have been unable to identify Totoca. Diderot mentions the first two in *Les Bijoux indiscrets* [The indiscreet jewels], 1748.

of their nuptials to offer him the *droit du seigneur.*[31] These two anecdotes doubtless suffice to show the origin and succession of a system of ritual that the despots must necessarily have gotten from an administration that had previously perverted morality and abused human nature.

With the source of despotism thus known, it remains for us also to complete the analysis of its history by stating what was its fate and destiny vis-à-vis the theocratic ministers who survived the ruin of their original power. The revolution that placed despots on the throne of the god-monarch could doubtless not have occurred without stimulating and bringing forth many disputes between old and new masters. The theocratic order had to view this as the cause of the interested god-monarch. The election of a king could be simultaneously regarded as rebellion and as idolatry. What powerful reasons to alarm kings and torment peoples! This order was the first enemy of emerging empires and human civilization. It never stopped speaking in the name of the invisible monarch in order to subject the visible monarch. It is since that epoch that the two supreme dignities have often been seen to fight for primacy, to struggle against each other in the plenum and the void, to set each other boundaries and ideal limits in turn, which they have alternated in transgressing, depending on whether they were more or less fortified by indecisive peoples wavering between superstition and the progress of knowledge.

Since a vestige of respect and habit had allowed the survival of the ancient symbols of stone and metal that should have been abolished, and since human symbols were to take their place, these ancient symbols remained under the direction of their ancient officers, who had no other task but to exploit them as much as possible, in order to use a religious worship to attract to their side peoples whom a new political worship was powerfully attracting to another object. Undoubtedly, the diversion must have been strong from the beginnings of royalty. But since the princes' disorders soon diminished the affection owed to their throne, men returned to the altars of the gods and to the other oracles, and restored to the theocratic order virtually all of its original authority. Soon these ministers dominated the despots

31. The lord's right to deflower the bride, also thought to be a feature of early medieval Europe; for the Libyan example, see Herodotus, *Histories*, IV.168 (vol. 2, p. 373 of the Loeb ed.).

themselves. The stone symbols commanded the living symbols. The constitution of states became double and ambiguous, and the reform that the people had thought they were bringing to their original government served only to place a political theocracy next to a religious theocracy—that is, to make them more miserable by doubling their chains with their prejudices.

The very persons of the despots showed only too much of the vice of their origins. If nations sometimes ventured to link the statues of their gods, they also did the same vis-à-vis human symbols. This is what we have already observed among the peoples of Saba and Abyssinia, where the sovereigns were the playthings and the victims of prejudices that had given them a pernicious existence through their false titles. Moreover, since the origin of the first despots and the origin of all the gods' idols was the same, the theocratic ministers often regarded them as sanctuary furniture. Considering them from the same perspective as those primitive idols that they decorated at their whim and that they caused to appear or disappear at will, they likewise thought they had a right to change those new images of the god-monarch—of which they thought themselves to be the only true ministers—on the throne, as on the altar. That's the claim that the idolatrous ministers of the temple of Meroë made particular use of against the sovereigns of ancient Ethiopia.

"[W]henever the idea comes to them," says Diodorus of Sicily, *bk. III.*, "[they] dispatch a messenger to the king with orders that he die. For the gods, they add, have revealed this to them, and it must be that the command of the immortals should in no wise be disregarded by one of mortal frame. And this order they accompany with other arguments, such as are accepted by a simpleminded nature, which has been bred in a custom that is both ancient and difficult to eradicate and which knows no argument that can be set in opposition to commands enforced by no compulsion. Now in former times the kings would obey the priests, having been overcome, not by arms nor by force, but because their reasoning powers had been put under a constraint by their very superstition; but during the reign of the second Ptolemy the king of the Ethiopians, Ergamenes, who had had a Greek education and had studied philosophy, was the first to have the courage to disdain the command." Our author continues, "For assuming a spirit which became the position of a king he entered with his soldier into the unapproachable place where stood, as it turned out, the golden shrine of the Ethiopians, put the priests to the sword, and after abolishing this custom thereafter ordered affairs after his own will."[32]

It is doubtless the experience of these sad excesses that led many peoples at the height of antiquity to recognize in their sovereigns both of the supreme dignities, whose division had only managed to produce disastrous effects. From the beginning of recorded time, in fact, the priesthood has often been joined to empire, and nations have often thought that the sovereign of a state ought to be their magistrates. Nonetheless, the union of the diadem and the altar was not without vice or drawback for those nations, because for many of them the throne was nothing but the altar itself secularized. And in all of them the titles of this union were sought in theocratic and mystical obsessions, all of them contrary to the well-being of societies.

We will bring our history of despotism to a close here. We have looked at its origin, its practice, and its false titles, and we have followed despots' crimes and calamities, which can be blamed only on the defect in the supernatural administration that had been given to them.

In its beginnings, theocracy took men as just; afterward, despotism regarded them as wicked. The former wanted to parade the heavens; the latter represented only the underworld. And these two governments, in assuming extreme principles that are not made for earth, have together brought on the misery of the human race, whose character they have changed and whose reason they have perverted. Idolatry came to seize the throne raised to the god-monarch and made it its altar; despotism usurped its altar and made it its throne. An unlimited servitude took the place of that precious liberty that men had wanted to parade and to preserve by supernatural means. That government is thus but a pagan theocracy, since it has all its customs, all its titles, and all its absurdity.

We have arrived at the point at which the abuse of despotic power will make republican government appear in various countries. It is here, in that multitude of ancient nations that have all been subjected to an absolute and unitary power, that we will recognize in some of them that agency of nature

32. Diodorus of Siculus, *Library of History*, trans. C. H. Oldfather (Cambridge: Harvard University Press, 1935), III.6.2–4, 2:101. For the last phrase, Boulanger paraphrases, stating simply that the ruler "reformed the worship."

that cooperates in fortifying or weakening the prejudices that normally command the earth's nations more imperiously than do their climates.

When the abuses of the original theocracy produced anarchy and slavery, anarchy was the lot of the Occident—whose peoples all became nomadic and savage—and servitude was the fate of the Oriental nations. The abuses of despotism then made humanity groan, and those abuses were introduced into Europe by the Asiatic colonies and legislation that spread their prejudices and false principles there a second time. Then, that part of the world also felt the force of its climate. It is true that it suffered for some time, but in the end, the spirit of the Occident overturned in Greece and Italy the seat of tyrants that had been raised there on every side. And to restore to the Europeans the honor and liberty that had been stolen from them, that spirit everywhere established republican government, believing it to be the one most capable of making men happy and free.[33]

In this revolution, one certainly does not expect to see the ancient prejudices of primitive theocracy reborn. Never have the Greek or Roman historians spoken to us of this mystical chimera, and they are in agreement in showing us the origin of the republics in the perfected reason of peoples and in the political knowledge of the profoundest legislators. In saying the opposite, we would be afraid of advancing a paradox if we were not supported and enlightened by the natural thread of that great chain of human errors that we have surveyed successfully up to this point, and that will likewise extend into the ages thought to be the wisest and most philosophical. Far from the theocratic prejudices being extinguished when the Peisistratuses were expelled from Athens, or the Tarquins from Rome, it was then that they were awakened more than ever;[34] they again had their influence on the scheme of the new governments. And just as they dictated designs for liberty imagined on all sides, they were also the source of all the political vices by which republican legislation was affected and disturbed.

The first act of the Athenian people after their deliverance was to raise a statue to Jupiter and give him the title of king, since they did not want

33. For the relationship between climate and liberty East and West that Boulanger seems to be referring to, see Montesquieu, *Laws,* 17.6.

34. Peisistratus (d. ca. 527 B.C.), a popular tyrant of Athens; Tarquin (r. 535–496 B.C.), the last of the kings of Rome before the establishment of the republic.

to have another king in the future. Thus, that people did nothing else but restore the reign of the god-monarch; theocracy thus seemed to them the sole true means of reviving that ancient golden age in which happy and free societies had no other sovereign but the god they were invoking.

The government of a theocratic king and the necessity of his presence in every society was so consistent at that time with the religion of the European peoples that, despite the horror they had conceived for kings, they nonetheless thought themselves obliged to preserve the shadow of kingship when they were annihilating its reality. The Athenians and Romans relegated its name to the priesthood. Both peoples—the former by creating a king of augurs, the latter a king of sacrifices—imagined they were thereby satisfying the prejudices that demanded that such and such functions be fulfilled only by theocratic images. It is true that they took great care to contain the power of these priest-kings within very narrow limits. They were given only a phony title and some vain distinctions. But it happened that, since the people recognized only the invisible gods as masters, they formed but one society whose unity existed only on the basis of a false speculation; each person wanted to be its master and its center, and since this center was everywhere, it was found nowhere.

We will also say that when these first republicans destroyed the kings while still preserving royalty, they were again led to this by a vestige of that ancient prejudice that had pushed primitive societies to live in expectation of the reign of the god-monarch, whose arrival the ruin of the world made them believe to be urgent and imminent. It was this false opinion that had led these societies to unite only under a figurative government and to give themselves only a provisional administration. Now, there is every reason to believe that the republicans had some similar motive in their time, because one again finds all the hints of this chimerical expectation among them. The Delphic oracle promised the Greeks a future king, and the Roman sibyls had also announced to them a king for the future, who would make them happy and extend their domination throughout the world. Indeed, it was only under the protection of that corrupt oracle that Rome always marched with a firm and certain step toward world empire, and that the Caesars took hold of that empire afterward. All these religious oracles had no other principle but the future unity of the reign of the god-monarch, a principle which had sown the kind of turbulent ambition throughout all societies that has so often ravaged the world, and that led all the ancient conquerors to regard themselves as gods, or as the children of gods.

After the destruction of the kings of Israel and Juda, and their return from captivity, the Hebrews acted pretty much like the other republics. They did not restore royalty or even the name of king, but they gave its power and authority to the priestly order. And what's more, they lived in the hope that they would one day have a monarch who would subject all the earth's peoples to them. But it was this false dogma that caused their complete ruin. They confused this chimerical and fleshly expectation with the special expectation they should have had of our divine Messiah, whose dogma had nothing to do with the follies of nations. Instead of hoping only for that sorrowful man and that hidden god promised to their forefathers, the Jews sought only a prince, a conqueror, and a great political king. After agitating the whole of Asia to find their phantom, they soon devoured each other, and the indignant Romans ultimately swallowed up those feeble rivals to their power and their religious ambition. Since that frivolous expectation of nations was in principle nothing more than an expectation of the god-monarch whose descent is due to occur only at the end of time, it subsequently did not fail to recall the other dogmas that are inseparable from it, and to revive all the ancient terrors concerning the end of the world. Thus, in the same circumstances, when the Roman republic was going to change into a monarchy, one sees the Tuscan soothsayers announcing, from the time of Sulla and Marius,[35] the approach of the revolution of the ages. One sees the false oracles of Asia scatter among the nations those alarms and false terrors that acted so powerfully on the first centuries of our era, and that then brought forth effects quite similar to those of primitive ages.

By this brief exposition of one of the great enigmas of the history of the Middle Ages, one may appreciate that the prejudices of ancient theocracy were far from being erased from the minds of Europeans. Thus, in proclaiming a god as the king of their nascent republic, they inevitably adopted all the abuses and all the customs that were bound to follow from that

35. The first half of the first century B.C.

first act. In renewing this act, they also attempted to bring societies back to that former golden age and to that supernatural reign of justice, liberty, and simplicity that had constituted its happiness. They did not know then that that state was in its time merely the consequence of the ancient miseries of the world and the effect of a momentary virtue and an extreme situation, which, since it is not the habitual state of the human race on earth, cannot be the basis of a political constitution, which should only be set up in a fixed and invariable environment.

It was thus from these principles—more brilliant than solid—that men were going to derive all the institutions that were to give liberty to each citizen, and they founded this liberty on equality of power because they had again forgotten that the ancients had only an equality of misery. Since they imagined that this equality, which countless physical and moral causes have always ruled out and will always rule out on earth—since they imagined, I say, that this equality was of the essence of liberty—all the members of a republic called themselves equal; they were all kings; they were all legislators or participants in legislation. To maintain these vainglorious and dangerous chimeras, there was no republican state that did not find itself forced to resort to violent and supernatural means. Contempt for wealth, community of goods, division of land, suppression of gold and silver money, abolition of debts, common meals, expulsion of foreigners, prohibition of commerce, forms of governance and discipline, the number and value of legislative voices, lastly a multitude of laws against luxury and in favor of public frugality occupied them and divided them constantly. They built today what they had to destroy a little later. Society's principles were always in contradiction with its condition, and the means employed were always misguided, because they took laws, or rather customs, that could only suit a mystical age and religious families, and applied them to populous and settled nations.

The republics called themselves free, but liberty fled before them; they wanted to be tranquil, but they never were; each person claimed to be equal, but there was no equality. In short, in taking as their reference point all the extreme advantages of theocracy and the golden age, these governments were constantly like those vessels which, in looking for imaginary countries, expose themselves on the stormy seas where they are long tormented by frightful tempests; finally, they run aground on the shoals and are dashed against the rocks of a deserted and savage land. The republican system likewise looked for a mythic country; it fled despotism, but everywhere it ended in despotism. Such was indeed the bad constitution of those governments jealous of liberty and equality that the very despotism they hated was their asylum and their support in difficult times. It was quite often that Rome's own preservation required it to submit voluntarily to sovereign dictators.[36] This drastic remedy, which suspended the operation of all law and all magistracy, was the recourse of that famous republic in all the wretched circumstances into which the defect of its constitution plunged it. The heroism of the early days at first made it salutary, but in the end, this dictatorship was fixed in one family; it became hereditary and no longer produced anything but abominable tyrants.

Originally, therefore, republican government was only a revival of theocracy. And since it had the same spirit, it also had all its abuses, likewise ending in servitude. Both governments had that essential defect of not giving society a visible tie and a common center to summon it toward unity and to represent it in aristocracy. This common center was nothing but the grandees of the nation, in whom authority resided. But since a title worn by a thousand heads could not represent this unity, the people was irresolute and always split in factions or subject to a thousand tyrants.

Democracy, in which the people were sovereign, was another government equally pernicious to society, and one does not have to have been born in the Orient to find it ridiculous and monstrous. At once legislator, subject, and monarch—now everything, now nothing—the sovereign people was never anything but a mistrustful tyrant and an indocile subject fostering society's constant disorders and dissensions, which in the end made it succumb to enemies from within and to enemies made abroad. Independent of the defect of their origins, the inconstancy of these various republics and their short durations would alone suffice to make us understand that this government is not made for the earth, or proportioned to the character of man, or capable of making all his possible happiness here below. The

36. The dictator was an office of emergency powers established ca. 501 B.C., shortly after the expulsion of the kings.

narrow territorial limit within which these republics have always had to be enclosed in order to preserve their constitutions also shows us that they are incapable of making large societies happy.[37] When they have wanted to live exactly according to their principles, and to maintain them without alteration, they have been obliged to separate themselves from the rest of the earth. In fact, a desert is as fitting around a republic as it is around a despotic empire, because anyone whose principles are in the supernatural must live alone and must separate himself from the world. But as a consequence of this inevitable abuse, the multitude of those republican jurisdictions meant there was less unity than the human race had ever had. Then, men saw anarchy from city to city as they had seen it in the past from individual to individual. The republics' inequality and mutual jealousy caused the shedding of as much and more blood than the cruellest despotism. The small societies were destroyed by the large ones, and the large ones in turn destroyed themselves.

The idolatry of those ancient republics again offers a vast domain in which we would easily find all the details and all the customs of that theocratic spirit they preserved. We will not linger here but will only observe that if, with the highest stupidity, they consulted sacred chickens and the flight of birds, if they never began any enterprise—public or private, in peace or in war—without the advice of their soothsayers and their augurs, this is because it was always their principle not to do anything without the orders of their theocratic monarch. It was only in that way that these republics were idolatrous, but the apostasy of reason that was the crime and the shame of paganism could not fail to perpetuate itself by their supernatural government.

Despite the unfavorable angle from which the republics have just been presented to our eyes, we cannot forget what their history has that is splendid and interesting in those astonishing examples of force, virtue, and courage that they have all given us, and by which they have all been immortalized. In fact, these examples still ravish our admiration and affect all virtuous hearts; that is the noble side of ancient Rome and Athens. Thus,

37. On the need for republics to be small in scale, see Montesquieu, *Laws*, 8.16, and the article FEDERAL REPUBLIC, in this volume.

let us expose here the causes of their virtues, since we have exposed the causes of their vice.

The republics have had their golden age, because all supernatural states have necessarily begun that way. Since theocratic speculation formed the basis of republican speculation, its first effects must have been to raise man above himself, assign him a more than human soul, and inspire in him all the sentiments that alone had previously been capable of supporting the primitive government that men now wanted to revive in order to again bring forth virtue, equality, and liberty on earth. Thus, for a time, the republican had to raise himself above himself. Because the outlook of his legislation was supernatural, he had to be virtuous for a while, since his legislation aimed to regenerate the golden age that had been the reign of virtue. But in the end, man had to become man again, because that is what he is made for.

The great motives that then gave such splendor to the generous efforts of humanity were also the causes of their short duration. The fervor of the golden age had been revived, but it was still transitory. Heroism had reappeared in all its luster, but it slipped away in the same fashion, because prodigies are not normal down here, and the supernatural is not made for the earth. Some have said that the virtues of these ancient republicans were only human and false virtues.[38] As for us, we say the opposite: if they were false, it is because they were more than human. Without this defect, they would have been truer and more enduring.

The condition of societies must in fact not be based on the sublime, because this is not the fixed point or the average character of man, who often cannot practice the virtue he is preached, and who even more often abuses it when he does practice it—when he has extinguished his reason and when he has overcome his nature. Up to now, we have always seen that man has done this only to raise himself above humanity; it is by the same principles that the republics were ruined, after producing monstrous virtues rather than true virtues, and delivering themselves to excesses contrary to their happiness and to the tranquility of the human race.

38. This was the position of many Christian thinkers, especially in the tradition of St. Augustine of Hippo (354–430); see also Jacques Esprit, *La Fausseté des vertus humaines* (1678; *The Falshood of Human Virtue,* 1691).

The sublime, that motive so necessary to republican government and to any government founded on outlooks that are more than human, is such a disproportionate resource in the political world that in those austere republics of Greece and Italy, the most sublime virtue was often punished and almost always mistreated. Rome and Athens have given us evidence of this that appears inconceivable to us because one never wants to take man for what he is. The greatest personage, the best citizens—all those, in a word, who had done most to oblige their country—either were exiled or they exiled themselves. They had offended that misunderstood human nature; their excess of virtue made them guilty in the eyes of public equality. From the extreme good and evil to which the ancient republics were susceptible, we will conclude that their government was wholly defective. Because it was preoccupied by theocratic principles, it could not but be very far removed from that middle state that alone on earth can fix the security, repose, and happiness of the human race at their true level.

The excesses of despotism, the dangers of republics, and the falsity of these two governments issuing from a chimerical theocracy will teach us what we should think of monarchical government, even if reason alone did not dictate it to us. A political state in which the throne of the monarch, who represents unity, has as its foundation the laws of the society over which he reigns is bound to be the wisest and happiest state of all. The principles of such a government are taken from the nature of man and of the planet that he inhabits. It is made for earth just as a republic and a true theocracy are made only for heaven, and as despotism is made for the underworld. Honor and reason, which have given it its being, are the true motives of man, just as that sublime virtue of which the republics could show us only passing rays will be the steadfast motive of the just in the empyrean, and the fear in despotic states will be the sole motive of the wicked in Tartarus.[39] Monarchical government alone has found the true means of enabling us to enjoy all the happiness possible, all the liberty possible, and all the advantages that man in society can enjoy on earth. It has not had to

39. The argument that honor animates monarchies, virtue republics, and fear despotisms was made by Montesquieu, *Laws*, bk. 3, esp. 3.3–3.9.

seek chimerical means as with the ancient legislation, which one cannot reliably use and which one can constantly abuse.

Thus, this government should be regarded as the masterpiece of human reason and as the port to which the human race, battered by storms in its search for an imaginary felicity, has finally had to return in order to find a felicity made for it. It is doubtless less sublime than the one that mankind had in view, but it is more solid, more real, and more true on earth. It is there that he has found kings who no longer make an exhibit of being divine, who cannot forget that they are men. It is there that he can love and respect them without worshipping them as vain idols, and without fearing them as avenging gods. It is there that kings recognize the fundamental and social laws that make their thrones unshakeable and their subjects happy, and that the people, without difficulty and without intrigue, follow the ancient and respectable laws given them by wise monarchs—under whom, for a long succession of centuries, they have enjoyed all the privileges and all the moderate advantages that distinguish sociable man from the Asian slave and the American savage.

The origin of monarchy has nothing in common with that chain of events and those shared defects that have up to now bound together all previous governments, and this especially is what makes for its happiness and its glory. As the ancient prejudices that everywhere remained the source of the world's misery expired in the icy North, our ancestors, coarse as they were, brought into our climes only a cold good sense, along with that sentiment of honor that has been passed down to us, to be forever the soul of monarchy. In principle, this honor has been and should still be merely the inner feeling of the dignity of human nature, which the theocratic governments have disdained and debased, which despotic government has destroyed, but which the monarchical has always respected, because its object is to govern men incapable of that lively imagination that has always led southern peoples to extreme vices and virtues. In this way, our ancestors found the truth,[40] which exists only in a golden mean. Far from recognizing supernatural gifts and a superhuman power in their leaders, they were content with crowning them to put them on a pedestal and carry

40. *Le vrai,* which may also mean the true government.

them on their shoulders, as if to make them understand that they would always be supported by public reason, guided by its spirit, and inspired by its laws. What's more: they placed beside them wise men whom they dignified with the name of *peers*—not to make them equal to kings, but to teach these kings that being men, they are equal to men. Their humane and moderate principles therefore did not require their sovereigns to behave like gods. Nor did these sovereigns require of those sensible people either that sublimity of which mortals are scarcely capable, or that abasement that revolts them or degrades them. Monarchical government took the earth for what it is and men for what they are. It allowed them to enjoy the rights and privileges attached to their birth, their status, and their talents. In each of them, it supported sentiments of honor, which make up the harmony and composure of the whole body politic. And in the end, what merits the highest praise is that in supporting this noble pride of humanity, it has been able to turn to the advantage of society human passions that have been so pernicious to all other kinds of legislation, which have sought less to guide those passions than to destroy them or exalt them. An admirable constitution worthy of all our respect and all our love! Each corporate body, each association, even each individual should see in it a situation all the more firm and all the more fortunate in that this situation is not established on false principles or founded on chimerical motives but on reason and on the character of things here below. What is even more estimable about this government is that it has not been a result of a particular legislation or a carefully pondered system, but the slow and belated fruit of reason, disengaged from those ancient prejudices.

It has been the work of nature, which should by rights be regarded as the legislator and the fundamental law of this happy and wise government. It is she alone that has provided legislation capable of following the genius of the human race in its progress, and of elevating the spirit of each government as the spirit of each nation is enlightened and elevated[41]—an

41. For the correlation between the general spirit of a nation and the spirit of its government, see, among others, "Of Refinement in the Arts," in Hume, *Essays, Moral, Political, and Literary*, ed. Eugene F. Miller, rev. ed. (Indianapolis: Liberty Fund, 1987), 273. The work was translated into French as *Discours politiques* by Abbé Le Blanc in numerous editions, beginning in 1754.

equilibrium without which those two spirits looked in vain for their repose and their security.

We will not go into detail on the variety among the present monarchies of Europe, nor the events that have produced this variety for ten or twelve centuries. In all of them, the primitive spirit is always the same. If it has sometimes been altered or changed, this is because the ancient preoccupations of the climates in which they came to be established have sought to subjugate them in those ages of ignorance and superstition that for a time plunged the good sense of European nations, and even the holiest religion, into sleep.

During this dark epoch, those same theocratic prejudices that had infected the ancient governments also undertook to subjugate the new monarchies; in countless different forms they were sometimes their scourges, sometimes their corruptors. But what is the use of recalling an age whose memory we detest today and whose false principles we despise? That it may at least serve to show us that the monarchies could be disturbed only by alien vices emerging from the breast of a calm and peaceful nature. The only connection they had with the theocracies—daughters of false terrors—was through the evils they received from them. Monarchies alone are capable of fulfilling the purpose of the science of government, which is to maintain men in society and effect the happiness of the world. They will always succeed at it by recalling their original spirit in order to dismiss false systems; by relying on an immutable governance and inalterable laws, in order to find their own security and that of society within them; and by placing theocratic prejudices, if any still exist, between reason and humanity, as if under a good and certain guard. Moreover, by operating on the powers[42] and on public reason, the progress of knowledge will continue to teach them what is important for the true good of society. It is reserved solely to this progress, which rules in an invisible and victorious fashion over every thinking being in nature, to be the legislator of all men, and to bring the new light effortlessly and imperceptibly into the political world, just as it is brought every day into the learned world.

42. *Les puissances,* which may mean either the holders of the highest dignities within a state, or the sovereign states themselves. See Translators' Note.

We think we would have omitted the most interesting of our observations and failed to give them the degree of authenticity of which they are susceptible, if, after following and examining the origin and principles of the various governments, we did not end by remarking on and admiring the sagacity of one of the great men of our time. Without having considered the particular origin of these governments—which, however, he would have seen better than we have—he began where we have just finished, and yet he prescribed to each of them its fitting motive force and its laws. We have seen that the republics took the golden age of theocracy as their model—that is, heaven itself. It is *virtue*, says M. de Montesquieu, that is bound to be the motive force of republican government. We have seen that despotism sought only to represent the avenging monarch of the theocracy of nations. It is *fear*, M. de Montesquieu said again, that is bound to be the motive force of despotism. It is *honor*, this legislator of our age said finally, that is bound to be the motive force of monarchy. And we have recognized indeed that it is this reasonable government made for the earth that, in leaving man all the sentiment of his condition and his existence, must be supported and preserved by honor, which is nothing else but the feeling that we all have of the dignity of our nature.[43] Whatever passion and ignorance may have been able to say against the principles of the sublime author of *The Spirit of the Laws,* those principles are as true as his sagacity has been great in uncovering them and in following their effects without having sought their origin. Such is the privilege of genius, to be alone capable of knowing the truth of a great whole, even when this whole is unknown to him or when he considers only part of it. *This article is by the late M. Boulanger.*

43. Boulanger again refers to Montesquieu, *Laws,* 3.3–3.9, as he had above at p. 444, n. 39.

Volume 12
(1765)

English Parliament
(*Parlement d'Angleterre*)

ENGLISH PARLIAMENT (*English history*). The *parliament* is the assembly and union of the three estates of the realm—that is, the lords spiritual, the lords temporal, and the commons—who have received an order from the king to assemble, to deliberate over matters related to the public good, and particularly to establish or revoke laws. It is normally in Westminster that the *parliament* of Great Britain assembles. The author of the *Henriade* speaks of it in these terms:

> *Three different powers at Westminster appear,*
> *And all admire the ties which join them there.*
> *Whom interest parts, the laws together bring,*
> *The people's deputies, the peers, and king.*
> *One whole they form, whose terror wide extends*
> *To neighboring nations, and their rights defends.*
> *Thrice happy times, when grateful subjects show*
> *That loyal, warm affection which is due!*
> *But happier still, when freedom's blessings spring*
> *From the wise conduct of a prudent king.*[1]

Permit me to elaborate on this powerful legislative body, since it is a sovereign senate, the most august of Europe, and in the country that has best known how to take advantage of religion, commerce, and liberty.[2]

This article can be found at 12:38–41 in the original edition of the *Encyclopédie*.

1. This passage comes from the first canto of Voltaire's *Henriade*. We use the early 1760's translation by Tobias Smollett reproduced in *The Works of Voltaire*, ed. and trans. Tobias Smollett et al., 43 vols. (New York: E. R. Du Mont, 1901), 38:20.

2. This last statement is an echo of Montesquieu, *The Spirit of the Laws*, 20.7.

The two chambers of *parliament* compose the great council of the nation and of the monarch. Up to the time of the Conquest,[3] this great council, composed only of the grandees of the realm, was named *magnatum conventus & praelatorum procerumque conventus*.[4] Spelman also informs us that the members were called *magnates regni, nobiles regni, proceres & fideles regni, discretio totius regni, generale consilium regni*.[5] In their language, the Saxons called it *witenagemot*—that is, an assembly of the wise. *See* WITENAGEMOT.

After the Conquest, around the beginning of the reign of Edward I (or, according to others, in the time of Henry I),[6] it was called *parliament*, perhaps from the French word *parler* [i.e., "to speak"]. But there is no agreement either on the power and authority of the ancient *parliaments* of Great Britain, or on the persons who composed it. And there will likely never be agreement on the origin of the House of Commons, given how divided the leading scholars themselves are on this score.

Some claim that *parliament* was composed only of the nation's barons or grandees until, under the reign of Henry III, the commons were also called to seats in *parliament*. Camden, Pryun, Dugdale, Heylin, Bradyd, Filmer, and others are of this opinion.[7] One of their principal arguments is that the first order, or circular letter, for convening in *parliament* a meeting of all the knight-citizens and bourgeois is not older than the 49th year

3. The Norman conquest of Anglo-Saxon Britain in 1066.

4. "Assembly of great men and of prelates, and an assembly of peers."

5. "Magnates of the realm, nobles of the realm, peers and faithful men of the realm, the distinguished of the whole realm, general council of the realm." The allusion is probably to the antiquary Sir Henry Spelman (1564–1641), *Two Discourses: i. Of the Ancient Government of England, ii. Of Parliaments; The Original of the Four Terms of the Year* (London, 1684).

6. Edward I (r. 1272–1307) and Henry I (r. 1100–1135).

7. William Camden (1551–1623), whose *Britannia* (1586) and *Annals* (in Latin) of the reign of Elizabeth cast a long shadow; William Prynne (1600–1669), Puritan writer imprisoned and divested of his ears in the 1630s, parliamentarian supporter during the civil war of the 1640s; Sir William Dugdale (1605–86), antiquary and author of *Baronage of England* (1675–76); Peter Heylin (1600–1662), English church writer, supporter of the Crown in the civil war, and author of a *History of the Reformation* and a life of William Laud; Robert Filmer (1588–1653), whose *Patriarcha* argued for absolute monarchy and prompted Locke to write his *Two Treatises on Government* when it appeared in 1680; Robert Brady (1627?–1700), physician, prolific historian, and member of Parliament who was a royalist during the civil war and a Tory later.

of Henry III's reign—that is, the year 1217.[8] To support their opinion, they add that the House of Commons was established during that prince's reign only after he had defeated the barons, because it is scarcely believable that beforehand, the barons would have allowed any power opposed to their own.

Nonetheless, the celebrated Raleigh, in his prerogatives of the *parliaments,* supports the idea that the commons were first called in *the 17th year of the reign of Henry I.* On the other hand, Sir Edward Coke, Duderidge, and other scholars have struggled to prove, by many facts of great weight, that the commons have always had a part in legislation and a seat in the great assemblies of the nation, albeit on a different footing than today.[9] For at present, they make up a distinct house composed of knights, citizens, and bourgeois. One thing is certain: in the reign of Edward I there was one House of Lords and one House of Commons, the latter of which was composed of knights, citizens, and bourgeois.

The *parliament* is signaled by a summons from the king. And when the parliamentary peerage was established, all the peers were summoned individually, which led Lord Coke to say that all lords spiritual and temporal of the required age should have a writ of summons *ex debito instituto.*[10] The form of these summonses will be found in *Cotton's records, iii.4.*[11]

Formerly, the holding of a fief created the right to a seat, and all who possessed holdings *per baroniam* [*as a baron*] were summoned to attend *parliament.* From this, it came about that the holding of a seat in *parliament*

8. Henry III (r. 1216–72); the event Jaucourt seems to refer to occurred in 1264, which would indeed have been the forty-ninth year of Henry's reign.

9. Sir Walter Raleigh, poet, adventurer, and author, among other works, of *The Prerogative of parliaments in England proved in a dialogue between a councellour of state and a justice of peace* (London: Sheares, 1661); Sir Edward Coke (1552–1634), leading theorist and practitioner of the common law during the constitutional struggles with Charles I, author of *Institutes of the laws of England* and other works; and Sir John Doddridge (1555–1628), jurist and author of *The antiquity and power of parliaments in England* (1679; of doubtful authenticity).

10. Coke uses "*ex debito justitiae,*" "established as a matter of right." See "The Fourth Part of the *Institutes,*" chap. 1, p. 1, found in *The Selected Writings of Sir Edward Coke,* ed. Steve Sheppard, 3 vols. (Indianapolis: Liberty Fund, 2003), 2:1062.

11. Sir Robert Cotton (1571–1631), English antiquary; the reference may be to *Cottoni posthuma: divers choice pieces of that renowned antiquary Sir Robert Cotton* (London: Seile, 1651, and many other editions).

made one a baron. But this holding was not sufficient for the other degrees of status above baron. For them, other ceremonies were required, unless they were dispensed with by duly registered letters patent.

The first summons of a peer to *parliament* differs from the summons that follow, in that in the first summons, the peer is called only by his baptismal and family name, since he is to hold the name and title of his distinction only after being seated; only then does the name of his distinction become part of his proper name.

The order of summons must emanate from the chancellery. It states that the king, *de avisamento consilii* [*on the advice of his council*] having decided to hold a *parliament*, desires *quod intersitis eum*, &c.[12] Each lord of the *parliament* must have an individual summons, and each summons must be addressed to him at least 40 days before the *parliament* begins.

As for the manner of summoning the judges, the barons of the exchequer, the barons of the king's council, the masters in the chancellery who have no vote, and as for the ways these summonses differ from those of a lord member of *parliament*, see the *Reg. 261. F.N.B. 229.4. Inst. 4.*[13]

Every order of summons must be addressed to the sheriff of each county in England and in the principality of Wales for the choice and election of knights, citizens, and bourgeois within the scope of their respective departments. Likewise, the order of summons is addressed to the lord governor of the Cinque Ports[14] for the election of the barons of his district. The form of these summonses must always be the same, without any change whatsoever, unless it has been decreed otherwise by act of *parliament*.

The king convokes, prorogues, and quashes *parliament*. This august body has the custom of beginning its sessions with the king's presence or his representation. The representation of the king occurs in two ways, either (1) by

12. "That you present yourself to him."

13. Coke, "Fourth Part," p. 4, in *Selected Writings*, 2:1069, also cites "Regist. 261. F. N. B. 229," meaning *Register* or *Register Brevium*, the oldest book of common law writs, and Fitzherbert's *Natura Brevium*, an early sixteenth-century legal reference book frequently reprinted.

14. Pronounced in English "sink" ports, these were five (*cinq*) seaports in southeastern England (originally Hastings, Romney, Hythe, Dover, and Sandwich, but also coming to include Rye and Winchelsea) that provided mutual support on maritime and defense matters starting in the eleventh century.

the lord guardian of England, *the guardian of England*,[15] when the king is out of the realm; or (2) by delegating the grand seal of England to a certain number of peers of the realm, who represent the person of the king when he is in the realm but cannot attend *parliament* because of some illness.

In the beginning, new *parliaments* were convoked every year. Gradually, their terms became longer. Under Charles II, they were held for a long time with large interruptions, but both of these customs were found to be of such dangerous moment that in the reign of King William[16] an act was passed by which the term of all *parliaments* would be restricted to three sessions, or three years, and for that reason this act was called the *triennial act*.[17] Since then, because of other considerations, the duration of *parliaments* has again been prorogued up to seven years, in the 3rd year of George I.[18] *Parliaments* are convoked by written order or letters of the king addressed to each lord, with the command to appear, and by other orders addressed to the sheriffs of each province, to summon the people to elect two knights for each county, and one or two members for each town, &c.

Formerly, the whole people had a voice in the elections, until it was decreed by Henry VI[19] that only proprietors of franc-fief[20] resident in the province and those who had at least 40 shillings of annual income would be allowed to vote. No one could be elected who was not at least 21 years old.

Every lord spiritual and temporal, knight, citizen, and bourgeois, who was a member of *parliament*, had to appear on the order of summons, unless he brought forth reasonable excuses for his absence. Otherwise he was condemned to a monetary fine—that is, a lord was condemned by the House of Peers,[21] a member of the commons by the lower chamber. But

15. Jaucourt puts the italicized phrase in English.

16. William III (r. 1689–1702).

17. Jaucourt refers to the Triennial Act of 1694 and not to the original act of 1641.

18. The Septennial Act was passed in 1716; some historians estimate that its effect was to reduce the number of contested elections and scale back the adult male electorate by roughly a fourth. See James Van Horn Melton, *The Rise of the Public in Enlightenment Europe* (Cambridge: Cambridge University Press, 2001), 22.

19. Henry VI (r. 1422–61).

20. Fiefs owned by commoners by special permission of the king (since only nobles could generally own fiefs), subject to a special tax.

21. The term "House of Lords" may be more familiar, but "House of Peers" was used for ceremonial purposes; it is Jaucourt's preferred term in this article.

at the same time, in order to increase attendance at *parliament,* there was a privilege for them and their domestics that shielded them from all sentences, seizures of property, physical arrest, *&c.*, for debts, offences, *&c.*, during the time of their travel, their stay, and their return. The only exceptions to this privilege were for treason, felony, and breach of the peace.

Although the rights and qualifications for election were generally established by various acts of *parliament,* it must nonetheless be observed that these rights and qualifications of the members of *parliament* for the towns, cities, and villages are founded since time immemorial on their charters and their customs. *Hobart, 120.126.241.*[22]

The king designates the place where the *parliament* must be held. Above, I named Westminster because for a long time, *parliament* has always assembled there. In that palace, lords and commons each have their separate accommodations. In the House of Peers, the princes of the blood are placed on private seats, the great officers of the state, dukes, marquesses, counts, bishops on benches, and the viscounts and barons on other benches from one side of the hall to the other—each one following the order of his creation and his rank.

The commons are higgledy-piggledy. The speaker alone has a distinguished seat at the top end. The secretary and his assistant are placed near him at a table. Before broaching any subject, all members of the House of Commons swear oaths and undersign their opinion against transubstantiation, *&c.*[23] The lords do not swear oaths, but they are obliged to undersign, like the members of the lower chamber. Every member of this latter house who votes after the speaker has been named, but without having sworn the required oaths beforehand, is declared incapable of any office, and is fined 500 pounds sterling by the statute 30. *carol. II. c.j.*[24] It is true however that the form of the oath of supremacy has been changed by the stat. 4. *an. c.v.*

22. The reference may be to Henry Hobart (1560–1625), *The reports of that reverend and learned judge, the right honorable Sr. Henry Hobart* (London: More, 1641, and many later editions).

23. The reference is to the Roman Catholic doctrine, anathema in Protestant England, that the Eucharistic host is transformed from bread into the body of Christ at its elevation during Mass.

24. The reference is to the Test Act of 1678.

The House of Peers is the sovereign court of justice in the realm, and the judge of last resort. The lower house makes the great inquests, but it is not a court of justice.

Since the most important object in the affairs of *parliament* concerns the manner in which bills or legislative acts are proposed and debated, we will linger here for a few moments.

The former method of proceeding with bills was different from that followed today. In the past, the bill was formed in the manner of a demand inscribed on the lords' register with the consent of the king. Next, at the close of *parliament,* the act was written up in the form of a statute and put on a register called the *register of statutes*. This practice lasted until the reign of Henry VI, when, after complaints that the statutes were not being faithfully inscribed as they had been pronounced, it was ordained that future bills, *continentes formam actûs parliamenti,*[25] would be lodged in the house of *parliament*. Today, then, as soon as a member desires to have a bill on a certain subject, and his proposition is accepted by the majority, he receives an order to prepare it and bring it forth. A time is fixed to read it out (the reading being done by the secretary), and the president asks if it will be read out a second time or not. After the second reading, the question is debated as to whether the bill will be seen in committee[26] or not. This committee is composed of the entire chamber, or a private committee formed by a certain number of delegates.

Once the committee is organized, a president is named who reads the bill item by item, and makes corrections according to the opinion of the majority. After the bill has been discussed and voted on in this way, the president makes his report to the bar of the chamber, reads all the additions and corrections, and leaves it on the table. Then he asks if the bill is going to be read a second time. If the chamber agrees, he again asks if said bill

25. "Keeping the form of an act of Parliament"

26. The French is *comité,* a new term in the late seventeenth century borrowed from the English, which itself had developed this new word in the early seventeenth century mainly out of parliamentary practice. Committees would be an important and conspicuous feature of the French Revolution; the twelve men led by Robespierre who presided over the Reign of Terror were called the Committee of Public Safety. The only similar usage of the term that I have found in the *Encyclopédie* is in the short article, also by Jaucourt, entitled RAPPORT [Report], in 13:798.

will be written out in large official form on parchment and read out a third time. Finally he asks if the bill will pass. When the majority of votes is for the affirmative, the secretary writes on top *let it be given to the lords,* or if it is in the House of Peers, *let it be given to the commons.* But if the bill is rejected, it can no longer be proposed during the same session.

When a bill is passed in one house and the other opposes it, then a conference is requested in the Painted Chamber,[27] where each chamber delegates a certain number of members, and there the affair is discussed—the lords being seated with heads covered, and the commons standing bareheaded. If the bill is rejected, the affair is moot. If it is accepted, then the bill, as well as the other bills that have passed in the two chambers, is placed at the feet of the king in the House of Peers. The king arrives, arrayed in his royal mantle and with the crown on his head. Then in his presence, the secretary of *parliament* reads the title of each bill, and as he reads, the secretary of the crown pronounces the king's consent or refusal.

If it is a public bill, the king's consent is expressed in these terms: *the king wills it.* If it is a private bill, *let it be done as is desired.* If the king rejects the bill, the response is, *the king will take it under advisement.* If it is a tax bill, the secretary responds, *the king thanks his loyal subjects, accepts their benevolence, and also wills it.*

A bill for a general pardon granted by the king is read only once.

It must also be observed that, for a bill's passage, the consent of the knights, citizens, and bourgeois must be shown in person, whereas the lords may vote by proxy. The reason for this difference is that the barons are thought to sit in *parliament* by right, in their status as peers of the king's court, *pares curtis.* Since they were allowed to serve in war by proxy, they likewise have a right to establish their proxy in *parliament.* But since the knights come to *parliament* only as representing the *minor barons,* and the citizens and bourgeois as representing the people of their city and town, they could not set up proxies, because they are themselves merely proxies and representatives of others.

Forty members suffice to form the House of Commons, and eight to form a committee. For the public good, each of these numbers ought to be

27. The Painted Chamber was a part of the royal palace at Westminster, where state ceremonies were held.

at least quadrupled in a body composed of more than 500 deputies. It would be fitting not to allow more than a few people to absent themselves, even from the private debates, because then cabals would be less easy and the discussion of all public matters would feature a more mature deliberation.

When speaking, a member of the commons stands, head uncovered, and addresses his speech to the speaker alone. If another member responds to his speech, the first is not allowed to reply the same day, unless it concerns him personally. The same person can speak only once on the same day on the same bill.

In the House of Peers, the members give their votes, beginning with the youngest and least-titled[28] baron, and continuing in rank order up to the most elevated. Each is answerable to his rank, either to approve or to disapprove.

In the House of Commons, votes are cast by yes or no, and when there is doubt over which side has the majority, there is a division of the house: if it's a matter of admitting something into the house, those who are for the affirmative leave; if it is something that the house has already seen, those who are for the negative leave.

In every division, the president names four orators, two for each opinion. In a committee of the whole house, it is divided by changing sides—those who agree take the right side of the rostrum, those who disagree take the left side, and then there are only two orators.

The number of members in the House of Peers is not determined, because it increases according to the good pleasure of H.M. The members of the House of Commons, when it is full, number 553—that is, 92 knights or provincial governors; 52 deputies for the 25 cities (London having four); 16 for the Cinque Ports; 2 for each university; 332 for 180 towns and villages; and finally, 12 for the principality of Wales and 45 for Scotland.

Lastly, the two houses must be prorogued together or dissolved together, because one house cannot exist without the other.

To these details, of which foreigners cannot perhaps have full knowledge, it is difficult not to add some reflections.

28. *Qualifié,* "titled"; by the mid-eighteenth century, however, the term is also being used to mean "qualified," in more like the modern meritocratic sense.

The House of Peers and the House of Commons are the arbiters of the nation, and the king is the superarbiter. This balance was lacking among the Romans.[29] The government of England is wiser because there is one body that is examining it constantly, and that is examining itself constantly. Its errors are such that they never last long, and by the spirit of watchfulness that they impart to the nation, they are often useful. A free state—that is, a state that is constantly subject to agitation—cannot last if it is not capable of being corrected by its own laws.[30] And such is the advantage of the legislative body that assembles from time to time to establish or revoke laws.

If need be, the kings of England can convoke a *parliament* at a time when the law does not oblige them to do so. The kings are, so to speak, on sentry duty. With great vigilance, they must observe the movements of the enemy and warn of his approach. But if the sentry sleeps, if he neglects his duty or maliciously tries to betray his city, don't those who have an interest in its preservation have a right to use any other means to uncover the danger that threatens them and protect themselves from it?

It was certainly up to the consuls or other principal magistrates of Rome to assemble and dismiss the senate. But when Hannibal was at the gates of the city, or when the Romans found themselves in some other pressing danger that threatened them with nothing less than complete destruction, if those magistrates had been drunk or insane, or if they had been captured by the enemy, no reasonable person could imagine being obliged in that case to adhere to the ordinary formalities.

On such an occasion, each individual is a magistrate, and whoever is first to perceive the danger and who knows the means of preventing it has a right to convoke the assembly of the senate or the people. The people would always be disposed to follow such a man, and would unfailingly follow him, just as the Romans followed Brutus and Valerius against Tarquin, or Horatius and Valerius against the decemvirs. And whoever does otherwise would without contradiction be as foolish as the courtiers of Kings

29. These lines are adapted from Voltaire, "On the Parliament," in his *Philosophical Letters;* see Voltaire, *Works,* 39:7.

30. This sentence comes from Montesquieu, *Considerations on the Causes of the Greatness of the Romans and Their Decline,* trans. David Lowenthal (New York: Free Press, 1965; repr. Indianapolis: Hackett, 1999), VIII, 88.

Philip III and Philip IV of Spain.[31] As the former was one day shaking with a fever, a furnace was brought into his room and placed so close to him that he was cruelly burned by it. One of the nobles cried out, "the king is burned!" Another nobleman responded, "that's very true." But since the person charged with removing the furnace had been absent, before he arrived the king's legs came to be in a pitiful state. When Philip IV was overtaken on the hunt by a storm of mixed hail and rain, he was attacked by a bad cold and a very dangerous fever because none of the courtiers in his retinue dared take the liberty of lending him a coat to protect him during the storm.

It is thus in vain for the *parliaments* to assemble if they are not permitted to continue their sessions until they have completed the business for which they assembled. And it would be ridiculous to give them power to assemble if they have not been permitted to remain in assembly until the dispatch of business. The sole reason for which *parliaments* assemble is to work for the advancement of the public good, and it is by virtue of the law that they assemble for this end. Thus, they should not be dissolved before they have terminated the items for which they assembled.

The history of the kings of England, and especially those who in the last century worked ceaselessly to seize despotic power, amply justifies Sidney's observations.[32] Indeed, it was mainly by refusing to hold *parliaments*, or by dissolving those that were assembled, that those princes attempted to establish their power. But these means, which they put in practice, were more harmful than helpful to them. In 1628, Charles I quashed the third *parliament* he had convoked, because he did not want to submit to its will—which Clarendon says demonstrates the strength of *parliament*. For unable to limit its power, the sovereign authority was inclined toward the harsh idea of abolishing it in practice. It thus belongs to *parliament* to repress the attacks of politics on liberty and to manage the authority of the prince by moderating it.

31. Lucius Valerius Potitus and Marcus Horatius Barbatus were consuls; the event was alleged to have occurred in 449 B.C.; Philip III (r. 1598–1621) and Philip IV (r. 1621–64). This whole paragraph is taken nearly verbatim from Algernon Sidney, *Discourses Concerning Government,* 3:38, second paragraph.

32. Here, the reference is to Sidney, *Discourses,* perhaps chap. 2, sec. 27.

"It is true," says M. de Voltaire, in his *Literary and Philosophical Miscellany*, "that the idol of arbitrary power has been drowned in seas of blood; nevertheless, the English do not think they have purchased their laws and their privileges at too high a price. Other nations have shed as much blood; but then the blood they spilled in defense of their liberty served only to enslave them the more. A city in Barbary or in Turkey takes up arms in defense of its privileges, when immediately it is stormed by mercenary troops; it is punished by executioners, and the rest of the nation kiss their chains. The French think that the government of England is more tempestuous than the seas which surround it; in which, indeed, they are not mistaken: but then this happens only when the king raises the storm by attempting to seize the ship, of which he is only the pilot. The civil wars of France lasted longer, were more cruel, and productive of greater evils, than those of England: but none of these civil wars had a wise and becoming liberty for their object."[33] (*Chevalier* DE JAUCOURT)

33. Voltaire, "On the Parliament," in *Philosophical Letters;* see Voltaire, *Works,* 39:7–8.

Country
(*Patrie*)

Throughout this volume, we have generally translated patrie *as "Country" with a capital* C, *to distinguish it from* pays, *generally a more geographical and less human term which we have translated as "country" with a lowercase* c. *Here, however, we leave the term untranslated, for convenience' sake and because of Jaucourt's etymological discussion. It is useful to recall the connection between* patrie *and "patriotism," a concept that was growing in importance in France and elsewhere at the time of writing, which was shortly after France's disastrous experience in the Seven Years' War (1756–63) had concluded.*

COUNTRY (*Political government*). The illogical orator, the geographer concerned only with the location of places, and the vulgar lexicographer all take *patrie* for the place of birth, wherever it is. But the philosopher knows that this word comes from the Latin *pater,* which represents a father and children, and consequently, that it expresses the sense we attach to the words *family, society, free state,* of which we are members and in which the laws assure our liberties and our happiness. There is no *patrie* under the yoke of despotism.[1] In the past century, Colbert also confused *royaume* [*realm or kingdom*] and *patrie*. Finally, a better-informed modern has brought forth an essay on this word, in which he has fixed with such taste and truthfulness the

This article can be found at 12:178–80 in the original edition of the *Encyclopédie.*

1. As Albert Souboul pointed out, this idea was expressed by La Bruyère in his 1688 "Du souverain ou de la République," in *Characters.* See Souboul, ed., *Textes choisis de l'Encyclopédie,* 2nd ed. (Paris: Editions Sociales, 1962), 178.

meaning of that term, its nature, and the idea we ought to have of it, that I would be wrong not to embellish—let us rather say fashion my article out of—the reflections of that witty writer.[2]

The Greeks and Romans knew nothing so lovable and so sacred as the *patrie*. They said that one owes oneself completely to her; that it is no more permissible to take revenge on her than on one's father; that one's friends must be her friends; that of all the omens, the best is to fight for her; that it is noble, that it is sweet to die preserving her; that heaven opens only for those who have served her. Thus spoke the magistrates, the warriors, and the people. What idea, then, did they form of the *patrie?*

The *patrie,* they said, is a land which all the inhabitants have an interest in preserving, which no one wants to quit (because one doesn't abandon one's happiness), and in which strangers seek refuge.[3] It is a nurse who gives her milk with as much pleasure as we receive it. It is a mother who cherishes all her children, who distinguishes among them only as much as they distinguish themselves; who readily accepts opulence and a middling condition but no poor; the great and the small, but no one oppressed; who even in this unequal division preserves a sort of equality, by opening to all the path to the leading positions; who suffers no evils in her family but those she cannot prevent, sickness and death; who, in giving existence to her children, would think she had done nothing if she had not added well-being. She is a power as ancient as society, founded on nature and order; a power superior to all the powers she establishes in her midst—archons, suffetes, ephors, consuls, or kings;[4] a power that subjects to her laws those who command in her name as well as those who obey. She is a divinity who accepts offerings only to spread them around, who demands more

2. The reference is to abbé Gabriel-François Coyer (1707–82), "Dissertation sur le vieux mot de patrie" [Essay on the old word *patrie*], in *Dissertations pour être lues: la première sur le vieux mot de patrie, la seconde sur la nature du peuple* [Essays to be read: the first on the old word *patrie,* the second on the nature of the people] (N.p., 1755), the first of which is reprinted in Edmond Dziembowski, *Ecrits sur le patriotisme, l'esprit public et la propagande au milieu du XVIIIe siècle* [Writings on patriotism, public spirit and propaganda in the middle of the 18th century] (La Rochelle: Rumeur des âges, 1997), 41–53; cited below as Coyer, *The old word "patrie."*

3. For this paragraph, see Coyer, *The old word "patrie,"* 44–45.

4. The suffetes were elected officials in Carthage; the others were Greek or Roman officials and rulers.

affection than fear, who smiles in doing good, and who sighs in unleashing a thunderbolt.

Such is the *patrie!* The love one bears her leads to good mores, and good mores lead to love of the *patrie*. This love is the love of the laws and of the success of the state, a love singularly attached to democracies.[5] It is a political virtue, by which one renounces oneself in preferring the public interest to one's own. It is a feeling and not a result of knowledge. The lowest man in the state can have this feeling as well as the leader of the republic.

The word *patrie* was one of the first words that children stammered among the Greeks and Romans.[6] It was the soul of conversation and the cry of war. It embellished poetry, it excited orators, it presided over the senate, it echoed in the theater and in the people's assemblies; it was engraved on the monuments. Cicero found the word so tender that he preferred it to any other when he was speaking of the interests of Rome.[7]

Among the Greeks and Romans, there were also customs that constantly called to mind the image of the *patrie* along with the word: crowns, triumphs, statues, tombs, funeral orations—these were so many motives to patriotism.[8] There were also truly public spectacles, in which all the orders relaxed together; rostrums at which the *patrie,* through the mouths of the orators, consulted with her children on the means of making them happy and glorious. But let us detail the facts that will prove everything we have just said.

When the Greeks defeated the Persians at Salamis,[9] men heard on one side the voice of an imperious master driving slaves into combat, and on the other the word *patrie* inspiring free men. Thus, the Greeks had nothing more dear than love of the *patrie;* to work for her was their happiness and their glory. Lycurgus, Solon, Miltiades, Themistocles, Aristides all preferred their *patrie* to everything in the world. In a war council held by the republic, one of these sees Eurybiades' baton raised over him; he responds with just these three

5. For this paragraph, see Montesquieu, *The Spirit of the Laws,* 4.5. See also DEMOCRACY, above.

6. For most of this paragraph, see Coyer, *The old word "patrie,"* 42.

7. For this sentence, see ibid., 43.

8. This paragraph draws on ibid., 48.

9. Ibid., 45.

words: strike, but listen.[10] After disposing for a long time of the forces and finances of Athens, Aristides did not leave enough to cover his own burial.[11]

Spartan women had just as much desire to please as our own do, but they counted on hitting the target with greater certainty by combining their charms with zeal for the *patrie*. "Go, my son," said one, "take arms to defend your *patrie*, and return only with your shield or on your shield—that is, victor or dead." "Console yourself," said another mother to one of her sons, "console yourself for the leg you lost; you will not take a single step that doesn't remind you that you have defended the *patrie*."[12] After the battle of Leuctra,[13] all the mothers of those who had died in combat congratulated themselves, whereas the others cried over their sons who came back defeated. They boasted of bringing men into the world, because even in the cradle they were showing them the *patrie* as their first mother.

Rome, which had received from the Greeks the image that should be formed of the *patrie*, engraved it very deeply into the hearts of her citizens. What was also distinctive of the Romans is that they mixed in some religious sentiments with their love for the *patrie*. That city founded under the most favorable auspices, that Romulus their king and their god, that capitol—eternal, like the city—and the city eternal like its founder, all this made an extraordinary impression on the Romans.

To preserve his *patrie*, Brutus had his sons beheaded, and that act will seem unnatural only to weak souls.[14] Without the death of the two traitors, Brutus's *patrie* was dying in the cradle. Valerius Publicola had only to utter the word *patrie* to make the senate more popular; Menenius Agrippa, to bring the people back from the holy mountain into the bosom of the republic; Veturia—for the women in Rome, as in Sparta, were citizens—to

10. The reference is to Eurybiades, a Spartan naval leader during the Persian wars, and to Themistocles (ca. 525–460 B.C.), his Athenian commander.

11. The other allusions in this paragraph are to Lycurgus (ca. 700–630 B.C.) and Solon (ca. 638–558 B.C.), lawgivers of Sparta and Athens, respectively; Miltiades (ca. 550–489 B.C.), adoptive Athenian leader in the successful Battle of Marathon against Persia in 490; and Aristides (530–468 B.C.), Athenian statesman and military leader. For this paragraph, see Coyer, *The old word "patrie,"* 50.

12. See Coyer, *The old word "patrie,"* 49, 47–48.

13. Battle of Leuctra (371 B.C.), where the Spartans were defeated by the Boeotians.

14. See Coyer, *The old word "patrie,"* 44.

disarm Coriolanus her son; Manlius, Camillus, Scipio, to defeat the enemies of the Roman name; the two Catos, to preserve the laws and the ancient mores; Cicero, to frighten Antony and to strike at Catiline.[15]

One might say that this word *patrie* contained a secret virtue, not only to make the most timid men valiant (according to Lucian's phrase), but also to generate heroes of all types and to work all sorts of wonders.[16] Or better yet: let us say that in those Greek and Roman souls, there were virtues that made them sensitive to the value of the word. I am not talking about those petty virtues that bring us cheap praise in our private circles. I mean those civic qualities, that vigor of the soul that makes us do and endure great things for the public good. Fabius was mocked, scorned, and insulted by his colleague and by his army. No matter: he made no changes in his plans, he still temporized, and yet he ended up defeating Hannibal.[17] Regulus, to preserve an advantage for Rome, dissuaded them from an exchange of prisoners even though he was a prisoner himself, so he returned to Carthage where death by torture awaited him. Three Deciuses distinguished their consulate by devoting themselves to a certain death.[18] As long as we regard these generous citizens as illustrious fools and their deeds as theatrical virtues, we will not have much understanding of the word *patrie*.

Never, perhaps, has this noble word been heard with more respect, more love, more advantage than in the time of Fabricius. Everyone knows what he said to Pyrrhus: "Keep your gold and your honors; as for us Romans, we

15. Marcus Junius Brutus (85–42 B.C.), a Roman senator and an assassin of Caesar; Publius Valerius Poplicola (ca. 560–503 B.C.), thought to be instrumental in overthrowing the Tarquin monarchy and establishing the republic; Menenius Agrippa (consul in 503), said to have persuaded the Plebs to return to work with a speech containing organic and patriotic imagery; Veturia's appeal to Coriolanus to call off the war against the Volscians is traditionally dated 488 B.C.; Manlius Capitolinus, thought to have turned away the Gauls at the Capitol in 390 B.C.; Furius Camillus, consul, tribune, and leader of campaigns against tribal enemies in the 390s and 380s B.C.; Cornelius Scipio Africanus (235–183 B.C.), a commander in the Carthaginian wars.

16. For the next three paragraphs, see Coyer, *The old word "patrie,"* 50–51.

17. Quintus Fabius Maximus Verrucosus (ca. 275–203 B.C.), a Roman statesman and military leader known for his delaying strategy.

18. Marcus Atilius Regulus (d. ca. 250 B.C.), a naval commander in the First Punic War, was taken prisoner after his defeat at the Battle of Tunis; Publius Decius Mus was the name of a father, son, and grandson who served as political and military leaders in Rome in the late fourth and third centuries B.C.

are all rich, because the *patrie* demands only merit to raise us to the highest positions."[19]

But everyone does not know that a thousand other Romans would have said the same thing. This patriotic tone was the general tone in a city in which all social classes were virtuous. This is why Rome appeared to Pyrrhus's ambassador Cyneas as a temple, and the senate as an assembly of kings.[20]

With a change in mores came a change in the reality. Toward the end of the republic, no one knew the word *patrie* any longer except to profane it. Catiline and his furious accomplices reserved death for whoever still pronounced the word as a Roman. Crassus and Caesar used it only to veil their ambition. And when this same Caesar later on said to his soldiers, in crossing the Rubicon, that he was going to avenge the injuries to the *patrie*, he was strangely misleading his troops. It was not in dining like Crassus, or building like Lucullus, or prostituting oneself in debauchery like Clodius, or pillaging provinces like Verres, or forming tyrannical plans like Caesar, or flattering Caesar like Antony that men learned to love the *patrie*.[21]

I know, however, that in the midst of this governmental and moral disorder, some Romans still yearned for the good of their *patrie*. Titus Labienus is a quite remarkable example of this.[22] Above the most seductive ambitions, friend of Caesar, companion and often instrument of his victories, he abandoned without hesitation a cause that fortune was protecting. Exposing himself to danger for love of the *patrie*, he embraced the party of Pompey, where he had everything to risk, and where even in success, he could only find very modest consideration.

19. Gaius Fabricius Luscinus, an early third century B.C. Roman political and military leader known for simplicity and incorruptibility; the story, though not the precise quotation, may be found in Plutarch's "Life of Pyrrhus," 20.1–3.

20. See Ibid., 19.4–5, for the apparent reference.

21. Marcus Licinius Crassus (ca. 115–53 B.C.), a general, political leader, and member of the First Triumvirate with Pompey and Caesar, known for his fabulous wealth and extravagant suppers; Publius Claudius Pulcher (ca. 92–ca. 52 B.C.), military and political leader and eventually nemesis of Cicero, known for his eccentric and plebeian conduct (hence his change of name to Clodius); Caius Verres (ca. 120–43 B.C.), a Roman magistrate and provincial governor, notoriously in Sicily; Lucius Licinius Lucullus (ca. 118–56 B.C.), a military and political leader, with political charges in Gaul and Cilicia, famous for retiring to a life of luxury and drinking bouts.

22. Titus Labienus (ca. 100–45 B.C.).

But at last under Tiberius, Rome forgot all love of *patrie,* though how would she have preserved it?[23] We see brigandage allied with authority, manipulation and intrigue disposing of offices, all wealth in the hands of a few, excessive luxury mistreating extreme poverty, the farmer regarding his field as but a pretext for vexation, each citizen reduced to abandoning the general good to concern himself only with his own. All the principles of government were corrupted, all the laws bent to the will of the sovereign. No more energy in the senate, no more security for individuals; senators who might have wanted to defend the public liberty would have been risking their own. It was nothing but a mute tyranny, carried out in the shadow of the laws, and woe to those who perceived this. To manifest one's fears was to redouble them. Tiberius, asleep on his island of Capri, left things to Sejanus, and Sejanus, worthy minister of such a master, did everything necessary to snuff out all the love the Romans had had for their *patrie*.[24]

Nothing brings more glory to Trajan than to have revived its remnants.[25] Six tyrants—equally cruel, almost all rabid, often imbecile—had preceded him on the throne. The reigns of Titus and Nerva were too short to establish the love of the *patrie*. Trajan intended to bring it about; let us see how he went about it.

While giving the praetorian prefect Saburanus the mark of this dignity (it was a sword [*épée*]), he began by saying: "receive this sabre [*fer*], and use it to defend me if I govern my *patrie* well, or against me if I behave ill." He knew what he was talking about.[26]

He refused the sums of money that new emperors were in the habit of receiving from the cities. He reduced taxes substantially and sold a portion of the imperial houses for the state's benefit. He gave gifts to all poor citizens. He prevented the rich from enriching themselves to excess. And those he put in office—the quaestors, the praetors, the proconsuls—saw only one way to keep themselves there: namely, to concern themselves with the well-being of

23. For this and the next three paragraphs, see Coyer, *The old word "patrie,"* 45–48.

24. Tiberius Claudius Nero (42 B.C.–A.D. 37) and Lucius Aelius Sejanus (20 B.C.–A.D. 31), his feared lieutenant.

25. Dziembowski suggests that Trajan may have had special iconographical resonance in the public representations of the reigning monarch, Louis XV. See Coyer, *The old word "patrie,"* 47 n. 1.

26. Dio Cassius, *Roman History,* LXVIII.16.1, for this story.

the people. He brought abundance, order, and justice back to the provinces and to Rome, where his palace was as open to the public as the temples—especially to those who came there to represent the interests of the *patrie.*

When the master of the world was seen to submit to the laws, to restore the senate's splendor and authority, to do nothing except in concert with it, to regard the imperial dignity as but a simple magistracy accountable to the *patrie;* when people in the final analysis saw the present good gain some credibility for the future—then, they no longer restrained themselves.[27] Women congratulated themselves for giving children to the *patrie;* young people spoke only of making her illustrious; old men recovered their energy to serve her; everyone cried out: "fortunate *patrie!* glorious emperor!" By acclamation, everyone gave to the best of princes a title that embraced all titles: father of his Country [*père de la patrie*]. But when new monsters took his place, the government fell again into its excesses; soldiers sold the *patrie* and assassinated emperors to get a better price for it.

After these details, I do not need to prove that there cannot be a *patrie* in servile states. Thus, those who live under Oriental despotism, in which no other law is known but the sovereign's will, no other maxims but adoration of his whims, no other principles of government but terror, in which no fortune, no head is secure—those men, I say, have no *patrie* and do not even know the word, a word that is the true expression of happiness.

In the zeal that animates me, says abbé Coyer, I have in many places put subjects of all orders to the test. Citizens, I have said, know the *patrie!* The common man has wept, the magistrate has knitted his brow while keeping a glum silence, the soldier has cursed, the courtier has made fun of me, the state budget official has asked me if this was the name of a new lease. As for the clergy who, like Anaxagoras, point to the sky with their fingertip when they are asked where is their *patrie,* it is not surprising that they do not celebrate it on this earth.[28]

27. Dziembowski sees this passage as a way for Coyer, with subtly republicanizing inflections, to take the side of the provincial parlements (sovereign courts) in their struggle with monarchy over the scope of centralized royal power; see Coyer, *The old word "patrie,"* 47 n. 2. On the scope of royal power, see also INTENDANTS, in this volume.

28. Anaxagoras (ca. 500–428 B.C.), a pre-Socratic philosopher from Asia Minor who settled in Athens.

A lord[29] as well known in letters as in diplomacy has written somewhere, perhaps with too much bitterness, that in his country, hospitality has changed into luxury, pleasure into debauchery, lords into courtiers, bourgeois into dandies.[30] If that is how it was, then soon—and what a shame!—love of *patrie* will no longer prevail there. Corrupt citizens are always ready to tear apart their country, or to excite disturbances and factions that are so contrary to the public good. (*Chevalier* DE JAUCOURT)

29. Jaucourt uses the English word here.

30. The reference is to Henry St. John, Viscount Bolingbroke (1678–1751), Tory leader and author of *Letters on the Spirit of Patriotism,* among other works; a major presence in France during his years of exile during Walpole's ministry and an influential friend of Voltaire and Montesquieu; see Coyer, *The old word "patrie,"* 51–52, as well as the entry PATRIOT, below.

Amor Patriae (Patriotism)

In foreground, a patriot with trophy, brazier, wreaths, weapons, and other symbols of civic spirit and patriotic achievement; in background, the Roman dictator Camillus, who broke his oath to the Gauls to save Rome.

Patriot
(*Patriote*)

After drawing on the Frenchman Coyer for his article COUNTRY, *Jaucourt turns almost exclusively to English authors for his related article* PATRIOT. *Much of this entry, as Dennis J. Fletcher has shown,*[1] *is drawn from Bolingbroke's 1736 "Letter on Patriotism," published in 1749 and translated into French in a 1750 edition.*[2] *Some is inspired by Joseph Addison's 1713 play* Cato, *which had a wide audience in the eighteenth century, especially but not exclusively in the English-speaking world. Jaucourt's deep familiarity with English political culture again provides a distinctive inflection to this French treatment of the subject.*

PATRIOT (*Government*). This is the one who in a free government loves his Country and zealously brings his own well-being and glory to its aid, according to his means and faculties.

"The *patriot* is one Who makes the welfare of mankind his care, Tho' still by faction, vice, and fortune crost, Shall find the generous labour was not lost."[3]

This article can be found at 12:181 in the original edition of the *Encyclopédie*.

1. Dennis J. Fletcher, "The Chevalier de Jaucourt and the English Sources of the Encyclopedic Article *Patriote*," *Diderot Studies* 16 (1973): 23–34.

2. See Henry St. John, Viscount Bolingbroke, *Letters, on the spirit of patriotism: on the idea of a patriot king: and on the state of parties, at the accession of King George the First* (Dublin, 1749), cited below as "Spirit of Patriotism" or as "Idea of a Patriot King," depending upon the case.

3. The quoted passage appears in English in Jaucourt's text. It is uttered by Cato upon the death of his son Marcus at the end of act IV, sc. 4, of Joseph Addison's *Cato* (1713).

Serving one's Country is not a chimerical duty but a real obligation. Any man who agrees that there are duties derived from nature's constitution and from the moral good and evil of things will recognize the duty that obliges us to do good for our Country, or else he will be reduced to the most absurd inconsistency. Once he has acknowledged this duty, it is not difficult to prove to him that this duty is proportioned to the means and occasions that he has to fulfill it, and that nothing can exempt us from what we owe to Country as far as it needs us and as far as we can serve it.

Ambitious slaves will say that it is very hard to renounce the pleasures of society in order to dedicate one's days to the service of one's Country. Base souls, you have no idea then of noble and solid pleasures! Believe me, there are truer and more delicious ones in a life occupied with procuring the good of one's Country than Caesar ever knew in destroying the liberty of his own; or Descartes in building new worlds; or Burnet in creating a world before the flood. In discovering the true laws of nature, Newton himself knew no greater intellectual pleasure than is tasted by a true *patriot* who extends all the force of his understanding and who guides all his thoughts and actions toward the good of his Country.[4]

When a state minister forms a political plan which he knows will bring the most seemingly independent parts together into a good and great design, he dedicates himself to it with as much ardor and pleasure as the geniuses I have just named dedicated themselves to their ingenious research. The satisfaction that a speculative philosopher derives from the importance of the subjects to which he applies himself is very great, I admit. But the satisfactions of a man of state animated by patriotism go even further. In executing the plan he has devised, his work and his pleasures enhance each other and become diversified. It is true that the execution is often impeded by unforeseen circumstances, by the perfidy of his false friends, or by the power of his enemies. But the faithfulness of some men compensates him

4. This paragraph is lightly adapted from Bolingbroke, "Spirit of Patriotism," 27, which also includes Montaigne on the list. René Descartes was the French philosopher (1596–1650) whose theory of vortices proposed a new scheme of the physical world; Thomas Burnet (1635?–1715) was an English theologian whose *Telluris Theoria Sacra, or Sacred Theory of the Earth* (Latin ed., 1681, English 1684) offered a new theory of the origins of Noah's flood. Isaac Newton's *Principia mathematica* appeared in 1687.

for the falseness of others. I will be told that, for whoever is involved in them, affairs of state are a type of lottery. Sure, but it's a lottery the virtuous man can't lose. If he meets with success, he will enjoy satisfaction proportional to the good he has done. If it's the opposite and the oppressive parties come to prevail, he will always be consoled by the testimony of his conscience and the enjoyment of the honor he has acquired.[5]

When fortune had prepared the circumstances for bringing down the Roman republic, Cato arrested its collapse for some time with his virtue.[6] If he couldn't save the liberty of Rome, he at least prolonged its survival. The republic would have been destroyed by Catiline, backed up by Caesar, Crassus, and their ilk, if it had not been defended by Cicero, supported by Cato and some *patriots*. I do think Cato showed too much severity for the mores of Rome, which for a long time had been abandoned to the greatest corruption. He was perhaps clumsy in his treatment of a worn-out civic body.[7] But if this virtuous and *patriotic* citizen was mistaken in his remedies, he has earned the glory he has acquired by the firmness of his conduct in consecrating his life to the service of his Country. He would have been more worthy of praise had he persisted to the end in defending its liberty. His death would have been nobler in Munda than in Utica.[8]

After all, if this great man balanced the power of fortune by his patriotism almost alone, then a fortiori can several good *patriots* by their courage and their labors defend the constitution of the state against the encroachments of ill-intentioned men who have neither Crassus's wealth nor Pompey's reputation nor Caesar's conduct nor Antony's skill, but at most Catiline's fury and Clodius's indecency.[9]

5. See Bolingbroke, "Spirit of Patriotism," 29.

6. This paragraph is adapted from Bolingbroke, "Spirit of Patriotism," 30–31; see the comments in Fletcher, "English Sources," 30.

7. Bolingbroke's phrase here is "a crazy constitution."

8. Utica, the city where Cato was born; Munda, the site in Hispania Baetica of an important victory by Caesar over Pompey's son in 45 B.C.

9. Marcus Licinius Crassus (ca. 115–53 B.C.), Gnaeus Pompeius Magnus (106–48 B.C.), and Caesar (d. 44 B.C.) were members of the First Triumvirate in the civil wars; Marcus Antonius (83–30 B.C.) was a member of the second. Lucius Sergius Catilina (102–62 B.C.) conspired against the senate. Publius Clodius Pulcher (ca. 93–52 B.C.) was a populist tribune. Both he and Catiline were enemies of Cicero.

As for me, who because of particular events has not had the good fortune to serve my Country in any public employment, I have at least dedicated my days to attempting to know the duties of *patriots.*[10] Perhaps today I am in a position to indicate them and depict them in their essence: *Non is solus reipublicae prodest qui tuetur reos, & de pace belloque censet; sed qui juventutem exhortatur, qui in tantâ bonorum praeceptorum inopiâ, virtute instruit animos; qui ad pecuniam, luxuriamque cursu ruentes, prensat ac reprehendit: is in privato publicum negotium agit.*[11] (*Chevalier* DE JAUCOURT)

10. The final paragraph, including the passage from Seneca, is adapted from the final paragraph in Bolingbroke's introduction to "Idea of a Patriot King" (65–66), where the author contrasts his public spirit with his present and future exile in another country. See also Fletcher, "English Sources," 32, for Jaucourt's editorial decisions.

11. The full passage, slightly altered by Jaucourt, would read: "For the man that does good service to the state is not merely he who brings forward candidates and defends the accused and votes for peace and war, but he also who admonishes young men, who instils virtue into their minds, supplying the great lack of good teachers, who lays hold upon those that are rushing wildly in pursuit of money and luxury, and draws them back, and, if he accomplishes nothing else, at least retards them—such a man performs a public service even in private life." See "On Tranquillity of Mind," in Seneca, *Moral Essays,* trans. John W. Basore (Cambridge: Harvard University Press, 1935), II.iii.3, 2:225.

Volume 13
(1765)

Population

Like David Hume's "Of the Populousness of Ancient Nations" (1754), which Damilaville had read, this lengthy essay on population addresses questions central to political observers of the eighteenth century: Is human population rising or declining? What determines the rise or decline of population? What are its implications for the health, strength, and prosperity of peoples?[1] *Like Hume, Damilaville relates population to policy and constitutional regime type among other factors.*

POPULATION s.f. (*Physics,*[2] *Politics, Morality*). This word is abstract, in its widest meaning; it expresses the product of all living things and their offspring; for the earth is populated not only by men, but also by animals of all kinds that live with them. Reproduction of one's own kind is in each individual the fruit of the power to procreate; the population is its result. But this expression most particularly applies to the human species; and in this particular sense, it designates the relationship of men to the land they occupy, which is a direct ratio relative to their number, and indirect relative to space.

This translation of POPULATION is based on the translation of an abridged version of the article by Odile Frank that appeared as part of "Diderot's *Encyclopédie* on Population" in *Population and Development Review* 15, no. 2 (June 1989): 342–57, and is reprinted and adapted with the permission of the Population Council. We have completed the translation of the full article, placing our contributions in brackets.

This article can be found at 13:88–103 in the original edition of the *Encyclopédie.*

1. For a preliminary discussion, see Hume, *Essays, Moral, Political, and Literary,* ed. Eugene F. Miller, rev. ed. (Indianapolis: Liberty Fund, 1987), 378 n. 2 and 382 n. 6.—HC

2. Here the rubric "Physics" is best thought of as concerning the physical or natural world.—HC

Was there a time when there existed only one human creature of each sex on earth? and the multitude of men distributed today on the surface of the earth: is it the product of a continual progression of generations for which this original and solitary people was the first limit?

That does not appear possible, if one considers with what prodigious abundance the human species reproduces itself; even though of all known living species, it is one of the least fertile.

In a table of progression given by Mr. Wallace, an English scholar and writer, in a work he published on the number of men, and which was translated into our language;[3] it is proved that, starting with this first couple, and assuming that they should have only borne, as have done all the couples who descended from them, six children each, half males and half females, the number of men should have grown in 1233 years, that is, from the creation to the eve of the flood, to the number of 412,316,860,416; by removing one-third of the children born for those who do not reach adulthood, and having couples procreate only to the age of 27 or so, and dividing the number of years of that epoch into 37 periods of 33 years each.

This calculation could appear specious, if real events were not otherwise. The number of children each couple is supposed to bear is not too large; it is more usual to see it exceeded in each marriage, than it is to see a lesser number come about. The subtraction of one-third of these children for those who die before growing up also seems sufficient. More than that number die, one might say: yes, but it should be noted that it's over a larger number born, which removes nothing from the total product resulting from Mr. Wallace's calculations. For, if in effect out of 15 or 16 children, which is not rare to come from the same father and mother, half perish, or even two-thirds, in childhood, the remainder will always be greater than the number that author assumes to be left to each couple.

If this propagation is believable, if together the number of children born in each marriage proves that the results determined by Mr. Wallace are not too large, with what number of men should then the earth be covered? It could no longer contain the multitude of its inhabitants. For if we calculate

3. Robert Wallace (1697–1771), *A Dissertation on the Numbers of Mankind, in Ancient and Modern Times* (Edinburgh: Hamilton, 1753); the work was translated into French by Elie de Joncourt in 1754.—HC

on the same principle the propagation since the flood, the quantity [of men] would be innumerable. It would still be uncountable if one reduced by one-half the hypothetical results in the work we have cited.

The three sons of Noah, saved with him from the flood, each had a wife. There were thus three couples who could multiply. The propagation must then have been much more rapid and more abundant than in the preceding era, when it had begun with only one couple; thus, as we have already said, by reducing it to a half of what Mr. Wallace assumes for the preceding interval, it would be still impossible to enumerate the quantity of men who would remain: since independent of the large number of multiplying units, there is also a greater time elapsed from the flood to the present, than from the creation to the flood, the era used in the calculation that contains only 37 periods of 33 and a third years each, whereas the fertile era is composed of 123 periods of the same duration.

M. de Voltaire says in the first volume of his *Essai sur l'histoire générale* "that erudite chronologists have estimated that a single family after the flood, continuing to be involved in procreating, and its children still involved in doing likewise, would in 250 years produce more inhabitants than the universe holds today."[4]

The human species is indeed quite far from being so numerous. Mr. Wallace himself showed on the basis of another calculation that, given the land surface of the earth as estimated by Thomas Templeton in his new review of the globe,[5] and taking the average size of the populations of the different states of Europe, and assuming the rest of the earth to be inhabited at the same rate, the earth must contain one thousand million men.

Whence does this prodigious difference come? Have men multiplied themselves at such a rate only for a time? If one set the progeny of each couple by common accord to only two children, they would be infinitely more numerous; by reducing the offspring to a single child, the human species would no longer exist. The cause of such an extraordinary effect amply deserves to be researched. To suppose, along with Mr. Wallace, that the human species is dwindling, and reduced in numbers: to claim to have found the cause of this

4. See chapter 1 of Voltaire's *Essay.*—HC

5. Thomas Templeman (d. 1729), *A new survey of the globe* (London: [Bowles], 1729?).—HC

in the physical and moral ills that afflict it, such as the temperature of climates that are more or less favorable, the barrenness of land in other cases, the inclemency of seasons, earthquakes, tidal waves, wars, pestilence, famines, disease; let us even add the dangerous work that men undertake; finally, the moral corruption and the vices of different governments: all this is to offer only accidental and proximate explanations in the face of a general problem.

All these hazards are indeed explanations for man's destruction, but, *primo,* the entire human species is not afflicted by them at the same time; only two examples are known of the entire earth being attacked by them. The first, which the spherical shape of the earth could make problematical, would be the universal flood; the second, a historical plague that was, so it is said, so generalized and so violent, that it shook the very roots of plants, that it was felt throughout the known world, even as far as the Empire of Cathay, says Mr. de Montesquieu;[6] with the exception of these two calamities, the others have always been particular, and had an influence on only a part of the human species, often on the smallest part.

Secondo, if we consider the moderateness of the number of men who can perish in these particular cases, and we compare them with the prodigious number of men that there should be, according to the aforementioned calculations, we can agree that those losses must have been negligible, and of the order of the ratio of a finite number to infinity.

It is therefore not among these explanations that we will find the reason for the difference between the real *population* and the population that would result from these suppositions. It is rather to be found in the incorrect opinions on which the suppositions are founded; it is in the truth of the invariable laws of nature, which no doubt has determined the number of human beings since the beginning.

Let us leave aside all the calculations; the suppositions with which they can be justified are too fantastic. It is too difficult to establish the manner in which and the time at which the human species began. Speaking philosophically, and ignoring for the moment all dogma, whether respectable or revelatory: *the origin of life is more remote than we think. Why should there*

6. See Montesquieu, *Persian Letters,* letter 113; he also discusses the issue in *The Spirit of the Laws,* bk. 23, esp. 23.19–29.—HC

have been an eternity during which it did not exist? But anyway, what is an eternity that has no duration? And what is duration outside existence?

Let us see nevertheless if it is possible that the earth was more abundantly peopled in distant centuries than it is today, and on what basis one could think so. “The grandeur of ancient monuments,” says Mr. Wallace, “presents us with a more vast and more magnificent setting, more numerous armies; which assumes a much larger human crowd than is apparent in modern centuries.” The tales of historians of ancient times justify that author’s opinion, and that of scholars who thought similarly.

According to Homer’s enumeration, *bk. II* of the *Illiad,* of the vessels used by the Greeks to transport troops for the siege of the city of Troy, and the number of men carried by each of those vessels, it would seem that their army consisted of 100,810 men; Thucydides noted in *bk. I* of his *history,* that the Greeks could have set up a larger army, had they not feared running short of food rations in a foreign land.

If we refer to Athenaeus’s reports of the number of inhabitants of Athens and Attica,[7] Greece, composed only of Epirus, Thessalonika, Achaius, and the Peloponnesus, must have comprised 14 million, evaluating them in proportion to the number of those who lived in Athens and in Attica.

If we believe Herodotus, Egypt at the time of Amasis, a little before the foundation of the empire of the Persians by Cyrus, was very populated; it contained 20,000 cities, all inhabited.[8] They sometimes had 410,000 soldiers on their payroll, all Egyptian-born. In proportion to this, the number of citizens must have been more than 30 million. It is true that Thebes and Memphis were cities of considerable size. The first was known to be one of the very largest ever; one may believe Tacitus, who speaks of it in those terms. But the remainder of the 20,000 cities of Egypt were at best large villages, unlike the city of Thebes.

[Diodorus of Sicily also noted that that part of the earth was the most populated land in the world in ancient times;[9] he relates a singular fact that would confirm it and that deserves to be mentioned.

7. See Athenaeus, *Deipnosophistarum* [The learned banquet], VI.103. The work was available in a 1680 French translation by Michel de Marolles.—HC

8. See Herodotus, *Histories,* bk. 3.—HC

9. Diodorus Siculus, *The Library of History,* I.58–59 and passim.—HC

The day, he says, that Sesostris was born, more than 1700 male children were born in Egypt. The father of this young prince, who reigned there then, had all these children raised with his son, and gave them the same education, hoping that having been fed and having lived with him from their earliest infancy, they would always be friends. Henry IV walking with his children in the streets of Paris, and enjoying watching the people kiss and pet his children can be compared to Sesostris's father. Only great kings know that their subjects' love is worth more than their fear. Sesostris had indeed many friends, wise advisors, great generals, and his reign was illustrious.

If as many male children were born each day in his lands, as were born the day he was born, and we add the same number of girls, Egypt must have been populated by 34 million inhabitants; but his father's act and even the observations of historians show that the birth of those 1700 males on one day was considered a very extraordinary event; thus this fact proves nothing with respect to the *population* of Egypt, any more than it explains the depopulation occurring there today.]

In the same historian's work, one reads that in his time, he already considered the earth depopulated; he did not want his reports about the numerous armies of ancient times to be judged on the basis of the very small size of the armies of his own time. He wrote that Ninus led against the Bactrians 1,700,000 infantrymen, 210,000 cavalrymen, 10,600 chariots, and that the king of Bactria faced this army with 40,000 men. At another point, he said that Semiramis assembled 2 million men to build Babylon; that that princess had in India an army of 3 million foot-soldiers, one and a half million cavalrymen, 100,000 chariots, and 100,000 men on camels decked out like elephants. Referring to an expedition of Medes against the Cadusians, he noted that they had an army of 800,000 men, and the Cadusians 200,000.

In Strabo,[10] one reads that many states and cities had declined in his time; that the Getes and the Daces, who could raise an army of 200,000 men in earlier times, were then able to bring together less than half that number.

[These historians, and all those who have referred to their work, attribute a greater population to Italy before the Romans conquered it. Their

10. Strabo, *Geography*, VII.v.1–2.—HC

accounts of the wars that Sicily had to wage against Carthage and other powers that attacked it, of the large armies with which that island confronted its enemies, particularly those led by the two Dions,[11] lead one to assume again that the number of inhabitants was prodigious.]

In his commentaries, Caesar estimated that Gaul, which consisted of France, a part of the Netherlands, and another part of Switzerland, comprised at least 32 million inhabitants.

According to Mr. Wallace, Palestine, a narrow and arid country, had 6,764,000 people; but to find so many Israelites in such a small space and on such poor soil, he himself admits that one has to resort to a supernatural explanation: otherwise, he cannot see why that country should be so populated relative to its neighbors; but one also sees to what extent the need to resort to such an explanation weakens the credibility of the facts.

The same author travelled around the islands of the Mediterranean, of the Aegean sea, in Asia Minor, the African coast of the Mediterranean, Colchidia, and the whole distance from the Black Sea and the Caspian sea, ancient Hircania, and the other countries toward the north and the northeast of Persia, and found that all those parts had been much more populated in ancient times than they are today; but he also acknowledges that England had been much less populated earlier. Couldn't we add that Germany, Denmark, Sweden, and the region of Moscow were also less populated earlier? At that time, we knew neither the African interior, nor America: it is probable that the nations of these vast regions had not grown as much as those whose fertility levels had been remarked.

We do not argue that these nations were much more populous than they are today; but of the entire earth's surface, they occupied only about three-quarters of Europe, a part of Asia, and a very little stretch of the African coast. Given the proposition, then, it would prove that these parts were more populated earlier, but not that the entire earth should have been so.

[These nations were the only ones that were civilized; the arts, the sciences, and trade that flourished there were entirely unknown to others; it is natural then that the *population* should have been larger there than it is now;

11. Dionysius the Elder (432–367 B.C.) and Dionysius the Younger (397–343 B.C.), tyrants of Syracuse.—HC

it would even appear certain that it should have been larger than in modern times in those countries that displaced them in possessing more arts, sciences, and trade. That is all the good that can be drawn by the partisans of the *population* of ancient times from their research; but this is only one comparison of a few nations with a few nations, and as such is incomplete; thus one cannot draw from it any convincing conclusion regarding the more favorable size of the ancient, as contrasted with the new, *population*.]

We know that a large number of scholars have thought that the human species suffered great declines. We saw that that was the opinion already held by Diodorus of Sicily, Strabo, and all the historians of antiquity, for whom all the passages to quote would take too much space here, and who, furthermore, only repeated each other. Vossius considers there to be an even larger difference between the numbers of men in ancient and modern times. The calculation for this that he published in 1685 is indefensible.[12] He reduces the number of inhabitants in Europe to 30 million, assuming that of that number there were only 5 million in France; we know that up to the Revocation of the Edict of Nantes, the population of the kingdom was always estimated at about 20 million: that is, the total enumerated by census at the end of the last century, and by the author of the royal levy, attributed to M. le Marechal Vauban.[13]

In his geography, Hubner, like Vossius, estimates the population of Europe to be only 30 million.[14]

M. de Montesquieu, in *The Spirit of the Laws* and in the 112th *Persian letter,* reports that after as exact a calculation as possible in these matters, he found that the earth held barely a tenth of the number of men who lived on it in earlier times; that what is amazing is that the earth is losing population every day, and that if this continues, in ten centuries the earth would be nothing but a desert.[15]

12. Isaac Vossius (1618–89), *Variarum Observationum Liber* [Book of various observations] (London: R. Scott, 1685); cf. Hume, "Of the Populousness of Ancient Nations," in *Essays,* 380 n. 3.—HC

13. Marshall Vauban (1633–1707), commander, royal official, developer of the French fortification system, and author of *Projet de dîme royal* [Plan for a royal tithe] (1706).—HC

14. [Johann Hubner (1668–1731)], *La Géographie universelle* (Basel, 1746, 1757). Originally published in German earlier in the century.—HC

15. The passage appears in Montesquieu, *Persian Letters,* letter 112.—HC

We could have allayed M. de Montesquieu's fears, which are the same as those of Strabo and Diodorus of Sicily who had expressed them earlier. The parts of the earth which he has travelled may yet lose more population; but it is highly probable that as long as the earth exists, men will continue to exist and inhabit it. It is perhaps as necessary for the earth to exist that there should be men, as it is for the universe to exist that there should be an earth.

We do not yet know the half of the earth's surface; we judge the remainder of the earth only in relation to what we know. We knew the earth even less in olden times; and yet it would appear that we have willingly believed at all times that there are fewer men than in earlier centuries. What is the basis for the conjectures that give rise to this opinion? What would be the causes of so substantial a dying off of the population? If the causes were only moral ones, they would be particular, and would exert their effect only on a part of mankind, which is not enough to depopulate the earth. These causes must therefore be physical and universal; with the exception of the two changes we mentioned earlier and whose effects must be long since remedied, assuming them to have been real, there have been no notable changes in nature; those that have occurred in the sky did not produce any measurable disturbance. There is barely a trace of the most recent earthquake that nearly buried the entire city of Lisbon, and that terrible convulsion was felt on only a small part of the globe:[16] besides, we have not seen a decline in the number of other living creatures in proportion to the supposed decline in the number of men. Why, if this be a real phenomenon, would the human species alone experience it? It is true that two cruel and devastating diseases have attacked man in particular in modern times. Without the remedies found for them, the human species would have perished at its root from one of them. It had been prohibited by law to save the victims of the second disease, which killed one twelfth of each generation, until theology decided that it was not contrary to religion nor displeasing to God to prevent men from dying of the smallpox. The fate of useful and beneficial things is to experience all the obstacles that should be reserved for evil, but that it never encounters. Man is governed by so many

16. The reference is to the earthquake that struck Lisbon, Portugal, on November 1, 1755, killing more than 50,000 people and destroying most of the city's buildings.—HC

purposes! Despite these defenses and despite the unceasing impediments of superstition, interest, bad faith, and stupidity to the advancement of knowledge and the other advantages that result from it for the public good, we must hope that the wise method of inoculation, of which all nations now feel the most fortunate effects, will finally stop the ravages of that disease, until now so deadly for humanity.

From now on, we can therefore consider that scourge, which is believed to be one of the principal causes of depopulation in modern times, as less destructive; there will even be the impression in centuries to come that it lasted only an instant, if reason and experience gain ascendancy over prejudice and preconceived opinion. But did there otherwise exist such generalized diseases in ancient times? Leaving aside all the diseases mentioned in history, and that are almost unknown to modern medicine; was leprosy, with which God's people have always been afflicted, and for which a cure has never been found, less destructive? All things considered, the sum total of pleasure and of pain that nature has attached to our existence is the same at all times; the universe also remains constant as far as we are concerned; if it is not incorruptible, if there was a beginning, if there must be progression, a dying off, it is not to beings whose duration is so short and whose vision is so weak, that it is given to see these gradual transformations. The world has existed, as far as we are concerned, only for a day, and yet we would wish to make out these changes in this brief moment that encompasses history and tradition; can we assert that the world has even undergone any such change?

Everything is in balance in the universe: it is a whole that persists only by the agreement and the correspondence of all its parts. Nothing exists within it, even down to the faintest aroma, that is not necessary to it. The bodies it comprises maintain their states only through the relationship of their masses and their motions. These bodies are subject to particular laws that emanate from the general law that governs them, and according to which they are supposed or not supposed to produce beings that inhabit them. May we not assume that in keeping with these laws the number of such beings is determined directly according to their mutual need of each other and of the globes whose surface they inhabit? that their number could not measurably decline lest the constitution of the globes, and consequently the harmony which they must all enjoy to maintain the universal order, be altered by it.

> [To the Existence of the Spider, that of the Fly is absolutely necessary. The heedless Flight, weak Frame, and tender Body of this latter Insect, fit and determine him as much *a prey*, as the rough Make, Watchfulness, and Cunning of the former, fit him for Rapine, and the ensnaring part. The Web and Wing are suted to each other. And in the Structure of each of these Animals, there is as apparent and perfect a relation to the other, as in our own Bodys there is a relation of Limbs and Organs; or, as in the Branches or Leaves of a Tree, we see a relation of each to the other, and all, in common, to *one* Root and Trunk.
>
> In the same manner are Flies also necessary to the Existence of other Creatures, both Fowls and Fish. And thus are other Species or Kinds subservient to one another; as being *Parts* of *a certain System*, and included in one and the same *Order* of Beings.
>
> So that there is a System of all Animals; an *Animal-Order* or *Oeconomy*, according to which the animal Affairs are regulated and dispos'd.
>
> Now, if the whole System of Animals, together with that of Vegetables, and all other things in this inferior World, be properly comprehended in *one System* of a Globe or Earth: [. . .] then is it in reality a PART only of some other System. And if it be allow'd, that there is in like manner a SYSTEM *of all Things, and a Universal Nature;* there can be no particular Being or System which is not either good or ill in that *general one* of the *Universe:* For if it be insignificant and of no use, it is a Fault or Imperfection, and consequently ill in the general System. *Essai sur le mérite & la vertu.*[17]]

It follows from these principles that the population at large must have been constant, and that it will remain so to the end; that the total number of all men taken together today is equal to the total in whatever other era in ancient times one wishes to choose, and is equal to what the total will be in centuries to come; and that, finally, with the exception of those terrible

17. Damilaville cites Diderot's translation of Shaftesbury's "An Inquiry concerning virtue and merit": *Principes de la philosophie morale: ou, Essai de M. S***. sur le mérite et la vertu, avec réflexions* (Amsterdam: Chatelain, 1745). See Shaftesbury, *Characteristicks of Men, Manners, Opinions, Times*, 3 vols. (Indianapolis: Liberty Fund, 2001), 2:11, for the original, which we have reproduced here.—HC

events when scourges have sometimes devastated nations, if there have been times when a greater or lesser scarcity of human beings has been remarked upon, it is not that the totality of humans had been diminished, but because the *population* moved about, which caused local reductions.

[The role of these movements is well underscored by what happened when conquering peoples and warrior nations laid waste the earth; one saw the peoples of the south retreat well to the north, and return to resettle the homeland they had left, or other sites with more favorable climates, as soon as the violence and oppression had ceased. It is clear that at the time only one part of the world was being depopulated in favor of another; and if one studies the issue carefully, one will see that this is what happens in nearly all eras. Times of devastation certainly cause great losses to the species; but whereas the species suffers these losses in one part of the world, it multiplies in others, and even compensates its losses with growth in the areas that have been devastated, in the calm that follows the calamity. Men never feel the need they have of others as much as after a disaster when the shared misfortune brings men together and rouses among them the feeling of affection that is so favorable to propagation.]

All the reports of the historians of antiquity, based as they are on instances and particular cases, have little weight in the face of eternal and general laws; besides, are the facts that they adduce incontrovertible? Herodotus himself, who was an eyewitness of what went on in Egypt, and even of the embalmings which he described so incorrectly, says that he cannot vouch for a large part of what he writes. How to reconcile the observation of Thucydides, who remarked that the Greeks brought only 100,810 men to the siege of Troy, because they feared running out of rations in a foreign country, with those millions of armed men that Diodorus of Sicily attributes to Ninus and to Semiramis? Was it easier to provide subsistence to these multitudes than to the 100,810 Greeks who besieged Troy? One reads in Xenophon that the army of Artaxerxes (against which he fought with the Greeks), who had joined the army of the young Cyrus, comprised 1,200,000 men: nowhere does he say that he saw the army himself, but only that it was reported to reach that number; and in the history of the retreat of the ten thousand, one sees that they crossed several immense deserts that formed part of the Persian empire.[18] Now one cannot say that a kingdom where there are such vast uninhabited regions is abundantly populated.

In his enumeration of the inhabitants of Gaul, Caesar seems to be less far from the truth; about the same number of people would be found there today, in the same regions he covered in his enumeration. That must serve to show how much one should be wary of the information left to us by other historians of antiquity. Indeed, should we not consider that Diodorus of Sicily and the others were misled by erroneous calculations and exaggerated accounts? Who in the future will not believe he can warrant that, according to the calculations of Vossius and Hubner's geography, in the sixteenth century, Europe had only 30 million inhabitants, supported as this estimate is by the deposition of the famous Montesquieu?

Let us agree nevertheless, as mentioned earlier, that the more civilized ancient nations might have been more populous than in modern times; we can judge by the Greeks and the Romans, about whom there is greater certainty regarding their situation. Another thing is sure, and that is that the nations that today have replaced them as guardians of the arts and sciences are themselves less populous now than they were in earlier times.

The reason for this difference is obviously the changes that have come about in religions, in political governments, in politics in general, and mainly in the moral tradition: were the laws and the customs of ancient times thus more favorable to propagation than are ours?

Mohammedanism and Christianity, which replaced the pagan religions, certainly work against propagation; today that is a truth demonstrated in the experience of several centuries, and which is no longer contested by those in whom superstition has forever darkened the light of reason.[19]

The first of these religions permits polygamy, which the other religions forbade; but the religion at the same time ordains that one should satisfy all the wives that one would take; this is tantamount to permitting and proscribing at one and the same time. The first part of the precept is observed,

18. The references are to Xenophon, *Anabasis,* I.vii.11; Diodorus Siculus, *Library of History,* II.5.4 and II.17.1; Thucydides, *History of the Peloponnesian War,* I.x.4; Herodotus, *Histories,* bk. II.—HC

19. The argument that appears in the following three paragraphs is similar to Usbek's in Montesquieu, *Persian Letters,* letters 114 and 116.—HC

but that is impossible for the second. A prodigious number of women are shut up in seraglios, and with them there are as many eunuchs to keep and to serve them; there is no place on earth where so few children are born with so many people designated to produce them. Yet we are told that a sultan had as many as two hundred children. If that is a fact, and if all sultans did the same, very few women would remain unoccupied; but for every sultan who keeps two hundred wives, two hundred sultans each keep only one. One would really need to fail to recognize the range of our affection not to know that tastes are limited. One has two hundred wives because it fulfills the requirements of magnificence to have that number; but in the end one sleeps with only one of them.

The objective of populating the earth is not characteristic of Christianity; its true objective is to populate heaven; its dogmas are divine, and one must agree that this sainted religion would achieve that objective if belief were universal, and if natural urges were not unfortunately stronger than are all dogmatic opinions.

This religion proscribes divorce that the ancients allowed, and in this it becomes an obstacle to the purpose of marriage; add to this that the purity of its moral code reduces the act of procreation to the insipidity of a physical need, and that it rigorously condemns the attraction embodied in the sentiment that incites it, and you will conclude that beings who are shackled by such irons will hardly be inclined to engender others; besides, if one spouse is not fit to have children, the faculty of the other to be prolific remains nil and is a net loss to society.

[Leaving aside as always things religious and respectable, can we not say, along with a famous Englishman, that any perversion of values that leads to the destruction of a reasonable emotion, or to an unjustified emotion, has a nefarious influence, and that there are no grounds to excuse such depravity; and that no one should respect any dogma that would lead to such gross transgressions of natural laws?

The dogma of the immortality of the soul, which originated far earlier than the Christianity that sanctified it, could have been useful to humanity. Yet experience shows that it has always been pernicious for mankind. The work of Plato on this doctrine had such a prodigious effect on the high and ebullient spirit of Africans that its reading had to be prohibited to prevent their being moved to kill themselves. This proves that given the meaning this dogma has acquired among men, its only effect has been to flatter their conceit; it makes them ungrateful toward nature; they think that all that nature offers is despicable and that they should seek neither to keep nor to pass on. What possible interest could beings with such benighted ideas have in the preservation and propagation of a society in which they feel they are only passing through, who look upon this world as a vast caravansary from which they hie to depart? In their minds, providence will take care of everything, and they will not need to concern themselves with anything.

The doctrine of Foë, relates a Chinese philosopher according to Du Halde,[20] to whom we owe the citation, "establishes that our body is our home, and our soul the immortal hostess who resides there; but if the body of our fellow creature is only a lodging, it is natural to look upon it with the same contempt as we should feel toward a clump of earth. Is it not tantamount to implying a need to wrench from the heart the virtue of love for one's fellow man? It incites even to neglect a body's needs and to withhold the compassion and feelings that are so necessary to its preservation. In this way the disciples of Foë kill themselves by the thousands." And so do men from all other peoples who are too imbued with this idea also destroy themselves little by little.

Finally, it is because they believed in life after death that the slaves, subjects, and loved ones of Indians sacrificed themselves on their death to go and serve them in the other world. This custom still exists today among several peoples.

Let us not tire to recall all that is to the good in humanity according to writings approved by honest people:

> In any postulate on religion in which hope and fear are granted as the principal and primary motivations behind our actions, particularist interest which is naturally only too strong within us is untempered, and must consequently become stronger each day from the exercising of

20. The reference is to the Jesuit Jean-Baptiste Du Halde, *Description géographique, historique, chronologique, politique, et physique de l'empire de la China* (Paris: Lemercier, 1735). The work was translated into English in 1736 as *The General History of China*.—HC

> our passions. In matters of such importance one should thus beware lest such a servile emotion should eventually triumph, and should rule all the circumstances of life; that an emotion habitually driven by particular interest should not diminish love for the general good, the more so the stronger the self-interest; and finally that the heart and soul should not shrink: a shortcoming, according to what is said in moral philosophy, that is remarkable among zealots of all religious persuasions.[21]

Indeed, men conduct their affairs according to opinion. The daughters of Millet were prevented from killing themselves only when they were threatened with having their naked bodies exposed to the public after death. Thus if the received opinion gives men the hope of great personal gain, they will take no interest in the general welfare; what modern religions hold out for their future afterlife renders this world disgusting to them; working unceasingly against nature, these religions forever demand that nature be sacrificed in order for men to deserve the rewards that they have been promised. It is impossible to live without laxity toward one or other of these demands, often both at the same time, and without continually jeopardizing one's eternal happiness. Under these circumstances, the best thing to do is to die promptly. The most religious and the best father is the one who will do the least to enlarge his family, and to guarantee the survival and subsistence of his children. To what would they not expose them in the effort to economize on the days they live? Such ideas can lead men to such terrible passes that heresiarchs of a certain sect grabbed their children by one foot, and smashed their heads on a rock in order to safeguard them from damnation, and to assure their eternal felicity;[22] and the church cooperated with civilian law to stop this violent rage.

The great lawgivers knew how to make better use of the facility with which men adopt beliefs regarding everything they least understand. A prince whom Europe admires, whose range of genius and knowledge and whose love of truth and science, which he successfully cultivates, will make even more admired in future ages than his military victories—a true

21. See Shaftesbury, "An Inquiry concerning virtue and merit," in *Characteristicks,* 2:33–34.—HC

22. See Psalm 137:9 for one of many possible references.—HC

philosopher king—found the means to make the doctrine of future rewards and punishments useful to his administrative authority. He would punish desertion from his army by death only on the second offense; but the second time, he deprived deserters and those who abetted them of spiritual consolation, or refused confessors to Catholics, and ministers to those of other faiths. One would not believe to what degree the fear of dying without being reconciled with one's maker keeps soldiers dutiful and loyal. It was thus that a great man, forced to submit his genius to the circumstances of the century, obliged to make use of what was available, unable to do all the good of which he was capable, did at least accomplish all that was possible.[23]

The Persians were so numerous, says M. de Montesquieu (and their country so cultured, I might add), only because the religion of the magi taught that the act most pleasing to God was to bear a child, till the land, and plant a tree.[24]

The gymnosophists of India wanted two children to be left to replace their father and mother; they abstained from knowledge of their wives as soon as they had had two children; but these good philosophers did not notice that in order to raise two men to the age of marriage, much more than two children were needed. Their dogma prevented their contribution to the *population;* they were debtors both to the human species and to society.

European religious practices have even more contrary effects. They lead men to isolate themselves, to distance themselves from the duties of civilian life. For them, the most perfect state is the one furthest removed from nature, and the most prejudicial to public welfare: celibacy.[25] A multitude of beings of both sexes go and bury themselves and their lost posterity in places of retreat; not to mention the ministers of religion and the rigorists who vow never to lend themselves to the propagation of the species; and this abstinence is the epitome of virtue in these religions. As if the greatest vice was not to cheat nature, and to live at the expense of a

23. The reference is probably to Frederick II (the Great), king of Prussia and a favorite of Voltaire and other philosophes. He drafted elaborate instructions on the prevention of desertion.—HC

24. See Montesquieu, *Persian Letters,* letter 119.—HC

25. See Diderot's article CELIBACY, above.—HC

species toward which one fulfills no obligation. A man whose virtue, moral values, and learning are uncontestable, the Abbot of ****, being greatly affected by his sense of duty to nature, devoted one day of the week to propagation.

The policy of the Greeks and of the Romans on this subject was quite opposite to modern customs; they had laws providing penalties for those who wanted to withhold themselves from marriage; and the Greeks conferred honors on citizens who had produced yet others for the republic: those who were not married were marked for infamy; they were excluded by the laws of Lycurgus from certain ceremonies, were obliged to walk naked in the middle of the market in winter, and to sing a song of shame; young men were relieved from owing them the respect they had to show their elders: "You must not expect from me, while I am young, an honor that your children cannot give me when I am old," a young Lacedemonian said in a public gathering to Dercylidas, a powerful man whom he refused to salute because he was celibate.[26]

These nations grew in strength while tolerating any number of religious persuasions. When it was attempted to reduce them to one common faith in Rome, the power of the Romans was destroyed. This example has been repeated only too often. Some countries of Europe will perhaps never make up for the losses incurred by one of them with the expulsion of the Moors, and by another with the revocation of an edict.[27] There is no better proof of the extent of these losses, states the famous historian of the tsar Peter the Great, than the number of refugees in the regiment that was being assembled in Russia at the time by General Le Fort.[28]

In China, the belief is so strongly held that the tranquillity and prosperity of the state, and the happiness of the people, depend on an administration that is tolerant in religious matters, that in order to become a mandarin,

26. The reference is to Dercylidas, the Spartan commander of the late fifth and early fourth centuries B.C., noted also for his bachelorhood.—HC

27. The Spanish government expelled the Moors in 1492; the French government revoked the Edict of Nantes granting limited tolerance to the Huguenots in 1685.—HC

28. Voltaire, *History of the Russian Empire Under Peter the Great* [1759]; see *The Works of Voltaire,* ed. and trans. Tobias Smollett et al., 43 vols. (New York: E. R. Du Mont, 1901), 34:95–96. The French version that Damilaville would have used, *Histoire de l'empire de Russie sous Pierre le Grand,* was published in Geneva by Cramer in 1759.—HC

and therefore also a magistrate, it is an absolute condition not to be attached to any particular religion.

Among the ancients, magistrates were no less enlightened and believed similarly. They were careful to avoid any suggestion of religious exclusivity, and would not suffer any religious allegation of pre-eminence over other religions. In this way the ancient religions made people neither cruel nor intolerant. They promoted man's preservation rather than his destruction, they encouraged men to multiply instead of diverting them from that purpose. The horrors of the wars of religion were unknown to them. Among us, the violent passions of dogma, the mad zeal of wars in foreign lands caused the slaughter of millions.

Gelon reduced the Carthaginians to the humiliating necessity of asking him for peace; the only condition he imposed on them was that they should no longer immolate their own children.[29] When Alexander defeated the Bactrians, he made them stop killing their fathers in old age. The Spaniards discovered the Indies, conquered them, and all of a sudden an entire people was wiped from the face of the earth, and this act became the glory of the religion that allowed it to happen. Those are the facts, one need only compare and judge.

We know what it cost one European power when it tried to destroy religious sects by violence. Its provinces remained uninhabited; vain and irrational beliefs prompted the ruler to see the number of faithful increased, but carefully protected him from seeing that he had fewer and fewer subjects, as they fled in large numbers into neighboring countries, taking their wealth and their industry with them.[30] This prince, who was deceived by piety while he devastated his dominions, believed that he was pleasing the supreme being: he was told that he was executing the divine will. The same motivation led his predecessor to enact a law that made slaves of all the Negroes in his colonies. It pained him greatly to follow it; he was persuaded that it was the surest way to convert them, and he acquiesced in that conviction.[31]

29. Gelon (ca. 540–478 B.C.), tyrant of Gela and Syracuse in Sicily.—HC

30. This seems to be another reference to the Revocation of the Edict of Nantes.—HC

31. Montesquieu, in *The Spirit of the Laws,* 15.4, writes, "Louis XIII was acutely distressed by the law that made slaves of the Negroes in his colonies, but when it had been fully impressed upon him that this was the surest way to convert them, he agreed to it."—HC

This mania of having all men subscribe to one religious form, and of forcing them all to think in the same way about a matter that we do not master well enough to know the way to think, is a scourge whose horrors were unknown to humanity under paganism. The ancient religions were so far from inspiring such cruelty that in Athens an Areopagite[32] was punished for killing a sparrow pursued by a hawk that took refuge in his breast. A child who showed promise of a ferocious character, as judged by the pleasure with which he poked out a bird's eyes, was put to death.

Finally, this spiritual despotism that would even subjugate thought to its iron sceptre has yet the further terrible effect of eventually producing civilian despotism. He who thinks he can mould consciences loses no time in convincing himself that he is all-powerful. Men are too inclined to want to strengthen the authority they have over others; they seek too much to equal what they see as superior to them, to resist the example that fanaticism shows in the name of divinity. Thus it is that we see liberty struggling unceasingly against absolute power on the one hand, while it has totally succumbed to Mohammedanism on the other.

Another drawback of the new religions that jeopardizes the multiplication of the species no less than all the foregoing is that they separate men not only spiritually, but also corporeally. They raise barriers between them that every effort of reason fails to break down. One would think that they are not composed of beings of the same species, nor denizens of the same globe. Each religion, each sect forms a separate people who do not mix with the others; and in the end one must admit that they are products of their systems; since if they did mix, they would have beside them examples of vices and virtues, common to all sects, which would infallibly lead them to reduce the importance they accord to the opinions that divide them to the low level it justly deserves. In the meantime, nature, which has inspired only one rite in the hearts of men, would bring about the birth of two beings in proximity to each other who would soon mutually feel an impulse stronger than all the religious interests that keep them apart. An innocent and pure, but violent, passion would compel them, and they would soon ignore the absurdity of their differences. If the dogmatic zeal of their parents prevented their union,

32. A member of the learned tribunal of the Areopagus.—HC

they would detest them; and unhappy for all time, they would curse the opinions that made them victims: but no, the bent of nature would prevail, and they would have to be married. Then the children they raise would not properly belong to any sect, but they would be honest; their affection for men would not be limited to the little circle of people of the same religious community; they would love all their brothers in general. The moral values particular to these sects might well lose something in the process, but the universal moral code and the *population* would gain a great deal, and they are both of quite another level of importance. Far from condemning them, the magistrate should encourage such unions; but our laws are still too much the product of their religious origin for proposals about such advantages to be entertained.]

It would be difficult to identify among all possible forms of government, excluding despotism of course, the one form under which absolutely nothing would run counter to the multiplication of the species; all have their advantages and their disadvantages. A government whose institutions are incorruptible, and that forever assures the survival and happiness of the society and the individuals that compose it, as well as their tranquillity and their liberty, has yet to be found: it is a masterpiece to which the human spirit will never dare aspire, and that its own inconstancy makes impossible. [The laws of China are perhaps the only ones in which one can find as much stability; they must be very wise, since they have not been modified, despite all sorts of dominations which the Chinese have experienced: they passed them on to all the nations they conquered; those who subjugated them received them and submitted to them. Yet however fertile that vast country is, it is barely large enough sometimes to feed two thirds of its inhabitants. This example is unique; generally, abuse of all kinds, the passage of time that wears and destroys, revolutions that are too frequent among men, the addition or loss of knowledge—these things make all political laws as variable as the rest, and will always leave large problems to solve on this important question. Solon, who was asked whether the laws he gave the Athenians were the best, answered that he had given them the best of all the laws that were appropriate for them.[33]]

33. The story is told in Plutarch's *Life of Solon,* XV.2; it is repeated in Montesquieu, *Laws,* 19.21.—HC

One can observe, however, that at all times and in all climates, the human species has been more fruitful under popular and tolerant governments, which generally cannot be very extensive for constitutional reasons, and in which citizens enjoy a greater religious and civilian liberty. Great populations have never arisen in the large states; and it is for this reason that modern governments are less likely to produce them than were governments in earlier times.

In the vast empires of today, public administration has to go through too many channels: it is a tree whose branches spread out too far and are too numerous; the sap dries before it reaches the extremities from the body. It is impossible to monitor all the provinces and all parts; a multitude of intermediate agents must be relied upon, whose personal interest is always their first rule, and who each approach the execution of the same task in a different spirit. One can see only through their eyes, and act only under their ministration. The ruler knows his people, their situation, their needs, only so far as his administrators wish him to; and he is unfortunate enough always to be ignorant of the truth. Often in their turn the people know him only through the harassments they are subjected to in his name.

[The spirit of conquest which is ordinarily that of large monarchies, the large numbers of troops that must be maintained for defensive and for offensive purposes; the discrepancies between the social classes and even more so in personal wealth; the ostentation of the ruler and his court; trade, the weight of which is concentrated in countries that are far away, and that will be only artificial; an unruly access to luxury, and the moral corruption that follows: these are so many obstacles to growth of the population, to which must be added the consumption in large cities, and especially capitals, that absorb every year a portion of the men born in the provinces.

Greece, which everyone agrees was the most populated country of antiquity, was divided into many small republics whose citizens were equal and free; the administration could supervise all the parts of the state and maintain the laws in their integrity, because no part was too far from the center. All contributed to the public prosperity, because it was everyman's, because there was no personal prosperity that one could prefer, and because everyone gained equally. Useful actions and the provision of services to the homeland constituted virtues there; merit and knowledge alone differentiated men, and the public esteem was their principal reward, obviating the necessity to draw upon the treasury.

The Romans were not so remarkable at any time, nor as numerous, as in the glory days of the republic, when they governed themselves with similar principles. At that time Rome swarmed with heroes and great men; as soon as it wanted to expand, it was necessary to give foreigners and slaves the rights of citizens, in order to compensate for the daily losses to the Roman race. Through its conquests that still impress us today, Rome was preparing its downfall; its power was weakening in proportion to its growth in size; its moral austerity was lost through association with foreign moral values; the conquests provided the wealth; their riches became the equivalent and the measure of everything, replacing all honorable and gratifying distinctions; any virtue, any talent, any merit soon became the unique ambition of the soul; the spirit of patriotism dimmed; luxury was born and luxury lost the empire: the empire eventually succumbed under the weight of its own grandeur: it had invaded every country; it was no longer possible to govern all of them. All the losses the human species suffered in the general disorder that followed the downfall of that great giant are well known. Its own subjects, being too far from the laws and authority to recognize them and fear them, helped to dismantle it. If Rome was always populated as long as it was the seat of the empire, it was at the expense of all the provinces, which were further devastated by the predations, the greed, the ambition, and the tyranny of those intendants known as *proconsuls*.

In all times, the same causes have produced the same effects: it would appear that there is a term to the grandeur and survival of empires, as there is for all of man's undertakings, that is impossible to exceed.

From Constantine to the last emperor of Constantinople, the world was devastated by the violent fury of conquest, and by religious opinions; there has been no other time perhaps when these opinions have cost so many men to Europe and to Asia, as during that period.

The empire of Charlemagne lasted a shorter time than that of the Romans, but was proportionately as destructive to the human species. One is moved to pity when one considers all the suffering that religious fanaticism and the glory of conquest have inflicted on it. Entire nations have been slaughtered several times over, and the wretched survivors have dragged themselves deep into the north in search of asylum from massacres at the hands of heroes who offered the victims of their ambition to the heavens.

The enormous power of Charles V had even more deadly consequences for humanity: a well-known author says, speaking of the prosperity of that prince, "that a new world opened up for him."[34] It was an additional misfortune for the human species, since what he did with this new world was to render it desolate. While he was conquering so many nations far away, and while they were being exterminated with a degree of cruelty that inspires horror at the telling, his own nation was losing population, his provinces were revolting, and the grounds for the dismemberment of his empire were being laid. Spain subsequently exhausted its population of males in order to repopulate America and the West Indies, which can never be repopulated and which Spain had laid waste.]

We need say no more to prove that the spirit of great monarchies is contrary to the growth of large populations. It is under mild, limited governments, where the rights of humanity are respected, that men will become numerous.

Liberty is such a precious good that, unaccompanied by any other, it attracts men and brings about their multiplication. We know the extraordinary acts of courage that the desire to preserve liberty has inspired in all times. It is liberty that pulled Holland from the ocean's bosom, that turned its marshlands into some of the most populated districts of Europe, and that holds the ocean back within tighter limits. It is liberty that explains that Switzerland, which will be the last surviving power of Europe, provides men to all the European powers without exhausting itself, and despite land that does not repay cultivation, and that appears to be incapable of producing anything else.

There is no government under which the same advantages will be had. Tyranny makes slaves and deserts; liberty makes subjects and provinces: the less liberty is hampered by laws and by sovereign will, the less these laws will be transgressed, and the more the ruler will be assured of the loyalty and obedience of his people. It is when authority demands things that are contrary to natural law, and to the conventions of a society, that

34. See Montesquieu, *Laws,* 21.21.—HC

obedience is onerous and is not forthcoming; then one feels obliged to punish disobedience, authority substitutes for law, the loyalty of subjects is questioned, and in their turn, the subjects are suspicious of authority. All the ties that bound society together break down, arbitrary power prevails, and the love of king and country fades away.

Men are not born where only servitude awaits them; in such places they only destroy each other. Let us look at the fate of the lands of despots; in order for them to multiply, their liberty should depend only on laws, they should fear only those laws, and should know that by observing them, each citizen is protected from being deprived of his liberty.

[It should not happen that many parts of society can be offended; it is too easy to become guilty or to be suspected of being guilty, when it is so easy to offend the laws, the prince, and religion. Superstition, ignorance, particular hatred, envy, calumny, and interest are so many dangerous and ever-present threats to the liberty of a good man; and the more worthy he is, the more he will be exposed to such dangers, as being the most fearsome to petty souls. No sooner are the latter blamed for some bad habit or shortcoming than the laws, the prince, and religion are threatened; it is these three powerful entities that are being attacked in their persons, and they have an interest in avenging themselves. "A man committed libel against the ministers of a king of England, it is said he spoke ill of the government; he was sentenced to the pillory. The king happened by, and asked the reason for the punishment; he was told it. 'The fool,' said the king, 'had he committed libel against me, nothing would have happened to him.'"[35] How many times has authority been used in this way to serve personal animosity? And how much must these abuses, which leave citizens with only a precarious freedom at the mercy of whosoever wishes to attack them, cause men to disperse?

Fairness and gentleness in a government will always make men more numerous. Because of human nature, the opposite can push them to excesses that would make humanity shudder. The women in America had abortions lest their children be subjected to masters as cruel as the Spanish.

The Saxons submitted to slaughters several times over to defend the natural rights of which Charlemagne wished to deprive them. His son Louis I

35. The passage seems to be adapted from Montesquieu, *Laws,* 6.16.—HC

restored those rights to them, and that was the most noble act of his reign: the Saxons remained loyal to him thereafter.

Those who have said that the poorer subjects are, the larger their families; that the more they are taxed, the more they are able to raise the funds to pay them, have blasphemed against humankind and the homeland; they have revealed themselves to be the cruelest enemy of one and the other by artfully introducing rules of conduct that have always provoked, and will continue forever to provoke the destruction of men and the ruin of empires. They should be reduced to the wretched indigence in which they wanted their fellows to be, in order to teach them that they had committed an atrocity with their lies that perhaps called for even greater punishment. To what excesses do self-interest and ambition debase men, since the level of vileness and flattery to which they stoop can degrade human nature to the point of self-inflicted outrage. Oh Henry! it is against your children that these homicidal sentences have been pronounced! No one would have dared even whisper them in your ear; the murderers of your subjects would not have dared approach you![36]

Excessive taxes annihilate liberty, dampen emulation and all patriotic feelings, discourage men and prevent them from reproducing themselves; extreme poverty leads to despair; despair to dejection, dejection to sloth and to indifference toward every good.

Just as society has advantages from which all its members benefit, it has its burdens which it is only fair that they all bear. It is the duty of each citizen to provide his contribution in labor, and his share of the taxes that maintenance of the community demands; he who excuses himself from these two contributions is a bad citizen, a useless member and an additional burden to society, which should not be suffered under a good administration; but the taxes must be commensurate with the wealth of the country, and distributed in fair proportion to the particular earning capacity of each citizen. When the needs of the state exceed this proper proportion, levy becomes difficult and evil begins; when taxes are enormously dispropor-

36. This paragraph suggests a contrast between a virtuous Henry IV (r. 1589–1610), whose minister Sully was viewed as a model frugal administrator, and Cardinal Richelieu, Louis XIII's chief minister (1624–42) known to describe the poor in the disparaging terms used here.—HC

tionate, levy becomes impossible, and that is when public calamities begin; all the springs are pulled as far as they will go, and the machine is ready to break apart at the first touch.

The Franks found the Gauls in this situation when they conquered them.

> They recognized (says M. de Boulainvilliers) that excessive taxes were the cause of the downfall of the Roman empire; that the financial draining of the provinces made tax collection impossible. The harsh financial subsidization of the state overwhelmed the people without relieving the state's finances, rendered the countryside desolate, prevented the cultivation of the land, kept men in a perpetual limbo between the horrors of famine and the worthlessness of crops, and made their situation so wretched in the end that epidemics were hailed as a favor from heaven that sought to release the chosen ones from the general desolation of that century. The monetary subsidies were beyond the capacity of those from whom they were being demanded; the people were reduced to selling what they owned to pay them; the land could not produce enough, or the price fetched for fallow land was not enough. The people were reduced to despair and called for outside help, submitting themselves to foreign government, and they found themselves more fortunate under this new slavery than in the enjoyment of the false sense of freedom with which the Romans left them.[37]

The same circumstances account for the surprising ease with which the Muhammedans conquered the empire of Constantinople.

Thus it is that the level of taxation should always be regulated on the basis of the earning capacity of the people. If the needs demand considerably larger revenues, such needs would not be those of the state, but particularist needs, because the needs of the state can be none other than those of the people, or rather those required in their interest. And the people cannot have needs they cannot fulfill, or else how could they arise?

If the people cannot raise the income to support extraneous expenditures, they will not engage in war. They will not create institutions if, in

37. Henri, count of Boulainvilliers (1658–1722), the author of *L'Histoire de l'ancien gouvernement de la France* [History of the early government of France] (The Hague, 1727) and *Essais sur la noblesse de France* (Amsterdam, 1732), and a proponent of a nobility-centered theory of the origins of the French monarchy.—HC

order to do so, they must draw on their subsistence. They will be content to repair their houses, and will not erect superb buildings, if, in order to do so, they must build from the ruins of their homes. They will not underwrite the vice and indolence of a vile and ostentatious court; the magnificence of the throne will be the happiness of the people; there will be fewer slaves and more citizens; their needs will never reduce them to selling the right for others to oppress them in all manner of ways, and even in the name of *justice;* they will not keep troops except for their own safety and the security of their property. Being able to speak directly with divinity, they will not keep large paralytic bodies in their midst that consume subsistence, and give nothing in return. Again and finally, they will eliminate all those needs that are not the state's. When the needs of the state are those of the people, then they will provide the necessary revenues. The revenues will be moderate, and the state will be strong, agriculture and trade will flourish there, and men will be numerous there, since they will grow in number because of the well-being they enjoy.

The opposite will follow from the opposite: if taxation absorbs the yield of land and labor, or there is not enough left over to provide the subsistence of the worker and the craftsman, the fields will remain uncultivated and all work will cease: it is then that old men will be seen to die without regret, and young men will fear bearing children. Will people who do not know when they will next eat expose themselves to the risk of giving life to more wretched human beings, when the impossibility of feeding them will only increase their despair? Will a breast that has dried up from misery provide them with milk? Will a father weakened by want support them and feed them through their youth? He would have neither the strength nor the capability. Public wretchedness would remove all possibility of his finding work; and what beings would still be born into such distress? Weak and debilitated children that do not grow up; the temperament of those who escaped the consequences of their poor constitutions and the common diseases, manages to be ruined by the bad food they receive. Those creatures who are virtually dead, so to speak, before they have lived, are later quite unfit for propagation. In this way, where people are wretched, the species degenerates and destroys itself; where abundance is general, it increases in strength and in number. Nature and well-being invite individuals to reproduce themselves.

When I gaze on a countryside where the well-cultivated land is lush with an abundant harvest, I do not ask if this land is happy and populated; I learn that this must be so from the beauties that nature offers. My soul is moved, and is filled with sweet and unadulterated joy as I admire the treasures that nature offers innocent men, and for whom she makes fruitful both the labor and the race. I feel suffused with tenderness and gratitude; I bless her and I also bless the government under which those treasures can multiply both the species and nature's gifts.

If honors be necessary to a society, they are owed to virtuous and useful men who enrich it without corrupting it. There have been such men under the most organized and celebrated governments. Romulus permitted free men to exercise only two professions, arms and agriculture. Cato the elder cultivated the land, and wrote a treatise on it.[38] In his *Dialogue Between Socrates and Cristobulus*, Xenophon has the young Cyrus say to Lysander that he never dined but after having engaged in training for battle or some work on the land until his brow sweated.[39] In China, working the land is even more honored. The emperor ceremonially opens the land every year; he is told each year which farmer has most distinguished himself, and makes him a mandarin of the eighth order, but without provision for him to leave his land. Father Du Halde informs us that Venty, the third emperor of the third dynasty, cultivated his land with his own hands: in this way is China the most fertile and populous country on earth.[40] One can also read in M. de Montesquieu that among the ancient Persians, on the eighth day of the month, called *chorrentruz*, the kings left their opulence behind to go and eat with the people who worked the land.[41] What moves me in these customs is not the sterile honor that the sovereign bestowed on the largest and most useful proportion of his subjects; but the sweet, justified conviction that he truly appreciated the full importance of their station, and that he did not overtax it. How much these customs must have encouraged

38. Romulus, the legendary founder of Rome with Remus; Cato the Elder (234–149 B.C.), a leading figure in the cultural and political life of Rome; the treatise was *De Agri Cultura* (*On Agriculture*).—HC

39. The work referred to is Xenophon, *Oeconomicus,* IV.24.—HC

40. See Du Halde, *General History of China,* 69. See p. 316 for a profile of Kang vang, who was the third emperor of the third dynasty.—HC

41. Montesquieu, *Laws,* 14.8.—HC

agriculture and *population!* How much our customs today must have exactly the opposite effect!]

The differences created among men by the inequality of rank and fortune that has prevailed in modern politics, are among the most important causes of their probable decline in numbers. One of the greatest disadvantages of such a humiliation is that it must extinguish in them all the natural and reciprocal feelings of affection that would be needed. There are such discrepancies in their lots that when they consider persons in one status or another, they have difficulty believing that they all belong to the same species. We have seen men, forgetting that they were born in abject poverty and that they owed all their dignity only to conventions, degrade other men to the point of employing them at tasks that they would not have animals perform; and convince themselves that their fellow men did not experience good and evil in the same way they themselves did.

[It is this inordinate conceit, and the desire to have the authority one has over others perpetuated, that led to the notion of primogeniture, which runs counter to nature and to the public welfare. In Athens, the concentration of assets was so feared that in order to prevent a union that consolidated two inheritances in the same family, it was possible for a man to marry a half-sister by the same father, but not a half-sister by the same mother, since she could inherit another fortune from her father.

These laws against inequality of wealth led to the prosperity and the abundant population of the Greeks and the early Romans. All were citizens, because all were landowners. For it is property that makes the citizen; it is the land that attaches him to his homeland. In those days, the burdens and benefits of society were common to all its members. Each enjoyed similar wealth and contributed equally to the growth of population. The obstacles of luxury and the debauchery of opulence, of discouragement and the weakness of indigence, were absent. It is a bad citizen, Curius used to say, who looks upon the size of land large enough for the survival of a single man as insignificant.[42]

When all the riches of the nation are amassed and owned by a small number of people, it follows that the multitude is wretched, and the burden

42. The reference may be to Manius Curius Dentatus (d. 270 B.C.), Roman soldier and consul known for his frugality and incorruptibility.—HC

of taxes overwhelms them. Indeed what difference is there between everything that is essential to the unfortunate masses and taken from them, and only a slight part of the enormous surplus of which the few deprive the rest? Their vast possessions are even more nefarious to society; these possessions invade all properties; their lands produce little, and the little they produce, they now produce only for themselves, and their possessions are inhabited only by slaves, or by day laborers that they employ in the fields. These expanses of land that belong to one person could provide an infinite number of families with enough land for their subsistence from generation to generation, and those families expelled from the nation by the acquisitions of the wealthy could people the provinces with inhabitants and citizens of which the homeland is deprived. The land would be better cultivated and more fertile, because they always produce in proportion to the effort that is expended on them; and the owner who had only enough land to meet his needs and those of his family would spare no effort to increase its yield as much as possible. A mass of people spread over the state, working for their own good, would contribute to the general welfare that vast landed possessions destroy through the murderous abundance they produce, which will always be large enough for those few who reap the benefit from it not to seek to expand it, which in any case would require care of which they are incapable given the indolence in which they live.

Nor is it in this state of apathy that they will multiply the species: rich people have fewer children than do the poor. It is the only source of sweetness left to them among the ills that overwhelm them; it is natural that they seek it out and that they enjoy it as long as they are not in the extreme misery that makes them insensitive to it. The others, however, immersed in pleasures of all kinds where choice is the only embarrassment, abusing everything in bursts of excess that extenuate them, exhausting nature before it is formed, have squandered and lost the capacity to be a father before reaching the age of fatherhood. If they become fathers later, their children are frail and debilitated as are those of the poor, but from different causes. They carry the burden of the debauchery of their father, and the fragility of his exhaustion. Besides, the right of primogeniture that assigns the entire estate to one child, and that provides nothing for all the others, even if they are born with the same rights, will prevent their being born:

being able to have only one wealthy child, the father does not want several children. If he does have them, they are as so many enemies within the family; self-interest produces animosities that never fade, and that break the sacred bonds of blood: brothers deprived by a brother of the affluence to which they have become accustomed in their paternal home, see in him only a thief who oppresses them, and who strips them of material goods to which they had had a common right. The oldest alone chooses the state of matrimony; the others, attracted by the leisure and the ease with which one can enrich oneself without trouble, toil, or labor, choose the ecclesiastical state. If they cannot attain it, then they go to live even more uselessly in cloisters, or they remain bachelors. The asylums to which the girls must repair are premature sepultures. Unnatural parents sacrifice more than the life of their children for the hubris of their eldest one. In the countries where this barbaric right has not been enacted, people go so far in their cruel designs as to use violence for lack of corruption in order to provide the idol of their vanity with the advantages that the law does not bestow on him.

Such are the consequences of inequality, and principally the inequality of fortunes under modern policies that are prejudicial to propagation. Such is also the utility, so touted by its advocates, of the deadly seclusion of children into which greed, ambition, and cruelty drag their victims, swallowing up their posterity.

The knowledgeable Mr. Hume, an English philosopher, in an essay on population that was full of learning, compares this custom of locking girls up in convents with the ancient custom of exposing children and gives many reasons to prefer the latter custom. Indeed, all the exposed children do not die; some are adopted, and the greatest number were not lost to nature and to society. In the former case, on the other hand, they are all lost to nature and to society.[43]

The law of Solon, which allowed children to be put to death, demonstrates far more ingeniousness and humanity. That great man, a philosopher and a legislator, sensed that it would be rare for a father to take the initiative to do what the law allowed him to; he considered that the option

43. Hume, "Of the Populousness," in *Essays,* 398–400, where the argument seems somewhat more complex than Damilaville suggests.—HC

to abandon or bury children alive might more often be chosen than to slaughter them.

Nature has only two great goals, the preservation of the individual and the propagation of the species. Now if it is true that everything promotes either life itself or the giving of life, if it is true that we were given life only to pass it on, we must agree that any institution that distances us from that goal is not a good one, and that it runs counter to the natural order.

Similarly, if it is true that all the members of a society must conspire and concur in the general welfare; if the best policy laws are those that leave no citizen and no worker idle in the republic, that will bring about a circulation of the wealth and that will know how to ensure that the society's momentum enhances things public, like so many springs providing energy for maintenance and prosperity, then we must agree that the establishments that remove a large part of its citizens from the state, that encroach on its wealth, without restoring them in kind or in value, are pernicious institutions that must undermine the state and eventually cause its ruin.

Our ancestors (said an emperor of the Tang family, in an ordinance that is cited in the work of Father Du Halde) lived by the principle that if there was one man who did not work, one woman who did not spin, somebody suffered from cold and hunger in the empire, and on this basis he ordered the destruction of countless fakir monasteries.

That principle will always be held by wise and well-ordered governments. These great bodies of single people produce a depopulation that is worsened beyond the fact that they abstain from giving nature her due and that they deprive society of citizens; it also follows from the rules of conduct that they follow, from their wealth and from the immense stretches of land that they own.

The wealth in mortmain, of the people who join the bodies and of these bodies in general, whose acquisitions take on a sacred character and become inalienable, is of no more use to the state than is a safe to a miser who only ever opens it to put something in.

A contemporary author, who is estimable otherwise if one judges by his intentions toward humanity, has advanced that the great landed estates of monks are the most successfully cultivated, because being rich, they can afford the expense, and in this at least they are useful to the state.

As if it were not enough to ignore and deceive nature's will in order to be devoid of all material goods, we saw from the foregoing on the disadvantages of large properties, that the author of the theory of taxation was wrong, and that in this matter as in all others, these establishments are such a burden to society that if one is not careful, they will manage in the end to destroy and invade all other assets.[44] Magistrates and public ministries have more than once had to put a rein on this cupidity.

Would it not be a greater benefit to the commonwealth that these vast lands provide as many families with work and a livelihood as they maintain single citizens and isolated individuals in idle leisure? I ask this of all right-minded people who are not superstitious, and I do not fear an answer in the negative. It is not necessary to repeat that these lands would be even better tended than they are now; again, the less one possesses, the more one seeks to enjoy its full value; and the land that will be the most productive is the land whose entire product is sufficient and essential to meet the needs of its owner and those of his family.

It is clear that as a result of this redistribution to citizens who are hardworking of the assets of those who are not, the society would grow in numbers; the financial responsibilities of the state would be shared by a larger number of people, and would be less onerous for each person; the state would be richer and individuals would be less oppressed.

All these effects are proved, and the evidence is before our eyes: there is no Protestant prince, says the author of *The Spirit of the Laws,* who does not levy many more taxes from his people than the sovereign pontiff levies from his subjects; and yet the latter are poor, whereas the former live in opulence; trade enlivens the economy in the first case, and monasticism brings death everywhere in the second.[45]

In the land of people of mortmain, the ministers of the national religious persuasion never furnish the state with anything; whatever they do

44. The author here criticizes the Physiocratic argument of Victor de Riquetti, Marquis de Mirabeau (1715–89), *Théorie de l'impôt* (Theory of taxation; n.p., [1761]), in favor of large landed estates. His first and most famous work was *L'Ami des hommes* [Friend of mankind] (1756). See Cereals by Quesnay, in this volume, for a sample of Physiocratic thinking.—HC

45. The reference is to Montesquieu, *Persian Letters,* letter 117.—HC

give the state, they had taken from it in the first place. It is not from their own funds that they pay the subsidies that they bestow, it is from those they borrow from other citizens; so that, aside from having to acquit themselves of their own personal taxes, the citizens support the taxes of these others through loans they provide for their payment; all tribute is always drawn from the same portion of wealth which is circulating between other classes of the society. The wealth of this other singular body which is largest by far remains untapped and increases continually rather than diminishing; in this way, with time it must totally absorb the entire wealth of the republic.

It is easy to see how this abuse influences the growth of population; everything is connected in politics, everything is related to everything else, just as in moral philosophy and in physics. If these people did not borrow from other citizens, the funds they drew from their own fortune to pay what they owe would be circulated into society. The funds they borrow would remain there nonetheless; some in circulation would benefit agriculture, some trade, some industry; and without agriculture, without trade, and without industry, there is no growth in *population*.

Our military institutions have the same drawbacks, and have a no less contrary influence on propagation than those we have discussed above. Our armies do not multiply themselves, they drain the population as much in peacetime as during war; our rules of conduct during war are less destructive, it is true, than were those of earlier times; that is to say, the manner of conducting war, the fighting, the pillage, and the massacres, which are far less frequent; but it would be self-deluding to believe that on that count alone our customs are any less destructive than were those of earlier times.

Our tactics, which spread troops out over a larger territory; the use of artillery and musketry, which more quickly determines the outcome of a battle—these things make battles less deadly than they once were. We lose fewer men in armed warfare, but more of them die through misery and exhaustion to which our troops are not accustomed.

The losses caused by ancient wars were greater, but momentary; ours are constant and continual.

Those armies were composed of citizens who cost the state nothing, or very little. They were married; they had assets in the republic and returned home after the war. Our armies are standing armies, even in peacetime;

their maintenance incurs surcharge taxes, which reduce the people who support them to a state of wretchedness, and thus remove them from conditions that favor propagation. They are composed of mercenaries, whose only asset is their soldier's pay; they are prevented from marrying, and that is reasonable. Who would feed their wives and children? Their pay is not enough for their own survival; they are a multitude of bachelors that perpetually exist, that do not reproduce, that must continually be renewed with more bachelors that are removed from the reproducing population; it is a monstrous form of anthropophagy that devours a portion of the human species in each generation. We must agree that we have some strange opinions and contradictions; we think it is barbarous to mutilate men in order to make singers of them, and that is right;[46] however, we do not think it so to castrate men in order to make homicides of them.

It is the desire to dominate; it is ostentation, luxury, and vanity, more than the security of states, that caused the introduction into Europe of the custom of preserving even in peacetime these multitudes of armed men who are useless, who ruin peoples, and who also exhaust the powers that maintain them of their men and wealth. The more people there are to command, the more titles there are; the more titles there are, the more dependents and courtiers there are to obtain them. No power has made gains in its security through the increase in costs that it has caused for itself. All of them have increased their troops in proportion to the troops their neighbors have kept on active duty. The armed forces are all at the same level, as they were before; the state that was protected with fifty thousand men is not better protected with 200,000 today, because the forces against which they sought to protect themselves were increased to the same level. The advantages of greater security, which were the excuse for this increased expenditure, are thus reduced to zero; only the expenditure and the depopulation remain.

Nothing compensates society for these expenditures; while Europe is quiet, the troops are held in a state of inaction that is deadly for them once war erupts. Being unused to working, they become enervated, and the least fatigue to which they are later subjected destroys them.

46. The reference is to the Italian *castrati*.—HC

The Roman armies were not maintained in this way, and were not susceptible to the same erosion. No sooner had they returned victorious than they engaged in large public works that were useful to the public good, and that have immortalized that nation as much as its victories have made it illustrious. The magnificence of those famous Ways that the Roman armies built during peacetime is well-known. And so it was that the strain that the Roman soldiers could endure in war seems today prodigious and almost unbelievable. It is surprising that we do not try to extract the same benefits from our armies, when there are so many ways in which they could be useful and perform work that could at least compensate for their sterility. The cruelest servitude of workers is the time they must provide corvée labor; this is a constant plague for them. It deters them from the cultivation of the soil, and often the animals that they must provide for the work die in the process, but there is no indemnity for them. They would be freed from this subjection, the lot of soldiers would be improved, they would be stronger and better able to withstand the strains they are destined to endure, if one engaged by turn a part of the troops each year to build the roads that the inhabitants of the countryside are forced to do in the gangs that cost them so dearly. If they could be excused from the task, there is not a man who would not make a small contribution to increase the soldier's pay, to make their subsistence easier, to keep them working, and to relieve the people of a burden under which they are groaning. It is said that this work would bend the backs of soldiers and deform them; I do not know if that is true, but apparently the Romans could be trim and fight bravely, even if they were deformed.]

Armies that are too large bring about depopulation; conditions in the colonies also bring it about. These two causes have the same origin, the spirit of conquest and of expansionism. It is never so true that this spirit ruins conquerors as much as it does the conquered as it is in the case of colonies.

It is said that manufacturing should not be envisaged until all the arable land is under cultivation, and that is a truth; colonies should be envisaged only when there is overpopulation and not enough territory. Since the establishment of Europe's colonies, the European powers have continually had to lose population in order to populate them, and there are still few inhabited colonies—if one excepts Pennsylvania, which was fortunate enough to have a philosopher as legislator, colonists who never take arms, and an administration that welcomes men of any religion as long as they submit to the rule of law.[47] Innumerable men have gone to the established colonies, whereas one can quickly count the number who have returned. The difference in climates, in staples, in the dangers and diseases of the journey, countless other causes make men perish. What advantages have there been for the *population* of America from the prodigious number of Negroes that were continually transported there from Africa? They all died; it is sad to admit that this was as much from the odious treatment they were subjected to, and the inhuman work they are put to, as by the change in temperature and food. Again, what did the Spaniards not do to repopulate the West Indies and America that they had made desolate? These regions are still deserted, and Spain itself has become desolate: its people extract gold from deep mines for us, and they die there. The more we amass gold in Europe, the more Spain will become a desert; the longer Portugal is poor, the longer it will remain an English province, without anybody being the richer for it.

Any place that men can live, it is rare to see none. When a country is uninhabited without there having been violence or force used to make people abandon it, it is a fairly sure sign that the climate or the land is not favorable to the human species. Why transplant it and expose it to certain death? Is man so insignificant that he should be subjected to the same risks as we might subject a young tree in a hostile terrain to test the quality of the soil? [The Romans, according to Tacitus, sent to Sardinia only criminals and Jews about whom they cared very little.[48]]

If the country one wants to take possession of is populated, it belongs to the people who inhabit it. Why strip them of it? What right did the Spaniards have to exterminate the inhabitants of such a large part of the earth? Where is our right to go rout people off the territory they occupy on this globe which they share with us? Isn't their possession of that territory the first right of property, and the most incontestable right? Do we know of any property rights that originate otherwise? We would reclaim our land if someone were to wrench it from us, and yet we deprive others of their possessions without scruple.

47. The allusion is to William Penn (1644–1718), English Quaker who founded the American colony.—HC

48. See Tacitus, *Annals*, II.85, for this episode.—HC

If only we had invaded their territory alone; but we made those inhabitants, and even the savages, espouse our hatreds. We brought them several of our vices and spirituous liquors that have destroyed them down to their posterity. These truths are countered with political exigencies; the interests of trade are especially brought into play. But are these principles wise, and is that trade as profitable as one thinks? [Switzerland, which will become as I said the most enduring government of Europe, is also the most populous and the least mercantile.

M. de Montesquieu reports that when the great Shah Abbas, wanting to stop the Turks from maintaining their armies on the border, transported nearly all the Armenians out of their country, he sent more than twenty thousand of their families into the province of Guilan, who almost all died in a short time.[49] Such is the effect produced by colonies. Far from increasing strength, they weaken it by dividing power; their armies need to be divided in order to preserve them, and how can conquests be defended and maintained from one continent to another? If the colonies are fruitful, a time comes when they want to free themselves, and remove themselves from the power that established them.

None of the populated nations of antiquity had similar institutions. The Greeks, according to Herodotus's account, knew nothing beyond the columns of Hercules. Their colonies do not merit the name if one compares them with ours; they were all, so to speak, within the field of vision of the metropolis, and so close by that they should rather be considered as extensions than as colonies. The Carthaginians discovered the coast of America. They noticed that the trade being carried out there was depopulating the republic, and so they outlawed it.[50]

These examples strongly challenge assumptions of the so-called advantages of these institutions and of trade that incites their creation. But maybe it is impossible to trade with nations without laying them waste, without depriving them of their country and of their liberty? If this is indeed so, far from being useful to men by allowing communication between them, trade would be one of the most nefarious of inventions for humanity! The

49. Montesquieu, *Persian Letters*, letter 121.—HC

50. For this story, see Aristotle, *On Marvellous Things Heard*, 84.—HC

way trade is now, it certainly contributes a great deal to depopulation. The wealth it procures, assuming that it is real, may have even more pernicious effects. We will examine them here only insofar as they relate to the growth or the decline in numbers of men. In fact, this means looking at the universality of their effects. Because what institution, what tradition, what custom does not influence these two phenomena?

One reads in the first volume of Father Du Halde's *Histoire de la Chine* that the third emperor of the twenty-first dynasty ordered the closing of a mine that produced precious stones, not wanting his subjects to tire themselves out working at something that could neither clothe nor feed them.[51] In this regard, I cannot resist recalling some words from the wise Locke: he said "that one should always preach our religion to the savages; that if they learned from it only as much as they needed to cover their bodies with clothing, it would at least do some good for the textile manufacturers of England." A colony is detrimental when it does not increase the industry and work of the nation that owns it.

Our travels in far-off countries where we go to fetch objects more or less akin to shiny stones, are much more destructive than would have been the work in the mine. Everything that keeps man away from man works against multiplication. The numerous carriage teams required to transport armaments overseas removes each year a considerable number of men from contact with women. A number of them perish from the long and arduous journey, the hardship, and disease. Others remain overseas, and it never happens that a vessel returns to Europe with as many people as it had when it left; the losses of each ship can even be estimated before its departure. But that is the least of the losses caused for humanity by the kind of trade to which we are most attached.

The more trade flourishes in a state, so it is said, the more men multiply there. This proposition does not apply to all cases. Nowhere did men multiply as much as in Greece, and the Greeks traded little. Nowhere do they multiply as much as in Switzerland, and the Swiss, as we noted earlier, are not at all mercantile. But it is also true, moreover, that the more men there are in a state, the more trade flourishes; it must therefore not destroy men,

51. See Du Halde, *The General History of China,* 455, for this episode.—HC

or else it would destroy itself, and that happens when it is not based on the natural foundation it should have. Let us add that in order to be really useful and favorable to *population,* trade must be proportional to and even depend on the country's production. It should stimulate agriculture and not cause its neglect; production should be the cause of trade and not an accessory to it; then we will have established, I believe, the true principles of trade for the nations whose soil produces tradable commodities.

These principles are not those that prevail in the majority of nations. Since the discovery of the New World and our settlements in the West Indies, all attention has focused on the riches contained in these lands; we have come to trade only in luxury and superfluity. We have abandoned the trade that was fitting for us, which could have brought us solid treasures.[52] What advantages have come from this? Where do we not instead see the harm it has wrought upon us?

By multiplying our needs, far beyond the means we have to satisfy them, all the riches drawn from all these parts of the world have made us three times poorer than we were before. A simple comparison of numerical values is enough to convince us: with twice as much gold and silver as we had before, prices are more than doubled. Is it usually the effect of abundance to increase the price of foodstuffs? Despite the greater amount, abundant specie is more scarce, since we were forced to have recourse to increasing its price; and whence does this scarcity come, if not from the fact that the quantity of wealth is far from enough to meet the need for it that has been fostered in us?

In general, any wealth that is not based on the industry of the nation, on the number of inhabitants, and on its agriculture, is illusory, detrimental, and never beneficial.

All the treasures of the New World and the West Indies did not prevent Philip II from declaring his famous bankruptcy.[53] With the same mines as Spain has today, it is depopulated, and its land lies fallow. The survival of Portugal depends on the English; the gold and the diamonds of Brazil have

52. For the contrast between a "commerce of economy" and a "commerce of luxury," see Montesquieu, *Laws,* 20.4–6.—HC

53. Philip II, king of Spain (1555–98), declared bankruptcy several times, the last in 1596.—HC

turned it into the most arid country, one of the least inhabited in Europe. Italy, which was once so fertile and so populous, no longer is since the commerce of luxury and foreign goods has replaced agriculture and its traffic in domestic foodstuffs.

In France, these effects are remarkable: since the beginning of the last century, this kingdom has grown by several large and populated provinces;[54] however, its inhabitants are less numerous by a fifth than they were before they were brought together, and its beautiful provinces, which nature seems to have destined to provide all of Europe with its food, are uncultivated. This decline must in part be attributed to the preference given to luxury trade. Sully, that great and wise administrator, knew of no beneficial trade for the kingdom, other than the trade in produce from its soil. He wanted to people and enrich the land by favoring agriculture: and that is in fact what happened under his ministry, which was too short for the fortune of the nation. It appears that he predicted all the harm that would occur there one day as a result of an opposing set of principles. "France," he said in 1603 to Henri IV, who was pressing him to applaud the establishments he planned to develop out of a few silk manufactures,

> France is generally better endowed than any kingdom in the world with so much good land that it can render productive, whose yield in cereals, vegetables, wines, forage, oils, ciders, salts, linens, hemps, wools, sheeting, swine, and mules is the cause of all the gold and silver that enters the kingdom. Consequently, the cultivation of these products, which keeps subjects in the wearisome and laborious occupations that they must exercise, is worth more than all the silks and manufactures of rich cloth that would make them acquire the habit of a meditative, leisurely and sedentary life, that would propel them into luxury, voluptuousness, idleness, and excessive spending, that have always been the principal cause of the downfall of kingdoms and republics, making them devoid of loyal, valiant, and courageous citizens, which Your Majesty needs more than all those gold- and crimson-clad snobs and braggarts of court and city. If for the time being [he added] you disdain these reasons, perhaps one day

54. The reference is to the provinces of Foix (1607), Béarn and Navarre (1620), Alsace (1648), Artois, Roussillon, and Cerdagne (1659), Franche-Comté and Flanders (1678–79).—HC

you may regret that you did not give them greater consideration. *Mém. de Sully, tom. I, pag. 180 & 181 de l'édition in-folio.*[55]

In addition to these inconveniences,] trade in luxury and related arts is dangerously seductive, as it offers men more benefits and less hardship than they find in farming. Who will toil to plow and furrow? Who with bent back from sunrise to sunset will cultivate the vines, harvest the fields, withstand the heat of summer and the rigor of winter while engaging in such hard labor when, quiet and sedentary, one could remain sheltered from the seasons spinning silk or doing something else in luxury manufacturing all day and earn more doing so? And so it is that these industries and this trade have attracted men into the cities, giving the cities an appearance of abundant growth in *population;* but go deep into the countryside and you will see that it is deserted and arid. As the fruit of the country is not the object of trade, only the amount of produce that is essential for local subsistence will be grown; there will only be the number of men necessary to provide that amount; for they do not multiply beyond that ratio.

It is thus that luxury trade depopulates the countryside and populates the cities; but that is only accidental. This *population,* as well as the wealth deriving from the trade, is precarious and dependent on events. The slightest circumstance makes it disappear; war, the establishment of competing manufacture, even the transportation of your products into other states, shortfalls in needed inputs, countless other causes can eliminate this trade, and bring the manufacturing to a halt. And then an entire people that has been removed from the cultivation of land becomes idle; they cannot make a livelihood, and the states must feed them. Suddenly there are many families begging for their daily bread, or leaving their country to search abroad for work that can no longer be provided for them. These men, who are now a burden to society, could have enriched it and populated it, if they had not been turned away from their true calling. They had a little property, which kept them attached to the land, and that made them citizens; by becoming simple day-laborers, they have ceased being patriots, because he who owns

55. Sully, *Mémoires de Maximilien de Béthune, duc de Sully* (London, 1747); the comments were made for the year 1603.—HC

nothing has no homeland; he takes his labor and his industry everywhere with him, and he settles where he finds a livelihood. This is how one ends up without trade, without wealth, and without people, because the true cause of these things has been neglected and abandoned.

[Another minister, whose administration was otherwise admirable, gave his full endorsement to opulence and none to utility; sacrificed real wealth to artificial wealth when he prohibited the export of grain from France, in order to favor the establishment of luxury manufacturing: it was a death sentence for agriculture and for the growth of *population.*[56]

With quite other institutions whose wisdom has quite opposite effects, the English had the wit to take over the treasure that a foreign minister was sacrificing for the wealth of vanity. That people seems to be made to give others a good example in all sorts of ways. By making basic needs the primary trading commodities, England has become the arbiter for Europe, the greatest sea power, the best-cultivated and most fertile homeland, and the largest trading nation.

Trade produces wealth, and wealth produces luxury; the arts and sciences are born from wealth and luxury. One can conclude that without luxury there is no trade, no wealth, no arts, no sciences; but that is a specious argument based on mistaking the effects of trade for its causes, making one conclude that the only thing that can give rise to arts and sciences is luxury, which is untrue.

There is no nation where arts and sciences flourished as much as among the Greeks, and their trade consisted only of exchanges of basic foodstuffs. *See* Thucydides, Isocrates, Demosthenes, Suidas and Heliodorus, whom he cites;[57] *see also* Xenophon and Plutarch. They will tell you that since the time of Solon, Greece was rich without this trade in superfluities. The arts and sciences are still very refined in China, and the Chinese do not leave their country to trade with foreigners.

56. The allusion is to Jean-Baptiste Colbert (1619–83), leading royal official for more than twenty years under Louis XIV.—HC

57. Thucydides (ca. 460–ca. 395 B.C.), Greek historian; Isocrates (ca. 436–338 B.C.) and Demosthenes (384–322 B.C.), Athenian orators; Heliodorus of Athens, who wrote on the Acropolis in the middle of the second century B.C.; Suidas or Suda, tenth-century Byzantine author of a historical encyclopedia.—HC

This is not the place to examine how far luxury can be necessary to sustain trade, and how far trade can concern luxury goods before it corrupts morals, or harms agriculture and the growth of *population.* It advances so quickly that it is difficult to preset limits; its effects are immediately intemperate, and they begin at that point to destroy the human species. The indolence, dependency, dissolution, futility, and excesses of all kinds into which it propels the opulent, ruin their physical capabilities as much as their moral qualities. It is not in order to become a father that one has forsaken the ability to be one; on the contrary, it is an outrage to nature to yield to one's urges, and what we should fear most is to give life while abusing the power to give life, which nature bestowed on us for that sole purpose.

It is luxury that keeps a mass of people in the service of one person—languishing in idle leisure, at loose ends, propelling themselves from sheer boredom and desultoriness into all sorts of debauches and perversities that are as deadly to propagation as the sought-after pleasures are to their masters. He goes far into the countryside to steal them away from useful production, and to use them up. A man who can occupy only one place wants to own immense lands that he will never inhabit; nothing is opulent enough for his taste in luxury; and as if he feared running out of space enough for himself, he drives away all those around him. Superintendent Fouquet bought three entire hamlets, and folded all that land into the gardens of his palace of Vaux. (*See tome VII of the Essai sur l'histoire générale*, by M. de Voltaire.) As the disruptions due to luxury multiply in all states, this murderous consolidation of land becomes almost customary. Countless people whose station is far below the Superintendent's follow suit and even outdo him. Newly acquired land, whatever its size (and size is no object), is immediately depopulated. New lords have been seen to become the sole owners of their entire parishes, expel all the inhabitants by buying their meager property at a high price, and take over all the land that these farmers rendered productive for the benefit of all society, in order to use it only to display an opulence that is insulting to this unfortunate people. But it is also through the same excesses that intemperate luxury leads from extreme opulence to extreme poverty, and that it also destroys the public welfare and the human species. Those who ruined the state, who wiped out the causes of its prosperity with exorbitant expenditures, become a burden to society when they fall into excessive wretchedness and drag down with them a mass of craftsmen and laborers who had provided their opulence, when they are no longer able to support them. They were bad citizens when wealthy, and they are even worse in poverty. According to Sallust, one saw in Rome a generation of men who could no longer preserve their own patrimonies nor allow others to preserve theirs.[58]

The multitude of beggars with which Europe has been flooded for several centuries and whose dissolute wandering existence is so contrary to the growth of *population* should perhaps be attributed to the pernicious effects of luxury. Luxury, as we have already said, destroys itself; it consumes itself; the exhaustion of wealth that it brings about becomes general and all the work it sustained ceases. Those who lived from this work remain without subsistence and without the means to provide it. Their inactivity leads to idleness, beggary, and all the vices that go with such an existence. The establishment of poorhouses, which can be regarded as a consequence of these effects, may have promoted the tendency that vile souls have to embrace the type of life that allows them to subsist in licentiousness, without greater sanction than the compulsion to beg. A sovereign was asked why he was not building poorhouses, to which he answered: "I will make my empire so rich that it will not need them." He should have added, "and my people so affluent from useful and productive work, that they will not need such relief."[59] A physician has even said that poorhouses are only good for physicians, because it is there that they sacrifice the poor to save the rich. If instead of being used to feed a mass of people in idle misery, the incomes allocated to these establishments were used for public works, on which each would occupy himself according to his strength and the ability he still has, there would certainly be fewer poor people. The poorhouses invite them to indolence, by guaranteeing them wherewithal when alms fall short, and for this reason they contribute to an increase in their numbers.

The question has been asked whether foundling homes do not have the same disadvantages, and whether rather than being favorable to the growth in *population,* they do not have the contrary effect, given that the facility

58. Sallust (86–34 B.C.), *The Histories,* 1.13 or 1.16, depending on the edition.—HC

59. The emperor referred to is Aureng-Zeb, Mughal ruler of India from 1658 to 1707, and the story is told in Montesquieu, *Laws,* 23.29. See also POORHOUSE, in this volume.—HC

with which they take the fruits of debauchery could encourage it. If moral values were not entirely corrupt, it would be a good thing to take into these homes only the legitimate children of parents who are virtuous, but too poor to raise them. But that institution was only created, just like all other institutions of the same type, when the evil had reached the greatest degree. At that point it is not dissolution that one wants to curb, it is too late for that; it is the even greater evils that begin to make themselves felt, and that one wants to prevent. Given the present state of moral values, it might be dangerous to undertake any reform in the administration of foundling homes. Libertine behavior would not cease simply because the children produced by it are refused, and at least they are preserved for humanity and for society; such a severe change could be criminal, and it would create a greater evil than the one we would have destroyed.]

It is mainly in cities, and especially in the capitals of the great empires, that the depravation of moral values is so excessive that the human species suffers from a measurable decline in numbers. They are colonies of a sort for the provinces that have each year to replenish their populations. In Rome, the population needed continually to be renewed with slaves. It is the same today in Constantinople; Paris, London, and the other European seats of monarchy demand considerable numbers of recruits. They are so many abysses that swallow up gold and the inhabitants of the provinces. One might say that the opulence of their appearance and the magnificence of the monuments they show off are composed of the debris of the countryside; but a man who would judge the wealth of a people by the brilliance of its capital is like one who would judge the fortune of a merchant by the richness of his clothes. Those who enjoy the opulence one sees in the city, and abuse it, die there and cannot reproduce themselves, because of the intemperance, the idle leisure, the heedlessness, the abnegation of all duty, the distance from productive work, the indifference toward all that is honest, the sumptuous and refined foods, and finally their indulgence of all the pleasures and their revolt against all the passions with which they live. Others do so because of the dangerous work they undertake and their sloth, indigence, and bad diet, which have effects contrary to *population*. The prodigious number of domestic servants that luxury assembles in these cities alone consumes a large quantity of the men in each generation. They are prevented from marrying, and they lose their position if they do. In this way, the only resource nature has in them is debauchery, the means most contrary to procreation. One might think that all modern customs are established to foil nature—which brings to mind the authors who have written, concerning the present growth of *population* and that of past centuries, that the practice of domestic slavery in earlier times was more favorable to the multiplication of the species than are the present circumstances of servants and the methods of providing assistance to the poor.

[It can make one think one is fit to act the master when one reasons so. On the opposite assumption, one would never fail to remember that no one has the right to acquire ownership of another individual; that liberty is an inalienable property of existence which can neither be sold nor bought; that the conditions of such a sale would be absurd; and that, finally, men belong to nature alone, and that they would desecrate it by a custom that debases them and degrades nature.

Were all the advantages attributed to that custom over those of the custom that replaced it as real as they are minor, one should praise for all time the institutions that abolished it, that restored humankind to its rights and lifted him from that infamy.

However awful civil despotism may be, it is less harsh and less cruel than domestic servitude. At least in the first, the condition is general, and the wretched are not constantly reminded of the invidious comparison of their lot with that of other members of their species who wield a tyrannical authority over them that nothing in the world could give them. We share slavery among all men, and human nature is trampled on by a single man.

Proof of the barbarism that that criminal custom inspires, says Mr. Hume, is in the fact that all the laws concerning slavery were against the slaves and there was not one to enjoin the masters to honor reciprocal duties of gentleness and humanity.[60] Demosthenes applauded an Athenian law that prohibited the striking of another's slave.[61] Can we conceive of anything more atrocious than the custom in Rome of exposing slaves who were no

60. See Hume, "Of the Populousness," in *Essays,* 384.—HC
61. Ibid., 390.—HC

longer able to work because of old age, illness, or debility on an island in the Tiber, there to die of hunger![62] And these are men who are treating other human beings this way!

But despite what is widely believed, these wretched people were far from contributing to the multiplication of the species. They populated the large cities by depopulating the countryside, just as today's domestic servants do. All the historians of antiquity tell us that Rome perpetually drew slaves from the furthermost provinces. Strabo asserts that in Cilicia, as many as ten thousand slaves were often sold in a day into the service of the Romans.[63] If these slaves had grown in proportion to their number, as is supposed, Italy would soon not have been large enough to contain them. However, the people in Rome did not increase in number; these levies were only to compensate for losses. Any interest their masters might have had to incite them to increase the *population* was unable to prevail over the rigor of the evils inflicted on them. Even without the same interest, instead of holding our servants to celibacy, why do we not encourage them to marry, by preferring those who are married? They would only be more honest and more reliable; and their children not having to be part of the master's patrimony, they would be more numerous than those of slaves, who must have trembled to associate any new victims of the ferocity of their tyrants to their torments. New links will keep these servants dutiful and loyal. It is rare that in becoming a father one does not become a better man. In the end it depends entirely on us to make them less a burden to society and to be more useful for propagation. They should not be paid so badly that they will be necessarily poor in old age. The idle leisure and the affluence of the moment close their eyes to the wretchedness that awaits them. M. le duc de la Rochefoucauld, the one who died most recently, gave other masters a good example to follow. He kept servants only ten years, during which the servant was fed and provided for, and drew none of his wages. At the end of that time, this charitable master and citizen paid his servant and forced him to buy a shop or a piece of land. He would not allow him to remain. This example of humanity and public spirit, so rare among the great nobles,

62. Ibid., 384.—HC

63. Strabo, *Geography*, XIV.v.2.—HC

deserves to be mentioned: there are families in which the practice of goodness and virtue seems to be hereditary.[64]

Beyond this,] the causes of the increase or decrease in numbers of men are endless. Since men are part of the universal natural and moral order of things, since they are the focus of all religious and civilian institutions, in all traditions, since all is done with reference to them in the end, everything also influences their ability to reproduce, favoring or suspending its effects. The nature of this work has not allowed us to go into detail on all of these causes, or to expound on the main causes that we have discussed, as much as the importance of the topic might demand. But from all we have said, one may conclude that the total number of men who inhabit the surface of the earth has been, is, and forever will be about the same in all times, dividing them into epochs that lasted for some time; that there are only a few places that are more or less densely settled, and that the difference will depend on the happiness or the hardship that the inhabitants find there; that all other things being equal, the government whose institutions work least against nature, where there is more equality between the inhabitants, a more secure liberty and livelihood, where there is more love of truth than of superstition, more morals than laws, more virtue than wealth, and where consequently the inhabitants will remain settled, will be that government under which men will be most numerous, and where they will multiply the most. (*This article is by* M. D'AMILAVILLE.)

64. The most recent duke at time of writing was Alexander, Duke of La Rochefoucauld (1690–1762), son of François VIII (1663–1728).—HC

Power
(*Pouvoir*)

For the difference between the topic covered by the anonymous author of this article, and the one covered by Jaucourt in LEGISLATIVE, EXECUTIVE POWER, *below, see the translators' note on* pouvoir *and* puissance, *above.*

POWER (*Natural law and politics*), the consent of men joined together in society is the foundation of *power*. That power which is established only by force can endure only by force. It can never confer title, and peoples always preserve the right to make claims against it. In establishing societies, men have renounced a portion of the independence in which nature brought them into the world only to assure themselves of the advantages that result from their submission to a legitimate and equitable authority. They have never sought to surrender themselves unreservedly to arbitrary masters, or to lend a hand to tyranny and oppression, or to entrust to others the right to make them unhappy.

The aim of every government is the good of the governed society. To prevent anarchy, to have the laws executed, to protect the people, to support the weak against the encroachments of the stronger—each society has had to establish sovereigns vested with *power* sufficient to fulfill all these objects. The impossibility of foreseeing all the circumstances in which society will find itself has made peoples resolve to give more or less latitude to the *power* they grant to those they charge with the task of governing them. Many nations, jealous of their liberty and their rights, have placed

This article can be found at 13:255 in the original edition of the *Encyclopédie.*

limits on this *power*. They have nonetheless felt that it was often necessary not to make the limits too narrow. That is why the Romans, in the time of the republic, named a dictator whose *power* was as extensive as that of the most absolute monarch. In some monarchical states, the sovereign's *power* is limited by the laws of the state, which set boundaries on it that he is not permitted to infringe. That is why in England, the legislative *power* resides in the king and in the two houses of parliament. In other countries the monarchs exercise an absolute *power* by the consent of the people, but that power is always subordinate to the fundamental laws of the state, which create the reciprocal security of sovereign and subjects.

However unlimited the *power* enjoyed by sovereigns may be, it never permits them to violate the laws, oppress the people, or trample on reason and equity. A century ago, Denmark furnished the unheard of example of a people conferring, by an authentic act, an unlimited power to its sovereign. Exhausted by the tyranny of the nobles, the Danes made the decision to deliver themselves without reservation—and, so to speak, hands and feet bound up—to the mercy of Frederick III. Such an act can only be regarded as the result of despair.[1] Thus far, the kings who have governed that people have not appeared to take advantage of this. They have preferred to reign with the laws rather than to exercise the destructive despotism which the conduct of their subjects seemed to authorize in them. *Nunquam satis fida potentia ubi nimia.*[2]

In speaking of Henry IV, Cardinal de Retz says *that he did not mistrust the laws, because he trusted in himself.* Good princes know that they are only the depositories of *power* for the happiness of the state.[3] Far from

1. By the revolution of 1660, Frederick III turned an elective into an absolute monarchy in Denmark. See Montesquieu, *Considerations on the Causes of the Greatness of the Romans and Their Decline,* trans. David Lowenthal (New York: Free Press, 1965; repr. Indianapolis: Hackett, 1999), XV, 138, for a similar critique.

2. The actual passage by Tacitus, which is slightly different, appears at *Histories,* II.92. Jaucourt may be citing Tacitus as interpreted by the English Whig Thomas Gordon, ed., *The Works of Tacitus. In Four Volumes. To which are prefixed, Political Discourses upon that Author by Thomas Gordon,* 2nd ed., corr. (London: Woodward and Peele, 1737), Discourse V, sect. III, note a.

3. The passage is from the memoirs of the important conspirator during the French Fronde (1648–52), Jean-François Paul de Gondi, Cardinal de Retz (1613–79), *Œuvres de*

wanting to extend it, they themselves have often sought to put limits on it, out of fear of the abuse that less virtuous successors might make of it: *ea demùm tuta est potentia quae viribus suis modum imponit.* Val. Max.[4] The Tituses, the Trajans, the Antonines used *power* for the happiness of humans; the Tiberiuses and Neros abused it for the misery of the world.[5] *See* SOVEREIGNS.

cardinal de Retz, ed. Régis de Chantelauze, Jules Gourdault, and Alphonse Feillet (Paris: Hachette, 1870–96), 1:274.

4. "Power is safe only if it imposes limits on its own strength." Although Jaucourt cites Valerius Maximus, *Memorable Doings and Sayings,* 4.1.8, he may also have gotten it from Gordon's *Discourses on Tacitus,* Discourse V, sect. V, note f, which again offers a version of the quotation identical to Jaucourt's.

5. The first-named Roman emperors reigned 79–81, 98–117, and 138–92, respectively; the last named, 14–37 and 54–68.

Press
(*Presse*)

It is useful to recall that the term "press" in the eighteenth century referred not only to journalism but to anything that came off the printing press. This was as true in America (see the first amendment of the United States Constitution) as it was in France.

PRESS (*Political law*). It is asked whether liberty of the *press* is advantageous or detrimental to a state. The response is not difficult. It is of the greatest importance to preserve this practice in all states founded on liberty. I say more: the drawbacks of this liberty are so trivial compared with its advantages that it ought to be the common right of the world, and that it is proper to authorize it under all governments.

We should not be apprehensive that freedom of the press will cause the harmful consequences that followed the harangues of the Athenians or the tribunes of Rome. A man reads a book or a satire in his office all alone and very coolly. It is not to be feared that he will contract the passions and the enthusiasm of another, or that he will be drawn outside himself by vehement ranting. Even if he were to take on a disposition to revolt, he never has occasions at hand to make his sentiments burst forth. Whatever abuses may be made of it, liberty of the *press* cannot excite popular tumults. As for the murmurs and secret discontents it may generate, isn't it better that, bursting forth only in words, it warns the magistrates in time to remedy them? It must be admitted that the public everywhere has a great disposi-

This article can be found at 13:320 in the original edition of the *Encyclopédie*.

tion to believe whatever is reported that is unfavorable toward those who govern. But this disposition is the same in countries of liberty and countries of servitude. Word of mouth can spread as fast and produce as big effects as a pamphlet can. This word of mouth itself can be equally pernicious in countries where people are not accustomed to think out loud and to distinguish the true from the false, and yet one should not be troubled by such speech.

Finally, nothing can so multiply sedition and defamation in a country in which the government exists in an independent condition as the prohibition of unauthorized printing, or the grant of unlimited powers to someone to punish everything he doesn't like. In a free country, such concessions of power would become an attack against liberty, so that one can be assured that this liberty would be lost in Great Britain, for example, the instant that the attempts to impede the *press* succeeded. Thus, they wouldn't think of establishing that kind of inquisition. (*D.J.*)

Property
(*Propriété*)

PROPERTY (*Natural and political right*). This is the right that each of the individuals composing a civil society has over the goods he has legitimately acquired.

One of men's main purposes in forming civil societies was to assure themselves of the tranquil possession of the advantages they had acquired or could acquire. They wanted no one to be able to disturb them in the enjoyment of their possessions. That is why each person consented to sacrifice a portion of these possessions in what is called *taxes* for the preservation and upkeep of the entire society. It was thereby meant to furnish the chosen leaders the means to maintain each individual in the enjoyment of the portion he had reserved for himself. However strong the enthusiasm of men might be for the sovereigns to whom they submitted, they never meant to give them absolute and unlimited power over all their possessions. They never planned on making it necessary to work solely for them. The flattery of courtiers, for whom the most absurd principles cost nothing, has sometimes sought to persuade princes that they had an absolute right over the belongings of their subjects;[1] only despots and tyrants have adopted such unreasonable maxims. The king of Siam claims to be the proprietor of all the possessions of his subjects. The fruit of such a barbarous right is that the first successful rebel is made proprietor of the king of Siam's possessions. Every power that is founded on force alone is destroyed in

This article can be found at 13:491 in the original edition of the *Encyclopédie*.

1. For intimations of this tradition in France, see Herbert H. Rowen, *The King's State: Proprietary Dynasticism in Early Modern France* (New Brunswick: Rutgers University Press, 1980).

the same way. In states where the rules of reason are followed, individuals' *properties* are under the protection of the laws. The head of a family is assured of both enjoying and transmitting to his posterity the goods he has accumulated by his labor. Good kings have always respected their subjects' possessions. They have regarded the public coffers that have been consigned to their care as but a trust, which it is impermissible for them to divert to the satisfaction of their frivolous passions, or the greed of their favorites, or the rapacity of their courtiers. *See* SUJETS [Subjects].

Legislative, Executive Power
(*Puissance Législative, Exécutrice*)

LEGISLATIVE, EXECUTIVE POWER, Legislative, executive, and the judging power (*Political government*). In a state, *power* is the name for the force established in the hands of one or of many.

In each state, three sorts of capacities or of *powers* are distinguished:[1] legislative *power*, the executive *power* over things that depend on the law of nations—in other words, the executive *power* of the state—and the executive *power* over things that depend on civil law.[2]

By the first, the prince or the state makes laws for a temporary or permanent period, and corrects or abrogates those already made. By the second, it makes peace or war, sends or receives ambassadors, establishes security, prevents invasions. By the third, it punishes crimes or judges disputes between individuals; that is why we call this latter the *power* of judging.

Liberty must extend to all individuals, as equally enjoying the same nature. If it is limited to certain persons, it would be better for it not to exist at all, since then it furnishes a dreadful comparison that aggravates the unhappiness of those deprived of it.

There is less risk of losing liberty when the *legislative power* is in the hands of many persons who differ by status and interest. But where it is at the discretion of those who are alike in these two things, the government is

This article can be found at 13:557–58 in the original edition of the *Encyclopédie*.

1. Jaucourt's distinction here is between *pouvoir,* which we translate as "capacity" because of its broader connotations, and *puissance,* which usually connotes a specifically human authority—whether familial, religious, or political. See the translators' note on this distinction, as well as POUVOIR, both above.

2. This definition, and the next paragraph, come from Montesquieu, *The Spirit of the Laws,* 11.6, on the English constitution.

not far from falling into the despotism of monarchy. Liberty is never more assured than when the legislative *power* is entrusted to different persons so happily distinguished from each other that, in working for their own interest, they advance the interest of the whole people—or, to use different terms, when there is not a single sector of the people that does not have a shared interest with at least a portion of the legislators.

If there is only one body of legislators, this is scarcely better than tyranny. If there are only two, one of them risks being swallowed up over time by the disputes that arise between them; they will need a third to tip the scales. There would be the same drawback with four, and a larger number would cause too much trouble. I have never been able to read a passage in Polybius on this score, and another in Cicero, without tasting a secret pleasure in applying them to the government of England, with which they are much more closely connected than with the Roman.[3] These two great authors give preference to government composed of three bodies—the monarchical, the aristocratic, and the popular. They doubtless had the Roman republic in mind, where the consuls represented the king, the senators the nobles, and the tribunes the people. These three *powers* that one sees in Rome were not as distinct or as natural as they seem in Great Britain's form of government. The governments of most ancient republics suffered this abuse: that the people were at the same time both judge and accuser. But since the legislative body is composed of two parts in the government of which we are speaking, one binds the other by its natural faculty of vetoing, and both are bound by the executive *power,* which is itself bound by the legislative *power. See* the details on this in the work *Spirit of the laws, bk. II, ch. vi.*[4] It is enough for me to remark in general that political liberty is lost in a state if the same man, or the same body of leaders or of nobles or of the people, exercise the three *powers*—that of making the laws, that of executing public resolutions, and that of judging crimes or private differences. (*D.J.*)

3. On the mixed constitution to which Jaucourt refers, see for example Polybius, *Histories,* 6.10–14; Cicero, *De Republica,* bk. 1.

4. The discussion appears in Montesquieu, *Laws,* 11.6.

Volume 14
(1765)

Representatives
(*Représentans*)

Generally regarded as one of the most sophisticated and original of the political entries in the Encyclopédie, *this article addresses a problem that was beginning to attract significant transatlantic attention. "Representatives" was published just three years after Rousseau's critique of the English representative system appeared in* The Social Contract *(3.15) and in the same year the Stamp Act crisis erupted in colonial America. Its author, Baron d'Holbach, who successfully preserved his anonymity until the twentieth century, draws on a combination of historical and philosophical resources to offer a specific new way of thinking about representation in the contemporary French monarchy, one that denies a special role for the two privileged orders that dominated contemporary society, the clergy and the nobility.*

REPRESENTATIVES (*Political right, Modern history*). The *representatives* of a nation are elected citizens who in a limited government are charged by society to speak in its name, to stipulate its interests, to prevent oppression, and to collaborate in the procedures of governing.

In a despotic state the head of the nation is everything, the nation is nothing. The will of only one man constitutes the law, society is not represented. Such is the form of government in Asia, whose inhabitants, sub-

Most of "Representatives" was translated by Stephen J. Gendzier in *Denis Diderot's "The Encyclopedia": Selections*, ed. and trans. Stephen J. Gendzier (New York: Harper and Row, 1967), 214–22, and is reprinted by permission of the translator. Text that we have added is in brackets, and we have also added some notes, as well as the headnote.

This article can be found at 14:143–46 in the original edition of the *Encyclopédie*.

jected for a great number of centuries to hereditary slavery, have not conceived of any way to sway the enormous power that constantly crushes them. It was not the same in Europe, whose inhabitants were more robust, hard working, and bellicose than Orientals, and who felt at all times the usefulness and necessity of having the nation represented by some citizens who would speak in the name of all the others and who would oppose the schemes of an authority that often becomes abusive when it does not recognize any restraint. The citizens elected to be the agents or the *representatives* of the nation, according to different times, different conventions, and diverse circumstances, enjoy certain prerogatives and rights that are more or less extensive. Such is the origin of those assemblies known under the name of *diets, states-general, parliaments,* and *senates,* which in almost all the countries of Europe participate in public administration, approve or reject the proposals of sovereigns, and were allowed to devise with them the measures necessary for the maintenance of the state.

In a purely democratic state the nation, to be quite accurate, is not represented: the people reserve for themselves the right to make their will known in the general assemblies, which are composed of all the citizens. But as soon as the people have chosen magistrates who have been made depositories of its authority, then these magistrates become their *representatives.* And according to whether more or less power has been reserved by and for the people, the government either becomes an aristocracy or it remains a democracy.

In an absolute monarchy the sovereign either enjoys by the consent of his people the right to be the unique *representative* of his nation, or else against their will he arrogates this right. The sovereign speaks then in the name of all people: the laws that he makes are, or at least are supposed to be, the expression of the wills of the entire nation that he represents.

In limited monarchies the sovereign is only the depository of the executive power: he represents his nation only in this domain; other *representatives* are elected for the other branches of the administration. Thus in England the executive power resides in the person of the monarch, while the legislative power is shared between him and the parliament, that is to say, the general assembly of the different orders of the British nation, composed of clergy, nobility, and commoners. The last mentioned are represented by a certain number of deputies elected by the cities, the boroughs, and the provinces of Great Britain. By the provisions of the constitution of this country the parliament cooperates with the monarch in public administration. As soon as these two powers are in agreement, the entire nation is reputed to have spoken, and their decisions become law.

[In Sweden, the monarch governs jointly with a senate, which itself is merely the *representative* of the general diet of the realm. This general diet is the assembly of all the *representatives* of the Swedish nation.

The German nation, whose leader is the emperor, is represented by the Imperial Diet—that is, by a body composed of sovereign vassals, or princes (whether ecclesiastical or lay), or deputies of the free cities, which represent the entire German nation. *See* DIETE DE L'EMPIRE [Imperial Diet].]

The French nation was formerly represented by the assembly of the states-general of the kingdom, composed of clergy and nobility, to which was subsequently associated the third estate, destined to represent the people. These national assemblies have been discontinued since the year 1628.[1]

[Tacitus shows that the ancient nations of Germany—albeit ferocious, warlike, and barbarous—all enjoyed a free or moderate government. The king or the chieftain proposed and persuaded, without having the power to force the nation to bend to his will: *Ubi rex, vel princeps, audiuntur autoritate suadendi magis quam jubendi potestate*. The great men deliberated among themselves over minor affairs; but the whole nation was consulted on great affairs: *de minoribus rebus principes consultant, de majoribus omnes*.[2] It is these warrior peoples, thusly governed, who emerged from the forests of Germany and conquered the Gauls, Spain, England, *&c.*, founding new kingdoms on the debris of the Roman Empire. They brought the form of their government with them. It was everywhere military. The subjugated nation disappeared. Reduced to slavery, it did not have the right to speak

1. The most recent Estates-General had taken place in 1614; the event to which d'Holbach seems to be referring was the Assembly of the Notables convoked by Louis XIII in 1626–27.—HC

2. D'Holbach edits the first of these passages: "then a king or a chief is listened to . . . , with the prestige which belongs to their counsel rather than with any prescriptive right to command." And: "On small matters the chiefs consult; on larger questions the community." "Germania," 11, in Tacitus, vol. 1, *Agricola. Germania. Dialogue on Oratory.* Loeb Classical Library 35 (Cambridge: Harvard University Press, 1914), 149.—HC

for itself. Its only *representatives* were conquering soldiers who, after subjecting it by arms, made themselves surrogates of the defeated nation.]

If we go back to the origin of all our modern governments, we shall find them founded by bellicose and savage nations who, having come from areas of severe climate, attempted to take possession of more fertile regions, created settlements under a more favorable sky, and plundered the rich and civilized nations. The former inhabitants of these subjugated countries were only considered by these fierce conquerors as a kind of cheap cattle that victory had pressed into their hands. Thus the first institutions of these happy brigands were usually the consequences of force overpowering weakness. We always find their laws partial to the victors and pernicious for the vanquished. This is why in all modern monarchies we see everywhere the nobles, the princes, that is to say, warriors, possessing the lands of the former inhabitants and investing themselves with the exclusive right to represent the nations. The latter, degraded, crushed, oppressed, had no freedom to express their opinions before their arrogant conquerors. This is without doubt the source of that pretension of the nobility, who long arrogated to themselves the right to speak exclusively to all the others in the name of the nations. They always continued to regard their fellow citizens as vanquished slaves, even a great number of centuries after a conquest in which the successors of that conquering nobility had no part. But self-interest supported by force soon produces rights for itself; habit makes the nations accomplices of their own debasement, and the people, in spite of the changes that have occurred in their circumstances, continue in many countries to be solely represented by a nobility who have always taken advantage of them because of the primitive violence displayed by some conquerors whose rights they claim to have inherited.

The barbarians who dismembered the Roman Empire in Europe were pagans. Little by little they were enlightened by the understanding of the Gospel; they adopted the religion of the vanquished. Immersed in ignorance which a warlike and agitated life helped to maintain, they needed to be guided and restrained by citizens more reasonable than themselves; they could not withhold their veneration of the ministers of religion, who combined a more gentle morality with more understanding and knowledge. The monarchs and the nobles, until then the unique *representatives* of the nations, were content therefore to have the ministers of the church called to the national assemblies. The kings, doubtless themselves tired of the continual enterprises of a nobility too powerful to be submissive, felt that it was in their own interest to counterbalance the power of their uncontrolled vassals with that of the interpreters of a religion respected by the people. Moreover the clergy, having become the possessors of great wealth, were interested in public administration and had thereby a claim to take part in the deliberations.

Under the feudal government the nobility and the clergy had for a long time the exclusive right to speak in the name of the entire nation or to be their unique *representatives*. The people, composed of farmers, inhabitants of the cities and the countryside, manufacturers, in a few words, the most numerous, the most laborious, the most useful part of society, did not have the right to speak for themselves. They were forced to accept without grumbling the laws that a few great men arranged with the sovereign. In that way the people were not considered; they were regarded only as a vile mass of contemptible citizens, unworthy of expressing their opinions before a small number of arrogant and ungrateful noblemen who enjoyed the fruits of their labor without supposing that they had thereby acquired a debt. To oppress, pillage, and harass the people with impunity, without the head of the nation being able to remedy this situation, these were the prerogatives of the nobility, who presumed that liberty consists in maintaining their own rights. Indeed, feudal government only shows us sovereigns without power and peoples crushed and degraded by an aristocracy armed equally against the monarch and the nation. It was only after kings had suffered for a long time from the excesses of a haughty nobility and from the enterprises of a clergy become too rich and independent that they exercised some influence over the nation in the assemblies that decided their fate. Thus the voice of the people was finally heard, laws were enforced, the excesses of the great men were repressed; they were forced to be just to citizens scorned until then. The body of the nation was thus opposed to an insubordinate and intractable nobility.

The imperatives of circumstance forced the political ideas and institutions to change; morality and manners became softer, iniquity prejudiced its own case; the tyrants of nations perceived in the long run that their follies were contrary to their own interests; trade and manufacture became necessities for all states, and peace a prerequisite for their existence; warriors less essential; and finally, recurring shortages and famine brought home at last the necessity of good farming, which was disturbed by the bloody strife of a few brigands. People wanted laws, respected those who were the interpreters of them, and considered these judges as the guardians of public safety. Thus the magistrate in a well-constituted state became an esteemed person who was more competent to adjudicate the rights of people than some ignorant nobles devoid of impartiality who were unacquainted with any other rights but those of the sword or who sold justice to their vassals.

It is only by slow and imperceptible degrees that governments settle down. Founded at first by force, they can, however, survive only with equitable laws that protect property and the rights of every citizen and shield him from oppression. Men are forced in the last resort to seek in the principle of equity the remedy for their own passions. If the formation of governments had not usually been the work of violence and irrationality, then people would not have felt that a durable society could not exist if the rights of each person were not sheltered from power constantly trying to misuse its prerogatives. In whatever hands power is placed, it becomes deadly if not kept within proper bounds. Neither the sovereign nor any order of the state can exercise a harmful authority over the nation if it is true that all governments have as their sole object the good of the people governed. The slightest reflection would therefore have been sufficient to show that a monarch cannot enjoy true power if he does not command happy subjects united in purpose. To make them this way, he must protect their possessions, defend them against oppression, never sacrifice the interests of all to those of a small number, and keep sight of the needs of all the orders composing society. No man, however enlightened, is capable of governing an entire nation without counsel or assistance; no order of the state can have the capacity or the will to know the needs of others. Thus the impartial sovereign must listen to the voices of all his subjects. He is equally interested in hearing them and in redressing their injuries, but in order to prevent the subjects from explaining their desires in a tumultuous manner, it is advisable for them to have *representatives,* that is to say, some citizens more enlightened than the others, more interested in the thing, whose possessions bind them to their Country and whose position enables them to be conscious of the needs of the state, the abuses which have crept in, and the remedial measures that are advisable to take.

In despotic states such as Turkey, the nation cannot have *representatives.* No nobility is found there; the despot has only slaves, equally contemptible in his eyes. There is no justice, because the master's will is the only law; the magistrate merely executes his orders. Commerce is oppressed, agriculture abandoned, industry annihilated, and no one thinks about working, because no one is sure of enjoying the fruits of his own labors. The entire nation, reduced to silence, either lapses into inertia or expresses itself only in revolt. A sultan is supported only by a wild army rabble, which itself submits to him only insofar as he lets them pillage and oppress the rest of the subjects. In the end, his janissaries often slit his throat and dispose of his throne, without the nation having an interest in his fall or disapproving of the change.

It is therefore in the interest of the sovereign that his nation be represented. His own safety depends on it: the affection of the people is the strongest bulwark against the outrages of evil men. But how can the sovereign gain the affection of his people if he does not enter into their needs, if he does not procure for them the advantages they desire, if he does not protect them from the enterprises of the powerful, if he does not try to relieve their woes? If the nation is not represented, how can its leader become acquainted with all those details of misery which from the height of his throne he only sees in the distance and which flattery always tries to hide from him? How, without knowing the resources and the strength of his country, could the monarch guarantee that they would not be abused? A nation deprived of the right to elect *representatives* is at the mercy of imprudent men who oppress it. The nation isolated from its masters hopes that any change will make its fate sweeter and often is in danger of becoming the instrument of any seditious passion that will promise assistance. A suffering people instinctively attaches itself to whoever has the courage to speak for them: they tacitly choose protectors and *representatives;* they approve of the complaints made in their name. When they are pushed to the breaking point, they often choose as their interpreters ambitious and dishonest men who seduce them into believing that they will take their cause in hand and then overthrow the state under the pretext of defending it. Guise in France, Cromwell in England, and so many other seditious men, under the pretext of preserving public welfare, have thrown their nations into the most frightful convulsions; and they were *representatives* and protectors of this type, equally dangerous for sovereigns and nations.[3]

To maintain the harmony and agreement that must always exist between sovereigns and their peoples, to shield both against the crimes of bad citizens, nothing would be more advantageous than a constitution that would allow each order of the citizens to have *representatives* and to speak in the assemblies dedicated to public welfare. These assemblies, to be useful and just, should be composed of those individuals who are citizens by virtue of their possessions and whose status and enlightenment enables them to know the interests of the nation and the needs of the people. In a word, it is property that makes the citizen: any man with possessions in the state is interested in the welfare of the state, whatever his station assigned by the particular social conventions: it is always as the owner of property, it is because of his possessions that he must speak or that he acquires the right to be represented.

In European nations the clergy, having become the owners of immense wealth donated by sovereigns and nations and thereby constituted a body of opulent and powerful citizens, seemed from that time to have a vested interest in speaking or in having *representatives* in the national assemblies. Moreover, the confidence of the people enabled them to see rather closely their needs and to know their wishes.

The nobleman, because of the possessions that tie his fate to that of the nation, has without a doubt the right to speak. If he had only titles, he would only be a man distinguished by the social conventions: if he were only a warrior, his voice would be suspect; his ambition and self-interest would frequently plunge the nation into useless and harmful wars.

The magistrate is a citizen by virtue of his possessions, but his functions make a more enlightened citizen whose experience teaches the advantages

3. The Guise family, from Lorraine, were leaders of the Catholic interest of France during the religious and civil wars of the late sixteenth and early seventeenth centuries; Oliver Cromwell (1599–1658) was leader of the English Puritan and Parliament party during the English Civil War and Commonwealth period in the 1640s and 1650s.—HC

and disadvantages of legislation, the abuses of jurisprudence, and the means to remedy them. It is the law that determines the welfare of the state.

Commerce is today for the states a source of strength and wealth. The merchant enriches himself as well as the state that encourages his enterprises: he continually shares its prosperity and its reverses: he cannot therefore be reduced to silence except by a miscarriage of justice. He is a useful citizen qualified to give his views in the councils of a nation whose affluence and power he increases.

Finally the farmer, that is to say, any citizen possessing land, whose work contributes to the needs of society, who provides for its sustenance, and on whom taxes are levied, must be represented. Nobody has a greater interest than he does in the public welfare. Land is the physical and political foundation of a state; and all advantages and misfortunes of a nation fall directly or indirectly on the landowner. It is in proportion to his possessions that the voice of a citizen must have more or less weight in the national assemblies.

These are the different orders of which modern nations are composed. As all cooperate in their way in the maintenance of the republic, all must be listened to. Religion, war, justice, commerce, and agriculture are administered in a well-constituted state so as to lend each other mutual assistance. The sovereign power is destined to preserve the balance among them; he will prevent any order from being oppressed by another, which is what would inevitably happen if one order had the exclusive right to legislate for all.

"There is no more equitable rule," said Edward I, king of England, "than that the things that are of interest to everyone, must be approved by everyone, and that common dangers must be fought by common efforts."[4] If the constitution of a state permitted one order of citizens to speak for all the others, there would soon arise an aristocracy under whom the interests of the nation and the sovereign would be sacrificed to those of a few powerful

4. Edward I (r. 1272–1307); the reference is to the Roman and canon law dictum, "Quod omnes tangit, ab omnibus approbari debet" ("What concerns all should be approved by all"), which Edward is known to have evoked. For the history of this dictum, which goes back at least to Justinian's *Code,* see Gaines Post, *Studies in Medieval Legal Thought: Public Law and the State, 1100–1322* (Princeton: Princeton University Press, 1964), 163–238.—HC

men who would inevitably become tyrants of the monarch and the people. This was, as we have seen, the state of almost all European nations under feudal government, that is to say, during that systematic anarchy of the nobles who tied the hands of the kings to use with impunity such license under the name of *liberty*. This is still today the government of Poland, where, under kings too weak to protect the people, the latter are at the mercy of an impetuous nobility who impede the sovereign power only to be able to tyrannize the nation with impunity. In fact this will always be the fate of a state in which one order of men who have become too powerful wish to represent all the others.

The nobleman or the warrior, the priest or the magistrate, the merchant, the manufacturer, and the farmer are men who are equally necessary. Each one of them serves in his way the great family of which he is a member; all are children of the state, the sovereign must enter into their diverse needs; but in order to know them it is necessary for them to be heard, and to be heard without confusion and turmoil each class must have the right to choose its agents or its *representatives*. In order for the latter to express the wishes of the nation, it is necessary for their interests to be indivisibly united to the nation's by the bonds of possession. How would a nobleman reared in combat know the interest of religion about which he is often only slightly informed, of commerce which he scorns, of agriculture which he disdains, of jurisprudence of which he has no idea? How could a magistrate, concerned with the difficult task of dispensing justice to the people, of probing the depths of jurisprudence, of guarding himself against the traps laid by deceit, of disentangling the snares set by chicanery, pass judgment on matters relative to war and useful to commerce, manufacture, or agriculture? How could a clergyman, whose mind is absorbed by study and the concerns of heaven, judge what is most advisable for navigation, war, or jurisprudence?

A state is only happy and its sovereign is only powerful when all the orders of the state lend each other a hand. To bring about such a salutary result the leaders of the political realm have an interest in maintaining among the different classes of citizens a just equilibrium that prevents any one of them from encroaching on the others. All authority beyond measure, placed in the hands of a few members of society, is established at the expense of the safety and well-being of all. The passions of men constantly produce dissension; and this conflict is only useful in providing them with various activities. It only becomes harmful to the state when the sovereign power forgets to preserve the balance so as to prevent one force from overwhelming all the others. The voice of a restless, ambitious nobility, only breathing forth war, must be counterbalanced by those of other citizens who believe that peace is much more necessary. If warriors decided by themselves the fate of empires, they would be perpetually on fire and the nation would even sink under the burden of its own success. The laws would be reduced to silence, the land would remain uncultivated, the countryside would be depopulated. In a word, we would see the reappearance of that misery which for so many centuries accompanied the license of nobles under feudal government. A preponderant commercial interest would perhaps neglect war too much; the state, to enrich itself, would not be sufficiently careful of its safety, or perhaps greed would often plunge it into wars that would frustrate their own purpose. In a state there is no indifferent concern or goal that requires only certain men to be exclusively preoccupied with it. No order of citizens could be capable of legislating for everyone; if they had the right, they would soon be legislating only for themselves. Each class must be represented by men who know their living conditions and their needs: these needs are truly known only by those who feel them.

The existence of *representatives* implies the existence of constituents from whom their power emanates, to whom they are consequently subordinate, and of whom they are only agents. Whatever current practices and abuses have been introduced in free and moderate governments, a *representative* cannot arrogate to himself the right to speak for his constituents in language opposed to their interests. The rights of the constituents are the rights of the nation: they are imprescriptible and inalienable. If reason is consulted, it will prove that the constituents can at all times contradict, disavow, and remove the *representatives* who betray them, who misuse their full powers against them, or who renounce for them certain inherent rights. In a word, the *representatives* of a free people cannot impose a yoke on them that would destroy their happiness. [No man acquires the right to represent another in spite of himself.]

Experience shows us that in the countries that flatter themselves that they enjoy the greatest liberty, those who are charged with representing the people betray only too often their interests and deliver their constituents to the greed of those who wish to plunder them.[5] A nation is right in distrusting such *representatives* and in limiting their powers. An ambitious person, a man hungering for riches, a squanderer, and a dissolute individual are all not fit to represent their fellow citizens. They will sell them for titles, honors, jobs, and money. They would then believe that they are interested in their troubles. What will happen if these infamous dealings seem to be authorized by the conduct of the constituents who will themselves be venal? What will happen if these constituents elect their *representatives* in a tumultuous and drunken manner, or if they neglect virtue, enlightenment, and talent to give the highest bidder the right to legislate their interests? Such constituents invite betrayal; they lose the right to complain, and their *representatives* will shut their mouths by saying, "I bought you at a very high price, and I shall sell you at the highest price I can get."

No order of citizens must enjoy forever the right to represent the nation. New elections are necessary to recall to the *representatives* that they hold their power from the people. A body whose members would enjoy without interruption the right to represent the state would soon become its master or its tyrant.

5. This was a common French criticism of the English parliamentary system at that time.—HC

Republic
(*République*)

REPUBLIC (*Political government*), form of government in which the people as a body, or only a part of the people, have sovereign power. *Republicae forma laudari faciliùs quàm evenire, & si evenit, haud diuturna esse potest*, says Tacitus, *Annal. 4.*[1]

When the people as a body have sovereign power in the *republic*, it is a *democracy*. When the sovereign power is in the hands of a part of the people, it is an *aristocracy*. *See* DEMOCRACY, ARISTOCRATIE [Aristocracy].[2]

When several political bodies join together to become citizens of a larger state that they want to form, it is a federal *republic*. *See* FEDERAL REPUBLIC.[3]

The most celebrated ancient *republics* are the *republic* of Athens, that of Lacedemon, and the Roman *republic*. *See* LACEDEMON, RÉPUBLIQUE D'ATHENES [Republic of Athens], and RÉPUBLIQUE ROMAINE [Roman Republic].

I must observe here that the ancients were not familiar with government founded on a corps of nobility, still less with government founded on a legislative body made up of the representatives of a nation. The *republics*

This article can be found at 14:150–51 in the original edition of the *Encyclopédie*.

1. The full passage, including an introductory sentence Jaucourt omits, reads, "Every nation or city is governed by the people, or by the nobility, or by individuals: a constitution selected and blended from these types is easier to commend than to create; or, if created, its tenure of life is brief." Tacitus, *Annals*, IV.xxxiii, Loeb Classical Library 312 (Cambridge: Harvard University Press, 1937), 57. John Jackson, the Loeb translator, has rendered *rei publicae* as "constitution," opting for a generic rather than specific interpretation. Jaucourt's interpretation is therefore doubtful. For ambiguity in "republic," see the translators' note, above.

2. DEMOCRACY is included in the present volume.

3. The next article in this volume.

of Greece and Italy were cities that each had their government, and that assembled their citizens inside their walls. Before Rome devoured all the *republics*, there were practically no kings anywhere—in Italy, Gaul, Spain, or Germany. It was all small peoples or small *republics*. Africa itself was subject to a large one. Asia Minor was occupied by Greek colonies. Thus, there was no example of city deputies or assemblies of estates. One had to go to Persia to find the government of one alone.

In the best Greek *republics,* wealth was taxed as much as poverty. For the rich were obliged to employ their money in festivals, sacrifices, musical choruses, chariots, racehorses, and magistracies, which alone created respect and esteem.

Modern *republics* are known to everyone. Their strength, their power, and their liberty are well known. In the *republics* of Italy, for example, the people are less free than in monarchies. Thus, to maintain itself, the government needs means as violent as the government of the Turks. Witness the state inquisitors in Venice, and the lion's maw into which an informer can at any moment toss his note of accusation.[4] Observe the possible situation of a citizen in these *republics*. The body of the magistracy, as executor of the laws, retains all the power it has given itself as legislator. It can plunder the state by its general acts of will, and since it also has the power of judgment, it can destroy each citizen by its particular acts of will. There, all power is one, and although there is none of the external pomp that reveals a despotic prince, it is felt at every moment. In Geneva, one feels only happiness and liberty.[5]

It is in the nature of a *republic* that it have only a small territory.[6] Otherwise, it can scarcely continue to exist. In a large republic, there are large fortunes, and consequently men's minds have little moderation. There is too much to be entrusted to the hands of a citizen; interests become particularized. At first, a man feels he can be happy, great, and glorious without his Country; and soon, that he can be great only on the ruins of his Country.

4. The argument of this paragraph is from Montesquieu, *The Spirit of the Laws,* 11.6.

5. This comment on Geneva, where Jaucourt was educated for several years, is the only sentence in the paragraph that does not appear in Montesquieu.

6. For this passage and the paragraphs to follow, see Montesquieu, *Laws,* 8.16.

In a large republic, the common good is sacrificed to countless considerations; it is subordinated to exceptions and dependent on accidents. In a small republic, the public good is better felt, better known, nearer to each citizen; abuses are less extensive and consequently less protected.

What made Lacedemon last so long is that, after all its wars, it always remained within its territory. Lacedemon's only goal was liberty; the only advantage of its liberty was glory.

It was in the spirit of the Greek republics to be as satisfied with their lands as they were with their laws. Athens was seized with ambition, and transmitted it to Lacedemon. But this was in order to command free peoples rather than to govern slaves; to be at the head of the union rather than to shatter it. All was lost when a monarchy rose up!—a government whose spirit tends toward expansion.

It is certain that a prince's tyranny does no more to ruin a state than indifference to the common good does to ruin a republic. The advantage of a free state is that there are no favorites. But when that is not the case—when it is necessary to line the pockets not of the prince's friends and relatives, but of the friends and relatives of everybody who participates in the government—all is lost. There is greater danger in the laws being evaded than in their being violated by a prince, because a prince, always being the foremost citizen of the state, has more interest in its preservation than anyone else. *Spirit of the laws.*[7] (*D.J.*)

7. Despite Jaucourt's final reference, this last paragraph is based not on Montesquieu's *Laws* but on his *Considerations on the Causes of the Greatness of the Romans and Their Decline,* trans. David Lowenthal (New York: Free Press, 1965; repr. Indianapolis: Hackett, 1999), IV, 44.

Federal Republic
(*République Fédérative*)

Although Montesquieu was often known later on for espousing the view that republics need to be small in order to survive,[1] he made an exception, which was less frequently noticed by contemporaries, for federal republics. Jaucourt, who had lived in the United Provinces for a while, offers here a brief article that draws on and highlights Montesquieu's arguments, arguments that would be of great interest to the American Founders some years later.

FEDERAL REPUBLIC (*Political government*), form of government by which several political bodies consent to become citizens of a larger state that they wish to form. It is a society of societies that make a new one, which can be enlarged by new associates that unite with it.[2]

If a *republic* is small, it can be destroyed by a foreign force; if it is large, it is destroyed by an internal defect. This dual drawback taints democracies and aristocracies equally, whether they are good or bad. The problem is in the thing itself; there is no form that can remedy it. Thus, it is very likely that men would ultimately have been obliged to live forever under the government of one alone if they had not devised a kind of constitution and of association that has all the internal advantages of republican government and the external strength of monarchy.

This article can be found at 14:158–59 in the original edition of the *Encyclopédie*.

1. Montesquieu, *The Spirit of the Laws*, 8.16.
2. This and the next five paragraphs are based on Montesquieu, *Laws*, 9.1.

Such associations made Greece flourish for so long. By using them, the Romans attacked the world, and by their use alone the world defended itself against them. And when Rome had reached the height of its grandeur, the barbarians were able to resist her by associations made beyond the Danube and the Rhine, associations created by fright. Because of them, Holland, Germany, and the Swiss leagues are regarded in Europe as eternal *republics*.

Associations of towns were more necessary in the past than they are today; a city without power risked greater perils. Conquest made it lose not only executive and legislative power, as today, but also everything men have a stake in—civil liberty, possessions, women, children, temples, and even tombs.

Able to resist external force, this sort of republic can maintain itself at its present size without internal corruption; the form of this association provides against every drawback. Whoever might want to be a usurper could scarcely enjoy equal credibility in all the confederated states. If he became too strong in one state, he would alarm all the others. If he subjugated a part, the still-free part could resist him with forces independent of those he had usurped, and overwhelm him before he had managed to establish himself.

If sedition occurs in one of the members of the confederation, the others can pacify it. If abuses are introduced somewhere, they are corrected by the healthy parts. This state can perish in one place without perishing in another; the confederation can be dissolved and the confederates can remain sovereign. Composed of small *republics*, it enjoys the goodness of the internal government of each one; as for the exterior, the force of association gives it all the advantages of large monarchies.

The *federal republic* of Germany is composed of free cities, and of small states subject to princes.[3] Experience shows that it is more imperfect than the federal republics of Holland and Switzerland. It lasts, however, because it has a leader; the magistrate of the union is in some sense the monarch.

All *federal republics* do not have the same laws in their constitutional form.[4] In the *republic* of Holland, for example, one province cannot form

3. This paragraph is based on Montesquieu, *Laws,* 9.2.

4. This paragraph and the next two are taken from Montesquieu, *Laws,* 9.3.

an alliance without the consent of the others. This law is very good, indeed necessary, in a *federal republic*. It is missing from the German constitution, where it would ward off the misfortunes that can come to all members from the imprudence, ambition, or avarice of one alone. A *republic* united by a political confederation has given itself entirely, and has nothing more to give.

It is clearly impossible for states that associate to be of the same size and of equal power. The *republic* of the Lycians was an association of twenty-three towns. The large ones had three votes in the common council; the medium-sized ones, two; the small ones, one. The *republic* of Holland is composed of seven provinces, large and small, each having one vote. The cities of Lycia paid taxes in proportion to their votes. The provinces of Holland cannot follow this proportion; they must follow the proportion of their power.

In Lycia, the judges and magistrates of the cities were elected by the common council, and in the proportion we have stated. In the *republic* of Holland, they are not elected by the common council, and each city names its magistrates. If one had to propose a model of a fine *federal republic*, the *republic* of Lycia would merit this honor.

When all is said and done, concord is the great support of *federal republics*. It is also the motto of the confederated United Provinces: *concordiâ res parvae crescunt, discordiâ dilabuntur*.[5]

History records that an envoy from Byzantium came in the name of his *republic* to exhort the Athenians to join a *federal* alliance against Philip, king of Macedon. That envoy, whose height was very similar to that of a dwarf, mounted the tribune to explain his official business. At the first sight of him, the people of Athens broke out laughing. Without being disconcerted, the Byzantine told them: "You have much to laugh at, gentlemen; I actually have a wife quite a bit shorter than I am." The laughter redoubled, and when it had stopped, the witty pygmy, who never lost sight of his subject,

5. "Small things grow in harmony and vanish in discord." The passage is based on Sallust, *Jugurthine War*, 10.6, where the latter phrase reads *discordiâ maximae dilabuntur*, "the greatest things vanish in discord." It seems to have been an official motto for the state of Zeeland from the late sixteenth century and was used by the Dutch East Indies Company in the seventeenth.

adapted to this episode and substituted for his prepared declamation the following simple words:

> When a woman such as I depict, and myself such as you see me, do not run a good household, we cannot get along together in Byzantium, however large it is. But as soon as we are in harmony, we are happy; the tiniest shelter is enough for us. O Athenians (he continued), turn this example to your advantage! Beware lest Philip, who threatens you nearby, soon profiting from your discord and your unseasonable gaiety, subjugate you with his power and his guile and transport you to a country in which you will have no desire to laugh.[6]

This apostrophe produced a marvelous effect. The Athenians withdrew among themselves, the proposals of the Byzantine minister were heeded, and the *federal* alliance was concluded. *Spirit of the Laws.* (*D.J.*)

6. The events occurred in the 340s B.C.; a less elaborate version of the anecdote can be found in Plutarch, "Precepts of Statecraft," in *Moralia,* 804b.

Rutland

D'Alembert tended to eschew biographical entries as being too traditional and dry, but Jaucourt was rather attracted to the genre. One solution to this editorial difference was that biographical material tended to be buried beneath articles with geographical rather than biographical titles. In this case, RUTLAND *provides an opportunity for Jaucourt to discuss the political philosophy of one of the most influential English theorists of the seventeenth century, James Harrington, whose* Oceana *Jaucourt calls a "profound work" below. As such, the article provides another example of the* Encyclopédie*'s extensive engagement with English political thought.*

RUTLAND (*Modern geography*), an inland province of England, in the diocese of Peterborough, with the title of duchy. It is the smallest province in England, for it is only forty miles in circumference. But it is very fertile, abundant in wheat and livestock. It has many woods and parks, and is irrigated by many little rivers, so that it feeds a goodly number of sheep, whose wool is ruddy like the land. Oakham is the main city in the province.

It owes its luster to the birth of James Harrington, son of the knight Sapcote Harrington. He was born in 1611, and from his tender youth he offered great expectations of what he might one day become. After studying at Oxford, he left the university to go travel in Holland, France, Italy, Denmark, and Germany, and he learned the languages of these various countries. When he returned, King Charles I made him private gentleman extraordinary, and he accompanied the monarch in this capacity in his first

This article can be found at 14:446–48 in the original edition of the *Encyclopédie*.

expedition against the Scots.[1] He always served that prince faithfully, and he employed his credit in bringing about a general compromise, which, however, did not work out. In 1661, after the restoration of Charles II, he was arrested on the king's order, having been accused of treason and misconduct.[2] But since the agents from the two houses could find nothing against him, he was set free. He died in Westminster in 1677, at the age of 66.

Among his political works, his *Oceana,* or the commonwealth, which appeared in London in 1656, *in-fol.*, is extremely famous in England.[3] When the author showed the manuscript of this work to his friends before it was published, he told them that since he had begun to think seriously, he had become dedicated mainly to the study of government, as a subject of the first importance to the happiness of the human race, and that he had succeeded (at least to his satisfaction) and had become convinced that there is no type of government that is as accidental as is commonly imagined, because there are natural causes in societies that produce their effects as necessarily as those of the earth and air.

Based on this principle, he maintained that England's disturbances should not have been absolutely attributed to the spirit of faction, the bad government of the prince, or the stubbornness of the people, but to the lack of equilibrium among the different authorities. The king and lords had lost too much since the time of Henry VIII,[4] and the balance was day by day tilting too much toward the commons. It is not that he meant to approve of the infractions the king had committed against the laws or to excuse the harsh manner in which some of his subjects had treated that prince, but he meant to show that as long as the causes of the disorder existed, they would inevitably produce the same effects.

He added that in one respect, as long as the king still looked to govern in the same manner as his predecessors, the people would surely do their utmost to procure new privileges and to extend their liberty as often as

1. Charles I (1625–49), king of England; the expedition referred to was the so-called first Bishops' War of 1639.

2. Charles II, king of England from 1660 to 1685; the arrest occurred on December 28, 1661.

3. See Harrington, *The Commonwealth of Oceana,* ed. J. G. A. Pocock (Cambridge: Cambridge University Press, 1992).

4. That is, 1509–47.

they could do so successfully, as the past demonstrated. His main purpose therefore was to find a means of preventing such troubles, or to apply the best remedies when they occurred.

He maintained that as long as the balance remained unequal, there was no prince who could remain beyond attack (however careful he was to make himself agreeable to the people), and that although a good king might do tolerably well at managing things during his life, that did not prove the government was good, since under a less prudent prince, the state could not fail to lapse into disorder, whereas in a well-ordered state, the wicked become good people, and fools behave wisely. He was the first to prove that authority follows property, whether it resides in the hands of one alone, of a few, or of many.

Having many acquaintances, he had no sooner begun to disseminate his system than everyone applied himself to examining its content, each according to his own prejudices. But many persons sought to argue with him over this content for the purpose of better informing themselves about it.

Harrington found it very difficult to bring his book out because all the parties—though opposed to each other—had joined forces, as it were, against him. The main obstacles came on the part of the defenders of Cromwell's tyranny,[5] especially since, in showing that a commonwealth is a government run by laws and not by military power, the author revealed the protector's violent administration by his major-generals. On another front, the *cavaliers* charged him with ingratitude toward the memory of the late king, and preferred monarchy, even under a usurper, to the best-ordered republic.

To these latter, he responded that it was enough that he had avoided publishing his opinions during the king's life, but that since the monarchy was now absolutely destroyed and the nation in a state of anarchy, or rather usurpation, he was no longer free but obliged—in his capacity as a good citizen—to communicate to his compatriots the model of government that seemed to him best-suited to ensure their tranquility, their happiness, and their glory. He added that there was no one who should like his plan more than the *cavaliers*, since if it were adopted, they would find themselves

5. A reference to the Commonwealth, or Protectorate, the republican government established in 1649 after the execution of Charles I.

freed from all oppression, because in a well-ordered commonwealth, there can be no distinction of parties, as the path to employment would be open to merit. Moreover, if the prince were restored, his doctrine of balance would enlighten the prince on his duties, which would put him in a position to avoid the mistakes of his father, since the system was no less fitting for a monarchy governed by laws than for a true democracy.

Nonetheless, when some courtiers learned that Harrington's work was in press, they did so much digging that they found out where it was being published. The manuscript was seized and brought to Whitehall. All the author's first initiatives to recover it were useless. At last he reflected that Lady Claypole, the Protector's daughter, who had much influence over his mind, had a character full of kindness for everyone, and that she very often took an interest in the unfortunate.[6] Even though this lady was unknown to him, he decided to turn to her; he presented himself in her antechamber and had himself announced.

While he was there, some of Lady Claypole's ladies entered the room, followed by her little daughter, around three years old. That child stopped near him, and he began to banter with her in such a way that she let him take her in his arms, which is where she was when her mother appeared. Harrington advanced toward Lady Claypole and placed the child at her feet, saying, "Madam, you have arrived just in time, otherwise I would certainly have stolen this charming young lady." "*Stolen!*" the mother replied with vivacity, "*but why, may I ask; for she is too young to be your mistress.*" "Madam," Harrington responded, "although her charms assure her of a conquest more important than my own, I confess that I would only have been led to this larceny by a motive of vengeance and not love." "*What harm have I done you, then,*" replied the lady, "*to oblige you to steal my child from me?*" "None," answered Harrington, "but this larceny would have been to engage you to bring milord your father to do me justice, by restoring the child he has stolen from me." Lady Claypole replied that this could not be, since her father already had enough children and was certainly not thinking of stealing any from any person in the world.

6. Elizabeth Claypole (1629–58), Cromwell's second daughter, depicted as Minerva, goddess of wisdom, in a portrait by John M. Wright.

Harrington then informed her that it was a question of the production of his mind, of which some false ideas had been given to his highness, and which had been kidnapped on his orders from the printer. She promised him right then and there that she would make him return the work, provided there be nothing contrary to her father's government. He assured her that it was a kind of political novel, which contained so few things detrimental to the Protector's interests that he hoped she would inform her father that he even had the intention of dedicating it to him, and he promised that she would have one of the first copies. Lady Claypole was so happy at his maneuver that she soon had his book returned to him.

As good as his word, Harrington dedicated it to Cromwell, who, after reading it, said the author had undertaken to strip him of his authority, but that he would not abandon for an act of the pen what he had acquired at the point of a sword. He added that no one disapproved of the government-of-one more than he did, but that he had been forced to take up the functions of a higher agent in order to maintain peace in the nation, convinced that if it had been left to itself, those who formed it would never have agreed on a form of government and would have employed their power to ruin each other.

To speak now of the work, it is written in the form of a novel, in imitation of Plato's Atlantis story. *Oceana* is England; *Adoxus* is King John; *Convallium* is Hampton Court; *Coraunus* is Henry VIII; *Dicotome,* Richard II; *Emporium,* London; *Halcionia,* the Thames; *Halo,* Whitehall; *Hiera,* Westminster; *Leviathan,* Hobbes; *Marpesia,* Scotland; *Morpheus,* King James I; *Mount Celia,* Windsor; the *Neustrians* are the Normans; *Olphaus Megaletor* is Oliver Cromwell; *Panopaea,* Ireland; *Pantheon,* the great hall of Westminster; *Panurgus,* Henry VIII; *Parthenia,* Queen Elizabeth; the *Scandians* are the Danes; the *Teutons,* the Saxons; *Turbo* is William the Conqueror; *Verulamius* is Lord Bacon.

This work is composed of three parts. The preliminaries are accompanied by a section entitled: *the council of the Legislators.* The program of the commonwealth—that is, the body of the work—follows, and finally, the corollaries, or conclusion.

The preliminaries contain the foundations, origin, and effects of all forms of government—monarchical, aristocratic, or democratic. He speaks of the corruption of these various kinds of government, and of how tyranny, oligarchy, and anarchy are born.

In the first part, he especially treats what he calls *ancient prudence*—that is, the most common type of government in the world until Julius Caesar's time. In the second part of the preliminaries, it is a question of modern prudence—that is, that type of government that prevailed in the world after Rome lost its liberty. The author is particularly interested in the laws established since the barbarian peoples began to pour into the Roman Empire. He gives a clear and accurate idea of the manner in which England was governed by the Romans, the Saxons, the Danes, and the Normans, until the complete ruin of that government under Charles I.

Next, one sees the council of the legislators, for the author, in laboring to offer the model of a perfect government, had studied the ancient and modern governments deeply in order to take up what seemed practicable to him and to avoid everything he found impracticable. With this intention, he introduced under fictitious names nine legislators perfectly versed in the various kinds of government that they must make known. The first is charged with explaining the government of the commonwealth of Israel; the second, the republic of Athens; the third, of Lacedemon; the fourth, Carthage; the fifth, the Achaeans, the Aeolians, and the Lycians; the sixth, Rome; the seventh, Venice; the eighth, Switzerland; and the ninth, Holland. He draws out what is good from these various governments, and in adding his own ideas, he forms the plan of his *Oceana*. The method in his plan of government is first to establish a law, then to add an explanation of it and accompany it with a speech that he has one of the legislators make.

The various bodies of the commonwealth (which he calls their wheels, *the orbs*[7])—civil, military, or provincial—are founded on the division of the people into four orders. The first, citizens and domestics; the second, old and young people. The third, those who have an annual income of 100 pounds sterling in land, money, or other effects—these make up the cavalry, while those who have less income, the infantry. In the fourth place, they are divided according to the places of their ordinary residence into parishes, centuries, and tribes.

7. The italicized words appear in English.

The people are the supreme tribunal of the nation, having the right to hear and decide appeals from all magistrates and from provincial or domestic courts. They can also call any magistrate to account when he has left office, if the tribunes—or any one of them—proposes it.

The author then details his ideas on the military, the army, and the polemarchs.[8]

Finally, he explains in the corollaries how one might manage to fashion his commonwealth. He is not content to develop what touches on the senate and the assembly of the people, the manner of waging war, and of governing in time of peace. He also talks about what concerns religious discipline, the means of assuring freedom of conscience, the particular form of government for Scotland, Ireland, and the other provinces of the commonwealth; the government of London and Westminster, which ought to be the model for the government of the other cities and communities.

He gives directions here for making commerce flourish and increase; laws for regulating the universities; advice on the education of youth; counsel for waging maritime war usefully, for establishing manufactures, for encouraging agriculture. He proposes regulations on law, medicine, religion, and especially on the manner of forming a finished gentleman. He speaks of the number, selection, duties, and income of the magistrates, and of all who hold office in the state; finally, he speaks of all the commonwealth's expenditures.

Contrary to my custom, I have expanded upon this profound work because it is little or not at all known to foreigners.[9] Along with the author of the *Spirit of the laws*, I myself think that M. Harrington, in examining the highest point of liberty to which the constitution of England could be brought, has built Chalcedon with the coast of Byzantium before his eyes.[10]

8. Polemarch, ancient Greek term for war chief.

9. Although Harrington's works were not translated into French until the Directory phase of the French Revolution (1795), they were brought together with the works of other English republicans such as Milton and Sidney by John Toland in the early eighteenth century. The Huguenot exile community in Holland, of which Jaucourt was temporarily a member, did its part to disseminate the views of Harrington and other republicans in their publications. See Rachel Hammersley, *The English Republican Tradition and Eighteenth-Century France: Between the Ancients and the Moderns* (Manchester: Manchester University Press, 2010).

10. The reference is to the closing sentence in Montesquieu's long chapter on the English constitution in *The Spirit of the Laws*, 11.6.

I don't know how he could expect his work to be looked at other than the way one looks at some lovely novel. It is certain that all the efforts to establish democracy in England have been useless. For after many movements, clashes, and agitations, they had to rely on the same government that had been banished—a government in which, as it happens, political liberty is established by the laws, and one should not seek more than that.

In any case, the author offered an abridgment in octavo of his *Oceana* in 1659. It is divided into three books, of which the first turns on the foundations and nature of all types of government. The second concerns the commonwealth of the Hebrews, and in the third, one finds a republican program appropriate to the condition in which the English nation found itself. At the end, he has placed a small essay entitled: *Discourse concerning an house of peers*.[11]

The compendium of all the works of this fine talent appeared in London in 1737, *in-folio;* on which, *see biblioth. Britan. tom. IX. part. II. art. 10.*[12]

Moreover, as M. Hume says, Harrington's *Oceana* was perfectly suited to the tastes of a century in which imaginary plans for republics furnished a constant subject for argument and conversation. Even in our own day, this work is credited with talent and inventiveness.[13] Nonetheless, perfection and immortality will always appear as chimerical in a republic as in a man. Harrington's style lacked ease and fluidity, but this defect is more than compensated for by the excellence of the content. (*Chevalier* DE JAUCOURT)

11. It is at the end of *The art of law-giving in III books* (London: Fletcher, 1659).

12. *The Oceana, and other works of James Harrington, esq.; collected, methodiz'd, and review'd, with an exact account of his life prefix'd,* ed. John Toland (London: A. Millar, 1737); see the *Bibliothèque britannique, ou Histoire des ouvrages des savans de la Grande-Bretagne* [British Library, or History of the works of the learned of Great Britain], edited by the Huguenot exile Pierre Des Maizeaux and others and published in the Hague from 1733 forward.

13. Hume's most extended discussion of Harrington appears in "Idea of a Perfect Commonwealth," *Essays, Moral, Political, and Literary,* ed. Eugene F. Miller, rev. ed. (Indianapolis: Liberty Fund, 1987), 514–16; the criticism cited by Jaucourt does not appear there, however, or anywhere else that I have found.

Savages
(*Sauvages*)

The dictionaries of the eighteenth century did not distinguish between "savages" and "barbarians." But Montesquieu, in The Spirit of the Laws,[1] *drew a political distinction between them that Jaucourt reproduces below. Both Montesquieu and Rousseau, though in very different ways, markedly qualified the pejorative connotation attached in contemporary language to both sorts of descriptions.*

SAVAGES (*Modern geography*). All Indian peoples who are not subject to the yoke of the land and who live apart are called *savages*.

There is this difference between *savage* peoples and barbarous peoples: the former are small, dispersed nations that do not want to join together, whereas barbarians often join together, as happens when one leader has subjected others.[2]

Natural liberty is the sole purpose of *savage* government;[3] along with this liberty, nature and climate almost alone dominate them.[4] Occupied with hunting or with the pastoral life, they do not burden themselves with religious practices, and they adopt no religion to organize themselves.

Many *savage* nations are found in America, because of the bad treatment they have experienced—and still fear—from the Spanish. Having

This article can be found at 14:729 in the original edition of the *Encyclopédie*.

1. Montesquieu, *The Spirit of the Laws,* 18.11.
2. This paragraph is a slight adaptation of Montesquieu, *Laws,* 18.11.
3. For this statement, see Montesquieu, *Laws,* 11.5.
4. Jaucourt relies here on Montesquieu, *Laws,* 19.4.

retreated into the forests and the mountains, they maintain their liberty and find the fruits of the earth there in abundance. If they cultivate a piece of land near their cabins, corn arrives immediately; eventually, hunting and fishing complete the task of bringing them into a state of subsistence.[5]

Since *savage* peoples do not dig canals for water in the places they reside, these places are filled with marshes where each *savage* band encamps, lives, multiplies, and forms a small nation.[6] (*D.J.*)

5. Where Montesquieu, *Laws,* 18.9, cites the terrain as the reason for the number of savages in America, Jaucourt cites Spanish oppression.

6. This sentence is an adaptation of Montesquieu, *Laws,* 18.10.

Volume 15
(1765)

Civil Society
(*Société Civile*)

This article is unsigned and of unknown authorship.

CIVIL SOCIETY means the political body that men from the same nation, the same state, the same city, or other place form together, and the political bonds that attach them to one another. It is the civil commerce of the world, the liaisons that men have together as subjects of the same prince, as fellow citizens of the same city, and as being subject to the same laws and participating in the rights and privileges common to all those who compose this same *society*. *See* CITÉ [City], CITIZEN, ETAT [State], NATION, PEUPLE [People].

This article can be found at 15:259 in the original edition of the *Encyclopédie*.

Sovereigns
(*Souverains*)

This entry is unsigned, and the identity of the author unknown.

SOVEREIGNS (*Natural and political law*), those on whom the will of the people has bestowed the power necessary to govern society.

In the state of nature, man knows no *sovereign*. Each individual is equal to another and enjoys the most perfect independence. In this state, there is no other subordination but that of children toward their father. Natural needs, and especially the necessity to combine forces to repulse the attacks of their enemies, caused several men or several families to come together to form but a single family called *society*. It did not take long to realize that if each person continued to exercise his will, to use his strength and his independence, and to give free reign to his passions, each individual's situation would be more miserable than if he lived in isolation. It came to be understood that each man must renounce a part of his natural independence to submit to a will that would represent the independence of the entire society, and that would be, so to speak, the common center and point of union for all its wills and all its forces. Such is the origin of *sovereigns*. Their power and their rights are clearly founded only on the consent of the people. Those who establish themselves by violence are merely usurpers; they become legitimate only when the consent of the people has confirmed the rights that the *sovereign* has seized.

This article can be found at 15:423–25 in the original edition of the *Encyclopédie*.

Men have only placed themselves in society to be happier. Society has only chosen *sovereigns* to attend more effectively to its happiness and preservation. The well-being of society depends on its security, its liberty, and its power to procure these advantages. The sovereign had to have sufficient power to establish good order and tranquility among the citizens, to assure their possessions, to protect the weak against the encroachments of the strong, to restrain the passions by punishments, and to encourage the virtues by rewards. The right to make these laws in society is called *legislative power. See* LEGISLATION.[1]

But in vain will the *sovereign* have the power to make the laws if he does not simultaneously have the power to have them executed. The passions and interests of men always make them oppose the general good when it seems to be contrary to their private interests. They see the former only in the distance, whereas they have the latter constantly before their eyes. The *sovereign* must thus be vested with the strength necessary to make each individual obey the general laws, which are the wills of all; this is called *executive power*.

Peoples have not always given the same extent of power to the *sovereigns* they have chosen. The experience of all times teaches that the greater men's power is, the more their passions lead them to abuse it. This consideration has caused some nations to put limits on the power of those they assign to govern them. These limitations on sovereignty have varied according to circumstances, according to the people's greater or lesser love of liberty, according to the scope of the drawbacks to which they found themselves entirely exposed with overly arbitrary *sovereigns*. This is what has given birth to the different divisions of sovereignty and the different forms of government. In England, the legislative power resides in the king and in parliament. This latter body represents the nation, which by the British constitution has thereby reserved itself a portion of the *sovereign power*, whereas it has left to the king alone the power of having the laws executed. In the German Empire, the emperor can only make laws with the cooperation of the states of the empire. And yet, the limitation of power must itself have some limits. For a *sovereign* to work for the good of the state, he must

1. That article by Diderot appears in the present volume.

be able to act and take the measures necessary for this end. For a *sovereign* to have power that was overly limited would thus be a defect in a government. It is easy to perceive this defect in the Swedish and Polish governments.[2]

Other peoples have not stipulated by express and authenticated acts the limits they fix on their *sovereigns*. They have been content to impose upon them the necessity of following the fundamental laws of the state, while entrusting them with the legislative as well as the executive power. This is what is called *absolute sovereignty*.[3] Nonetheless, right reason reveals that it always has natural limits. A *sovereign*, however absolute he may be, does not have the right to touch a state's constitutive laws any more than its religion. He may not alter the form of government or change the order of succession, except with formal authorization from his nation. And in any case, he is always subject to the laws of justice and reason, with which no human force may dispense.

When an absolute *sovereign* arrogates to himself the right to change at will the fundamental laws of his country, when he claims an arbitrary power over the persons and possessions of his people, he becomes a despot. No people has ever been able or willing to grant a power of this nature to its *sovereigns*. If they have done so, nature and reason still give them the right to cry out against the violence. *See the article* POWER. Tyranny is nothing but the exercise of despotism.

Sovereignty that resides in a single man, whether it be absolute or limited, is called *monarchy*. See *that article*. When it resides in the people themselves, it exists in its fullest extent and is not susceptible of limitation; this is called *democracy*.[4] Thus, among the Athenians sovereignty resided wholly in the people. Sovereignty is sometimes exercised by a body or an assembly that represents the people, as in the republican states.

In whatever hands *sovereign* power may be vested, its purpose must be solely to make the people subject to it happy. Any sovereign power that

2. The reference is to the Swedish Rikdsag, representing the clergy, nobility, burghers, and peasantry, and dominant through much of the eighteenth century, and the Polish Sejm, representing king, lower house, and upper house, in which the nobility held a *liberum veto* by which one dissenting member could block legislation.

3. The reference is to France.

4. POWER, MONARCHY, and DEMOCRACY have all been included in this volume.

makes men unhappy is a manifest usurpation and an overthrow of the rights that man has never been able to renounce. The *sovereign* owes his subjects security; it is only with this in view that they submitted to authority. *See* PROTECTION. He must establish good order by salutary laws. He must be authorized to change them, as circumstantial necessity demands. He must repress those who would disturb others in the enjoyment of their possessions, their liberty, or their persons. He has the right to set up tribunals and magistrates to render justice and punish the guilty according to known and unvarying rules. These laws are called *civil* to distinguish them from the natural laws and the fundamental laws that the *sovereign* himself cannot contravene. Since he can change the civil laws, some persons believe that he should not be subject to them. Nonetheless, it is natural that the *sovereign* himself conform to his laws for as long as they are in force; this will contribute to making them more respectable to his subjects.

After seeing to the internal security of the state, the *sovereign* must occupy himself with its external security. The latter depends on the state's wealth and its military forces. To achieve this goal, he will cast his eyes over agriculture, population, and commerce. He will seek to maintain peace with his neighbors, but without neglecting military discipline or the forces that would make his nation respectable to all those that might endeavor to harm it or to disturb its tranquility. Thus is born the right of *sovereigns* to wage war, conclude peace, form alliances, *&c. See* PAIX [Peace], GUERRE [War], PUISSANCE [Power].

Such are the principal rights of sovereignty; such are the rights of *sovereigns*. History furnishes us countless examples of prince-oppressors, laws violated, subjects in revolt. If reason governed *sovereigns,* peoples would not need to tie their hands or live with them in a constant state of mistrust. Content to work for the happiness of their subjects, the leaders of nations would not seek to usurp their rights. By a fate attached to human nature, men make continual efforts to extend their power. Whatever dikes the people's prudence has sought to oppose to them, there are none that ambition and violence don't end up smashing or evading. *Sovereigns* have too great an advantage over peoples: the depravity of a single will suffices in the *sovereign* to endanger or destroy the felicity of his subjects, whereas the latter are hardly able to put forth the unanimity or cooperation of wills and forces necessary to oppose and repress these unjust attacks.

It is an error disastrous for the happiness of peoples—and one to which *sovereigns* succumb only too commonly. They believe that sovereignty is debased as soon as its rights are restricted within limits. The leaders of nations who work for their subjects' felicity will assure themselves of their love, will encounter prompt obedience, and will always be fearsome to their enemies. Lord Temple used to say to Charles II "that a king of England who is a man of his people is the greatest king in the world; but if he wants to be more, he will no longer be anything." "I want to be a man of my people," answered the monarch.[5] *See the articles* POWER, AUTORITÉ [Authority], PUISSANCE [Power], SUJETS [Subjects], TYRAN [Tyrant].

5. Sir William Temple (1628–99), diplomat and author of *Observations upon the United Provinces, Essay on the Original and Nature of Government,* and *Miscellanea.* He was a frequent consultant to Charles II.

Switzerland
(*Suisse*)

One of the genres that some contributors resorted to was what might be called the dramatic-historical set piece, often wedged inside an entry that seemed to be innocently geographical in nature. In this article, in the "modern geography" category, Jaucourt traces the constitutional history of Switzerland, with special emphasis on the story of William Tell—a subject that provides more occasion for reflection upon republicanism, its conditions and possibilities. (For another example, see the treatment of Selden in the article SUSSEX *below.) In 1761, a few years before this entry appeared, a Swiss cleric wrote an anonymous, debunking pamphlet tracing the legend of Tell to twelfth-century Denmark, an account favored by many historians today. But the work stirred a hornet's nest at the time, showing its resonance for contemporary Swiss self-understanding. For the present volume, the first eight paragraphs of the article, which offer mere geographical description, have been omitted.*

SWITZERLAND (*Modern geography*). They lived under Roman domination until that empire itself was torn apart by the inundation of northern peoples, and new realms arose on its ruins. One of these realms was Burgundy, of which *Switzerland* was a part until around the end of the twelfth century. At that time, it happened that the realm was divided into several petty sovereignties under the counts of Burgundy, Maurienne, Savoy, and Provence, as well as under the dauphins of Viennois and the dukes of Zähringen.

This article can be found at 15:646–48 in the original edition of the *Encyclopédie*.

Libertas (Liberty)

In the foreground sits a female figure for liberty, with various symbols of liberty, victory, and peace. In the background the story of William Tell is depicted.

Because of this dismemberment, Switzerland never again found itself united under the same leader. Some of its cities were made into imperial cities. Emperor Frederick Barbarossa gave others, along with their territory (in order to possess them as fiefs of the empire), to the counts of Habsburg, from whom the house of Austria is descended.[1] As for other Swiss cities, at least their hereditary government was granted to the duke of Zähringen. This ducal race died out in the thirteenth century, which provided the occasion for the counts of Habsburg to expand their power throughout the country. But what most endangered liberty in Switzerland was the schism that so rent the empire in the same century, when Otto IV and Frederick II were emperors at the same time, and were alternately excommunicated by two popes in succession.[2] In this disorder, all government was in upheaval, and the cities of *Switzerland* in particular felt the dreadful effects of that anarchy. For since the empire was filled with nobles and powerful ecclesiastics, each one exercised his dominion and tried to grab now one city, now another, under any pretext possible.

This oppression prompted many cities of *Switzerland* and Germany to enter together into a confederation for their mutual defense. It was for this reason that Zurich, Uri, and Schwyz concluded a close alliance in 1251. Nonetheless, since that union of cities was not a sufficient barrier against the violence of many lords, most of the free cities of *Switzerland*—and among others the three cantons I have just named—placed themselves under the protection of Rudolph of Habsburg, while reserving their rights and liberties.[3]

When Rudolph had become emperor, the nobility made a formal, legal accusation against the cantons of Schwyz, Uri, and Unterwalden for having revolted against their feudal domination and demolished their castles. Rudolph, who in the past had fought with danger against these petty tyrants, ruled in favor of the citizens.

1. Frederick Barbarossa, German king and Holy Roman Emperor (r. 1152–90).

2. Otto IV (1175?–1218) and Frederick II (1194–1250), called "stupor mundi" ("wonder of the world") for his linguistic, scientific, and other intellectual abilities. The events recounted by Jaucourt occurred from 1212 to 1215.

3. King Rudolph I (1218–91) was crowned in Aachen in 1273.

Albert of Austria, instead of following in the footsteps of his father, conducted himself in an entirely opposite manner as soon as he was on the throne.[4] He strove to extend his power over lands that did not belong to him, and lost by his violent conduct what his predecessor had acquired by moderation. Having a large family, that prince formed the design of submitting all of *Switzerland* to the house of Austria, in order to establish it as a principality for one of his sons. With this intention, he named a certain Grisler[5] sheriff or governor of Uri, and one named Landerberg governor of Schwyz and Unterwalden; these were two men devoted to his will. He decreed that they subject the three cantons to him, either by corruption or by force.

When these two governors gained nothing by their artifices, they employed all kinds of violence and inflicted so much horrific and barbarous treatment that the exasperated people, obtaining no justice from the emperor and finding no safety except in their own courage, devised measures fit for liberating themselves from the frightful slavery under which they were groaning.

Three men from these three cantons, each of whom was the most respected in his canton, were for this reason the principal targets of the governors' persecution. They were named Arnold Melchtal, from the canton of Unterwalden; Werner Stauffacher, from the canton of Schwyz; and Walter Fürst from Uri. They were good and honest peasants, but the difficulty of pronouncing such respectable names has perhaps damaged their celebrity.

These three naturally courageous men—equally mistreated by the governors, and all three united by a long friendship that their common misfortunes had reinforced—held secret assemblies to deliberate over the means of emancipating their Country, and for each to attract into their party all the men of his canton that he could trust and that he knew to have enough heart to contribute to the execution of the decisions they might make. Consistent with this agreement, they each engaged three reliable friends in their plot, and these twelve heads became the leaders of the enterprise. They confirmed their alliance by oath, and resolved, on the arranged day,

4. Albert II of Austria (1298–1358), son of Albert I (1255–1308), himself son of Rudolph I.

5. Also written Gesler.

to cause a general uprising in the three cantons, to demolish the fortified castles, and to expel from the country the two governors along with their protegés.

All the historians inform us that this conspiracy acquired irresistible force by an unforeseen event. Grisler, the governor of Uri, got the idea of inflicting a kind of barbarism that was at once horrible and ridiculous. He had a pole planted with his hat on it in the marketplace of Altorff, capital of the canton of Uri, and ordered everyone on pain of death to salute this hat while removing their own and to genuflect with the same respect as if the governor were there in person.

One of the conspirators, an intrepid man named William Tell who was incapable of servility, did not salute the hat. Grisler sentenced him to be hanged, and by means of a tyrannical nicety, he gave him his pardon, but only on condition that this father, who was known as a very skilled archer, hit an apple placed on his son's head with one arrow. The father fired and was lucky enough or skillful enough to hit the apple without touching his son's head. The whole populace exploded with joy and clapped their hands in general acclamation. Noticing a second arrow under Tell's clothes, Grisler asked him the reason for it and promised to pardon him, whatever intention he might have had. "It was designed for you," Tell responded, "if I had wounded my son."

Nonetheless, frightened by the risk he had run of killing his dear son, Tell waited for the governor at a place where he was to pass several days later. Spotting him, Tell aimed at him, shot him in the heart with that same arrow, and left him dead right there. He informed his friends of his exploit on the spot and kept himself in hiding until the day of their plan's implementation.

On the appointed day, the first of January 1308, the confederates' measures turned out to be so well executed that simultaneously, the garrisons of the three castles were arrested and expelled without bloodshed, the fortresses razed, and by a moderation quite incredible in an angry people, the governors were simply led over the border and released, after swearing an oath that they would never return to the country again. Thus, four men—deprived of the goods of fortune and of the advantages provided by birth, but smitten by love of Country and animated by a just hatred of their tyrants—were the immortal founders of Helvetic liberty! The names of these great men ought to be engraved on the same coin with the names of Mons, the Dorias, the Nassaus.[6]

Informed of his disaster, Emperor Albert resolved to take vengeance, but his plans evaporated upon his premature death. He was killed at Konigsfeld by his nephew John, whom he had stripped, contrary to all justice, of the duchy of Swabia.

Seven years after this adventure, which gave the inhabitants of Schwyz, Uri, and Unterwalden time to provide for their security, the Archduke Leopold, who was heir of the states and the feelings of his father, Albert, assembled an army of twenty thousand men, with the intention of sacking those three rebellious cantons and laying them waste. Their citizens conducted themselves like the Lacedemonians at Thermopylae.[7] Up to five hundred men lay in wait for the greater part of the Austrian army at the Morgarten pass.[8] More fortunate than the Lacedemonians, they threw the archduke's cavalry into disorder, raining a frightful shower of stones down upon them. Profiting from the confusion, they threw themselves with such bravery at their terrified enemies that their defeat was complete.

Since this remarkable victory had been won in the canton of Schwyz, the two other cantons gave that name to their alliance, which, becoming more general, still evokes by its name alone the brilliant successes that won them their liberty.

In vain did the house of Austria try for three centuries to subjugate those three cantons. All its efforts had so little success that instead of bringing the three cantons back to obedience, the latter detached other territories and other cities from the yoke of the house of Austria. Lucerne was the

6. The reference seems to be to William the Silent of Orange-Nassau (1533–84), known as the "father of the fatherland" in the Netherlands because of his role in leading the revolt against Spain in the 1560s and 1570s, and perhaps to the capture of the strategically important city of Mons in 1572 by the Dutch patriot cause during that campaign; and to Andrea Doria (1468?–1560), soldier of fortune, naval commander, and, on more than one occasion, defender of the Genoese republic against French and Habsburg domination, for which he was eventually styled *Liberator et Pater Patriae* [Liberator and Father of his Country]. For another reference by Jaucourt to William of Orange, see LAW, n. 10, above, pp. 342–43.

7. Against the Persians in 480 B.C.

8. The battle occurred in November 1315.

first to enter the confederation in 1332. Zurich, Clarus, and Zug followed Lucerne's example twenty years later; Berne, which is to Switzerland what Amsterdam is to Holland, reinforced the alliance. The number of cantons was increased by the addition of Fribourg and Solothurn in 1481, Basel and Schaffhausen in 1501. That makes twelve. The little territory of Appenzell, which was incorporated in 1513, made the thirteenth. Finally, the princes of the house of Austria saw themselves forced by the Treaty of Münster to declare the *Swiss* an independent people.[9] They have acquired this independence by means of more than sixty battles, and by all appearances they will preserve it for a long time.

Reasonably well-informed persons agree that the Helvetic body should be called the *confederation* rather than the republic of the *Swiss,* because the thirteen cantons form as many independent republics. They govern themselves by entirely different principles. Each of them preserves all the attributes of sovereignty and deals with foreigners at will. Their general diet has no right to make regulations or impose laws.

It is true that there are such tight connections among the thirteen cantons that if one of them were attacked, the other twelve would be obliged to come to its support. But this would be because of the relations two cantons might have with a third, not by a direct alliance each of the thirteen cantons has with the others.

Since the Swiss do not want to sacrifice their liberty to the desire for aggrandizement, they never meddle in the disputes that arise among foreign powers. They observe an exact neutrality, never make themselves the guarantors of any commitment, and draw no other advantage from the wars that so often desolate Europe than to furnish men to their allies indiscriminately, and to the princes who have recourse to them. They think they are strong enough if they preserve their laws. They inhabit a country that cannot excite the ambition of their neighbors. And I dare say they are strong enough to defend themselves against the league of all those same neighbors. Invincible when they are united, and when it's a matter of merely closing off access to their Country, the nature of their republican

9. The Treaty of Münster (October 1648) was part of the larger Treaty of Westphalia ending the Thirty Years' War.

government does not permit them to make advances abroad. It is a pacific government, whereas the whole people is warlike. Equality, the natural lot of men, exists there as far as possible. The laws are mild; such a country is bound to remain free!

It must not be thought, however, that the republican form of government is the same in all cantons. There are seven in which the republic is aristocratic with some mixture of democracy; six are purely democratic. The seven aristocratic ones are Zurich, Berne, Lucerne, Basel, Fribourg, Solothurn, and Schaffhausen; the six democratic ones are Uri, Schwyz, Unterwalden, Zug, Glarus, and Appenzell. This difference in their governments seems to be the result of the condition in which each of these republics found itself before they were set up as cantons. For since the first seven each consisted of only a city with little or no territory, the entire government naturally resided in the bourgeois, and once it had been restricted to the corps of bourgeois, it continued there for good, notwithstanding the large acquisitions of territory they have made since then. On the other hand, since the six democratic cantons had no cities or villages that could claim preeminence over the others, the country was divided into communities. And since each community had an equal right to sovereignty, there was no alternative to admitting them to an equal share of it and establishing pure democracy.

It is known that *Switzerland,* taken for the whole Helvetic body, includes *Switzerland* proper, the allies of the *Swiss,* and the subjects of the *Swiss. Switzerland* proper is divided into sixteen sovereignties—namely, thirteen cantons, two petty sovereign states (i.e., the county of Neuchâtel and the abbey of St. Gall), and one republic (i.e., the city of St. Gall). The allies of the *Swiss* are the Grisons, the Valaisians, and Geneva. The subjects of the *Swiss* are those who are outside of *Switzerland* or those who obey several cantons that hold them jointly.

There are Catholic cantons and Protestant ones. In the cantons of Glarus and Appenzell, the two religions reign equally without causing the least trouble.

I have been expansive on *Switzerland* and haven't said two words about the great realms of Asia, Africa, and America. This is because all those realms bring only slaves into the world, but *Switzerland* produces free men.

I know that while nature is so liberal elsewhere, she has done nothing for that country; and yet the inhabitants live happily there. Solid wealth, which consists in the cultivation of the earth, is reaped by wise and industrious hands. The graces of society and sound philosophy, without which society has no durable charms, have penetrated the parts of *Switzerland* where the climate is most temperate and where abundance prevails. Religious sects are tolerant there. The arts and sciences have made admirable progress there. In fact, these previously rustic countries have in many places managed to combine the politeness of Athens with the simplicity of Lacedemon. Let these lands be careful today not to adopt foreign luxury or to let the sumptuary laws that prohibit it become dormant!

Those curious about the history of the vicissitudes of *Switzerland* will consult the memoirs of M. Bochat, which make up three volumes in-4°. Gesner, Scheuchzer, and Wagner have offered the natural history of Helvetia.[10] (*Chevalier* DE JAUCOURT)

10. Charles-Guillaume Loys de Bochat (1695–1754), whose *Memoires critiques, pour servir d'eclaircissemens sur divers points de l'histoire ancienne de la Suisse* [Critical memoirs, to serve in illuminating various points in the early history of Switzerland] came out in numerous editions from 1727 to 1749; Johann Jakob Scheuchzer (1672–1733), *Helvetiae historia naturalis* [Natural history of Switzerland] (1716–18); Conrad Gesner (1516–65), author of many works on natural history.

Sussex

Like the articles on Rutland and Switzerland, above, this entry contains a pointed piece of history buried beneath a seemingly harmless, if obscure, geographical description. For Sussex was the home of the Englishman John Selden, a man whose political and intellectual activities Jaucourt wished to single out for attention. The first thirty-eight paragraphs, containing geographical and historical material, have been omitted here; only the final portion of the article, which concerns Selden's life and career, have been reproduced.

SUSSEX (*Modern geography*). *Selden* (John) is regarded by foreigners as one of the learned men of Europe. But in general, they do not know about the glory he acquired in his country as a member of Parliament and the role he played there—without, however, discontinuing his cultivation of letters, and without the reversals he suffered defending the rights of the nation managing to shake the strength of his soul. For his motto, he took these Greek words: *περι παντὸς τὴν ελευθεριαν, liberty over all things.*

He was born in 1584, studied at Oxford, distinguished himself there, and soon made a great reputation by the writings he brought forth one after the other on various subjects. In 1621, King James I, unhappy with Parliament, had Selden arrested along with several members of the House of Commons. In 1625, he was elected deputy to the first Parliament convened under Charles I, and there he spoke out clearly against the Duke of Buckingham. In 1627 and 1628, he was again very actively opposed to the court party.[1]

This article can be found at 15:704–5 in the original edition of the *Encyclopédie*.

1. James I (r. 1603–25), Charles I (r. 1625–49), and George Villiers, First Duke of Buckingham (1592–1628), a favorite of James and an advocate of an aggressive and expensive foreign policy.

> I do not take the floor (he said) in the debates that have taken place concerning the liberty of subjects; I do not take the floor to make an argument on this point, the most important that has ever been debated. This liberty, which I trust is recognized by everyone as well as by the lawyers, has been violated, though not without complaint. But I do not believe the violation has ever been legitimated, except in the most recent instance. The privilege of *habeas corpus* has been demanded; the case has been referred by the King's order; notification has been made by the council. Argument was made; seven parliamentary acts were cited, and all this has done no good; authority alone has acted, it was decided that whoever is imprisoned by order of king or council cannot be released. I have always seen that in great affairs, the custom has been to publicly advance the reasons for one's action. Here, it is a case where his Majesty and his Council are interested parties. I desire only that some of the council instruct us on what might establish such an extensive power.[2]

In 1629, Selden again distinguished himself against the court when there was agitation in the lower house to vote on whether customs officials taking the effects of members of Parliament wasn't a violation of their privileges. The speaker refused to propose the question, by reason of the king's prohibition. Selden told him:

> It is surprising, Mr. Speaker, that you dare not put the question when the chamber commands you. They who come after you will therefore declare in all cases that they have the King's command not to put the question. But do be aware, sir, that this is not how to fulfill your duty. We are assembled here for the public good by commandment of the King and under the great Seal. And it is the King himself who, sitting on his throne and in the presence of the two houses, has named you our Speaker.[3]

2. A slightly different version of this March 25, 1628, speech can be found in *Commons Debates: 1628*, ed. Robert C. Johnson and Maija Jansson Cole (New Haven: Yale University Press, 1977), 2:99–100.

3. For a slightly different version of this March 2, 1629, speech, see *Commons Debates for 1629*, ed. Wallace Notestein and Frances Helen Relf (Minneapolis: University of Minnesota Press, 1921), 103; upon these words, the House locked the doors and drafted a protestation, precipitating the constitutional crisis that led Charles to disband Parliament.

Once the king had dissolved Parliament, Selden was arrested and incarcerated in the prison of the King's Bench, where his life was at risk because of the plague that prevailed in the neighborhood. He recovered his liberty some time afterward, and Parliament gave him five thousand pounds sterling to compensate him for the losses he had incurred on this occasion.[4]

In 1630, he was again imprisoned with some lords, accused of having distributed a libelous work entitled *Propositions for the service of the king, to bridle the impertinence of parliaments.*[5] The birth of Charles, Prince of Wales, persuaded the king to order that Selden and the other prisoners be set free.

In 1634, a dispute arose between England and Holland over the herring fishing off the coasts of Great Britain. Grotius having published his *Mare liberum* in favor of the Dutch,[6] Selden responded with his *Mare clausum, seu de dominio maris, libri duo*, London 1636, *in-8°*.[7] This work put him on such good terms with the court that it was entirely up to him whether to rise to the highest offices, but he preferred the pleasure of dedicating himself completely to study. The king himself, having decided to take the seals from Mr. Littleton, had some desire to give them to Selden. But Lords Clarendon and Falkland declared to His Majesty that Selden would refuse this post.[8] He accepted only the position of keeper of the Tower archives, which Parliament entrusted to him, and some time afterward he was made one of the twelve commissioners set up for the administration of the admiralty.[9]

4. This latter event occurred much later, in 1647.

5. The 1629 manuscript, apparently intercepted before publication, was entitled *A proposition for His Majesty's service to bridle the impertinence of Parliament,* and the case went to Star Chamber.

6. See Hugo Grotius, *The Free Sea,* trans. Richard Hakluyt, ed. and intro. David Armitage (Indianapolis: Liberty Fund, 2004). The work originally appeared in 1609.

7. The work was translated by Marchamont Nedham (London: Dugard, 1652) under the subtitle *Of the dominion, or ownership, of the sea;* James Howell revised the translation two years later by the subtitle *The right and dominion of the sea.*

8. Edward Littleton (1589–1645), Lord Keeper of the Great Seal in 1641; Lucius Cary, Second Viscount Falkland (1610–43), organizer of an intellectual society at Great Tew in the 1630s who ended up fighting, with some ambivalence, for the king in 1642; Edward Hyde, First Earl of Clarendon (1609–74), political leader and historian who also became a moderate royalist during the Civil War. The event Jaucourt describes occurred in 1642.

9. These two events occurred in 1644–45.

His health weakened at the beginning of 1654, and he died on the following December 16. The executors of his will generously relinquished his library, to make a gift of it to the University of Oxford. Doctor Burnet said that this library was appraised at several thousand pounds sterling, and that it was regarded as one of the most intriguing in Europe.[10]

All of Selden's works have been collected by Doctor David Wilkins in three volumes, *in-folio*, in London in 1726. The first two volumes contain the Latin works, and the third the English ones. In front, the editor has placed an extensive life of Selden and has added some other pieces by the same author that had not yet appeared—among others, letters, poetry, *&c.*

It is quite surprising that the editor has not inserted in his collection the work entitled *Historical and political researches* on the laws of England, from the earliest times to the reign of Queen Elizabeth. This work is by Selden and was published under his name in London in 1739, *in-fol.*, fourth edition. Its principal purpose is to prove by historical deductions that the kings of England have never been vested with arbitrary power. This book was published for the first time *in quarto* in 1649, shortly after the death of Charles I.[11]

Selden's learning is known to everyone. Doctor Hicker observes nonetheless that he did not have a profound grasp of Anglo-Saxon. His erudition was extraordinary, always changing and full of useful observations. But his works lack method and clarity of style. His *Analecta anglo-britannica* do not reveal as much as might be desired about the religion and government of the Saxons, or the revolutions they experienced.[12]

His famous treatise *De diis Siriis* has three great defects, which he shares with most of those who have written on the idolatry of Oriental peoples:[13] (1) very few quotations; (2) among these quotations, most of those who have written about the gods of the Orient are constantly confusing the Greek

10. Bishop Gilbert Burnet (1643–1715), author of *History of the Reformation of the Church of England* (1679, 1682, 1714) and *History of my own Times,* published posthumously by his request in 1723.

11. *An historical and political discourse of the laws and government of England* also appeared in 1689 and 1760.

12. *Analecton Anglobritannicon* [Anglo-British fragments] (1615).

13. *De dis* [or "*diis*"] *syris* [On the Syrian gods] (London, 1617, and Leiden, 1629).

gods with those of barbarous peoples; (3) the allegorical interpretation of myths, which Selden has not always avoided.

His *History of tithes* was extremely offensive to the clergy and was attacked on all sides.[14] This work's purpose is to prove that tithes are not of divine right, although the author does not want to contest the ecclesiastics' possession of them, for that is founded on the laws of the country.

His labors on the *marbles of Arundel* brought him much honor and were worth the fine editions of Prideaux in 1676, *in-fol.* and of Mattaire in 1732.[15]

His *Titles of honor* have been reprinted separately three or four times.[16] Nicholson says that, concerning the high and petty nobility of England, she must confess that one must read this book in order to acquire a general idea of all the different degrees of distinction, from emperor to country gentleman.

His *Mare clausum* is highly praised by the English, who constantly maintain that as opposed to Grotius, the author has used old historical monuments to demonstrate the dominion of the English over the four seas, and that the French, the Flemish, and the Dutch have no right to fish there without their permission. But for his part, Grotius has the vote of foreigners. In any case, the English nation so esteemed the work of Selden that by express order of the king and council, this book was brought publicly to the barons of the Exchequer, to be deposited in the archives like an invaluable document among those that concern the rights of the Crown.

His *Fleta, seu commentarius juris anglicani* appeared in London, *in quarto*, and it is a prized monument for the nation. A second edition was offered in 1685, in which the mistakes that Selden himself had indicated were to have been corrected.[17]

14. *Historie of Tithes* (1618), written in English.

15. The *Marmora Oxoniensis ex Arundellianis, Seldenianis, aliisque* [The Oxford Marbles from Arundel, Selden and others], brought out by Humphrey Prideaux in 1676 and Michel Mattaire, under a slightly different title, in 1732.

16. *Titles of honor* was brought out in editions of 1614, 1631, and 1672, and is more recently available from the Lawbook Exchange in a 2006 edition.

17. The work, whose title may be translated as *Fleta, or a commentary on English law*, was the first-ever printed edition of a late thirteenth-century manuscript of the same name—so called because the anonymous author stated in the preface that he wrote the work while in Fleet prison. It appeared first in 1647, in a corrected but still imperfect edition of 1685, and later in numerous twentieth-century reprints; it was translated into English as *The*

The book *De jure naturali, & gentium* received great praise from Pufendorf, but Messrs. Le Clerc and Barbeyrac think differently.[18] The former criticizes him for his rabbinical principles, built on uncertain assumptions about the Judaic tradition. The latter adds that Selden was content to cite the decisions of the rabbis, without taking the trouble to examine whether they were right or not. It is certain that in a work of this nature, his principles ought to have been derived from the pure light of reason, and not solely from precepts given to Noah that are of highly uncertain number and are founded only on a dubious tradition. Finally, this work of Selden's contains a great deal of disorder, and especially obscurity, which is noticeable in his writings in general. (*Chevalier* DE JAUCOURT)

Dissertation of John Selden, Annexed to "Fleta," in a London edition of 1771, six years after this article appeared.

18. Pufendorf discusses Selden sympathetically in *Of the Law of Nature and Nations,* VIII.iii.4 (and perhaps elsewhere). In the same place, Jean Barbeyrac (1674?–1744), the French Huguenot jurist and émigré to Holland whose translations and extensive commentary of Grotius and Pufendorf became influential in the eighteenth century, draws on Locke to defend Grotius from Pufendorf's reliance on Selden; Jean Le Clerc (1657–1736) was a Genevan theologian, Old Testament scholar, and journalist who also lived in Amsterdam, where Locke was among his friends and correspondents.

Volume 16
(1765)

Temples of Liberty
(*Temples de la Liberté*)

TEMPLES OF LIBERTY (*Roman antiquity*). A people as rightly idolatrous of liberty as the Roman people could not fail to make a divinity of it, and to consecrate its *temples* and altars. Thus, this goddess, who was invoked to preserve that same liberty which the extinction of royalty had procured, had many temples in the city.

Cicero, *bk. II De nat. deor.*, mentions one of these *temples*.[1] Publius Victor had had one constructed on the Aventine hill, with a vestibule named *the vestibule of Liberty*. The ancients, who often spoke of this vestibule, do not inform us of its intended use. But one may believe that public sales took place there, as in the others. Referring to the *temple* that Tiberius Gracchus had consecrated to the same goddess, Titus Livy says that its columns were made of bronze and that very fine statues were seen there. When Cicero departed for his exile, P. Clodius, his persecutor, dedicated the house of that great man to *Liberty*.[2]

Finally, Dio informs us that by public decree, the friends of Antony had a *temple* to the same goddess built on behalf of Julius Caesar[3]—a deed quite worthy of those last Romans, who raised a *temple* to Liberty in honor of the man who had made them lose the remnants of that precious prerogative, which the Mariuses and the Sullas had still left them, and of which they had hitherto been so jealous. (*D.J.*)

This article can be found at 16:75 in the original edition of the *Encyclopédie*.

1. Cicero, *On the Nature of the Gods* [De natura deorum], II.xxiii.61, in *On the Nature of the Gods. Academics.* Loeb Classical Library 268 (Cambridge: Harvard University Press, 1933), 181–83.

2. See Cicero, *De domo sua* [On his own house], 44.116, and Plutarch's *Life of Cicero*, xxxiii.1.

3. Dio Cassius (ca. 155–235?), *Roman Histories*, XLIII.44.1, for this episode. The temple was voted by the Senate in 46 B.C.

Toleration
(*Tolérance*)

This article by Jaucourt was deleted by the censor and therefore suppressed by the publisher Le Breton before it would have appeared in print at 16:383. It was restored by Douglas H. Gordon and Norman L. Torrey in their edited work The Censoring of Diderot's "Encyclopédie" and the Re-established Text *(New York: Columbia University Press, 1947), 95–106. An article on the same subject had been written for the* Encyclopédie *by Romilly, and in the margins to the Jaucourt entry, Le Breton wrote, "[delete] this article. It is a weak repetition of the first and does double duty; moreover, agreed by M. Did[erot]." Jaucourt indicates at the end of the article that his entry draws heavily from John Locke's 1692* Epistola de Tolerantia *[A letter on toleration]. Much of the text can also be found verbatim in Jean Barbeyrac, "What has been said about Gregory of Nazianzen," in* Traité de la morale des peres de l'Eglise *[Treatise on the morality of the Church fathers] (Amsterdam: Pierre de Coup, 1728), 180–82 and passim. Barbeyrac, the natural law professor, translator, and prolific Protestant journalist, edited the Amsterdam-based* Bibliothèque raisonnée, *to which Jaucourt seems to have contributed in the early 1730s.*

The text on which the present translation of "Toleration" is based is in the public domain. It is used courtesy of the *ARTFL Encyclopédie Project*, which created the text from images of the original French page proofs borrowed from the Small Special Collections Library at the University of Virginia. (See "Censored Articles: Tolérance" in "The 18th Volume," University of Chicago: *ARTFL Encyclopédie Project*, Spring 2011 Edition, ed. Robert Morrissey, http://encyclopedie.uchicago.edu/.)

Tolerance (*Religion, Morality, Politics*), support of the church or state for those who profess the opinions that they believe true in matters of religion without disturbing civil society.

I say church or state, because two types of toleration are distinguished, ecclesiastical toleration and civil toleration. The first consists in bearing with those who have some peculiar sentiment within the same ecclesiastical society; the second in leaving freedom of conscience in the state to those who are not of the dominant religion, or who have separated themselves from it, or who have been excluded from it because of certain peculiar opinions.

There is as much difference between the former sort of toleration and the latter as there is between ecclesiastical society and civil society. Each of these societies has its own laws, and laws that are different in nature: force is essential to civil laws, whereas everything that smacks of constraint is incompatible with the legitimate goal of ecclesiastical laws.

The common purpose of ecclesiastical associations and of associations for the human sciences should doubtless be to search painstakingly for the truth, and to convince those who are ignorant of it. To reasonably claim to have discovered the truth, one must have good reasons for the opinions one believes to be true, and one can persuade others of these opinions only by making them sample these reasons. The only means of making others sample them is to put them forward with all the clarity and force one can muster. If, notwithstanding, they do not yield, it is through lack of perspicacity—or by bias, or if you will, by willful stubbornness. For I will not quibble over the question of whether there are any such reasons on which one can be certain. To whichever of these causes one attributes a person's obstinacy in persisting in opinions one believes to be false, it is always certain that the ways of force are entirely unsuitable for bringing him back on track.

Violence does not enlighten; it does not possess the property of changing the character, or the disposition of mind or heart, of anyone at all. A stupid man will not become more perspicacious because of it.[1] It is

1. For this argument, see John Locke, *A Letter Concerning Toleration*, ed. James H. Tully (Indianapolis: Hackett, 1983), 46.

to attempt the impossible to make him understand something beyond his reach; it is to act as a tyrant to coerce him to recognize as true what he is not capable of understanding. In a man biased in whatever fashion toward ideas that prevent him from being impressed by the strongest reasons you can adduce against them, the more you want to force him to sample these reasons, the more he will stiffen up and hold firm in his opinions. This is the nature of bias; it can be attacked successfully only from covert paths, in engaging and indirect ways. A willfully stubborn man, if that is what we are dealing with here, will begin to become stubborn in good faith. The reasons for his opinion, which he perhaps had mistrusted, will seem strong to him as soon as the partisans of the opposite opinion evince a mistrust in their own opinions by calling on the aid of violence. One is led naturally to think that way about those who use such means, and this judgment is very well founded. When we feel strong enough with the arms of truth, we have no desire to borrow alien ones.

Up to this point, I have assumed that the religion of those who want to force others into line is the only true one, or at least is more orthodox than that of the people being coerced. But sometimes this assumption is far from being indubitable, so that it could be used reasonably to justify the use of violence—if it were not by nature absurd and unjust. This is just what is at issue: whether you, who want to coerce me, belong to a better religion than mine, or else have more orthodox opinions than mine on particular points of a religion we have in common. This is what will always be subject to dispute among men, none of whom are infallible and whom God has given no visible judge to resolve it with full power.

I say more: there are even opposing opinions of which one cannot be assured that one or the other is necessarily true, since they might both be false. Such are the opinions concerning the depths of the divine nature, the essence of God, the extent and proportion of his attributes, his decrees, his manner of acting, etc. God has only revealed things to us in a very obscure manner, whether because they completely surpass the feeble reach of our minds or because he did not want us to know more about them. It is over the questions related to such matters, however, that Christians of all times have been most impassioned and most divided. They recognize that these are mysteries, but they give themselves license to want to penetrate them—

similar to blind people who would argue amongst themselves about colors and fight to support their opinion.

From this small number of observations, it follows that one ought to leave each person the freedom to believe and profess what seems true to him in religious matters. No one may undermine this freedom without manifestly encroaching upon the rights of God, who alone is master of our consciences. Though a man may be as mistaken as you like on this, it is certain that he must nonetheless act according to his lights until he is disabused of his errors.[2] It is up to the examiner of hearts to see whether these errors come from negligence or from some other bad source. It is only to him that one is obliged to account for them, just as it is only he who can judge them.

Nonetheless, one must not infer from this that every type of sect and religion has to be tolerated in the same ecclesiastical society. Not to allow into the society, or to exclude from it, those who are not of such and such an authorized opinion is a different thing from persecuting them to force them to abandon their peculiar opinions or not to profess them.[3]

There are certainly fundamental truths in Christianity which its different parties have agreed upon at all times, because they are clearly contained in Scripture and so often repeated that one cannot avoid acknowledging them.

Ecclesiastical toleration does not extend to those who would like to deny such indubitable truths.[4] And yet, all one can do against them is to declare that they cannot be recognized as members of the same church. Besides, far from persecuting them in any manner, one ought to have compassion for them and put in effect the most engaging methods of persuasion in order to dissipate their blindness. Both the interests of their salvation and the interests of the truth demand that one abstain from every appearance of vexation toward them; this would serve only to confirm them in their errors and make it easier for them to spread these errors. The persecuted, who are only so because of their religion, inspire pity for themselves in those who have some humanity, and at the same time aversion for the persecutors. From there, one passes easily to having a less bad opinion of the sentiments

2. Locke, *Letter,* 26.
3. Ibid., 30.
4. Ibid., 49ff.

of the persecuted, and a less good one for those of the persecutors. Persecution can make proselytes for error as well as for truth.

One persecutes men by involving the civil power, but this power, reduced to its just limits, has no more right in this area than do the leaders of ecclesiastical society. For the civil power as such acts and operates only by force. Now force, put in practice against the wayward in religious matters, is by itself both absurd and unjust. The sovereign's authority certainly cannot make it just and reasonable.

Nor does this use of force have any connection with the purpose of civil societies, which is what determines the extent of sovereign power. Every religion considered in itself, however erroneous it may be, is absolutely beyond their jurisdiction, unless those who profess it use this pretext to do and teach things that are either contrary to morals or prohibited by reasons of public utility. For then, the error can hardly be in good faith. And even assuming it is, it is still not excusable, even before the human tribunal. The sovereign has an incontestable right to repress those who do things that are certainly bad, by whatever maxim they may do them.

But this is not the case with errors that are innocent in relation to public order and tranquility, however dangerous they are thought to be to the salvation of those preoccupied by them. It is their business, and not the business of the sovereign considered as such and acting by the power appropriate to him.

Men have not come together as a body in civil society to establish or preserve, by common agreement, a certain religion that they believed to be the only true one. In the independence of the state of nature, they had nothing to fear from that quarter. No one had yet gotten the idea of coercing others, or insulting them, in order to bring them back to the opinions that he himself had of the divinity, or to the manner in which he thought he was obliged to serve the divinity. Each person thought only of finding some support, in the union of wills and forces of a large multitude, to compensate for his impotence in defending himself alone; as well as public protection by which his life, his possessions, and his temporal rights would be as secure as possible. To this end, men divested themselves of a part of their natural liberty. And they were as jealous of the part they retained as they would otherwise have been glad to hold on to all of it. One of the most substantial rights inherent in the liberty they retained, for anyone who took religion at all to heart, was doubtless that of serving the divinity in the manner they believed most agreeable to him.

But even if men were foolish enough to submit their judgment and their will in religious matters to the judgment and will of the sovereign, the latter would not thereby acquire more right in this respect, because this is not one of the things that each person is at liberty to dispose of at his whim. A man can never give another man arbitrary power over his life, since he is not the master of that. He is still less the master of his conscience, whose dominion belongs so much to God that other men, whatever they want and whatever they do, cannot truly exercise any dominion over it.

The greatest efforts of violence only end up leading men to pretend to believe, not to truly believe. Indeed, whatever desire we have to believe, we cannot convince ourselves of the opposite of what seems true to us, unless some reason capable of convincing our minds is presented to us.

Far from an external force producing this effect, it produces one that is just the opposite. Here, even God himself uses his infinite power solely in a manner that is proportioned to the nature of religion and of our understanding. If he takes our captive thoughts and subjects them to the obedience of J. C., if he triumphs over our errors, this is only by the victorious brilliance of the truth, by unearthly arms. It was the apostle St. Paul, who before his conversion had employed earthly ones, who afterward declared loudly that they are not suitable for his army, and that he needed all the mercy of God for having been a persecutor, even though he acted then out of ignorance and in good faith.

Every sovereign as such is committed to do what is beneficial for the state and to avoid what may be harmful. Now generally speaking, there is nothing more beneficial to a state than increasing the number of subjects, nothing more pernicious than what tends to decrease its number.[5] But experience has borne out that civil intolerance is the plague of states in this

5. The populationist argument for religious toleration can be found, among other places, in seventeenth-century Dutch republican authors such as Pieter de la Court; see his "Political Maxims of the State of Holland," chap. 14, reprinted in Henry C. Clark, *Commerce, Culture, and Liberty: Readings on Capitalism Before Adam Smith* (Indianapolis: Liberty Fund, 2003), 25–30.

respect, as in every other. The Inquisition has reduced the finest countries in the world virtually to solitary spaces. And if we wanted to talk frankly about other places, we would recognize how much it cost them to reduce countless people to the necessity of leaving everything in order to go elsewhere to serve God peaceably according to the lights of their conscience.[6] On the other hand, look at the countries in which each person has an honest freedom of conscience; it will be found that this freedom contributes to making those countries flourish, in proportion to how far it is provided.

Thus, let us not believe that religious diversity in itself causes tumults and disorders in a state. The sovereign has only to keep the scales equal—as he can and must—so that he leaves no party with the means of oppressing another one. Everything will soon be calm, and religious diversity will bring forth no more discord, no more disorder, than different tastes in any other thing.

This is not a prophecy based upon a schematic system. Without going back to paganism, one has only (as I have just said) to glance over the countries where each person is permitted to serve God in his own manner, and to profess the religion he thinks best. It will be noticed that the more scrupulously toleration is observed, the more peace prevails there, notwithstanding the diversity of religions.

Before the United Provinces gave England a fine example of toleration, few people thought such toleration was compatible with good government. It had been regarded as an impossible thing for a large number of religious sects to live together in profound peace, and even to be able to bear each other and assist each other out of a motive of love of Country. Experience has opened everyone's eyes.

In essence, even if some disadvantages were to arise from religious diversity, this would not suffice to sanction civil intolerance. It would still be necessary to get around to examining whether one has the right to employ such an expedient to prevent these disadvantages. Some of these arise by accident out of a virtual totality of effects that are more legitimate. *Nihil est ab*

6. Probably a reference to France after the Revocation of the Edict of Nantes (1685), withdrawing limited religious toleration for French Protestants (Huguenots) and leading to their mass exile. Jaucourt himself was born into a Huguenot family.

omni parte beatum.[7] Here, moreover, we have disadvantage set against disadvantage. For a superior force, as long as it exists, may well close the mouths and tie the hands of the persecuted, but since it cannot change their minds, only one occasion is needed to enable the latter to get the upper hand with all the more vigor in that the weight under which they groaned was crushing. The least zealous on the religious essentials are then the most ardent in compensating themselves for the violence they have suffered in relation to the freedom of their opinions. And the wise have a great deal of trouble restraining fervor that believes itself authorized by the injustice it has endured.

I know there exist individuals who are afraid that if each person were accorded freedom of conscience, there would be as many religions as there are people, and this apprehension disturbs them. But experience does not confirm this fear in the countries in which many religions are tolerated. Almost all men are disposed to remain in the religion in which they were raised, and to content themselves with the wisdom of their forefathers, as with their land and their sun.

On the contrary, the establishment of toleration seems the most fitting way of uniting the different Christian sects, or at least of reducing their number. Once the truth has some elbow room, once each person is free to examine it without constraint, you will see it make rapid progress. Men will at least learn to familiarize themselves with the different opinions, and especially with those who profess them. They will become accustomed to suffering others and to being suffered. Peace and truth will open their arms to each other—sometimes peace and error, but peace is such a big advantage! From mutual support, the greatest possible uniformity of sentiments will emerge (for after all, complete uniformity can never exist). Providence has intended the diversity of sentiments to serve in the exercise of the greatest virtue of a Christian: toleration. To say that in the diversity of opinions, God authorizes the use of violence to maintain or advance the interests of the truth that each person thinks he has on his side would be to say that the Supreme Being wanted to throw the entire human race into tumult.

For political reasons, a sovereign may admit or not admit foreigners of such and such a religion into his domain. In his state, he may render dominant

7. "Nothing is happy altogether." Horace, *Odes,* II.xvi.27–28.

the religion that he professes and thinks the best; these are the attributes of sovereignty. But he may not coerce the consciences of his own subjects, or deprive them, by reason of their nonconformity with the dominant religion, of the rights those subjects have as men and citizens. Thus, it is right to regard as tyrannical the laws from the Theodosian and Justinian codes that strip heretics, by the sole reason that they are heretics, of the capacity to inherit or make a will.[8]

The most zealously orthodox fathers of the church were quite far from approving the laws of the two emperors we have just named; they preached only toleration. "It is," says Tertullian, "a species of impiety to deprive men of liberty in religious matters, to prevent them from choosing a divinity, not to allow them the one they want, to force them to worship the one they do not want. No God, no man even, would want one to serve him in spite of himself." Here is the Latin text: "*Videte enim, ne et hoc ad irreligiositatis elogium concurrat, adimere libertatem religionis, et interdicere optionem divinitatis, ut non liceat mihi colere quem velim, sed cogar colere quem nolim. Nemo se ab invito coli volet, ne homo quidem." Apologet. ch. xxiv. p. 237. ed. Havercamp.*[9]

The same Tertullian says elsewhere: "All men have a natural right to serve whatever divinity they like, and the religion of one does neither good nor harm to another. Nor is it fitting for religion to coerce people into embracing one divinity rather than another, because every religion ought to be embraced voluntarily and not by force." "*Tamen humani juris et naturalis potestatis, est unicuique, quod putaveris, colere: nec alii obest, aut prodest, alterius religio. Sed nec religionis est cogere religionem, quae sponte suscipi debeat, non vi,*" etc. *Ad Scapulam*, cap. ii., p. 69.[10]

8. The reference is to the Code of Emperor Theodosius (379–95), XVI.i.2, and to the policies of Justinian (529–65) as well as to the Justinian Code, I.v.12, I.xi.9–10, among others.

9. The Loeb translation by T. R. Glover reads, "Look to it, whether this also may form part of the accusation of irreligion—to do away with freedom of religion, to forbid a man choice of deity, so that I may not worship whom I would, but am forced to worship whom I would not. No one, not even a man, will wish to receive reluctant worship." Tertullian, "Apology," xxiv.6, in *Apology. De Spectaculis. Minucius Felix: Octavius,* Loeb 250 (1931), 133.

10. "It is the law of mankind and the natural right of each individual to worship what he thinks proper, nor does the religion of one man either harm or help another. But, it is not proper for religion to compel men to religion, which should be accepted of one's own accord, not by force," etc. See Tertullian, "To Scapula," in *Tertullian: Apologetical Works,*

The reader will exempt me from producing similar passages here from St. Cyprian, epist. 59, pag. 130. ed. Fell, Brem. epist. 4. p. 9. epist. 54.[11] From *Lactantius,* Inst. div. bk. V. ch. xiii. num. 18.19. c. xix. num. 12. 17. 23. ed. Cellar.[12] From Arnob. lib. I, p. 11. Lugd. B. 1651.[13] From *Saint Hilary,* ad constant. lib. I. p. 1221 ed. Benedict, et lib. contr. Auxeut, cap. iii and iv. pag. 1264, 1265.[14] From *St. Athanasius,* epist. ad solitary. vit. agent. vol. I. p. 830. 852. 855. etc. edit. 1686. Colon. (or Lips.).[15] From *Optat de Mileve,* Contra Permenian. lib. II.[16] From *St. Ambrose,* in Luc. lib. VII. cap. x.[17] From *St. Chrysostom,* homil. 47. in Matth. t. II. pag. 297. edit. savil. Eton. serm. de anathem. et alib.[18] From *Sulpicius Severus,* sacr. hist. bk. II. c. xlvii ff.[19] From *Salvian,* de gubern. Dei. bk. V. c. ii p. 100 101. ed. de Baluz.[20] From *the pope Gregory the Great,* bk. II. ep. ind. ii. epist. 52. ad Joann. Hierosolym.[21] From *Isidore,* chron. Gotth. and Vandal. p. 224. ed. Vulcan.[22] From *the Council of Toledo,* can. 4. *See* dist. 45. ch. v. in jur. can.[23] From *St. Bernard,* in cantic. Canticor. serm. 64. etc.[24]

---

trans. Rudolph Arbesmann et al. (New York: Fathers of the Church, 1950), 152. Jaucourt's text has "putaveris" for "putaverit."

11. Cyprian (ca. 200–258), Bishop of Carthage, *Letters.*

12. Lactantius (ca. 240–ca. 320).

13. Arnobius of Sicca (fl. late 3rd century), *Arnobii Afri Adversus gentes libri VII* [Arnobius of Africa against the pagan nations] (Lugduni Batavorum, 1651).

14. St. Hilary of Poitier (ca. 300–367), *Ad Constantium Augustum liber secundus* [To Constantius Augustus, book two] and *Contra Arianos vel Auxentium Mediolanensem liber* [Against the Arians or Auxentius of Milan].

15. Saint Alexandrinus Athanasius, Bishop of Alexandria (ca. 296–373), *Sancti patris nostri Athanasii archiepiscopi opera quae reperiuntur omnia* [All the works of our father the Holy Athanasius, archbishop, that have been discovered] (Coloniae: Weidmann, 1686).

16. Saint Optatus, Bishop of Mileve (4th century), *De schismate Donatistarum* [On the schism of the Donatists], including an attack on Parmenianum, Bishop of Carthage (d. 391–92).

17. Saint Ambrose, Bishop of Milan (ca. 340–97), the reference is to his commentary on the Gospel of Luke.

18. Saint John Chrysostom (ca. 354–407), Bishop of Constantinople, *Homilies on Matthew.*

19. Saint Sulpicius Severus (ca. 360–ca. 425), *Historia sacra* [Sacred histories].

20. Salvian (ca. 405–after 470), *De Gubernatione Dei* [On the government of God].

21. Saint Gregory I, or Pope Gregory the Great (ca. 540–604), *Letters.*

22. Saint Isidore of Seville (ca. 560–636), *Chronica Gotthorum, Vandalorum, & Langobardorum* [The chronicles of the Goths, Vandals, and Lombards].

23. The Third Council of Toledo (589), hosted by Isidore's brother Leander, Bishop of Seville, which settled the Arian controversy and brought Christianity to Spain.

24. Saint Bernard of Clairvaux (1090–1153), *Cantica canticorum* [Song of songs].

Since the lack of ecclesiastical toleration always leads to the lack of civil toleration, it follows that the former is no less necessary than the latter. And yet it has happened in all sects, not excepting the Protestant one, that there have been times when men have strayed but too far on this point from the principles of the Gospel. But today, every Protestant rejects Beza's ideas and abhors Calvin's conduct.[25] Thus, the blame must fall on the person of that reformer, not on religion, which condemns him as it condemns the inquisitors.

The passage where St. Paul says to Titus, cap. iii. v. 10., "avoid the heretic after one or two warnings," encourages neither civil nor ecclesiastical intolerance.[26] For to avoid and to persecute are not synonymous words in any language. Moreover, this passage concerns people of bad faith who in the time of the apostles formed a sect apart, and who out of pure mischief had separated themselves from the churches that those holy men had founded. And yet Saint Paul recommends that Titus inform them charitably of their mistake, and ultimately abandon them in the event they persist in their conduct.

I said above that the sovereign had the right not to admit foreigners of such and such religion in his domain. But it is still asked whether the worship of many religions is a beneficial thing in a state. The author of *The Spirit of the Laws* was in no doubt: one notices (he says in one of his works)[27] that those who live under tolerant and tolerated religions normally make themselves more useful to their Country than those who live under the dominant religion. This is because, distant from men and able to achieve distinction only by their opulence and their wealth, they are led to acquire this by their work, and to embrace society's hardest jobs. Moreover, since all religions contain precepts useful to society, it is good for them to be observed with zeal. Now what is more capable of animating this zeal than their multiplicity?

25. The allusion is to Theodore Beza (1519–1605), Calvin's lieutenant in Geneva and author of the 1554 *De Haereticis a civili magistratu puniendis* [On the punishment of heretics by the civil magistrate] (French translation, 1560), which defended Calvin's 1553 burning of the anti-Trinitarian Michael Servetus in Geneva.

26. Titus, 3:10: "As for a man who is factious, after admonishing him once or twice, have nothing more to do with him."

27. For this and the next four paragraphs, see Montesquieu, *Persian Letters,* letter 85.

These are rivals that pardon each other nothing; the jealousy descends even to individuals. Each person keeps himself on guard, and is afraid of doing things that would dishonor his party and expose it to the contempt and the unpardonable censure of the opposite party. Moreover, it has always been noticed that the introduction of a new sect within a state was the surest means of correcting the abuses of the old sect. It is in vain to say that it is not in the interest of the prince to allow many religions in his state; if all the sects in the world were to come and gather there, this would not be at all detrimental to it, because there are none that do not prescribe obedience and preach submission.

It is true that the histories are full of wars of religion. But if one looks closely at them, it is not the multiplicity of religions that has brought forth these wars, it is the spirit of intolerance that animated the one that thought itself dominant. It is this proselytizing spirit that the Jews picked up from the Egyptians and that passed from them, like a popular and epidemic disease, to the Mohammedans and the Christians. It is this spirit of madness whose progress can only be regarded as a complete eclipse of human reason.

Finally, even if there were no inhumanity in afflicting the consciences of others; even if such an act did not cause those bad effects to sprout up all over, it would still be foolish to take up this idea. Whoever would have me change my religion undoubtedly does this only because he would not change his own; thus, he finds it strange that I will not do something that he himself will not do, perhaps for all the world.

What most ruined the political condition of Justinian's government, M. de Montesquieu says elsewhere, was the plan he conceived of reducing all men to the same opinion on matters of religion, a plan whose success can only belong to God.[28]

Just as the ancient Romans strengthened their empire by leaving alone the diversity of worship, Justinian reduced that empire to nothing by cutting down, one after the other, sects that were not dominating. These sects were entire nations; he exterminated them by the sword or by his laws. He

28. Montesquieu, *Considerations on the Causes of the Greatness of the Romans and Their Decline,* trans. David Lowenthal (New York: Free Press, 1965; repr. Indianapolis: Hackett, 1999), XX, 190–92.

thought he had increased the number of the faithful, but he had merely decreased the number of men.

What made things desperate is that, while the emperor was carrying intolerance so far, he himself did not agree with the empress on the most essential points in their manner of thinking. He followed the Council of Chalcedon, but the empress favored those that were opposed to it—whether in good faith or by design, says Evagrius.[29]

It only remains for me to say a word about the religious assemblies that people in some realms believe cannot be tolerated. I wish to speak about the conventicles, temples, churches of the condemned sects, because they are regarded as dangerous to the state and to public tranquility. But aren't all the people allowed to crowd into the marketplaces for their temporal needs, and into the law courts for their trials, without any harm resulting from it?[30] You will respond that these latter assemblies concern only the civil, whereas the others have the spiritual in view. I agree, and it is for that very reason that spiritual assemblies cannot be breeding-grounds for revolt, because their purpose is entirely opposed to this. What would one say (setting aside the religious dimension) if a prince were to distinguish his subjects by differences in complexion or facial characteristics, so that those who had black hair or blue eyes could not engage in commerce, and would be deprived of the care and education of their children? Wouldn't we find this political scheme unfavorable to the good of the state? If the desire for wealth and profit engages everyone to form societies for subsistence, religion likewise leads everyone to attend various temples to worship the divinity. But, you will say, these churches, these temples that the magistrate would very much like to permit will swarm with condemned sects that will multiply every day. But in fact, these condemned sects are so many subjects who pay taxes, who populate the state and enrich it by human industry and commerce. You will reply that, being so numerous, they will create factions and revolts. But their religion is opposed to this; it preaches only submission

29. Evagrius Scholasticus (ca. 535–ca. 600), aide to the Patriarch of Antioch and author of a Church history that covered the years 431–594; for the anecdote in question, see *The Ecclesiastical History of Evagrius Scholasticus*, trans. Michael Whitby (Liverpool: Liverpool University Press, 2000), IV.10, 209.

30. Locke, *Letter*, 51.

to power and rendering to Caesar what belongs to Caesar. In the end, tranquility prevails wherever the government is mild. Oppression alone can produce disorders, and it will produce this result equally in subjects of the dominant religion and in the tolerated religions.

Let us conclude that the enlightened, just, and beneficent ministry will not heed the cries of the intolerant, because its purpose is to protect all the citizens, whose cooperation and multiplication are the pillar of a state.

Grotius, Barbeyrac, and other learned men deserve to be consulted here;[31] but especially Mr. Locke, who in 1692 brought to light a little work on this subject. It is so full of energy and truth that it has convinced his country that the greatest heresy of Christianity is intolerance. (*Chevalier* DE JAUCOURT)

31. See Grotius, *Rights of War and Peace;* Barbeyrac, *Traité de la morale des peres de l'Eglise* [Treatise on the morality of the church fathers], chap. 12.

Traffic in Blacks
(*Traite des Nègres*)

Although the abolitionist movement did not begin in earnest in either England or France until the 1770s and 1780s, with the founding of organizations such as the French Société des amis des noirs *(Society for the Friends of Blacks) and the English Society for the Abolition of the Slave Trade (1787), the subject had begun to attract the attention of writers and commentators. In 1748, Montesquieu had offered a scathingly ironic attack upon the European slave trade in* The Spirit of the Laws *(15.5), and Voltaire had revised his 1759* Candide *to include a mordant episode on slavery in Surinam (chap. 19). Diderot himself helped give edge to Raynal's critique of the slave trade in his* Philosophical and Political History of the Settlements and Trade of the Europeans in the East and West Indies, *a best-seller that began to appear in 1770. Jaucourt also seems to draw on Locke for his ideas.*

Traffic in Blacks (*African trade*). This is the purchase of blacks that Europeans make on the coasts of Africa, to employ those poor wretches in their colonies as slaves. This purchase of blacks, in order to reduce them to slavery, is a trade that violates religion, morality, natural laws, and all the rights of human nature.

A modern Englishman full of enlightenment and humanity says blacks have not become slaves by right of war. Nor do they commit themselves voluntarily to servitude, and consequently their children are not born slaves.

Below, we translate the word *nègre* as "black." For a related entry, see Slavery, above. This article can be found at 16:532–33 in the original edition of the *Encyclopédie*.

No one is unaware of the fact that they are bought from their princes, who claim to have the right to dispose of their liberty, and that the traders have them transported in the same manner as their other merchandise, whether to their colonies or to America, where they declare them to be for sale.

If a trade of this kind can be justified by a principle of morality, there is no crime, however atrocious, that cannot be legitimated. Kings, princes, and magistrates are not the proprietors of their subjects; they do not have a right to dispose of their liberty and to sell them as slaves.

Likewise, no man has a right to sell them or to make himself master of them. Men and their liberty are not articles of trade; they cannot be sold, bought, or paid for at any price. From this, it must be concluded that a man whose slave escapes must not go after him himself, since he had acquired illicit merchandise by money, and this acquisition is prohibited by all the laws of humanity and equity.

Thus, there is not a single one of these wretches—whom men claim to be but slaves—who does not have the right to be declared free, since he has never lost his liberty, since he could not have lost it, and since his prince, his father, and anyone else anywhere had no power to dispose of it. Consequently, its sale is null and void in itself. That black man is not divesting himself—and can never divest himself—of his natural right. He brings it with him everywhere, and everywhere he can demand to be left to enjoy it. It is therefore a manifest inhumanity on the part of judges in the free countries where he is transported not to emancipate him immediately by declaring him free—since he is their fellow man, possessing a soul just as they do.

There are authors who, posing as political jurisconsults, come to tell us boldly that the questions relative to the condition of persons must be decided by the laws of the countries to which they belong, and that therefore a man who is declared a slave in America, and who is transported from there to Europe, must be regarded in Europe as a slave. But this is to decide the rights of humanity by the civil laws of a gutter, as Cicero said.[1] Must the magistrates of one nation, by its tactful treatment of another nation, have no regard for their own species? Must their deference to a law that obliges them in nothing

1. It is possible that the reference is to Cicero, *On the laws,* I.iv., though the gutter image does not appear there; Montesquieu cites the same passage in a different context in *The Spirit of the Laws,* 26.16.

make them stomp on the law of nature, which obliges all men in all times and places? Is there any law that is as obligatory as the eternal laws of equity? Can one problematize the question of whether a judge is more obliged to observe these laws than to respect the arbitrary and inhuman practices of the colonies?

It will perhaps be said that these colonies would soon be ruined if the enslavement of blacks were abolished there. But even if that were true, must it follow that the human race must be horribly injured[2] in order to enrich us or supply our luxury? It is true that the purses of highway robbers would be empty if theft were absolutely suppressed—but do men have the right to get rich by cruel and criminal means? What right does a brigand have to rob passersby? Who is permitted to become opulent by making his fellow men miserable? Can it be legitimate to deprive the human species of its most sacred rights solely to satisfy one's avarice, one's vanity, or one's private passions? No. . . . Then let the European colonies be destroyed rather than create so many poor wretches!

But I believe it is false that the abolition of slavery will entail their ruin. Commerce will suffer for a certain time. I admit it. This is the effect of all new arrangements, because in this case the means to pursue another system cannot be found on site. But many other advantages will result from this abolition.

It is this *traffic in blacks,* this practice of servitude that has prevented America from becoming populated as promptly as it would otherwise have done. Set the blacks free, and in a few generations that vast and fertile land will count innumerable inhabitants. The arts and talents will flourish, and in places populated almost exclusively by savages and wild beasts, there will soon be only industrious men. It is liberty and human industry that are the real sources of abundance. As long as a people preserves this industry and this liberty, it should fear nothing. Industry, like need, is ingenious and inventive. It finds countless different ways of procuring riches. And if one of the channels of opulence is blocked, a hundred others open up immediately.

Sensitive and generous souls will no doubt applaud these arguments in favor of humanity. But avarice and cupidity, which dominate the earth, will never want to hear them. (*D.J.*)

2. The French term is *lésé,* which at that time can have either a legal resonance (as in tort law) or a medical one (as in surgery, whence the English word *lesion*).

Tyranny
(*Tyrannie*)

TYRANNY (*Political government*), all government unjustly exercised, without the restraint of the laws.

The Greeks and Romans gave the name *tyranny* to the intention of overturning power founded by the laws, and especially democracy. It seems, however, that they distinguished two sorts of *tyranny:*[1] one real, which consists in government violence; and one based on opinion, when those who govern establish things that offend a nation's manner of thinking.

Dio says that Augustus wanted to have himself called Romulus, but that, having learned that the people were afraid he wanted to make himself king, Augustus changed his mind.[2]

The first Romans did not want a king, because they did not want to endure his power; the Romans of Augustus's time did not want a king, so as not to endure his manners. For although Caesar, the triumvirs, and Augustus were all genuine kings, they had kept up the exterior of equality, and their private lives contained a kind of opposition to the kingly pomp of that time. And if the Romans did not want kings, this signified that they wanted to keep their manners and not take up those of the African and Oriental peoples.

Dio adds that the same Roman people were indignant at Augustus because of certain overly harsh laws he had passed, but as soon as he recalled the performer Pylades—exiled by the city's factions—the discontent ceased.[3]

This article can be found at 16:785–86 in the original edition of the *Encyclopédie*.

1. For this distinction, and for the three paragraphs that follow, see Montesquieu, *The Spirit of the Laws,* 19.3.

2. Dio Cassius, *Roman Histories,* LIII.16.7–8, for this episode.

3. The episode appears at Dio Cassius, *Roman Histories,* LIV.17.4.

Such a people felt the *tyranny* more acutely when a dancer was exiled than when all their laws were eliminated. It was indeed inevitable that they succumb to the domination of a real *tyranny,* and this event was not long in coming.

Since usurpation is the exercise of a power to which others have the right, we define *tyranny* as the exercise of a power that is both unjust and excessive, to which no one—whoever he may be—has a right in nature. Or else *tyranny* is the use of a power exercised against the laws to the public detriment, in order to satisfy one's private ambition, vengeance, avarice, and other disordered passions harmful to the state. It unites extremes, and on the backs of a million men that it crushes, it raises the monstrous colossus of some unworthy favorites who serve it.

This degeneration of governments is all the more fearsome in that it is slow and weak at the beginning, rapid and brisk at the end. At first it shows only a helping hand, but then it oppresses with boundless brawn.

I say this degeneration or corruption of governments, not—like Pufendorf—of simple monarchy, because all forms of government are subject to *tyranny.*[4] Wherever the persons who are raised to supreme power in order to lead the people and preserve what belongs to them as property employ their power for other ends and tread on people they are obliged to treat in a completely different manner—there, certainly, is *tyranny,* whether it be a sole man vested with power who acts in that way, or whether it be many who violate the rights of the nation. Thus, history tells us of the thirty tyrants of Athens, as well as of the one in Syracuse. And everyone knows that the domination of the decemvirs of Rome was but a true *tyranny.*

Wherever the laws cease or are violated by brigandage, *tyranny* exerts its dominion. Whoever is vested with supreme power and uses the forces at hand without any regard for divine and human law is a true tyrant. Neither art nor science is necessary to manage *tyranny.* It is the work of force, and is altogether the grossest and most horrible manner of governing. *Oderint dùm metuant;* this is the tyrant's motto. But this execrable maxim was not that of Minos or of Rhadamantus.[5]

4. The reference is perhaps to Pufendorf, *Of the Law of Nature and Nations,* VII.v.11.

5. "Oderint dum metuant" ("Let them hate, as long as they fear"). Originally attributed to the tragic poet Lucius Accius (170–ca. 86 B.C.), it was a favorite expression of the Emperor

Plutarch reports that Cato of Utica, being still a child and under a firm hand, went often (although always accompanied by his master) to see Sulla the dictator, because of the proximity and kinship connecting them.[6] One day, he saw that in this great house of Sulla's, in his presence or on his orders, some men were being imprisoned; others were being sentenced to various punishments: this one was being exiled, that one stripped of his property, a third one strangled. To get to the point, everything was happening not as it would before a magistrate but before a tyrant of the people. This was not a tribunal of justice; it was a cavern of *tyranny*. Indignant, that noble child turned sharply to his preceptor.

> "Give me a dagger," he said; "I'm going to hide it under my cloak. I often enter that tyrant's bedroom before he gets up. I'm going to plunge it into his breast and deliver my Country from that execrable monster."

Such was the childhood of that grand personage whose death placed a crown on virtue. When Thales was interrogated as to what thing seemed to him the most surprising, he said, "it's an old tyrant, because tyrants have as many enemies as they have men under their domination."[7]

I do not think there has ever been a people barbarous enough and imbecilic enough to submit to *tyranny* by an original contract. Nonetheless, I know very well that there are nations over which *tyranny* has been introduced either imperceptibly, or by violence, or by prescription. I will not set myself up as a political casuist on the rights of such sovereigns and the obligations of such peoples. Men must perhaps content themselves with their lot, suffer the disadvantages of governments as they do those of the climate, and endure what they cannot change.

But if one were to speak to me of one people in particular who have been wise enough and fortunate enough to found and preserve a free constitution of government, as for example the people of Great Britain have done,

---

Caligula. Minos, the mythic son of Zeus and Europa, and his wise brother Rhadamanthus sat in judgment over the souls of the underworld; Socrates evoked them on the eve of his death. See the final four paragraphs of Plato's *Apology*.

6. Plutarch, *Life of Cato the Younger*, 3.

7. Thales of Miletus (ca. 624–ca. 546 B.C.), pre-Socratic philosopher. The story can be found in Diogenes Laertius, "Thales," in *Lives of Eminent Philosophers*, I.36, and in Plutarch, "On the Sign of Socrates," in *Moralia*, 578d.

it is to them that I would freely say that their kings are obliged, by the most sacred duties that human laws can create and that divine laws can authorize, to defend and maintain—in preference to every other consideration—the liberty of the constitution at whose head they are placed. That was the opinion not only of Queen Elizabeth, who never spoke any other language, but even of King James himself. Here is the manner in which he expressed himself in the speech he gave to parliament in 1603.

> I will ever preferre the weale of the Body and of the whole Commonwealth, in making of good Lawes and Constitutions, to any particular or private ends of mine, thinking ever the wealth and weale of the Commonwealth to be my greatest weale & worldly felicitie: A point wherein a lawfull King doeth directly differ from a Tyrant.[8]

It is asked whether the people—that is, not the rabble but the sounder portion of the subjects from all the orders of a state—may escape from the authority of a tyrant if he mistreats his subjects, exhausts them with excessive taxes, neglects the interests of government, and overturns the fundamental laws.

My first answer to this question is that a clear distinction must be made between an extreme abuse of sovereignty, which degenerates manifestly and overtly into *tyranny* and which tends to the ruin of the subjects, and a moderate abuse such as may be attributed to human weakness.

In the first case, it appears that the people have a full right to retake the sovereignty they have entrusted to their leaders, which the latter have abused excessively.

In the second case, it is absolutely the people's duty to suffer something rather than to rise up by force against their sovereign.

This distinction is founded on the nature of man and government. It is just to suffer patiently the bearable faults of sovereigns, and their light injustices, because that is a just support owed to humanity. But as soon as the *tyranny* is extreme, one has a right to wrest the sacred trust of sovereignty from the tyrant.

8. King James's accession speech of March 19, 1603, in *The Kings Maiesties Speech . . .* (London: Robert Barker, 1604), p. 18 of an unpaginated pamphlet. The passage is also cited in Locke, *Second Treatise,* chap. 18, par. 200.

This is an opinion that can be proven (1) by the nature of *tyranny,* which in itself degrades the sovereign's condition, which ought to be beneficent. (2) Men have established governments for their greatest good; now it is evident that if they were obliged to endure everything from their governors, they would find themselves reduced to a much more deplorable state than the one from which they meant to shelter themselves under the wings of the law. (3) Even a people who have submitted to absolute sovereignty have not, for all that, lost the right to have their own preservation in mind, when they find themselves reduced to the lowest misery. Absolute sovereignty in itself is nothing but the absolute power to do good, which is quite contrary to the absolute power to do evil, which in all probability, no people have ever had the intention of entrusting to any mortal. Suppose, says Grotius, one had asked those who first handed down civil laws whether they meant to impose on the citizens the harsh necessity of dying rather than taking up arms to defend themselves against their sovereign's unjust violence; would they have answered yes? There is every reason to believe that they would have decided that one should not endure everything—unless, perhaps, when things are found to be such that resistance would inevitably cause greater disturbances in the state, or would consign a very large number of innocents to ruin.[9]

In fact, it is indubitably the case that no one would renounce his liberty this far. That would be to sell his own life, his children's lives, his religion—in a word, all his advantages, which is certainly not in man's power.

Let us even add that strictly speaking, the people are not obliged to wait until their sovereign has completely forged the irons of *tyranny,* and made them powerless to resist him. For them to have a right to show due regard to their preservation, it is enough that every step taken by their leaders tends manifestly toward oppressing them, and that these leaders march, so to speak, flags unfurled, toward the violence of *tyranny.*

The objections made to this opinion have been so often resolved and by so many fine talents—Bacon, Sidney, Grotius, Pufendorf, Locke, and Barbeyrac[10]—that it would be superfluous to respond to them again.

9. Grotius, *Rights of War and Peace,* I.IV.vii.

10. Francis Bacon (1561–1626), English statesman, chancellor, and philosopher; Sidney, *Discourses;* Barbeyrac was the influential translator and commentator of the natural-law theorists Grotius and Pufendorf.

Nonetheless, the truths that have just been established are of the first importance. It is appropriate that they be known for the happiness of nations and for the advantage of sovereigns who abhor governing against the laws. It is very good to read the works that instruct us about the principles of *tyranny,* and about the horrors that result from it. Apollonius of Tiana went to Rome in Nero's time to see for once, he said, what kind of animal a tyrant is.[11] He could not have done better. The name of Nero has become proverbial as designating a monster in government. But unfortunately, Rome no longer had within her but a feeble vestige of virtue, and since she possessed ever less of it, she became ever more enslaved. All the blows went against tyrants, none against *tyranny.*[12] (*Chevalier* DE JAUCOURT)

11. Apollonius of Tiana, charismatic Pythagorean sage and miracle worker of the first century; see Flavius Philostratus (ca. 170–ca. 247), *The Life of Apollonius of Tyana,* 4.387.
12. See Montesquieu, *Laws,* 3.3, for this remark.

Volume 17
(1765)

Five Percent Tax
(*Vingtième*)

Perhaps the last truly important political essay in the Encyclopédie, *this book-length entry, most of which appears here, translated for the first time, was attributed to Boulanger, who had conveniently died in 1759, six years before the article appeared. It is now thought to have been mainly the work of Damilaville, though with perhaps significant contribution from Diderot at certain points. The title, as is often the case, is misleading. The* vingtième, *or "twentieth," probably an echo of the ancient Roman* vicesima, *was a universal tax levied on Frenchmen without regard to special geographical or social privilege; beginning as the* dixième, *or "tenth," which had been a temporary expedient under Louis XIV, the "twentieth" was established in 1749 and made more or less permanent.*

The entry contains a lengthy hypothetical calculation of the productivity of a parish, and of the resulting tax revenues therefrom. But the core of the article is a wide-ranging discussion of the nature of government, of civil society, and of the economy. Like Montesquieu, the author agrees that taxation is to be viewed primarily in its relation to liberty and the philosophy of government. Especially noteworthy is his clear distinction between the state, as the collectivity of the people in a society, and the government. In addition, the treatise contains a lengthy argument for tax simplification, a typology of different kinds of taxes and their social justifications, and a long critique of Montesquieu's normative typology of taxation in The Spirit of the Laws, *book 13, among other subjects. The work was reprinted both in the 1782 Lausanne edition (vol. 7, pt. 1, pp. 321–82) and in*

This article can be found at 17:855–81, 889–90, in the original edition of the *Encyclopédie*.

Pancoucke's 1784 Encyclopédie Méthodique: Finances *(1:246–92) under the more comprehensive and conspicuous title* charges publiques *("public burdens"). In short, this entry will serve as a fitting conclusion to the present anthology. All notes are by the present editor.*

FIVE PERCENT TAX, a charge (*Political economy*). In this particular sense the term means a portion of revenue that all citizens give the state for public needs, whose quota is determined by its own appellation.

This manner of contributing to the expenses of society is quite old. It has a closer connection than any other to the nature of the obligations contracted toward society by the citizenry. It is also the most just, the least susceptible to arbitrariness and abuse.

On Plutarch's account, it seems this is how the Persians imposed taxes.[1] He says that when Xerxes' father Darius had fixed the amounts the people had to pay on their income, he assembled the leading residents of each province and asked them if these amounts were not too high. "Somewhat," they answered. Immediately the prince cut them by half. The people would be happy if the prince were in that way to model his needs on their own.

In Athens, taxes were levied in proportion to the yield from the land. The people were divided into four classes: The first, composed of *pentacosiomedimni*,[2] who enjoyed income of five hundred measures of dry or liquid fruit, paid one talent.

Those from the second class, called *knights*, who had only three hundred measures of income, paid a half-talent.

The *zeugitae*, who formed the third class and possessed only two hundred measures of income, gave ten minae, or a sixth of a talent.

Finally, the *thetes*, who had less than two hundred measures of income and who composed the fourth class, paid nothing.

It is clear that the proportion of these tax burdens lay not in the ratio of their respective incomes but in the ratio of the taxes to what should remain free to the taxpayer for his sustenance. And this exempt portion was

1. The reference is to Plutarch (ca. 46–127), "The Sayings of Kings and Commanders," in *Moralia*, 172f.

2. The "five-hundred bushellers"; the law dates to Solon.

estimated in the same way for all. Back then, it was not thought that being richer meant having more needs; only what was superfluous was taxed.

In Sparta, where everything was in common, where all goods belonged to all, where the people and not their officers were the state, and where they paid no one to govern or defend them, taxes were not necessary. They would have been superfluous and impossible to levy. Precious metals were proscribed there, and with them the avarice they produce and the dissensions they entail. For as long as poverty ruled Sparta, Sparta ruled nations; the most opulent nations came there to look for legislators.

Until Constantine, called *the Great,* taxes in the Roman Empire consisted mainly of levies on real estate. They were fixed at a tenth or an eighth of the yield from plowable land, and at a fifth of the yield from fruit trees, livestock, *etc.* Other contributions were also levied in kind, in grain, in all sorts of foodstuffs that the people were obliged to furnish independent of the monetary taxes called *daces.*[3]

In virtually all current governments in Europe, and mainly in those that are agricultural, the majority of taxes are applied equally to landed properties. The practice of levying them by the *twentieth* of the yield still exists in Artois, in Flanders, in Brabant, and it seems that it likewise takes place in most of the provinces that make up what used to be the duchy of Burgundy. There, people pay one, two, three, four, up to five *twentieths,* according to what the needs and will of the sovereign demand.

In France, there are taxes of all kinds—on land, on persons, on foodstuffs and consumer merchandise, on industry, on the rivers, on the highways, and on the freedom to frequent them. The *twentieth* or *twentieths* of the citizens' income are also collected there. These latter charges are only established in exceptional circumstances; they were unknown before 1710. Louis XIV was the first to decree the levy of the tenth along with the head tax, which has not been abolished since then. The tenth was abolished after the last war that prince had to support. Under the regency of the Duke of Orleans, they wanted to replace it with the fiftieth, which did not last. In 1733 and in every war thereafter, the tenth has always been restored and

3. *Dictionnaire de Académie Française* (Paris, 1694) defines *dace* as "a tax levied on the people," though the term seems to die out thereafter.

abolished. Finally in 1750, the *twentieth* replaced it for the payment of state debts, and up to three of them were levied during the war begun in 1756 between this crown and England.[4]

In treating this tax, my intention has been to enter in some detail into the nature and obligation of public charges. There are few topics more important than this part of political administration. It is not for the multitude. The people see only the necessity to pay, the statesman only the outcome, the budget official only the benefit. The philosopher sees the cause of the prosperity or ruin of empires, of the liberty or slavery of the citizenry, of their happiness or misery. There is no subject more interesting to him, because there is no subject so close to humanity and because he cannot be indifferent toward anything that affects him so intimately.

Before examining these various types of current taxes or duties and unfolding the disadvantages or advantages that result from their different natures and the various ways of levying them, I will show:

(1) that public charges are just and legitimate in proportion as they are founded on social conventions, and as the existence and preservation of society depends on them;

(2) that they are a form of tribute that all citizens owe society, for the advantages they enjoy under its protection;

(3) that they have as their purpose the general good of the commonwealth and the individual good of each of those who compose it;

(4) that unable to govern itself alone, society needs a continually active power [*puissance*][5] to represent it, to unite all its forces and put them in motion for its utility; that this power is government, and that in furnishing it the individual contribution of forces he owes society, each citizen does no more than discharge his obligations toward society and toward himself;

(5) finally, that society or the government representing it has the right to demand this contribution in its name, but its standard must be public utility

4. The allusions are to the War of the Spanish Succession (1701–14), the War of the Polish Succession (1733–38), the War of the Austrian Succession (1740–48), and the Seven Years' War (1756–63).

5. For this passage and others throughout the essay, see the translators' note on "power." Generally, the term Damilaville uses in this essay is "puissance"; we have highlighted the exceptions where necessary.

and the greatest good of the individuals. Otherwise, it can be excessive under any legitimate pretext.

I. The passage of men from the state of nature to the civil state is like their extraction from nothingness into existence—it is what people talk about most and understand least. Was this passage made by a sudden and noticeable transition? Or has it been brought about by gradual and imperceptible changes, as men became aware of a better way of being and adopted it; as they have perceived the disadvantages of their customs and rectified them?

If we believe the example of all peoples and even what is seen in our day, this is how societies have founded and perfected themselves. The Russians were a people before the reign of Czar Peter. The prodigious changes that the talent of that great man brought forth in his nation have made a more civilized people out of them but not a new one.[6]

Before their conquests, the Goths lived as a community and practiced the great principles of humanity, which seem to be destroyed as men become civilized. The beneficence and affection they showed toward foreigners made the Germans give them the name *Goths*, which means *good*.[7] They were good in fact, whereas the rest of Europe groaned under desolation and barbarism, in which the violence and oppression of the most civilized governments had plunged it. We see Theodoric, one of their earliest kings, making the laws and justice prevail in Italy and offering the model for an equitable and moderate government. It's a pity he has to be blamed for the deaths of Symmachus and Boethius, whom he unjustly sent to their demise on false reports. They were philosophers; someone must have slandered them to the prince.[8]

Those people and so many others no longer resemble what they were but have only become more civilized. Even among those savage nations that are closer to the state of nature than anyone has ever discovered, one

6. Peter I (the Great) (r. 1696–1725).

7. *Gott*, "God," which becomes "good" in terms such as *gottlob*, "thank goodness."

8. Theodoric the Great (454–526), king of the Ostrogoths and regent of the Visigoths, who had the philosopher Boethius, his erstwhile head of government offices and services, executed in 525; Symmachus was Pope (498–514) but had a tempestuous relationship with both the senate and Theodoric.

finds a type of union that is certainly the germ of a more perfect social state that time and custom could develop without the aid of examples. The hospitality that those nations practice with such piety proves that they feel the need men have for one another. This need is the source of natural law, and the state of nature is itself a social state governed by this law. Finally, the inclination of one sex for the other (which is not contained solely in the human species) plus the long infirmity of childhood furnish strong evidence, against the opinion of an original state absolutely isolated and solitary,[9] that the present form of society proves nothing more than that the coordination of the world does not presuppose a void.

In any case, and however they may have arrived at the state we now see them in, civil societies have a fundamental source, all the more incontestable in that it is and always will be the source of societies currently in existence, in whatever form they may exist.

This source is the defense and common preservation for which each person has joined it, and from which the mutual obligations of citizens, the obligations of all toward society and of society toward all, arise.

On the citizens' part, these obligations consist in combining all their forces to constitute the general power, which in turn must be employed in protecting and preserving them. Such is the purpose of societies: each person, placing his forces in common, increases them by means of others' forces and assures his own existence by the full existence of the body politic of which he makes himself part.

Since society is formed only from the united forces of all, it follows that each person owes it a part of his own. By "force," I do not mean only the physical quality ordinarily designated by this term but all physical and moral power that men enjoy as beings and as citizens. Without this total union of the members that compose it and all their power, the body politic can no longer exist except as a whole without parts. Thus, in this association each belongs to all and all belong to each.

By this commitment, I do not mean that each citizen has renounced his ownership of himself or his possessions, or that these have become public

9. Perhaps a reference to Jean-Jacques Rousseau, *Discourse on the Origins of Inequality Among Men* (1755).

property. I am far from insinuating such maxims. This renunciation would be contrary to the spirit of the social pact, whose purpose is to preserve these possessions; it would even be detrimental, not advantageous, to society.

The Romans, who created the most powerful republic in the known world, never allowed the government any rights over their persons or property in whatever did not concern order and public security. They enjoyed these with the greatest freedom and immunity and in the fullest extent of rights that confer the title of *property*. This is what they called "to possess *optimo jure*," or *jus quiritium*,[10] which was only abolished under Justinian and which Cicero recommended that rulers observe. "The principal thing that they must be careful of," he says (*de off.*),[11] "is that the property of each individual be preserved for him, and that public authority not encroach upon it."

But their property and their persons were only too devoted to the republic. When its defense, its glory, or its utility were at issue, each person saw his private interest in the general interest. Liberty is an inestimable good, and the more one has to lose, the more zeal one has in defending oneself. Thus the Roman armies, composed of unpaid citizens, were for a long time only (if one may put it this way) armies of confederates. Without depending on the others, each man bore all the expenses and strains of war.

This proves that by preserving in all its integrity the original and inviolable right that citizens have over themselves and everything that belongs to them, they impose only more forcefully upon themselves the obligation of providing the state with everything necessary for its support and preservation. Thus, if this obligation were not already contracted through the conventions of the social contract, it would arise from the individual interests of the members who have subscribed to it and who find themselves in reciprocal dependence on this point and in a mutual relationship with the common interest.

But I have shown that the only purpose of civil union is the establishment of the general power. The public burdens from which it draws its existence are thus legitimate, since they constitute that power which effects

10. The law of full Roman citizens (*Quirites*).

11. See Cicero, *De Officiis* [On duties], II.xxi.73.

the preservation of society—and consequently that of the individuals who compose it. And these burdens are just, since they are common to all and since each has necessarily submitted to conditions he has imposed on the others.

II. To the justice and legitimacy of public burdens must be added the fact that they are also a personal tribute[12] that all citizens owe society for the advantages it procures them. Is it not under the safeguard of the common power or the body politic that they enjoy civil liberty, as much for their persons as for their property?

Originally, this tribute was on everything the citizens possessed, even their personal service. At that time, the general forces were too limited and required the union of all private forces. As societies expanded, their power was increased by the power of the individuals who joined it, and their wealth by the largest territories they occupied. The totality of individual forces was no longer necessary for defense and common security; it was enough to furnish part of it to create the general and supreme power. The obligations of all toward all were reduced to this.

This personal tax is levied under different forms and different names, but these variations have produced no changes in its nature. It is still the same contribution of forces that all citizens have committed themselves to furnish for the maintenance of the body politic of which they are the parts. It is thus clear that no one can be freed from them and that all immunities and exemptions which do without them are null by the original and unalterable right of each citizen against all and of all against each; that these things are so many attacks upon public security and the social union, whose destruction would result from the spread of these exemptions.[13]

It is worse if those who enjoy these exemptions also possess the largest portion of the goods of the state—if, in contributing nothing to the maintenance of society, they alone profit from all its advantages and bear none of its burdens. Such citizens cannot but be regarded as its enemies, and the state cannot be too hasty about effecting their ruin if it wants to avoid its own.

12. *Tribut,* a tribute, a contribution, a monetary payment as in a tax.

13. The reference is mainly to France, which at this time had a tax system larded with exemptions.

But we will have occasion elsewhere to talk about the dangers of this abuse. After establishing the legitimacy, the obligation, and the justice of public charges, let us demonstrate that their purpose is only the general good of the community and the private advantage of those who compose it.

III. In their relationships with each other, societies are in the same condition that men are assumed to have been in before those societies were formed—that is, a state of war.[14] But this state has become much more real and more widespread ever since the right of some to everything has replaced the right of all, and since ambition and the passions of one or several, rather than need or individual physical appetite, can determine attack and compel defense.

This constant and universal state of war obliges each civil government, whose principal function is to assure public peace, to be perpetually on guard against its neighbors. Troops must be maintained on the border, always ready to oppose invasions the latter might attempt on its territory. In fact, defense often obliges one to wage war, whether to repulse an attack or to prevent it.

The constitution of ancient states and their limited extent did not require the immense and ruinous precautions taken in this regard under the present system of Europe, which do not allow it to enjoy even the appearances of peace. The government could supervise all the republic's dependencies, gather their forces with ease, and bring them promptly to wherever defense was necessary. They did not employ mercenary troops; they did not keep vast standing armies. The state would not have been up to their expense, and they would have endangered public liberty. The citizens defended the Country and their possessions.

As soon as Marius introduced paid troops, Rome was no longer free.[15] It was possible to buy them, and the republic soon had a master.

Feudal government was also destroyed when the use of paid troops was established among the nations founded on the ruins of the Roman empire.[16]

14. The reference is especially to Hobbes, *De Cive,* chap. 1; *Leviathan,* chap. 13.

15. Marius (157–86 B.C.), general, statesman, and seven times consul; the reference is to the civil wars begun in the 80s against Sulla.

16. The reference is to the widespread use of mercenary troops, often of foreign extraction, in the late Middle Ages and into the sixteenth century by European monarchies and Italian rulers.

Power cannot long be shared when the salary and rewards of a multitude depend on one alone.

These new practices exempted the citizens from military service but subjected them to the contributions necessary for the upkeep of those who undertake this service on their behalf. Their own tranquility, the state's tranquility, and the preservation of their property depend on these troops. The burdens they bear for this purpose thus procure both the general good and their private advantage.

But external enemies are not the only ones society has to fear. An exacting administration must also ensure its internal peace and that of its members, so that it be undisturbed by factions and so that its members and their possessions be secure under the power of the laws.

Indifference as to worship and equality of conditions and fortunes, which prevents the equally pernicious effects of the ambition of the wealthy and the despair of the poor, were highly favorable to this tranquility. Everywhere that men are happy and free, they are numerous and tranquil. Why wouldn't they be? We want to change our condition only when it cannot become harder. Thus, it is less by regulations and punishments than by religious toleration—so loudly demanded by natural and positive law—and by equity and mild government that one maintains peace within a state and harmony among its citizens. Making justice, virtue, and mores reign is what creates its prosperity.

Multiplicity of laws produces multiplicity of infractions and of guilty parties. *Lycurgus* made few laws, but he gave mores to his Country, which preserved it and rendered it powerful for a long time. *Et in republicâ corruptissimâ plurimae leges,* says Tacitus.[17]

It is especially dangerous that there are laws citizens think they should prefer that are contrary to civil law and that have greater authority over them. The Christians of Ireland, the Christians of the League,[18] and so many others misunderstood the civil laws and lost all natural sentiments and all social affection as soon as their superstition decreed contempt for these laws and fanaticism commanded them to slaughter each other.

17. Adapted from Tacitus, *Annals,* III.27, "when the state was most corrupt, laws were most abundant." Lycurgus was the legendary Spartan lawgiver of the seventh century B.C.

18. The Catholic League, founded in 1576 to reverse the advances of the Protestants (Huguenots) during the French wars of religion.

It has been said of the Jesuits that they were a dangerous body within the state because they depended on a foreign power, and this is true. Another truth is the assurance by the dogmas and beliefs of modern religions that there is not one state that does not also create a dangerous body against itself, a body whose alien and fantastic interests are bound to bring about its moral and political destruction: *omne regnum contra se divisum desolabitur*. Elsewhere, one finds, *nolite arbitrari quia pacem venerim mittere in terram: non veni pacem mittere sed gladium . . . Veni enim separare hominem adversus patrem suum, & filiam adversus matrem suam, & nurum adversus socrum suam . . . & inimici hominis domestici ejus*.[19] The passages are positive, but there is not an enlightened Christian today who does not reject their consequences.

When Montesquieu advances the proposition, against Bayle, that "true Christians would be citizens enlightened about their duties and greatly zealous about performing them; that they would know very well the rights of natural defense; that the more they believed they owed religion, the more they would think they owed their Country," etc.,[20] Montesquieu says things that are true, although they seem difficult to reconcile with the ideas of some Church Fathers. Tertullian, wanting to justify the Christians against the ambitious designs imputed to them (which it would have been more reasonable to suspect them of under Constantine), expresses himself this way: "we cannot fight to defend our possessions, because in receiving baptism we have renounced the world and everything that is of the world; nor to acquire honors, believing there is nothing less fitting for us than public employments; nor to save our lives, for we regard their loss as a good fortune." *Nobis omnis gloriae, & dignitatis ardore frigentibus, &c.* (Tert. ap.)[21]

19. The first passage is from Matthew 12:25, where Jesus says to the crowd, "Every kingdom divided against itself is laid waste, and no city or house divided against itself will stand." The second passage comes from Matthew 10:34–36, where Jesus sends forth his disciples with these words: "Do not think that I have come to bring peace on earth; I have not come to bring peace, but a sword. For I have come to set a man against his father, and a daughter against her mother, and a daughter-in-law against her mother-in-law; and a man's foes will be those of his own household."

20. See Montesquieu, *The Spirit of the Laws,* 24.6.

21. "We, however, whom all the flames of glory and dignity leave cold, have no need to combine; nothing is more foreign to us than the state." See Tertullian, *Apology,* chap. 38; the same passages, it may be noted, are cited in Sidney, *Discourses Concerning Government,* chap. 3, sec. 8, known in France partly through a 1702 translation by Peter A. Samson.

This doctrine is certainly not suitable for creating defenders of the Country. But Tertullian's doctrine is that it will always be possible to return to a sentiment more consistent with the public interest, by the distinction so often made between precepts and counsel, between orders for the establishment of Christianity and Christianity itself.

Now by these distinctions, everything is reduced to the morality of the Gospel. And what else is that but the universal morality engraved on all hearts by nature and recognized in all men by reason?

Whoever has the social virtues without belonging to any sect will be a just and reasonable man, steeped in the duties that nature and his status as citizen impose upon him, faithful in fulfilling them and in rendering everything he owes to humanity and to the society of which he is part.

But if you make no chronological distinctions and if you confuse counsel with precepts, then the same man will be but a stranger exiled on earth where nothing can bind him. Intoxicated by eternal felicities, he has no desire to spend his time on whatever would ruin these felicities for him. The best citizen will be divided between this interest, which rules over him, and that of his Country. It is already quite something if he weighs them in the balance; which will he prefer? To contribute to the peace and preservation of the civil society of which he is a member, to fulfill his commitments toward it and his fellow men, will he sacrifice the infinite happiness that awaits him in the celestial Country and in losing it, risk exposing himself to such lengthy miseries? To obtain one and avoid the other, he will thus abjure all human and social virtues. And one cannot blame him, for this is his best option.

> "An Expectation and Dependency, so miraculous and great as this," says a philosopher,[22] "must naturally take off from other inferior Dependencys and Encouragements. [. . .] Other Interests are hardly so much as computed, whilst the Mind is thus transported in the pursuit of a high Advantage and Self-Interest, so narrowly confin'd within our-selves. On

22. What follows in the text is Damilaville's nearly exact transcription from Diderot's *Principes de la philosophie morale: ou, Essai de M. S*** sur le mérite et la vertu, avec réflexions* (Amsterdam: Chatelain, 1745), itself a quite loose translation of Shaftesbury's "An Inquiry Concerning Virtue or Merit." We use the original English from Shaftesbury, *Characteristicks of Men, Manners, Opinions, Times* (Indianapolis: Liberty Fund, 2001), 2:39.

> this account, all other Affections towards Friends, Relations, or Mankind, are often slightly regarded, as being *worldly*, and of little moment, in respect of the Interest of *our Soul*. And so little thought is there of any immediate Satisfaction arising from such good Offices of Life, that it is customary with many devout People zealously to decry all temporal Advantages of Goodness, all natural Benefits of Virtue; and magnifying the contrary Happiness of a vitious State, to declare, 'That except only for the sake of future Reward, and fear of future Punishment, they wou'd divest themselves of all Goodness at once, and freely allow themselves to be most immoral and profligate.' From whence it appears, that in some respects there can be nothing more fatal to Virtue, than the weak and uncertain Belief of a future Reward and Punishment."

One may add that this belief is no less fatal to the tranquility and preservation of empires. It must reduce the finest men to the cruel alternative of being irreligious, or else denatured, and bad citizens.

But let it not be said that religion demands this total and pernicious abandonment of human duties. If one reads: "*Et omnis qui reliquerit dominum, vel fratres aut patrem, aut matrem, aut filios, aut agros propter nomen meum, centuplum accipiet & vitam aeternam possidebit. (Matt. ch. xix. V. 29, & Luk., ch. xiv:) Si quis venit ad me & non odit patrem suum, & matrem, & uxorem, & filios, & fratres, & sorores, adhuc autem & animam suam, & venit post me, non potest meus esse discipulus,*" it is certain that these words are addressed mainly to those whom J. C. called to the apostolate, which in fact demands all these sacrifices.[23]

To presume to subject everyone to these things indiscriminately is to transform society into a monastery. And then we have a right to ask who will restrain men, what authority will prevent them from being denatured and indifferent to all social ties? And what will become of the commonwealth if one lives apart from the commerce of women in order to make oneself even more worthy of the promised rewards; and if fasts and

23. Matthew 19:29: "And every one who has left houses or brothers or sisters or father or mother or children or lands, for my name's sake, will receive a hundredfold, and inherit eternal life." Luke 14:26: "If any one comes to me and does not hate his own father and mother and wife and children and brothers and sisters, yes, and even his own life, he cannot be my disciple."

mortifications are combined with infractions of all natural and civil laws to accelerate its ruin by a more rapid destruction of the species?[24]

Society cannot exist without combining the forces of all those who compose it. What would become of it if, as would be prescribed and as the importance of the matter would demand, they were solely occupied with the care of their salvation; if they lived in the way they ought to according to Tertullian, in abnegation of all public interest, in contemplation and idleness and refusing all work, which alone produces the wealth and power of the body politic?

The ancients deified only men who had rendered distinguished service to their Country. They thereby invited others to be useful to her. The moderns seem to have reserved this honor only for those who have tried to be harmful to her and who would have caused her ruin if their example had been followed.

Thus, when the magistrate employs force to subject people to these destructive opinions, force of which he is the depository solely for the purpose of using it for their benefit, this is a man lending his sword to another in order to kill him, or using it to assassinate himself.

Salus populi suprema lex esto.[25] The most stable and most fortunate governments have been those in which nothing has overridden this maxim, in which the civil law has been the only rule for the actions of men, and in which all have been subject to it and to it alone. What does it matter to the government or the city how a citizen thinks about abstract and metaphysical matters, provided that he do good and that he be just toward others and himself! Citizens have reciprocally guaranteed their temporal and civil preservation; that's the important thing for each person to fulfill. Someone has made himself the guarantor of another's salvation? But who has the right to prescribe to my conscience what it must believe or reject? I alone have that power through reason.[26]

My conscience is even less persuaded by violence. As Montaigne put it very well, having a man cooked alive is putting a very high price on one's

24. See also Diderot's article CELIBACY, above, on these themes.
25. "The public good is the supreme law."
26. See Jaucourt's article TOLERATION, in this volume.

conjectures.[27] Dionysius, the scourge of Sicily, put to death a certain Marcias who had dreamed of assassinating him.[28] I understand that Dionysius was a tyrant; but what had those Vaudois dreamed about whom the Lord of Langey pointed out to Francis I: "These are the folks who for 300 years have cleared the land and enjoyed the use of it by means of rent they pay to the landowners, and who by assiduous labor have made it fertile; who are industrious and sober; who, instead of employing their money in lawsuits, employ it in the relief of the poor; who regularly pay taille to the king and taxes and duties to their lords; whose frequent prayers and innocent mores attest that they fear God"?

What had they done, I say, these virtuous, faithful, and industrious citizens, to be massacred with cruelty that one cannot read about in P. de Thou without being gripped with horror and compassion?[29] And the sovereign who had the misfortune to underwrite such cruelty: what was he? Alas, a man otherwise filled with the most worthy qualities but shamefully deceived by superstition and blinded by fanaticism.

There is one thing that deserves to be noticed and that I don't believe has been, as of yet. To the impossibility of denying the atrocity of these crimes, their authors dare to add the further atrocity of blaming the policy of princes for them. They say it is because of this policy that millions of men have been exterminated; religion has had no part in it. One of these apologists of crime—those types who, to applaud the detestable rage of their fellows, would remorselessly steep their pens in the human blood they have caused to flow—has not been afraid to outrage nature and sovereigns simultaneously by supporting this reprehensible assertion in a work that excites indignation and that would certainly have attracted public vengeance on the author if that author had not prudently left the country. It is no thanks to him if the soil of that country has not yet been strewn

27. See "Of Cripples," in *The Complete Essays of Montaigne,* trans. Donald M. Frame (Stanford: Stanford University Press, 1958), 790.

28. Dionysius I the Elder of Syracuse (ca. 432–367 B.C.), prototype of the tyrant.

29. Jacques-Auguste de Thou (1553–1617), historian and *president à mortier* in the Parlement of Paris (1595) who helped negotiate the Edict of Nantes with the French Protestants (1598). English translations of his Latin work on the St. Bartholomew's Day Massacre appeared as *The history of the bloody massacres of the Protestants in France in the year of our Lord, 1572* in 1674 and afterward.

with the cadavers of its inhabitants. *See the apol. of S. Bartholomew, by abbé Caveyrac.*[30]

True religion doubtless condemns these abominable murders. But since this is not a question of true religion, it is a deception to want to exculpate the other kind at the expense of the civil power—a deception all the more criminal in that it tends to render sovereigns odious by shifting the blame onto them for the horrors of which it is guilty.

Interest has said that religious prejudices were useful or even necessary for the people, stupidity has repeated it, and men have believed it. If theft were not punished by the civil law, these prejudices would not repress it any more than they repress adultery, which they condemn equally strongly and which they threaten with the same punishments. Thus, other opinions are needed for commonwealths to be happy and tranquil, for they undoubtedly could not be that way with unjust and wicked citizens.

In *The Spirit of the Laws,* one reads: "Not much integrity is needed for a monarchical or despotic government to maintain or sustain itself. The force of the laws in the one, the prince's ready arm in the other, rule or contain the whole. But in a popular state, there must be an added spring, namely virtue."[31] Taken in a strict and narrow sense, this proposition does not appear to be either accurate or advantageous to monarchical government, and it is with reason that M. de Voltaire has noted that virtue is all the more necessary in a government in which there is more seduction than in any other.[32]

But he who elsewhere said: "the mores of the prince contribute as much to liberty as do the laws; like the laws, the prince can make beasts of men and men of beasts. If he loves free souls, he will have subjects; if he loves base souls, he will have slaves. Does he want to know the great art of ruling? Let him bring honor and virtue close to him; let him call forth personal merit.

30. Abbé Jean Novi de Caveirac (1713–82), musical historian, demographic theorist, religious polemicist (he was exiled for defending the Jesuits in print), and author of *Apologie de Louis XIV et son conseil sur la révocation de l'Edit de Nantes* [Apologia for Louis XIV and his Council on the Revocation of the Edict of Nantes] (1758), a work Voltaire called a justification of the St. Bartholomew's Day Massacre (August 1572).

31. Montesquieu, *Laws,* 3.3.

32. Perhaps a reference to Voltaire, "Etats," in *Philosophical Dictionary* (1764).

Let him win hearts, but let him not capture minds."[33] I say that he who has so well grasped the power and utility of virtue could not think it was less necessary in one place than in another. What difference is there between the sword of the law and the sword by which the prince is armed? Both are threatening, and the obedience that results is equally the result of fear. If this fear produces tranquility in despotic states, that is because brutalized men have lost their sense of dignity and even of their existence. To use an expression whose energy cannot be improved upon, they are dead bodies buried next to each other. But everywhere else, fear will never produce more than an uncertain and anxious tranquility. It is to the soul what chains are to the body: both soul and body are striving constantly to free themselves from them.

Was the law less threatening after Caesar, Tiberius, Caius [i.e., Caligula], Nero, Domitian? *If, however, the Romans became more slave-like, this is because all the blows fell against tyrants, none against tyranny.*[34] Was the empire strengthened by this? Its progressive weakening followed its progressive loss of virtue. What made Rome incapable of receiving liberty when Sulla offered it to her also made the Romans incapable of perceiving their enslavement, and prevented them from defending and supporting the empire. All the authority of the law could not prevent its ruin, just as it could not prevent the ruin of virtue and morals.

Greek politics knew of nothing so powerful as virtue to support republics. In vain will the law—and force along with it—issue commands; it will not assure either the peace or the continuance of the state if fear and not love of justice causes the observance of its decrees. When the Athenians allowed Demetrius of Phalereus to have them counted in a market like slaves and when they fought with so much difficulty and so little courage against Philip, they were as numerous as when they defended Greece alone against the great monarch of Asia and when they performed so many heroic deeds.[35] But they were less virtuous and less affected by honorable

33. This passage is adapted from Montesquieu, *Laws,* 12.27.

34. The italicized material comes from Montesquieu, *Laws,* 3.3. The same passage was cited by Jaucourt at the end of TYRANNY, included above in this volume.

35. Demetrius of Phalereus (ca. 350–280 B.C.), orator, Peripatetic philosopher, and despot of Athens (317–307); Philip, king of Macedon (r. 359–336 B.C.). See Montesquieu, *Laws,* 3.3, for this example.

things. A nation that passes laws condemning to death whoever proposes to put to a different use money destined for public entertainments is preparing its hands for the chains, and is only awaiting the moment to receive them in order to wear them.

At all times and in all sorts of governments, the same cause has produced and will always produce the same effects. Someone said, *no monarch without nobility; no nobility without monarchy*.[36] I would rather say, *no monarchy without morals; no morals without a virtuous government.*

All is lost when gold is the price of everything, and credit, respect, dignities, and the esteem of one's fellows have become a function of wealth. Who would prefer virtue, what is just, or what is honorable to the desire to acquire wealth, since without wealth one is nothing and with it one is everything? *quis enim virtutem amplectitur ipsam, praemia si tollas?*[37] Then, it is no longer the merit of the actions that leads one to engage in them; it is their price. In Rome, the triumphal and civic crowns—that is, the most illustrious ones—were made of laurel leaves and oak leaves; the others were of gold. What then! Were those who obtained the former not sufficiently rewarded for having increased the glory of their Country or for having saved a citizen for it? But this is no longer what moves us; it is no longer crowns that are needed any more; it is piles of gold. When morals remain to a people, honor alone moves them. This is so true that the crowns of ivy that Cato distributed were preferred to his colleague's crowns of gold.[38] This is because if the crown is gold, it has lost its value.

By depraving morals and multiplying needs to extremes, excessive luxury has brought forth the greed that is so pernicious to virtue and to empires' prosperity.[39] How to satisfy such vast superfluities with an honorable

36. The statement is based on Montesquieu's discussion of intermediary powers at *Laws*, 2.4.

37. "After all, who embraces goodness for itself, if you remove its rewards?" The passage is from Juvenal, *Satires*, ed. and trans. Susanna Morton Braund (Cambridge: Harvard University Press, 2004), X.141–42, 379; it was cited the year before this article by Voltaire in his article "Virtue," in *Philosophical Dictionary*.

38. The contrast between Cato the Younger (95–46 B.C.) and the aedile Favonius in their management of the public entertainments is found in Plutarch, *Life of Cato the Younger*.

39. Compare the discussion of luxury throughout this essay with that in the important article LUXE by Saint-Lambert, which appeared in *Encyclopédie*, 9:763–71, and which is translated in Henry C. Clark, *Commerce, Culture, and Liberty: Readings on Capitalism Before Adam Smith* (Indianapolis: Liberty Fund, 2003), 477–501.

reward! Marks of distinction and the esteem of one's fellow citizens are devalued. Rather than being admired for one's virtue, one wants to astonish by one's magnificence. One wants to strip away respect along with one's clothes, as Herodotus said women stripped away shame along with their tunics.[40]

Neither reason nor experience, but luxury's very disorder has offered the complacently repeated maxim that great luxury is necessary in a great state. Cato the elder maintained that a city in which a fish sold for more than an ox could not last, and Cato was right.[41] All disorders arise from that fact and there are none that, taken in isolation, are not destined to cause the ruin of states.

To speak here only of that disorder most analogous to the subject I am treating: what evils don't arise from the excessive taxes by which the people must be crushed in order to satisfy the greed of those whose only acquaintance with greatness and goodness is with their own enormous superfluities?

Those lavish people don't know the painful cost of the gilt that covers them. Go then, sumptuously perverse and arrogantly inhuman men: enter that cottage; look at your fellow man exhausted by hunger, no longer having the strength to defend his subsistence, which has been wrested from him to braid your valets' costume. Like Saturn, or rather like beasts that are even more ferocious, you devour the state's children. If all natural affection is extinguished in you, if you dare do this without dying of shame, then look at those innocent victims of your debaucheries—clinging to a breast that you have shriveled through poverty. You nurture them with blood, and you make their mothers pour forth their tears. You will answer to nature for the destruction of so many beings, who see the light of day only to be sacrificed to your murderous opulence. You will answer for all those who will not have been brought forth, and for the descendants whose ruin you will have caused by desiccating through want the generative sources in those by whom they were to be engendered.

40. When Kandaules, king of Lydia (r. 735–718 B.C.), urged his bodyguard Gyges to see Kandaules's wife naked, so as to confirm the latter's reports of her beauty, Gyges balked, saying, "in the stripping off of her tunic a woman is stripped of the honour due to her." Herodotus, *Histories*, I.8.

41. For this anecdote, see Plutarch, *Life of Cato the Elder*.

For the present, it is not my intention to carry these reflections on the effects of luxury any further. Nor will I examine how far luxury might be necessary. But I will always believe that in any well-administered state whose extent, position, and fertility of soil allow it to produce abundantly and beyond all needs, the measure of luxury must be the consumption of surplus. If it exceeds this point, then you have a torrent that nothing can stop. Let me develop these ideas further.

The laws will not repress luxury any more than they repress mores. Censorship could maintain mores in Rome as long as they existed, but it would not have restored them once depravity had destroyed them. Virtue does not regulate itself. Example, and the esteem accorded it, make us love virtue and invite us to practice it. If the prince grants distinction only to personal merit, if he welcomes only those who are honorable and modest, then men will become these things. Under the Antonines, it would have been difficult to be perverse and lavish.[42] It would also be difficult under a prince of our time who is justly the admiration of Europe because of the many qualities he brings together, after having astonished it.[43]

For anyone with the wherewithal to satisfy only the necessities, it is rare to dream of superfluities. The taste for expense and sensual pleasures comes only with the means of satisfying them. These means have two principal sources at their origin: wealth acquired at the expense of public revenues, and wealth procured by the profits of commerce.

But the trade in superfluities, which alone produces gains substantial enough to stimulate luxury, presupposes a preexisting luxury that has given it being. Thus, the gains of commerce that support it and increase it are only secondary and incidental means. Bad management of public revenues is the primary cause of this support and this increase, just as it is the primary cause of the original existence of luxury.

A wise and well-ordered administration—one which permitted no depredations in the receipt or expenditure of its revenues, which left no pos-

42. The term "Antonines" usually refers mainly to the Roman emperors Antoninus Pius (r. 138–61) and Marcus Aurelius (r. 161–80).

43. Probably Frederick II (the Great), king of Prussia (1740–86), who began his reign by invading Silesia, triggering the War of the Austrian Succession in 1740, but became a celebrated reformer and patron of the arts and sciences, hosting Voltaire among others.

sibility for those immense, illegitimate, and scandalous fortunes made by handling them—would dry up the source and channels of luxury without further regulation. Since luxury always increases at a rate of double, triple, quadruple its means and then some, the profits from trade would soon become inadequate for it. Since fiscal wealth would no longer serve to renew the wealth this luxury dissipates, it would consume itself and end up destroying or at least moderating itself. The grandees alone would support it by their ostentation. But this would be the affair of one generation, at most; the next would not be in a position to have to deal with it. They would leave only bankrupt descendants, and perhaps this would not be a great evil. Brought closer to the other citizens, they would have a better sense of their resemblance to them, which wealth causes its possessors to ignore. Solon used to say that *whoever has dissipated his wealth is a commoner.*

The efficacy of these means is not to be doubted, especially if example is joined to them; nor can it be doubted that everything august is simple. In wise governments, men have been no less careful to repress the luxury of superstition than the luxury of vanity. The laws of Lycurgus and Plato are admirable in this respect.

Magnificence in public worship stimulates that of private individuals. One always wants to imitate what one most admires. When one says this magnificence is necessary to inspire people with the veneration they should have for the object of their faith, one offers a quite petty idea of it. It seems to me the early Christians had a larger one: Origen says they were horrified by temples, altars, and idols.[44] In fact, whoever one believes to be the author of all spaces, all bodies, and all beings should be worshipped in the midst of the world. A stone altar raised on top of a hill, from which the view is lost in the vast expanse of a distant horizon, would be more august and more worthy of his majesty than those human edifices which seem to restrict his power and grandeur within four columns and which represent him as decorated like a vain and ostentatious being. The people become familiar with pomp and ceremonies all the more easily in that these things are closer to them and less apt to impress them, being conducted by their

44. Origen of Alexandria (ca. 185–ca. 254), Christian theologian and philosopher; see *Contra Celsus,* VII.62, VIII.17, and passim for this sentiment.

fellow men. Soon these ceremonies become a simple object of curiosity, and habit ends up making the people indifferent to them. If synaxis were celebrated only once a year and if people assembled from various places to attend it as they did the Olympic games, it would have a very different importance among those who practice this rite.[45] It is the fate of all things to become less venerable by becoming more common and less marvelous by growing older.

Moreover, wealth buried away in the state treasury is entirely lost to society and to the people who furnish that treasury one more surcharge from which they derive no utility. At least the golden clothing that Pericles arranged to be made for the Pallas Athena could be removed—in order, he said, to use it in time of public need.[46]

Whatever its object, then, luxury is fatal to public prosperity and to the security of societies. Purity of mores is doubtless their firmest support. But if it were possible to prevent society's general degradation, it is those creatures born to misfortune who would need the strongest bridle. And public honor would not suffice without the fear of the laws and of the punishments they pronounce in order to contain malefactors.

Both the common and individual security demand magistrates who are constantly vigilant about executing the laws. For life not to be at the mercy of an assassin and for property not to be prey to a plunderer, a strict and constant administration must remove the brigands from city and country. To go about our affairs and communicate in all the places where those affairs oblige us to betake ourselves, the routes must be convenient and secure. The highways have been opened up and bridges built at great expense. That is not enough. If they are not maintained, and with them the troops to guard them, people will be unable to frequent them without risking loss of life or fortune. And in each place or in each canton, there must be civil judges who protect you against the bad faith of a debtor or an unjust pleader, and who guarantee you against the assaults of the wicked.

45. Synaxis was a communal liturgy in the early church as well as a generic term for assembly; a possible contemporary source for Damilaville was Voltaire, *Essai sur l'histoire universelle* (Geneva: Cramer, 1756), chap. 12, a work he expressly names below.

46. Pericles (495–429 B.C.), Athenian statesman; the gold statue of Athena was to be built by his friend, the sculptor Phidias (ca. 480–430 B.C.).

To prevent the corruption of the air and the diseases that arise from it, cleanliness must be maintained in the cities. And in a word, countless things at once useful and convenient for the public must be carried out.[47] Since the public is the sole object of these precautions, it is just that it support their expense. Thus, the contribution each person furnishes again has its origin and effect in the general advantage and private utility of the citizens.

IV. We have said that the fundamental cause of the establishment of every society is the defense and common preservation of all, and of its members individually. We have just seen how many (always active) means are used to direct the state's forces toward this end. But the state is only an abstract being that cannot itself make use of its forces and that needs an agent to put them in action to the benefit of the community. Society cannot itself watch over its preservation and that of its members. It would have to be assembled constantly, which would be not only impractical but even contrary to its purpose. Men have joined together and combined their power solely for the purpose of enjoying as individuals a greater moral and civil liberty. And besides, a society that watched ceaselessly over all its members would no longer be a society. It would be a state without people, a sovereign without subjects, a city without citizens. The surveilling and the surveilled cannot be the same; if all citizens were on watch, whom would they be watching? That's why all those who have written on politics systematically[48] have established that the people alone have the legislative power, but that they could not at the same time have the executive power. The power of having someone execute the conventions of the civil association and of maintaining the political body in the relationships it should have with its neighbors must be in continual exercise. Thus, a corresponding capacity must be introduced by which all the state's forces are combined, in order to be a central point where these forces come together, to make them act according to the common good—in short, to be the guardian of the civil and political liberty of the entire body and each of its members.

47. For a contemporary survey of the proper scope of government action, see Boucher d'Argis's article PUBLIC LAW, above.

48. *Avec quelques principes,* which can refer to moral principles as well as to the intellectual principles evoked in our translation.

The intermediate power [*pouvoir*] is what is called *government,* whatever type or form it may be, whence one may conclude that the government is manifestly not the state but a particular body constituted to manage it according to its laws.

Thus, without being the state, the supreme administration represents it, exercises its rights, and discharges its obligations toward the citizens. Powerless by itself but a depository of the general power, it has the right to demand from everyone the contribution which must establish that general power. And in satisfying the duties the government imposes in this respect, each person does nothing but discharge toward himself and toward society the tribute of the forces he has promised to furnish, either by joining together to form society or by remaining united to perpetuate it and to live in security under the protection of arms and the laws.

V. But the sum of public needs can never exceed the sum of all forces. It cannot even be equal. Nothing more would remain for the private preservation of individuals. They would perish, and the state with them.

A general preservation that reduced individuals to a miserable existence would resemble that of a being whose limbs were removed to make it live: it would be chimerical. If it demands more than the surplus of their necessities, what interest would people have in such a preservation that annihilates them? The preservation of oneself is the first duty imposed upon men by nature, and even by society's interest. Government is established only to guarantee society and optimize the condition of each person—a condition, however, that is bound to vary ceaselessly according to circumstances. Thus, it may demand nothing that is prejudicial to that individual preservation antecedent to it, but only what is indispensable to assure it in everything that ought to contribute to it. Otherwise, it would act in contradiction to the nature and purpose of its establishment.

These ideas about the power [*pouvoir*] exercised over citizens in the name of society are not arbitrary. It is impossible to formulate any ideas about society without having these at the same time. The more liberty deteriorates, the more obscure these ideas become. Where authority is absolute and therefore illegitimate, they are entirely lost. That is where we see the absurd quarrel of the stomach and the limbs and the ridiculous league of the limbs against the stomach.[49] There, leaders command, they do not govern. Whence it arises that in despotic states, everyone thinks himself capable of governing, and even honesty is sacrificed to the ambition to achieve this. With the power to have it done, only the will is necessary. And who is lacking will when it comes to dominating over others?

If one saw in ministerial dignities only the constant solicitudes that are inseparable from them, the extent and multiplicity of the arduous duties they impose, the superiority of talents and universality of knowledge necessary to fulfill them; if it was only the craving for domination and for the acquisition of wealth that made one desire them, then far from seeking them with such avidity, there is no one who would not tremble at the prospect of yielding under the weight of such a heavy burden. There isn't a vizier who would want to do so.

It is a terrible responsibility to have to answer to an entire people for their happiness and tranquility. Seleucus felt its weight when he stated that if one knew how painstaking the cares of governance were, one would not deign to pick up a diadem found by the roadside. And Roquelaure said a very sensible thing to Henry IV when he answered that for all his treasures, he would not want to have the job that Sully had.[50]

Civil societies and governments do not exist, as some have thought, because there are beings especially destined to march at the head of others. Grotius, and those who have dared to join him in advancing this proposition—a proposition as absurd as it is injurious to the human species—has abused what Aristotle had said before him. No one has received from nature the right to command his fellow creature. No one has the right to buy him. The slave who sold himself yesterday has so little power to do so that according to natural right, he could today tell who-

49. See Livy, *History of Rome,* II.xxxii, where the story is told by Menenius Agrippa to defuse plebeian animosity against the patricians, a problem then solved by establishing "tribunes of the people."

50. The reference to Seleucus I (ca. 358–ca. 280 B.C.) is from Plutarch, "Whether an Old Man should engage in Public Affairs," in *Moralia* 790b. Antoine, Baron of Roquelaure (1544–1625), was an officeholder and confidant of Henry IV (r. 1589–1610); Sully (1559–1641), the minister under Henry IV revered for his frugality. See discussions of him in POLITICAL AUTHORITY, SAVINGS, and POPULATION, in this volume.

ever bought him that he is his own master if he had the strength to back it up.

One deplores the yoke that reason and truth have been under at all times when one reads in Grotius: "If a private individual can alienate his liberty and make himself the slave of a master, why couldn't an entire people do this?" One is distressed to hear this good and talented man assert "that all human power [*pouvoir*] is not established for the happiness of those who are governed."[51]

Doubtless not, if he judges by the facts. But by rights, what would then be the motive causing men to submit to authority if its purpose were not the common happiness?

Aristotle said that men are not naturally equal, that some are born for slavery and others for domination. But it was not to be concluded from this that slavery accords with natural law. Aristotle's idea must be explained by the diversity of faculties that nature grants men. Some are born with loftier talent and qualities more fit for governance, others with the need to be governed and with the inclination to let themselves be ruled. According to the illustrious author of the *Essay on universal history,* it was in this way that Marshall Ancre's wife came to respond to her judges that she had governed Catherine de' Medici by the power strong souls ought to have over weak ones. In his tragedy on *fanaticism,* too, this noble genius in all genres has Mohammed say that he wants to dominate by *the right that a vast mind, firm in its designs, has over the gross minds of vulgar humans.*[52]

Such are the sole natural rights of authority over one's fellow creatures; the others depend on civil conventions, and it cannot be suspected that they had the enslavement of society as their purpose.

This strange government, where the prince is a pastor and the people a flock, where nature is outraged constantly and in cold blood—in short, despotism—was never inspired by her. Men have derived the example of it from her, but not the idea.

51. The passage is from Grotius, *The Rights of War and Peace,* I.iii.8.

52. Leonora Dori, Maréschale d'Ancre (1571–1617), was tried and executed for bewitching the queen regent Marie de Medici, whom Damilaville seems to be confusing with Catherine de' Medici. The trial is described in Voltaire's *La Pucelle d'Orléans* [The maid of Orleans] (Louvain, 1755), 30ff.; the other reference is to Voltaire's *Mahomet, ou le fanatisme* (1742), act 2, sc. 5.

After men had imagined beings of a species above their own to which they attributed effects whose causes they did not understand, they made these their sovereigns. And it must have seemed more natural to submit to them than to their fellow beings, from whom they had neither the same evils to fear nor the same goods to hope for.[53]

The period of the infancy of the human species—that is, when it was reproduced in nature if it had not had a continuous existence—or else every time societies renewed themselves after being destroyed by their antiquity, these periods (I say) were the times of perfect equality among men. Force dominated, but one could flee if it were not possible to resist. Thus, the first general subjection must have been to the authority of the gods. Only time and the habit of seeing this authority exercised by a man in their name could defeat the natural repugnance toward the power of some over all.

The proof that the first ones who attempted to claim this power did not believe that they were authorized, or that others were disposed to obey them, is that all the earliest legislators had recourse to some divinity to cause the laws they gave the peoples they founded to be accepted under their auspices. In the traditions of the world's most ancient nations, one finds the reign of the gods and the demigods—as if, says Montaigne, every polity is headed by a god.[54]

The leader was merely his minister. He announced his will and transmitted his orders but gave none of his own. These orders were often cruel, and a learned antiquarian has judiciously observed that theocracy pushed tyranny to the most horrible excesses that human madness can reach; that the more this government called itself divine, the more abominable it was.[55]

That is how one of the earliest legislators reigned and how 20,000 men let themselves be massacred without resistance for having worshiped an idol that one of their intimate associates had raised up for them.[56] Again, it

53. Compare Boulanger, POLITICAL ECONOMY, above, on the themes of the next several paragraphs.

54. See "Of Glory" in Montaigne, *Essays*, 477.

55. The reference is to Boulanger's posthumously published *Recherches sur l'origine du despotisme oriental* (1761; translated by John Wilkes as *The Origin and Progress of Despotism* in 1764), a work much discussed in the circles around Diderot, d'Holbach (who helped publish it), and others.

56. The episode of the golden calf is recounted in Exodus 32.

was because people thought they heard the Great Being order these bloody sacrifices that twenty-four thousand others were slaughtered without defense, because one of them had slept with a foreign woman from the same country as the lawgiver's wife.[57]

The divine monarch's representatives imperceptibly put themselves in his place. They had only one step to take: it became customary to confound them, so the representatives remained in possession of the absolute power that until then they had exercised on only a proxy basis.

But this error of peoples regarding their despots, who allowed the appearances of theocracy to remain in order to be more despotic, managed to come to an end. Men were able to perceive that they were no longer obeying anyone but a fellow creature, and that it would be better to confine themselves to a more solid and less flashy opinion.

Men were content to have received from the divinity an absolute power over the lives and properties of their fellows; this division was still fine. Samuel made Saul's allotment in giving him to the Hebrews as king.[58] Men were found base enough and low enough to make their masters understand that this depiction of Saul contained the portrait of the sovereign's rights. "The illustrious Bossuet," says the count of Boulainvilliers (even more illustrious than he), "abused the texts of Scripture by bad faith to create new chains for the liberty of men and to increase the luxury and harshness of kings. That bishop's political system is one of the most shameful testimonies to the disgracefulness of our age and the corruption of our hearts."[59]

I am not saying that the count of Boulainvilliers was right in this accusation and that the views of the bishop of Meaux were the ones he criticized. But one has to be ignorant of the main facts of history not to admit that as soon as they could, the promoters of superstition—as eager for wealth as

57. See Numbers 25:6–9 for this episode.

58. The reference is to 1 Samuel 10.

59. The reference is to Jacques-Bénigne Bossuet (1627–1704), whose *Politique tirée des propres paroles de l'écriture sainte* [*Politics drawn from the very words of Holy Scripture*], ed. and trans. Patrick Riley (1709; Cambridge: Cambridge University Press, 1990), was perhaps the most influential argument for divine-right monarchy in France. It was criticized by Henri, Count of Boulainvilliers (1658–1722) in letter three of his *Lettres aux Parlements*, contained in his *Histoire de l'ancien gouvernement de la France* [History of the former government of France] (The Hague, 1727), 253.

for authority, and looking to acquire both by the ruin and slavery of all—strove to persuade people to accept unlimited power for sovereigns, whom they themselves attempted to subjugate after using them to raise up their own power, and whom they exalted as much as they needed them, preaching to everyone an absolute obedience to one, provided the one be subject to them; making everything depend on him, provided he depend on them.

That is what all the authority Constantine gave them by his laws and all the authority they had under the Visigoth kings was worth to them. In *Suidas*, in *Mezeray*, and in many other authors, one can see how, under these princes, they abused that maxim, *all power comes from on high,* to the ruin of society.[60] It's a maxim that would relieve those who would take advantage of it from every bridle, free them from every remorse, and dispense them from even the appearances of justice.

One would have thought more justly and spoken more sensibly, and sovereign authority would have been more solidified, if one had said: *all power comes from nature and from reason, by which every man must regulate his actions*. For every power is only established, and must only be exercised, by nature and reason. It is reason that has decreed that men, joined in society and unable to be governed by the multitude, confer upon one or several the power of governing them—according to their number and the extent of the possessions they have to preserve, and following the conventions and laws of the society they have formed.

It is again reason that decrees that those to whom this authority is conferred use it not according to the force of which they are the custodians but in conformity with those same laws—which in reality limit all their power [*puissance*] to the capacity of having them executed. Archidamus was asked who governed at Sparta. *It's the laws,* he said, *and then the magistrate following the laws*.[61] One should be able to give this response about all the governments in the world.

60. Suidas, or Suda, a tenth-century Byzantine historical encyclopedia; François Eudes de Mézeray (1610–83), historiographer of France and member of the French Academy, author of *Histoire de France,* in 3 vols. (1643–51). For the cited maxim, see John 19:11.

61. The reference is to Archidamus II (r. ca. 469–427 B.C.), son of Zeuxidamus and king during the Peloponnesian Wars; see Plutarch, "Sayings of Spartans," in *Moralia,* 218c, for this anecdote.

I am well aware that Grotius has not been the only one to think in a manner contrary to these principles. Hobbes seems no more favorable to them. But what he says that is seemingly analogous to the former's maxims should be attributed only to his personal misfortunes and to the necessitous circumstances in which he found himself. That philosopher veiled himself; it is the same with his political works as with *Machiavelli's* prince: those who have seen only the obvious meaning that these works present have not understood their true meaning.[62]

Hobbes had a different purpose. In looking closely at it, one sees that he presented an apologia for the sovereign solely as a pretext for presenting a satire of the divinity to which he compares him and whom no honorable man would want to resemble.

This luminous and exact idea would not be presented here if it had occurred to one of the finest geniuses of this century, namely, the author of the *article* HOBBES in this dictionary.[63] It explains all the apparent contradictions in one of the strongest logicians and most decent men of his time.

In fact, how can we presume that such a profound reasoner believed that any being whatsoever could give an indefinite power over himself to another being of the same species, and that as a result of this concession, the latter could indeed be evil but never unjust? How to imagine that he believed that the man whom the law of war permitted to engage in killing in the state of nature would submit to all sorts of services and forms of obedience to the man who is happy to preserve his life on that condition, and that this obligation covers everything he wants without restriction?

This proposition announces several contradictions very distinctly. (1) According to this frightful system, the victor could demand that the vanquished deprive himself of his own life or that he deprive his father, his wife, or his children of theirs—in short, that he sacrifice what is most dear to him. He would be submitting to this shameful slavery solely to preserve himself.

62. See MACHIAVELLIANISM, above, where Diderot interprets Machiavelli's work in a similar fashion.

63. The reference is to Diderot, although the article in question is entitled HOBBISME. For Diderot's unsatirical treatment of Hobbes's political theory criticized here by Damilaville, see 8:240.

(2) If it is true in nature that the stronger kills the weaker when the latter resists, it is not true in nature that he makes him a slave; this would not be seen in the state of nature. What would be done? Nature allows killing because she is quite indifferent about the form in which a being exists. For her, it is merely a question of one modification more or less, which is always done without any trouble or expense on her part. But she cannot endure slavery because it is of no use to her and because she has given this right to no being over another.

Where obligations are not reciprocal, agreements are null; this truth is no less true for having already been stated. Is it not an abuse of words and of the rational faculty to say: *the magistrate who holds his power* [pouvoir] *from the law is not subject to the law?* Despite St. Augustine's affirmation of this, and despite all the sophisms one may engage in to support this inhuman assertion, it is clear that in transgressing the law that gives him authority, the magistrate overturns the foundations of his power. In substituting his will for the law, he puts both himself and others back in the state of nature in relation to each other. Each person then reclaims against him, as against all, the right to have nothing but his own will as a rule, a right which had only been renounced because he himself had renounced it. Finally, in violating the social pact, he dispenses others from its execution in his own case and forces all those who have submitted to it to return to natural right to provide for their defense. They had only alienated this natural right to substitute the law that punishes infractions against society, being a less violent and more certain means of assuring their general and individual preservation.

If Hobbes had really meant, as he said and as Grotius seriously thought, *that a people that hands over its right to a tyrant no longer exists*, could it not be answered that in this case, the tyrant no longer exists himself? On what basis would he exist? *The multitude* (as Hobbes calls them after this right has been handed over) would say to the tyrant: "I am no longer the people from whom you hold the *right* that you mean to exercise, since your election annihilates me. Since I am no longer what I was when I contracted with you, being a different person, I am no longer bound by any of the conditions." And this reasoning would be just.

Can the powers with which dethroned sovereigns contracted state obligations while on the throne require their fulfillment of these agreements once they are only private persons? If France had made a treaty with King James while he was reigning in England, by which he engaged to cede her some port in that realm, wouldn't it have been ridiculous to want to force the same King James and his pensioner in Saint Germain to fulfill the treaty's conditions by handing over the promised port once he was but a simple individual?[64] It is the same with *the multitude* if they cease to be a people as soon as they have conferred the right of governing them to another.

But we see Hobbes reveal himself and agree with this principle. "The first of the means (he says in another chapter) by which one may acquire domination over a person is when someone, for the good of peace and for the interest of the common defense, has willingly placed himself under the power of a certain man or a certain assembly, *after having agreed on some articles that must be observed reciprocally*." It must be noted that he adds, "it is by this means that civil societies have been established."[65]

Thus, behold the rights of peoples recognized as well as the obligations of sovereigns toward them, and by the very man who was refusing those rights and denying those obligations. In laying down everything they had in common, men placed themselves under the power of society in order to maintain it and be protected by it. In entrusting its right to one or several, society has done so only on the condition that the entrusted ones lighten society's burden by fulfilling the obligations that bind it to the citizens. Thus, it is not true that the sovereign in whom the people have entrusted the power [*pouvoir*] to govern them is no longer bound in any way toward this same people. He owes them everything society itself would owe them, and what society would owe them is to govern them according to the express or tacit conditions to which each person subscribed in forming it. But this is too much discussion of a truth so evident it needs no demonstration.

Thus, if on the one hand (as we have already made clear), citizens owe the state everything necessary for its defense and preservation, then on the other, society or the government that represents it may demand nothing beyond that nor make any other use of that which the citizens provide to it.

64. The reference is to James II (r. 1685–88), dethroned during the Glorious Revolution and exiled during his last years (1690–1701) in St. Germain, outside of Paris.

65. See Hobbes, *Leviathan,* chap. 17, and *De Cive* [On the Citizen], chap. 5, for general discussions of this theme.

Someone observed to one of the greatest kings that France has ever had that his power was limited. "I can do everything I want," responded the equitable and beneficent monarch, "because I want only what is just and good for my subjects." This response is splendid; it's a shame that it should be noteworthy. It ought to be the response of all sovereigns.[66]

In every state governed by these principles, taxes will be moderate because public utility will be their measure. In other states, they will be excessive because the imaginary needs that the passions and the illusion of false glory will produce in those who govern are insatiable, and excessive taxes will be the rule.[67]

In pocketbook laws,[68] one finds that public revenues are the prince's revenues and that his debts are those of the state. It's impossible to overturn principles more advantageous to the government or more ruinous to the state. Thus, in states where these maxims are allowed to be published, one might say that they are enemies of each other and that the interest of the government is to annihilate the state—as if, in destroying the state, it was not itself destined to be buried under the ruins.

Once this astonishing neglect of all order and all public good has been reached, one no longer serves the state but the government—for its money. Rapacity puts an enormous price on all services. The exhaustion of the people, even the complete alienation of the state, does not suffice. Since you have to buy—and not cheaply—even the baseness of the courtiers, who think the shame of their opulence erases the shame of their degradation, you must also sell with one portion of authority even the right to trade that authority and to traffic in justice. This is a monstrous right that subjects truth, reason, and knowledge to error, ignorance, and folly; that abandons life, liberty, and the citizens' honor and fortune to fanaticism, cruelty, arrogance, and all the passions of whoever has the means to pay for this dreadful right, which is at once the opprobrium and the terror of humanity.

66. This anecdote is told by Boulainvilliers in *Histoire de l'ancien gouvernement de la France,* 156, where the king also goes unnamed.

67. See Montesquieu, *Laws,* 13.1, for similar language.

68. The term is *lois bursales,* meaning edicts to exact extraordinary levies from the *bourse,* or pocketbook, of the subjects.

When the government resorts to such pernicious expedients, it consults only its always-greedy and always-improvident needs. Is the fate of men so unimportant that the power of disposing of it can be given over to chance in this way? The princes who have been most worthy of the human race have not thought so. Alexander Severus raised up no one to the magistracy or to public office without publicizing it beforehand, so that anyone could oppose him if there were some criticisms made of those he designated. He used to say that whoever buys must sell, and he never allowed dignities to be a prize for money.[69]

During the heyday of the Roman republic, the customs were even more favorable to the citizens' liberty and security. Judges were named for each case, and with the consent of the parties, too. Dionysius of Halicarnassus writes that when the magistrates[70] judged alone, they rendered themselves odious. Titus Livy says a public gathering of the people was needed to inflict capital punishment on a citizen.[71] Only in the great assemblies could they decide about his life.

Murders committed with the sword of justice were not seen there. The orphan's inheritance was not a reward for dishonor obtained by the seduction of the judge, and justice was not sold to iniquity. Hypocrisy and false zeal did not insult merit and outrage virtue. Finally, there was nothing resembling all the kinds of venality that were practiced against the citizens and against the state itself.[72] For if this venality is pernicious to individuals, it is no less so to the good order and tranquility of commonwealths.

A truth demonstrated by the experience of all times is that the more divided the general administration is, the more weakened it is and the less well-governed the state. Partial interests, always opposed to the total interest, multiply in proportion to the number of subsidiary administrations.

69. Alexander Severus, Roman emperor (r. 222–35). For the anecdotes in question, see "Severus Alexander," in *The Scriptores Historiae Augustae*, XLV.6 and XLIX.1.

70. *Tribuns*, or "tribunes," elected officials in Rome.

71. Dionysius of Halicarnassus (ca. 60 B.C.–ca. 7 B.C.); the passage Damilaville cites is from *Roman Antiquities*, 11.39.1. It is cited to identical effect by Montesquieu in *Laws*, 11.18; see also Livy, *History of Rome*, I.xxvi.

72. Damilaville probably means later on in Roman history, although the grammatical construction *s'est pratiqué* is consistent with a reference to recent France, well known for its widespread venality of offices. See also the next paragraph for a standard complaint about France.

The more substantial their number is, the less coherence there is in the general administration, and the more difficult it is. Independent of individual wills, each corporate entity has its own will according to which it wants to govern, and which it often opposes to the will of others and almost always to the supreme authority. They all attempt to encroach upon and take advantage of the latter. A portion has been bought and the rest is in dispute, so the general power, being too divided, becomes exhausted. The state is poorly defended externally and poorly led internally. Disorder is introduced. Interests clash. Passions, prejudices, ambition, and the whims of a swarm of administrators take the place of principles. Rules become arbitrary, local, and variable by the day. What was prescribed yesterday is proscribed today. Under this multitude of authorities colliding with each other, the people are no longer governed but oppressed. They no longer know what they have to do nor what obedience they owe. The laws fall into contempt and civil liberty is weighted down with chains.

Let us add that the more numerous the magistrates are, the more private needs there are to satisfy and consequently the more vexations to be borne by the people.

In Thebes, the judges were represented with a blindfold and no hands. All they have kept is the blindfold; it is not for the sake of being what the rest of this symbol signifies[73] that they gain the possibility of selling what is already no longer justice as soon as it has a price. Woe betide anyone who is obliged to have recourse to this justice. It would have been better to suffer the damages from the unjust person. It is not enough to pay one's judges; one must corrupt them, without which the innocent is surrendered to the criminal behavior of the guilty and the weak to the oppression of the strong. The celebrated Chancellor de l'Hôpital wrote to Olivier, "It is impossible to appease this ardor for accumulation that is devouring our tribunals, and that no humane respect or fear of the laws can curb."[74] While

73. Handless; according to the *Emblemata* of Andreas Alciatus (1492–1550), judges were depicted with no hands "so that they should take no bribes, or let themselves be swayed by promises or gifts." See Alciatus, *Emblems in Translation,* vol. 2 of *Andreas Alciatus,* ed. Peter M. Daly (Toronto: University of Toronto Press, 1985), 145.

74. Michel de l'Hôpital (ca. 1505–73) succeeded François Olivier (1487–1560) as chancellor under King Francis II in 1560, at the outset of the French religious wars. The cited

speaking to judges on another occasion in the presence of the sovereign, he said, "You are accused of much violence; you threaten people with your judgments, and many are scandalized by the manner in which you do your business. There are some among you who have been made provisions officers[75] during the late disturbances and others who take money to have audiences given." The memoirs and letters of that great man are full of similar criticisms he made to the tribunals.

Whoever serves the state should be paid by it, no doubt. His upkeep and subsistence must be provided for; that is the price of his work. Along with mores, the price of merit and of virtue is only esteem and public consideration. After the battle of Salamis, Themistocles said he was paid for his labors and for the pains he had endured for the salvation of Greece by the admiration the people displayed for him at the Olympic games.[76]

Such rewards do not burden the state with debt. They elevate men; money debases them. It is shameful deeds that should be paid for, to make them even more debased—if it were permissible to endure them for any reason whatsoever.

But as for what ought to be paid to those whom the state employs, the citizens have already furnished it by the taxes whose purpose is in part these expenses. Why are the citizens also obliged to make a special purchase of their labor and their favor? This is to surcharge the same thing many times, and always more expensively than the last time. Even the author of the *Political Testament,* attributed to Cardinal de Richelieu,[77] was unable to avoid admitting its injustice, however partial he was toward venality.

The public good does not give rise to these surcharges. The utility of society cannot be a disaster for those who compose it; that which produces

---

passage was well known, appearing in *L'Année littéraire* (1764), 3:156, and Jean Simon Lévesque de Pouilly, *Vie de Michel de l'Hôpital* (London: Wilson, 1764), 64, for example.

75. *Commissaires de vivres,* widely suspected of skimming significant sums in the sixteenth century.

76. Themistocles (ca. 525–460 B.C.), Athenian statesman and military leader during the Persian wars, including the naval battle of Salamis in September 480 B.C. For the episode in question, see Plutarch, *Life of Themistocles,* XVII.2.

77. Damilaville here sides with Voltaire, *Essay,* chap. 144, rather than with Montesquieu, *Laws,* 3.5, that the work was not by Richelieu. Modern scholarship has concluded that the work was in fact by the cardinal-minister.

nothing but society's ruin and the people's misery is what costs the most. Out of all the causes that have this effect, superstition is the principal one. This is the most terrible scourge of the human race, just as it is the heaviest burden on societies—and the most useless.

Plutarch says that priests do not make the gods good or the dispensers of good; the gods are that way all by themselves.[78] Everyone thinks like Plutarch but acts the opposite. This pile of incoherent ideas that the human mind gives and receives is one of its strangest contradictions. Nothing better proves that it understands none of them and that it will never have the least notion of the thing of which it thinks it is most certain.

Not to mention all those ideas that are mutually exclusive. It must be admitted that our passions turn us into extraordinary magicians: once they have made us exceed the limits of reason, nothing costs us anything, nothing surprises us, and nothing stops us. Inflamed by self-interest or seduction, the imagination sees and makes others see truths in the most monstrous absurdities. And as Tacitus observes, men add more faith to whatever they do not understand. The human mind is naturally led to believe incomprehensible things more willingly. *Majorem fidem homines adhibent iis quae non intelligunt: cupidine obscura creduntur. Hist. bk. I.*[79]

It is an impiety toward the gods, says Plato, to believe that they can be appeased by sacrifices.[80] It is an even greater impiety to plunder the goods of society on this pretext. This is a spiritual fraud more reprehensible and pernicious than the civil fraud which the laws punish with such rigor.[81]

Severus condemned Vetronius, whom he loved most among his favorites, to die of suffocation in smoke. He said this was for having sold smoke—that is, the graces and favors that he was able to obtain from him. By dint of being just, Severus was cruel. But when Tchuen-Hio declared, according to Fr. Du Halde's account, that in the entire empire, he alone

78. The passage is based on Plutarch, "That a philosopher ought to converse especially with Men in Power," in *Moralia,* 778f.

79. The author paraphrases Tacitus, *Histories,* I.xxii; Montaigne had cited the same passage in his essay "Of Cripples," in *Essays,* 789.

80. See Plato, *Republic,* bk. 2.

81. *Stellionat,* which we translate as "fraud," is a sale of what one does not own, or of the same thing to different persons, or of something as unencumbered when there is still debt on it.

had the right to offer sacrifices to the sovereign lord of heaven, he freed his subjects from the heaviest of vexations.[82]

It is said that the prince to whom the Chinese are indebted for this good, which they still enjoy today, had a count made of the number of those making a living this way at the expense of the commonwealth, without bearing its burdens and without giving back anything equivalent to the burdens it was causing. He found that they amounted to 300,000, who were costing the citizens at least 40 *sols* each per day in our money,[83] which meant that those useless people levied 219 million each year on the people who supported the state by their labors and their tax contributions. The emperor was not collecting that much for the needs of the empire, and he decided that he would be making himself an accomplice of these vexations by tolerating them. It seems the sovereigns of that vast country feared nothing except not doing enough good for their subjects.

Under the same pretext, powerful and numerous corporate entities have come into being in Europe's leading countries. Like the rat in the fable, they are fattening themselves on the substance of the body politic that contains them.

Self-defense against their cupidity has been necessary from the beginning. In 370, fifty years after Constantine, Valentinian the Elder was obliged to publish a law prohibiting them from profiting on the simplicity of the people, and especially of their women. The law prohibited them from receiving either by will or by living donation any inheritance or furniture from virgins or from any other women. And he banned them by this law from any conversation with the sex that they had only too much abused.[84]

Twenty years later, Theodosius was forced to renew these prohibitions.[85]

In France, Charlemagne, St. Louis, Philip the Fair, Charles the Good, Charles V, Francis I, Henry II, Charles IX, Henry III, Louis XIV, and

82. On Severus, see note 69, above; Du Halde, *The General History of China,* trans. Richard Brookes, 4 vols. (London: Watts, 1736), 1:280, for Tchuen-Hio.

83. At 20 *sous* per pound, this would be two pounds per day.

84. Valentinian I (r. 364–75); Constantine I the Great (r. 306–37); the law referred to is sometimes called the law against clerical legacies.

85. Emperor Theodosius I (r. 379–95).

Louis XV, and in England, Edward I, Edward III, and Henry V have made similar laws against the acquisition of folks in a state of *mortemain*.[86]

Narbona & Molina cite the prohibitions made in Spain, in Castile, in Portugal, and in the kingdom of Aragon.[87]

Guilo, Chopin & Christin report similar laws that have taken effect in Germany.[88]

There are some laws from William III, count of Holland, for the Low Countries; from Emperor Frederick II for the kingdom of Naples; and *Giannone* mentions those passed in Venice, Milan, and the rest of Italy.[89]

In short, the dominant spirit of these bodies has always and everywhere been to encroach upon everything. Where the precautions have been less severe and less numerous, they have managed to succeed. Where more obstacles have been set against their greed, they still possess a large portion of the state's wealth:

(1) At least a third of all property.

(2) A third of the other two-thirds in rents, of which the capital of this portion is taxed to their benefit. This is a way of becoming a landowner without being obliged to maintain the land and of reducing the possessor to nothing more than a leaseholder.

(3) From this same portion, they also deduct the tithe on all production. This is antecedent to all rents, so that one revenue stream will not be detrimental

86. People in a certain condition of servitude. The references were to Charlemagne (768–814), Saint Louis (Louis IX, 1226–70), Philip IV the Fair (1285–1314), Charles IV the Fair (1322–28), Charles V (1364–80), Francis I (1515–47), Henry II (1547–59), Charles IX (1560–74), Henry III (1574–89), kings of France; and Edward I (1272–1307), Edward III (1327–77), and Henry V (1413–22), English kings.

87. Luis de Molina (1535–1600), Spanish Jesuit and theologian mainly at the University of Madrid; the other reference may be to Diego Narbona (1605?–50), author of *Annales tractatus juris de aetate ad omnes humanos actus requisita* [Histories: A legal treatise on adulthood (and) on whatever is necessary for all human actions] (Rome: Corbi, 1669).

88. Perhaps the legal expert Renatus Choppinus (1537–1606); the other references remain unidentified.

89. Pietro Giannone (1676–1748), the Neapolitan historian whose *Storia civile del regno di Napoli* [Civil history of the kingdom of Naples (1723)] influenced Montesquieu's *Laws* and Edward Gibbon's *The Decline and Fall of the Roman Empire;* William III of Hainault (William I, Count of Holland, 1304–37), and Frederick II (1194–1250), Holy Roman Emperor and King of Sicily.

to another and the landowner who cultivates for them will find these more burdensome.

Now a third, plus a tenth, and a third of the other two thirds, makes very close to half of all wealth. Most of the titles of these immense donations begin as follows: *Given that the end of the world is going to arrive*, &c.

You would at least think that those who enjoy so much wealth would render very important services *gratis* to society. But you would be mistaken. Nothing they do serves toward the food, shelter, and clothing of men. And yet, they do nothing—not a single act, not a single step, they exercise no function—without demanding an enormous price.

A memoir published in 1764, in a trial[90] whose scandal alone should have been enough to liberate society forever from that swarm of insects gnawing at it, informs us that just one of their houses levies 1200 pounds of bread per week on the most straitened inhabitants, a quantity whose common assessment assumes 114 consumers at the rate of one and a half pounds each per day.

But these men do not feed only on bread or quench their thirst only on water. If their diet were reckoned at even thirty *sous* per day including clothes, it would be found that this house alone levies 62,412 pounds per year on the public—not counting the value of the land they occupy, the construction and maintenance on the building, as well as everything necessary for the decoration and service of the altars.

Thus, assuming even as few as thirty houses in a city, of men as well as women—which, like this one, must subsist only on public contributions by express condition of their statutes—the capital will bear 1,872,450 pounds in taxes per year for this sole purpose. One can extrapolate from the enormity of these levies to the rest of the entire realm, and to what these people are leaving alone by which the useful citizens are to support the state's burdens.

90. It was becoming more common in France to publish briefs (*mémoires*) concerning ongoing trials, as a way of appealing to public opinion. Some of these involved civil trials concerning the Catholic Church. A typical specimen of the genre, which may or may not have been Damilaville's reference, is *Mémoire pour René Le Lievre, prétendu chanoine-régulier de la Congrégation de France, appelant comme d'abus et demandeur, contre les abbé, procureur-général & autres supérieurs majeurs de la même Congrégation* (A Memoir for René Le Lievre, would-be canon-regular of the Congregation of France, as plaintiff against the abbé, solicitor-general and other major superiors of the same congregation; Paris: Desprez, 1764).

I'm well aware that I am saying monstrous things, and that I might be suspected of false allegations if they were less well known. But I am speaking the truth, and like Montaigne, *not my fill of it.*[91] Whoever takes the trouble to read the memoir from which these facts are drawn will not accuse me of passion or partiality.

They will even see that I have brought only necessary expenses into the valuation, in order to avoid any notion of partiality.

It must be repeated: one is amazed that an abuse so detrimental to society still exists, when the disorders and misconduct of those who cause it furnish such a favorable occasion to free society from it, and to protect mores from an example so apt to corrupt them.

This is how the people adore the cause of their miseries in the object of their veneration, and prostrate themselves before the hand that squeezes them. It is by one part's violation and the other's ignorance of the most sacred and inviolable of natural and positive laws that everything in the subjects' civil society becomes a crushing burden, that its service and utility are only pretexts for vexation. Far from being a state of security for the individuals who compose it, it becomes a state of destruction more miserable than would be the state of nature, where at least they would have the right to provide for their own preservation—a right which, judging by the abuse made of it, they seem only to have conferred in order to arm against themselves those who exercise it.

I can hear from a distance those docile-minded people disapproving the harshness of these reflections, citing received practice against them and claiming that an abuse that has prevailed is consecrated, that it was inevitable once it existed. I would respond that in those maxims, custom takes the place of equity. I am not so apathetic toward the miseries under which humanity groans. *Populari silentio rempublicam prodere.*[92]

I am not unaware of the fact that I will reform nothing. Error has such attraction for men that truth itself would not prevent them from being its victims. But I also know that abuses owe their origin and their perpetuity to the fear of attacking them. Moreover, they are not imprescriptible, and

91. "Of Repentance," in Montaigne, *Essays*, 611.

92. "Popular silence forsakes the republic." For the context see Livy, *History of Rome*, II.xxvii.10.

their continuity is not a sanction. To claim otherwise would be to condemn the human species to misery. The authority of abuses can do nothing against the natural, universal, inalienable right that all recognize and whose annulment depends on no one.

It is a truth that cannot be repeated too often, and never will my mouth or my pen contradict my heart and betray it. Nature has not made men for other men, as they think she has made animals for them. Societies are not established for the felicity of some and the desolation of all. Every public expense whose sole and direct purpose is not the general and particular utility of the citizens, or that exceeds what is demanded by this utility, is unjust and oppressive. It is an infringement on the fundamental laws of society and on the inviolable liberty that its members should enjoy.

It would be a lot for those public expenses to be reduced to such legitimate contours, namely, to what is truly necessary for the good of all. But it would not be enough. What would also be needed are:

(1) that they not be arbitrary; this is the most important condition of all;

(2) that they be distributed equally and borne by all citizens without exception or difference, except for the difference resulting from an inequality in particular strength or faculty, and then, it should be in proportion to the greater or lesser share of the advantages of society that they derive from their participation in it;

(3) that their method of payment not be contrary to the natural and civil liberty the citizens are to enjoy for their persons and their property;

(4) that the levy be simple and easy; that the yield reach the public treasury with ease and by passing through the fewest possible channels;

(5) that the return to the people be prompt, so that they not be too impoverished by these levies and that they be able to continue bearing them;

(6) that the regulations concerning each person's payment not depend on anyone's will but on a fixed law superior to all authority, so that payment be rather a voluntary tribute than an exaction;

(7) and finally, that these regulations cause neither interceptions nor obstacles in the commerce of the earth's produce, of labor, or of the inhabitants' industry, whose circulation constitutes wealth and always produces that wealth in proportion to the liberty it enjoys.

There you have the outline of a problem that the public good has long presented for resolution; it seems it can be reduced to this statement:

Find a form of taxation which, without altering the liberty of the citizens or of commerce and without vexations or disturbances, assures the state sufficient funds for all times and all needs, and by which each person contributes in just proportion to his particular faculties and to the advantages which benefit him in society.

Until now, this problem has remained insoluble. Of all the parts of public administration, that of tax collection has been the most neglected, despite having become the most important. I believe I know the reason.

Among the ancients, it was a matter of indifference how taxes were borne. In the Greek republics, they were not up to the choice or fancy of those who governed; their usage and necessity were known. It was known that the good of the state was always their sole object. There was nothing to prescribe to those whom love of Country made always ready to sacrifice even their lives. Was she in danger? Was her glory or her interest at stake? No one engaged in calculation; even the women divested themselves. It was enough to show the need; the aid was just as prompt and more abundant. Anything the legislator could have done would never have produced the effect of that enthusiasm of patriotic virtue. Thus, very few regulations on this matter are found in those peoples' political institutions.

This does not contradict what was said at the beginning of this article. There, it was a question of ordinary taxes; here, it is clearly understood that I am speaking of circumstances in which more substantial ones are needed.

We observed above that the Romans, in the splendor of the republic when they were absolute masters of their persons and their property, shared both of these unreservedly in the common defense and the common interest. No regulation was yet necessary for the distribution of public offices.

But when wealth and luxury had corrupted everything, the desire to dominate, which always arises from extreme opulence, gave birth to cruel citizens who tore their Country apart in order to enslave it. Rome had its masters and, as we have said, other needs besides those of the republic. So the authorities established taxes and multiplied them.

What then happened is what we have since seen. Men thought only of bringing in the taxes, not at all of regulating their collection. Each new tax was a usurpation. Measures ensuring equal treatment of all citizens could have announced their duration and alerted the citizens against oppression; these measures weren't taken. When tyranny had carried taxes to excess, it was still less the time for distributive justice; taxes accumulated with the same disorder. One never does differently what one is not obliged to do.

One proof of this is that the Roman right of *optimo jure* still existed under Justinian, who in completely abolishing it declared that it was no longer anything but an empty phrase with no advantages.[93] Thus, while destroying it in fact, men had been afraid to abolish its expression. They left the phantom of liberty while crushing the people with vexations.

The nations which founded today's European states on the ruins of that immense empire brought over from their former countries the principles and form of the feudal government they set up there. As long as that constitution existed, taxes were useless. All the costs of public administration and of internal order and policing were at the expense of the fief owners. Each one was obliged to maintain them throughout his jurisdiction.

All combined their forces for the general external defense. The kings were merely chieftains—*primus inter pares*,[94] the one that had the greatest capacity for command. As the excellent author of a new history of Scotland, Mr. Robertson, has very well put it, a feudal government was properly speaking the camp of a large army.[95] Military talent and subordination held sway. Possession of the soil was the payment for each soldier, and personal service was the remuneration he gave in return. The barons possessed a quantity of some land or other, on condition of leading and maintaining a certain quantity of men in war. By the hands of the king-general, they took on these mutual obligations with an oath. On the same conditions,

93. *Optimo jure* refers to the full or perfect protection of legal right, not only private but public as well. See also p. 629, n. 10, above.

94. "First among equals."

95. William Robertson (1721–93), leading Moderate divine, principal of Edinburgh University, and one of the premier historians of the late eighteenth century; the passage cited is in *History of Scotland: during the reigns of Queen Mary and King James VI* (London, 1759), 1:13. The work was translated into French in 1764.

they committed a part of these possessions to vassals less powerful than themselves—and there you have the origin of the service of fiefs.

The majority owed this service to the royal fiefs, which themselves conveyed it to the state. These royal fiefs were substantial; the leading personages always had the lion's share in the distribution of conquered lands. The yield from these lands sufficed for their support; they had nothing beyond that. Even Charlemagne had the yield from his fruit gardens sold for his personal expenses, and he put the surplus from his receipts in the public treasury. In that era, the voraciousness of the flatterers had not yet made a hash of fiscal claims. A very clear distinction was made between the needs and revenues of the prince, composed of his domains, and the needs and revenues of the state, composed of the assemblage of services from all the fiefs, of which his own formed a part.

In the work of history that I have just cited, one reads that in Scotland, the first tax on land was established only in 1555.[96] For a long time in France, only three kinds of claims were known aside from the service from the fiefs: the first was due when the vassal's eldest son was made knight; the second, at the marriage of his eldest daughter; and the third, when the king or lord suzerain was made a prisoner of war. The vassals were obliged to contribute to the payment of his ransom.

But these claims, as well as several other vassalage claims that were owed to kings, were marks of dependence rather than taxes. In very urgent situations, the people made extraordinary but instantaneous gifts, as rare as they were modest and always out of pure will, which led them to be called *gifts of benevolence*. Clovis's father, Childeric, was expelled for intending to raise taxes on his subjects. Childeric was killed by Badillus, a gentleman whom he had had flogged for representing to him that he had no right to do so. Badillus was never able to forgive that offense in the prince that he assassinated.[97] So true is it that men can bear death but not ignominy.

96. Robertson, *History of Scotland*, 1:130–31; it is perhaps worth noting that Robertson reports such resistance on the part of the Scottish nobility that Queen Mary felt obliged to deny any association with the provenance of the proposal.

97. Childeric II, Frankish chieftain and ultimately king of the Franks (673–75). Damilaville seems to confuse him with Childeric I (ca. 437–82), father of Clovis (ca. 466–511), founder of the Frankish monarchy. His assassin's name is sometimes spelled Badillo or Bodilo.

Philip Augustus nearly provoked the people when he attempted to impose a tax. Under Philip the Fair, the main cities of the realm revolted for the same reason. It is said that Louis IX recommended to his son that he never exact anything from his subjects without their consent. The assembly of notables under Louis the Headstrong decreed that sovereigns could levy no extraordinary revenues without the approbation of the three estates and that they would swear an oath to this effect at their coronation ceremony.[98]

It was only in the calamitous confusion of a foreign invasion under Charles VI that the taille was introduced.[99] The wars Charles VII had to wage in order to reconquer the realm gave him the means to perpetuate that tax—whose long-lasting effects made it even more pernicious than the invasion that had prompted it.[100] Sully's memoirs show us the successive progression of this tax. What is worse is that it still exists—with all the arbitrariness that makes it destructive; with the same diversity of principles in its distribution; with all the vices inseparable from an imposition done on the fly, in a time of trouble, and in the midst of the disasters that were afflicting France; and for which assistance was urgent but momentary.

The edicts published in Europe are not like the ones issued by the Asian sovereigns. The goal of the latter is merely to remit tax payments,[101] the goal of the former to ordain them. They have left nothing free for men on earth; one might say men have no right to their dwelling or to what it produces. Men are sold the gifts that nature creates for them *gratis,* even what they obtain by virtue of work; it's the sweat that is levied. Everything is taxed—even their actions, even the space they occupy, even their existence. They have to pay for the right to enjoy it.

98. Philip II Augustus (r. 1180–1223), Philip IV the Fair (r. 1285–1314), Louis IX (1226–70), Louis X the Headstrong (r. 1314–16), the son of Philip the Fair. The need for the consent of the three estates, which was finally agreed to in 1788 when the king convoked the Estates General for the first time since 1614, was an idea gaining currency in the second half of the eighteenth century. It was the 1788 assembly that led to the outbreak of the French Revolution the next year. See also REPRESENTATIVES, in this volume.

99. For the introduction of the taille as the key source of the longer-term political corruption of the old regime, see Tocqueville's classic account in *The Old Regime and the Revolution in France,* trans. Alan Kahan, intro. François Furet and Françoise Mélonio, 2 vols. (Chicago: University of Chicago Press, 1998), 1:164.

100. Charles VI (r. 1380–1422), Charles VII (r. 1422–61).

101. Compare Montesquieu, *Laws,* 13.18.

Those who are best informed about this could not expect to understand and enumerate with precision such an astonishing mass of taxes that have been added to the taille and multiplied over all things in general and each one in particular—at first in its original state, then in all its possible modifications, and always by the same cause; with equally little concern that they be borne in proportion to individual capacities; seeking only the yield and thinking that they have foreseen everything and done everything as long as the people are forced to pay.

More harm arises from this endless number of taxes and from the state of disorder in which their levy occurs than from the tax burden itself—however enormous that is. Thus, a method of collecting them that rooted out this disastrous diversity would by this fact alone be a great good, even if it produced no others. But it would also have this advantage: it would free the people from the vexations of which that diversity is the source; it would guarantee their freedom and the freedom of trade against these constant encroachments on them; it would at least relieve them of everything they are obliged to bear beyond what the government exacts for the expenses of a multitude of tax administrators and collectors, for the benefit of the tax farmer (for those taxes that are farmed out); and finally, it would free them from the persecutions to which they are constantly exposed in the prevention of fraud.

It must be agreed that the science of levying taxes—which should never have been created—has become more vast and complicated than people think. On this subject, it is easy to offer reveries instead of solid systems, and that is what we have seen in countless writings published on this topic recently.[102]

If all I had to propose were those vague speculations formed from uncertain ideas and drawn from common and superficial notions, I would keep quiet. I am not unaware of all the evils that may arise from the adoption of a faulty plan. Humanity will never have the occasion to criticize

102. Probably a reference to the polemic unleashed by the anonymous publication in 1763 of *Richesse de l'état* [The state's wealth] by the parlementary official Roussel de la Tour. On this polemic, see James C. Riley, *The Seven Years' War and the Old Regime in France* (Princeton: Princeton University Press, 1986), 194–207; Riley notes (206) a near consensus among the participants that taxes should be paid in money and on the basis of a flat tax rate.

me for intending to cause these evils. But I have been working at it, I have collected facts, I have meditated over them, and I will say nothing that is not the result of a serious calculation. I believe I am in a position to respond to all the reasonable observations that one might put to me, and to resolve them; it is up to those more skilful than I to judge whether I am mistaken.

All taxes, whatever their nature and from whatever perspective they may be viewed, are divided into three categories: taxes on land, on persons, and on merchandise or consumption commodities.[103]

Taxes on land I called *imposts,*[104] because to furnish the state a portion of landed produce for common protection is a condition imposed[105] on its possession.

Personal taxes I name *contributions,* because they are without exchange—that is, the citizen receives nothing in return for what he pays in these taxes; and also because, since they have no principle except the will of those who decree them, they are analogous to what a general exacts from the inhabitants of an enemy country that he has entered, and that he forces to contribute.

Finally, I call *rights*[106] the taxes on merchandise and consumption commodities, because it seems in fact that it is the right to sell them and to make use of them for which people are being made to pay the public.

Here is what the most enlightened of those who have written on this matter have thought:

In his republic, Plato decrees that when it is necessary to impose taxes, they should be levied on consumption. Grotius, Hobbes, and Pufendorf think you can use all three kinds. Montesquieu does not reject this, but he observes that the form of taxation natural to moderate governments is the tax on merchandise: "This tax," he says, "actually paid by the buyers although the merchant advances it, is a loan the merchant has already made

103. See Montesquieu, *Laws,* 13.7.

104. *Impôts,* a term for "tax" usually used more broadly than Damilaville is doing here.

105. *Imposée,* hence, the etymological link with *impôt.*

106. *Droits,* a term that we have above translated as either "duties" or "taxes and fees" or "fiscal claims," depending on the context. Despite Damilaville's rationale here, below we will usually translate the term as "duties" or as "excise taxes" whenever it specifically refers to duties on merchandise, rather than invite confusion by opting for the word "rights," as the author demands here.

to the buyer. Thus, the trader must be regarded as both the state's debtor and as the creditor of all individuals, &c."[107]

Elsewhere I will take up the propositions contained in this reasoning.

The author of the *article* ECONOMIE OU ŒCONOMIE[108] in this dictionary is of the same opinion concerning the nature of this tax [*impôt*]. But he does not want it to be paid by the merchant, claiming it ought to be paid by the buyer. I confess that I see in this distinction only chains added to the citizens' liberty, and one more contradiction in the man who calls himself its greatest defender. Nero decreed nothing but the reverse of what M. Rousseau proposes, and Tacitus says he seemed to have abolished the tax. This was the four percent tax, levied on the price of the sale of slaves—so true is it that form counts for something, and that the citizen of Geneva's proposed form is not the best.[109]

I know what I owe to the enlightenment of the celebrated men whose opinions I have just reported. If mine is different, I am only more aware of the difficulty of my subject, but I am not discouraged by this.

Taxes—whatever they are, and wherever and however they are collected—can be levied only on wealth, and wealth has only one source. In states where the soil is fertile, it is the land; in states where the soil produces nothing, it is commerce.

The tax on merchandise is therefore the one that suits the latter states, for there is nothing else on which to base it.

The tax on land is the most natural one and the only one that suits the former states, since in these, it is land that produces all the wealth.

Now here I am already in contradiction with Montesquieu, but not as much as one thinks. You may set up as many taxes[110] as you want and on

107. Montesquieu, *Laws,* 13.14. The other references may be to Plato, *Republic,* bk. 1, 343d, or *Laws,* bk. 12, 955d–e; Hobbes, *De Cive* (*On the Citizen*), chap. 13, sect. 10–11, and *Leviathan,* chap. 30 (though he seems to argue for a consumption tax); Grotius, *Rights of War and Peace,* I.ii.7, or II.ii.14; Pufendorf, *Of the Law of Nature and Nations,* VIII.v.4–6.

108. Rousseau's discussion of taxes can be found in *Encyclopédie,* 5:346–49; today the work is more commonly known as *Discourse on Political Economy.*

109. The criticism here is of Rousseau, ECONOMIE OU ŒCONOMIE, 5:348–49; the reference is to Tacitus, who recounts the abolition of the *quadragesima* in *Annals,* XIII.31. Montesquieu, *Laws,* 13.7, cites this abolition.

110. *Droits;* see note 106, above.

anything you want: they will always be connected to these two original sources of all proceeds. All you will have done is multiply receipts, costs, and difficulties.

I am not speaking of despotic states; taxes by head are suitable for tyranny and for slaves.[111] Since slaves can be sold, they can certainly be taxed; this is also what is done in Turkey. Thus, whoever thought he had found the state's wealth in a single capital tax was proposing the taxes of servitude for his nation.

Thus, it is a single territorial tax that I propose for agricultural states,[112] and a single one on merchandise at the point of entry and exit for those that are only commercial states. I will speak only of the former, because everything I will say can be applied to the latter by substituting a single tax on merchandise in place of the one on the soil.

These ideas are so far from the common ideas that those who judge things without deeply examining them will not fail to regard them as paradoxes. To make the land bear all public expenses! All people talk about is the need to relieve landowners and cultivators of them. No one is more convinced than I am of this necessity; but what's chimerical is to think you are relieving them by taxes and surcharges on other items.

Everything is connected in civil society as it is in nature, and my ideas are also connected, but I must be given the time to develop them.

Because one of the parts constituting the body politic is extremely distant from another, it is thought that no relationship exists between them; I would be as ready to say that a line in geometry can exist without intermediate points that correspond to those that terminate it.

People do not think it is burdening the land to tax state rentiers. Nonetheless, I assume only two types of citizens: the ones possessing and cultivating land, and the others having no other property but state funds [*rentes*]. I further assume all public charges assigned to the latter. I assert that in that case, it

111. This statement echoes Montesquieu, *Laws*, 13.14.

112. The uniform territorial tax had been proposed on and off in France for at least a few generations. It had recently been revived by the Physiocrats; see Quesnay's article CEREALS, in this volume. See also Anne-Robert-Jacques Turgot (1727–81), "Memorandum on Local Government" (1775), an abridged version of which can be found in Keith Michael Baker, ed., *The Old Regime and the French Revolution*, Chicago Readings on Western Civilization 7 (Chicago: University of Chicago Press, 1987), 97–118.

is only the landed proprietors who would bear them, even though they seem to be exempt from them; no great effort of logic is needed to conceive of this.

Land has value only through the consumption of its produce. Setting aside the substance of the cultivators, the value of the surplus would be nil if the rentiers did not consume it. As it happens, the more the state takes out of the latters' income, the less they will consume. The less they consume, the less the land will produce. Thus, those who possess the land will bear the tax in full, for their income will be less by the full amount that the tax will have cut from the consumers' income.

In the present situation of things imposed upon public rentiers, it is not their frugality that is drawn upon. The excesses of luxury long ago banished this from all the status groups of society; matching expenses with receipts makes one quite prudent. Thus, the tax will fall only on their consumption. And it is bad reasoning to say that these rentiers will not be the less for it. The cause cannot be diminished without the effect being less. Either they will reduce their consumption to satisfy their tax obligations, producing a reduction in landed income; or else they will continue their consumption but on credit, in which case it will be a negative consumption, even more detrimental than the real reduction. He who has none of his income left will only continue to spend as much by not paying the retailer who supplies him. The latter will not pay the merchant who sells to him and so on back to the first buyer of commodities who, not being paid, will not pay the cultivator from whom he buys them, and for whom that portion of the fruits of the earth is lost even though it is consumed.

Taxes by head are neither more distant nor more alien than the ones here at this common source where all of them must meet. They cause the same reaction and the same effects, which is enough for us to conclude that taxes always fall on land, by whatever means the return may be effected. But since this truth is fundamental, I will seek to prove it again in a stronger fashion. First, it will not be useless at this point to refute a sophism by which people have been accustomed to minimize the harm that results from excessive taxes. This is the place to do it, because one might otherwise use it against me, thus abusing my principles.

"Government," one might say, "does not hoard. Everything it levies on the people it spends, and this spending produces either its own consumption or that of the people who profit from it. Taxes therefore do not diminish general consumption. Consumption merely shifts position to some extent, just like the nominal wealth or signs of value that merely change hands. Since the general consumption remains the same, it follows that the produce of the land that is its subject does not diminish. Thus, taxes do no harm here; thus, land does not support taxes."

Here, I believe, you have the argument in all its force. This is what ought to result from it if it is accurate:

However excessive the taxes of whatever kind may be that are exacted by government, society in general will not be the less rich for it, the land less cultivated, or commerce less flourishing. They will produce only local and private harm; whatever they take away from those who pay beyond their capacity will be passed on to others. The state will lose nothing, yet the sum of all fortunes will nonetheless be the same.

This line of reasoning is insidious; it has been perhaps only too often adopted as a way of seducing those who were not distressed at being abused in this way. But aside from the fact that these variations in fortune among private individuals are already a very great evil which always causes a greater depravity of mores—and a revolution in each family—of which the state as a whole never fails to feel the effects, this is not at all the way the state will get a surplus. The facts prove it, and their testimony is stronger than all the reasoning in the world.

Never have such exorbitant sums been levied on the people; a murderous ingenuity has exhausted all means of fleecing them. Never, therefore, have governments been obliged to engage in—and in fact have engaged in—so much expense and consumption. And yet, the countryside is sterile and deserted, commerce languishing, subjects and states[113] ruined.

Let those who have betrayed truth, justice, and humanity by insinuating or claiming that inordinate taxes would have the opposite effect state the explanation for this. Their interest, which is not that of others, and their indifference toward the public calamities in which they find their good, have not instructed them about this explanation. I will state it for them.

113. *Etats,* so "status groups" could also be the intention.

(1) It is not true that consumption by government, or by those who profit from the depredations committed in its revenue-collection and expenses, takes the place of the consumption that unbearable taxes force individuals to cut from their own. Large general consumption[114] results only from the multiplicity of small ones. The surplus of a few—however sumptuous we may suppose it to be—never replaces what it absorbs from the necessity of all, which it ruins. Two hundred individuals with 400 thousand pounds each in funds, and 100 domestics that they don't have, do not consume as much as 80 thousand persons whose income is divided along the lines of 1000 pounds each among them. In a word, give one person the income of 100 citizens, and he can consume only for himself and a few others that he employs in his service. The number of consumers and the quantity of consumption will always be at least four-fifths less. Whence it is seen (to state it in passing) that all other things being equal and the sum total of wealth being the same, the country in which this wealth is most divided will be the richest and most populous. This shows the advantages conferred by equality of fortunes on the ancient governments over the modern.

Let no one cite against me the dissipation of the rich, which absorbs not only their income and capital, but even the salaries of the poor, from whom vanity still exacts work even when it is no longer in a position to pay for it.

The luxury that produces this dissipation—that raises fortunes, overturns them, and ends up devouring them—does not encourage the consumption I am speaking of, which is consumption of necessary things produced by the state. On the contrary, such luxury restrains that consumption in proportion to its profusion of other things.

Things must be this way, because there has never been a time when men have found such abundant use for everything that is useful or agreeable to them, and yet never has national produce been less cultivated. Whence one may infer that the more people spend in a state, the less use they make of their harvested foodstuffs.

Two great disadvantages result: first, public charges, being the same and often higher, are distributed over fewer products; second, those who

114. In modern terms, "aggregate demand" is close to what Damilaville means.

contribute the most to them have less capacity to afford them, whence it follows that they are overwhelmed by them.

(2) The more the government spends, the less restitution[115] it gives the people. This proposition is in part a consequence of the preceding one, whatever assumptions may be made by people with an interest in persuading us of the contrary. One will always calculate accurately by taking as a value of one of these terms the inverse ratio of the other.

The dissipation of public revenues arises from the wars waged abroad, the alliances paid for, the inordinate rewards agreed to (which are always more excessive in proportion to being less merited)—in short, from the disorder and corrupt practices of all kinds in the administration of these revenues.

No consumption of the country's foodstuffs results from all this; thus, there is no return to the state of the sums that have been levied from it.

The sums that war and treaties cause to exit do not return. Luxury is either the cause or the effect of the wasting away of the other sums, which also do not return.

It's the cause, on account of all the expenses that are personal or relative to the sovereign and to the splendor that surrounds him; it's the effect, because the prodigality of his gifts and the pillage of the finances generate it or increase it enormously in those who profit from them.

Now for every country in the world, luxury is but the use of foreign materials. Its consumption is thus not to the benefit of the state but to its ruin; this causes the constant extraction of the state's monetary wealth, without replacement. This shows that, far from having the advantage attributed to it of correcting by circulation the disadvantages of the extreme disproportion in fortunes which is said to be inevitable in modern governments and especially in monarchies, it actually impoverishes the commonwealth and diminishes the means of subsistence for the poor, in the same proportion as it does the wealth of the opulent.

115. *Restitue,* a verb the *Dictionnaire de l'Académie Française* (1694) defines as "to return what was taken or possessed unduly or unjustly." We will flag this verb throughout the remainder of the essay, since it carries a more normative inflection than other possible verb choices the author might have made.

I know very well that if those who possess everything spend only on necessities, those who possess nothing will not get the necessities; but what I know even better is that the latter are in fact lacking these necessities.

Once again, it is not that the rich do not spend—even, as I have said, far beyond their means, although these are immense—but that neither the poor nor the state gain anything by it. It is the foreigner who benefits from all this expense. In calculating his own expense, each person can easily recognize that the consumption of national materials makes up the smallest part of it. The taste for other materials is so extravagant that for real needs and even things of the most ordinary usage, foreign materials are employed to the exclusion of domestic ones, which are not used any more even though they are perhaps more useful and convenient—so pleased have men been to increase their poverty through this imaginary need for everything they do not have.

I am saying nothing vague. Everything that surrounds us attests to it. Who is not dressed and furnished with silk, where silk does not grow? Only whoever is dressed differently seems extraordinary; that is, the perversion is so general that it is now only whoever is honorable, modest, and useful to society who is remarkable, just as Cato's integrity was remarkable in Rome.[116]

How many people are there whose finery alone would suffice to assure the subsistence of an entire family, and on whom it would be hard to find a single thing produced by the native soil? One wouldn't find perhaps half of these native goods on even the least lavish person.

In considering the nature and price of everything that composes this finery, I have often been astonished at what it costs the state to decorate a smug narcissist who overburdens it in turn with his uselessness. There is indeed enough to be astonished at, but it doesn't occur to us to observe it. Do we have eyes to see and heads to think? For that matter, the universality of the evil prevents it from being perceived.

Again, if this unbridled taste for display and this taste for foreign things existed as strongly in all nations, then by ruining themselves equally in order to procure them, their relative wealth would remain the same and

116. Cato the Younger.

their political power would not change, relatively speaking. But the folly of some is one more means for others to increase their fortune and strength, so that the formers' loss is doubled. The prosperity of the English proves it. Enlightened on their true interests by the freedom to think and write, they have not cut the wings off the talent that has been instructing them. Instead of threats against those who could give them useful lessons, they have invited these to become involved in public affairs. Whoever knows the good is afraid of neither the examination nor the censure of those whose task is to judge it. For Drusus's benefit, workers offered to prevent his neighbors from seeing what was going on in his house if he would give them three thousand gold crowns. "I will give you six," he responded, "if you make it so they can see in from all sides."[117]

Fitness of mind[118] gives the English the superiority they have acquired in all areas, but especially in their wisdom in engaging in the commerce of luxury only for their neighbors, whose needs they constantly seek to increase while striving to diminish their own.[119] They are economizers in materials and prodigal in the money they procure. Their luxury consists in dispersing over the poor the immense profits they make. More useful to humanity and less dangerous to the state, this luxury will never impoverish them—consuming not at all (or very little, and only for their greater convenience) the merchandise whose traffic composes their wealth. They preserve its source while using up only its product. Others, on the contrary, exhaust this merchandise and deny themselves the means of renewing it. Our entire trade consists in facilitating the entry of foreign merchandise and the exit of our money.[120]

"But," it will be said, "the fabrication of these materials within the country employs a large number of workers whom it provides the means of consuming its foodstuffs." This is again a frivolous objection.

117. The reference is probably to Marcus Livius Drusus, famous for his austerity. He was killed in 91 B.C. after protracted attempts to enfranchise the Italian landowners. See *Velleius Paterculus*, II:xiii–xiv; the story is also told in "Of Repentance," Montaigne's *Essays*, 613–14.

118. *Bon esprit;* see Littré for the idiom.

119. For the terms "commerce of luxury" and "commerce of economy," see Montesquieu, *Laws*, 20.4ff., and for the English, 19.27. See also pp. 519, n. 52, and 380, n. 1, above.

120. *Argent*, also "silver."

(1) Most of them reach here fully made; independent of raw materials and edible items, don't the most precious and expensive trinkets come entirely finished from China, Japan, the Indies, *etc.?*

The luxury that corrupts everything touching it consumes the benefits it procures. The worker who employs the materials used in this luxury soon uses them for himself. His expense exceeds the proportion of the profit. Without improving his condition, therefore, he worsens that of the state by increasing the consumption of foreign merchandise and the extraction of legal tender.

(2) But even if this work were profitable to some individuals, far from enriching the state, such profit gained by citizens from other citizens would work to its detriment. Without bringing the state any benefit, this would always cost it the value of the materials, not counting the value of the national foodstuffs that would have been employed instead—and in addition, the profit from the circulation of those assets that would have resulted from such use. President Montesquieu partly attributes the first devaluations effected in Rome to a similar error over this supposed benefit.[121]

Such are the true effects of luxury as concerns the consumption, the industry, and the internal work that it produces. Let us again stop for a moment to consider the effects of its external commerce, and we will see that it is no more advantageous. The importance of this topic carries me along and I cannot leave it.

By this trade, I mean the re-export of foreign materials after they have been manufactured. Only the worker's labor is furnished from the harvest. However expensive one may suppose it to be, it is difficult to believe that it is expensive enough to make amends [*restituer*] for the cost of one's own lavishing of these materials. One would have to say that the price of artisanal labor would be so disproportionate to the principal asset that the sale of a very small quantity would suffice to pay for the sale of everything, and this cannot be the case.

Moreover, it is a principle founded on experience that no commerce is advantageous if it is not an exchange. Republics engage in the commerce of economy only because they occupy sterile terrain that forces them to do so.

121. The reference is to Montesquieu, *Laws,* 22.11–13.

It is much more for this reason that such commerce is natural to them than because of a governmental constitution that seems favorable to it.[122]

Liberty is never where abundance is found; they are incompatible.[123] Tyre, Sidon, Rhodes, Carthage, Marseilles, Florence, Venice, Holland were and are barren soils that produce nothing. It is indeed necessary to traffic in others' foodstuffs when you possess none yourself, if only to procure those necessary ones that the terrain refuses. But this position is perilous, holding the nations that find themselves in it in a constant equilibrium and perpetually inclining them toward destruction.

In fact, a state whose subsistence depends entirely on the will of others can have only an uncertain and precarious existence. People will refuse to sell it their foodstuffs; they will not want to buy these back; conventional wealth[124] will dry up. Such a state will be prey to ambition or need; without anyone taking the trouble of subjugating it, extreme poverty will force the people to accept or take on a master in order to have bread. The Lacedemonians would have subjugated the inhabitants of Smyrna if, in abstaining from eating one day, they had not preferred the glory of giving them succour while they were in dire straits to the glory of profiting from their situation by becoming their sovereign.

Holland has seen this extremity up close. Without closing off the ports of Spain and Portugal to them, which reduced their inhabitants to despair and forced them to go to the Indies to acquire establishments whose possession procured them the exclusive sale of the spices by which they replace the other products of the earth they lack, perhaps Holland would already have ceased to be an independent republic.[125]

But an even more imminent danger threatens republics that are obliged to engage in this commerce of economy, namely, the luxury that it brings

122. For the constitutional argument that Damilaville is downplaying here, see Montesquieu, *Laws,* 20.4.

123. Cf. Montesquieu, *Laws,* 18.1.

124. Gold and silver money, as opposed to "real wealth," meaning agriculture and industry. For this distinction, see especially Forbonnais's *Encyclopédie* articles COMMERCE, 3:691, 695, 698, CULTURE DES TERRES [Cultivation of the Earth], 3:552, and ESPECES [Specie], 4:959, 961, which is an excerpt from his 1754 work *Elemens du commerce* [Elements of commerce].

125. The reference is probably to Don Felipe I's policy in 1590 of closing Portuguese ports to Dutch (and English) vessels.

in. Lycurgus found no other means of protecting his own republic from this danger than by instituting a currency that could not circulate among other peoples. An English philosopher, Mr. Hume, regrets that Lycurgus did not know the use of paper.[126] He does not consider that paper represents a debt and is only the obligation to pay off this debt. For this reason, such paper might have become a commercial asset receivable by foreigners, to whom it would have given rights over the very territory of the republic. On the other hand, once the pieces of metal invented by that legislator were accepted, there were no other claims to make against Lacedemon. Luxury was thereby all the more certainly prohibited, and the absolute lack of exchange made the commerce of luxury impractical.

Perhaps Switzerland, whose government seems destined to be the most durable, will owe its preservation to the same impossibility, albeit from a different cause. Its situation renders it inaccessible to others' merchandise trade. Its natural production is men. It traffics in them with all the powers of Europe, and never runs out of them. Nature grants men abundantly to the liberty and equality that cultivate them.

Finally, it is a truth repeated by Montesquieu, following Florus whom he quotes: republics come to an end because of luxury, monarchies because of poverty.[127]

Thus, to abandon the exchange of one's natural products in order to devote oneself to the commerce from which these dangers are inseparable is to accelerate these effects and to place oneself voluntarily in the constricted situation to which necessity reduces others. The nations in which this commerce has prevailed resemble wholesalers who, with inexhaustible stores of every kind of merchandise as well as a secure market, have abandoned them to go sell their neighbors' merchandise and become their agents and day laborers. This is to reason quite badly, even in politics and especially within governments that are supposedly absolute. For take away their property, and nothing will now stop men whose liberty is attacked.

To be sure, it may well be the case that with these principles, one has everything of a rare, perfect, and agreeable nature that the arts of vanity

126. Hume, "Of the Balance of Trade," in *Essays, Moral, Political, and Literary,* ed. Eugene F. Miller, rev. ed. (Indianapolis: Liberty Fund, 1987), 318.

127. Montesquieu, *Laws,* 7.4.

can produce. But one no longer has provinces; one has only deserts. One sacrifices reality for illusion and brings on a state all the evils that it can withstand.

The countryside remains barren because the value of what can be obtained from it—beyond what is necessary for internal consumption, already much reduced by luxury consumption—would be nil.

It is abandoned because people can no longer procure their subsistence by work, and because rich manufactures elsewhere invite them to leave it by offering less arduous and more lucrative work.

The needs of the state increase and its wealth decreases. A people of landowners is reduced to a mercenary condition; poverty disperses them and destroys them. A frightful depopulation and the ruin of the body politic are the results.

You can extol Colbert's ministry all you want, but this is what he produced and what he was bound to produce. No doubt he was brilliant and worthy of the greatest praise, but you have to be quite bedazzled not to see that his regulations on commerce, of which agriculture was not the basis, are regulations of destruction.[128] Perhaps with the aim of flattering a luxurious nation, a nation seduced by false glitter, he preferred the glory of being a model of futility for all peoples and of surpassing them in all the arts of ostentation to the more solid and always more certain advantage of supplying their natural needs, which do not depend on the whims of fashion or the fantasies of taste but which are the same at all times for all men.

France possesses subsistence foodstuffs and is in the most fortunate situation for distributing them. All nations could have been dependent on her, but Colbert made her dependent on them all. He lavished riches and rewards to build and maintain sumptuous workshops and manufactures. He did not have raw materials; he spurred their import with all his might and prohibited the export of domestic materials. This was to fashion a treaty entirely to foreigners' advantage; it was to say to them, "I impose upon myself the obligation of consuming your commodities and of never being able to have you consume mine." This was to annihilate France's own

128. Jean-Baptiste Colbert (1619–83), Louis XIV's leading official and author of many French "mercantilist" policies, including a preference for luxury manufacturing exports.

natural wealth, the agriculture and population of her provinces, in order to multiply in the same proportion all these things to foreigners' benefit.

It is clear that if a conqueror had dictated these conditions, they would not have been harsher to the one accepting them.

One sees the possible consequences of such a system in the example of Sardinia, so rich and flourishing when Aristaeus gave it laws.[129] On pain of death, the Carthaginians prohibited the inhabitants of that island from cultivating their land. It has never been repopulated since. It is known that the English dominate in Portugal from a similar administrative viewpoint, and that this realm seems attractive to the English only for the treasures of the new world.

The fruits of this policy in France do just as much to show how disastrous it can be. During Colbert's entire ministry, the price of grains did not stop falling until, no longer sufficient to pay for the costs of their cultivation, people ended up suffering scarcity.[130]

He did all he could to correct this problem, but he did not do what he should have done; he persisted in his principles. Reductions in the taille and encouragements granted to population and agriculture corrected nothing. What would the landowners have done with any foodstuffs they might have harvested? These foodstuffs were without an outlet, and consequently without value. To engage the owners in their cultivation was to commit them to become poorer by the entire expense of the cultivation.

One mistake of this kind does not remain isolated; all branches of administration are bound to feel its effects. I would abstain from retracing the sequence of miseries that followed this one if I did not believe it is useful to know them in order to avoid them—and if, moreover, they had less connection to the topic I am treating.

With the natural wealth destroyed,[131] the subjects found themselves in no condition to endure the necessary taxes. The government was obliged to resort to the creation of bonds and offices, to the multiplicity of excise taxes

129. Aristotle, "On Marvellous Things Heard," 838b; cited in Montesquieu, *Laws*, 18.3.

130. Encouraging high grain prices was a staple of Physiocratic doctrine. Laverdy's edict of 1764 freeing the internal grain trade was largely a result of their advocacy. See the article CEREALS by Quesnay, in this volume.

131. See the discussion of "conventional wealth" above, p. 680.

(which reduce consumption proportionally), to loans, to tax farmers, and to all those destructive expedients that devastate the people and ruin empires.

Colbert himself consumed the revenues through anticipation.[132] The progress of the evil whose beginnings he witnessed accelerated at such a pace that in 1715, a mere thirty-two years after his death, we find the principal revenues of the state committed in perpetuity—the excess spent in advance over many years, all circulation destroyed, the country houses dilapidated, the livestock dead, the land fallow, and the realm inundated with all sorts of exactors who, through the most bizarre claims, had acquired the right to oppress the people under every possible pretext.

As I have already stated, it is with regret that I retrace this portrait. I do not deny this minister the tribute of gratitude that the arts and letters owe him, but even less can I deny the tribute one owes to truth, when the public good depends on its testimony.

Without the traffic for its wines and some coarse manufactures that Colbert despised, who knows how deplorable a situation France might have found herself in?

What proves that his commercial establishments were ruinous is that after his death, as soon as men broke off expenditures for their support, most crumbled and could not survive.

Sully, who saw his master's glory only in the happiness of the people and who knew that his master[133] found it only there, much better understood the source of this happiness and of French wealth in believing that it was in the extent and fertility of her soil. He said land produces all treasures, both necessary and superfluous. It is only a matter of multiplying its production, and for this, all that is needed is to make its commerce sure and free. "Your people, and consequently your Majesty, would soon be without money if each official acted this way," he wrote to Henry, speaking of a stupid magistrate who had prohibited the transport of wheat.[134]

132. The *Dictionnaire de l'Académie Française* (1762) and Littré indicate that *anticipation* may connote a usurpation upon someone's property, an inflection that Damilaville may intend here; the 1798 *Dictionnaire* adds that secret loans mortgaged on part of the public revenue were also sometimes involved.

133. King Henry IV (r. 1589–1610).

134. The passage appears in Sully's *Mémoires* in a letter by Sully to the king, dated April 27, 1607; Damilaville has rearranged the sentence structure. The Physiocrat Quesnay

It is known that with the help of these maxims, his frugality, and especially his moderating of taxes, he rescued the realm from the state of desolation to which cruel and bloody wars had reduced it. It is curious to read in Bolingbroke the prodigies of public good effected by this minister—still greater because of his integrity than his enlightenment—in the short space of the fifteen years that his administration lasted.[135] It seems that since then, men have been afraid to share his glory by imitating it.

A great love of the public good is a prodigious step toward governing well. This sentiment dominated Sully. Perhaps he did not grasp the full scope of his views. But he had accurate ones on commerce, for he understood that it only truly produces wealth to the extent that people possess its materials. In going further, he might have recognized that the more necessary these materials are, the more secure and profitable the commerce will be.

I again find an example of this in the English. While Spain, Portugal, and Holland were invading all the mines of the Indies and America, the English became more powerful than all of them solely by their wool manufacturing. And this trade raised their navy to such a superior level that it ruined all the forces of Spain and made them the arbiters of Europe.[136]

Every other traffic is disadvantageous, even with one's colonies. Whatever wealth may be drawn from them, they will impoverish the home country if she is not in a position to send them commodities from her harvest in exchange. It is even worse if she lacks subsistence commodities for herself. For then, it is only for nations that possess the latter that she will have brought in these treasures. Look at what this wealth has produced in Spain. No power possesses colonies so rich; no power is so poor.

---

noted this passage in Sully with approval; see *Encyclopédie,* 7:820, a section of the article CEREALS not reproduced in this volume.

135. Henry St. John, Viscount Bolingbroke (1678–1751), leading Tory man of politics and letters, author of *The Idea of a Patriot King* (1738), among other works. For his praise of Sully, see "Some Reflections on the Present State of the Nation, Principally with Regard to her Taxes and her Debts," in *The Works of the Right Honourable Henry St. John, Lord Viscount Bolingbroke* (London: Johnson, 1809), 4:369–72. The work seems to have been published for the first time posthumously in 1753. A French translation was published separately in 1754 and sometimes bound with the Le Blanc translation of Hume's *Political Essays.*

136. The reference may be to the defeat of the Spanish Armada in 1588.

All this leads to a reflection: every nation that can have an abundant surplus of materials of prime necessity should only engage in trade and procure the foreign merchandise that she lacks by exchanging what exceeds her needs. The entry of that merchandise into the country should be permitted only on condition of exporting what the country produces at a similar value.

There, perhaps, you have the true measure of luxury and the only laws to be made against its excesses. This idea would be worth the trouble of developing at greater length than I can do here. I will only say that then, with the consumption of surplus becoming the measure of the progress of luxury, the greatest possible level of luxury would be the greatest possible quantity of this surplus and the universal cultivation of the whole surface of the state. This luxury would thereby contribute to multiplying instead of destroying natural wealth, which is the only real wealth.

I say *natural wealth* because the conventional type, being limited to returns in kind, would add nothing to one's wealth. You would only be exchanging commodity for commodity; not even one more gold crown for the state would ensue, though there would also not be one less. But what would be acquired via *natural wealth* is of a quite different value. The earth would everywhere multiply its treasures and men, agriculture, and commerce would be finely balanced, offering men in all situations the means of subsistence and reproduction and always increasing together at the same pace, while leaving nothing barren, nothing uninhabited—in a word, creating the grandeur and prosperity of the state by means of the multitude and ease of the citizens, especially by means of the purity of mores resulting from the habitation of the countryside. For only there is wealth innocent and stable.

It would also follow that the power of empires would no longer be made by money but only by the number of men. That empire with the greatest space for cultivation would have the most men. If after working them up, this empire also happened to re-export a portion of the foreign materials it had received or sent a greater quantity of its own, it would find itself even richer because of all the profit from this re-export or because of the whole value of the commodities it had transported beyond what others' commodities had been brought to it.

If one wanted to ignore these advantages (most of which I am merely summarizing) by claiming that in prescribing the nature of exchange, I am imposing on commerce an obstacle contrary to its progress and even conducive to its interruption, I would respond at the outset with two things.

First, I am proposing these exchanges only for superfluous merchandise that is of no real utility, that is not consumed through natural needs but is lavished by vanity and fancy—for that merchandise, in a word, which the state could forego without suffering any harm if it ceased to be brought in, and which has no value (despite its enormous price range) except the caprice of those who use it.

Second, the interest of those who possess this merchandise is not in keeping it. There would always be more advantage for them to truck this merchandise for subsistence commodities, whose sale is much more secure. Thus, far from being afraid of falling short, the import of these commodities could be so abundant that the surplus would not suffice and precautions would be needed so that the exchanges would never be substantial enough to exceed the surplus.

It is clear that these arrangements would not be entirely suitable to all nations. For many, they are feasible only in part, according to what they have and what they lack; for others, they are not at all feasible. The latter have very harsh laws against the use of luxury merchandise; it would be better to prevent the evil than to have to punish it. Laws get old and lapse into disuse. Commerce produces opulence, which introduces luxury, and the materials are employed despite the prohibitions.

I would think it more sound for these nations to prescribe a rigorous proportion between the import and export of these materials, and to allow entry only for those quantities equal to those that exit, so as to be certain that none of these materials remain in the country. In this regard, the body politic should be considered like a private merchant who buys only as much as he sells. If he consumes it himself, he is lost. And everything that is received and not re-exported is either consumed or will be.

I cannot stop people from regarding what I am going to say as a reverie. Only humanity will lose thereby. If justice, beneficence, and concord existed among men, then only those peoples whom strength and love of liberty have relegated to arid countries whose soil produces nothing should be left the task of distributing among nations the reciprocal surplus of those that have some of it. They would limit themselves to taking it up and selling it to others coming to seek it, and the goal of exchange would be to procure for everyone the necessities of which they are being deprived.

But a treaty in favor of the human race is not the first that will be made. The opinions dividing the earth have expelled general equity, replacing it with private interest. Men are much closer to slitting each other's throats over chimeras than to getting along with each other for the sharing of their wealth. Thus, I'm quite aware that I am proposing something the majority would find ridiculous.

It is time to return to my subject. I have perhaps too much digressed from it. But if these reflections on a matter as important as luxury and all it brings forth are useful, if they are once and for all able to determine its effects, then they will be neither out of place nor too extensive.

I promised to demonstrate, in a more general and definite manner than I have done thus far, that all taxes revert to the land, wherever they may be imposed. Even those taxes to which luxury merchandise is subject—despite its being foreign—would have this effect. And it would be a mistake to conclude the opposite from what I have just said.

The foreigner who brings in this merchandise will increase the price in proportion to the tax [*impôt*]. Thus, it is not the aforementioned foreigner who will incur the tax, but the citizen who consumes the merchandise and who will pay more for it by the total amount of the duty [*droit*].

Now, if I have proven that luxury expense is harmful to the consumption of the necessities that the soil produces, it is evident that the greater that expense is, the less one will consume of those products. What results is a proportional reduction in the cultivation of the land and therefore in its yield. Thus, these taxes will revert to cultivation. And so on for all the rest. Let's give some other examples.

When in their final stage of consumption, leather and all the merchandise of the leather trades, the tanners, the fur trades, and glove trades (which come from animal skins), seem to be least related to the soil. No one thinks there might be any relation between the soil and a pair of gloves. And yet, what does the price the consumer pays for them include? The price of all the produce of the land employed for the food and living expenses of all the workers who have worked on them in all the forms through which they have passed; all the taxes[137] these workers have borne personally, and even those levied on their subsistence, plus the duties collected on the skins at each of the modifications they have undergone.

It is said that in imposing a new tax on the last of these modifications, only the consumer really pays it. Not at all; it reverts to the produce of the land, directly or indirectly:

Directly by affecting the pasture on which the livestock that furnish this merchandise are raised—pasture that would become less productive if the tax, by reducing the consumption of skins in their final preparations, reduces the amount of feed that gives value to these stocks.

Indirectly, by affecting manual labor, which is nothing but the price of the commodities employed by the workers. And where do these commodities come from?

The same can be said of lace, and of all merchandise that demands the greatest preparation, in which the multitude of tailoring has caused, so to speak, the disappearance of the materials of which it is composed, leaving no trace of its origin.

It is thus true, and these examples prove it invincibly, that however roundabout their collection may appear, duties always go back to the source of all items of consumption, which is land. It is also true that taxes on land are charged to all citizens. But their distribution and collection are established in a simple and natural manner, whereas that of the other taxes is done with inconvenience, expense, confusion, and a welter of surprising redundancies.

For example, what an immense variety of taxes for the merchandise that I have just discussed!

(1) Those paid by the owner of the land used for feeding the livestock, as much for him personally as for these stocks.

(2) Those levied on the livestock herded into various places at various times.

(3) Duties on the skins, in the various forms these skins are taken.

(4) The personal taxes of all the laborers who have worked on the skins.

137. *Taxes,* a generic term similar to *impôt.*

(5) Those of the different manufacturers who have sold them, to the extent they have been worked up.

(6) Those borne by the final artisans, who bring them into use.

(7) The fee for the exclusive privilege of manufacturing them.

(8) All the duties that were collected on the commodities that all these persons have used for their subsistence and their upkeep, which are unlimited.

(9) And finally, a portion of those borne by the people who have furnished these commodities, which are not less.

This sequence is horrifying. It is inconceivable how such a complicated machine whose springs have proliferated so much can exist.

What chains for commerce in this multitude of collections! How often has a commodity been stopped, controlled, subjected to visitation,[138] appraised, and taxed before being consumed!

What false calculations, double counts, mistakes, errors, and abuses of every kind do the tax farmer's greed and his subordinates' unfaithfulness or ineptitude not make the citizens endure!

All must contribute to the public charges, that is true, but what is not true is that all must pay them. Whoever possesses nothing can pay nothing; it is always another who pays for him.

Taxes on the poor are duplicates of those on the rich. To understand this clearly, we must define the public charges more correctly than has hitherto been done. They are of two sorts: the work and the wealth it produces.

This definition is complete: without work, no wealth; without wealth, no taxes.

It follows that the manual laborer's contribution to the charges of society is work. Wealth's contribution is a portion of the wealth that results from this work, and wealth makes this contribution to the state in order to enjoy everything—minus this portion—peacefully.

138. *Visitée,* the reference is to domiciliary visits conducted by French authorities during this period, especially in enforcement of the state's monopoly on salt and tobacco; see George T. Matthews, *The Royal General Farms in Eighteenth-Century France* (New York: Columbia University Press, 1958), 110–12 and passim. For the more general policy against smuggling, see Michael Kwass, *Contraband: Louis Mandrin and the Making of a Global Underground* (Cambridge: Harvard University Press, 2014), chaps. 2–4.

It is thereby clear that taxes [*taxes*] on the manual laborer, assuming he has to pay them, would be an enormous injustice, for it would be a double counting on all the work he has already furnished the state.

But my servant's head-tax is levied on me; I must pay for him or else I must increase his wages.

The artisan, the worker, or the day laborer that I employ adds to the price of his effort or his industry everything exacted from him—and always even more than that. Each of these will be more expensive if his subsistence and his upkeep become more expensive due to the excise taxes imposed on the things useful to him.

This is because, in fact, there can only be three sorts of taxpayers: landowners, idle consumers, and foreign traders who pay the duties imposed on them along with the core price of your commodities. Then he will sell you his own commodities in proportion to what he has bought of yours. This remits to your charge the duties he will have paid. Strictly speaking, it is thus only the landowners and the unoccupied consumers who truly incur the taxes.

Everyone works for the latter, and they work for no one. They therefore pay for everyone's consumption, and no one pays for theirs. They have no means of recuperating what they have paid out for themselves and others, for these others provide them with nothing at a price capable of achieving this. The succession of reimbursements for all the duties imposed on merchandise and on the laborers who have fashioned it from its origin until its final consumption ends with them.

A proprietor is taxed for his person and his land; his tenant farmer is taxed the same way, and the commodities they consume are as well.

The farmer's valets are taxed for themselves, and for everything that serves to feed and clothe them.

The livestock, the materials, and the plowing tools are taxed.

All this is charged to the proprietor. The tenant farms his property only after deducting all these different duties that he has to bear. He bears these duties directly for those that are personal to him and indirectly by the increase he will have to pay for the cost of the workdays, the livestock, the materials, and the tools he needs. The proprietor receives from the produce of the land or from any property whatsoever only the excess over the farmer's expenses and profit, on which basis all these duties are rightly calculated. Thus, it is the proprietor who bears them and not those on whom they are levied. Were it otherwise, he would do more to farm his property.

Thus, the endless multiplication of taxes on all persons and all things has done nothing but uselessly multiply the tax farms, the collections, and all the instruments of the ruin, desolation, and slavery of the people.

What, then, has made the best minds think that the duties on consumption, from which this disastrous diversity infallibly arises, are the least onerous for the subjects and the most suitable to mild and moderate government?[139]

Wherever these duties exist, there is a constant civil war against them: a hundred thousand citizens, armed for the preservation of these duties and for the prevention of fraud on their account, constantly threaten the liberty, security, honor, and fortune of the rest.[140]

A nobleman living in the provinces has retreated to his home; he thinks he is at peace in the midst of his family. Thirty men, with bayonet at rifle's end, surround his house,[141] violate its asylum, scour it from top to bottom, and forcibly penetrate the most secret interior. The tearful children ask their father what crime he is guilty of; he has committed none. This attack on rights respected by the most barbarous nations is committed by these disturbers of the public peace to ensure that the home of this citizen holds no merchandise of a kind whose exclusive sale the tax farmer has reserved for himself—in order to resell it at a profit of seventeen or eighteen times its value.

This is not rhetoric, this is fact. If this is enjoying civil liberty, I would like someone to tell me what servitude is. If this is how persons and property have security, what does it mean not to have it?

It will be only a matter of luck if these police hunters,[142] who have an interest in finding guilty parties, do not themselves create some, bringing into your home what they came to look for. For then your ruin is assured,

139. The reference is probably primarily to Montesquieu, who wrote in *Laws*, 13.14, that "the tax natural to moderate government is the tax [*impôt*] on commodities."

140. Kwass calculates in *Contraband* (48) that three-quarters of tax farm officials were armed agents around the time Damilaville was writing.

141. *Investissent*, has a military inflection.

142. *Perquisiteur*, "perquisitor," rare term for someone carrying out a search, usually of a domicile.

and it is in their hands. Unique procedures, convictions, fines, and all the methods that the cruelest vexations can muster are authorized against you.

I would prefer to dissimulate the even greater and more shameful evils of which these taxes are the source. The enormous disparity between a thing's price and the duty on it renders fraud highly lucrative and invites men to engage in it. People who could not possibly be regarded as criminals lose their lives for attempting to preserve their lives. But the tax farmer, whose interest repulses all remorse, pursues from the comfort of his murderous opulence all the rigor of punishments inflicted by the law upon the wicked against those whom his own illegitimate gains have often reduced to the cruel necessity of exposing themselves to such punishments. I do not like it, said Cicero, that a people dominating the world should at the same time be its agent.[143] There is something more distressing than what displeased Cicero.

I know that not all duties on consumption expose citizens to such terrible dangers. But all are equally contrary to their liberty, their security, and all natural and civil rights, because of the surveillances, the inquisitions, and the searches—as oppressive as they are ridiculous—that they occasion. They even bring the misfortune of constricting the sentiments of humanity itself.

They make me very careful about assisting the good man whose cabin abuts my dwelling. He is poor and sick; a little wine would fortify his old age and call him back to life. It is an efficacious remedy for those who do not make a regular practice of it. I won't bring him any; I won't go and wrest him from death. He who has the strange right of micromanaging my needs and prescribing just how I ought to use what belongs to me would make me regret it, and my ruin would be the price of my act of commiseration. The good man perishes; I have not performed a deed that would have been so sweet to my heart; society loses a citizen who perhaps leaves others in its care—to whom he had given life and whom his death deprives of subsistence.

It is not the best administration where you have beneficence repressed as a crime and where nature is forcibly opposed to nature and humanity to humanity.

143. Cicero, *De Republica,* 4.7; see also Montesquieu, *Laws,* 20.4, for the same citation.

Nor will commerce flourish where that mass of duties exists. We do not give enough consideration to the harm commerce suffers and the harm this causes for the state, when, for the interests of the fisc, it is overwhelmed with all the hindrances caused by these diverse collections. It is time, nonetheless, to think about this. Commerce has become the measure of imperial power. The eagerness for gain produced by the excess of luxury expense has substituted the spirit of traffic, which enervates the soul and slackens courage, for the military spirit that has been lost along with frugality of mores.

People for whom reasoning is always an offense have accused philosophy of this change and have wanted to blame her for the disasters that have ensued. This proves that they have not had the good fortune of understanding philosophy or of appreciating the energy with which she inspires the taste for good, the love of one's duties, and the enthusiasm for things that are grand, just, honorable, and virtuous—especially the horror at injustice and calumny.

Whatever false imputations folly and wickedness may lavish on good people and on virtue, it is certain that commerce's ruin is the necessary result of taxes on merchandise: (1) by causes that are inherent in them; (2) by the means they furnish to the tax farmers' rapacity to engage in every vexation it can imagine. And when we realize what this rapacity is capable of, we shudder at that liberty which makes for the enslavement of commerce and the constant torment and perplexity of those who engage in it.

All these movements are spied upon and constricted. Formalities beyond number are so many dangers across which this commerce treads, if I may so express myself, into traps that are set for good faith constantly and on all sides. If one either ignores them or inadvertently neglects any of them, that's enough; one is ruined.

From the entry of foreign merchandise, from its departure out of the land—and even before, for those things produced by the soil—until its complete consumption, it is surrounded by guards and exactors who never leave it alone. At every step, there are customs, barriers, tolls, bureaux, declarations to make, visits to endure, measures, weights, unintelligible tariffs, arbitrary assessments, discussions to have, duties to bear, and vexations to suffer.

Whoever has seen the receipts for everything that one commodity has paid for, in all forms and in all the places it passed through, is well aware that I am saying nothing exaggerated or unattested by the wording of those documents.

Along with the multitude of these duties, one sees their confusion. The purest intention on the part of those who collect them does not guarantee them against uncertainty and injustice. What errors and misappropriations can they not be obliged to charge to their principals, but which always fall on the public's charge! What means of bringing order to so many duties which are themselves mostly indeterminable!

If the item's value is the criterion, then the principle is impractical. How to fix the price of a piece of merchandise? It varies constantly; the merchandise does not have the value today that it had yesterday. It depends on its abundance or its rarity (which depend on no one), on the will of those who use it, and on all the revolutions of nature and commerce, which cause commodities to be more or less common and outlets to be more or less favorable.

The tax [*impôt*] does not lend itself to any of these circumstances; it would be constantly changing and would only be a new source of difficulties.

If the criterion is quantity without regard to quality, it no longer has any relation with the real value of the commodities; all those of the same kind are taxed equally. It thus happens that the poor person who consumes only the lowest quality pays as much in duties for what is worse as the rich person pays for what is more excellent, which makes the condition of the former doubly unfortunate. Excluded by his poverty from the use of the better foods, he also bears part of the taxes on those foods lavished by the pride and sensuality of the others. Given equal quantities, the idle opulent person does not furnish the state with more by indulging his taste in an exquisite wine than the indigent manual laborer does by consuming the most common wine to restore his forces after they have been depleted by work.

There is not only injustice here, but cruelty as well. For this situation weighs down the most precious portion of the citizenry; it makes them feel with only too much inhumanity their excessive humiliation and the horror of their destiny, which might be that of anyone else.

It would take too long to go through all the vices essential to the nature of these taxes. We already have more than enough to prove that their effects are not those attributed to them. Let us move on to the gravest detriments that arise from the necessity of farming them.

Since the tax farmer's interest is to increase the duty instead of assimilating it to all the vicissitudes of commerce, which might cause its reduction, he seeks only to expand it by twisting the meaning of the law. He tries by specious interpretations to subject what had not been subjected to the law. I have known some who have pored over an edict for months at a time until they were blue in the face, in order to find in some equivocal expressions—which are not lacking there—whatever it takes to support a higher exaction.

A new duty is established, presumably to give him more latitude and more violations to punish. The tax farmer brings legal action against himself under an assumed name, leads astray a judgment that he obtains all the more easily because there is no real opponent contradicting him, and prevails in the end. It's an advance condemnation of those whom ignorance of these supposed frauds will render guilty of them. Never has the spirit of ruse and cupidity invented anything so subtle. Those who conceive of these sublime expedients are then called *great laborers* and *good workers*.

In addition, I think I am obliged to indicate that this is not a satire. Most of the numerous tax-farm regulations are composed of nothing but anticipatory judgments of this sort, which have the force of law even for those who have rendered them. When a serious occasion puts them in position to decide the contrary, they are made to see that the question has already been judged. Laziness authorizes it and pronounces likewise. Thus, the man who did not imagine he could be guilty is simultaneously accused, convicted, and sentenced before even being aware that he could be.

All these plots hatched against the security of commerce and the citizenry are joined with outlandish appraisals when it comes to setting the duty. Whence arises that mass of difficulties, contestations, and trials that cause obstacles and delays in the transport and sale of merchandise, which in turn occasion its withering away—often its complete loss—and the ruin of those who own the merchandise.

True enough, one may abandon one's commodity to the tax farmer for the price he has imposed on it. But while this expedient is thought proper to contain his greed, it is merely a means of concentrating commerce and government finance into his hands. If he wants to, he will grab all the merchandise and consequently come to dominate prices, becoming the sole merchant in the state. This will happen all the more easily and advantageously in that, since he has to bear only that portion of the duties that reverts to the sovereign, he will always be able to offer the merchandise at a better price than the other merchants, who will not be able to withstand this competition. Witness the sale of brandy in Rouen, of which the tax farmers have in this way become the exclusive vendors.

Moreover, these renunciations[144] are always ruinous for those who make them if the tax farmer disdains to profit from them. Since he did not count on someone leaving him the commodities for the price to which he had unjustly raised it, he exhausts the resources of chicanery to dispense with paying it and ends up obtaining a decree in his favor, which obliges the proprietor to take back his rotting merchandise, after having been deprived of its value for the whole duration of a long and arduous legal process. This in turn means he bears the loss not only of a part of his capital but of the interest that this capital would have yielded during the interval.

One cannot deny any of the damage caused by consumption taxes without ignoring truths that are unfortunately only too clearly grasped. To say, with the author of *The Spirit of the Laws,* that they are the least onerous for the people and the ones they endure with the most mildness and equality is to say that the more they are weighed down, the less they suffer.[145] The inordinate profits of the tax farmers and the immense costs of all the collections and levies are so many surcharges on the people which, without any profit for the prince, add more than a quarter to what they would have had to pay if their contributions passed directly from their hands into his own.

As for the mildness and equality of these taxes, Herodian writes that they are tyrannical and that Pertinax abolished them for this reason.[146] It has just been seen that in fact, it would be difficult to imagine taxes that had

144. *Abandons,* has a legal connotation meaning a debtor's relinquishment of goods into a creditor's hands.

145. The target here is Montesquieu, *Laws,* 13.14, though he qualifies his judgment somewhat in 13.15.

146. Herodian (ca. 170–240), author of *History of the Empire from the Death of Marcus;* book 2 concerns the reign of Publius Helvius Pertinax (r. 192–93).

fewer of these characteristics. It is useless to remark that, with the freedom not to consume, one has the freedom not to pay. This is merely a sophism. I know of no other "freedom" to exempt oneself from paying these taxes but that of ceasing to live. Is it up to oneself to abstain from what is required by real, physical needs? Since the things most necessary to existence are taxed, the necessity to live imposes the necessity to pay; none other is more pressing.

It is also a quite strange illusion to imagine that these taxes are the most advantageous ones for the sovereign. What advantage can he garner from the oppression of his subjects and of commerce?

Many Asian cities raised statues to Vespasian's father Sabinius with this inscription in Greek: *to an honest tax collector:*[147] Temples ought to be raised with this one: *to the liberator of the Country,* to whoever brings together into a single territorial tax all those taxes whose multiplicity and diversity make the people groan under such cruel oppression.

To insist at present on the advantages of this tax would be to want to demonstrate a truth so palpable that one can neither ignore it nor challenge it.

Everything comes back to the land, no matter how circuitous the route. I have proven this by an exact analysis of the circuits that seem the furthest removed, even the personal taxes.

Thus, fixing them all at once at the source to which they must somehow return would only make their collection shorter, simpler, easier, and less murderous, because the land alone brings forth all the things on which these taxes are levied.

Benefits as numerous as they are invaluable would result from this:

(1) A single collection that would pass directly from the citizens' hands into the sovereign's.

(2) The abolition, to the people's benefit, of everything presently in the hands of the intermediaries to support their armies of officials, the expense of the direct taxes (which is not mediocre), the costs of collections (which are substantial), and—still more—their enrichment.

147. Titus Flavius Sabinus, a respected customs official in the Roman province of Asia (roughly, modern southwestern Turkey) and father of the Roman emperor Vespasian (r. 69–79). See Suetonius, *Life of Vespasian,* 1.2, for this claim.

(3) The monuments, the apparatus, and all the instruments of servitude—annihilated; the regulations—which are nothing more than declarations of war against the people—abolished; the customs laid low; the bureaux demolished; the tolls closed; the barriers overturned; a multitude of citizens—today the terror and scourge of others—returned to the social affections they have abjured, to the cultivation of the lands they have abandoned, to the military and mechanical arts they should have pursued; in a word, becoming useful to society by ceasing to persecute it.

(4) No more means of getting rich that are not honorable, rather than those involving the ruin and devastation of one's fellow creatures.

(5) Personal liberty reestablished, that of commerce and industry restored [*restituée*], each person disposing—at his will, not another's—of what belongs to him as the fruit of his sweat and toil, able to transfer them without obstacles, trouble, or fear wherever his interest or his will might determine to take them.

(6) A just proportion between the duty and the real value of things, resulting on the one hand from their quantity, and on the other from their quality. To prove this, I use a common example, because it is more familiar and easy to apply.

I have said that under current practice, the lowest-priced wines are taxed equally with the more expensive wines. If all the taxes borne by this commodity were combined into one tax on vines, it would at first become higher on those vines that produce the best.

Later on, it would generally be more or less on each unit of wine, depending on whether its production has been more or less abundant. If, in a common year—which would set the baseline for the tax—the tax amounted to one gold crown per unit, then in a fertile year in which the quantity doubled, the tax would be less by one half apiece. The price of the commodity would be less by the same proportion. The opposite would have the opposite effect: the quantity being less, the per-unit tax would be higher, and the price as well.

In generalizing this example, we see that the same proportion would be established in relation to all other types of commodities, which would no longer bear taxes except at the rate of their real value, determined by their quality and quantity. And this would happen naturally, without appraisers or controllers.

(7) Another, no less important, proportion would result. Bearing the public charges only by his consumption, each person would contribute to them only in just relationship to his private capacities. The poor would no longer pay as much for commodities of inferior quality as the rich do for the better ones. The duties each bears would be exactly relative to the quality and quantity of what he could consume.

I will show that this manner of levying the public charges would assure the necessary funds at all times for the state's needs, and that their return to the people would be easy and faster. Now these and the preceding conditions are the conditions of the problem that I have laid out. The territorial tax is thus its solution. Let's confront the objections that may be made to it.

(1) The landowner would have to pay an advance on it.

This is what the merchant does, and as President Montesquieu observes, this advance makes him the debtor of the state and the creditor of private individuals. As we have seen, it is one of the things that seduced him in favor of consumption taxes.[148]

I do not deny this advantage. But it really lies in the territorial tax, and without any of the disadvantages inseparable from it in the other taxes.

In place of the merchant, the proprietor will become the debtor of the state, and the creditor of private individuals. He will add the tax he has disbursed to the price of his commodity. He will do so one time only, instead of doing so on several occasions, with all the confusion that results from this. The first buyer will effect the reimbursement, the second will reimburse the first, and so on all the way to the consumer, where these restitutions will be definitively terminated. It does this without any new collection to undergo during this interval, which leaves the commodity free to follow all the destinations that commerce may provide it. Its price at the end point and at all intermediate points will be the same as at the first point—plus only the manual labor, the profit of those who trade it, and the transport costs for those commodities consumed at a distance from their production site.

(2) This advance would be onerous for the cultivators.

Yes, for the first year; but soon accustomed to being promptly reimbursed, it would no longer seem any more of a burden to them than it is to

148. Montesquieu, *Laws*, 13.14.

the merchant. They would know that it is only a loan they are making for a short time to the buyer.

Moreover, no longer having to bear any but this tax, their emancipation from the others would render the advance less noticeable. Perhaps it would not even much exceed what they pay today, without return, for all those that remain on their charge.

Again, I do not know why one would require this advance or what would prevent one from waiting to do the collection at the moment of sale of the commodities. This would procure the tax sum along with the price of the commodities for the landowners. This is the practice in the collection of current taxes in different places, and no harm results from it. For the government, it is just a question of combining the period of payments with that of receipts, which entails no confusion or difficulty. Then the need for advances by the landowners becomes nil and the objection disappears.

Thus, there is no reasonable objection to make against the territorial tax as concerns collection; on the contrary, one has to be strangely biased not to agree that its collection would be simpler and therefore easier and less burdensome to the people.

It could be even more useful to them by more quickly procuring them the return of the sums they had paid. And this advantage would not be the only one brought about by the method I am going to discuss.

Among the taxes exacted by government is everything necessary for expenses on the clothing, the food, and everything useful in the upkeep of the armies (except the soldiers' pay)—and along with the value of these things is added the immense fortunes made by the contractors who furnish them.

These taxes also include the price of all those products of the soil consumed for the personal service of the sovereign and for the service of the establishments under state charge.

Instead of employing people who get rich paying for these products very cheaply from the citizens and selling them very expensively to the government, couldn't one start by arranging for the sums that each province ought to bear out of the totality of the tax, then fix the quantity of commodities from each province's harvest, to be provided in descending amounts for the different uses I have just discussed?

All the national products that the government consumes would be levied in kind, and by that much less in money on the people. Nonetheless, the contribution as a whole would still be established on a monetary basis. But the levy would occur solely by means of the exchange made of one portion of these products for commodities of equal value, determined from their current prices. One must also be careful to arrange these exchanges in inverse proportion to the outlets of each canton—that is, they should be more substantial where they are less easy. With less consumption of specie, a greater consumption of commodities that now oftentimes remain unsold would occur, and this would be a double advantage.

Not only is this method not impractical, but the operations it requires are easy. I assume that the sum total of taxes taken together is two hundred million,[149] and of this sum, the outlay of commodities from the soil is sixty million. It is clear that in levying this latter item in kind, no more than a hundred forty million in nominal currency will leave the provinces, which would be a very large good.

The less people must disburse, the less they will be exposed to the rigorous prosecutions of the receivers, the costs of which often double the people's main contribution and which they sustain only because the impossibility of selling their commodities makes it impossible for them to pay. It is quite a country in which one does not count in nominal wealth the equivalent of several years of taxes for which the people are charged, and for which the distance of the capital renders any return impractical. It is thus very important in these cantons to consume the yield from the taxes, without which they would soon be exhausted and in no condition to continue bearing them.

With each province having to furnish its share of commodities, all would participate in the advantages of this method of contributing in proportion to their extent, their production, and their favorable location relative to market outlets. In the current system, on the other hand, the only provinces that benefit are those in closest proximity to the places where the contractors must deliver these commodities. Their interest is opposed to distant purchases; transportation would absorb a part of their profits.

149. French pounds (*livres*); see the note on currency, above.

These contractors would become useless, and the immense gains they make would come back to lighten the burden on the people making provision in their place, who would have less to bear.

Under this arrangement, the territorial tax would also simplify public expenditure as much as it would collection. Those intermediate hands through which both pass, and which retain such substantial portions that do not reenter circulation, would no longer be open except for legitimate gain, the product of useful work. The sums levied on the people would go directly to the public treasury and would likewise leave from there, returning to the people. With people's capacities constantly being renewed, the taxpayers would always be in a position to bear the tax, because they would not be exhausted by it.

I am well aware that there would have to be stewards and agents for the preservation of the merchandise and commodities that the provinces furnish in kind. I also know that the loss of what is entrusted to them is ordinarily the result of their mismanagement. But if the first to engage in corrupt practices were punished with all the severity appropriate for a public sacrilege (to express myself like Plutarch), the others would have no desire to imitate his example.

Besides, it is not a chimera that I am proposing. This method of levying taxes in money and in kind was long that of the Romans, who knew about it just as we do. All the provinces of that vast empire furnished the clothing for the troops, the cereals and all necessary commodities for their food, the fodder for the horses, *&c.* Titus Livy and Polybius inform us that the tax payments of Naples, Tarentum, Locri, and Reggio were armed vessels, asked of them in time of war.[150] Capua provided soldiers and maintained them. The practices so advantageously engaged in then cannot be impractical or harmful today.

But relative to what I have just examined, the problems over collection are not the only objections to be made against a single territorial tax. There are others of a different kind and of greater importance which I must resolve:

150. See Livy, *The History of Rome,* XXXV.xxvi; I have found no discussion of this subject in Polybius.

(1) With all the taxes being brought together into one and falling on the land, no further differences exist in the prices of commodities. They will be the same universally, with the result that subsistence goods and all items of consumption will be equally expensive everywhere, even though the price of labor is not. The artisan, worker, or day laborer from the city earns less than his counterparts from the country; those from the provincial cities earn less than those from the capital. Nonetheless, they will all be obliged to spend as much to live. This disproportion between profit and cost would be unjust and too detrimental to be allowed.

I acknowledge the force and interest of this objection. But it is in no way insurmountable.

The difference in the prices of commodities from one place to another, setting aside that which results from their quality, their rarity, or their abundance, arises from four causes:

The costs of their transportation.

The expense of the manual labor for those commodities finished or converted into different forms.

The profits made by the workmen and merchants who manufacture, buy, and sell them.

Finally, the successive duties levied on top of them, which more or less increase the main price in proportion to their quantity and to the different places the commodities have passed through. If one thinks carefully about it, one will find no other causes.

The territorial tax changes nothing in the first three; they exist in their entirety. The prices of the commodities will always be more expensive by their transport cost, their manufacture, and their finishing, as well as by the profit of the workmen and of those who trade it.

Thus, it is merely a matter of restoring the difference destroyed by the unity and equality of the territorial tax. And for this, all you need is to make it higher for town houses that are to be subject to it than for land. Due to the scale of the tax and of their earnings, for example, if the town houses were to be taxed at a quarter of their income, this tax would be brought to a third, a half, or more, according to the requirements of the ratio between profit and expense, as that ratio is applied to the comparison between their inhabitants and those of the countryside. The extra that the city dwellers would bear for their lodging would compensate for the lesser amount they would pay for their consumption. This increase in the tax on houses, which would lighten the burden on land, would restore [*restitueroit*] the condition of both to the relationship it ought to be in. Thus, this objection, one of the most specious and the most likely to seduce at first sight, is not an obstacle to the establishment of this tax.

The objection that derives from the privileges of certain bodies and certain provinces, which claim to have the right either not to contribute to the public charges or to do so in a manner different from their fellow citizens, is no better founded.[151]

In speaking of the obligation to bear them, I have made clear that all exemptions from these charges are infractions against the fundamental laws of society; that they tend to bring forth its ruin; that they are null and abusive, because of the inalienable and indestructible right that all members of the body politic possess to require of each, and each of all, the reciprocal contribution of forces which they have committed themselves to supply for the common expense and security.

No power in the commonwealth can exempt anyone from this obligation; no power can bestow privileges or make concessions to the detriment of this right. Society itself does not have this power because it does not have the power to do what would be contrary to its preservation; a fortiori for the government that represents it and that was established solely to look out for it.

The state was not founded so that one part enjoy and the other suffer. Wherever the burdens and advantages are not shared, there is no more society. Thus, the body or individual that refuses to participate in society's burdens renounces its advantages, declares that he no longer belongs to it, and should be treated as a foreigner to whom nothing is owed since he thinks he owes nothing to anyone.

Whoever wants to incur these burdens only in a lesser proportion and in a different form from other citizens also ruptures the civil association in what concerns him. He attests that he separates himself from this association

151. In eighteenth-century France, different provinces had different methods of handling their royal tax obligations, as did different bodies such as the clergy, the nobility, and privileged professional or municipal corporations. See INTENDANTS, above, for a discussion.

and that it does not suit him to be placed with those who compose it. He puts himself in the situation of being considered as no longer belonging to it. Each person can deny him what he denies to all and not think himself more obliged toward him than he claims to be toward others.

Those are the disadvantages of the lack of uniformity in the administration of the same state. The bodies or provinces ruled by principles and interests different from those of the body as a whole cannot be subject to the same obligations; they are so many private societies in the midst of the general society. It is no longer the same society but many, bound solely by a confederation in which each person finds his interest to dwell—an interest, however, that these private societies prefer and promote to the detriment of the interest of all. Thus, we see these bodies and provinces constantly seeking to free themselves from public charges at the expense of the others, and to unscrupulously shift onto them the shortfall in their own burdens by not contributing in the same proportion as the whole citizenry.

The territorial tax excludes all these distinctions and all these privileges, which are as unjust as they are demoralizing for those who do not enjoy them. Far from this being an obstacle to its establishment, it is one more advantage, which only makes its necessity even more palpable. Anacharsis says the best commonwealth[152] is the one in which, all things otherwise equal among the inhabitants, preeminence is measured by virtue and the dregs by vice.[153]

This preeminence is the only one of which it is fitting for the nobility to be jealous. They distinguish themselves from others by doing good and by their utility, not by overburdening others with needs that they themselves occasion without wanting to contribute toward fulfilling them. Following the count of Boulainvilliers,[154] who will not be suspected of wanting to

152. *La chose publique,* "the public business," which Féraud describes as "an old expression, renewed in our time," and "à la mode."

153. Anacharsis, sixth-century B.C. Scythian philosopher who acquired Athenian citizenship and charmed the Athenians with his blunt, homespun insights into Greek culture; author of a book, now lost, paralleling the laws of the Greeks and the Scythians. The Jesuit abbé Jean-Jacques Barthélemy (1716–95) made a huge impact with his fictionalized history, *Voyage du jeune Anarcharsis en Grèce* [Voyage of the young Anarcharsis to Greece] (1787).

154. On Boulainvilliers, see notes 5, 26, and 29, above. This reference seems to be to his *Essais sur la noblesse de France* (Amsterdam, 1732).

weaken its rights, the nobility must found these rights on principles other than violence, arrogance, and exemption from the taille.

In Sparta, the kings and magistrates bore the public charges in common with all the citizens and were only the more respected for it. It is the same in Venice, where the nobles and the doge himself are subject to it. Amelot de la Houssaye, who has written the history of that city's government,[155] observes that the people are more attached to its administration and its nobility. They do not refuse to submit to what their leaders decree, because what they decree concerns themselves as well as the others. This historian adds that they do not see their tyrants in those who govern.

Although liberty and austere mores were lost in Rome under the emperors, no one was exempt from taxes. Even the prince's lands contributed to them, and Diocletian laughed at a favorite who asked him for an exemption.[156]

Under the republic, the distribution was even stricter. The share of public burdens was fixed in proportion to the share one had in the government. It thereby happened, says Montesquieu, that high taxes were endured because of one's high reputation[157] and that one consoled oneself for one's low reputation with low taxes.[158] According to Titus Livy, the poor paid nothing; it was thought that they were furnishing enough to the state by raising their families.[159] In fact, if one calculates what it must cost them in work and sacrifice to bring their children to the age at which they can provide for their own subsistence, one will find they have rendered an outsized contribution when they have reached the point of giving society useful citizens who populate it and enrich it with their work. Relative to their situations, richer people have furnished much less to the state, however high the burdens they have discharged.

155. Abraham Nicolas Amelot de la Houssaye (1634–1706), historian, diplomat, student of Tacitus, and translator of Machiavelli's *The Prince* and Paolo Sarpi's history of the Council of Trent. When his highly critical *Histoire du gouvernement de Venise* appeared (1676), the Venetian ambassador protested, the author spent a short time in the Bastille, and the work became a best seller.

156. Diocletian, Roman emperor (284–305) whose policies included an increase in taxes.

157. *Crédit,* meaning "creditworthiness"; the 1762 *Dictionnaire de l'Académie Française* adds a broader sense of authority, esteem, even power.

158. The passage appears in Montesquieu, *Laws,* 11.19.

159. Livy, *The History of Rome,* II.ix.6.

Equity existed in the Roman republic; the contrary is found in modern governments,[160] where the burdens are borne in inverse proportion to the share one has in them, to the reputation and wealth one possesses.

But the privilege of exemption from taxes that the nobility used to have in these modern governments no longer exists, because its cause is destroyed and no pretext remains for it.

This exemption, which was not even an exemption,[161] took place because the nobles were burdened with the whole of state service. They defended it, governed it, and administered justice at their own expense. It was then just for them to be exempt from the taxes borne in exchange by those who were exempt from all these burdens.

It would no longer be just today, now that the nobility are not bound by any of these obligations; now that the nobility are paid very handsomely to go to war alone instead of leading troops to war, feeding them, and maintaining them at their own expense; now that even the excessive rewards they demand from government for the least useful things—often those most contrary to the public good—cause an excessive burden on the people. It would involve not only enjoying all the advantages of an agreement without fulfilling its conditions, but also turning all the burdens it imposes on us to their benefit.

One thus sees that by rights,[162] the necessity of contributing to the public charges like the other citizens which would result from the establishment of the territorial tax in no way injures the privileges of the nobility.

It injures those privileges even less in fact. Doesn't the nobility bear all current taxes and duties? The exemption from the taille on some of the properties they possess is only a fiction. If the nobility are not charged nominally for these properties, the tenant farmers are charged in their stead, and they farm the property that much less. The only difference between the nobility and the other taxpayers is that instead of paying the tax collectors,

160. In this and the next paragraph, Damilaville seems by "modern governments" to mean those established upon the ruins of the Roman Empire starting in the early Middle Ages, a not uncommon usage in his time.

161. What Damilaville seems to mean is that there was at that time no general practice or even conception of taxing the nobility, from which any individual or group of nobles might be exempt.

162. The phrase is "dans le droit," so "legally speaking" might be an alternative rendering.

they pay their tenants. If they pit their prerogatives against the territorial tax, which affects only the real estate while enfranchising persons by abolishing the head taxes to which the nobility had submitted without difficulty, couldn't one conclude that they are making more of an issue of their property than of nobility itself and that they are less afraid of the marks of servitude for their persons than for their property?

But this opposition would be as contrary to their true interests as to their dignity. If all the taxes were brought together into one on the land, then the nobility, like everyone else, would be less burdened by everything levied above and beyond this for the cost of its collection and for the enrichment of those who engage in the collection. Being less burdened, their tenant farmers would do more to farm their property; their income would be more substantial and their expenses less so. And what ought to affect them infinitely more than anyone else: they would be emancipated from the yoke of cupidity and from all the infractions committed against civil liberty in the levy of the current duties, of which they are no more exempt than the multitude of citizens.

If noble privileges are not an obstacle to this establishment, certainly the privileges of the folks in mortmain[163] would be much less so. One of the earliest of them (St. Cyprian) says, "It is in vain for those whom reason and justice alike prohibit from enjoying privilege to respond with possession, as if custom and practice could ever have more force than truth and were destined to prevail over it."[164]

The precautionary measures taken by these bodies do not even have the advantages of possession. They were unknown before 1711; at no time before then were these bodies exempt from public charges. In the past, they even bore the charge of giving citizens to the state.[165]

163. *Mainmorte,* in this context, properties that cannot provide the duties or services otherwise required by the fief; inalienable and immutable properties; in practice, it refers to ecclesiastics.

164. Saint Cyprian (ca. 200–258), wealthy pagan, convert to Christianity, bishop of Carthage (248), influential writer on church matters, who was executed in 258. French editions of his works appeared in 1672 and 1716. Voltaire discusses him similarly in *Essay,* 56.

165. On October 27, 1711, the government of Louis XIV gave formal recognition to ecclesiastical immunity from royal taxes, while ensuring a periodic source of *dons gratuits,*

If the ministers of the ancient priesthood, with which they claim parity, did not contribute to their charges, this is because they possessed no property in the society and lived only on the alms they received from it under the name of *tithes*. Would the ministers of the modern priesthood want to be reduced to the same condition?

The priests bore taxes in the Roman Empire, and Constantine himself, who had so many obligations toward them and showered them with so many favors in gratitude, did not exempt them from these. In vain did St. Gregory of Nazianzen say to Julian, who had been appointed to arrange the taxes of that city, "that the clergy and the monks had none for Caesar, and that everything was for God." Julian imposed them anyway.[166]

Clotaire I did the same, despite the audacity of Bishop Injuriosus of Tours, who dared tell him, "If you are thinking, sir, of taking from God what is his, God will take your crown from you." Clotaire obliged them annually to pay the state a third of the income from ecclesiastical properties. And Peter of Blois, even though he maintained with the greatest violence "that princes must exact from bishops and the clergy only continual prayer for them, and that if they want to make the church tributary, whoever is son of the church must oppose them and die rather than allow it," could not prevent his colleagues and himself from being subject to the Saladin tithe.[167]

I will not go into more detail on the facts proving that at all times, those subject to mortmain have borne state charges without distinction, that they have even contributed—and with justice—at a higher proportion than others. Those who have some knowledge of history do not doubt it, and

that is, free gifts, which continued up to the Revolution. See Marcel Marion, *Dictionnaire des institutions de la France aux XVIIe et XVIIIe siècles* (Paris: Picard, 1923), 103.

166. Saint Gregory Nazianzen (329–89), bishop of Sasima and then of Constantinople (378), who had studied at Athens, where he became acquainted with the future emperor Julian the Apostate (r. 361–63), so called because he attempted to restore pagan culture and religion against the state-sponsored inroads of Christianity.

167. Clotaire I (ca. 497–561), son of Clovis and king of the Franks; Injuriosus, bishop of Tours (529–46); Peter of Blois (ca. 1130–ca. 1203), statesman and theologian in service to the archbishop of Canterbury and then to Eleanor of Aquitaine; the Saladin tithe was a tax imposed in England and in parts of France in response to the capture of Jerusalem by Saladin in 1187.

whoever would like authorities will find countless ones in the abbé Fleury's *Eccles. hist.*[168]

I will only note that it is quite strange that privileges which men knew how to appraise so well in ages of darkness and ignorance, when the bishops assembled at Rheims wrote to Louis the German "that saint Eucherius, in a vision that stole him from heaven, had seen Charles Martel tormented in the lower reaches of Hell by order of the saints destined to attend the last judgment with Christ, for having stripped the churches and thus rendered himself culpable for the sins of all those who had endowed them"[169]—it would be quite strange, I say, that in a more enlightened time, when the bishops themselves are too enlightened not to know all the injustice and all the illusion in these claims, those privileges would appear of greater importance than they were then.

I will not waste time refuting them. Is it necessary to demonstrate that he to whom another has entrusted his property would not have the right to refuse to give it back to him, or to want to return to him only what he sees fit and in the manner that suits him? Mortmain property is a substantial portion of the forces of society; it is not up to the possessors to shield it from society. In passing into their hands, it has not changed its nature. It does not belong to them; they have not acquired or earned it; it belongs to the poor, and consequently to the commonwealth. If such a body intends to constantly deplete her of wealth and subjects, without equivalent and without any utility for her; if it finds it to be undignified to belong to her—to contribute to her burdens in proportion to the property that it possesses and in the same form as the others; to honor the vows of those who have made it the depository of these properties; to reserve for itself only what is needed to live in modesty and frugality; to return [*restitue*] all the rest to the poor, and to distribute it to them not for them to exist in idleness and in all the vices this always engenders, but to obtain their subsistence from it through

168. Claude Fleury (1640–1723?), *Histoire ecclésiastique,* a respected multivolume work that appeared frequently from 1691; an English translation appeared in 1727–32, and a German one in 1752–56.

169. Charles Martel (686–741), Frankish mayor of the palace, victor at Tours against Muslim invaders (732), and grandfather of Charlemagne; Saint Eucherius (687?–743), bishop of Orléans, who opposed Charles's taxing of church property to fund the war against the Moors.

work—how many families that are now burdens to the state would become useful to it, and would render it the tax that others refuse it! How many of them would I establish over these vast possessions! How many men would be produced by these lands, thus cultivated by a greater number of hands!

But it is said that these bodies furnish contributions. Yes! But there is a double injustice in their method:

(1) In doing so much less than others do and than they ought to do.

(2) In doing so by loans, so that the other citizens are always really contributing for them.

It is in the interests of everyone, and of the state that is the guarantor of these loans, to reform this flawed administration. The clergy's property is going to become insufficient even for the interest on their debts. They have complained for a long time about being in debt; these debts fall to the burden of society. What is called the *pensions on the former clergy,*[170] reduced to half, are an example. Nothing proves better than this example how advantageous it would be for this body itself to be subject to annual and proportional contributions, and consequently, how the territorial tax would be more useful for them than for others—independent of the fact that it has no right to oppose this, as I have shown.

A final difficulty: if one were to object that the provinces I have discussed have an incontestable right to administer themselves in the manner they judge appropriate and that this is the condition on which they have submitted to the government, I answer that even if their administration were the best, which I will show in a moment is not the case, they must conform to that of others because there must not be any difference in the obligations and in the lots of subjects within the same state. Either these provinces belong to society or they do not.

If they belong, nothing could alter the right that society has over them, as over everything that composes it. The government, which was instituted solely for the preservation of this right, could make no agreement contrary to it; in any case, it could not destroy it.

170. *Rentes sur l'ancien clergé* were established for private individuals in exchange for contributions made by the clergy to the royal treasury. The French clergy resorted to some of the same expedients to pay its growing bills as the monarchy—creation of venal offices, for example. See Marion, *Dictionnaire,* 106.

If they do not belong, the general society can refuse them its advantages and treat them as foreign societies whose support is not of interest to them and which they must provide for themselves without assistance.

After recognizing the inadequacy of these objections, it will be said (as some have done) that in truth these objections create no obstacles to this establishment [i.e., the single territorial tax], but one fears that all the taxes it brought together would be reestablished one by one afterward, while still existing in the land tax. If this reflection is not solid, it is at least distressing. It proves that the people are unfortunately accustomed to dread even the good that one might want to do for them. I can respond to such a difficulty only by regretting that one could think of raising it. But since the territorial tax includes all the charges it is possible to impose on the people, the impossibility of adding anything to it is assured by the impossibility of bearing it.

It is no great thing to have resolved all individual objections and left none that one could reasonably make against the territorial tax. There remains one task more difficult to fulfill: showing that the assessment of this tax is not impractical, as has been imagined up to now, and to offer the means of achieving this.

I am not unaware of either the extent or the difficulties of the operations demanded by such an establishment. One must know all the properties in the state, their exact quantity, and their real value. How to acquire this knowledge?

Cadastres have been undertaken; the few that have been done have cost immense sums, and they are defective. An enumeration of properties is requested; it is thought that the municipal officers are in a position to provide this for each of their communities, but they are incapable of it. Will you survey an entire realm acre by acre? The time and expense would be endless, and yet you would still have only quantities. And even if they were assumed to be certain, you would have nothing. Measurement does not provide value; but how then to determine this value?

I have seen people cut through these difficulties—which they found no means of escaping—and propose, without going into all these details, to distribute the sum total of all taxes over all the provinces according to their number and without regard to their extent or to the value of the real estate that composes them. Their claim has been that balance would reestablish itself over time by the increases and decreases that would arise in property values. The overcharged properties in one province would have to be sold for much less and vice versa, so that after a complete turnover in all the properties, the level would end up being restored [*restitué*]. No longer would anyone be either too much or too little neglected, since each would have acquired in proportion to the tax.

There is a host of cruel injustices here which, even if they turned out to be momentary, would suffice to reject this expedient regardless of what good might otherwise arise from it. In waiting for this turnover, families and even whole generations from countless provinces would be ruined without recourse, since the surcharge is bound to fall mainly on those who possess properties of lesser value. I cannot abide the idea of so many victims sacrificed on the altar of an advantage far removed and more than uncertain, for who would buy bad estates weighed down with taxes? And who would sell many good ones that carry few taxes?

Moreover, fixing the sums to be borne respectively by all the provinces is not all there is to be done. These sums must also be fixed for each parish, city, or community, and then for each quantity of real estate. Who will make these subdivisions and arrange these individual taxes, where it is so easy and so dangerous to be unjust? Will it be the public magistrates and the municipal officers? We know in advance how that will turn out.

I mean to exalt municipal administration and its effects, but they are not understood. I believe it is excellent in republics, where it is the administration of the state itself. But in the other types of government, the popular magistrates—even those the Marquis d'Argenson proposes to establish[171]—will never be more than people of little intelligence, who will dominate by their petty talents and who will use those talents solely to procure relief for themselves and all those they are attached to, at others' expense. Those destined to succeed to office will always be known; authority

171. René-Louis de Voyer, marquis d'Argenson (1694–1757), *Considérations sur le gouvernement ancien et présent de la France* [Considerations on the past and present government of France] (Amsterdam: Michel Rey, 1764). Conceived at the meetings of the Club de l'Entresol in Paris in the 1720s, completed (probably) by 1737, this posthumously published work of comparative government argued that most modern European governments are of "mixed" constitution and advocated a "democratic monarchy" for France based on decentralization and local reform. On this theme, see also INTENDANTS, above.

will rest within a small circle of families. The poor man without support or protection will never have a share in it; he will be crushed—especially since the freedom to vary and change the form of the collections will be left to the popular magistrates. In this form of administration, even in that of the much esteemed *pays d'état*,[172] I have never seen anything but the weak man being surrendered to the power of the strong who oppresses him.

This leads to countless evils, seeds of disorder and division which constantly foster hatreds, animosities, private vengeance, the habit of injustice and of resentment among the inhabitants—in the end, the general corruption and ruin of the villages, by the very persons set up to maintain order and make equity reign there.

Another disadvantage in the economy of this system[173] is solidarity;[174] that species of cruelty was unknown in ancient governments. Fortunately, it is little known in modern ones where it is practiced. Emperor Zeno said it offends civil law and natural equity to pursue a man for the crimes of others.[175]

Thus, this administration is not the best. Nor is this one, or any of these expedients, the one that I have proposed. In all things, I would like to deliver men from the authority of other men and for them never to be subject to any authority but that of the law.

Men have passions and interests; the law does not. Men are partial and subject to error; the law never is. It does not recognize relatives, friends, protectors, protegés, considerations, motives. What it decrees, it decrees for all and for all circumstances.

I don't know whether the operations necessary to establish such an administration are impossible. But what follows is what has been done and

172. Provinces with regular meetings of their local estates, as opposed to *pays d'élection*, which are administered by royal officials. For a fuller discussion of the differences, see INTENDANTS, above, which comes to a quite different conclusion.

173. *Système économique*, where "économique" carries the older meaning of resource management, originally in the household but figuratively to the "political body" (*Dictionnaire de l'Académie Française*, 1762).

174. *Solidité*, or *solidarité*, the old-regime practice of imposing collective debts or obligations on villages, guilds, or other corporate entities rather than on individuals.

175. Emperor Zeno (ca. 425–91), Eastern Roman Emperor (474–91). See *Code of Justinian*, bk. 10, title 56, no. 1.

what I am proposing. It is not an ivory tower speculation that I'm offering here. It is a project that was implemented before my eyes, while I was occupied on the great highways of Champagne and the Soissonnais. Its result is imitated in a large number of parishes and cities in different provinces, not only without complaint on the part of the inhabitants but underwritten by them and demanded by many, as soon as they learned of its utility. It must not be thought that this operation demands a substantial amount of time; I have seen it done in less than two months by just one person in a parish comprising more than three hundred souls.

If it could be put into effect in several, it cannot be said that it could not be done in all.

[*Several pages follow, 17:881–89, in which Damilaville provides sample calculations (clearly of Physiocratic inspiration) of the production and taxation of various kinds of landed property in a specific parish, to illustrate the foregoing. These have been omitted.*]

No one will disagree that, with similar operations for all parishes, cities, or communities, I will soon have the cadastre, and by extrapolation the general picture of all the estates in each province—their nature, their quality, and their value. I'll therefore have the entire enumeration, and by extrapolation, I'll again have the picture of all estates in the realm as a whole and of their produce.

I now ask what can prevent one from recording the amount of all the burdens of the state and all the costs of government:

(1) for an ordinary year, chosen based on one common year out of several;

(2) for one year out of the first five years of war;

(3) for one of the five following years;

(4) and lastly, for one of the five other years after the preceding ones.

This gradation is necessary. War expenses increase in proportion to its duration, and pretty much according to the progression of these three periods. This calamity has afflicted the human race for so long that it ought to be easily within our capacity to define a normal year out of the expenses that war occasions in each of these periods. But war cannot exceed these periods. After fifteen years of it, one must make peace, either from one's own inability to continue on or from others'.

In adding to these variously set rates a reasonable and proportionate surplus for unforeseen things and for the public treasury never to be without some advances, one will have the sum total of all state and government costs, in all possible circumstances. And this total will be the total tax for each of these circumstances.

Presently, where is the difficulty in distributing this total and regulating what each acre or each type of property ought to bear?

With these proportional calculations, it will be distributed as often as it can change—that is, four times at first over all the provinces, in proportion to their mass and their particular strengths. The yield will be the portion of each one.

This yield will be distributed in the same proportion over all the cities, parishes, or communities of the province, and this will give the sum total of each one's contribution.

This total will eventually be distributed over all the properties that compose the territory of the cities, parishes, or communities, in a proportion composed of their quantity, their yield, and the sum total to bear. This will result in the quota that each unit of these properties will have to bear.

Thus, you have the tax for each acre (or whatever type of property it may be) determined for all possible times in exact proportion to its value and to the sum total of the public charges that all the needs of the state and the government may exact.

In what I have proposed to add for unforeseen cases, I have not included those which might cause bad debts, such as the accidents that deprive proprietors of their harvests and their income. It would therefore be necessary to arrange a separate surplus that had nothing in common with the first, and to distribute it in the same way over the provinces, communities, and properties. But this would be distinct from the main tax, so that each person would know what his burden is for both of them. The reason for this arrangement is that such surplus should never be carried over to the prince's treasury or elsewhere. (We know what happens to those levied today.) It would remain in trust in the community responsible for it, and in the care of the parish priest and twelve of the leading inhabitants.

If it happened that this surplus became so substantial as to make up the total amount of the tax imposed for one year, it would be employed to pay this off. The estates would not be taxed that year, so that it would always redound to the taxpayers' benefit. No other use could be made of it except when necessary to pay on behalf of those who had found it impossible to pay because of accident.

Instead of this surplus, I would have been happy to propose fixing the tax rates on the basis of a normal year's yield, by which the losses would be appraised and deducted; they would still have to be paid when these losses occurred. But men are not sensible enough to base their expenses on an ordinary year of their income. And even if they had benefitted in years when they have suffered no loss, they would nonetheless be in no position to pay for those losses when they do take place.

Finally, uncultivated lands that had been cleared would be taxed according to their class. But for the first ten years, they would enjoy an exemption from the tax. For the next ten years, their taxes would be half for the benefit of the community and for the discharge of all the other estates, which would pay that much less for a period of time. All inhabitants would thereby have an interest in ensuring that cleared terrain was known and taxed when it ought to be.

What is left to do? A solemn law that fixes all these taxes unalterably, and that likewise prescribes all these arrangements. I am convinced that the prosperity and durability of an empire would depend upon the stability of this law. For the people's happiness and the government's tranquility, one must be able to give this law a sacred pledge. For as strong a pledge as any human institution can receive, the sovereigns and the nation must at least swear to observe it and to prevent it from ever suffering any innovation.[176] I would like it to be decreed with such solemn authority that, whoever were to propose abrogating it or changing it could do so only with a rope around his neck, in order to be punished on the spot, even if he proposed only things less good and less useful to the state and the citizens.

This law would be deposited in each community as the expression of the general will of the people,[177] as their safeguard and as the title deed to

176. The verb is *innover*, which carries a more pejorative connotation than modern English equivalents might.

177. For the idea of a "general will," see Diderot's entry Droit Naturel, above. Its most elaborate formulation is in Rousseau's *Social Contract* (1762). Here, the French word used for "the people" is plural: *les peuples.*

public liberty and tranquility. Every year, the extract from this law containing the list of taxes for all the properties attached to the parish—according to whether it was a time of peace or war—would be published and posted without need to ordain it by any new law. Each person would read there on any given day what he has to pay, and would not learn this from anyone.

There is nothing arbitrary in this—no personal exceptions, no subordinate authority. There is no privilege, no privileged, no protectors, no protected. The taxpayer depends only on the law and on himself. He does not have to hope for the favor or fear the animosity of anyone. He does not answer for others. He can dispose of his entire property as he sees fit, cultivate it after his fashion, consume or sell his commodities as he wishes and without anyone at all having the right to punish him for it. If he is well off, he will dare to let this fact appear. He will never have to pay anything except what the law decrees. He makes an advance on his payments; the consumer reimburses him without complication and without oppression for either of them. All the funds necessary for public expenses are assured for all times and all needs. The syndic of each parish conducts the collection and entrusts it to a public tax collector, who transmits it directly to the state treasury. The funds move easily and without cost; they come back in the same way in returning to their source.

There you have the whole business of state finance—without vexation, without publicans, without intrigue, and without all those expedients that are as offensive to the dignity of government as to the public faith and honor. *Frustra fit per plura quod aeque commode fiere potest per pauciora.*[178]

It is easy to recognize that this cadastre could also be the one for the national debt—but only once in the entire lifetime of a state; a second would liquidate it.[179]

This article is drawn from the papers of the late M. BOULLANGER, *state roads and bridges engineer. The connections between the operations he was assigned and those that have just been displayed had situated him to be well informed on*

178. "It is pointless to do with more what can be done with less." This is the "law of parsimony," or "Ockham's Razor," associated with William of Ockham (ca. 1285–ca. 1348), the English late Scholastic philosopher. See his *Summa totius logicae* (ca. 1323), I.12 for this passage.

179. The debt, not the state.

them. For a mind like his, this knowledge could not be useless. He had intended to make it the subject of a substantial work on financial administration. The materials for this work were found scattered around; someone assembled them with as much order and connection as possible. If one finds some things that seem to stray from the subject and to form extensive digressions, this is because we did not want to lose anything and perhaps because we do not have the art of employing these as the author had intended. But we thought we would make ourselves useful to society by publishing them in this Dictionary, designed specifically to be the depository of human knowledge.[180]

180. But see our introductory note at the head of this article, as well as the entry on Damilaville, the probable author of this article, in the Contributors, above.

Bibliography

What follows is a combination of some but not all of the works cited in the text and some but not all of what is necessary for a basic orientation to the very large topic at hand. Wherever possible, English translations of original French texts have been indicated.

Primary Sources

The *Encyclopédie*

d'Alembert, Jean Le Rond. *Preliminary Discourse to the Encyclopedia of Diderot.* 1751. Translated by Richard N. Schwab. Indianapolis: Bobbs-Merrill, 1963.

Diderot, Denis. *Choix d'articles de "l'Encyclopédie"* [Selection of articles from the *Encyclopédie*]. Edited by Marie Leca-Tsiomis. Paris: CTHS, 2001.

Diderot, Denis, and Jean Le Rond d'Alembert, eds. *The Encyclopedia of Diderot and d'Alembert Collaborative Translation Project.* Ann Arbor: Michigan Publishing, University of Michigan Library. An ongoing partial translation hosted by MPublishing, a division of the University of Michigan Library, available online at: http://quod.lib.umich.edu/d/did/.

———. *Encyclopédie, ou Dictionnaire raisonné des sciences, des arts et des métiers, par une Société de gens de lettres* [Encyclopedia, or critical dictionary of the sciences, arts and trades, by an Association of men of letters]. 28 vols. Paris: Briasson, David, Le Breton, Durand, 1751–72. Available in electronic form at the ARTFL website: http://encyclopedie.uchicago.edu.

Donato, Clorinda, and Robert M. Maniquis, ed. *The "Encyclopédie" and the Age of Revolution.* Boston: G. K. Hall, 1992.

Gendzier, Stephen J., ed. and trans. *Denis Diderot's "The Encyclopedia": Selections.* New York: Harper and Row, 1967.

Hoyt, Nelly S., and Thomas Cassirer, ed. and trans. *The Encyclopedia: Selections [by] Diderot, d'Alembert and a Society of Men of Letters.* Indianapolis: Bobbs-Merrill, 1965.

Le Ru, Véronique. *Subversives lumières: L'Encyclopédie comme machine de guerre* [Enlightened subversives: The *Encyclopédie* as a war machine]. Paris: CNRS, 2007.

Lough, John, ed. *The "Encyclopédie" of Diderot and D'Alembert: Selected Articles.* Cambridge: Cambridge University Press, 1954.

Lough, John, and Jacques Proust, eds. *Diderot: "Encyclopédie."* Vols. 5–8 of *Denis Diderot: Œuvres complètes,* edited by Hans Dieckmann and Jean Varloot. Paris: Hermann, 1976.

Pons, Alain, ed. *Encyclopédie: ou Dictionnaire raisonné des Sciences, des Arts et des Métiers, 1751–1772.* Paris: J'ai Lu, 1963.

Soboul, Albert, ed. *Textes choisis de l'Encyclopédie.* 2nd ed., revised and expanded. Paris: Editions Sociales, 1962.

Other Primary Sources

Addison, Joseph, and Richard Steele. *The Spectator.* London: Buckley, 1711–13. Translated into French as *Le Spectateur; ou le Socrate moderne.* 3 vols. Paris: Merigot, 1755.

Ainsworth, Henry. *Annotations upon the five bookes of Moses.* London: Bellamy, 1627.

Alciatus, Andreas. *Emblems in Translation.* Vol. 2 of *Andreas Alciatus,* edited by Peter M. Daly. Toronto: University of Toronto Press, 1985. Based on the 1621 edition of the original 1531 work.

d'Argenson, René-Louis de Voyer, marquis. *Considérations sur le gouvernement ancien et présent de la France* [Considerations on the past and present government of France]. Amsterdam: Michel Rey, 1764.

Baker, Keith Michael, ed. *The Old Regime and the French Revolution.* Vol. 7 of *University of Chicago Readings in Western Civilization,* edited by John W. Boyer and Julius Kirshner. Chicago: University of Chicago Press, 1987.

Barbeyrac, Jean. *Traité de la morale des peres de l'Eglise* [Treatise on the morality of the Church fathers]. Amsterdam: Pierre de Coup, 1728.

Barrow, Henry. *A True description out of the Word of God of the visible church.* Amsterdam, 1589.

Bayle, Pierre. *Dictionnaire historique et critique.* 2 vols. Rotterdam: Leers, 1697.

Bolingbroke, Henry St. John, Viscount. *Letters, on the spirit of patriotism: On the idea of a patriot king: and on the state of parties, at the accession of King George the First.* Dublin, 1749.

———. *The Works of the Late Right Honourable Henry St. John, Lord Viscount Bolingbroke.* 8 vols. London: Johnson, 1809.

Bossuet, Jacques-Bénigne. *Politics drawn from the very words of Holy Scripture* [Politique tirée des propres paroles de l'Écriture sainte]. 1709. Edited and translated by Patrick Riley. Cambridge: Cambridge University Press, 1990.

Boulainvilliers, Henri. *Essais sur la noblesse de France* [Essays on the nobility of France]. Amsterdam, 1732.

———. *L'Histoire de l'ancien gouvernement de la France* [History of the former government of France]. 3 vols. The Hague, 1727. Translated by Charles Forman in 1739 as *An historical account of the antient parliaments of France or States-General of the kingdom.*

Brucker, Johann Jakob. *Historia Critica Philosophiae* [Critical history of philosophy]. Leipzig, 1742–44. English translation in 1791.

Burlamaqui, Jean-Jacques. *The Principles of Natural and Politic Law.* 1747. Edited by Petter Korkman. Indianapolis: Liberty Fund, 2006. Translated into English by Thomas Nugent in 1748, revised and corrected in 1763.

Chambers, Ephraim. *Cyclopaedia, or, an universal dictionary of arts and sciences.* 2 vols. London, 1728. 2nd ed., corrected and amended, 1738.

Child, Josiah. *A Discourse About Trade wherein the reduction of interest in money to 4.l. per centum, is recommended.* London, 1690.

Clark, Henry C., ed. *Commerce, Culture, and Liberty: Readings on Capitalism Before Adam Smith.* Indianapolis: Liberty Fund, 2003.

Colbert, Jean-Baptiste. *Testament politique de messire Jean-Baptiste Colbert.* The Hague: H. van Bulderen, 1693.

Commons Debates: 1628. Edited by Robert C. Johnson and Maija Jansson Cole. 6 vols. New Haven: Yale University Press, 1977–83.

Commons Debates for 1629. Edited by Wallace Notestein and Frances Helen Relf. Minneapolis: University of Minnesota, 1921.

Corneille, Pierre. "Sertorius." 1662. In *Moot Plays of Corneille,* translated by Lacey Lockert. Nashville: Vanderbilt University Press, 1959.

Cotton, Sir Robert. *Cottoni posthuma: divers choice pieces of that renowned antiquary Sir Robert Cotton.* London: Seile, 1651 and many other editions.

[Coyer, abbé Gabriel-François]. "Dissertation sur le vieux mot de patrie" [Essay on the old word *patrie*]. 1755. In Gabriel-François Coyer and Jacob-Nicolas Moreau, *Ecrits sur le patriotisme, l'esprit public et la propagande au milieu du XVIIIe siècle* [Writings on patriotism, public spirit and propaganda in the middle of the eighteenth century], edited by Edmond Dziembowski. La Rochelle: Rumeur des âges, 1997.

Davenant, Charles. *Discourse on the publick revenues, and on the trade of England.* London: Knapton, 1698.

Dictionnaire de l'Académie Française. Paris, 1694, 1762, 1798. Available in the ARTFL database at: http://artfl-project.uchicago.edu/node/17.

Diderot, Denis. *Political Writings.* Edited and translated by John Hope Mason and Robert Wokler. Cambridge: Cambridge University Press, 1992.

——. *Principes de la philosophie morale: ou, Essai de M. S***sur le mérite et la vertu, avec réflexions.* Amsterdam: Chatelain, 1745. French translation of Shaftesbury's 1711 work *An Inquiry Concerning Virtue and Merit,* in vol. 2 of *Characteristicks.*

Duclos, Charles Pinot. *Considérations sur les mœurs de ce siècle.* 1751. Translated anonymously into English in 1752 as *Memoirs illustrating the manners of the present age.*

Du Halde, J. B., S.J. *Description géographique, historique, chronologique, politique, et physique de l'empire de la Chine et de la Tartarie chinoise.* Paris: Lemercier, 1735. Translated into English by Richard Brookes in 1736 as *The General History of China.*

Féraud, Jean-François. *Dictionnaire critique de la langue française* [Critical dictionary of the French language]. Marseille: Mossy, 1787–88. Available in electronic form in the ARTFL database at: http://artfl-project.uchicago.edu/node/17.

Furetière, Antoine. *Dictionnaire universel.* Paris, 1690. Available electronically at the Lexilogos website: http://www.lexilogos.com/francais_classique.htm

Godinot, Jean. *Manière de cultiver la vigne et de faire le vin en Champagne.* 1722. [The way to cultivate vineyards and make wine in Champagne]. Langres: Guéniot, 1990.

Gordon, Thomas. *The Works of Tacitus. In Four Volumes. To which are prefixed, Political Discourses upon that Author by Thomas Gordon.* 2nd ed., corr. 4 vols. London: Woodward and Peele, 1737.

Grimm, Friedrich Melchior. *Correspondance littéraire.* Edited by Maurice Tourneux. 16 vols. Paris: Garnier frères, 1877–82.

Grotius, Hugo. *The Free Sea.* 1609. Translated by Richard Hakluyt. Edited by David Armitage. Indianapolis: Liberty Fund, 2004.

——. *The Rights of War and Peace.* 1625. Edited by Richard Tuck. From the edition by Jean Barbeyrac, translated into English in 1738. 3 vols. Indianapolis: Liberty Fund, 2005.

Harrington, James. *The Commonwealth of Oceana.* 1656. Edited by J. G. A. Pocock. Cambridge: Cambridge University Press, 1992.

Histoire abregée des provinces-unies des païs bas [Abridged history of the United Provinces of the Low Countries]. Amsterdam: Malherbe, 1701.

Hobart, Henry. *The reports of that reverend and learned judge, the right honorable Sr. Henry Hobart.* London: More, 1641.

Hobbes, Thomas. *De Cive* [On the citizen]. 1647. Edited by Richard Tuck and Michael Silverthorne. Cambridge: Cambridge University Press, 1998. First translated into English by the author in 1651, and into French by Samuel Sorbière in 1657.

———. *Leviathan*. 1651. Edited by Richard Tuck. Cambridge: Cambridge University Press, 1996.

Hübner, Johann. *La Géographie universelle*. 1746. New ed., Basel, 1757. Originally published in German in 1706; also translated into English in 1746.

Hume, David. *An enquiry concerning the principles of morals*. London: Miller, 1751. Translated into French in 1760 by Jean-Baptiste Robinet as *Essais de Morale ou Recherches sur les principes de la morale*.

———. *Essays, Moral, Political, and Literary*. Edited by Eugene F. Miller. Rev. ed. Indianapolis: Liberty Fund, 1987. The 1752 edition was translated into French by abbé Leblanc in 1755 as *Discours politiques*. The anonymous German translation of 1754–56 was entitled *Vermischte Schriften über die Handlung, die Manufacturen, und die andern Quellen des Reichthums und der Macht eines Staats* [A mixture of writings on commerce, manufacturing, and the other sources of a state's wealth and power].

Isambert, François-André, Athanase-Jean-Léger Jourdan, and Alphonse-Honoré Taillandier, eds. *Recueil général des anciennes lois françaises* [General collection of former French laws]. 29 vols. Paris, 1822–33. Reprint, Ridgewood, N.J.: Gregg Press, 1964.

Johnson, Francis. *Certayne reasons and arguments proving that it is not lawfull to heare or to have any spirituall communion with the present ministerie of the Church of England*. Amsterdam: Thorp, 1608.

La Bruyère, Jean de. *Characters*. 1688. Translated by Henri Van Laun. Introduction by Denys C. Potts. London: Oxford University Press, 1963.

La Mothe le Vayer, François de. *L'Economique du prince*. Paris, 1653.

Laslett, Peter, ed. *The Earliest Classics: Natural and political observations made upon the bills of mortality (1662) [by] John Graunt; Natural and political observations and conclusions upon the state and condition of England, 1696 (1804); The L.C.C. Burns journal, a manuscript notebook containing workings for several projected works (composed c. 1695–1700) [by Gregory King]*. Farnborough, England: Gregg, 1973.

[Lévesque de Pouilly, Jean Simon]. *Vie de Michel de l'Hôpital, Chancelier de France*. London: Wilson, 1764.

Locke, John. *Epistola de tolerantia* [A Letter Concerning Toleration]. 1689. Edited by James H. Tully. Indianapolis: Hackett, 1983. Translated into German in 1710 and into French, by Jean Le Clerc, in 1732.

——. *Two Treatises of Government.* 1690. Edited by Peter Laslett. Cambridge: Cambridge University Press, 1960. The 1690 edition was translated by David Mazel in 1691 as *Du gouvernement civil.*

Loys de Bochat, Charles-Guillaume. *Memoires critiques, pour servir d'eclaircissemens sur divers points de l'histoire ancienne de la Suisse* [Critical memoirs, to serve in illuminating various points in the early history of Switzerland]. Lausanne: Bousquet, 1747–49.

Melon, Jean-François. *Essai politique sur le commerce* [Political essay on commerce]. N.p., 1734. The English translation by the Irishman David Bindon appeared in 1738.

Mirabeau, Victor de Riquetti, Marquis de. *Théorie de l'impôt* [Theory of taxation]. N.p., [1761].

Montaigne, Michel de. *The Complete Essays of Montaigne.* 1588. Translated by Donald M. Frame. Stanford: Stanford University Press, 1958.

Montesquieu, Charles de Secondat, baron de. *Considerations on the Causes of the Greatness of the Romans and Their Decline* [Considérations sur les causes de la grandeur des romains et de leur décadence]. 1734. Translated by David Lowenthal. Indianapolis: Hackett, 1999.

——. *Persian Letters* [Lettres persanes]. 1721. Translated by George R. Healy. Indianapolis: Hackett, 1999. This translation is based on the 1758 edition.

——. *The Spirit of the Laws* [L'Esprit des loix]. 1748. Translated and edited by Anne Cohler, Basia Miller, and Harold Stone. Cambridge: Cambridge University Press, 1989.

More, Thomas. *Utopia.* 1516. Edited and translated by George M. Logan, Robert M. Adams, and Clarence H. Miller. Cambridge: Cambridge University Press, 1995.

Moréri, Louis. *Le Grand dictionnaire historique.* Many editions in French and English from 1674 and well into the eighteenth century, sometimes with Pierre Bayle or Jeremy Collier listed as co-editor.

Narbona, Diego. *Annales tractatus juris de aetate ad omnes humanos actus requisita* [Histories: A legal treatise on adulthood (and) on whatever is necessary for all human actions]. Rome: Corbi, 1669.

Petty, Sir William. *Five Essays in Political Arithmetick.* London: H. Mortlock, 1687.

Piarron de Chamousset, Claude-Humbert. *Œuvres complettes de M. de Chamousset* [Complete works by M. de Chamousset]. Edited by abbé Cotton Des-Houssayes. 2 vols. Paris, 1783.

Pollux, Julius. *Onomasticon.* Edited by J. H. Lederlin and T. Hemsterduis. 2 vols. Amsterdam: Wetsten, 1706.

Pufendorf, Samuel. *Of the Law of Nature and Nations: Eight Books.* 1672. 4th ed., notes and preface by Jean Barbeyrac, edited and translated into English by Basil Kennett, 1729. Clark, N. J.: Lawbook Exchange, 2005.

———. [Severinus de Monzambano, pseud.]. "De Republica irregulari," in *Dissertationes Academicae Selectiores.* Upsala, 1677.

———. [Severinus de Monzambano, pseud.]. *De Statu imperii Germanici.* Genevae: Columesium, 1667.

———. *The Whole Duty of Man According to the Law of Nature.* 1673. Translated by Andrew Tooke in 1691. Edited by Ian Hunter and David Saunders. Indianapolis: Liberty Fund, 2003.

Raleigh, Sir Walter. *The Prerogative of parliaments in England proved in a dialogue between a councellour of state and a justice of peace.* London: Sheares, 1661.

Retz, Jean-François Paul de Gondi, Cardinal de. *Œuvres de Cardinal de Retz.* 1679. Edited by Régis de Chantelauze, Jules Gourdault, and Alphonse Feillet. 10 vols. Paris: Hachette, 1870–96.

Robertson, William. *History of Scotland during the reigns of Queen Mary and King James VI.* 2 vols. London, 1759. Translated into French by Besset de la Chapelle in an edition bearing a London imprint in 1764.

Rousseau, Jean-Jacques. *Discours sur l'économie politique* [Discourse on political economy]. Geneva: Villard, 1758. This was the first stand-alone version of the article Rousseau contributed in 1755 to the *Encyclopédie.*

———. *Discours sur les arts et les sciences* [Discourse on the arts and sciences]. Geneva: Barillot, 1750. First translated anonymously into English as *The Discourse Which Carried the Praemium . . .* in 1751.

———. *Discours sur l'origine et les fondemens de l'inégalité parmi les hommes.* Geneva: Philibert, 1754. First translated into English as *A Discourse on the origins and the foundations of the inequality among men* by John Farrington in 1756.

———. *Le Contrat social.* Amsterdam: Rey, 1762. First translated into English by William Kenrick in 1764 as *A Treatise on the Social Compact.*

Saint-Pierre, Charles-Irénée Castel, abbé de. *Ouvrajes de politique* [Political works]. 17 vols. Rotterdam: Beman, 1733–40.

Savary des Bruslons, Jacques. *Dictionnaire universel de commerce.* 1723. Geneva: Cramer and Philibert, 1744.

Selden, John. *De dis syris* [On the Syrian gods]. London, 1617; Leiden, 1629.

Shaftesbury, Anthony Ashley Cooper, Earl of. *Characteristicks of Men, Manners, Opinions, Times.* 3 vols. 1732. Indianapolis: Liberty Fund, 2001.

Sibrand, Johannes. *Urbis Lubecae et Anseaticarum* [On Lübeck and the Hanseatic cities]. Rostock, 1619.

Sidney, Algernon. *Discourses concerning Government.* 1698. Edited by Thomas G. West. Indianapolis: Liberty Fund, 1996.

Smith, Adam. *An Inquiry into the Nature and Causes of the Wealth of Nations.* 1776. Edited by R. H. Campbell and A. S. Skinner. 2 vols. Oxford: Clarendon Press, 1976. Reprint, Indianapolis: Liberty Fund, 1982.

Soret, G. Jean, and Jean-Nicolas-Hubert Hayer, eds. *La Religion vengée, ou Réfutation des auteurs impies* [Religion avenged, or Refutation of impious authors]. 21 vols. Paris: Chaubert, Hérissant, 1757–63.

Spelman, Sir Henry. *Two Discourses: i. Of the Ancient Government of England, ii. Of Parliaments; The Original of the Four Terms of the Year.* 1614. London, 1684.

Sully, Maximilien de Béthune, duc de. *Mémoires des sages et royalles œconomies d'estat* [Memoirs on prudent royal management of the state]. Amsterdam, 1638.

Temple, Sir William, *Œuvres postumes de chevalier Temple.* Utrecht: Van de Water, 1704. A translation of some of the works, mainly political in nature, from *Miscellanea,* a collection first published in 1680 and reedited by Jonathan Swift in 1701. Also translated into Dutch in 1704.

Templeman, Thomas. *A new survey of the globe: or, an accurate mensuration of all the empires, kingdoms, countries, states, principal provinces, counties, and islands in the world.* London: Bowles, 1765.

Turgot, Anne-Robert-Jacques. *The Life and Writings of Turgot: Comptroller-General of France, 1774–76.* Translated and edited by W. Walker Stephens. London: Longmans, 1895.

Velthuysen, Lambert van. *Epistolica dissertatio De principiis iusti et decori: continens apologiam pro tractatu clarissimi Hobbaei, "De Cive"* [On the principles of the just and proper: containing an apology for Hobbes's "De Cive"]. Amsterdam: Elzevier, 1651.

Voltaire, François-Marie Arouet de. *Essai sur l'histoire universelle.* Geneva: Cramer, 1756. The work was translated into English by Thomas Nugent as *An Essay on Universal History* in 1759. It is commonly known in modern times as *Essai sur les mœurs* [Essay on manners].

———. *La Pucelle d'Orléans* [The maid of Orleans]. Louvain, 1755.

———. *The Works of Voltaire.* Translated and edited by Tobias Smollett, John Morley, William F. Fleming, and Oliver Herbrand Gordon Leigh. 43 vols. New York: E. R. Du Mont, 1901.

Wallace, Robert. *Dissertation on the Numbers of Mankind, in Ancient and Modern Times.* Edinburgh: Hamilton, 1753. Translated into French by Elie de Joncourt in 1754.

Wilkinson, William. *A very godly and learned treatise, of the exercise of fasting*. London: Daye, 1580.

Secondary Sources

Blom, Philipp. *Enlightening the World: "Encyclopédie," The Book That Changed the Course of History*. New York: Palgrave Macmillan, 2005.

Buck, Peter. "Seventeenth-Century Political Arithmetic: Civil Strife and Vital Statistics." *Isis* 68 (March 1977): 67–84.

Darnton, Robert. *The Business of Enlightenment: A Publishing History of the "Encyclopédie."* Cambridge: Harvard University Press, 1979.

Delia, Luigi. *Droit et philosophie à la lumière de l'Encyclopédie* [Law and Philosophy in the Light of the *Encyclopédie*]. Oxford University Studies in the Enlightenment 2015:06. Oxford: Voltaire Foundation, 2015.

Edelstein, Dan. *The Enlightenment: A Genealogy*. Chicago: University of Chicago Press, 2010.

———. "Humanism, *l'Esprit Philosophique*, and the *Encyclopédie*." *Republics of Letters: A Journal for the Study of Knowledge, Politics, and the Arts* 1, no. 1 (May 1, 2009). http://rofl.stanford.edu/node/27.

Edelstein, Dan, Robert Morrissey, and Glenn Roe. "To Quote or Not to Quote: Citation Strategies in the *Encyclopédie*." *Journal of the History of Ideas* 74 (April 2013): 213–36.

Fletcher, Dennis J. "The Chevalier de Jaucourt and the English Sources of the Encyclopedic Article 'Patriote.'" *Diderot Studies* 16 (1973): 23–34.

Furbank, P. N. *Diderot: A Critical Biography*. New York: A. A. Knopf, 1992.

Garrard, Graeme. *Rousseau's Counter-Enlightenment: A Republican Critique of the Philosophes*. Albany: State University of New York Press, 2003.

Gay, Peter. *The Enlightenment: An Interpretation*. 2 vols. New York: Knopf, 1966–69.

———. *Voltaire's Politics*. Princeton: Princeton University Press, 1959.

Goodman, Dena. *Criticism in Action: Enlightenment Experiments in Political Writing*. Ithaca: Cornell University Press, 1989.

Gordon, Douglas H., and Norman L. Torrey. *The Censoring of Diderot's "Encyclopédie" and the Re-established Text*. New York: Columbia University Press, 1947.

Grimsley, Ronald. *Jean d'Alembert (1717–83)*. Oxford: Clarendon Press, 1963.

Haechler, Jean. *L'Encyclopédie de Diderot et de . . . Jaucourt: Essai biographique sur le chevalier Louis de Jaucourt*. Paris: Champion, 1995.

Hammersley, Rachel. *The English Republican Tradition and Eighteenth-Century France: Between the Ancients and the Moderns.* Manchester: Manchester University Press, 2010.

Hubert, René. *Les Sciences sociales dans l'Encyclopédie: la philosophie de l'histoire et le problème des origines sociales.* Paris: Alcan, 1923.

Kafker, Frank A. *Notable Encyclopedias of the Late Eighteenth Century: Eleven Successors of the "Encyclopédie."* Oxford: Voltaire Foundation, 1994.

———. *Notable Encyclopedias of the Seventeenth and Eighteenth Centuries: Nine Predecessors of the "Encyclopédie."* Oxford: Voltaire Foundation, 1981.

———. "The Recruitment of the Encyclopedists." *Eighteenth-Century Studies* 6 (Summer 1973): 452–61.

Kafker, Frank A., and Serena L. Kafker. *The Encyclopedists as Individuals: A Biographical Dictionary of the Authors of the "Encyclopédie."* Studies on Voltaire and the Eighteenth Century 257. Oxford: Voltaire Foundation, 1988.

Kors, Alan Charles. *D'Holbach's Coterie: An Enlightenment in Paris.* Princeton: Princeton University Press, 1976.

Littré, Emile. *Dictionnaire de la langue française.* 2nd ed. Paris: Hachette, 1872–77. Available online at the ARTFL website: http://artfl-project.uchicago.edu/node/17.

Lough, John. *The Contributors to The "Encyclopédie."* London: Grant and Cutler, 1973.

———. *The "Encyclopédie."* New York: McKay, 1971.

———. *Essays on the "Encyclopédie" of Diderot and d'Alembert.* London: Oxford University Press, 1968.

Lynn, John. "The Treatment of Military Subjects in Diderot's *Encyclopédie.*" *Journal of Military History* 65 (2001): 131–65.

Marion, Marcel. *Dictionnaire des institutions de la France aux XVIIe et XVIIIe siècles.* Paris: Picard, 1923.

McMahon, Darrin M. *Enemies of the Enlightenment: The French Counter-Enlightenment and the Making of Modernity.* Oxford: Oxford University Press, 2001.

Morris, Madeleine F. *Le Chevalier de Jaucourt: un ami de la terre* [Chevalier de Jaucourt: a friend of the earth]. Geneva: Droz, 1979.

Post, Gaines. *Studies in Medieval Legal Thought: Public Law and the State, 1100–1322.* Princeton: Princeton University Press, 1964.

Proust, Jacques. *Diderot et l'Encyclopédie.* Paris: Albin Michel, 1995.

Riley, James C. *The Seven Years War and the Old Regime in France: The Economic and Financial Toll.* Princeton: Princeton University Press, 1986.

Rosso, Jeannette Geffriaud. "Montesquieu, Diderot et l'*Encyclopédie.*" *Diderot Studies* 25 (1993): 63–74.

Rowen, Herbert H. *The King's State: Proprietary Dynasticism in Early Modern France*. New Brunswick: Rutgers University Press, 1980.

Savonius, S.-J. "Locke in French: The *Du Gouvernement civil* and Its Readers." *Historical Journal* 47, no. 1 (2004): 47–79.

Schwab, Richard N., Walter E. Rex, and John Lough. *Inventory of Diderot's "Encyclopédie."* Studies on Voltaire and the Eighteenth Century, vols. 80, 83, 85, 91–93, 223. Geneva: Institut et Musée Voltaire, 1971–84.

Shusterman, Noah. *Religion and the Politics of Time: Holidays in France from Louis XIV Through Napoleon*. Washington, D.C.: Catholic University Press, 2010.

Spurlin, Paul Merrill. *The French Enlightenment in America: Essays on the Times of the Founding Fathers*. Athens: University of Georgia Press, 1984.

Walters, Gordon B. *The Significance of Diderot's "Essai sur le mérite et la vertu."* Chapel Hill: University of North Carolina Press, 1971.

Wilson, Arthur M. *Diderot*. New York: Oxford University Press, 1972.

——. "Why Did the Political Theory of the Encyclopedists Not Prevail?: A Suggestion." *French Historical Studies* 1 (Spring 1960): 283–94.

Index

Titles of articles in the *Encyclopédie,* whether or not they appear in this volume, are indicated by SMALL CAPS. Page numbers for the text of articles that do appear in this volume are in **bold.** Page numbers in *italics* indicate illustrations.

(This page constitutes an extension of the copyright page.)

Illustrations in the text are reproduced from Cesare Ripa, *Baroque and Rococo Pictorial Imagery: The 1758–60 Hertel Edition of Ripa's "Iconologia" with 200 Engraved Illustrations*, ed. Edward A. Maser (New York: Dover Publications, 1971), *Amor Patriae* (Patriotism), 26; *Libertas* (Liberty), 62; *Industria* (Industry), 147; *Res Domestica* (Frugality), 148; *Ars Politica* (Statecraft), 199.

The newly translated articles in this volume (exceptions noted below) are based on the following French-language source: Denis Diderot and Jean Le Rond d'Alembert, eds. *Encyclopédie, ou Dictionnaire raisonné des sciences, des arts et des métiers, par une Société de gens de lettres* [Encyclopedia, or critical dictionary of the sciences, arts and trades, by an Association of men of letters]. 28 vols. (Paris: Briasson, David, Le Breton, Durand, 1751–72). Available in electronic form on the University of Chicago's *ARTFL Encyclopédie Project* website (Spring 2011 Edition), Robert Morrissey (ed.), http://encyclopedie.uchicago.edu/.

The text on which the translation of "Toleration" is based is in the public domain. It is used courtesy of the *ARTFL Encyclopédie Project*, which created the text from images of the original French page proofs borrowed from the Small Special Collections Library at the University of Virginia. (See "Censored Articles: Tolérance" in "The 18th Volume," University of Chicago: *ARTFL Encyclopédie Project*, Spring 2011 Edition, ed. Robert Morrissey, http://encyclopedie.uchicago.edu/.)

The articles "Masterpiece," translated by Malcolm Eden, "Child," translated by Emily-Jane Cohen, and "Machiavellianism," translated by Timothy Cleary, are from the University of Michigan's website *Encyclopedia of Diderot and d'Alembert: Collaborative Translation Project*, http://quod.lib.umich.edu/d/did. Articles reprinted by permission of the translators.

All or part of "The Divine Voice," "Political Authority," "Natural Right," "Natural Equality," "Legislator," and "Representatives" are translated by Stephen J. Gendzier, in *Denis Diderot's* The Encyclopedia: *Selections*, ed. and trans. Stephen J. Gendzier (New York: Harper and Row, 1967). Articles reprinted by permission of the translator.

The article "Population," translated in abridged form by Odile Frank, is from her "Diderot's *Encyclopédie* on Population," in *Population and Development Review* 15 (June 1989): 342–57. Reprinted and adapted with the permission of the Population Council.

This book is set in Fournier, a font based on types cut by Pierre Simon Fournier circa 1742 in his *Manuel Typographique*. These types were some of the most influential designs of the eighteenth century, being among the earliest of the transitional style of typeface, and were a stepping stone to the more severe modern style made popular by Bodoni later in the century. They had more vertical stress than the old style types, greater contrast between thick and thin strokes, and little or no bracketing on the serifs.

Printed on paper that is acid-free and meets the requirements of the American National Standard for Permanence of Paper for Printed Library Materials, z39.48-1992. ♾

Book design by Louise OFarrell
Gainesville, Florida
Typography by Graphic Composition, Inc.
Bogart, Georgia
Printed and bound by Edwards Brothers Malloy
Ann Arbor, Michigan